AFFIRMATIONS
coloring book for kids

With Autism

Introduction

Welcome to your world of affirmation and creativity! In this special coloring book, you are not just an artist, but a storyteller of your own unique journey. Choose colors that resonate with your feelings, your joys, and your dreams

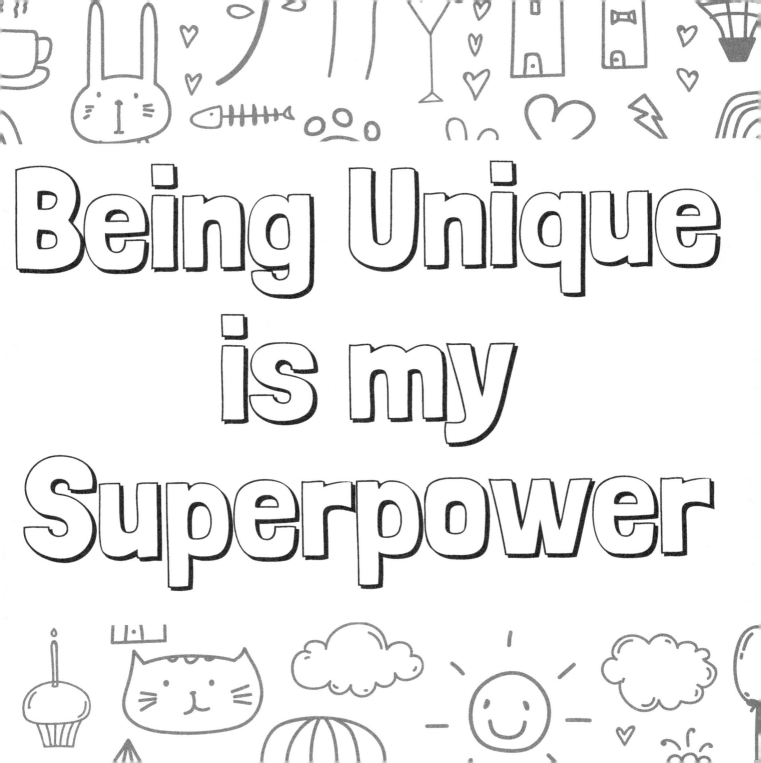

Being Unique is my Superpower

I can Learn and Achieve anything

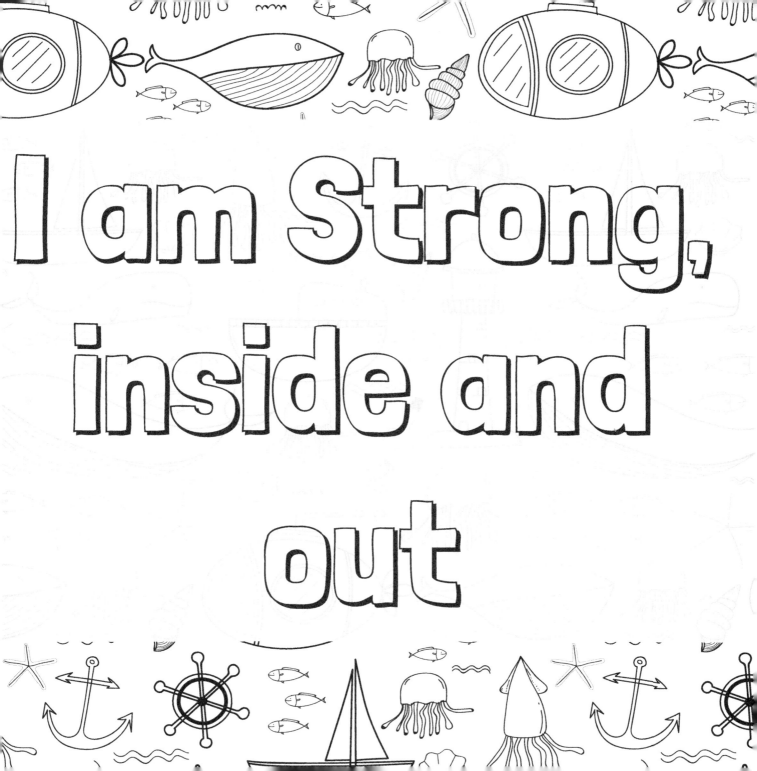

I have a Bright and Creative mind

I am a
Problem
Solver

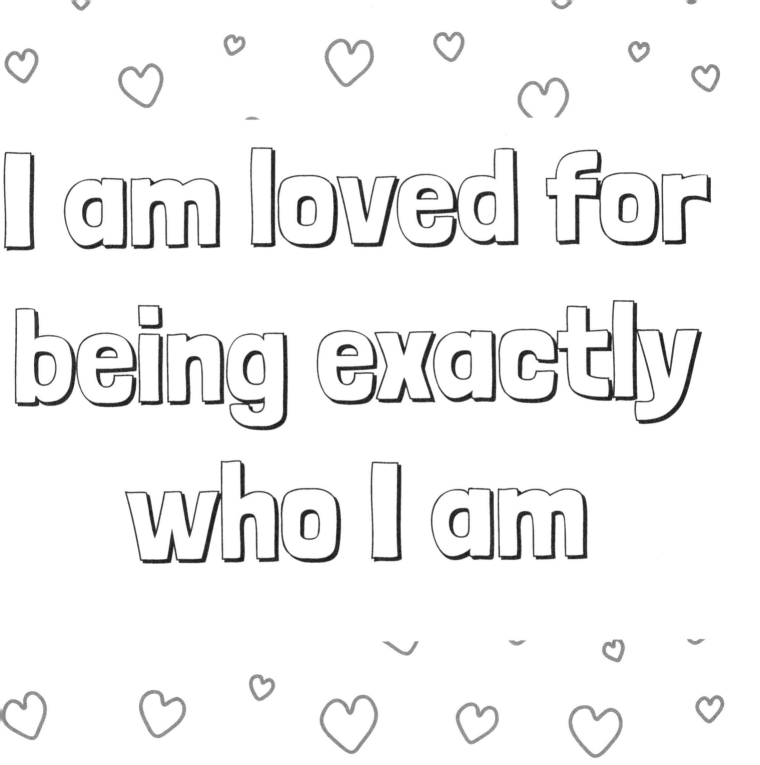

I am a Great Friend to Others

I am safe and cared for

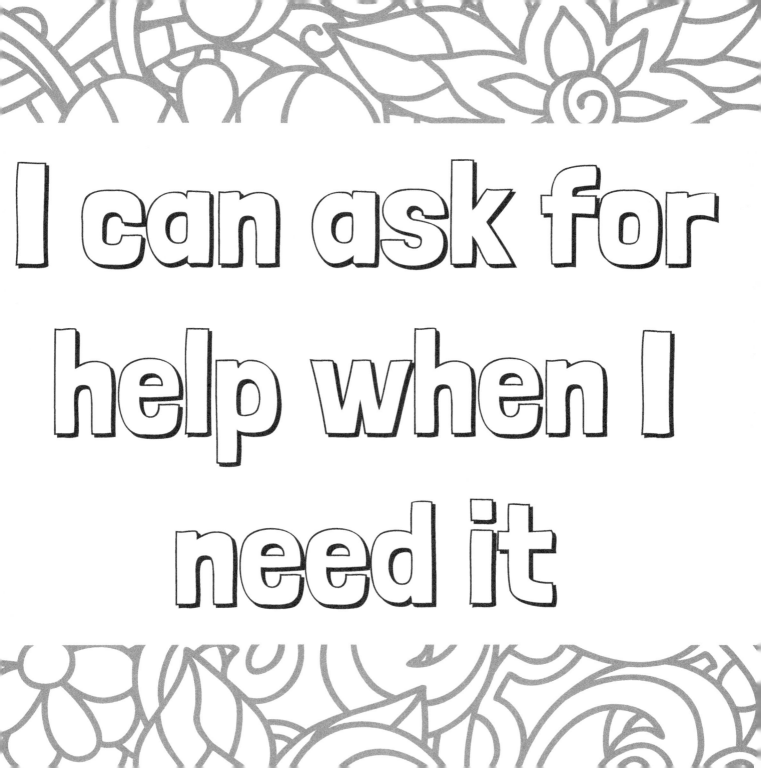

I Have a Big loving heart

My future is bright

Life is a lot of fun

I can do better next time

My challenges help me grow

Today I'm a leader

I forgive my self for my mistakes

I care about others

I have big
dreams

I keep my body healthy

I am here for
a purpose

I am a good brother/sister

Growing Like a Flower

I have a positive attitude

Mistakes help

me learn

I talk about my feelings

I enjoy learning new things

My differences make me special

Every day is a fresh start

I surround myself with positive people.

I can take
deep breaths

Printed in Great Britain
by Amazon

Growing Pains

Brentford FC's
2015/16 Season

Greville Waterman

BENNION
KEARNY

Whilst we all wait impatiently for the new season to start, I would highly recommend Greville Waterman's excellent new book *Growing Pains* to every Brentford supporter. He has written wisely and entertainingly on pretty much everything that happened on and off the field at the club last season, good and bad alike, and whilst I do not agree with all his conclusions he has written a most entertaining account.

So I hope you enjoy reading his book and recollecting some of the key moments in what was a real rollercoaster of a season.

Matthew Benham

About Greville Waterman

Greville Waterman with Cliff Crown

I have been a Brentford supporter for around fifty years and I have enjoyed all of the good and bad times at Griffin Park and totally relished the last couple of years in The Championship, a level of the game that pre-Matthew Benham I could only dream of the club returning to.

I was a director of the club for a brief spell in 2005 (don't ask) and remain on the board of *Bees United*.

I owned a sponsorship consultancy for many years and now teach Autogenic Therapy, a Mind/Body relaxation technique that helps people who are suffering from anxiety, stress and mild depression (please visit *www.howtobeatstress.co.uk*).

I certainly needed the help of AT after suffering from the effects of our eight unsuccessful playoff campaigns since 1991!

I still dabble in sponsorship consultancy amongst other things, and I am constantly looking for fresh challenges that will stretch and challenge me.

I am married to the beautiful and wonderfully talented artist, Miriam whose creativity takes my breath away and we both take massive pride in the accomplishments of our two children Nick and Rebecca, and, just like last year I dedicate this book to the three of them.

Growing Pains covers the rollercoaster that was Brentford's 2015/16 season and is a follow up to *Ahead Of The Game* which dealt with the tumultuous events of the previous campaign.

Both are published by *Bennion Kearny* and my thanks and eternal gratitude go to James Lumsden-Cook for taking a chance on me and my writing.

Acknowledgements

I would like to thank everybody who read, commented on, or responded to any of my articles on the *BFC Talk* blog throughout the 2015/16 season.

I want to make the blog as interactive as possible and I really enjoy reading all your comments and feedback and they have given me so many new insights and different perspectives into all matters relating to the one passion that we all share in common – Brentford FC.

A special thank you too to all those friends and colleagues from both inside and outside Brentford FC who went the extra mile and took note of my entreaties, begging and pleading and somehow found the time to write their own contributions and articles.

They will all be found within the covers of this book, and I am grateful and in total awe of all of you for the quality of your writing and depth of your passion, knowledge and thought which have added immeasurably to this book.

About Mark Fuller

The images in this book are the work of **Mark D. Fuller**. Mark is Brentford FC's Official Photographer, and the season featured in this book was his ninth season fulfilling the role. He has covered in excess of 500 games during that time. Shooting around a thousand frames each game, each season he racks up 100,000 shots and

18,000 miles of travel. To keep up with these demands he uses an ever-expanding collection of Canon professional photography equipment and a battered Audi A6.

Mark's Brentford FC work can be viewed at: *officialbfcpics.co.uk*. Official Brentford Pictures updates are on Twitter: *@BFCPics*.

Mark also undertakes product photography for a number of clients including Premier League and Championship football clubs. Other photography work undertaken includes Corporate & PR work along with the occasional wedding.

If you need a photographer then Mark can be contacted by email: *mark@markdfuller.co.uk* and followed on Twitter: *@TheMarkFuller*.

Table of Contents

Introduction

Last year I wrote a book about Brentford FC's incredible first season in the Championship. *Ahead Of The Game* covered an amazing and totally unexpected journey that took them to the brink of the Premier League until reality took over and they fell foul of their customary playoff hoodoo.

Was 2014/15 a dream or a one-off? Could Brentford perhaps maintain or even build on their success or was it a one-off and would they fall away into obscurity?

Given all these imponderables, I decided to continue telling the story and record and analyse all the events of the 2015/16 season and *Growing Pains* is the result, and what a rollercoaster season it turned out to be.

I hope you come along for the ride with me.

Greville Waterman

The Roll Of Honour – 21/6/15

I read a fascinating article on the Brentford FC website yesterday which totally grabbed my attention and highlighted and confirmed just what an exceptional season we have all just enjoyed. It simply listed everyone involved and associated with the club – players, management and coaches, back room staff and indeed supporters whose incredible achievements have been recognised and marked with awards both from within the club and also from outside.

Let's start by perusing the entire list of Brentford FC's Roll Of Honour 2014/15:

- Family Excellence Award: Brentford FC
- *Sky Bet* Championship PFA Team of the Year: Alex Pritchard
- *Sky Bet* League Two Player of the Year Top Three: Alfie Mawson (on loan at Wycombe Wanderers)
- *Sky Bet* Championship Player of the Year Top Ten: Alex Pritchard
- *Zoo Magazine* Sky Bet League Two Player of the Year: Alfie Mawson
- *MATCH Magazine* FL Wonderkid: Alex Pritchard
- *FourFourTwo* Top 50 Players in the Football League: Jota, Alex Pritchard
- *MATCH Magazine* Top 100 Players in the Football League: Andre Gray, Jota, Alex Pritchard
- Brentford FC Club Hero: Roger Crook
- London Manager of the Year 2014: Mark Warburton
- Special Awards: Mark Warburton (to mark his time at Brentford FC) and Richard Lee (to mark his retirement)
- Special Achievement Award: Roger Crook (for his work for Brentford FC Community Sports Trust, the Club and Brentford Women's and Girls FC)
- Supporters' Player of the Year: Toumani Diagouraga
- Players' Player of the Year: Alex Pritchard
- Goal of the Season: Stuart Dallas (v Fulham 3 April 2015)
- Community Player of the Year: Jake Bidwell
- *Bees Player* Moment of the Season: Jota (for winning goal against Fulham on 21 November 2014)
- Bees Travel Club Player of the Season: Toumani Diagouraga
- Junior Bees Player of the Season: Toumani Diagouraga
- The Brentford Football Club Norwegian Supporters' Player of the Season: Alex Pritchard
- Irish Brentford Supporters Club Player of the Year: Alex Pritchard
- Player of the Season for 2014/15 from Brentford's Italian supporters: Alex Pritchard
- Social Media Player of the Season: Alex Pritchard
- Goal of 2014: Jota (v Cardiff City 20 December 2014)
- Youth Team Player of the Year: Nik Tzanev
- *Sky Bet* Championship Manager of the Month November 2014: Mark Warburton
- *Sky Bet* Championship Player of the Month November 2014: Andre Gray
- LMA Performance of the Week: Brentford (v Wolverhampton Wanderers 29 November 2014)

- Hottie of the Year: Andre Gray

- British Legal Awards Property Team of the Year: Taylor Wessing (for work securing planning permission for a new stadium for Brentford FC)

- Brentford FC Nominations for Football League Team of the Decade: Wojciech Szczęsny, Michael Turner, Jonathan Douglas, Lloyd Owusu

- Graham Haynes Trophy: Dave Morley

- Alfie Mawson won six awards from Wycombe Wanderers – Supporters' Player of the Year, Players' Player of the Year, Official Wycombe Wanderers Supporters Association Player of the Year, Young Player of the Year and Away Travel Player of the Year, Wycombe Wanderers Independent Supporters Club Player of the Year

- Lewis Macleod won the Rangers Goal of the Season Award

- International Honours while with Brentford this season:
    - Stuart Dallas: Four Northern Ireland caps and one goal
    - Moses Odubajo: Six England Under 20 caps
    - Alex Pritchard: Six England Under 21 caps
    - Will Grigg: Two Northern Ireland caps (while on loan at Milton Keynes Dons)
    - Liam Moore: One England Under 21 cap
    - Daniel O'Shaughnessy: Five Finland Under 21 caps and one goal, One Finland Under 20 cap
    - Nik Tzanev: Three New Zealand Under 20 caps
    - Julius Fenn-Evans: Three Wales Under 16 caps
    - First Team players Alan Judge (Republic of Ireland) and Chris Long (England Under 20) and Academy players Kyjuon Marsh-Brown (Antigua and Barbuda) Harry Francis (England Under 15), Ross McMahon (Scotland Under 16) and Josh Bohui (England Under 16) were also called up to training camps or squads

- The following players were named in the Football League Team of the Week: Alfie Mawson (three times), Jota (twice), Alex Pritchard (twice), Jake Bidwell, David Button, Jonathan Douglas, Andre Gray, Alan Judge, Jon Toral, Mark Warburton, Will Grigg and Nico Yennaris (from Wycombe Wanderers)

- The following were inducted in to the Brentford FC Hall of Fame this season: Terry Evans, Bob Booker, Peter Gelson, Keith Millen, Alan Nelmes, Danis Salman, Kevin O'Connor and Marcus Gayle

- The following were inducted in to the Brentford FC Hall of Fame posthumously this season: Harry Curtis, Gerry Cakebread, Ephraim Rhodes, Fred Monk, George Bristow, Jimmy Bain, Jimmy Cartmell, Arthur Bateman, Patsy Hendren, Ernie Muttitt, David McCulloch, Austin Underwood, Allan Jones, Chic Brodie, Jimmy Jay, Bill Gorman, Arthur Charlton, Fred Halliday, Jack Lane, Jack Holliday, Leslie Smith, Billy Scott, Jim Towers and Johnny Rainford

An impressive list as I am sure that you will agree, and one that bears testimony to the enormous success that we enjoyed both on and off the field throughout what was in my opinion our best season in living memory. I also doubt whether we have ever previously received so much recognition from external sources and media groups.

The only addition that I would suggest to what is already an exceptionally thorough and comprehensive list is that of Tom Higginson, dear beloved *Higgy* to the Brentford FC Hall of Fame, as, unless I have got it wrong, and if so I apologise unreservedly to the club, then he has perhaps fallen through the cracks – an oversight that I am sure will be speedily rectified once the facts are checked.

This seems a perfect way of drawing a line under the 2014/15 season and starting to look forward with a mixture of optimism, trepidation and excitement to what awaits us next season.

It has certainly been a close season which has already seen much change with a completely new football management structure at the club and the arrival of two players to date, a number which is likely to increase exponentially shortly after the beginning of July.

Stan Is Still The Man – 22/6/15

Like everybody else, I was shocked and distressed to hear the sad news over the weekend that Stan Bowles has unfortunately developed a form of Alzheimer's disease. There was a picture of Stan on his *Facebook* site celebrating Fathers' Day and thankfully he looked to be in good spirits. It was good to see him with a smile on his face as he gave such pleasure to untold millions of football fans with his skill, *joie de vivre* and overall approach to life.

The term *genius* is thrown around with gay abandon and is often applied to merely the very good rather than the rare one-offs and special ones, but nobody could ever quibble or complain at Stan being so described. He had a wonderful career that spanned the best part of twenty years and he played nearly six hundred games, testimony to the fact that he was not a luxury player who picked his games, as he loved to play and was a tough competitor.

Immaturity, massive competition for places and some dodgy off-field connections cost Stan the opportunity of early stardom at Manchester City but he rehabilitated himself in the nether regions of the Football League at Crewe and Carlisle and whilst other teams dithered, Gordon Jago took the gamble and signed him for Queens Park Rangers in September 1972 for what turned out to be a bargain fee of £110,000. Rodney Marsh had long been the idol of all QPR fans who had bemoaned his transfer, ironically to Manchester City, of all places, but Stan proved to be the perfect replacement and became an instant hero at Loftus Road and the hallowed number ten shirt soon had a worthy new owner.

Stan stayed seven years at QPR and was in his pomp during that period, but despite his ability and consistency and excellent goal scoring record he failed to convince successive England managers of his temperament and played only five times for his country – a terrible waste of talent and an indictment of the cautious and puritanical establishment running the game at the time who could not cope with free spirits like Stan. He joined fellow mavericks such as Frank Worthington, Alan Hudson, Charlie George, Peter Osgood and Tony Currie who were treated with suspicion and were never allowed to fulfil their undoubted ability at international level.

Stan was not the first footballer to fall out with the mercurial Tommy Docherty and was sold to Nottingham Forest – out of the frying pan, into the fire – where he also fell foul of Brian Clough, ruling himself out of playing in the 1980 European Cup Final. His career looked like it was drifting towards its conclusion when his next move to Leyton Orient left him treading water but he was revitalised and enjoyed one last hurrah when Fred Callaghan and Martin Lange persuaded him to join Brentford in October 1981 for what proved to be a giveaway £25,000 fee.

It was an inspirational move for the club as Stan refound his enthusiasm for the game and energized players and supporters alike with his sparkling presence and twinkling feet. Despite his advancing years, he provided marvellous value for money and played nearly one hundred games for the Bees, scoring seventeen times in all and assisting on countless others. He has also gone down in Brentford legend by forming the final leg in what became perhaps our finest midfield trio since the Second World War.

Terry Hurlock was passionate and aggressive and took no prisoners, Chris Kamara was a tireless box-to-box runner who also provided goals and heading ability and Stan was just Stan. He didn't do a lot of running, confining himself to the left side of midfield, but he didn't really need to as the other players did it for him. He simply conserved his energy and sprayed the ball around and cut helpless opposition defences to shreds with his rapier-like passes.

The fans adored him and a season's best attendance of nearly seven thousand crammed in to see him make his debut at home to Burnley. Three days later he pulled all the strings as the Bees destroyed Swindon with a convincing win at The County Ground and he maintained his consistency for the next eighteen months. He also scored regularly, six times in 1981/82, and he managed a remarkable eleven goals the following season when he played over fifty times and laid on goals aplenty for the rampaging forward line of Tony Mahoney, Francis Joseph and Gary Roberts although sometimes he was too clever for them and they could not read his intentions.

Stan could seemingly do anything on the pitch, he was the complete master of the football and his left foot was like a wand. He scored eleven out of twelve times from the penalty spot, languidly strolling up and sending the goalkeeper and the crowd behind the goal one way before stroking the ball effortlessly into the other corner of the net. I still cannot believe that he actually missed one kick and remain sceptical, as no photograph seems to exist of that rare happening one Friday night at Wrexham. Would that he could provide some expert tuition in the long-lost art of penalty taking to the hapless Brentford players of today who seem to find the task of scoring consistently from the spot totally beyond them.

Not content with that, Stan also produced his party piece of scoring direct from a corner kick against Swindon and he was naturally deadly from long-range free kicks as Wimbledon's Dave Beasant could attest. Stan was a star and you simply could not take your eyes off him, but he also mucked in and was just one of the lads and was universally popular with everyone at the club. There were no airs and graces, he always played to win and gave everything that he had rather than merely going through the motions and playing only when the mood took him.

Stan provided full value and lit up Griffin Park with his wonderful ability and ever-present smile and the fact that he had been a hero at our massive rivals QPR was soon forgiven and forgotten as he so obviously gave everything to the cause throughout his spell at Brentford. Everyone associated with the club fondly remembers him and we all salute him and send him and his family our best wishes today.

Catching Up – And What Lies Ahead – 29/06/15

So what's been happening over the course of the past month or so in and around Brentford FC as we begin to prepare for a long and exciting season ahead?

Well, quite a lot actually, and the purpose of this article is simply to provide everyone with a quick update and catch-up as well as look forward to the excitement of the next few weeks as the players return for preseason training and the transfer market begins to hot up.

Given that our involvement in the playoffs meant that last season ended later than anticipated – but perhaps earlier than hoped – on the 15th May, there has been a hive of activity at Griffin Park over the last six weeks or so. The new backroom team has now been assembled and is hard at work with new Head Coach Marinus Dijkhuizen arriving after a successful spell in charge at Excelsior who he led to promotion, before, against all the odds, consolidating their position in the *Eredivisi*e and gaining an excellent reputation for innovation, youth development and a determination to play good football despite limited resources.

His achievements and approach certainly ticked all the boxes for Matthew Benham, as did his willingness to embrace the management structure and analytics based system that the Brentford owner intends to implement at the club, where the Head Coach has an important say, but no actual veto, on incoming players.

Fellow Dutchman Roy Hendriksen, a former playing colleague of Dijkhuizen, is the new Assistant Head Coach and it will be fascinating and illuminating as well as a little bit concerning, if truth be told, to see how well the players respond to their ideas, tactical innovation and man management skills after the overwhelming success and popularity of their predecessors, Mark Warburton and David Weir who presided over a totally united and motivated dressing room.

As for the Two W's themselves, I wish them both nothing but success and good fortune for the future given how brilliantly they served us, but I have spent the last month since their departure worrying that their shadow would loom over us, particularly if they had decided, as at one time appeared a distinct possibility, to move on to another Championship team.

Thankfully they are now both out of sight and out of mind, facing a massive new challenge over the border at Glasgow Rangers, and with respect to my feelings towards Mark and David, I can only echo the immortal blessing from *Fiddler On The Roof*: *May God bless and keep the Tsar – far away from us.*

Rasmus Ankersen and Phil Giles have come in to job share as Co-Directors of Football with responsibility for player recruitment and for ensuring that the runes are properly examined, fresh gems identified and polished and that there is a constant supply of new talent to enhance the strong squad already *in situ* at the club.

The final piece of the jigsaw saw the appointment last week of experienced coach Flemming Pedersen as Head of Football Philosophy and Player Development. He will assist in coaching the first team as well as being responsible for setting out Brentford's football philosophy and structuring individual development plans for players. I assume he will be acting as a Technical Director and will liaise with coaches at all levels of the club, as well as the Academy Director, in order to ensure uniformity and that the same approach and style of football is employed throughout the club.

Only Brentford could actually use the word *philosophy* in a job title for a football coach and this just highlights that we are marching to our own drum and doing things rather differently to the rest of the football world – and long may that remain the case if we are to maintain or even expand our competitive advantage over clubs far less enlightened, ambitious, or forward seeking than ourselves.

The tabloid media in the shape of *The Daily Mirror* took a cheap shot in a puerile and superficial article that poked fun at us regarding Flemming's unusual and original job title, but this is now par for the course.

Throughout the course of history, innovative and original thinkers across all spheres of activity have been universally mocked and ridiculed for propagating ideas and practices that break new ground and are outside the accepted rules and methodology. It is far easier and less taxing on the brain to mock, jeer and make fun of something new rather than take the time, trouble and intellectual challenge of examining it, breaking it down into its component parts and then analysing and evaluating it in greater detail.

The mainstream football media is gunning for us and it is now open season on Brentford FC. There are many people both within the game and who also commentate upon it who would like nothing better than to see us fall flat on our backsides and speedily return from whence we came with our tail firmly between our legs. *Those cocky little upstarts at Brentford need to be put back in their rightful place* goes their thinking. Not only are they unwilling to take the time and trouble to get their head around the way in which we are now running and structuring the club, there is also a massive residue of sympathy remaining towards Mark Warburton given the outside perception of how *unfairly* he was *rewarded* by us despite being responsible for bringing so much unexpected success to the club.

Last season we were media darlings until *Timesgate* in February, but this year will almost certainly be different and we need to be prepared to batten down the hatches and await the onslaught and ideally defend our position. The best way to throw negative comments back from whence they came is simply by proving that they are inaccurate and erroneous and in that regard it would be enormously helpful if we are able to hit the ground running and get off to a fast start to the new season, clearly demonstrate that we remain on course for greater things, that our progress and development continues apace and that we are remain in the vanguard of a new era for football.

No pressure then on what is pretty much an entirely new team behind the first team. There is continuity in the welcome presence of Kevin O'Connor and Simon Royce with Lee Carsley remaining in charge of the Development Squad and thankfully there has been no news of any departures from amongst the valued ranks of our highly prized analysis, fitness and medical support staff.

Given the changes, it might well take a little while for things to gel, who knows, but given the quality of personnel that we possess and the level of planning that has gone into every major decision that we have taken, I remain fully confident about our prospects. In my next article I will take a look at the Brentford squad, examine the new arrivals, speculate on who might be coming or going and eagerly look forward to the exciting few weeks that lie ahead as we build our squad for the new season.

July

The Season Starts Here – 1/7/15

There has been a lot of recent speculation and concern amongst Brentford supporters about the future of some of our best young players and our ability to hang onto them. The rumours abound and continue to grow, linking the likes of David Button to Aston Villa, Moses Odubajo to Everton, Tarky to Fulham, Jota to Swansea and Leicester, Andre Gray to Hull or QPR and Stuart Dallas to Glasgow Rangers.

Despite all the rumours as of today only two players have left the club with misfit Nick Proschwitz returning to SC Paderborn 07 and promising defender Alfie Mawson joining Barnsley.

The trickle of transfers is now about to become a veritable torrent as we enter July, a time of the year when contracts have expired and players are free to move on to pastures anew. Speculation is rife as rumours abound in the press, on social media and message boards alike of moves actual and mooted, likely and ludicrous – football is back on the agenda with a vengeance, and we await the next ten months with relish, excitement and not a little foreboding too.

Yes, there certainly have been rumours about any number of our players leaving but that was ever the case. Remember two years ago when Harry Forrester and Simon Moore decided to move on, and last season when we lost star assets in Clayton Donaldson and Adam Forshaw?

That is simply the way of the game as players are led by the nose by rapacious agents who are programmed to sniff out more lucrative opportunities elsewhere and many is the time when players seem to be ruled by their bank balance rather than by their head.

It would be hard to make a strong case that any of the four aforementioned former Brentford favourites have made good footballing moves even though they have undoubtedly benefited financially and I suspect that deep down perhaps a couple of them regret their impetuosity in deciding to leave Griffin Park.

It is no use my bemoaning the situation, as one has simply to accept that the days of loyal one club heroes like Peter Gelson and Alan Hawley and indeed Kevin O'Connor are dwindling as players can now enjoy the benefits of freedom of contract and have little or no compunction in feathering their nest by moving on a regular basis to the highest bidder.

Brentford are not high payers by Championship standards, and neither should they be, given our lack of income relative to the competition and the club understandably prefers to incentivise players more through a generous bonus scheme that rewards players for actual achievement rather than for merely turning up.

It is therefore inevitable that until our revenue base grows exponentially with a combination of sustained success as well as the enhanced revenue streams emanating from our new stadium at Lionel Road, we will run the risk of losing players, perhaps even over the next few weeks, as richer clubs higher up the food chain jockey for position and attempt to divest their less fortunate brethren of their star assets.

If the predators do come sniffing around us then there are a few things that are certain:

- They will be looking to sign one or more of our top players – the likes of Jota, Gray, Odubajo, Tarks and Button rather than players sitting like wallflowers at the end of our bench

- If a player really wants to leave because he and his representative believe that the grass is greener elsewhere, then in truth there is little that can be done to salvage the situation even if the player is safely in contract particularly given the problems caused by the demands of Financial Fair Play

- We are no longer a soft touch, encouraging external approaches and keen to sell our family heirlooms for a song and a fraction of their true value as was the case for time immemorial

- We will only sell on our own terms when we are ready to do so even if the player's departure becomes inevitable, and we will extract top dollar for him

- Whoever leaves us will be replaced by another promising player identified by our impressive team of analysts who are scouring the football world and crawling under rocks to discover new gems to ensure that we are continually able to replenish our squad

I look at the current situation as a backhanded compliment to us, as we now possess so many young, talented players who are only going to improve and appreciate in value and I would far prefer that other clubs covet our assets and might even possibly succeed in spiriting some of them away, rather than our having a squad full of mediocrities and journeymen as has so often been the case in the past.

I remain firmly of the opinion that we are on our way to the Premier League, it is simply a question of when, rather than if we get there, however it might well be that for players of the calibre of Odubajo and Jota, that incredible day might not come soon enough for their immediate ambitions to be fully realised and we might simply have to accept that the time might well come, sooner rather than later, when they decide to leave us.

At the other end of the spectrum there are several valuable and highly experienced squad players like Tony Craig, Sam Saunders and Alan McCormack who, given our recent progress, we have outgrown and whose time might well have come to move on to a new home where they can play every week, a privilege that is likely to be denied them if they remain at Brentford.

Players of that calibre and loyalty deserve better than to wither on the vine and should be treated with respect and allowed to find a new home where they can inspire a fresh generation of young players albeit at a lower level of the game.

Like time, football waits for no man and it might also be that several regulars from last season's team also begin to feel the hot breath of fresh challengers for their shirt. Harlee Dean, Jonathan Douglas and Toumani Diagouraga might be particularly vulnerable and Jake Bidwell would also benefit from having a new competitor breathing down his neck and fighting him for possession of his place.

One of the complaints justifiably levelled against Mark Warburton last season was his undoubted loyalty to his squad, and all eleven of those who started the first match of the season also featured in the squad for the final game over nine months later.

I anticipate a larger and deeper squad this season with more and tougher competition for places as well as increased squad rotation. With that will come the problem of keeping the non-playing members of the squad onside and this will be a massive task for the new coaching staff. We were a happy and tight-knit unit last season, a factor that contributed greatly to our success, and we need to ensure that this positive state of affairs remains if we are to be successful over the coming months.

One of my great pleasures over previous years has been trying to work out who we were likely to sign, and very often it was possible by applying a bit of logic, a keen nose for clues and a reasonable knowledge of the UK football scene, to make a decent stab at guessing who was going to arrive. That is certainly no longer the case.

In those days, which now seem so distant, we were shopping in a totally different market, and given the way that we now operate and how our analysts interpret the data they receive from around the world, I suspect that new British players will be the exception rather than the rule.

This is a situation that I fully accept given that we need to be smarter and better informed than our richer competitors but it isn't as much fun for me given that I had not previously heard of any of our new foreign imports!

We have already signed Akaki Gogia, a Georgian winger from the German lower leagues, Yoann Barbet, a highly promising left sided central defender from Chamois Niortais and, more familiarly, midfielder Ryan Williams from Morecambe.

Quite frankly I know nothing at all bar what I have researched online about the first two and as for Williams, who I have seen play, I regard him as a decent each way bet as he has shown real skill on the ball throughout his career as well as the ability to put the ball on a sixpence from free kicks, whilst also demonstrating that his slight build and skills set is not best suited for the hustle and bustle of lower league football. Maybe he will make it with us, maybe not, but he is an inexpensive gamble well worth taking.

It is also likely that we will imminently be announcing the signings of Austrian box-to-box midfielder Konstantin Kerschbaumer and potential club record signing Danish international defender Andreas Bjelland who is expected to arrive from FC Twente in return for a fee of over two million pounds, a figure that quite frankly I still struggle to get my head around when talking about Brentford,

Of course we are now entering another stratosphere and if we have done our homework correctly then players of this ilk will be a massive upgrade on what we have seen previously. I hope also that they will all fit in off the field, engage with supporters and not merely prove to be mercenaries looking for another payday.

We must not expect too much too soon as they will all need time to settle down in a new environment.

We must not lose our sense of identity and community and we should ideally keep a solid British base to the team. This is also where the likes of Kevin O'Connor, who fully understands the history, heritage and tradition of Brentford FC and what it represents, will be truly crucial.

I am not complaining, far from it, as I welcome ambition, progress and evolution, traits we were sadly lacking for decades, but I also recognise that with them come potential problems and we must not throw out the baby with the bathwater.

Given the intelligence and perspicacity of those running the club I doubt that I have anything to worry about, but I am a supporter and that is what fans do!

Interesting times ahead!

Tony Craig – An Appreciation – 5/7/15

There was a universal reaction amongst all Brentford supporters to the news that broke yesterday that captain and inspiration Tony Craig had left the club and returned for yet another spell – his fourth including an earlier loan – to Millwall where he will become team captain.

It was simply one of thanks and gratitude to *TC* for the three years of exceptional service he gave us, as well as pleasure and delight that he will now be given the opportunity to play every week, a privilege that would surely have been denied him if he had remained at Griffin Park.

Tony made his reputation at Millwall as a tough and committed central defender or left back and he led his team to promotion to the Championship. His arrival at Griffin Park in the summer of 2012 for a fee reputed to be around one hundred and fifty thousand pounds was seen as a real coup for the club and Uwe Rösler soon recognised his leadership ability and named him as captain. Tony played a prominent part in our success over the past three years. He was a real and visible presence on the field – you knew that he was in charge and he set a wonderful example as he never knew when he was beaten.

I will always remember him in the pre-match huddle, with jaw set, eyes blazing and with his head bobbing up and down like a metronome as he exhorted his teammates to greater efforts and forcefully reminded them of their personal responsibilities. He made it perfectly clear who was in charge on the pitch and what winning the match meant to the club. Woe betide anyone caught shirking or falling short in his task.

Once the whistle went he was a human dynamo and set a massive personal example. He never gave up or accepted that the cause was lost and that long left leg would sneak out to save the day when all otherwise looked lost. Not the tallest of defenders, he timed his leaps well and won far more than his fair share of aerial challenges.

Most importantly, he read the game brilliantly and could anticipate potential danger and snuff it out before any serious damage occurred. He was indestructible and was rarely injured and shrugged off fearsome assaults that left him covered in blood or cinder rash and would have resulted in lesser men leaving the field. He was our bionic man and a total inspiration.

No wonder that his three seasons saw the club rise to almost unprecedented heights of achievement with a promotion and two appearances in the playoffs to add to his already impressive CV. This was no accident and *TC* played a massive part in ensuring our promotion to the Championship and his central defensive partnership with either Harlee Dean or James Tarkowski was mean and effective.

Tony had played previously in the Championship with Millwall and initially he made a seamless transition to the higher level. He also embraced the club's newfound patient and short passing approach to the game and demonstrated calmness and a previously unsuspected and unseen skill on the ball. His left-footedness provided a much needed balance to the back four and he changed the direction of our attack by pinging any number of accurate long range passes to an appreciative and generally unmarked Jota or Odubajo on the right wing.

Tony started last season well and was consistent and competent and fully earned his contract extension. He made an inspirational return to his old stamping ground where he received a rapturous welcome from the otherwise subdued Millwall fans and he stood up bravely and brilliantly to Millwall's aerial bombardment and helped steady the ship and cement our victory after we had conceded two quick goals.

However as the season progressed a few chinks began to appear in Tony's armour as he came up against a seemingly never-ending series of canny, strong and experienced strikers. He struggled and came out second best in his personal battles against exceptionally talented players like Danny Graham, Grant Holt, Rudy Gestede and Daryl Murphy, looked vulnerable to balls played over the top which forced him to turn and Mark Warburton began to rotate his three central defenders as he sought to establish his best pairing. Tony finally lost his place and fittingly made his last appearance for the club in a thrilling victory over eventual title winners, AFC Bournemouth before being forced to settle for a cheerleader's role on the bench.

That was no place for such a legend and with two new central defenders already having arrived at the club in the last couple of weeks, it was obviously best for all concerned that he was allowed to move on, and it remains to be seen whether similar experienced players like Alan McCormack, Sam Saunders and Jonathan Douglas, like Craig, mainstays of the promotion team, decide to remain at the club and fight for the opportunity to play against increasingly strong competition, or also recognise that their time has time and that our levels of success and progress have overtaken them.

Tony's disciplinary record was also good although he saw red three times during his spell at the club. An assistant referee bizarrely concluded that he had struck Dave Kitson at a crucial stage in that momentous match at Sheffield United, a decision endorsed by our old friend Keith Stroud. Despite video evidence that seemed to exonerate him, Craig received a devastating three-match ban and missed the last two league matches as well as the first playoff game against Swindon. Had he been on the pitch I wonder whether we might have got over the line without recourse to the dreaded playoffs and I am certain that he would have had something to say about Marcello Trotta's fateful decision to take *that* penalty kick against Doncaster Rovers!

He took one for the team with a last man red card against Carlisle and then fell foul of *Mad Madley* when he got on the wrong side of Clayton Donaldson and compounded his error by clutching at his former colleague, conceding a penalty kick and earning an early bath.

The most amazing statistic about Tony is that he never scored – and barely looked like doing so in his three seasons at the club. He came the closest when his rasping long-range effort was brilliantly saved by the Peterborough keeper and a header from a corner against Leyton Orient was blocked on the line. He was also clumsily pulled down by Adam Barrett, earning us a spot kick against Gillingham, otherwise his efforts were invariably high, wide and not very handsome.

He will best be remembered for his heroic defending against Oldham Athletic in Mark Warburton's first match as manager when a swift breakaway from a corner left him alone facing five opponents as they bore down on the home goal, but Tony was calmness personified and saved the day against seemingly insurmountable odds.

Then there was his wide-eyed celebration in front of a jubilant Ealing Road terrace after scoring a perfectly taken and utterly crucial penalty kick, thrashed high into the roof of the net in the Swindon playoff second leg shootout, a feat he repeated in a less frenetic atmosphere last season at Dagenham & Redbridge!

We forgave him for his lack of prowess and threat in front of the opposition goal, we even overlooked the three own goals he scored in his first season at the club, one of them a perfectly placed unstoppable header from a corner which arched beyond the reach of the helpless Simon Moore and gifted Hartlepool an unlikely last minute equaliser at Griffin Park.

Tony Craig epitomises all that is good about professional football. He gave us everything throughout his three years at the club and inspired his teammates to greater heights of achievement. He has returned to his first love and I suspect that he will lead Millwall to promotion – and I will celebrate and raise a glass to him if he does so.

Tony Craig will live long in our memory and I thank him and wish him nothing but joy and success in the future.

Splashing The Cash – 7/7/15

The news that Brentford had broken the two million pound transfer fee barrier when they signed Danish international defender Andreas Bjelland from FC Twente last week shook me to the core, as I am sure it did every other long-established Bees fan, brought up as I was supporting a club with a well-deserved reputation for caution and parsimony in the transfer market.

This is the club that in recent times eagerly snatched the money on offer for star strikers such as John O'Mara, Andy McCulloch, Dean Holdsworth, Nicky Forster and DJ Campbell and *replaced* them instead with cheap nonentities and journeymen like Stan Webb, Lee Holmes, Murray Jones and Calum Willock. Oh, and in Nicky Forster's case the stupendously idiotic decision was taken not to replace him at all.

That was then and this is now as the Bees have in the last year paid three transfer fees in excess of a million pounds for Moses Odubajo, Jota and the aforementioned Bjelland and I suspect that there is more to come too.

In order to highlight just how much our approach towards investing in emerging young talent has changed since Matthew Benham took over control of the club, it is illuminating to look back over the past century and see how our record transfer fee gradually and slowly increased in value with a few blips along the way.

Middlesbrough was the first club to pay a four-figure sum for a player in 1905 when they signed Alf Common from Sunderland. Brentford took twenty years to match them when they invested one thousand pounds, or forty thousand pounds at today's equivalent value, on centre forward Ernie Watkins from Southend. This was rightly seen as a massive sum for an impoverished and struggling club, but the gamble paid off as the threat of re-election was averted and he scored a club record twenty-four goals in the following season.

The wonderfully named fullback, Baden Herod, cost fifteen hundred pounds from Charlton three years later but Harry Curtis quickly cashed in on him when Spurs offered four thousand pounds for him in 1929, or one hundred and seventy-seven thousand pounds at today's value.

Despite Brentford's meteoric rise in the mid-to-late 1930's the highest fee paid at that time by Harry Curtis was a mere six thousand pounds to Hearts for star striker Dave McCulloch, or just under three hundred thousand pounds in today's figures. He also provided massive value for money, scoring ninety times for the club in three years and playing for Scotland, before surprisingly being sold to Derby County for a fee of nine and a half thousand pounds – a sum not far short of the then British record transfer fee.

So even at the time of Brentford's greatest success, money still talked and our star asset was sold and then not properly replaced. How many times since then have we seen that self-same scenario repeat itself?

Jackie Gibbons and Ron Greenwood were brought in soon after the Second World War for eight and nine thousand pounds respectively and both were fine players, and the five-figure barrier was finally broken in 1952 with the astonishing signing of the legendary centre forward Tommy Lawton for an eye-watering sixteen thousand pounds from Notts County.

Lawton had scored almost a goal per game in twenty-three England internationals, but at thirty-two years of age he was well past his best. He was still a massive attraction though and the chance to watch a fully-fledged star saw gates soar, with thirty-one thousand watching his home debut against Swansea. He performed decently on the pitch and became player-manager before a decline set in and he resigned before making a surprise return to the First Division with Arsenal.

Relegation back to the Third Division in 1954 saw the beginning of a near-decade of austerity where the club, particularly under the astute management of Malcolm MacDonald relied upon a conveyor belt of local youngsters and cheap imports from junior football in MacDonald's native Scotland and transfer fees were a rarity. Despite the lack of investment he twice almost led his team back into the Second Division but fell just short, and with the end of the maximum wage and money in short supply a weakened and depleted squad dropped into the bottom division in 1962.

New Chairman Jack Dunnett blew out the cobwebs around Griffin Park and determined to spend in order to buy the club back to respectability and perhaps also see his political ambitions benefit from the reflected kudos. An all-international forward trio of Johnny Brooks, Billy McAdams and John Dick supported by other expensive purchases in John Fielding, Matt Crowe and Mel Scott, reversed the slump and saw the Fourth Division title won in 1963 with a massive ninety-eight goals scored.

John Dick became Brentford's record signing when we splurged seventeen thousand five hundred pounds on the experienced thirty-two year old Scottish international forward who had been West Ham's top scorer in Division One just the year before. The football world was bemused at how the Bees had managed to persuade Ron Greenwood to sell him and suspected that the old-boy network had come into play, but the West Ham manager knew that he had a young converted wing half called Geoff Hurst ready and waiting in the reserves to fill the vacancy upfront! Whatever happened to him, I wonder?

Over sixty thousand pounds had been spent in the transfer market in order to build a team that won promotion back to the Third Division and the spending did not end there, as within the next eighteen months additional major signings such as Dai Ward, Mark Lazarus, Allan Jones, Chic Brodie, George Thomson, Jimmy Bloomfield, Joe Bonson, Billy Cobb and Ian Lawther took the total expenditure on players since Dunnett took over to a sum in excess of one hundred and fifty thousand pounds, a figure that would have been significantly increased if an audacious forty thousand pound bid for former international striker Gerry Hitchens, now playing for Torino, had been accepted.

Brentford had gone from famine to feast and to put all this expenditure into context, Dunnett spent the equivalent at today's prices of over two million pounds on transfer fees, predominantly on a series of undoubtedly talented but in the main, experienced players whose best days had long since gone and who had little or no resale value. Indeed we did not recoup our investment on any of the players that he brought into the club. He gambled on getting the club back into the Second Division but after a narrow miss in 1965 an appalling decline saw the Bees back in the bottom division in 1966.

His gamble had failed, these were the economics of the madhouse and it was a policy that came within a whisker of destroying the club in 1967 when, scenting blood, QPR mounted an abortive takeover bid. Disaster was narrowly averted but we were holed beneath the waterline and the next few years after Dunnett decamped to Notts County saw budgets slashed, squad numbers reduced and austerity rule. With priority naturally given to paying off the now massive debt, transfer fees would become a distant memory for the foreseeable future.

The fallout from the QPR affair in 1967 left Brentford in a parlous financial position which resulted in a series of drastic cuts and the adoption of the new motto – *Economy with Efficiency*. Attendances had plummeted, sponsorship, hospitality and merchandising revenues were unheard of and non-existent and we relied totally on the income generated from gate money, director loans and the begging bowl.

Multi-tasker supreme, Jimmy Sirrel, took on the unique role of Manager/Coach/Trainer/Scout and was left with a squad of thirteen players with no reserve or junior teams. Balding striker Dennis Edwards did become the club's first ever loan signing but when we tried to make his move permanent, Portsmouth's asking price of five thousand pounds was far too rich for us and he joined Aldershot instead.

Stringent economies ensured that the overall debt was slowly whittled down and with the side struggling for results and reeling from the body blow of losing to non-league Guildford City in the FA Cup, twelve thousand pounds was scraped together to bring in Ron Fenton and Allan Mansley – a sum recouped when John Docherty was sold to Reading. The priority was simply survival with results on the field of far less importance.

1968/69 saw the emergence of Mansley as our own version of George Best and bigger clubs began to take notice of him. A large fee was in prospect before opponents, outclassed by his pace and effervescence slowed him down the only way they could, by kicking him, and he was never the same player again. George Dobson was another promising youngster whose career was blighted by injury after looking like he had a bright future.

A run to the Third Round of the Football League Cup raised spirits and put some cash into the coffers and with another injury crisis looming, ten thousand pounds was found from somewhere to bring in Arsenal winger Gordon Neilson. He had played at the top level and was tricky and a goal threat but he failed to establish himself and did not stay long at the club. Not the best use of the funds made available.

The cuts were having a beneficial effect with an eighteen thousand pound profit achieved, but at a cost given that Brentford entered the new decade still boasting a squad of only fourteen players. We might have been short in numbers but with the likes of Jackie Graham, Chic Brodie, Gordon Phillips, Alan Hawley, Bobby Ross and Peter Gelson, we were long in character, loyalty, grit and determination.

Things slowly improved on the pitch under a talented manager in Frank Blunstone, with promotion just missed in 1970, a wonderful run to the fifth round of the FA Cup the following year and then a return to the Third Division in 1972.

The Man From Uncle, former manager Billy Gray's young nephew, John Richardson, raised a welcome ten thousand pounds when he left for Fulham and twelve thousand pounds was invested in the elegant Roger Cross, he of the white boots, long throw and venomous shot, who more than justified his fee and was eventually sold for thirty thousand pounds, again to Fulham, who were happy to pick off our best players.

But old habits died hard when, despite scoring freely throughout a massively successful loan spell, the directors were content to allow Alex Dawson to return to Brighton when personal terms could not be agreed with the burly striker – a short-sighted decision in the extreme, although one which perhaps paved the way for John O'Mara to join the club later that same season.

Stewart Houston was well known to Frank Blunstone from their time together at Chelsea and the fifteen thousand pounds invested in him, a massive sum that was only raised with difficulty and after much discussion, was entirely justified when he moved back from striker to full back and was signed by Manchester United in December 1973 for a club record fifty thousand pound fee and he went on to play for Scotland.

Brentford also hit the jackpot when the board decided to back manager Frank Blunstone's judgement and paid an initial seven hundred and fifty pounds – chicken feed even by Brentford's standards – on a tall, raw striker playing for Wimbledon in the Southern League. John O'Mara took time to settle down and initially looked awkward, clumsy and ungainly, but the ugly duckling turned into a swan by dint of his own hard work and Blunstone's coaching ability.

His ability to hang in the air combined with his power and subtle skills on the ground led to a twenty-seven goal season and promotion back to the third tier. Instead of investing for the future, the board reverted to type and a few weeks into the next season, just as the Bees looked like they were beginning to find their feet in the new division, O'Mara was ludicrously sold to fellow Third Division Blackburn Rovers for a paltry fifty thousand pounds, much to the dismay of manager and supporters alike – a disastrous and myopic decision that set the club back years, particularly when his replacement, Stan Webb, signed for a not insignificant ten thousand pounds, despite a decent goalscoring record at his former clubs, Middlesbrough and Carlisle, proved to be a total damp squib.

With relegation looming on the horizon the board finally relented and paid around twenty-five thousand pounds to bring back Roger Cross and sign tricky winger Barry Salvage from QPR, too little – too late as the Bees fell straight back down to the bottom division and were almost forced to seek re-election the following season. Money was found to sign Dave Simmons, Willie Brown and Terry Johnson who all did well for the club, although Brown was mystifyingly sold to Torquay at a time when he was still scoring freely for the Bees.

But otherwise the chequebook was firmly locked away as austerity ruled again at Brentford in the mid-70's until new manager John Docherty arrested the rot and a club record twenty-five thousand pounds was lavished in March 1976 on Andy McCulloch, an injury ravaged striker from Oxford United suffering from bad knees.

It took almost a year to get him properly fit but Andy eventually proved to be a talismanic signing as he formed a deadly fifty-eight goal *Little and Large* partnership with Steve Phillips – himself a four thousand pound giveaway from Northampton Town. McCulloch was eventually sold for a club record fee of sixty thousand pounds to Jack Charlton's resurgent Sheffield Wednesday team, a figure that was ridiculously low for a player of his ability, and far less than Wednesday were actually prepared to pay for him if the Bees, as always, happy to cash in, had negotiated far harder than they apparently did.

Bill Dodgin built a team that won promotion in 1977/78 through playing exuberant and entertaining attacking football. He had a real eye for a player and built his team for a song. Playmaker Dave Carlton cost a mere three thousand pounds, stalwarts Paul Shrubb and Doug Allder were free transfers and only Len Bond (eight thousand pounds), Barry Tucker (ten thousand pounds) and Pat Kruse (twenty thousand pounds – a club record fee for a defender) cost real money.

The sale of goal machine, Gordon Sweetzer for thirty thousand pounds to Cambridge United midway through the promotion season, went a long way towards balancing the books, but we shrugged off his loss and maintained our impetus.

Chairman Dan Tana was prepared to support his manager and as the Bees struggled to cope with the higher level Dodgin was permitted to make a record double transfer swoop with fifty-eight thousand pounds being spent on defender Jimmy McNichol, who cost a new club record fee of thirty-three thousand pounds from Luton Town, and striker Dean Smith from Leicester City. McNichol was a tough defender with a powerful long-range shot who performed consistently over a number of years at the club but Smith flattered to deceive, never made the most of his abundant talent, fell out with Dodgin's replacement, Fred Callaghan and eventually died tragically young in 2009.

The loss of McCulloch was a serious blow as he was bizarrely replaced by Lee Holmes, a part-timer from Enfield who unsurprisingly never really looked the part and it was not until March 1980 that the chequebook came out again and the club record was smashed when striker Tony Funnell arrived from Gillingham for a massive fifty thousand pound fee. Funnell was the total antithesis to McCulloch as he was small and nippy and found space in crowded penalty areas, but he was a strange choice by a manager now under pressure for results. Funnell struggled initially although he scored the winning goal on the last day of the season that ensured survival.

Many thanks to Mark Croxford and Paul Briers for their help in jogging my memory and providing me with crucial facts regarding our record signings over the ages.

Get Him Off! – 11/7/15

There have been a lot of comments over the past few days on the main fans' message board, *The Griffin Park Grapevine,* regarding the players who we loved to hate – the ones who came in for regular and vituperative abuse whatever they did on the pitch, good or bad.

Personally I can't abide any of our players being subjected to constant and systematic criticism from so-called Brentford supporters. What's the point of it, it only encourages the opposition and barracking is hardly going to inspire the recipient to redouble his efforts and perform better.

I can understand the odd harsh or unsavoury comment slipping out in the heat of the moment if a player is guilty of committing a particularly flagrant error – an open goal spurned, a soft goal conceded, after all football is a game of heated emotions, but anything more sustained is unnecessary, uncalled for, unhelpful and totally unacceptable.

Given the quality of all the players currently at the club and their obvious and total commitment to the cause, I would be absolutely flabbergasted if anyone was to suffer any abuse next season but I'm afraid that I cannot say the same about a small minority of our players from previous years who were either less technically or physically gifted and suffered at the hands of a minority of the crowd who were not prepared to give them the benefit of the doubt and forgive them for their perceived inadequacies.

So why were certain players singled out for abuse? Generally because it was felt that they were not up to the requisite standard, a pretty tough verdict given that we have had to endure a plethora of average (or worse) journeymen over the years given our regular shortage of funds, or, more unforgivably, a perceived lack of commitment when a player who generally possessed a decent level of ability was thought not to have been putting in sufficient effort or demonstrating enough passion for the game.

To put things into context, I was fortunate enough to play at a reasonable standard of football as a teenager and sometimes came up against opponents who had played in the Football League and can therefore testify from personal experience that there is a vast chasm between the ability of decent amateurs and actual professionals, so it has to be accepted that anyone fortunate enough to have pulled on a Brentford shirt must have been a pretty decent footballer by anyone's standard.

Having given that caveat I have cast my mind back pretty much as far back as it goes regarding all things Brentford – about fifty years or so – and here are some of the players who were given a particularly hard time by the supporters.

Firstly though I vaguely recall one of my earliest games which saw a thumping five-nil home defeat to a rampant Bristol Rovers team inspired by an Alfie Biggs hat trick. This was an abject Brentford performance best summed up by an own goal of appalling violence from central defender Mel Scott with a diving header perfectly placed into the roof of his own net. The boos echoed across the rapidly emptying stadium as the whole team got it in the neck for a performance of total incompetence and lack of effort and as a highly impressionable young boy I probably joined in.

Keith Hooker was a chunky young midfielder who failed to establish himself in the team soon after the 1967 financial crisis, when by necessity many youngsters were thrown into the deep end and unfortunately not all of them managed to swim. Hooker did manage to score a freak winning goal with a sliced cross from way out on the left wing against Notts County, a feat greeted with laughter and sheer incredulity by disbelieving fans who had already cruelly made it clear that for all his willing running they did not believe that he had what it takes to make the grade.

Stan Webb was the unwitting replacement for departed hero John O'Mara. It would have been an uphill task for anyone to replace such a legend and he got off to an unlucky start when he fell foul of the rugged Dick Renwick on his debut and was carried off. Things could surely only get better for him but they really didn't and he became the butt of the fans' displeasure. His career at Brentford never took off but as soon as he returned to his native North East the goals started flowing again. Perhaps a bit more patience might have borne fruit as Stan proved to be a regular marksman at every other club that he played for except Brentford.

Barry Lloyd was a skilful midfielder brought in by Bill Dodgin after spells at Chelsea, Fulham and Hereford. He had played under his new manager at Craven Cottage where he had scored a memorable televised volleyed goal against Leicester's Peter Shilton. Barry scored on his debut against Northampton but for all his subtle skills he never won the approval of the masses that barracked him relentlessly.

Maybe he appeared to be too laid back in his approach and he certainly wasn't as tough in the tackle as Jackie Graham, but few were. Perhaps his Fulham past went against him too? I was saddened because I used to play cricket with him sometimes for Hayes and knew just what a decent man he was but his spell at Griffin Park was short.

Lee Frost was a real enigma. He had a wonderful loan spell in 1978 as a marauding winger who terrorised opponents with his pace. Two years later he signed on a permanent basis and was switched up front to partner Gary Johnson. Not a good move as he appeared to be a totally different player who was languid, easily knocked off the ball and peripheral to the action. The crowd reacted accordingly as they had high hopes and expectations for him which were sadly unrealised.

Inexperienced young keeper Paul McCullough was unfairly thrown into the fray when Fred Callaghan fell out with first choice, Len Bond and his performances were riddled with costly errors. He did his best even though he was well out of his depth and he earned the nickname *The Kamikaze Kid* for his reckless bravery but it was a blessing for all concerned when he was taken out of the firing line after the welcome arrival of Dave McKellar.

Keith Bowen was another lightweight striker who struggled to make an impact and earned the constant wrath of the home fans. Yet away from Griffin Park and the hectoring voices he could appear a different player and on one memorable night at Swindon he tore their defence apart and was totally unplayable. A lesson maybe for supporters to be more patient and perhaps avoid self-perpetuating prophecies.

Graham Wilkins also failed to live up to expectations and never really cemented his place after arriving from Chelsea and was not well treated by fans who expected more from a player with top-level experience.

Ian Bolton was a similar case. A player who had been an inspiration at Watford and who was expected to steady the ship at Griffin Park. He proved to be an utter disappointment and the fans felt let down by him given his pedigree.

Tom Finney was a tough tackling midfielder who was subjected to loud barracking when his own supporters reacted vehemently to his performance against Bishops Stortford in an FA Cup tie when he was seen to be needlessly aggressive in a match long since won, and he was soon on his way.

George Torrance and Steve Butler were both bought out of the army and initially neither really adjusted to the pace of league football. Torrance tried hard but was out of his depth but Butler's languid style did not impress and he lost what few friends he had made amongst supporters when his errant penalty kick ended up closer to the corner flag than the goal. Neither stayed long although Butler, like many before and after him, emerged as an exceptional lower league striker, but not of course with us.

Ian Holloway was another who impressed on loan but who looked a different player when signed on a permanent basis. He was peripheral and anonymous in midfield and received terrible stick from frustrated supporters. Later it became known that he was suffering from glandular fever at the time and also had serious family problems to deal with. No wonder he was distracted and he recovered his appetite and form soon afterwards, but not at Griffin Park.

Wayne Turner arrived from Coventry for an eye-watering thirty-five thousand pound fee and was immediately made captain by Frank McLintock. Again, I believe that our hopes were falsely raised as for that money we expected a Maradona rather than a ball winner with limited passing ability or creative vision.

Experienced striker David Geddis also had a short loan spell at the club and his inept performance against Middlesbrough when he missed any number of clear chances did not endear himself to his new supporters and he was soon on his way.

Eddie May had the thankless task of replacing Andy Sinton and also had the millstone of a record fee on his back when he arrived from Hibernian. He had skill in abundance but did not take games by the scruff of his neck and he appeared hangdog and hesitant. His body language was negative in the extreme and he scampered back over the border as fast as he possibly could.

All Brentford supporters of a certain age are already well aware of the details of the Murray Jones fiasco so I will not take up any more of your time by repeating the story of that entire sad and sorry episode that cost us so dear.

Given the subject matter of this article, all I would say at this point is that given how utterly appalling the hapless striker turned out to be, he was treated remarkably gently by the Brentford faithful who were left struggling to come to terms with quite how incompetent the long awaited replacement for departed legend Dean Holdsworth had turned out to be.

I suspect that their silence was caused as much by stunned disbelief at what they were seeing rather than simple good manners. We felt sorry for someone so patently out of his depth.

The same was the case with poor Ashley Bayes who proved to be an accident waiting to happen whenever called upon in our goal. I'm as guilty as everyone else for giving him a hard time when he committed yet another bungling error, punching a cross into his own net whilst seemingly defying the laws of geometry or dropping the ball at the feet of a waiting opponent.

It was hard to take at the time but I now realise that just as had been the case with Paul McCullough before him, the fault really lay with the managers who exposed someone to potential ridicule who was patently unready to play first team football. Something similar happened years later to Clark Masters and we lost a potentially valuable asset far too soon.

Ian Benjamin was yet another non-striking striker with an abysmal goal scoring record. David Webb tried to talk up his ability to hold the ball up and act as a target man but we fans saw straight through this and recognised that we were watching yet another slow, superannuated over the hill journeyman.

Webb appeared to have pulled off a real coup when he persuaded former England Under 21 international Paul Davis to step down to join us. The thirty-three year old midfielder had played over four hundred times for Arsenal and it was expected that he would revitalise our fairly sedate and prosaic style of football. The reality was totally different as Davis found it impossible to adapt to football at the sharp end and could not cope with the culture shock of seeing balls fly over his head rather than being played to his feet.

That being said he gave the impression that he was just going through the motions and never demonstrated any real enthusiasm or relish for the task at hand. It really looked as if he did not want to be at the club and he played a mere five matches for us and eventually departed with the fans' disapproval ringing in his ears. Wrong player – wrong time.

Winger Dean Martin initially looked a tricky customer but never recovered from a nightmare performance one Boxing Day on an icy pitch against Brighton. The Braemar Road side of the pitch was frozen and tricky in the extreme and Martin couldn't keep his feet and suffered accordingly. The supporters got on his back and he soon drifted out of the reckoning. This was a real shame and a waste of a good player, as he possessed real ability.

Leon Townley was a rare Eddie May signing from Spurs but the central defender was awkward, slow and cumbersome, and tried to play football in all the wrong areas. I remember with a shudder Townley struggling in vain to cope with the pace and strength of Barry Hayles who showed him no mercy – neither did our fans who called him *The Dancing Bear* and were not impressed with what they saw.

Goalkeeper Andy Woodman also fell foul of the fans who expected him to be more positive and dominate his area and thought him to be too tentative and reactive. He played out of his skin in the title clincher at Cambridge but otherwise rarely justified his record fee for a goalkeeper of one hundred thousand pounds.

Ron Noades brought in striker Steve Jones on loan from Bristol City with a view to paying an astronomical four hundred and seventy-five thousand pound fee for somebody patently past his best. The fans were up in arms at his below par performances and thankfully the mooted deal was not concluded and the money was not squandered.

Mark McCammon was yet another misfit who cost a significant fee. Despite looking every inch a footballer he signally failed to deliver. He is best remembered for his cataclysmic miss from a free header at Loftus Road, which might have changed our recent history had he scored, as he surely should have done. And yet for all the criticism he faced, he eventually became a sort of anti-hero as fans recognised that he was always giving everything he had and appreciated his efforts even though they knew that he was just not up to scratch.

Eddie Hutchinson was another who eventually gained the grudging respect of the fans who were won over by his relentless energy and passion and were able to overlook his lack of technique. Two other hard tackling midfielders, Jamie Fullarton and Ricky Newman, were not so fortunate or well treated as they were considered to be too aggressive by far as well as distinctly average on the ball.

Darren Pratley was a different kettle of fish as the elegant midfielder on loan from Fulham became a crowd favourite before burning his boats after an unsavoury post-match row with fans after a shambolic defeat at Gillingham.

Homegrown defender Karleigh Osborne took a lot of unfair criticism from impatient supporters who were not prepared to allow him to develop and learn from his mistakes. He eventually won them over but it was an uphill struggle for the talented youngster who understandably moved elsewhere.

Paul Brooker was another who flattered to deceive and throughout his career never did justice to his vast ability. He scored a goal of sheer brilliance after running the length of the pitch at Swindon, but on other days he appeared to be lethargic, disinterested and peripheral to the action. He did not take criticism well either from fans, or indeed, his manager, Terry Butcher, and reacted badly before having his contract cancelled.

That leads onto another point. Fans feel that it's perfectly acceptable for them to have a pop at players, but woe betide the footballer who responds in kind! Unfair – certainly, but that's just the way it is.

Peterborough striker Calum Willock was brought in at the last moment to replace the prolific DJ Campbell but never looked the part as our promotion drive petered out at the last hurdle. He never provided any real goal threat, proved to be a total waste of money, and the fans were, to say the least, not happy with the quality of his contribution.

John Mackie also never lived up to expectations after being brought in by Terry Butcher and being immediately named as captain. He had been inspirational at Leyton Orient but the spark had been extinguished, he looked old before his time and he did not last long at Brentford – another Ian Bolton, perhaps?

Given the quality of player brought in over the past few seasons and the success we have achieved over that period, perhaps constant barracking of players will become a thing of the past and it is hard to remember anyone receiving regular criticism under the regime of either Uwe Rösler or Mark Warburton, except perhaps for Niall McGinn who sometimes tried supporters' patience with some tentative displays.

What It Is Like To Be Booed – A Player's View – 16/7/15

I wrote a couple of articles recently that, slightly tongue-in-cheek, recalled some of our former players who we loved to hate – or maybe more accurately – hated to love. In response I received many suggestions of a whole raft of other players, many thankfully long since forgotten, who had also earned the displeasure of my fellow Brentford supporters and, as a result, got it in the neck.

One key question that bugged me and remained unanswered was how does it feel as a footballer to be booed, barracked and abused from the terraces, particularly by your own so-called supporters?

Does it inspire you to greater heights in order to try and stuff the critical words back down the throats from whence they came, or do players retreat into their shell and play less expansively, more cautiously and try to eliminate risk from their game determined not to make another mistake that could bring about even more criticism?

I decided to ask former Bee Richard Poole for his view on this contentious subject, as I thought that his opinion would be particularly apposite given that he played for the club during the early to mid-70s, an era when Brentford FC was not blessed with a plethora of talent and, with budgets stretched, generally had to make do and mend with whatever combination of players could be scraped together. Performances were inconsistent to say the least and veered from one extreme to another, and the fans were not slow to express their wrath and disapproval at some of the substandard fare that they were forced to endure.

Here is what Richard had to say:

I was really interested in your comments about Stan Webb as I watched him particularly closely during his spell at Griffin Park given that we both played in the same position. I really felt sorry for him as he was onto an absolute hiding to nothing from the moment he signed for us. His move turned out to be a poisoned chalice as he had the near impossible task of replacing a living legend in John O'Mara.

The fans were furious at the lack of ambition shown by the club when they sold him just after we had won promotion and saw poor Stan simply as a cheap replacement. They certainly took their frustration out on him. I thought that he was a good influence around the club and he was really not a bad player at all by the standards of the time. He had scored goals regularly in the Second Division at both his previous clubs and given half a chance I am sure that he could have done the same for the Bees.

I remember that he would stay behind with us apprentices for extra training in the afternoon and give us some advice, but maybe he was too nice and sensitive a person which can be a bad failing for a footballer, whatever division you play in.

He was strong and could certainly mix it but he was affected by the constant barrage of criticism he was subjected to, his performances suffered and he lost confidence, which made him play even worse – a vicious circle.

Given more time and a more sympathetic response from the Brentford supporters I am sure that he would have done much better at the club and he must have been delighted and seen it as suitable revenge when he scored a crucial goal against us after he had moved on to Darlington, where, of course, he regained his touch and confidence and became a regular goal scorer again!

I also experienced some very harsh comments from Brentford supporters when I came back to play in a reserve game for Watford a couple of months after I had left Griffin Park. My parents were watching the game in the stands and were really upset by all the abuse I received. It was so bad that some of my new teammates asked me what on earth was going on. The supporters who were giving me such a hard time lived really close to my family and that was very upsetting.

There was certainly no love lost between Brentford and Watford supporters, but I needed a job, Brentford had released me, which almost broke my heart, and Watford were now the team putting the food on my table and enabling me to support my young wife.

I have far happier memories of turning out for the Bees and being roared on by our loyal fans, something that always inspired me! I stayed a year too long at my beloved Brentford and in my last season I only seemed to be selected to play in tough away games at the likes of Tranmere Rovers and Northampton Town when we had players out injured or sick and had very little chance of winning.

You do hear all the comments from the crowd, good and bad, particularly when there are not too many supporters in the ground, and it certainly has an effect on your game. When I first came into the side as a youngster my concentration was exclusively on the game to such an extent that I really only heard the crowd noise when there was a lull in play just before a corner or free kick.

I do remember an important home game against Colchester United at Easter on a Tuesday evening with Griffin Park full to the brim with almost seven and a half thousand fans packed inside. I was waiting for a corner kick to be played into the penalty area and I heard a voice behind the goal shouting, "Come on Richard!" This really got through to me, inspired me, and made me feel ten feet tall. I looked straight at him and saw that it was an old school friend of mine and it seemed just like yesterday when we were in class – or detention together!

As for being booed by away fans, that was fine with me as it simply meant that I must be doing my job properly and getting something right! I clearly remember a game at Lincoln in April 1975 when I came on at halftime to replace fellow striker, Micky French (so much class but there was something missing) to partner Roger Cross up front. I remember we grabbed an unexpected draw against one of the division's top teams with Roger scoring the equaliser. Well afterwards in the bar their centre half, the massive Sam Ellis came up to me and told me that I had always been a handful against them and even apologised for marking me so hard! He said all this right in front of my manager at the time, John Docherty, and given what a tough competitor Sam Ellis was, that made me feel really proud of myself.

I suppose that's why the following Tuesday Mr. Docherty put me straight in the side up front with both Micky and Roger in an end of season game against Southport. But he took me off at halftime and replaced me with a defender in Alan Nelmes! That really hurt and upset me and it was my last official game for the Bees. I suppose it was easier to take off an eighteen-year-old in his first year as a professional rather than a more established player who might have given his manager a hard time about his decision.

Going back to far happier times, I do so remember scoring that goal of mine against Bradford City at Griffin Park. I saw everyone standing up and applauding and for me it was like there were thousands and thousands of fans cheering me on and supporting me, and even now, over forty years later, writing this sentence I am getting goosebumps just thinking about that magic and unforgettable moment.

I got almost as much pleasure making goals for others, something that I think I was quite good at, but it's true, when you are a local boy and you are encouraged and cheered on it gives you such a boost.

I can only remember that horrific reserve match for Watford against Brentford when I was booed and it really affected my game. I also played in that remarkable match against Brentford for Watford at Easter at home when (thanks to Paul Priddy) we somehow lost and also missed those two penalty kicks. I wasn't booed that day, maybe because Brentford won!

"Ahead Of The Game" – Book Review – 19/7/15

Many apologies for the blatant self-promotion but I hope that you all can forgive me for enclosing this wonderful review of **Ahead Of The Game**, which was written by Tim Street – obviously a really talented and observant book critic – in today's online newspaper **Get West London**.

Many thanks, Tim for your kind and perspicacious words! I am really knocked out by them.

Brentford blogger documents a season to remember!

BY TIM STREET

New book covers Bees' most exciting season in decades – and more is to come

It all started by trying to kill some hours on a flight home from Spain by writing about his favourite football club.

A year later, the end result was a book documenting Brentford's most exciting season in living memory, as they took the Championship by storm and so nearly landed a top flight spot for the first time in 70 years.

Over the course of the season, Greville Waterman, who was, by delightful chance, celebrating his fiftieth year following the Bees, wrote more than two hundred online blogs which he has now put into print with a book, **Ahead of the Game**.

He said: *I was sitting on a plane back from Spain last June with some time on my hands and just started writing, and the words began to flow.*

There weren't any times I struggled for inspiration. Frankly, it was harder to stop writing than start as I wrote over 225 blogs, and nearly 300,000 words, over the course of the season.

My favourite was one I wrote one last December about what Griffin Park means to me and how it has become part of my life, which I am pretty proud of.

As for my least favourite, I could have done without all the articles immediately after Timesgate last February (when the fact that popular manager Mark Warburton would be leaving at the end of the season whether the Bees were promoted or not was leaked to The Times.)

And yes, last season would have been too soon to go up both on and off the pitch, but carpe diem, when the chance comes you need to grasp it and we let it slip. Harsh but true.

If you read **Ahead of the Game**, *you will see that my expectations changed after the Bournemouth away match in August. I was concerned until then, but after we had totally outplayed the ultimate champions on their own turf I knew that we would do far better than establish ourselves.*

I have to confess that on the long drive back from Leeds in February (Brentford won 1-0 at Elland Road) I allowed myself to dream of the promised land of the Premier League – and then Timesgate broke a few days later.

One of the consolations for failing in the play-offs was two more derbies against QPR, relegated from the Premier League, next season, which are bound to bring the memories flooding back for Waterman of his debut season half a century ago – when Brentford's last glory era was coming to an end and years of decline were about to set in.

He said: *My first game was in 1965 as a callow youth, and we beat QPR 5-2. On my second visit we beat them 6-1. I thought Brentford were world-beaters. Not for too long though!*

No other era in the past 50 years can come anywhere close to what we are so privileged to witness now. It's as if someone up there has said to me and others like me "you've suffered so much for so long, now it's your time in the sun."

As for next season, with so many changes on the pitch and behind the scenes, I suspect that it might take us a little time to gel. As long as the players buy into the new coaching team and we retain the amazing team spirit and will to win of last season we will do just fine. Maybe even better than last season as we are certainly bringing in quality players.

But will next season – under the new era of Marinus Dijkhuizen as head coach, with players scouted using, alongside more traditional methods, a ground-breaking stats-based approach – be blogged and documented too?

Waterman added: *I have started writing articles already this preseason, and my blog, BFC TALK, can be found at* **bfctalk.wordpress.com**. *I hope to write a new book the same length next year as I am sure that there will be lots of new material both on and off the pitch.*

"Ahead of the Game", by Greville Waterman, is available in the BFC Superstore and can also be obtained as a paperback or eBook on Amazon. The book is 408 pages long and includes a paragraph of endorsement from Brentford owner Matthew Benham.

The Season Starts Here – 20/7/15

It was a beautiful lazy and sunny Sunday afternoon in Boreham Wood and even the short walk from the car park was hard work in the blistering heat. The sun beating on my back made a mockery of the fact that the football season was fast approaching but despite the sweltering conditions there was a spring in my step if not a song in my heart as Brentford's first preseason friendly in the UK was a milestone that I was certainly not going to miss.

But this was far more than just a mere football match, this was a rite of passage marking the beginning of another nine months' worth of – who knows what, and also the long-awaited opportunity to meet up with lots of old friends and acquaintances, compare suntans, swap tall stories about the happenings of the past couple of months without our regular football fix and look forward with relish and anticipation to what lies ahead of us over the coming season.

Boreham Wood has become a regular fixture on our preseason calendar over the past couple of years and it is always a pleasure to visit this ambitious and friendly club, particularly as their excellent Meadow Park stadium is no more than a relative hop, skip and jump from my North London home.

The afternoon was an enjoyable and successful one as Brentford strolled to a comfortable three – nil victory against a Boreham Wood team which, as always, tried to play positive and pleasing football without exhibiting any killer touch. The presence of the willing but limited Ricky Shakes in the home team, a Brentford regular no more than eight years ago, gave further evidence, if it was really needed, of just how far we have come in the intervening period.

Neither David Button nor Jack Bonham were greatly extended in the Brentford goal with Button's comfortable first half diving save from a long-range Montgomery effort the nearest that either of them came to being brought into serious action.

If truth be told, Brentford did not create too much themselves, but were far more clinical when their opportunities arrived. Andre Gray was a livewire up front, with his pace and movement far too much for his more cumbersome opponents who were left with twisted blood after his sinuous turns. Gray it was who converted from the spot with a shimmy and half stop to deceive the keeper and then a side foot neatly into the corner after Nunn panicked and upended the striker as he was running harmlessly into a blind alley following his air shot in front of goal – shades of Reading at Griffin Park last season when Pritchard seized upon Gray's similar aberration to score our second goal.

Stuart Dallas was a lonely and peripheral figure largely starved of possession on the left wing, but he showed just how lethal he could be when he emerged with assists for the other two goals. First he passed inside, Douglas dummied cleverly, thus creating some space for Jota who needed no second invitation to control the ball and send it searing unerringly into the top corner of the net with a twenty-five yard thunderbolt with, naturally, his left foot.

James Russell was left clutching thin air and the keeper was beaten for a third time on the stroke of halftime when Judge's long diagonal cross was miscontrolled by the hapless Nunn who will surely today be praying for divine absolution after his two ghastly errors and Dallas passed the ball inside for Gray to poke home without fuss from close range.

That completed the scoring although Gray came close to a hat trick when substitute keeper Preston Edwards just managed to block his sharp angled effort at the near post.

The victory and three goals scored were the icing on the cake, and such a comfortable victory even against second-rate opposition will certainly help to boost confidence, but what really mattered and was the subject of close scrutiny from the Brentford masses in attendance was the quality of their team's performance, the formation employed and the players who took part.

After a slow start Brentford gradually captured their rhythm, kept possession well and calmly played the ball around the back four whilst probing for openings. Surprisingly the two left footers Bjelland and Barbet formed the first half central defensive partnership with Bjelland looking completely comfortable on the right hand side whilst Barbet was strong and positive on the left.

It is far too early to make any sort of accurate prediction concerning the makeup of the team for the first league fixture on the eighth of August but in my initial analyses of all the potential permutations I was fully expecting that Bjelland and one of Tarkowski or Dean would probably get the nod in central defence against Ipswich next month, but yesterday changed my thinking as it was plainly evident that Bjelland and Barbet could also play together given that Bjelland was more than happy to use his right foot.

Yennaris and Bidwell were efficient if largely untroubled at fullback. Diagouraga sat in front of the back four allowing Douglas to move forward and they dovetailed well and used the ball effectively. Jota and Dallas hugged the touchline, with Jota encouragingly showing as much energy in defence as he did in the opposition half of the field and Judge was given a free role acting as the playmaker feeding the bullets for Gray.

Practically an entirely new team took the field for the second half and the new back four of Odubajo, the freshly clean-shaven Dean, O'Connell and McCormack was barely tested with Moses offering us a welcome attacking outlet when he overlapped menacingly.

Diagouraga and McEachran played as a screen in front of the defenders and Josh still looked a pace behind the others but gradually grew into the game. Jota and the lively Courtney Senior played out wide with Kerschbaumer operating from box to box and Gray up front. The Austrian looked an excellent addition to the squad with his nonstop running and energy as well as his good touch on the ball.

The fun started with twenty minutes to go when the three players remaining from the first half, Diagouraga, Jota and Gray wearily left the field after a job well done. Tarkowski went into an unfamiliar holding midfield role and Aaron Greene replaced Jota but the referee refused to allow the already substituted Yennaris to return to the field and Brentford were forced to play out the match with ten men, gaining experience for a situation that hopefully they will rarely find themselves in throughout the course of the forthcoming season.

The Bees took up a 4-2-3-0 formation, which, with the pacy Greene valiantly attempting to fill two gaps and play right wing and centre forward simultaneously, looked strangely symbolic and symptomatic of our current struggle to fill the striker role adequately. With the recent sale of Will Grigg to Wigan, a decision with which I totally concur, Andre Gray is pretty much the only striker left at the club barring a few promising youngsters who are not yet considered to be in the first team reckoning.

It is far too early to start panicking as I am sure that there is frenetic activity going on behind the scenes to fill the gap but I am also well aware of how hard it is to acquire strikers of the requisite standard at a realistic and reasonable cost. Brentford also play with only one genuine striker, which is a difficult role to master, so it is essential that the correct decision is made about who we eventually bring in, both as potential first choice and as cover.

Even more worrying have been the rumours that refuse to go away regarding the possibility of Gray leaving for pastures anew. Who knows if it is necessary for us to sell any of our prize assets in order to keep within the draconian requirements of Financial Fair Play and, if that is, indeed, the case, we will only sell from a position of strength and ensure that our valuations of players are met before they leave the club, and anyone leaving will also be replaced. The potential loss of Gray, in particular would create a massive problem given the lack of an obvious replacement. At this point last season we had already acquired Gray and Scott Hogan and we eventually found our third striker, Nick Proschwitz, immediately before the first game of the season.

Football supporters are never happier than when they have something to worry and moan about so I make no apologies for focusing on a potential problem as well as highlighting the many positives that came out of yesterday's match.

Football is back and all is well with the world!

Jonathan Douglas – Will He Stay Or Will He Go? – 22/7/15

There have apparently been some unsubstantiated rumours flying around over the last day or so suggesting that Brentford might be prepared to allow midfielder Jonathan Douglas to leave the club and find a new home. As of yet I have neither seen nor heard anything that fully convinces me that there is any truth in this suggestion, but sometimes there is no smoke without fire and it has got me thinking about the player and how much of a role he is likely to have at Griffin Park next season.

Firstly let's look back at his contribution over the past four years. It can simply be summed up in one word – *massive*.

Uwe Rösler persuaded him to leave Swindon Town, where he had spent a couple of successful seasons, been voted Player of the Year and was an established member of the team, in order to spearhead his new project at Brentford. Swindon fans reacted to his departure with vitriol and fury, just as they were to do subsequently when Alan McCormack and loanee Alex Pritchard also joined us after spells at the County Ground. We simply cherry picked their best players by convincing them that there was a far better future to be had at Griffin Park and subsequent events have proved us right.

Douglas has played over one hundred and sixty games for us, averaging over forty appearances per season and when fit has been an automatic first choice selection under both Rösler and his successor Mark Warburton. Not bad for a Bosman free transfer. He is perhaps best remembered for his crucial last minute headed goal against Oldham which gave Mark Warburton a winning start in his first match as Brentford manager, took away any uncertainty that might otherwise have crept in, and ensured that our promotion challenge remained on track. In fact it is hard to isolate too many individual stand out moments for Douglas as he rather eschewed the spectacular for the massively reliable and consistent.

He was voted Player of the Season by the supporters in his first season at Brentford and also captained the side on many occasions despite his assertion that he did not see himself as a natural leader. He led more by example and became a source of inspiration to his teammates by dint of his swashbuckling and buccaneering performances in midfield which combined non-stop effort and energy, an engine strong enough to cover almost every blade of grass on the pitch, hard tackling, the unerring ability to read the game and snuff out danger as well as an eye for a pass and a goal. He possessed almost every attribute required for a midfield player in today's game, bar pace, but given that the first yard is said to be in the head, he was rarely left trailing, so well did he read the game.

In other words he never accepted second best and was tough on fellow players who fell below his own high standards. He was an alpha male and a powerful presence in the dressing room who was not slow to make his opinions heard and he had strong views that he was quick to express. This trait, I would surmise, did not always make him the most popular player with either management or directors but he was always true to himself as well as being searingly honest.

In his first three seasons at the club he proved that he was amongst the top midfielders in the third tier but doubts remained as to whether he could raise his game and adapt to the challenge and requirements of the Championship. Predominantly a defensive midfielder, did he have the skill on the ball and vision to hold his own against the better players he would be facing at the higher level?

The statistics speak for themselves. In all Jonathan Douglas played four thousand and forty-three minutes last season, more than any other outfield player at the club, and missed only two games, one through suspension, and the other when he was rested to eliminate the risk of a second suspension at a crucial stage of the season. He seemed to be inspired by the challenge and demonstrated a skill on the ball and a subtlety of passing that had previously lain dormant.

As soon as Toumani Diagouraga won his place back into the team Douglas knew that he had someone to watch his back and with the defensive gaps filled behind him, he was given the freedom to advance forward with the ball and he became a potent attacking force, scoring a career high tally of eight goals, including four headers, and assisting on four more. It is rare that a player of his age and experience improves and develops new skills but *Dougie* was the exception that proved the rule.

He made a habit of sneaking late and generally unmarked into opposition penalty areas where he found pockets of space and he should really have notched an unprecedented double figure goal tally given the opportunities that fell his way. His confidence was boosted by a wonderfully taken goal against Crystal Palace in preseason with a perfectly placed curling effort that proved that he was far more than a mere destroyer. He became more flamboyant and ambitious on the ball attempting any number of subtle flicks in and around the opposition penalty area that sometimes came off and created chances for the likes of Gray and Jota. He made no less than forty-six passes per game with an impressive eighty-two percent accuracy rate.

Perhaps his acknowledged value and indeed, indispensability to Mark Warburton proved to be his undoing. He was played too often and for too long as he missed only two league matches and was taken off early only three times all season. He was overworked and at his age this took its toll. It often seemed in the latter part of the season that the spirit was willing but the flesh was weak as he was just that split second too late to spot an opening or make an interception. Douglas celebrated his thirty-third birthday during the season and given his seniority, I believe that he should have been used more sparingly and that over four thousand minutes of action was too much for him.

I am not carping or criticising as he had a quite exceptional season and proved that he more than belonged at Championship level.

The Middlesbrough playoff matches, however, proved to be an eye-opener as Jonathan gave everything but there was nothing left in the tank and he and Diagouraga were left chasing shadows by the roadrunners Leadbitter and Clayton who combined vision and subtlety on the ball with a level of energy and a dash of ruthlessness that we simply could not match.

They demonstrated quite clearly the gulf between the exceptionally good players that we possess and the real elite at this level and that leads onto where we find ourselves now. It is crucial that we keep improving, raising our standards and enhancing and developing our squad. New players have already arrived with the expectation of more, and stalwarts such as Tony Craig, Sam Saunders and Alan McCormack have sadly begun to be left behind and I suspect that Jonathan Douglas is next on the list. Such is the cruel and inexorable way of football.

All would be fine and good if he was able to reconcile himself to the inevitability of the situation and the fact that given the increased competition for places he is no longer likely to be an automatic choice next season and give us perhaps twenty games of top quality performance. Maybe that is what will happen as the likes of Josh McEachran and Konstantin Kerschbaumer are vying for his position, however I believe that Jonathan is such a competitive and proud individual that he will find it extremely hard if not impossible to accept not playing every week and if that is indeed the case it might well be in everyone's best interests for him to be allowed to move on to another club where he can become the fulcrum of the team and play as often as a player of his stature, experience and talent deserves to do.

I am sure that the truth will be revealed over the next week or so and I find myself rather conflicted by the situation. I fully support the desire to upgrade and have real competition in every position and time waits for no man; however I also worry at the prospect of losing good, solid, proven professionals like Douglas, Craig, Saunders and McCormack as you know exactly what you will get from them. They will fight for the cause with skill and passion, give everything and never accept defeat until the final whistle. I can only hope that our new recruits share their work ethic and will to win.

Such is progress but time will tell.

More Of The Same – But Even Better – 26/7/15

Results in preseason friendly matches can be notoriously misleading but we saw more than enough from Brentford in a comfortable two-nil victory over Premier League Stoke City to be reassured that the transition from Mark Warburton to Marinus Dijkhuizen's leadership will be a seamless one and that the season looming ahead is one to look forward to with relish.

Stoke fielded a team packed with first team regulars with international fullback Glen Johnson making his debut, but they were made to look second best in all departments by a rampant Brentford team which included the rump of last season's team and saw only three of their eight newcomers make the starting eleven.

There were certainly tweaks and improvements to be seen particularly in terms of our set pieces which saw us actually score a goal from a corner, and also in our defensive organisation where we funnelled back in two solid banks of four and denied them space whenever Stoke threatened us. Button made an excellent full length save from Odemwingie's free kick and Walters lobbed narrowly wide with our heart for once in our mouth as an equaliser looked on the cards, but we otherwise kept them at bay and it was the Bees who created the lion's share of the chances.

Andre Gray started upfront in an unchanged 4-2-3-1 formation and he more than held his own against the experienced Ryan Shawcross, using his upper body strength to brush off the challenge of the far bigger man before forcing an excellent tip over save from Butland, and he never gave the visitors' defence a moment of rest. He was well supported by Jota whose seemingly languid approach belied his committed and positive display and he was a constant danger to the unfortunate Cameron who was often left trailing in the Spaniard's wake.

The real surprise came from one of the newcomers. This was our first opportunity to see Andy Gogia, an unheralded signing from the lower reaches of German football who had missed the Boreham Wood match through injury, and we were left boggled and awestruck by his trickery, as were the Stoke defence who could not get anywhere near him. A veritable box of tricks with a constant series of feints and back heels he led them a merry dance, but he was not a show pony, never tried to do too much on his own, and he played with his head up and was always looking to set up one of his team mates.

One piece of defensive work when he tracked back and left Johnson standing with a perfectly executed back heel was worth the price of admission on its own. He too forced a desperate save from Butland before scoring the opener soon after the half hour. He drove infield from the left wing with the ball glued to his right foot and his thirty yarder was on target but hit Shawcross on the edge of his penalty area and the ball arched over Butland in an unstoppable parabola into the roof of the net.

Toumani Diagouraga and the second new signing, Konstantin Kerschbaumer dominated the midfield and after a slow start the Austrian grew into the game and looked the perfect all-energy box-to-box midfielder. He was everywhere on the pitch, winning the ball, running with it and invariably finding a Brentford player with his careful selection of passes. Alan Judge was the spark plug, with a license to roam, and he simply got better and better as the game progressed, showing a real vision with his passing and relishing the freedom he was given to create.

The back four were solid and undemonstrative and played the ball around between them in what we now recognise as the Brentford way of doing things. Moses and Jake Bidwell rampaged up and down the field as auxiliary wingers in support of the elusive Jota and Gogia but never neglected their primary defensive responsibilities and Bjelland and Dean were imperious in central defence. Andreas Bjelland bestrode the pitch like a colossus, always a move ahead of his opponent Walters, always there first to snuff out any danger, calm and serene and skilful on the ball. He went off on the half-hour with a slight strain but had done more than enough to convince us that we have massively upgraded our central defensive resources.

Harlee Dean looked a different player, lean, clean-shaven and re-energised, he relished the extra responsibility of being named captain and the penny seemed to have finally dropped and he simply let his game do the talking. Like many others, I fully expected Harlee to have gone through the exit door by now, but perhaps he has finally realised that this is a truly exceptional club to be with and I hope that he remains to fight for his place as on Saturday's performance it will be hard to leave him out of the team.

Yoann Barbet replaced Bjelland and the young Frenchman wowed the supporters with his strength both in the air and on the ground combined with the unerring ability to find a teammate with his passes. He roared forward on a couple of occasions to support his attack and looked a real danger to the opposition. Barbet is another example of our scouting and analysis department hitting the jackpot and is yet another unknown gem for us to nurture and cherish.

Stoke started the second half on the front foot but we managed to keep them at arm's length before regaining control. The newly arrived Lasse Vibe was given a run out and looked sharp and fit and twice shot narrowly wide. Others also impressed in their cameo roles. Stuart Dallas had a point to prove given the two new forward arrivals and more than stated his own impressive case for selection. Fast and direct he ran past and through defenders, almost set up Judge for a tap-in and then sent a perfect volley screaming into the net after a Judge corner was allowed to bounce in the box and go through a crowd of players congregating at the near post. Dallas is such a clean striker of the ball and adds so much to the team when on the pitch.

Alan McCormack and Nico Yennaris both slotted in as fullbacks late on and it has not gone unnoticed how impressive Yennaris has been in every appearance he has made this preseason. He looks solid and clever on the ball and perhaps he will yet establish himself at the club after looking a near certainty to move on. Jack O'Connell was calm and measured when he came on and the newly arrived Philipp Hofmann gave us something different up front once he replaced Andre Gray. He offered us a focal point and the ball stuck to him as he brought the midfield into play. He also brooked no aggression from the porky looking Charlie Adam who soon backed down when faced by an irate giant German.

Yesterday proved that we have a squad to be reckoned with as well as a plethora of options in every position. The euphoria was slightly tempered by the sad news that Josh McEachran has broken a foot in training and will apparently miss the first three months of action. He will certainly be missed but we have more than enough strength in depth to cope without him in the meantime.

There are still worries that with over five million pounds spent on incoming transfers there might be players leaving to help balance the books. There will also be a number of quality players who will be unable to force their way into the starting eleven. Whether players leave or not will be revealed over the next couple of weeks, but as things stand, the squad has been greatly improved and enhanced both in depth and in quality, the football is as positive and effervescent as ever but there seems also be a massive improvement in our defensive nous, solidity and organisation.

There is still a lot of hard work to be done before the season starts and this was, admittedly, just a preseason friendly and not too much should be read into it, but our future looks bright, our appetite has been whetted, and there is so much for us all to look forward to.

Heroes – 28/7/15

Back in the late 60s and early 70s I used to spend most of my school Summer holidays at Lord's cricket ground where, like many youngsters of a similar age I spent the day not watching the cricket and glorying in the achievements of the stars of the time in the Middlesex team such as Peter Parfitt, John Murray (an ex-Brentford Junior), Mike Brearley, John Price and Fred Titmus but instead, I remained glued all day to the back door of the Members' Pavilion in the hope and anticipation of actually meeting the players in the flesh.

An MCC steward, an ex-military type in full commissionaire regalia would guard the pavilion door seemingly with his life and suspiciously look down his nose at us lest one of us urchins should attempt to enter the hallowed and forbidden ground which was the province of lords and gentry rather than a bunch of ragamuffin kids like ourselves. He would establish a *cordon sanitaire* and we were not allowed to come within a few yards of the entrance in case we obstructed the path of our elders and betters.

Players would come and go throughout the day, some of them would sign our dog-eared autograph books with lordly disdain, others would engage us in a bit of patronising banter and small talk and we would barely manage to stammer our replies so overwhelmed were we that they had actually deigned to speak to us, a few (and one day I shall name and shame them) would ignore us and haughtily push past the beseeching pack of schoolboys as we clamoured for their signature.

One sweltering hot summer morning Lancashire came to town and we boys salivated at the prospect of obtaining the cherished autographs of the likes of stars like Clive Lloyd, Jack Simmons and Peter Lever. They drove into the ground in a convoy of vehicles and we surrounded them in the car park in search of their signatures. One of the players was struggling under the weight of his massive cricket coffin and I instantly zeroed in on him. It was the wicketkeeper, Farokh Engineer, an Indian Test player of massive ability, charm and flamboyance. Wicketkeepers always seem to accumulate more equipment than their teammates and he was desperately looking for some help.

I seized my opportunity and without being asked, I grabbed hold of one end of his case and together we laboriously manhandled it towards the pavilion door where the jobsworth steward awaited us.

He can't come in here he roared with relish as he pointed at me scornfully, and to my undying surprise and pride Farokh said *he's with me and I have invited him in.* Stunned, the steward stood back and I accompanied Farokh inside the holy of holies and together we puffed our way up the stairs to the away dressing room bent double with the weight of his case – now I know where my bad back came from!

I expected to be peremptorily dismissed once we had arrived but instead Farokh sat me down and took the time and trouble to engage me in a long and detailed conversation about myself, my schooling and whether or not I played cricket. He, an established Test player and superstar treated me, a young kid whom he had never met before and would never see again, with interest and as an equal, and I have never forgotten his kindness and encouragement.

Forty-five years or so on, and I still have the pictures that he autographed: *To Greville with Best Wishes from Farokh Engineer* and he inspired me to become a wicketkeeper.

You will not be surprised to learn that to this day Farokh Engineer, now a portly man of seventy-seven years, and long since retired, remains an absolute hero to me and always will do.

As I hope you will understand from that convoluted story, given the example he set and how wonderfully Engineer behaved towards me, since that occasion sportsmen do not earn the sobriquet of hero very easily from me and in fact there is only one other sportsman who has ever come up to the mark.

I have been watching Brentford, man and boy, for fifty years now and however much I have liked and admired so many players there is only one who I would actually class as a hero, and he and the others who come very close to earning that accolade all come from the same era – the late 60s and early 70s, a time when I was still young and impressionable and in those more innocent days I still saw some of the Brentford players in an heroic light.

My first couple of years watching the Bees passed by in a blur, as the players were largely faceless and indistinguishable to me as I was still earning my spurs as a supporter and was not yet able to identify them as the individuals that they were.

Allan Mansley was the first Brentford player who truly stood out to me initially as much for his looks, as he had the long flowing locks and sinuous gait of a George Best, as for his ability. In an era of plebeian mediocrity when players with real flair and talent were the exception rather than the rule – particularly at Brentford, *Ollie* Mansley completely broke the mould. He played with passion and effervescent joy, galloped down the left wing with gay abandon and beat his opponents by virtue of a combination of pace, body swerves, dribbling ability, trickery and the precocity of youth.

He had an *annus mirabilis* in 1968 when he was touched by the Gods and scored goals of every hue – swerving free kicks, rasping volleys, solo runs, clinical angled finishes, even a looping twenty-yard header over a mesmerised Halifax goalkeeper. I followed him with the rapture of a starstruck thirteen year old and he could do no wrong in my eyes and I ached to be as talented and handsome as he was.

However like all the best heroes, his fame was glittering but transitory and short-lived as he was irrevocably hobbled by the thuggery of the pantomime villain, Chesterfield's Keith Kettleborough and never truly recovered his pace and verve and within a year or so he was gone and his career withered on the vine.

Allan Mansley remains a hero to me to this day because he was the first Brentford player who stirred my emotions and made me realise that football was a beautiful art form as well as a sport and that there was room for guile and intelligence as well as organisation and brute strength.

The fact that despite his outrageous ability his career never reached the heights that had once looked likely, was truncated through injury and that he also died tragically young, makes him even more of an heroic figure to me, if a more tragic one. I never spoke to him – I never dared to do so, and can only hope that the man himself lived up to the image. Thankfully I am reliably informed by others who knew him that he was indeed a lovely young man and I am glad to hear so.

There were others of that same long-past generation who I also revered although not to the same extent that I hero-worshipped Allan Mansley. The likes of Chic Brodie, Gordon Phillips, Peter Gelson, Alan Hawley, Alan Nelmes, Jackie Graham, Roger Cross, John O'Mara and Bobby Ross were all talented players who gave the club long, loyal and dedicated service. I admired them all but none moved me as much as *Ollie* had.

Over the years the club has boasted many more players of massive ability and personality including such personal favourites like Francis Joseph and Stan Bowles but as I grew up and the players indeed, became younger than me I knew that the day for heroes had both come and gone and had now long since passed.

As an adult my eyes have been well and truly opened and I see the players for what they are – good honest professionals doing a job, generally to the best of their ability, living separate lives off the field and possessing the foibles, weaknesses and shortcomings of all men.

I know that their loyalty to the club that I have supported for nigh on half a century and will do for the rest of my life, will last for the duration of their stay with us and not a jot longer – and nor should we expect anything else. Brentford, in most cases, is simply a staging post in what they hope will be a long, varied and successful career.

The nearest I came to feeling any different was when we launched *The Big Brentford Book Of The Seventies* four years ago and Dave Lane, Mark Croxford and I invited some of the most popular players from that decade to a launch event at the club and Alan Hawley, Alan Nelmes, Jackie Graham. Peter Gelson, Terry Scales, Pat Kruse, Andy McCulloch, John O'Mara and Paul Bence all graced us with their presence.

They were without exception a delight to be with, reminiscing happily about the club to which they had all devoted so great a proportion of their footballing career. Icons they, and the likes of Kevin O'Connor, most certainly are, but real heroes, in the true sense of the word are thin on the ground and I have only had two sporting heroes and I will be forever grateful to Farokh Engineer and Allan Mansley for providing me with so much joy and inspiration.

It Was Just A Friendly! – 29/7/15

Going to Kenilworth Road is like travelling back to Dickensian times. A horrid, squalid, filthy stadium half hidden amongst the maze of terraced houses, the decrepit Lego-like DIY hospitality boxes strung erratically all along one side of the ground, the ghastly cramped away end with no leg room and that dark, dank, narrow alley behind the stand where you anxiously watch out for Bill Sikes lurking in the shadows.

Luton is never the friendliest or most welcoming of venues and Brentford contributed to the gloom by subsiding to a disappointing two – one defeat in last night's friendly match.

In truth, there wasn't too much wrong with the actual performance with the Bees enjoying plenty of possession, fizzing the ball around comfortably where it didn't really count, but there was a lack of devil, precision and penetration in the final third and when chances were created they were squandered and busy keeper Elliot Justham brought off a series of acrobatic saves to earn a narrow and hard-fought victory for his team.

The goals conceded were sloppy in the extreme. An unopposed simple far post header from a corner by Luke Wilkinson and then, late on, veteran Calvin Zola was allowed to bustle his way, elbows jutting, to the edge of the box and slide a well-placed shot into the corner of the net. Poor defending and perhaps a wakeup call for a Brentford team, which, up to tonight, had been sailing serenely through the preseason with three consecutive clean sheets.

The rump of the squad featured last night but the big guns in Gray, who received a rapturous reception from his former supporters, Judge, Dean, Bidwell, Diagouraga and Jota did not see action until the dying embers of the game and it was a mixed squad which competed for most of the proceedings. Several other likely first teamers such as Button, Kerschbaumer, Odubajo and Vibe were nowhere to be seen.

This game epitomised what preseason matches should be all about, gaining match fitness, shaking out the cobwebs, getting used to playing with new teammates and most importantly, allowing the team management to assess the quality and depth of every member of the squad.

It is generally accepted throughout football, except apparently at Bashley where the manager has already lost his job after some poor preseason performances, that the actual results are of secondary importance.

Nobody likes losing, particularly at lower league opposition but if last night helps us improve our learning curve and some of the weaknesses that were clearly demonstrated are also eradicated before they become costly, then that is fine by me.

I am sure that our complete first team, whatever that is, would have defeated Luton but that would surely have proved little as our new Head Coach needed to see some of the so called lesser lights in action against what turned out to be a more than decent Luton team which played crisp football and pressed and covered like demons. This was a good workout and Dijkhuizen must have been left with much to chew over.

Some of the squad did their prospects no harm but others unfortunately did not fare so well.

Bonham and Smith were relatively untroubled, had no chance with either goal and both looked the part in goal. Yennaris was always involved and overlapped eagerly but he never entirely convinced. I see him as a benchwarmer at best, valuable to have around but unlikely to start. Barbet looked every inch a footballer, calm, composed and powerful with a hint of pace and a real eye for a pass. He looked really at home at left back.

O'Connell played the entire match and did his prospects no harm. He is probably nearer the back of the queue than the front but he looked an exceptional defender in the making with the advantage of being left footed. Tarkowski and Bjelland also each had a decent run out and were under little pressure. Quite who starts at centre half is still an utter mystery to me – a nice problem to have.

Williams is slight with a low centre of gravity but busy and always on the move and looking to bring others into the game. He lacked some sharpness, but this will come. He also came close with a swerving free kick that forced a full length save. I would best describe him as a sleeper, he's not ready to start for us yet but one day, in the not too far distant future, he could well be.

Tebar and McCormack, neither of whom really advanced their case for selection, partnered him in midfield. Tebar was peripheral and lightweight and Alan had one of those nights when he lost touch and concentration and gave the ball away far too often.

Dallas was dangerous when fed the ball but was too often starved of possession and Gogia always looked to be positive and forced a great save from the keeper, however he needed some reminding about his defensive responsibilities.

The Hoff scored his first goal for the club, turning in a Gogia cross with such lack of fuss and economy of effort that the two hundred and forty-two Bees fans scattered behind the goal far away in the Stygian gloom at the other end of the pitch barely realised that the ball had gone in. Hofmann was determined and clever on the ball and always shot on sight. He will be a danger, score goals and create chances for others, but he lacks the dynamism and sheer pace and energy of Andre Gray.

Gray terrorised the opposition and we looked far more potent once he came on. Only a brilliant save denied him a goal with his first touch and he miscontrolled with the goal yawning right at the death.

Yes, the result was disappointing, as were some of the individual performances too but the peripheral squad members all got some valuable match practice and the Head Coach is now surely far closer to deciding who will be included in his first choice starting eleven.

Saturday's team against Norwich will certainly be close to the one that will begin the first game of the season against Ipswich but valuable lessons were learned last night and whilst I hate losing any game this was a mere skirmish – the real battle commences on Saturday week.

Philipp Hofmann after scoring at Luton

Warburton Already Winning Over The Doubters – 30/7/15

I have been talking recently to some Rangers fans who were seeking some background information regarding their new manager, Mark Warburton. I was happy to provide them with an article which set out his managerial style and approach at Brentford last season, which was very much one of positive reinforcement and encouragement and asked them in return to let us know how Mark and David Weir were settling into their new posts in Glasgow.

Jordan Campbell of *The Rangers Report* blog has kindly obliged and provided a fascinating update, which summarises, as if we ever doubted it, just what an impact Mark has already made on the supporters of his new club. Here is what Jordan had to say:

It has been just forty-one days since Mark Warburton was appointed as the fourteenth permanent manager of Rangers Football Club, and just thirty since the heavily depleted squad he inherited returned to the training ground in Auchenhowie for the start of preseason. But last Saturday, his new-look side put on a rampant second-half performance, which could have fooled you into thinking, that he had been implementing his footballing philosophy for a whole lot longer.

Although we are very much in the infancy of his tenure, the last thirty minutes' showing must have proved to the doubters that his Ibrox transformation is well and truly underway. It is far too premature to judge whether he will be a success in the long run (challenging Celtic within two years and then progressing on the European front – not much to ask for) but if I were to grade his report card so far there would be no other option than to give him top marks; he is yet to put a foot wrong.

Since our financial collapse in 2012 we have had to endure three and a half years of torture with the chronic football on the park providing little escape from the drama in the boardroom. However, it seemed like last Saturday finally heralded the start of a new chapter of success as the supporters witnessed the most entertaining ninety minutes of football served up in three seasons.

I was a huge admirer of Warburton's work while he was at Brentford and even earmarked him as a potential candidate for the managerial position as early on as March. His style of play and the bond he had established with the fans, combined with Weir's knowledge of the club made it the perfect partnership in my opinion. But even with high expectations of what he and Davie were capable of, I cannot help but be impressed with how they are managing every aspect of the club whether that be the recruitment, the youth structure or the media.

They were exactly what was needed in our situation: strong figures who wouldn't be fazed by the spotlight or by the fact that they had to imprint their footballing vision from virtually a blank canvas.

It has to be put into perspective just how mammoth the task they faced was – and still is. Having to rebuild every department of the club and ensure that we win promotion, all the while playing a brand of football which will fill Ibrox is no mean feat when you have to face forty-odd thousand expectant supporters every second week. And when I said he had to rebuild every department I really meant it.

When he took charge, the club had just released eleven out of contract players who were part of the side that lost heavily to Motherwell in that humiliating playoff final. That left him with a nineteen-man squad consisting of mainly academy graduates and existing players who had woefully underperformed. There was no scouting system in place whatsoever which meant the board had to trust in his extensive knowledge of the market down south in the hope that he could identify value for money himself.

The club had no footballing identity either. Ally McCoist's long ball tactics and refusal to promote youth players had consigned our modern training facility to a state of redundancy as the conveyor belt of talent lay dormant with no direction or pathway into the first-team.

Warburton has gone about addressing every one of these points in an efficient and diligent manner, which is what the supporters have come to expect from him in the short space of time he has been here.

Eight players have since come through the door but there have been no panic buys. Some managers may have come in and decided that there had to be an entire clear-out but Warburton took the sensible option of assessing the squad for himself before he made wholesale changes. Goalkeeper Wes Foderingham, defenders Danny Wilson, Rob Kiernan and James Tavernier, midfielders Andy Halliday, Jordan Thompson and Jason Holt along with striker Martyn Waghorn have all been brought in while John Eustace trains with the squad hoping to secure a deal.

All of these players have had up-and-down periods so far in their short careers with most of their CV's littered with loan moves around the country. Six of them were plying their trade in League One last season which is why some fans were sceptical of Warburton's recruitment policy, but the vast majority of them showed up really well on their debut which has put to bed some of the initial worries.

But he has been unequivocal in his desire to bring in players who still have years ahead of them to develop. Rangers are no longer in the position where they can spend millions on established internationals, bringing in young, British talent with sell-on value is the only viable option going forward. At a total cost of around seven hundred thousand pounds, the six players he has signed look as if they will go on to represent great value for the club.

Whereas McCoist repeatedly spoke of the need to add "experience", Warburton stresses the need for any signings to "add value" and reiterates the need to keep the core of the squad "young and hungry." This fresh outlook has been exactly what the fans have been crying out for and it was evident on Saturday as the average age of the starting eleven had been reduced to twenty-four compared to twenty-nine in the reverse fixture last year.

He has taken a holistic approach to overhauling the youth department along with the recently appointed Head of Youth Development, Craig Mulholland. Every age group will now play with the exact same system (4-3-3) making the transition for players progressing through the ranks smoother and allowing them to seamlessly slot into the first-team when the time comes.

He has made it abundantly clearly that he has no qualms about putting youngsters in if they are good enough and it seems to have acted as a source of motivation for the Under 20s as they have been flying in preseason, beating senior outfits such as Tynecastle and Arbroath by comfortable margins.

Warburton's handling of the media has been superb so far, but the increased spotlight was never likely to trouble a man who turned over hundreds of millions of pounds per day as a city trader, was it? However, the animosity shown towards Rangers from the majority of Scottish football is at an all-time high and the reaction to the club's pursuit of Hibs midfielder Scott Allan typified the sort of response the club have become accustomed to in recent years.

Rangers had two bids turned down for Allan last Thursday and Friday which saw a BBC journalist question Warburton over the morality of bidding for a player that would be facing his side just a day later – yes, that's right, how immoral of him to bid for a player during the transfer window!

Don't get me wrong, the timing of the bids was clearly tactical as Allan informed Hibs that he wanted to join less than twenty-four hours before the match which prompted manager Alan Stubbs to drop him to the bench. But his handling of the situation has been exemplary, as he has remained calm and dignified, refusing to speak about another club's player when he could have easily taken exception to those questioning the ethics of himself and the club. His open and candid media persona presents a great image of the club.

It is the product on the park that is the main focus though and is ultimately what he will be judged upon. It will inevitably take time for his new style of play to bed in and for the newly assembled squad to gel, but in his first two games there have been clear signs that his ideas are speedily getting across to the players.

Being brave on the ball and playing out from the back are two prerequisites of his philosophy which incorporates a high-energy approach to the game revolving around "dominating the ball" – a phrase we have become familiar with. The fullbacks are pushed on very high and the whole team presses as a unit, which, while it can leave us exposed at the back makes for an open game.

The most refreshing aspect of the game was that when we went two goals up he didn't allow us to drop deeper and deeper and rest on our laurels, instead he brought on Kenny Miller and Dean Shiels who helped further increase the winning margin. I can envisage there being a number of high-scoring games this year where it may be a case of "if you score four, we'll score five" or if Saturday is anything to go by, "if you score two we'll score six!"

It seems that he has created a real togetherness within the squad and the players have already struck up an affinity with the fans, which had been sorely lacking. This was shown as he ordered each and every one of the squad to march over to the travelling supporters to thank them for their support.

It's the little things that make a huge difference to the overall feel of the club. On day one he held a team meeting where he outlined what was expected of them. Honesty and respect were the traits that seem to have been stressed as the key principles on which the season will be based upon. He has even given the players the task of producing their own code of conduct, which ties in with his preference to give them more responsibility, as he is a firm believer that they should give their opinion in tactical meetings.

The quality of the training sessions seem to be the biggest difference that the players have noted. Triple sessions have been a regular feature and all the endurance training has been with a ball compared to the aimless running, which they have been used to under Head of Sports Science Jim Henry. He, along with first team coach Gordon Durie have subsequently left the club as Warburton and Weir say they prefer to do all of the coaching themselves.

Even Warburton's demeanour on the touchline gives off a more positive vibe. In keeping with tradition he was suited and booted and was animated from the first whistle to the last, barking out instructions. Not satisfied with the four-goal margin of victory, he lamented his side's poor start to the game in his post-match interviews and demanded that they meet the high expectations they have set themselves.

He also showed what a gentleman he is when he made the effort to travel to Ibrox to meet the club's oldest season ticket holder on his one hundredth birthday to present him with his new season ticket on the pitch.

With Warburton and Weir at the helm, it feels like the club is in safe hands. They have a clear direction in which they are heading in and as the weeks and months roll on I can only see the team going from strength to strength as the players familiarise with themselves with the new set-up. The feel-good factor surrounding the club has given birth to a wave of optimism which was can only be compared to when Dick Advocaat arrived in 1998 and even has some fans talking about potentially winning a domestic trophy which seemed a long way off just a couple of months ago.

In everything he has done so far, he has shown that he possesses the managerial nous and the level of class required to be a Rangers manager. His professionalism and the way he went about things is clearly what endeared him to the Brentford support and it seems that the fans up here have taken to him too as the magic hat song has proved a big hit with him.

Good luck to the Bees this season and I'm sure all Rangers fans will be keeping a close eye on how you get on with your new statistical approach to the game. Oh, and if it doesn't work out with Lewis Macleod, feel free to send him back up the road!

Thank you Jordan for this wonderful incisive article and I am sure that all Brentford fans will be delighted to hear that Mark has settled down so quickly in his new home and it sounds as if he is establishing firm foundations at Rangers and replicating many of the systems and philosophies that he implemented at Brentford.

We all wish him and Rangers every success over the coming months and most importantly of all, we would really welcome your suggestions regarding how on earth we can get Lewis Macleod back onto a football pitch at some time soon?

The Rangers Report can be found at therangersreport.com.

We Know He Is Good! – 31/7/15

It certainly came as no surprise to me and every other Brentford supporter to learn from our new friends up at Glasgow Rangers that the partnership of Mark Warburton and David Weir has already made a massive impression in the first few weeks of their reign and that they have started to both revitalise and restore pride to what was a faltering club. The real surprise would have been if Rangers fans felt anything other than delight and renewed confidence at their appointment and how they have begun to tackle the massive task that awaits them.

It is surely the ideal appointment given that Weir is steeped in the history and tradition of the club, and, it must also be said, the recent chaos that has ensued there, and Warburton is simply an excellent all round manager, or as I have described him before a *Renaissance Man* who is a wonderful motivator, communicator and man manager as well as an excellent and positive coach who also has an excellent eye for unearthing and then placing his faith in young, vibrant talent.

If they are given the necessary support then I really cannot see them failing in their task and I look forward to Rangers returning in triumph to the top flight of Scottish football at the end of the season.

Several other Brentford fans shared my pleasure in hearing yesterday's positive update. **Patrick Sutton** commented succinctly:

Well that's a mighty fine assessment of Mark's start at Rangers and I wish him all the best. It would be fantastic if he succeeds north of the border as well as he did in the south, if only to prove he is no fly by night merchant but indeed a good young manager who is not only able to create a positive attitude but to also get results.

Alan Bird looked at his broader management skills:

The assessment of the excellent start that Mark Warburton seems to have made at Rangers suggests to me that if he ever left football he'd make an excellent CEO somewhere.

He seems to have the knack of making people happy in their roles and positions and they seem to want to work for him and do a good job. I really liked and was impressed that he asked the players to write their own Code of Conduct, so if there are any future issues and he can say "They're your own rules not mine."

I wonder if that is something that he wishes he'd tried to do at Brentford.

Rebel Bee was also impressed:

Thank you for reaching out to the Rangers supporter who has written an excellent piece on Mark Warburton's early days in the hot seat up there. I watched the highlights of their six-two win at Hibs and it was vintage

Warburton – you get two goals we'll just keep coming at you and get six, even the odd not so good bit had his DNA all over it. He will do brilliantly up there, and given time and support he will totally revive Rangers – I'm sure of it.

Also thank you for avoiding the temptation felt by some Bees fans, to move on so quickly from the Warbs era that his incredible achievement is now overlooked or at worst devalued. This type of piece doesn't in any way undermine the new team at the helm, but serves to remind us of the talent and ongoing progress of our finest post war manager.

Matthew Benham and Mark Warburton working in partnership provided my best memories as a lifelong supporter of our great club, I will never forget Warbs and his legacy – and it was also nice to see the interesting comments from Alan Bird who would know more than most.

Matthew Benham continues to back the club to an incredible level, and we have a new coach in Marinus who I'm warming to day by day. Who knows where we'll end up, maybe the best is ahead, but for now I'll look back on the Benham/Warburton period at Brentford as the best ever.

Good luck to the Gers too.

Former Brentford striker **Richard Poole** also had some astute comments to make:

Well Greville your recent words about Warburton going far away and not coming back to haunt us ring true with me! I have a strong feeling that we have not heard the last of somebody who I am quite certain will be an excellent manager at whatever club he works at. What he achieved in so short a period at Brentford clearly reminds me of what Frank Blunstone started to do in my time at the club, but as we all know he was not given the time even with the pitifully small resources he had to play with.

I await fresh news and updates from Glasgow with relish and anticipation. Mark Warburton is a young manager in terms of his experience in the position and he is still learning and developing new skills. He appears to be one of those rare multitalented individuals who can turn his hand and use his common sense to adapt to most new situations and opportunities.

I am glad that the Brentford blueprint and framework seems to be working for him there too and like my fellow Brentford fans I can see nothing less than continued success for him wherever he goes.

August

Will They Go? – 2/8/15

The fans' message boards and social media have both been red hot over the last couple of days and filled with vituperative comments regarding the potentially imminent sales of up to three of Brentford's star players, Moses Odubajo, Andre Gray and Stuart Dallas. I wanted to wait and see whether any of them played in the final friendly match against Norwich City on Saturday afternoon before providing my viewpoint on the situation, and given that only Andre took part then that perhaps provides further evidence that at least a couple of deals might well be in the offing.

Everything in the garden was looking rosy for Brentford just a few short days ago with eight high quality new players coming in to provide additional options and compete for places and the remainder of the squad had remained intact with the exception of Tony Craig rejoining Millwall and the inevitable decision to allow Jonathan Douglas to leave.

Now, seemingly in the twinkling of an eye, things have changed dramatically and the general feeling of confidence has swiftly evaporated and many supporters are feeling concerned, unsettled and uncertain about what might be about to happen and how that will affect the strength of our squad and our prospects for the new season.

Let's look in some detail at the situation regarding each of the three players who are rumoured to be on the move so that we can see why they might possibly be considering a transfer away from Griffin Park and how, indeed, the club should respond.

Many eyebrows were raised when it was announced that Brentford had managed to sign winger Moses Odubajo a year ago for what was the first ever seven-figure transfer fee paid by the club. Spurs were just one of several Premier League clubs rumoured to be sniffing around the highly-rated youngster and, quite frankly, it was a surprise when he chose us rather than other potentially more attractive options.

Whilst the Bees had won promotion to the Championship, it could be argued that for a large proportion of the 2013/14 season Leyton Orient had looked the more likely club to go up and that joining Brentford was really not such a massive move given the other interest in him from bigger fish.

Of course he bought into the project at Griffin Park as he could clearly see the potential of the squad that Matthew Benham and Mark Warburton were building at Brentford. Perhaps he saw the move as a stepping-stone and a way of putting himself into the shop window whilst proving himself at Championship level?

Whatever transpired in the negotiations between Odubajo's agent, Hootan Ahmadi of *CSM*, and Brentford, we now learn that a buyout clause of three and a half million pounds was incorporated into his contract. There is much criticism about the club allowing such a clause to be included but this is arrant nonsense! It was simply an agent doing his job for his client and I well suspect that this was the only way that we could persuade Moses to join the club, as from his point of view, it protected his upside should he perform to his true potential. From Brentford's perspective it might well have seen a long shot at the time, despite his obvious talent and potential, that Moses's stock would improve by such a massive margin in so short a time.

As it happened, everything that Moses touched last season turned to gold. He started well as a winger but he really flourished when he replaced Alan McCormack at right back after Macca's unfortunate injury at Bolton. Moses never looked back, became almost two players in one as an overlapping, attacking fullback and combined brilliantly with Jota. It is not an exaggeration to say that he looked like a future England international in the making and he also impressed when playing for the England Under 20 team this summer.

Given the circumstances, and I am sure that Mr. Ahmadi made it his business to ensure that the buyout figure became widely known within the game, it is hardly a shock that Hull City have agreed to meet the terms of the clause, indeed what is more surprising to me is that bigger fish than Hull haven't done the same, as the fee now looks an absolute steal.

Release clauses have become increasingly popular in the game and you only need to look at the example of current international Fabian Delph who recently left Aston Villa for a measly eight million pounds when Manchester City exercised a similar clause. Like the situation at Brentford, Aston Villa were forced to accept such a clause if they were to persuade the player to extend his contract.

Moses has now made it perfectly clear that he wants to further his career by leaving the club and if that is the case and he has rejected any approaches from Brentford to perhaps sweeten his contract and stay for another year, then there is really absolutely nothing that we can do about it.

Just over a year ago Moses's agent described Brentford as *a Premiership club in the Championship*. It is just a shame that he seems to have changed his opinion so quickly and feels that his client can now do better for himself – such is the way of football!

From Brentford's point of view the best possible outcome if the player has irrevocably decided to leave, is for Moses to go as soon as possible so that we can get on with anointing his successor, whether it be a new signing or one of Nico Yennaris and Alan McCormack who are vying for his position from within the club. That being said Moses in my view has easily been our best player, our *X Factor*, and the one who might well be the most difficult for us to replace.

From Moses's perspective it would be good if a Premier League club also decided to swoop for him, although I do feel that he would benefit from another year spent learning his trade in the Championship.

There is still some confusion as to the contents of the release clause. Is three and a half million pounds merely the opening gambit and the starting point to be allowed to talk terms with the player, in which case perhaps Brentford can encourage an auction and get the price raised significantly closer to his real value? Or is it the final agreed sum at which he will be allowed to leave the club?

Leyton Orient will also be due a fairly heavy slice of the profit we have made and the other query I would have about the deal is whether we can insert a sell-on clause into any transfer deal or whether it will be the initial fee and nothing more? Another possibility, although surely a slim one is to sell him to a Premier League club and then loan him back.

Looking at the bright side, whilst it is now plainly obvious that Moses is already worth a lot more than the buyout figure and will likely be transferred for a massive sum in the future, we will have more than tripled our investment in him and realised what will be easily be a club record fee.

At the moment we are still a selling club which looks to use our analytical expertise and proprietary player data to uncover and then bring in emerging young talent and unhewn nuggets from either the lower divisions or abroad, develop them into the finished article, or as close to it as we can do, and then sell them on at a massive profit.

We have already done this with the likes of Simon Moore and Adam Forshaw who arrived for nothing and left for huge transfer fees. Despite the continued investment from Matthew Benham, without which we would be playing the likes of Forest Green Rovers rather than Ipswich Town next weekend, we have to be realistic and accept that there is no other option given our own particular circumstances.

We play in the smallest stadium in the division and our average attendance of 10,822 last season was higher than only two other teams in the Championship. Our commercial income streams are therefore restricted given the lack of suitable facilities at Griffin Park and we have never had the benefit of the massive parachute payments lavished on clubs relegated from the Premier League. No wonder we are competing with one or even both hands tied behind our back!

A lot of our supporters have been openly sneering at the prospect of Moses and maybe also Andre Gray joining Hull City and suggesting, rightly or wrongly that we are on an upward curve whereas they are in decline and are maybe another Wigan Athletic in the making given their recent relegation and the current uncertainty over their ownership. Hopefully, when Lionel Road comes on stream we might well in time become a so-called *bigger* club than them, but at the moment it is fanciful in the extreme if not utter nonsense to suggest that that is the case.

Just look at the facts; Hull City have spent four of the past seven seasons in the Premier League and have benefited accordingly. In 2012/13, in the Championship, the club's accounts state that they received just over two million pounds from Football League TV and other league-related income. The following season, after promotion to the Premier League, that sum immediately increased more than thirty-fold, to over sixty-eight million pounds, an increase of over sixty-six million pounds as a result of being promoted.

Last season they had to make do with a mere sixty-six million pounds and their disappointment at being relegated will be partially allayed by an initial parachute payment of twenty-four million pounds. In fact they will receive a massive sixty-four million pounds split over four years – the aforementioned twenty-four million pounds this season, then nineteen million three hundred thousand pounds in 2016 followed by nine million six hundred thousand pounds for each of the next two years.

What a ridiculous reward for failure and you can see how uneven the playing field is in the Championship. Looking at these figures perhaps makes it clear just how incredible Brentford's achievement was in managing to finish fifth last season whilst overcoming seemingly insurmountable odds. We spent our limited resources far better and far smarter than pretty much every other rival Championship team but we have to keep doing the same every year if we are to even maintain our position let alone continue our progress to even higher strata.

It is therefore fanciful in the extreme to suggest that we can outbid clubs such as Hull City who have had recent Premier League experience – we are dwarfed by their resources, also bearing in mind that their average attendance last season was well over double the figure we achieved, twenty-three thousand five hundred and fifty-seven, filling ninety-two percent of their stadium capacity.

No wonder a player's head can be turned. I am not for one moment suggesting that this is the case with any of the Brentford trio we are discussing, but very often impressionable young footballers are egged on by unscrupulous agents who benefit financially, often by massive sums, from encouraging their client to move. Leaving aside any footballing reasons, and, maybe naïvely, I honestly believe that a strong argument can be made for choosing Brentford over Hull City in that regard, it is quite another case when you come to consider wages as Moses and Andre can expect to cash in significantly should they decide to move as Brentford cannot get anywhere near matching what they might be offered elsewhere.

I have already mentioned Simon Moore and Adam Forshaw, two other high profile departures from Griffin Park in the recent past. They joined the likes of Harry Forrester and Clayton Donaldson in deciding to move on. Financially I am sure that they have all benefited significantly, although they might perhaps rue missing out on the more than generous bonuses paid out for reaching the playoffs at the end of last season.

In footballing terms they have all had mixed fortunes. Simon Moore's career has disappeared into a black hole and he has gone backwards owing to a lack of opportunity. At the moment he reminds me of Paul Smith, so promising a young keeper whose career was stymied after he left the club and who never went on to fulfil his massive potential. First choice Cardiff keeper, David Marshall, is apparently, on the verge of joining West Bromwich Albion so perhaps Simon's time has finally come – I certainly hope so, but so far his move has been a disaster for him in footballing terms.

Harry Forrester is also treading water at Doncaster and must surely regret his terrible decision to leave Brentford. The jury is still out on Adam Forshaw. Will he become a first team regular at Middlesbrough next season and become the player he promised to do whilst at Brentford? Clayton Donaldson, in truth, had an exceptional season at Birmingham and has earned a contract extension until 2018, so he can perhaps justify his move, although those missed bonus payments might have come in handy too!

It is clear from these examples that leaving Brentford, its exceptional coaching and support staff and an environment that is positive, supportive and nurturing is not necessarily a good thing and that there is no guarantee of success for players, however talented, who choose to follow this route.

The situation with Andre Gray is totally different as this time, unlike with Moses, the club holds the aces. Of course he is in demand, he is a young player of immense talent and potential who has proved that he can score the best part of twenty goals in the tough environment of the Championship.

What is there not to like about him? He is quick, strong and brave, he can score goals of all shapes and sizes and has responded well to the help and support he has received at the club. He can only get even better and frankly, I am surprised that Hull City are the only club that has been linked with him in a serious way as I would have expected that many other teams would have been trying to extract him from our clutches.

I have heard no whispers of unhappiness behind the scenes or any agitating for a move on the part of his agent and he has two more seasons left on his contract so for another year at least, Brentford can control his destiny. In that case the situation is totally clear, for all the reasons given earlier, Brentford currently remain a selling club, but, as demonstrated with Adam Forshaw, we will only allow him to leave on our terms and at a price that we feel is acceptable as we are under no immediate pressure to sell him.

Of course we have no desire to lose our best, and, indeed, only proven striker at this juncture but if a club overwhelms us with its offer then he, like every other player will have his price. The asking price is unknown but is rumoured on social media to be in the region of around seven million pounds plus significant add-ons related to appearances and achievement. This would represent our receiving over ten times what we paid for him just over a year ago.

This is an eye-watering sum and should Hull City, or indeed any other club match it, then I am sure that he will be on his way. Such a figure would also go a long way towards solving any potential problems with Financial Fair Play in a stroke and the fact that we would even contemplate selling Gray in my opinion demonstrates a massive confidence in our ability to unearth another gem to replace him.

Personally I hope that he stays with us and increases his value even more by scoring the goals that enable us to reach the heights of the Premier League, but this is probably wishful thinking on my part. His form this preseason has been awesome and he has looked sharp and already scored four times including a brilliantly taken effort at Norwich yesterday. I expect Andre to have a great season and score over twenty goals – ideally for Brentford and not another club!

Andre Gray hungry for goals at Norwich

Stuart Dallas is also rumoured to be on the verge of joining his former manager Uwe Rösler at the madhouse that is Leeds United. A fee of almost one hundred times the fifteen thousand pounds we paid for him to Crusaders has been discussed and apparently agreed and in this case I can see the virtue of him moving on.

Stuart is now an established international footballer with Northern Ireland but at twenty-four years of age, his place is still not guaranteed at his current club. He scored eight times last season including that incredible double at Fulham and improved us whenever he came onto the pitch with his pace, power, directness and shoot-on-sight policy. He played in thirty-eight of the forty-six Championship games but only started twenty-three of them. That is surely not enough for a player of his quality, age and experience and maybe he feels that with the recent arrival of both Gogia and Vibe his chances of starting every week have been further diminished. He is quite good enough to be a first team regular but his pathway has been blocked at Griffin Park and perhaps he feels that it is time for him to move on.

Whether the new Head Coach is right to prefer others is a matter of opinion and the success or otherwise of that decision will be revealed over the coming months. Managers and coaches are paid to make such judgements and it is conceivable that players also decide that they would rather play somewhere else in a different environment and in this instance I can quite understand why Stuart might perhaps prefer to seek a fresh opportunity elsewhere. Uwe Rösler certainly knows the player and his capabilities although it is perhaps slightly perplexing that Dallas might be prepared to play for a manager who it is reputed that he did not totally get on with in the past, but perhaps those rumours are unfounded. Maybe Stuart also wants a fresh start where he will be welcomed as an international footballer and go straight into the starting eleven.

We are at a crossroads and it remains to be seen what happens over the coming days and weeks. The fact that three of our players are so desired by other clubs pays a glowing testament to our growing reputation and success in finding and developing players, and larger clubs find it easier to allow us to do the hard work and then attempt to pry our stars from our grasp. If that turns out to be the case then they will have to pay top dollar to do so and whilst I look forward to the day when we are able to refuse any offer for our players I am also pragmatic and realistic, and accept that we will have to wait until we are at Lionel Road before we are in a position to do so.

What is also certain is that we will only keep players who are committed to the club and the cause and that anyone who wants to leave will be allowed to do so – but only when it best suits us and for a price that is deemed acceptable and meets our valuation of him. Moses, however, is a special case because of his release clause and, to a large extent, our hands are tied.

Should we lose any of the three aforementioned players then they will be replaced quickly and properly, ideally by players who have the potential to become even better than the ones who went before them.

Of course it is unsettling but the era of the loyal one club player – the Peter Gelson's and Alan Hawley's – has long since gone. We are now in the big time and are perhaps a victim of our own success and we also have to adapt to changing circumstances. I am sure that we will do so and every Brentford supporter will just have to accept things as they are and trust in the club to get things right. Something they do more far more often than not.

Welcome to the new world of Brentford.

RIP Professor Adrian Woods – A Tribute – 4/8/15

Like everyone else on *The Griffin Park Grapevine* fans' message board, I avidly looked forward to the next contribution from **ade211**. He wrote exclusively about statistics, analytics and even mathematical modelling, subjects of massive relevance to all Brentford fans nowadays.

For someone that struggled with the intricacies of Maths O Level far too many years ago this could have been a step too far for me but he always made a difficult subject fresh and interesting. Rather than just concentrating on and getting bogged down by the actual numbers, he instead demonstrated how to interpret them, what they really meant and the benefit they could bring in terms of understanding the game and how players perform.

What's more, it was obvious that he was a man of vast intelligence who had an open mind and was keen to embrace new concepts and ideas.

His words were clear, concise, illuminating and often self-deprecating and witty. He never patronised his audience but he was a wonderful teacher and communicator with his obvious bubbling enthusiasm for the subject and clarity of expression. In short he was an absolute jewel.

A couple of weeks ago I approached him and asked if he would be prepared to write a longer article on the subject which would serve as a general introduction to the convoluted word of statistics, analysis and mathematical modelling and how best to gain a competitive advantage through their usage. He immediately agreed but stated that he had not been in the best of health and it might take him a little time.

I was therefore terribly shocked and saddened to hear about his sudden death yesterday and only then learned that his real name was **Professor Adrian Woods**. I contacted his son Anthony to discuss the article and he kindly gave me his permission to use it so I am enclosing it today as a heartfelt tribute to a man who I never met but greatly admired.

It is only recently that the application of statistics to football has become widely known and broadly accepted. Today clubs purchase data from companies like Opta using back room staff to analyse the data. If you look at the back room staff involved at say Chelsea or Manchester City you will see the massive resources they have in this growing area. Brentford are now investing heavily in both the acquisition of data and the staff qualified to analyse it and have quickly gained a reputation as being in the vanguard of this move towards the systematic use of stats to help predict performance.

While most football supporters know about the use of statistics, many remain confused about how they are best applied and are sceptical about their value. One of the key objectives is to reduce a manager and coach's subjective evaluation of a player and replace it with a cold, clinical and more objective one based on statistics. So how does this work? A simple illustration may help to demonstrate.

For players it is possible to report on their shot accuracy as well as the number of shots they take. Let's take two Brentford players as an example. Last season Andre Gray took 2.68 shots every ninety minutes he played with an accuracy level of 54%. Alan Judge in comparison took 2.35 shots every ninety minutes he played with an accuracy level of 38%. Is it possible to delve further into this?

Of Gray's 2.68, 2.37 were within the box. Of Judge's 2.35 shots only .65 were within the penalty area. So the difference between their accuracy may be explained in part by the fact that Gray takes more of his shots in the box (88%) than Judge does (28%).

Now if we look at Stuart Dallas too we see that he had a shot accuracy of 55%, took 1.74 shots per game with half in the box and half outside. In terms of goals, Gray scored .43 goals every ninety minutes he played, with 93% of them scored in the box. Judge scored 0.09 goals every ninety minutes he played with 67% within the box. In fact this is misleading for Judge as he only scored three goals in total of which two were in the box. Dallas scored 0.24 goals per ninety minutes he played with 50% scored from inside the penalty area.

This exercise could be repeated for each player, broken down by home games and away and for different parts of the season. These are objective statistics, however they still need interpreting by experts to uncover any coaching insights that may arise. Other statistics could also be looked at, such as passing, tackles and chance creation, in order to give a fuller picture of a player's contribution to the team. It is interesting to note that Judge created 2.41 opportunities per game compared to 0.98 for Gray and 1.31 by Dallas. Judge was also fouled more often per match than both Gray and Dallas. The figures are 2.09, 0.71 and 1.23 respectively per ninety minutes

The analysis used by Matthew Benham and his team uses very good data, analysed by excellent statisticians to provide the manager and his coaches with insights into players that are objective and not biased by subjective opinion.

The profiles of Judge, Gray and Dallas used data in the public domain and even then used only a small part of it. Brentford have access to much more in-depth data and have the people skilled in interpreting it. This should at least in the Championship provide the club with a competitive advantage.

Using statistics guards against us suffering from confirmation bias. This is when we believe something to be true then filter evidence to support this viewpoint. We tend to remember instances when an event supported our view and forget or undervalue evidence when it does not.

My own favourite example is from watching pundits on television argue for putting a man on the post at corners. Now I have no idea if this is a good or bad thing to do, but I do know that most corners do not result in goals, only a very few do. Yet by selective editing it is possible to find the minuscule number of corners out of all the corners taken over a weekend where a man on the post would have prevented a goal. These then get shown ad infinitum on television to substantiate an incorrect assertion.

In an entire season what percentage of goals from a corner would have been prevented by a player on the post, and if the player had been deployed elsewhere would this have prevented more goals, or if a player had been sent forward at corners as Brentford invariably do, would the team have scored more goals from opposition corners? I have no idea of the answers but I think many suffer from confirmation bias on this topic, remembering dramatic goal line clearances and forgetting all the other times it made no difference at all. By looking at the statistics for this a manager or a coach can be better informed on whether to use a player this way or not without being influenced by their own confirmation bias.

What other ways can statistics can be used?

The most common use of statistics in football is to assist in the analysis of a player and his value. If the market for players was efficient every player would have a value that accurately represented his actual worth to their team. But as we know this is not the case. What statistics on players help to do is to identify players that the market otherwise ignores or undervalues. In the past scouts would spend time going to games, watching players to see who might represent good value. By using statistics a wider field of players can be searched at a much lower cost and the subjective element in player acquisition minimised. Also scouts watching a player in the flesh may by influenced by chance. They could, by chance, pick the rare occasion when he has a great game. The opposite could also happen. Now players can be identified from their statistics, drawn from many games, before being watched. Looking at the players we have acquired recently clearly demonstrates the work that the background analysts have done in identifying players.

From what Matthew Benham has said, the model used by Brentford has propriety algorithms embedded in it to make the choice of player even more efficient than by our just using other more readily available statistics. As this is not in the public domain given its commercial sensitivity we do not know what it consists of. At the centre though is the certainly that subjective assessment on potential players has been substituted by more objective analytical tools.

The players we have acquired recently are the fruits of this approach. We now search a much wider area than others in our league and it is safe to assume that we consider many more players in order to find latent value. In the future other areas of Europe will be searched I suspect, as well as the USA and even Asia. Benham is apparently keen to establish links with the KGH Sports Football Academy based in The Gambia. So perhaps The Gambia will be the next place Brentford looks for new players!

Another way statistics can help is by giving players and coaches data on areas of weakness that need attention, as well as ensuring that strengths are maximised. This allows more individual sessions to be planned and their results monitored in game situations. The use of a player's heat map can show whether they have had the discipline to play exactly how and where the manager wanted. Deviations from this can be discussed and steps taken to rectify errors in positional play. A player's statistics can also be used to assess whether a player's impact is declining in so a plan can be drawn up to replace him and also help him find a new, more suitable club to join.

A lot of us, I suspect, will find the use of stats in player acquisition and player improvement not that controversial or difficult to assimilate. Other aspects of the use of statistics most certainly are.

There is a wealth of statistical analysis based on large amounts of data that look at, for example, the probability of scoring from a corner, or from a cross or from shots outside of the box. Most find the low probability of scoring from these quite surprising. With the appointment of a specialised set piece coach our success rate should improve to become, hopefully, above average for the league. One early and well-known piece of statistical work was undertaken for Manchester City regarding corners. The manager felt they were not scoring enough from corners. The statistics drawn from across the Premiership found that in-swinging corners aimed at just past the penalty spot had a higher probability of leading to a goal. Even though the manager favoured away-swingers, in-swinging corners were used and more goals occurred. Work also has been done on the distance covered by a team in a match. The consensus being, at present, is that the team covering the most ground is more likely to win.

One observation that causes controversy can be expressed by "goals wins matches but defences win leagues." This emphasises the importance of keeping clean sheets. Under Warburton Brentford played an expansive style but some have argued that defensive weakness caused by over-attacking left us short at the back, resulting in losing points and detracting from our chances of promotion. In about 23% of our games we kept clean sheets, this compares badly to the near 45% of matches in which Middlesbrough kept a clean sheet. Two of the promoted teams, Norwich and Watford, managed 31% and 33% respectively.

One area that has attracted serious work is penalties. Several studies have shown that the keeper staying still in the middle of the goal increases the chance of the penalty being saved. The reason why keepers dive is that we all prefer action to inactivity. So there is a bias at work that psychologically nudges the keeper to dive.

Interestingly the taker should focus solely on where he wants the ball to go. If he looks at the keeper in the moment before the kick he tends not to hit the ball cleanly and often it goes high or wide of the goal. This gaze effect has been documented in other sports. Just having someone stand in the middle of the goal, even if not a professional keeper is often enough to disrupt the taker's ability to strike the ball correctly. I have to say I find that hard to believe but there are several pieces of work on this now that substantiate this view.

At present the Holy Grail is to develop statistics that predict accurately how many goals a team will score in a match. People working on this for obvious reasons are loath to put this into the public domain. Also predicting match outcomes has produced a lot of work of which only a proportion reaches a wider audience.

There are also models where league position is predicted. Typically these look at wage bill, then injury, then suspension, then managers. The remainder being down to luck. Running these models from what can be ascertained, means that after about twenty games luck has pretty much evened itself out and a team's league position reflects the other factors. Some have put the manager's impact on performance at only about 20%. Evidently Brentford has a very good model for this, which was used recently to identify candidates for the Head Coach position. It may even be able to factor out random events in order to uncover how well the team is doing and if random events had a neutral impact on performance. This militates against taking rash decisions based too much on luck and random events.

The experiment being undertaken by Brentford is actually not so radical. The owner is a leading figure in football odds making, building up resources over several years to produce models that predict match outcome better than his competitors. What I think is new is that he actually understands the statistics and what they can and what they can't do, as well as having some of the best models available and, crucially, some of the best people to analyse the statistics.

He is an astute businessman who has made a considerable personal fortune out of this. In doing so he has acquired excellent skills in running a business. One skill he clearly demonstrates is his strategic ability. Since it became public knowledge exactly how he wanted the club to be run, new managerial and coaching staff have been employed, as have new players. These have not been acquired overnight but are the clear end result of having a vision and from that a plan.

His majority shareholding in FC Midtjylland and the way he has tested his approach there with great success also demonstrates his single-mindedness and determination to break new ground. He has succeeded where others failed in the imminent building of a new ground, something the club has been trying to achieve for years. Again, a crucial part of his long-term vision.

On the whole we are now seeing the outcome of decisions made quite a long time ago. At present he, his board and managerial team are planning for what will be required in the Premier League. Just as players emerged from outside of our radar I suspect this will happen again. The use of better statistical analysis will be introduced as will other more specialised coaches and analysts. At present we supporters are focused solely on the season ahead. I reckon he is thinking five years ahead. Just as with hindsight we can now see what he has been up to for the last few seasons, hopefully in time individual decisions will form a coherent pattern to solidify our place in the Premier League. We may struggle at times to see the big picture but there will be one.

While he is the owner of Brentford I can't see us going back to the good old days of jumpers for goalposts and day trips to Hartlepool where the ball is just belted by us up and down the pitch without rhyme or reason.

RIP Professor Woods and our sincerest condolences to his son, Anthony, and all of his family.

What Brentford Means To Us All – 6/8/15

Towards the end of last season, along with several club directors, staff members and many other Brentford supporters I was interviewed so that I could express my own feelings and sentiments regarding the football club.

What did it mean to me? What made it stand out? Why did I continue to support the club and return week after week to the shrine that is Griffin Park? What was so special and unique about Brentford?

There was also a lot of discussion about the Brentford brand and what it stood for. As the fan base continues to grow and more and more people begin to take an interest in Brentford, was the club being introduced and presented to supporters, both new and old, in the right way? What values best personified the club looking back to the past as well as now, in the present, and most importantly, to what extent would these remain the same in the future?

How could the club retain its traditional positive character traits and not alienate long-term supporters yet still remain relevant and contemporary to the younger fans now being attracted to the club by virtue of its recent success and growing reputation for playing vibrant attacking football?

A lot of work was conducted by the club who then drilled down even further through a series of online questionnaires to season ticket holders and members and finally a working party was established with a group of fans of all ages and backgrounds who analysed and reviewed the initial findings and acted as one last sounding board.

The salient points and learnings from this research project will, I am sure, become evident over the coming months by virtue of changes and ideally improvements in how the club presents its public face through communication channels such as its website and all areas of social media and, on Tuesday, as a first step the club released a brand new video which allowed fans of all ages to tell their own stories about Brentford, what it means to them, their mood regarding the current state of the club and how they felt about the immediate future.

It can be found on the Brentford website and I commend it to you all as it is three minutes and forty-five seconds of pure gold dust which made the hair stand up on the back of my neck, and I have to say it also gave me goose bumps. It is a truly excellent piece of work which is evocative, pulls at the heart strings but is also confident and forward thinking and it has accurately portrayed what the Brentford brand represents, retrospectively, in the present, and ideally, moving forward.

Through a series of short, sharp *vox pops* it clearly communicates the values of the club and helps to explain what makes us different and unique.

Brentford surely means different things to every supporter but each and every interview had one thing in common that clearly shone through – a feeling of unity and belonging. We are all in this together as one extended family and there is not the dissonance and void that exists in many bigger clubs where there is a clear separation and divide and a feeling of *them* and *us.*

Brentford is part of and also serves a vibrant local community and must never lose sight of that fact and however high we rise in the football food chain, we cannot ever allow ourselves to fall into the trap of becoming a soulless, amorphous and clinical conglomerate. The intimacy, charm and, frankly, ramshackle nature of Griffin Park is the glue that binds us all together and Lionel Road must, and surely will, replicate that sense of warmth and togetherness.

Many of the comments, viewpoints, memories and assertions expressed by the fans included in the video will strike a chord with all Brentford supporters and here are some of my favourites:

- *The walk to the ground through streets of terraced houses*
- *The only ground with a pub on all four corners*
- *It feels like being at home*
- *Brentford is at the heart of its community*
- *There is a closeness – a real community spirit*
- *We have a close-knit bunch of fans*
- *I see people I have known for fifty years*
- *It is what you call a friendly club*
- *There is a community spirit and sense of togetherness that other London clubs do not possess*
- *It is my spiritual home*
- *Wherever you go on a match day you are always going to bump into a friendly face*
- *Brentford is part of my family, it is part of me*
- *Saturday would not really be the same without going to Griffin Park*
- *Coming through the gates at Griffin Park just makes you buzz*
- *The people here are all in it together*
- *The atmosphere is electric*
- *I love the fact that it is an old-style stadium*
- *It is one of the few remaining ones with terracing*
- *The fans are close to the pitch and it is very, very intimidating for the opposition*
- *I get an adrenalin rush when I go there*
- *The quality of the football over the past couple of seasons has been second to none*
- *What I am seeing is a football team that is evolving and progressing*
- *We have grown together almost out of adversity and from being an underdog*
- *The owner is very forward thinking*
- *The investment that the owner and staff have put in is all about making this club fit for the future*
- *These are really exciting times*
- *Who knows what the next ten years can bring*
- *This is a club that is going places*
- *We have always been a bit innovative*
- *It's been a rollercoaster ride but finally people can believe that this club will be successful for years to come*
- *You can have contact with Brentford, you feel like you are a part of the club*
- *We are a London club, but we are also a local club, it is the best of both worlds*
- *I am prouder than I have ever been in my life to walk around West London wearing red and white*
- *We are traditional but progressive*

I am sure that all these words will make you feel just as proud and emotional as they did me when I first watched the video. The club is to be commended and has done an excellent job in capturing the mood and spirit of its supporters and I feel proud of our past, delighted about the present and confident about the future.

The Way Of The World For Brentford – 7/8/15

Southampton totally surpassed expectations a couple of seasons ago by establishing themselves in the Premier League and playing a highly effective and positive brand of football based upon patient possession and pressing high up the field. Their football was easy on the eye was and rewarded with a fully deserved eighth place finish, equalling their best ever Premier League position. Their manager Mauricio Pochettino marshalled his troops efficiently and effectively and incredibly, three players from such an unfashionable team, Adam Lallana, Luke Shaw and Rickie Lambert were named in England's World Cup squad.

Everything in the garden seemed rosy with the club on the crest of a wave – and then the vultures pounced. Lallana, Shaw and Lambert were the first out of the door, swiftly followed by star defender Dejan Lovren and the impressive young Calum Chambers, all for vast sums. Manager Pochettino left for Spurs and it seemed only a matter of time before two of the remaining stars, Morgan Schneiderlin and Jay Rodriguez joined him.

The fans wailed and gnashed their teeth, the club was accused of greed and lack of ambition and were nailed on favourites for relegation last season. So what happened? Dutch manager Ronald Koeman seamlessly replaced Mauricio Pochettino and The Saints made a number of astute signings in the summer, including winger Dušan Tadić, striker Graziano Pellè, goalkeeper Fraser Forster, attacking midfielder Sadio Mané and loanee centre back Toby Alderweireld. None of these players were as heralded or expensive as the stars they replaced yet the newly built squad improved on the previous season and finished seventh.

This close season has yet again seen the departure of even more high profile players in Schneiderlin, Alderweireld and Nathaniel Clyne but players of apparently comparable ability at far less cost have replaced them all. Schneiderlin's replacement, Jordy Claisie, was signed for well under half the twenty-five million pounds the club received for their departing midfielder, as was the case with Clyne's likely replacement at right back, Cedric Soares.

Southampton's business model is brave and innovative and should be examined closely by every other far-sighted club in the country. Everyone has his price and can go if that price is achieved. Nobody is irreplaceable. Every football market around the world is scrutinised for emerging talent and potential bargains not yet spotted by less astute rivals. New recruits are carefully identified and scouted before being brought in at under market value and they all ideally have massive development and resale potential.

The structure and system is far more important and long-lasting than any one individual and analysis and knowledge are the keys to success as they enable the club to buy low and sell high.

I hope that the Brentford fans reading this have had the patience to stay with me to this point as I am sure that they will fully recognise the massive similarities between what Southampton have achieved over the past couple of years and how they have done it, and what is happening now at Griffin Park.

I am writing this article on the eve of a new season and am trying to assess the evidence as to how Brentford will do over the coming months. Can they match or even surpass their incredible fifth place finish of last season or will we become also-rans or, perish the thought, return in ignominy from whence we came so triumphantly in 2014?

We have lost a number of players from last season's tight-knit squad. Tommy Smith and the underperforming Nick Proschwitz were both gently ushered out of the door. Alex Pritchard and Jon Toral returned to their parent clubs after jobs extremely well done. Young defender, Alfie Mawson, understandably preferred the prospect of immediate first team football at Barnsley rather than an uncertain future at Brentford. Striker Will Grigg was deemed not to be up to scratch and was despatched to Wigan in return for a seven-figure fee. Tony Craig returned to Millwall with our heartfelt best wishes and thanks for providing us with three years of unblemished service. Stalwarts Richard Lee and Kevin O'Connor both retired and Jonathan Douglas moved to Ipswich when it was made clear to him that after four good seasons he was now surplus to requirements.

Stuart Dallas wanted the opportunity to play every week, something that was likely to be denied him at Brentford and rejoined Uwe Rösler at Leeds United for a fee of well over a million pounds. More contentiously, star full back Moses Odubajo left this week for fellow Championship rivals Hull City who met his release clause fee of three and a half million pounds.

The supporters have understandably been disturbed and unsettled by the loss of so many players as well as the Andre Gray saga, which still remains unresolved. Hull have been banging on the door for the past week or so but have not matched our asking fee which is reputed to be in the region of eight million pounds, along with another two million pounds in add-ons. Whether the deal is resurrected or another club comes in for him is unknown at this stage but the star striker, so impressive in preseason with four goals to his name, is expected to lead the attack against Ipswich on Saturday. The situation there is quite simple, the club currently holds all the aces and Gray will only leave if we are overwhelmed by an offer and another player of a similar ilk would of course, replace him.

We are in a confusing new world where players will regularly come and go, with the ones that either surpassed themselves or even fell short of expectations being replaced by cheaper, younger and ideally more promising new arrivals from off the conveyor belt that hopefully never stops.

Odubajo made it clear in his interview today that he considered Hull to be a bigger club than Brentford, and however much it hurts and angers us to hear such comments, I am afraid that they are the unpalatable truth for the time being, until we identify and obtain new revenue streams. I fully suspect that Moses has at least tripled his salary after his move and unfortunately money talks and Hull City, bloated and replete with Premier League television money and now parachute payments, have far, far more of it than us.

Let's look on the bright side; we have brought in eight new recruits with, I am sure, more to come before the end of the transfer window. Andreas Bjelland and Yoann Barbet look as if they will strengthen our central defensive options. Konstantin Kerschbaumer has impressed as an all-action midfielder, Andy Gogia has shown pace and trickery on the flanks and strikers Philipp Hofmann and Lasse Vibe both have excellent track records. Midfielder Ryan Williams is a promising low cost gamble in midfield and unfortunately Josh McEachran has broken his foot and is *hors de combat* for the foreseeable future.

However unsettled our supporters are feeling, they need to take comfort from the fact that no less than eight of the members of the successful team that began our last few matches last season remain at the club with only Odubajo, Douglas and Pritchard having departed. Moses will undoubtedly be replaced shortly and stringent efforts are being made to identify a playmaker that can replicate or even better Pritchard's achievements of last season. Perhaps Jota will be given the chance to play in the middle where he could well prove to be more influential than he is when isolated on the wing? Players like David Button, Jake Bidwell, Harlee Dean and Alan Judge can also only improve after the experience and confidence they gained last season.

How will they gel as a team? The jury is still out as the preseason preparations were hampered by injuries and uncertainty. Premier League Stoke City were well-beaten as we demonstrated our full potential but we were similarly outplayed last weekend at Norwich City. There is also a totally new management and coaching team settling down in their new surroundings.

Plus ça change, plus c'est la même chose. This needs to be our motto and mantra for the foreseeable future. Let's simply look at the Southampton model, acknowledge its success and then replicate and even adapt it. It will take some time to get used to the new way of the world and it might well be a little while before our new squad finds its feet but I am certain that this season will ultimately prove to be as exciting, fulfilling and successful as last year.

Get Out Of Jail Card For Brentford – 9/8/15

Brentford fans have learned that you leave Griffin Park early at your peril. Last season the Bees scored twelve times in the ninetieth minute or later and from the evidence of yesterday afternoon it would appear that little is going to change over the coming nine months given that Brentford got out of jail and secured the most unlikely of points against Ipswich Town with goals in the ninety-third and ninety-sixth minutes respectively.

Brentford certainly dominated the possession and shots statistics but this was a curate's egg of a performance – good in parts but otherwise substandard although there were extenuating circumstances that we will deal with later.

Ipswich were their customary tough and solid selves but they had also added some pace and flair to their brawn with two tricky wingers in Fraser, so impressive for Bournemouth at Griffin Park last season, and Maitland-Niles, on loan from Arsenal. They tormented us down the flanks and McCormack and Bidwell were too often left trailing in their wake. Given that the surprise central defensive partnership of Dean and Tarkowski also looked slow and uncertain and were dominated by Sears and Murphy, we creaked ominously at the back and but for the immaculate David Button Ipswich could have been out of sight before our Lazarus-like resurrection, rather than merely two goals ahead.

And yet it had all started so well for Brentford who initially overcame the massive handicap of an abominable Griffin Park surface, which cut up from the opening whistle. It had been liberally sanded but this did not prevent a constant flow of divots and the bumpy and uneven surface did not allow us to play our normal free-flowing style of football with any confidence that the pitch would not misbehave.

The Bees dominated the opening half-hour with Judge and Gogia prominent. Andy was a live wire, always looking for the ball, cutting inside at will and debutant fullback Emmanuel could not live with him. Jota was too hot to handle, streaking past his fullback with ease but with a frustrating lack of end product. For all Brentford's possession there were far too few actual chances created with some flurries from set pieces, which have been vastly improved this season, and Judge also shot narrowly wide from a free kick. Hofmann was a surprise choice to play upfront instead of Andre Gray who, given all the recent transfer speculation surrounding him, was apparently not in the correct frame of mind to start the match, and he worked hard and showed clever touches on the ball without overly threatening the Ipswich goal.

The big opportunity came and went when Judge's brilliant control allowed him to kill a difficult pass instantly and his accurate cross was met by Jota lurking unmarked in front of goal but his firm close range header hit Bialkowski and somehow stayed out and instead of the net billowing and the confidence boost that a goal would have provided, we immediately lost the initiative.

The visitors grew into the game as our midfield was pushed back by the hardworking Skuse and Bru and we started to retreat deep in our half and but for Button's wonderful point-blank save from Sears we would have fallen behind earlier than we did as Ipswich dominated the last ten minutes of the half.

We looked to have escaped unscathed and we longed for the break and the chance to reorganise but instead we conceded a soft and eminently avoidable goal right on the interval when we backed off and dozed in the sunshine as the ball was passed square to Fraser who advanced unchallenged and picked his spot from long-range. The ball pinged off the post and ricocheted across goal to the right wing from where the ball was quickly crossed in by Emmanuel and Bru was totally unmarked and scored with a clever acrobatic over the shoulder volley.

The Bees left the field disconsolate and up against it as for all their clever play early on they were not incisive enough and when the chance came it was spurned. Surely we would come out for the second half reinvigorated and take the game to Ipswich? We all thought that would be the case but the total opposite happened. An enormous long throw from Knudsen was ridiculously allowed to bounce in our box without penalty but we were slow, torpid and sluggish and were swiftly punished again when Ipswich broke quickly from our corner and Bru's perfectly timed through ball beat our naïve offside trap and Sears was left in ample time and space to roar in on goal unchallenged, draw the helpless Button and slip the ball to the unmarked Fraser who scored easily in front of the Ipswich supporters now bouncing up and down in triumph behind the Brook Road goal.

What followed then was not easy to either watch or describe as Brentford visibly disintegrated in the heat. Kerschbaumer disappeared after a reasonable start and Diagouraga went deeper and deeper. Judge was left to probe alone, like a whirling dervish, but the harder he tried, the less came off for him.

Jota dribbled into blind alleys and Hofmann and Gogia were totally starved of possession. Ipswich probed and jabbed at our overworked defence and but for Button a third goal would have come.

Midfield was our strength and joy last season but now ours had been overwhelmed, outplayed and had totally gone missing. Maybe it was the pitch that did not allow us to play our normal quick, short passing game, perhaps it was the lack of the likes of Odubajo and Pritchard who used pace and guile to open up defences but our challenge and poise evaporated and we were visibly wilting in the sun as Ipswich bossed the proceedings.

Last season Mark Warburton relied solely on Plan A but now Marinus Dijkhuizen shuffled his pack and brought on two strikers in Gray and Vibe who replaced the invisible Kerschbaumer and Alan McCormack who had used the ball well and almost put a brilliant curling cross on the head of the straining Jota but had struggled defensively. The Bees changed formation and went to three at the back in a 3-4-1-2 formation with Vibe playing just behind Gray and Hofmann – and nothing really changed at first.

Gray was a spark plug, strong, rangy and fast and he almost got in behind as Brentford finally adapted their play to the vagaries and limitations of the pitch and went long ball. We won very little up front and even fewer second balls but gradually we regained control, perhaps as much because Ipswich funnelled backwards thinking that the job had been done and withdrew both their wingers. Jonathan Douglas came on to a hero's ovation – not something that I really approved of, as he is now the enemy and applause and an acknowledgement of his achievements for the Bees could and should have waited until the final whistle.

Chances finally started to come but they appeared to be too little too late as Gray set up first Vibe who shot weakly at Bialkowski's leg and then Judge who fired wastefully high, wide and none too handsome. The game drifted towards its conclusion, Ipswich tried to play out time but soon after the five minutes of injury time where signalled, Tarkowski hoofed the ball forward and Gray was away beyond the clutches of Smith, he could not be caught and finished clinically. We perked up and Ipswich looked rattled. The ball pinged around the Ipswich goal and a last gasp corner was earned. Button lumbered forward and Judge swung the ball in. The keeper flapped and the ball hit a defender and rebounded onto the crossbar and Tarky reacted quicker than anyone else and poked home the unlikeliest and most undeserved of equalisers.

The crowd bellowed its approval in a mixture of delight and incredulity as we had stolen a point right at the death. Credit must go to the new Head Coach who had not had the easiest of weeks as his squad visibly disintegrated in front of him as he lost the services of Douglas, Moses and Dallas. He also had the uncertainty of the Gray situation to deal with as well as some so-called supporters who were quick to call for the return of Warburton when things began to go pear-shaped. He made good substitutions and changed our shape and his efforts received their reward.

There is much to learn from yesterday. The back four was nowhere near good enough and Bjelland, Barbet and O'Connell saw nothing to make them feel that they will not challenge for a place. Moses too needs replacing as we missed his pace and interplay with Jota. The pitch was a great leveller and needs immediate attention as it did not allow us to play as we like so I reserve any judgement on our midfield. As for Gray, his situation must and surely will be resolved over the next seven days. He was immense when he came on and probably added another million pounds to his burgeoning value. If he goes, then he goes and he will be replaced.

We did well to emerge with a point given the problems we faced. A week is a long time in football and I am sure that much will have changed before we run out for our next Championship match at Bristol City next Saturday.

Who's On First? – 10/8/15

I spent some of yesterday afternoon relaxing on the sofa and perusing all the team lineups from Saturday's first matches of the new season. I always enjoy looking at what has taken place at all ninety-two clubs over the summer and checking out who has joined them in the close season and who, indeed, has left. Time was when the same names reassuringly appeared on teamsheets year after year but things have changed as with freedom of contract, the influence of agents, cost-cutting and natural wastage there now appears to be a much more rapid turnover of players at all levels of the game. There are also more and more unknown trialists from across the globe that seem to appear from out of the blue, have their brief moment in the sun and then rapidly disappear without trace.

Brentford are a prime example as ten players have left Griffin Park and eight have arrived since the end of last season. No wonder it is hard for supporters to keep up with all the comings and goings.

The Daily Telegraph used to publish a list of all the transfers in and out of each club, which was regularly updated throughout the summer, but it does not seem to have been produced this year so it took me quite some time to discover more about some of the new names I unearthed during my research.

As is my custom, I was looking to see how many former Brentford players, both permanent and loanees I could find still plying their trade elsewhere in the football pyramid. Given the rapid recent turnover of players at the club I expected to find quite a few, and I wasn't to be disappointed.

There were slim pickings in the Premier League and I was only able to unearth Lewis Grabban who missed an early open goal when playing for Norwich against his old club, Crystal Palace, former loanee Jeffrey Schlupp now a regular at Leicester City as a marauding left back and Steve Sidwell who came on as a late substitute for Stoke City and was turned with embarrassing ease by Philippe Coutinho before he smashed in Liverpool's winning goal. I had been hopeful that Alex Pritchard would use his wonderful season at Brentford as a springboard to at least secure a place on the Spurs bench but injury has so far scuppered his chances. Hopefully Saido Berahino will play for West Brom tonight and bring the number up to four.

More and more former Brentford players are now at rival Championship clubs, proof indeed of our own rising standards, and yesterday's live Championship bore draw at Preston saw Adam Forshaw dozing gently on the end of the Middlesbrough bench before he was roused from his torpor to play out the last few moments of a dreadfully uninspired match.

Clayton Donaldson helped Birmingham to a victory over Reading and it was his cross, which led to a fine headed goal by debutant Jon Toral. I had hoped that we could entice Toral back to Brentford this season but he obviously felt that he would receive more opportunities at Birmingham. Simon Cox almost saved the day when he won a last minute penalty for Reading but it was squandered. Surprisingly, Jordan Rhodes is still at Blackburn Rovers despite several offers from Middlesbrough and Darren Pratley also started for Bolton Wanderers. Two very recent former Bees also featured, in Jonathan Douglas, a late Ipswich substitute at Griffin

Park and Stuart Dallas who almost marked his debut for Leeds with goal with a brilliant effort that was pushed onto the crossbar by Burnley keeper Tom Heaton. Tom Adeyemi also made his debut for Leeds on Saturday.

Simon Moore flubbed his lines when given a rare chance to start for Cardiff City, misjudging a Ben Pringle cross which allowed Matt Smith to score a gift goal for Fulham. Dean Bowditch's goal also helped MK Dons to a comfortable win at Rotherham watched by Lee Hodson on the bench.

Brentford were also well represented in League One. John Mousinho led Burton to an opening day victory over Scunthorpe but Alfie Mawson's debut for Barnsley was less memorable as they subsided to defeat at Chesterfield. Harry Forrester scored for Doncaster with a perfectly judged thirty yard lob, but unfortunately his technique let him down as he had simply been trying to return the ball to the Bury keeper after an injury break and Doncaster manager Paul Dickov sportingly ordered his defence to allow Leon Clarke to walk through them for an immediate equaliser. Myles Weston also helped Southend to a point at Fleetwood. Million pound striker Will Grigg made his debut for Wigan but missed a good opportunity to equalise at Coventry.

Stuart Nelson was back in goal for Gillingham who hammered promotion favourites Sheffield United, aided and abetted by an early poacher's goal from Luke Norris. Josh Wright also made a late appearance from the bench. Kyle Vassell was forced to endure Peterborough's dismal defeat at Rochdale from the bench. Tony Craig skippered Millwall to an excellent win at Shrewsbury and Nathan Byrne was the star of the show with a sixteen minute hat trick for Swindon against Bradford City for whom Billy Clarke missed a vital penalty kick, and James Wilson played at centre half for Oldham Athletic.

In League Two, Jake Reeves and Karleigh Osborne were unable to prevent AFC Wimbledon slumping to a home defeat by Plymouth Argyle. Nicky Adams helped Northampton to a win at Bristol Rovers and Leon Legge made his debut for a totally revamped Cambridge United team for whom Robbie Simpson scored a late goal. Craig Woodman is still at Exeter City, as is Clinton Morrison, and they beat a Yeovil team for whom Marc Laird and Ryan Dickson played and Ryan was tripped for a penalty kick.

Leyton Orient had Sammy Moore in midfield as they defeated Barnet for whom John Akinde led their attack. Matt Harrold is at Crawley and came off the bench at Oxford United. Goalkeeper Liam O'Brien was an unused Dagenham substitute at Portsmouth. Dean Wells had a brief first team career at Brentford over a decade ago and remains a regular at Stevenage for whom Fraser Franks now plays.

Four former Brentford players remain at Wycombe and Aaron Pierre, Sam Wood, Marcus Bean and Paul Hayes all played against York City and James Spencer who had a brief loan spell for the Bees back in 2012 is still at Notts County.

I also must not forget the Scottish contingent in Shay Logan, Farid El Alagui and now Rob Kiernan.

One day I will try and repeat the exercise and identify as many ex-Bees as I can within the non-league pyramid – if I can find enough hours in the day!

Shambles – 11/8/15

Despite the unexpected and remarkable fillip of two goals on Saturday against Ipswich so late that they arrived almost at the end of the classified football results on *Sports Report*, there was still an almost perceptible sense of foreboding before tonight's Capital One cup tie against Oxford United.

Head Coach Marinus Dijkhuizen had also announced that he would make extensive team changes and give valuable match practice to his previously unused squad members as well as some deserving members of the Development Squad.

Supporters with only a short memory could recall recent matches in the same competition when a similar course was followed without much success.

Two seasons ago, a young team, naïve and wet behind the ears, was massacred by a full strength Derby County who, thankfully and mercifully, declared at five after lessons had not been learned when a mixed squad had barely squeaked through in the previous round against Dagenham.

Last season another weakened side played out that remarkable six-all draw against a plucky Dagenham team which was almost allowed to win a game in which we had threatened at times to run riot.

The Griffin Park pitch, so lush and true last season was another massive concern as despite extensive close season attention, it now resembled nothing more than a sandy beach painted green and the uneven, lumpy and bumpy surface was a ticking time bomb which threatened ankles and cruciates alike and had defied Brentford's best efforts to play our customary brand of incisive one touch football on Saturday, and stymied by the vagaries and inconsistencies of the surface, the Bees had resorted to an inelegant and untypical long ball game.

There had also been an ominous silence regarding Andre Gray. Perhaps no news was good news but we remained in total ignorance about his future and whether he would be in the right frame of mind to be included in the starting eleven.

The injury list was also growing on a seemingly daily basis with Alan Judge, Jota and Harlee Dean, Josh McEachran and of course, Scott Hogan all unavailable and, as for Lewis Macleod, mention of his name brought about a bemused shrug as the current whereabouts and state of fitness of this elusive young man remained a closely guarded secret.

Well, however concerned we were at the prospect of the match, the reality was far worse than even the greatest pessimist could have envisaged as a ludicrously weak Brentford team which treated the competition, the opposition and, indeed, our supporters with utter disrespect and contempt was hammered by an experienced and committed and crucially, unchanged Oxford United team which barely had to go through the motions or break sweat to stroll to an easy four goal victory. And we were lucky that it was only four.

Oxford were a team who played as a cohesive unit, Brentford were a disparate rabble, a cobbled together collection of strangers and callow kids who lacked leadership and frankly were a disgrace to the shirt.

In the club's defence, the Head Coach had stated that he would rest players but nobody could have expected the eleven players who actually started to have rested to the extent that they did throughout a first half which saw them lethargically chasing shadows and falling three goals behind within ten minutes.

All three were the result of staggering and almost laughable defensive howlers by Bjelland and Bonham which were ruthlessly punished by Sercombe, Hylton and, spectacularly with a forty-yard lob into an empty net by the exceptional Kemar Roofe after the hapless Bonham went walkabout.

There were eleven, yes, eleven team changes from Saturday with none of the starters against Ipswich being named in the team. We fielded seven debutants in Bjelland, Barbet, O'Connell, Williams, Udemaga, Laurent and Senior and the team was completed by Bonham, Clarke, Vibe and the most experienced player on view in Yennaris.

Indeed the entire team had played less than a dozen first team matches for Brentford between them. No wonder the performance was shambolic as such a scratch eleven who had never played together before and surely never will again could not be expected to succeed against a team of hardened opponents who played to win. Surely our team of analysts had scouted our opponents and realized that they were a more than decent team? As it was we totally underestimated them and paid the penalty for doing so.

Just to make things even worse Bjelland limped off before the interval with a serious knee injury and then your correspondent was hit flush on the head by an errant Brentford shot from Alan McCormack during the half time break and knocked over, thus ending his active participation as a spectator.

A suitable ending to a terrible evening and I would like to express my grateful thanks to the club's paramedics who were helpful, kind and solicitous to me as I felt extremely dazed, sick and shocked – and not just as a result of our appalling performance!

I am told that the second half was another non-event for Brentford who finally lost by four clear goals.

Squad rotation is one thing, what Brentford did tonight is quite another. We have lots of promising players with massive potential and tonight will have done them no good whatsoever as they were hung out to dry and perhaps some budding careers have even taken a backwards step.

Play a couple of them, certainly, but surround, protect and encourage them with a coterie of first teamers. To make eleven changes and field a team with so little experience was a disaster waiting to happen and a catastrophic decision by the new Head Coach who fully deserves the criticism he is sure to face although perhaps he should have received better advice from others behind the scenes?

This was a night of shame and embarrassment for the club coming at the worst possible time just when a new regime is seeking to establish itself with the fans.

Dijkhuizen has inherited a tough enough job with all the raised expectations after last season's achievements and the massive success of Mark Warburton, without making it even harder for himself, something that he has now done after the disappointing events of tonight. He desperately needed that first victory in charge of the team and this match offered him the perfect opportunity to get his reign off to a good start but he spurned it.

I am going to bed now feeling lousy and the blow on the head, nasty as it was, is not the sole cause of my pain and discomfort.

Time To Move On – 14/8/15

It is time for every Brentford supporter to put the last couple of weeks behind us. The past fortnight has seen a series of misfortunes and setbacks both on and off the pitch which have been allowed to snowball and caused even the most optimistic of us to look into our glass and see it as half empty rather than full to the brim, but now we need to put an end to all feelings of negativity and look forward and not back.

But first let's just get everything off our chest one last time before we move on:

- A patchy end to the preseason with unconvincing performances and defeats at Luton and Norwich

- Being hit by an injury jinx that now affects Josh McEachran, Scott Hogan, Lewis Macleod, Jota, Marcos Tebar, Nico Yennaris and Andreas Bjelland with our record signing looking likely to miss the entire season

- Harlee Dean and Alan Judge falling foul of a bug

- A seemingly settled looking squad losing the services of Jonathan Douglas, Stuart Dallas and Moses Obubajo

- The *will-he – won't-he* Andre Gray saga which is still being played out in front of us

- *Pitchgate* and how the club has been made to look bumbling and incompetent by its failure to provide an adequate surface, resulting in the postponement of our next home game against Birmingham

- The Oxford United Capital One cup fiasco and how we shot ourselves in the foot by fielding seven debutants before subsiding to an appalling four goal home defeat to a club two divisions below us who took the tie seriously

- Murmurings of discontent from some of the faithful, culminating in the over-the-top applause for the returning Jonathan Douglas and the ludicrous cries in support of the departed Mark Warburton

- Some totally uncalled for and highly unpleasant abuse of goalkeeper Jack Bonham on Tuesday night. Admittedly he had a shocker but I cannot see how belittling him is going to improve his performance

Is that everything or have I missed anything out? If so then let's just acknowledge and accept everything that has happened, put our negativity behind us and instead concentrate on the immediate future and on all the positive things that are happening in and around the club.

A quick search on *YouTube* will reveal a wonderful new documentary made by *Copa 90* on the similarities in approach between both Brentford and FC Midtjylland. It features our Co-Director of Football Rasmus Ankersen and a number of supporters discussing how the clever and innovative use of statistics and mathematical modelling has transformed the fortunes of both clubs and made them the talk of the football world.

Watching the film reinvigorated me and totally renewed my faith in what we are doing and how we are doing it.

We are only one game into what will be a marathon Championship season. There are still forty-five matches to go, plenty of time for us to have bedded in our new players, sorted out our best team, established our optimum pattern of play and given our new management and coaching team sufficient opportunity to understand the harsh realities of the league in which they are now competing.

Marinus Dijkhuizen has already come in for some sniping and criticism from supporters who are quick to find fault and compare him to his predecessor. Given the management structure now in place behind the scenes Marinus is possibly feeling the heat and taking the blame for decisions taken by others, although he was naïve in the extreme to underestimate the quality of the challenge that Oxford United would pose and decide to field a team that was so lacking in experience.

Rather than damn him with criticism or at best, faint praise, I would instead commend him for his actions last Saturday when, fully aware that his team was being outplayed and was offering little or no threat to an Ipswich team that was totally dominating the midfield, he was brave and flexible enough to make changes early in the second half, bring on Gray and Vibe who revitalised a flagging team and go to three at the back which allowed more players to pour forward until we had five attackers on the pitch by the end.

I honestly do not think that Mark Warburton would have responded to a tough situation as bravely as Marinus did and his tactical flexibility and positivity received its due reward with two late goals that earned an unlikely point.

Today also saw the arrival of a replacement for the departed Moses Odubajo, and is now the custom, nobody outside the magic circle within the club could have guessed his identity, heard of him or known anything about his capabilities. Twenty-three year old right back Maxime Colin has arrived from Belgian side Anderlecht for a fee rumoured to be around nine hundred thousand pounds, or about a quarter of the sum we received from Hull for Moses. This is yet another example of our selling high and replacing far cheaper. French Under 20 international Maxime is another total mystery to us supporters but is reputed to be skilful on the ball and quick and will therefore fit in perfectly with the way we intend to play.

Maxime is our ninth signing of the summer and with the exception of Ryan Williams, who is a cheap anomaly, Josh McEachran and the experienced Andreas Bjelland, the other six in Andy Gogia (Hallescher), Yoann Barbet (Chamois Niortais), Konstantin Kerschbaumer (Admira Wacker), Philipp Hofmann (Kaiserslautern), Lasse Vibe (Goteborg) and now Maxime Colin (Anderlecht) all fit the same pattern being young foreign players with bags of room for improvement, reasonably priced, totally unknown to us and not apparently on the radar of any of our rivals. This last named fact means to me that we are both identifying and scouting prospects far better, widely and more thoroughly than our competition, or else we are signing players that have already been considered and rejected by everybody else! My money is on the first option. Last season Brentford and Wigan seemed to share an identical shopping list, now we appear to be streets ahead of most other teams with far greater resources than us.

Our new arrivals will take time to settle down and there is no guarantee that they will all prove to be a success but the chances are that we will have some new heroes to enjoy as the season develops. As for Andre Gray, hopefully he can now get his head down and concentrate on scoring goals for us, and if he does so then his move will come, perhaps sooner rather than later, and given his rapid rate of improvement, I am sure that he will end up playing for a far bigger fish than Hull City, and if and when he does leave us then his replacement, who I am pretty certain has already been identified and his club approached, will shortly arrive in his place, and he will also fit the pattern of the rest of our new signings in terms of his age and development potential.

We simply have to believe and trust in the process. Of course there will be some bumpy roads ahead and lots of teething problems for us to overcome, and quite a bit of patience might well be called for on our part as we bed in new players, staff and systems, but our basic premise and business plan is sound and is surely the only one that allows Brentford, a veritable minnow in comparison with the giants in the Championship, to compete on an almost even playing field.

We have a tiny budget compared to the rest of the league, many of whom are buttressed by massive parachute payments. Last season was miraculous and our success was due to our having a number of good players who were well managed and prepared and who took the opposition by surprise. We were generally underestimated and the other teams will not make that mistake again.

We can do the same or even better this season but we supporters need to recognise just how tough it will be for us to do so as we need to keep progressing merely to stand still and we also have to try to manage our expectations which have become inflated and in my view unrealistic.

Perhaps we need to consolidate for a year before we push on again? It just remains to be seen and maybe a finish halfway up the league might in the circumstances be just as impressive as finishing in the playoff positions was last season?

Tomorrow will be another tough test at a revitalised Bristol City team still on a high from their promotion to the Championship last season. We will have to keep a careful eye out for their most dangerous attacker in central defender Aden Flint, scorer of a quite glorious own goal the last time the two teams met at Griffin Park but he has since proved to be far more lethal at the other end of the pitch and we will concede set pieces at our peril.

Hopefully our nemesis Keith Stroud will also have one of his less combustible days and decide that he has already done us far more than our fair share of damage in recent years and not for once be an influence on proceedings. If we can impose ourselves on the game early on and silence the crowd then three points are well within our grasp and I am hopeful of a successful outcome.

I look forward to seeing you all there tomorrow!

A Topsy-Turvy Day! – 16/8/15

Visiting a team that has just won promotion for their first home game in their new division is a journey always fraught with peril and the vagaries of the fixture list decreed that that was Brentford's fate yesterday as the Bees attempted to beard Bristol City in their den.

Not unexpectedly after Tuesday night's disaster against Oxford United, Marinus Dijkhuizen made eleven changes for the second match running, reverting to the same team that began against Ipswich Town the previous

Saturday with the exception of Andre Gray replacing the injured Jota who is yet another addition to Brentford's long-term injury list and will be a massive loss to us.

I had previously remarked in my match preview how crucial it would be for the Bees to start well and silence the crowd and they obviously heeded my wise words and for a whole one hundred and fourteen seconds we totally dominated the proceedings and never gave the home team a look-in let alone a sniff at goal.

Job done, surely, but things then took a sudden turn for the worse when Button was pressurised and, shades of Sheffield Wednesday last season, Brentford gave up possession far too easily from his fly kick, Ayling ran with the ball from halfway, our entire midfield and defence evaporated and new signing Jonathan Kodjia was left with the time and space to slot the ball into the net for a well-worked goal from their point of view, but one of total disorganisation and incompetence from ours.

Our well-laid plans had gone up in smoke and a long, tough afternoon seemed to be in prospect as the invigorated home team with their tails up with a rabid crowd screaming encouragement took total control. We had set up in a 4-3-3 formation with Gray and Gogia on the flanks and whilst they were both supporting Hofmann, Gray, in particular was doing nothing to assist the beleaguered Alan McCormack who was constantly faced with his ultimate nightmare – two speedy players in Freeman and the overlapping Bryan running at him in tandem. Our right side was lopsided and overwhelmed and all the danger came from the City left wing.

We were in deep trouble but somehow we regrouped and an incisive attack saw Kerschbaumer's clever back heel release Diagouraga who found space and slipped Gray through on the left but his instant lobbed volley from the edge of the area was weak and poorly executed and even looked as if it was dropping wide before Ben Hamer, making his home debut for his new club, made a total hash of his save and pat-a-caked the ball straight into the path of Alan Judge who was left with an open goal and he calmly accepted the gift.

This unexpected equaliser did nothing to change the way the game was going as a rampant Bristol City simply battered us, creating chances at will as they waltzed through a non-existent midfield and defence and only a combination of Button's saves and appalling finishing kept us level until a left wing corner was headed in comfortably at the near post by Aaron Wilbraham as our zonal marking system broke down and he got in between two straining defenders. Another shocking goal to concede and I just hope that our set-piece coach will also spend some time working on how best to defend corners as well as score from them.

Not content with two, Bristol City went close on several occasions to putting the scoreline well out of our reach as we continued to flounder and chase shadows in the heat. Ashton Gate was a cauldron and the Bees were simply trying to keep in the game when out of the carnage came salvation when, soon after the half-hour Luke Freeman launched himself into a ludicrous and totally unnecessary Kung Fu-like aerial challenge with Harlee Dean. The ball was at head height, but so was Freeman's foot, which poleaxed the Brentford defender and Keith Stroud, for once, took his time and consulted his assistant before eventually producing his red card.

The crowd seethed with anger and disbelief and the tide turned. McCormack was no longer pressurised and Bristol City fell back in disarray. Brentford took full advantage and equalised just before the interval when Bidwell and Judge kept possession well near the left corner flag and Judge curled the ball in perfectly and with Gray and Williams stretching for the ball it was deflected through the hapless Hamer's legs into the net. Whose goal was it? Gray was awarded it initially but it was then debited to the defender however Alan Judge has also claimed it – another mystery that remains to be solved.

The biggest mystery, though, was why Wilbraham did not suffer an identical fate to his teammate Freeman as his assault on Tarkowski left the Brentford defender with a smashed and broken nose, however this time the referee saw no evil.

The equaliser dashed the spirits of the home team and took the wind out of their sails and the second half saw a procession of Brentford possession and chances as the Bees turned the match on its head and totally dominated the proceedings. Button was forced into a decent save from Pack and there were a few flurries and breakaways but most of the action was at the other end.

Bidwell forced a decent save from Hamer with a long-ranger, Gray turned well and found space but skied his effort and McCormack also went close as Brentford used their extra man well and made Bristol City work hard and they soon ran themselves out in the energy sapping conditions. The goal had to come and it eventually arrived on the hour when Gogia and McCormack worked space on the right and Gray hammered home the fullback's low centre – he is a man on a mission and is already looking twice the player he was last season.

He and Hofmann are beginning to forge an effective partnership and they combined well ten minutes later when the ball was played into Hofmann's feet and he was far too strong for Williams as he turned the defender and swept the ball imperiously into the bottom corner for a goal of true international class.

A Brentford team that had regained its Mojo passed the ball around with growing confidence and played out the remainder of the game quietly and efficiently.

It is impossible to assess yesterday with any degree of accuracy or certainty. We won and scored four goals away from home. Gray and Hofmann impressed and were a constant danger. Judge too was a massive influence and is growing into his new role as an advanced midfield playmaker and inspiration. Jack O'Connell also opened some eyes with a defensive performance of calmness, strength and composure when he replaced Tarkowski and McCormack recovered well and was a massive influence in the second half.

To counterbalance the positives, we could easily have been dead and buried if City had taken their early chances and had Freeman not had his rush of blood. The midfield provided flimsy cover at best to a defence that was overrun early on and we lacked balance and organisation. Diagouraga grew into the game but Kerschbaumer is still finding his feet and the wingers need to understand and adhere to their defensive responsibilities as well as just bomb forward.

Given the appalling few days that the club had suffered both on and off the pitch and an ever-growing injury list that now sees the addition of Tarkowski and the loss of Jota for three to four months, the team showed tremendous grit and determination and no small amount of skill to recover from what looked like a desperate position.

The win is more than welcome, as it will further build confidence and a sense of togetherness amongst a squad that is still settling down and is very much a work in progress. The Andre Gray situation also hangs over us like a sword of Damocles and in that regard the end of the Transfer Window cannot come soon enough. At the moment we simply cannot afford to lose him unless our hand is forced.

The new Head Coach heard his name being serenaded by the fans for the first time yesterday and he responded with a wave of acknowledgement. That is good news too as a bond is beginning to be forged between him and the supporters. There is much hard work that is required over the coming weeks and I, for one, am delighted that Tuesday's match has been postponed particularly given the lack of our current resources.

Three Development Squad players in Senior, Udumaga and Clarke found themselves on the bench yesterday – it was either them or pick somebody at random from the crowd. Maxime Colin will join the squad next week and hopefully Sam Saunders will also be fit for selection but fresh faces are needed to replenish our squad given the quite ridiculous number of injuries that we are currently suffering.

With four points from two games we now find ourselves with an excellent platform to build from and with hard work, good management and some new blood we can soon settle down into a cohesive and effective unit.

Happiness is an Alan Judge equaliser at Bristol City

One Week In – 18/8/15

Mark Croxford is a long-established and well-respected Brentford supporter and author who is an astute observer of the Brentford scene and he has produced a fascinating overview and his own personal viewpoint regarding our start to the season which was published yesterday on *The Griffin Park Grapevine* fans' message board and Mark has kindly agreed to allow me to reproduce his article here as it deserves the widest readership possible:

One week in ... and it's far too early to make assessments, but here goes!

Our new Head Coach has shown naïvety and bravery in equal measures over the course of the three games. I can't say that's entirely unexpected but Marinus's success or failure will no doubt be somewhat based on how well he balances these two traits.

I wrote some weeks back that I felt that the two Sporting Directors had not lived up to their summer promises and I still subscribe to that view, as so much emphasis was based on having a big squad allowing Dijkhuizen to be able to rotate.

I know that injuries have hampered their efforts but – even allowing for the long-term losses of Bjelland, Jota and McEachran, we are still left with a squad of just nineteen (and that's assuming Andre Gray stays). We have to assume that this season's planning took place with the names of Hogan and Macleod on a separate piece of paper.

Ron Noades said little that I concurred with but I do recall one of his comments being that one should always assume that between ten to fifteen percent of the playing squad will be unavailable through injury at any one time. So that's about par for the course then – the huge drawback being that this batch is predominantly long-term absentees. By the way, that figure of nineteen also includes the likes of Tebar, Yennaris and Saunders who we may not have expected to see play for us too often.

So how great an impact will all the injuries have on us? I reckon Bjelland is a massive loss. His brief forty minute display against Oxford was uninspiring to say the least, but he was clearly brought in to be the mainstay of a back four which was hoped and intended to be far less porous than last season. Can O'Connell and Barbet fill his boots? Who knows, but over the course of a whole season the prospect of one of these two talented but inexperienced youngsters playing such a key role is a big, big gamble.

I don't for one moment believe that anyone really expected Dean and Tarkowski to form our central defensive partnership for the start of the season and I'd be amazed, and frankly disappointed, if they are there for the duration.

Jota's loss for up to four months is also a major blow. Aside from the entertainment value he provides, the goals he contributes are priceless. Personally, I don't think his assists are anywhere near frequent enough – he has so much possession in dangerous areas but delivers such a small percentage of assists – but just look at last season's goal-scoring credits.

We scored seventy-eight goals in the Championship. Take away the thirty-seven goals netted by Jota, Pritchard, Douglas, Dallas and almost half have disappeared. If Gray's sixteen were to go too, I reckon that's practically three quarters of last season's goals that need to be found from elsewhere! I'm not saying it's impossible to achieve, but what a monumental ask!

McEachran's absence is a frustrating one. Maybe he was meant to be the holding midfielder and yet from the very, very limited view that we've had of him in preseason, he doesn't look to be someone to provide the defensive shield that the back four is crying out for. We've seen already that Toumani probably doesn't play that role either and the failure to have acquired a player like Mokotjo might prove to be the biggest mistake of all.

What of the other newcomers who have so far remained fit and healthy? Gogia is a more exciting winger than Dallas but far less effective in providing a left-sided attacking/defensive partnership with Bidwell. That might change as he gets used to English football but will he be able to contribute the goals and assists that Dallas did? Hopefully so.

Kerschbaumer has got potential without doubt. So far he's shown himself to be a willing worker and hard-runner but, and as is only to be expected in his early days, he alternates between impressive and invisible and does not influence the game in the way that Douglas was able to do. Maybe the loss of Douglas was inevitable and welcome off the field, but on the pitch his replacement is not obvious at the moment.

Yoann Barbet looks promising but it has to be remembered that this time last year, he'd never kicked a ball in anger in a first-team professional game so patience will be a necessary virtue in his development.

Jack O'Connell looks the real deal – and it's not beyond the realms of possibility that he'll turn out to be the unexpected star of the season. He certainly played well on Saturday when he replaced Tarkowski – yet another addition to the injury list!

And so to the front men. The Andre Gray scenario changes so rapidly that by the time I've finished typing this, he might have gone elsewhere! If he does, I genuinely fear for the season ahead. It has taken him a year to develop into the player he is and ready-made replacements within budget may not exist.

Philipp Hofmann will score goals I believe, but maybe not as many as the tally that Gray notched last season. Lasse Vibe may score goals too, but he looks to be someone who firstly needs a bit more time to become accustomed to the pace and strength of Championship football and then needs to find a suitable role for himself within the team framework.

Going back to where I started and the activities of the Sporting Directors and the recruitment team, I can't see much likelihood of a late influx of players to boost the ailing numbers, so perhaps this really will be a genuine season of transition and stability with the January window proving to be the busiest we've seen since the Andy Scott days.

I reckon the shopping list so far reads: a replacement for Bjelland (on and off the field), a strong and effective defensive midfielder (six steps up from Alan McCormack) and a true number ten or playmaker as have we got anyone within the squad who can currently play that role effectively?

A couple of loans wouldn't go amiss either – a wide player to cover for Jota's absence and a left-sided player to compete with the only two currently at the club (Bidwell and Gogia).

And as for Andre Gray? Who knows what will happen and if so, when? But don't forget all those goals that need to be made up! I'm not thinking about that any more – it's too frightening.

Thanks, Mark for taking the time to provide so cogent and well thought through an article. He makes many good points in particular about the missing goals that we will have to replace from midfield as well as the potential implications of losing Andre Gray and as always he has carefully researched his facts before he makes his opinions known.

Personally I think that the jury is still out and that it is far too early to make any judgements about how this season will progress.

The Head Coach appears to favour a 4-3-3 formation and ideally to play Gray and Hofmann together. Will the extra goals that such an exciting attacking partnership provides, rather than last season's lone striker policy, make up for the lack of defensive cover from midfield that was exposed as such a major weakness at Bristol City last Saturday? I have my doubts on the limited evidence to date.

The relentless procession of injuries has come as an unwelcome and unexpected blow, they have already hit us hard and their impact could well be long-term and far-reaching. I remain hopeful that swift action will be taken in the transfer market to help redress the problems that Mark has so clearly outlined, but it remains to be seen, and perhaps this season will be far tougher than a lot of supporters have envisaged and in that case consolidation in the Championship should be regarded as acceptable progress in its own right and a triumphant progress to the giddy heights of the Premier League might have to wait for another year or so?

What's Going On? – 20/8/15

So what's going on at Griffin Park as bemused Brentford supporters anxiously await the puff of white smoke that will finally confirm the departure of Andre Gray and the inevitable conclusion to what has developed into a seemingly never-ending saga that has dragged on for several weeks now?

On the face of it the evidence is damning, as Gray will be just one more addition to what now seems to be a massive and increasing exodus of players from Griffin Park since the end of last season.

Alex Pritchard, Jon Toral, Richard Lee, Tommy Smith, Alfie Mawson, Nick Proschwitz, Will Grigg, Stuart Dallas, Tony Craig, Jonathan Douglas, Moses Odubajo are the others who are no longer with us, and there have now been massive changes and upheavals to the settled squad that ended the season just a few short months ago in May.

However it is only when you look at all the departures in greater detail and analyse the reason for each one that you can obtain a full understanding of what has been going on.

Richard Lee retired, as also did Kevin O'Connor and Smith and Proschwitz were both deemed surplus to our requirements. Grigg too was not thought to be the answer to our needs up front despite his rehabilitation at MK Dons last season and to obtain a cool million pounds from Wigan for a player who has never found his feet at our club was surely good business on our part – even if he did not prove to be an inspired purchase in the first place.

Alex Pritchard's future was simply out of our hands as the loanee returned in triumph to his parent club, Spurs. Would that we were able to find a way to spirit him back to Griffin Park as his influence is sadly missed which is hardly surprising given how talented he is and how effective he was at playing the killer pass that opened up the opposition defence.

Jon Toral also returned to Arsenal after his loan spell, although there were certainly rumours that we had tried to retain his services either on loan or a permanent basis and I confess that it came as a real surprise to me when he joined Birmingham. It is open to question whether he would have played sufficiently often for us as a loan player to keep Arsenal happy but I was half expecting that he would become a permanent Brentford player as he would have been an excellent addition to the squad.

Alfie Mawson simply and understandably felt that he would not get a look-in at Griffin Park and joined Barnsley for whom he scored his first goal at Millwall on Tuesday night.

Stuart Dallas was another who felt that he would receive more opportunities elsewhere given that he was seen more as a valuable substitute rather than as an automatic first choice at Brentford. The fee of around one and a quarter million pounds represented a massive return on the sum paid by the club to Crusaders but I suspect that his value might well increase in coming years as he gains more experience, and hopefully our interests are protected with a sell-on clause.

The Jonathan Douglas situation has been discussed to death on message boards recently and I would agree that his influence was waning on the pitch and that he was unlikely to reconcile himself to becoming a bit part player. His departure was therefore the best solution for all parties although I still feel that he has yet to be replaced adequately particularly given Josh McEachran's injury. Tony Craig was another who needed to leave with our gratitude for services rendered over the past three years.

Our hands were then completely tied regarding the loss of star fullback Moses Odubajo to Hull City as a three and a half million pound release clause had been inserted into his contract in order to ensure that he joined us in the first place from Leyton Orient a year ago, at a time when bigger fish were also sniffing around him.

Hull offered us the money and we could not get anywhere close to competing with them in terms of the wages they were able to pay him given the income they have received from their spell in the Premier League plus the massive and iniquitous Parachute Payments that they are currently in receipt of.

It pains me to admit it but we are still small fry and remain well down the football totem pole. We are totally stymied and our growth is restricted by the limited capacity and lack of resources of Griffin Park and I understand that our income is in the bottom three of all twenty-four Championship teams.

No wonder we are losing our stars to clubs who can pay them more than us. We might say that we are *bigger* than say Hull City or even Bristol City, but we are deluding ourselves to even think that that is really the case. Maybe in years to come once we have moved into our new stadium at Lionel Road and reached the Premier League, or even stabilised in the top half of the Championship, we can then match what others are offering to our top players but for the time being we simply have to accept facts as they are.

We are no more than a stepping-stone and a proving ground where players receive a platform and the necessary support and encouragement to thrive, shine and improve. Bigger clubs than us who will certainly offer higher wages and perhaps even a better professional opportunity will then pick off the best of them.

Footballers have a short career and an even shorter window of opportunity. Today's budding star is tomorrow's broken leg or free transfer and I would never blame any footballer for chasing the main chance and following the money trail.

Let's assume that Andre Gray is earning around four thousand pounds per week at Brentford. This is a guess and I might well be miles out in my figure. Bristol City then come in and offer to pay him perhaps sixteen thousand pounds per week. What can he be expected to do in the circumstances? What would *you* do if you were offered the same choice?

I will tell you what will happen with Gray if you haven't already worked it out for yourself – he will quickly get his agent to see if a higher profile club is prepared to pay Brentford the required fee and either match or better the salary on offer.

If nothing else is forthcoming then he will surely sign for Bristol City as he cannot afford to allow such an incredible financial opportunity to perhaps quadruple his salary to slip through his hands. Nor should he be expected to. Loyalty for, and love of the club is for us supporters, not professional footballers. They have to look after Number One.

Let's now look at the situation for Brentford. Bristol City have apparently had an offer of nine million pounds accepted, perhaps seven million pounds down and an additional two million pounds dependent upon performance. Let me just repeat those figures and allow them to sink in. **Seven million pounds down and an additional two million pounds dependent upon performance**.

This for a player we bought for around six hundred thousand pounds a year or so ago. Ideally there is also a sell-on clause included too as well as an additional promotion bonus payment. This is double the previous record fee received for a player!

If we turn down an offer of this magnitude we risk having a disgruntled player on our hands whose value could quickly spiral downwards.

Similarly, promising young players are happy to join us, as they are secure in the knowledge that they will be in the shop window at Griffin Park and it becomes a win/win situation for all parties. We sign players who might otherwise have spurned us and we also benefit from the transfer fees that we eventually receive when they move on.

Should the Gray deal go through then we will have taken in over twelve and a half million pounds in transfer fees this summer with the potential of further payments to come.

The Brentford model is very simple and straightforward. We utilise our proprietary statistics and mathematical modelling techniques to identify hot young prospects that have either been ignored or undervalued by our rivals. We buy low then sell high once another club has reached our valuation of the player. Every player without exception is for sale assuming we receive adequate compensation.

The key though is what we do with all the money we receive. We are not asset stripping or hoarding the cash as some critics have asserted, and the money taken in is not siphoned off to pay off debt. Yes, some will go to ensure that we remain within the stringent requirements of Financial Fair Play but the majority is reinvested in the squad. The more money we bring in from player sales the more we can spend on investing in new talent.

Last year we sold Adam Forshaw and spent over a million pounds each on Moses Odubajo and Jota and around half that sum on Gray and Scott Hogan. Now we have upgraded exponentially as the money we have received from our outgoing players has enabled us to invest around six million pounds on the likes of Andreas Bjelland, Lasse Vibe, Philipp Hofmann, Josh McEachran, Yoann Barbet, Maxine Colin and Konstantin Kerschbaumer. There is also talk of us trying to bring in another four players before the Transfer Window shuts at the end of the month. That is a very tight deadline and we will do well to get suitable players in by that time and other clubs will also try and take advantage of our situation and charge us a premium.

The more we bring in, the more we can spend – it is a very simple formula. This year we spent over two million pounds, easily a club record fee, on Bjelland, and maybe very soon, given the extra transfer sums that have been received, we will be in a position to spend even more money on a player.

The problem is that the pressure is always on us to keep unearthing more and more uncut gems so that the conveyor belt can keep moving. It is far too early to say how successful any of our new signings will turn out to be and it is perhaps one of the cheaper newcomers, Andy Gogia, who might well turn out to be the most valuable, if he meets our expectations and turns out to be as good as is anticipated. With serious expenditure comes serious risk. Not all our signings will come off and some will fail to perform as well as expected.

Will Grigg turned out to be a total bust for us, but in the end we succeeded in more than doubling our total investment in him when we sold him to Wigan. It was a close run thing though, as at one time it seemed that we might well lose a significant sum on him, but thankfully he performed well on loan at MK Dons last season which enabled us to set and obtain a fee for him that a year or so ago seemed highly improbable.

We have now spent heavily on seven players in recent weeks, and the more we spend the more we can lose as well as gain. Thankfully the analysts seem to have got it right far more often than not up to now but there will be increasing pressure on them to keep doing so as the stakes get even higher.

There is also concern that there are too many moves and changes taking place in too short a time, particularly when you also take into account the number of injuries we have recently been incurring – and not just any old minor injury, but serious long-term ones that have incapacitated the likes of Bjelland, McEachran and Jota.

To some degree there has been little that we can do as most of the injuries occurred late on in the close season or in the first couple of matches of the new season at a time when most of the player sales, with the exception of Moses and perhaps now Gray, should he finally leave us, had already been completed. I see that as bad luck rather than poor planning however I feel for the new Head Coach as in many ways he has been handed a poisoned chalice as well as a massive opportunity.

Marinus Dijkhuizen has certainly got excellent support off the field in terms of his coaching and specialist staff and he has indubitably been provided with all the potential tools with which to do the job, in terms of the number and quality of new players who have arrived. However his planning must have been hindered firstly by the unprecedented number of injuries, secondly by the Griffin Park and Jersey Road pitch fiascos and now by players being sold around him, admittedly for all the good reasons previously provided, at a time well after he had presumably completed his preseason preparations with his original squad and had already made decisions upon his best team.

Assuming Gray leaves and given the current injury crisis, it is anticipated that there will be yet a further influx of new players, plus of course Maxime Colin, into the squad over the next couple of weeks. All well and good certainly, as we are really short of numbers at present and this will also provide evidence indeed of the club's determination to keep strengthening but it falls on the Head Coach to integrate yet more players into his squad – no easy task once the season has already started and the games come thick and fast.

The supporters are slowly warming to Dijkhuizen and appreciate his tactical flexibility, phlegmatic approach in accepting how things are and his bravery in terms of switching players and formation when things are not initially working out on the field. He will need patience and an understanding of the task and obstacles that he is currently facing but the omens are good for him and I feel that he has made an excellent start in what is a challenging new job.

We have to trust in the strategy employed by the club as it is the only sensible one given our financial constraints and it is surely the one that will continue to allow us to punch well above our weight and outperform clubs who are far richer but perhaps not as smart, brave or well informed as we are.

Given less radical changes since the end of last season and a bit more stability I would have been confident that we could have kicked on from even last season's incredible fifth place achievement. Now I think we will need to retrench, regroup and allow our new group of players and coaches to bed in and settle down. We hoped for promotion, and still do, but now I think, despite what must obviously be a far higher playing budget than last season, that we will probably have to settle for consolidation.

It is still far too early to say whether we will be successful this season, or if we have perhaps bitten off more than we can chew. We have certainly been single-minded and relentless in pursuit of our goal but I would question whether we have attempted to do too much too soon and if evolution rather than revolution might have paid greater dividends. Matthew Benham is certainly a risk taker but he is only a taker of considered and educated gambles and we must believe in him and his team, accept a few growing pains and the vicissitudes of ill fortune and hope that the season turns out well.

Good communication is also essential. It really helps to reassure us when we are kept in the loop by the club. We were recently given helpful updates regarding the pitch repair and also the current injury situation that helped inform us and set minds at rest. I understand that a Fans' Forum is planned for the near future. I appreciate that Matthew Benham is never one to seek the limelight and make public utterances but in this case, given the circumstances, his presence would be massively reassuring as it would be extremely helpful to hear things straight from the horse's mouth.

Tipping Point – 23/8/15

Did as well as could be expected given what limited resources were available to us, might be a fair description of Brentford's performance at Turf Moor yesterday.

Burnley were tough, well-organised and uncompromising and proved hard to break down, but in all honesty they were pretty dour and uninspired and were really there for the taking, particularly as they were lacking in confidence given that they were still searching for their first victory of the season.

Brentford more than matched them throughout the first half when we pinged the ball out to both wings with pace and accuracy with Diagouraga linking the play skilfully, and but for some pretty insipid finishing from the otherwise lively Vibe, a good save by Heaton from Judge's well-placed free kick and Hofmann not gambling and anticipating a couple of opportunities from penetrative balls into the area, we would have been comfortably ahead.

As it was, the home crowd was already beginning to moan and mutter and get on the back of their team when Brentford unforgivably gave away the initiative at a time when they were in total control and conceded yet another soft goal from Burnley's first corner kick when Jones's excellent delivery left Hofmann floundering at the far post, he lost his man and Keane headed home easily without much of a challenge. Maybe there had been a foul on Hofmann, who claimed that he'd been pushed, but he was guilty of ball watching and we need to show better organisation and far more determination when defending set pieces or we will continue to suffer the consequences. Surely our set piece coach should also be looking at how we defend them as well as helping us to take advantage of our own opportunities.

Our heads went down at this self-inflicted blow and Burnley gratefully took control without ever seriously threatening a second goal.

Our threat also disappeared for long spells, but we improved when Colin made an excellent debut as a second half substitute. He is quick, plays with his head up and uses the ball intelligently and he looked to be an excellent replacement for Moses Odubajo. Finally some good news!

We flitted in and out of the game throughout the second half and went close with a long range effort from Kerschbaumer whistling narrowly over the crossbar and auxiliary striker Harlee Dean, easily our man of the match, almost getting on the end of a loose ball in the area during a late but abortive flurry.

As it was Burnley just about deserved the victory on the overall balance of play but had the Bees scored in the first quarter of the match, as they surely should have done, then Burnley heads would have gone down and Brentford would likely have emerged victorious.

In all honesty Brentford were totally hamstrung through lack of options. With the late sale on Friday of Andre Gray, who was an interested onlooker from the main stand cheering on his new team mates, and the injury list still biting deep into our limited resources, pretty much every fit senior player was included in the squad and, as for the bench, it was utterly threadbare, and more resembled a kindergarten than being fit for purpose for a purported Championship promotion contender, with Senior, Udumaga and Clarke all included, and as Alan Judge ruefully admitted afterwards, it contained a mixture of defenders and kids and gave us no flexibility to change things.

Hofmann in particular needed a break as he had run himself out with little support but he was forced to lumber on given the lack of a suitable alternative.

I have written at length over the past week about our approach and provided a rationale for why we have allowed so many players to leave. I have to admit it hurt me to watch Stuart Dallas make such an impact and create the Leeds equaliser against Sheffield Wednesday and he would have made a real difference for us up at Turf Moor, it was similarly galling to see Jon Toral look so lively for Birmingham against Derby (I did try and refrain from mentioning how impressive Clayton Donaldson looked too but I failed dismally) but we have made our bed and we now have to lie in it.

We were promised an increased depth and size of squad with adequate cover in every position but so far that has proved to be a chimera. Injuries and sales, forced and otherwise, have meant that we have been reduced to using raw Development Squad recruits just to fill the bench and ensure that we have the requisite number of seven substitutes.

To be frank, I did not expect there to be quite the level of upheaval that has taken place recently and that we would pretty much be looking for an entirely new team.

A reported opportunity to earn the thick end of ten million pounds for Gray from Burnley when the add-ons are included made the deal inevitable, and we have almost doubled our record sale figure in less than a fortnight. I have no complaints about any of the sales as long as those who have left us as well as the long-term injured are adequately replaced – and quickly.

Without Moses, Gray and the injured Jota we have lost all of our pace and dynamism and much of our guile and we look a pallid and lethargic shadow of the exciting, speedy and vibrant team of last season that cut opponents to ribbons, but I fully realise and pray that things can change very quickly if we are able to complete deals for our prime targets and they then settle down quickly into a new team and pattern of play. Big *ifs* though!

Max Colin (great name) made an encouraging start at Burnley but Vibe, Hofmann and Kerschbaumer have, quite understandably, yet to find their feet in the hustle and bustle of the Championship. All have contributed little cameos to date with Kerschbaumer's wonderful back heel at Bristol last weekend which helped set up our opening goal and his beautifully weighed pass yesterday that created a massive chance for Vibe that he spurned. Vibe and Hofmann have also had their moments, particularly with the fourth goal at Bristol, but they have been pretty rare and spasmodic.

We have played some excellent football in spurts in each of our opening three league matches but we have looked disorganised, disjointed and open in defence, vulnerable at set pieces and lacking cover from the midfield and without Gray, pretty toothless up front.

The loss of Douglas has nowhere near been covered adequately and with the departures of Pritchard, Dallas, Douglas and Gray, and Jota's injury we now have to replace nearly three quarters of the goals we scored last season, and frankly I cannot see where they are going to come from.

It is hard to overestimate the impact that the injuries, combined with player transfers have had on us. As we came into the last couple of weeks of the preseason I fully expect that Dijkhuizen was planning on starting with the following team – until fate intervened:

Button | Odubajo | Dean | Bjelland | Bidwell | Diagouraga | McEachran | Jota | Judge | Gogia | Gray

Five of that likely starting eleven have either left the club or are currently unavailable for the long-term and with Douglas and Dallas also departed we are really creaking at the seams. Midfield was our strong point last season with a combination of goals, pace, flair and flexibility and several selection options too, whereas now we are struggling for bodies and balance.

The season has barely begun but what happens over the next week or so up until the end of the transfer window in my opinion will set the tone for how the remainder of the season will pan out. Yes, of course we can sign loan players from early September too but we need to get some semblance of a settled team as well as strength in depth and give Marinus a realistic chance to build and develop his squad.

We are a bit of a shambles at the moment – understandably so, given all the circumstances, and yesterday I hope we reached our nadir and the tipping point as I do not expect to see such a weak squad again for the foreseeable future.

We drastically need reinforcements, but they have to be of a suitable calibre and character, and players who are ideally not just short term solutions intended merely to paper over the cracks.

It would be a gross overstatement to say that we are currently in crisis mode regarding the size, quality and battle readiness of our squad but we are certainly cash rich and player poor – a horribly dangerous combination that could lead us to be held to ransom and perhaps have our pockets picked as the dreaded deadline approaches. The international break also cannot come quickly enough as it will allow us the time to regroup and ideally integrate new players into our system.

We are running out of time and much has to happen over the next week or so and this is the time when our joint Directors of Football need to earn their spurs. Gentlemen – it is over to you.

Reasons To Be Cheerful – 25/8/15

Queens Park Rangers – nil, Brentford – three. Doesn't that score line have a lovely ring to it? It slides off the tongue so smoothly and perfectly. Just try saying it for yourself and see!

No matter that the victory came in a Development Squad tussle rather than in a first team match. Any victory over the old enemy at whatever level, and yes, despite any suggestions to the contrary regarding the likes of Fulham or even Birmingham City, QPR are certainly Brentford's traditional rival and *bête noire*, must be savoured and luxuriated over.

Just in case our friends from Shepherd's Bush think that yesterday's result was an aberration, fluke or anomaly let me just remind them that we did the double over them last season too, scoring six times in the two matches and dominating proceedings to such an extent that even *The Invisible Man*, the immortal Betinho, managed to get himself on the scoreboard.

Oh, and if that still isn't enough we also beat the Ra Ra's by four goals to two last Saturday in the Under 18 Youth League.

Have I done enough gloating? No, not yet by a long chalk. I've barely got started.

My good friend, Mark Croxford, watched yesterday's match which was dominated from start to finish by a young, vibrant, confident, exciting and talented Brentford team who could and should have scored at least six times and afterwards he spoke to a Rangers fan who ruefully and despondently admitted that it was the second time in only a couple of days that his team had been totally outplayed by a Brentford team. What wonderful words and doesn't it make you feel good to read them particularly given the source of the comment?

There were lots of noteworthy performances and Lee Carsley and his coaches must have been purring with a mixture of pride and pleasure given how well the team had played on the day. I also suspect that he was feeling a lot more sanguine than he was a couple of weeks ago after the Capital One Cup hammering by Oxford United. On the one hand he must have been proud at the fact that so many of his best prospects were named in the Brentford first team, but on the other, he would not have been happy at the way in which Josh Clarke, Josh Laurent, Courtney Senior and Jermaine Udumaga were thrown to the wolves and hung out to dry by being totally exposed in an horrendously weak team that lacked any real first team experience or seemingly even the will to compete.

Jack Bonham had the confidence boost of a long-awaited clean sheet yesterday, which included an excellent penalty save. He had an awful night against Oxford United when he could do little to prevent a torrent of goals and also fell foul of a fickle crowd who treated him appallingly, but hopefully he is now well on the road to recovery.

He has all the ability in the world and he has been well coached, but success as a goalkeeper at Football League level is as much about intangibles such as sound judgement, good temperament and the ability to make instantaneous and correct decisions. I have long held the view that Bonham needs to gain experience by means of a loan spell away from Griffin Park and from playing games every week in which there are points and bonuses at stake rather than rusting on the bench and playing Development Squad matches which generally lack the necessary bite and passion.

Josh Clarke has also managed to rehabilitate himself from being a winger whose career was stalling to becoming an exciting attacking right back who now looks as if he could make a name for himself. He was one of the few players who enhanced his reputation against Oxford United and he must surely have taken inspiration from the example of Moses Odubajo who set such high standards last season.

Aaron Greene has pace, height, power and dribbling ability and was deeply impressive throughout the preseason period. He too has a real chance of making the grade.

Josh Laurent had a brief taste of first team football against Oxford and has now also made his Football League debut whilst on loan at Newport County. He too has much to learn and will certainly have his eyes opened throughout his loan spell but he has real ability and could go far. As an ex-QPR prospect whose departure from the club was greeted by massive outpourings of anger and frustration on their message boards, he must have been upset to have missed yesterday's thrashing of his old team but I am sure he is happy to be where he is for the time being.

Daniel O'Shaughnessy is also finally settling down and developing into an effective central defender who might soon benefit from a loan spell and first team football elsewhere.

Midfielder Jan Holldack has also caught the eye with some encouraging midfield performances playing just behind the main striker in which he has demonstrated a real eye for goal from long-range.

We are also blessed with real talent up front with Jermaine Udumaga, who made his Championship debut at Turf Moor last weekend and by no means looked out of place, Courtney Senior who has already made his first team debut whilst on loan for Wycombe Wanderers last season and Montell Moore who has much to prove after last season's off-field indiscretions but is blessed with massive ability.

There is also a plethora of players coming through at an even younger age group and the likes of Tom Field, James Ferry, Zain Westbrooke, Reece Cole and Gradi Milenge are all expected to improve further this season.

Brentford have gained much publicity and even notoriety over the last few months from their oft-stated policy of using a statistically based approach towards player identification and recruitment.

That is all very well but unless that strategy is underpinned and supported by a successful Academy system that also produces players who come into first team contention then all our efforts are likely to end in failure. We have lavished care, attention and monetary support into a Category Two Academy and hopefully it will start to bear fruit shortly.

We also need to ensure that there is a tried and tested pathway from the Academy, but first team places have to be earned on merit and the Oxford United experience when far too many youngsters were thrown together at one time clearly demonstrated that young players, however promising they are, need to be eased into the first team gently and in small numbers and also surrounded, encouraged and supported by more experienced team mates.

That being said, I would love us to be in a position before the end of this current season to introduce a policy or protocol whereby there has to be at least one Academy or Development Squad product on the bench for every first team game, with every effort, if not a directive, to be made to ensure that some of them actually play in the Championship and that we continue to give them pitch experience in all cup matches.

Yesterday was good news, firstly for the boost that any victory over QPR brings us, but, just as importantly because it provided further firm evidence that we are a long way ahead of our rivals in terms of our youth development – and that is really a reason to be cheerful.

No Cheering In The Press Box! – Tom Moore Speaks – 27/8/15

I grew up relishing and poring over the words of the late, great, legendary George Sands, the writer *sans pareil* for *The Middlesex Chronicle*. Those were gentler, less hurried and frenetic times when he could spin out an elegant, witty and erudite match report to at least a couple of thousand words and he had the time and opportunity to do so given that he had pretty much the whole week to hone and refine his words until the publication of the one weekly edition. He was not required or expected to interview players, or ferret out stories regarding transfer rumours or behind the scenes manoeuvrings – only the games mattered with perhaps a brief respectful comment from the team manager of the time.

George held the title of Sports Editor at the newspaper for thirty-five years and is best remembered for attending a total of one thousand one hundred and twenty-six consecutive Brentford games between December 1953 and May 1976, and his incredible achievement is listed in *The Guinness Book of Records*. He was so well regarded within the local community that he served so wonderfully that a testimonial match was held for him in 1980, surely an unparalleled mark of respect for a journalist. One day perhaps *The Middlesex Chronicle* will mark his memory by publishing an anthology of his columns which have easily stood the test of time and remain a wonderful read to this day.

The life of a journalist today has totally changed given the ever changing and evolving media landscape, the emergence of social media and the overwhelming need for immediacy with news having to be disseminated instantly and accurately before it passes its sell-by date. I therefore went to one of the best and most popular local exponents of this art, **Tom Moore**, and asked him to describe the role of a local football reporter in 2015.

1. Please describe you current role and job

My current role is sports writer for Get West London and our local papers. My main tasks are to cover Brentford, Barnet and Wealdstone as well as local sport in Hounslow but, depending on what the team needs, I will help out regarding covering our other clubs (Chelsea, Fulham, QPR, AFC Wimbledon and Wycombe). I also report on Middlesex CCC.

When it comes to reporting on Brentford, I see my role as someone who is a bridge between the fans and the club. On press conference day, I'll always put out question suggestions for Marinus Dijkhuizen on my Twitter page (@TomMooreJourno), which is why I end up asking about Lewis Macleod most weeks. He won't be fit before the international break, so forgive me if I don't ask about him this week!

I also report on local sport in the borough of Hounslow. If you have a sports story, please email me (tom.moore@trinitymirror.com).

2. How did you get there? Where did you work previously?

I studied English at the University of Salford before enrolling in News Associates' journalism course. After passing my exams and gaining experience, I started at London24 and worked there between October 2011 and December 2014 before taking on a role at Get West London in February.

3. Did you always want to become a journalist?

Everything from my A-Level choices onwards was geared to becoming a journalist.

4. Are you a Brentford fan? If so is supporting Brentford a help or a hindrance?

I am a Brentford fan. It is a help in that I know where the club has come from, having stood on the terraces for ninety long minutes to watch us suffer a seven - nil defeat and I know all about the players of different eras. It is also a hindrance when you have to remain professional after tough defeats (Doncaster, Yeovil) or the great moments (Preston.)

5. No cheering in the press box! Do you remain impartial and is it easy to do so?

I will talk to other journalists and offer my opinion about the performance. Cheering in the press box – as a rule, no, although it may have failed on certain occasions like against Chelsea. Normally a smile will have to suffice. When it comes to copy, I believe honesty is the best policy, whether people like it or not.

6. What are you favourite and worst memories of following Brentford?

My favourite memories as a fan normally revolve around the day out. Walsall in 2010 was a dire game but I had a great day with a mate. Leeds away last season was special. My favourite away day as a fan remains Darlington in 2009. The worst has to be losing seven-nil at Peterborough – a seven hour round trip and a lot of money spent for a disgraceful showing. Barrow away in the cup was also grim.

7. Any favourite players – or ones you hated?

I'm not going to reveal my favourites in the current squad. My first favourite player was Jay Tabb; the last one was Tony Craig. My least favourite player was Thomas Pinault. I wasn't a fan of Sam Sodje by the end. I thought the hype had gone to his head.

8. Talk us through a week in the life of Tom Moore

Monday – Send a fair few emails regarding the previous weekend and produce stories from whom I have spoken to the previous weekend. Have a think about print coverage.

Tuesday – The paper takes more priority as I compile the local sport content for print. I'll keep an eye on what's going on at the Football League clubs I specialise in.

Wednesday – Finish off the paper and prepare web copy.

Thursday – Ring managers and attend Brentford's media day, typing up stories from them ahead of the weekend.

Friday – Day Off (or help out colleagues if needed)

Saturday – Game

Sunday – Day Off (it can include a swim to provide me with some relaxation time, alternatively I'll try and prepare for the following week)

9. How much pressure are you under to get scoops and unearth your own stories?

I put pressure on myself to do that.

10. How hard is it to get information from the new regime at the club? Was it easier in the past?

Not dramatically different.

11. How would you describe the attitude towards the club now from the national media? Are they hoping our new approach totally succeeds or fails?

It depends on the person.

12. Can you compare your dealings with the current Head Coach and previous managers?

The first manager I dealt with was Uwe Rösler. *It took time to build a relationship with him but we got on well by the time he left for Wigan. I had plenty of time for Mark Warburton and spoke to him regularly. He'd always pick up the phone when I needed to ring him. As for Marinus Dijkhuizen, it's early days so it's just a case of working out how he ticks.*

13. Do you have much contact with the players and how easy are they to deal with? Most/least helpful?

I speak to a player or two at least once a week on Thursdays and after games. Most are easy to deal with. George Saville was not always the most forthcoming. Compared to other clubs I've reported on it is easy.

14. No names but do you have your sources within the club who give you off the record information?

Yes.

15. Are you aware of any of the greats who came before you like George Sands?

I'm aware of George Sands. My direct predecessor, Jake Murtagh, did an exceptional job covering the club so I know I have big shoes to fill.

16. How do you feel about Brentford's raised profile in the national media?

A raised profile means an increase in competition for stories etc. Reporting on the club in the League One/League Two days had its advantages.

17. Your favourite football journalist?

I'll always read Jonathan Liew's articles. I'll also make sure I read stuff by people I get on with, whether football or not. Tim Wigmore is an excellent cricket/politics journalist.

18. How would you describe Brentford's current strategy?

If Brentford tried to do what every other club did we'd lose out every time. It's a novel approach. Whether it works, time will tell.

19. How would you describe Brentford's playing style?

I loved the Mark Warburton style of football of just pure all-out attack but I do feel it went slightly too far at times. I want to see positive football as in every decision made is a positive one.

20. How do you feel about all the changes in personnel on and off the field and the recent spate of player sales?

I view Brentford players and staff in a different way to supporters; namely on how good an interviewee they are. Some players, not naming names, are better talkers than others. I had a good relationship with Mark Warburton. I interviewed him over the phone soon after the announcement was made that he was going to leave the club. So, from that perspective, it was sad to see him leave. I knew how to work with him. Others were less helpful so it didn't matter to me on that score that they left.

21. Are the foreign players different/easier to deal with than the English ones? How do they differ in approach or professionalism?

It all depends on the player. Jota's English, for example, is not at interview standard so I've yet to speak to him since his arrival. Others know English so can talk. Lasse Vibe and Marcos Tebar speak excellent English.

Thanks again, Tom, for providing all of us with such a detailed insight into your work and explaining so cogently how you operate and what is expected of you every week.

Nothing To Say – 30/8/15

As *Thumper's Law* so memorably states – *If you can't something nice, don't say nothing at all,* so here is my verdict on Brentford's performance yesterday against Reading…

Too Soon To Tell – 31/8/15

I thought long and hard before writing yesterday's article.

Saturday's match left me as angry, bemused, disappointed and concerned as I am sure it did every other Brentford supporter.

The easy option would have been to give in to my emotions and vent my spleen and write something highly negative and critical about what is currently happening both on and off the pitch at Griffin Park.

That would most certainly have been the easy option and knee jerk reaction but I resisted the temptation, not without some difficulty, and instead I wrote the quickest and shortest article of my life, only twenty-eight words in length, that took me all of thirty seconds to compose and yet it was read by more people than anything else that I have written for the last few months – indeed since news of the Mark Warburton crisis broke in February!

Go figure! Maybe there is a lesson in that fact for me too! Perhaps less is more and the least time I take and the shorter the article the more popular it will be! Perhaps that is something for me to ponder and deliberate about for the future! Believe me anything that reduces the amount of time I generally spend most days thinking through, researching, analysing and finally writing each article would be greatly welcomed by me!

I received several replies from readers who were far less restrained than me

Michael Ohl was brief and brutal:

Very disappointing. My expectations have been adjusted to staying up. What a terrible ref and ugly opponents. Vibe looks like he might be a good signing. Clarke may also develop into something useful. Button was outstanding. At least the new pitch gave a good account of itself.

Rebel Bee gave a more studied, if sardonic view of the situation:

Totally inept from all involved perhaps bar Button, and it was a game with no redeeming features at all. Good to see all the new coaches are working their magic! Maybe the sleep coach is doing his thing – most of the players and crowd seemed to be having a nap in a shambolic first half where we could have been four down. As poor a midfield quartet as I've seen since the days of Butcher.

This is exactly what happens when good players leave, to be replaced by inadequate cover from lower levels across Europe. There are huge questions over the competence of Marinus Dijkhuizen with his big decisions all going badly wrong for him.

We have huge problems – and it is time to face facts.

That is fairly close to what I might well have written immediately after the match if I had given way to temptation and it is quite natural to let off steam after what was, in truth, a totally inept performance but, as I will say later, I think it might well be more reasonable, fair, accurate and beneficial if we wait for a little while longer before we come to any firm decision and pronounce our verdict.

Steve Houlihan was also not too impressed with what he had seen:

Marinus has to work with what he is given and on yesterday's show that will not be enough. The game reminded me of a League Two performance when MK Dons beat us three-nil at Griffin Park. On that day a faster and stronger team made us look like a development squad.

We are simply not at Championship level at the moment. I fear for the team with two tough northern away days coming up.

Gary Manning was disappointed that I had not given my immediate viewpoint:

Well Greville sometimes one word is too many and a thousand not enough. I was hoping for some comforting words today to cheer me up! Did you ghostwrite Len Shackleton's chapter on football directors, in his autobiography?

No I didn't, I am not nearly that old and plead not guilty to writing that famous blank page which provided chapter and verse on Shackleton's opinion on the average football director's knowledge of the game.

Dave Hodson also had a gentle dig at me:

Come on Greville I don't expect sulky heads-dropped performances from the players and I certainly don't expect one from our mercurial correspondent. I expect you in early tomorrow and want those fingers clattering away at the keyboard until there's smoke coming out of them. Keep the faith.

Well Dave, I hope you are feeling a bit better now.

Alan Dally was also concerned at the current state of affairs:

Greville, you are right. Least said soonest forgotten, as my old Granny used to say. One observation from me is that, despite what many think, we miss Dougie big time. Or at least Toums does. He is a mere shadow of the player who played alongside Douglas. The worrying thing from my point of view is that the togetherness that was apparent under Warbs has disappeared out of the window. Maybe that should not surprise me as the massive changes since May seem to have torn the place apart.

It is still very early days, but nevertheless the warning signs are there. My initial thoughts on Marinus are not totally positive, but I'll be the first to admit he has been dealt a tough hand up until now. As I said, it is still very early days, but my Bournemouth mate who took a 20/1 bet on us being relegated is smiling at the moment. He took this bet as he was convinced that the Bees totally lost the plot in February and will pay a heavy price for their stupidity. Personally I think we will still finish around mid-table, but the doubts are now creeping in.

Gary Hennell was more positive in his comments:

I am from a family that goes back over a hundred years supporting Brentford, we all live in Kettering these days but travel as much as possible to Griffin Park when we can afford to. Dad, my sons and I were there yesterday and I can't help feeling that Marinus hasn't figured his best system out yet for the players he has. Diagouraga will never be a centre midfield distributor in a 4-3-3 formation, Warbs knew this, and I think we all know McCormack is better equipped for that role all day long. However, what I really liked was that he spotted it and had no hesitation in taking him off, just a shame we were two down before he acted.

As soon as we switched to 4-4-2 Brentford were transformed and Vibe came alive – he needs to be in the middle not out on the wing, he has a great attitude, works hard and produced some fantastic flick-ons and clinical finishing – he will be a great buy!

Sadly, my view is that Brentford look totally disorganised this year and lack pace in transition to attack, Hoff looks out of his depth and lacked any support. I liked Colin a lot, he looked composed, quick and with good distribution – an upgrade in my opinion, so I think Benham and his statto's are getting it right on the whole.

I just wish we had more time to get this system sorted and had not sold our only natural left winger, which I put money on will cost us big time against Leeds.

Anyway, fingers crossed for Jota, McEachran, Judge and Vibe – now there's a Championship attacking front line I can't wait to see in action.

Will we go down? No, not with these all fit, only if Marinus takes too long to figure out 4-3-1-2 is the only system he can play at the moment and I would put Judge in the middle to create the lovely passing moves we saw at Griffin Park last year. Up the Bees!

There are some conflicting opinions there and the message boards and social media have also been red hot with vituperative comments, in-depth questioning of our approach and expressions of doom and gloom leavened with some isolated pleas for more patience and understanding.

So where do I stand?

I really do not want to regurgitate what I have already written at great length over the past few weeks, but the key points and questions that are flashing repeatedly through my mind are as follows:

1. Brentford are and will remain a selling club until our income levels increase and are more in line with the requirements of a competitive Championship team

2. Without the largesse and continued support of Matthew Benham we would have a National League budget at best if we were forced to live within our means

3. We are also hindered by the need to adhere to the stringent Financial Fair Play restrictions

4. Players follow the money and there is very little you can do about it particularly if they have release clauses in their contract

5. They also get distracted when they learn what the market rate is as well as how much their former colleagues are earning elsewhere

6. All players have their price and if another club meets our valuation then they will be sold

7. All players who are sold will ideally be quickly and adequately replaced

8. Have we sold too many players too quickly and allowed evolution to become revolution through trying to integrate too many new players at one time

9. Marinus Dijkhuizen's plan have been totally stymied and hamstrung by having his squad decimated by injuries to key players and late sales

10. It seems ridiculous for him to have taken one squad to Portugal, bedded them down and then having pretty much had to start again given the loss of so many players who were sold around him

11. Homegrown players are proving to be too expensive, however is the squad blend correct or are we now relying on too many new foreign players who have no experience or understanding of the daunting requirements of the Championship

12. Are we in desperate need of leaders both in the dressing room and on the pitch

13. Will our analytics and stats based player recruitment prove to be successful and will our new players prove to be up to the required standard once they have settled in to their new surroundings

14. How many of our new recruits will blossom and become saleable assets in the near future as we need to keep selling players at a massive profit to afford better replacements

15. Have our new Co-Directors of Football enough experience and suitable contacts to ensure that, as has been the case for the past couple of years, we obtain privileged access to Premier League loanees of massive talent and potential like Alex Pritchard

16. We pride ourselves in thinking outside the box but do we have enough basic football experience and contacts in the boardroom and behind the scenes

17. Given that our playing budget has surely been increased substantially from last season's figure, has this extra money been well spent

18. Have current prime assets such as Button and Judge, whose departure would be massively harmful to us, been offered enhanced contracts commensurate with their value, given that they are obviously now well aware of what they could perhaps earn elsewhere

19. We have now lost more than enough of last season's squad and cannot afford to lose any more key starters particularly given the current injury jinx

20. We were promised a squad enhanced both in quantity and quality. Injuries have taken their toll and the jury is out about the quality of all our newcomers but to be reduced to a situation where we have untried

youngsters on the bench, no spare forwards, McCormack as our midfield playmaker and Harlee Dean playing an auxiliary striker is unacceptable and hard to accept

21. We need at least two more strikers, a playmaker, a midfield enforcer and perhaps even another centre half

22. Is the dressing room a happy place and are the players buying into the new methods as well as the training routines introduced by the new Head Coach

23. The Head Coach has received a baptism of fire and I hope that there is no disconnect between him and the recruitment side of the back room team and that he is being given a reasonable say in all player movements

24. It must be particularly galling for Marinus to receive constant questions from the media about ins and outs when neither are his responsibility

25. The new pitch played perfectly on Saturday, but did the previous abomination provide further problems for the squad and backroom staff

26. Have we been too zealous in adhering to a totally new way of running the club rather than trying to combine the best of the old with the best of the new

27. There were articles in the match programme from the Chairman and Chief Executive who both made excellent points regarding the problems we have faced and they tried to manage expectations and urge a sense of realism towards the outcome of this season

28. They may well be correct but their comments do beg the question that given the enhanced budget is it reasonable for us to spend far more money to at best stand still but more likely go a fair way backwards when it might be thought that Matthew Benham was perhaps looking for us to kick on this season

29. There is also talk that Miguel Rios has left the club, which is also worrying news given how well he is regarded in academy and youth circles

Dijkhuizen's comments after Saturday's game were telling, honest in the extreme and extremely concerning and they pretty much sum up what every Brentford supporter is thinking:

I didn't recognise my team in the first half. There was no organisation and we were poor on the ball. We are not the strongest and most physical side so if you are bad on the ball then we have no chance. But I know we have to be patient because some of our players are only having their second game in the Championship.

It is difficult to adapt but we need to get used to the tempo because players coming from Germany and Holland are not ready. We have had too many changes in the preseason and now have had some big injuries to players. We also have a bench with no strikers on it and the side looks to be lacking leadership. Hopefully we will be able to bring one or two more players in before the window closes.

He actually expressed himself far more clearly and cogently than any supporter and given his position and insider's view, it is obvious that he feels that matters are serious and need immediate attention. Perhaps he has also been more far more open, honest and straight talking than his superiors would have wished!

Marinus has also received a lot of flak – totally unjustified in my opinion, for his apparent detachment and lack of emotion on the bench during matches. If that is your opinion of him then perhaps you should take note of this quotation from the excellent and thoughtful Exeter City manager Paul Tisdale which comes from Michael Calvin's wonderful new book on the psyche of football managers – *Living on The Volcano:*

I was criticised for about a year at Exeter for not having any passion, because they expected something different. I live this. I'm consumed by it. Try thinking about a really important decision and screaming at the same time. It doesn't work, does it?

Keep quiet, think clearly. I'm taking everything out of my mind and concentrating on one big decision, the thirty seconds out of ninety minutes when I have to get everything right.

There are a lot of questions that still need to be asked about the situation at Brentford, both on and off the pitch, and quite frankly there are still very few answers yet to be had. The transfer window closes tomorrow night and we need to see what strengthening has taken place before that time, given the two exciting loan arrivals of Sergi Canos and Marco Djuricin today, and indeed if we lose any more of our assets too, and we should not discount that possibility either.

Of course I am concerned. I had hoped that with our new mould-breaking strategy and increased investment we would progress even from last season's miraculous achievements but I remain fully realistic and aware of the time it takes for new systems, approaches and, indeed, players to settle down and bed in, and we now have a welcome and much needed gap of a fortnight before our next game where a lot of hard work will doubtless be carried out.

Let us see where we are at the beginning of October when we go into the next international break and I am sure that the situation will look a lot clearer by that time.

Position	Team	P	W	D	L	F	A	GD	Pt	Form
1	Brighton and Hove A	5	4	1	0	8	4	4	13	W W D W W
2	Hull City	5	3	1	1	8	4	4	10	W D W L W
3	Ipswich Town	5	3	1	1	10	7	3	10	D W W W L
4	Queens Park Rangers	5	3	1	1	10	8	2	10	L D W W W
5	Cardiff City	5	2	3	0	8	5	3	9	D D D W W
6	Middlesbrough	5	2	2	1	7	3	4	8	D W D L W
7	Birmingham City	4	2	2	0	7	4	3	8	W D D W
8	Charlton Athletic	5	2	2	1	6	4	2	8	W D D W L
9	Burnley	5	2	2	1	6	6	0	8	D D L W W
10	Leeds United	5	1	4	0	6	5	1	7	D D D D W
11	Milton Keynes Dons	5	2	1	2	5	4	1	7	W L W D L
12	Wolverhampton Wndrs	5	2	1	2	7	8	-1	7	W D L L W
13	Reading	5	1	3	1	5	4	1	6	L D D D W
14	Fulham	5	1	2	2	7	7	0	5	D L L D W
15	Sheffield Wednesday	5	1	2	2	6	7	-1	5	W L D D L
16	Nottingham Forest	5	1	2	2	4	5	-1	5	L W D D L
17	Preston North End	5	1	2	2	2	4	-2	5	D W D L L
18	Brentford	4	1	1	2	7	8	-1	4	D W L L
19	Derby County	5	0	4	1	4	5	-1	4	D D D D L
20	Bristol City	5	1	1	3	6	10	-4	4	L L D W L
21	Blackburn Rovers	5	0	3	2	3	5	-2	3	L D D L D
22	Huddersfield Town	5	0	3	2	3	6	-3	3	L D D D L
23	Bolton Wanderers	5	0	3	2	1	5	-4	3	D L L D D
24	Rotherham United	5	0	1	4	5	13	-8	1	L L D L L

[28th August 2015]

September

A Good Day! – 2/9/15

There were quite a few comments from my fellow Bees supporters about my last article, which set out all the myriad of questions that I still feel need answering after Brentford's rickety start to the season. I urged patience and for everybody to allow the squad time to gel on the pitch given the large number of additions and subtractions to the squad and also for the massive and fundamental root and branch changes made off the pitch ideally to start to take beneficial effect.

Dave Washer agreed with this approach but still bemoaned the upheaval that has taken place in recent months:

Another excellent article, as always. When the view of other Brentford fans is either one of complete and utter apathy or a kind of "support the team at all costs otherwise you're not a real fan" attitude, your insightful writing serves as a refreshing and honest alternative.

I too was at the Reading game and I, like many, thought we were abysmal. Uncomfortable on the ball, lacking ideas, very little going forward and, most worrying of all, absolutely clueless at the back. When Reading scored their third right at the death, I somewhat rakishly said, at the top of my voice, "Statistically speaking, we're losing 3-1." A fellow Bees fan close to me in the Ealing Road stand took exception to this and things became a bit heated. But are we not allowed to express discontentment when we play as badly as that? According to some people, no. Which is frustrating. Because on Saturday we were bad. Very bad indeed.

The worst thing is the comparison with last season: assured, measured, confident, totally comfortable in possession. Brilliant going forward, solid (more often than not) in defence. I still wake up in a cold sweat when I think about Benham's (misguided) decision to let Warburton go. In hindsight, could he not have put his Moneyball plans on hold, signed Warbs up for two or three more years and gone again this season with the existing (and very successful) management structure in place?

But that's all hypothetical. We are where we are and we have to deal with it. All the main points have been made, so I don't have to go over them again. Suffice to say, the club were massively naïve when it came to players wanting to depart. Warburton was a leader, and a great one at that. Once the club decided he was out, it was inevitable that many of his team would want out too. And so we are left with a load of new players, none of whom have Championship experience, all of whom need time to adjust to the rigorous demands of one of the most competitive leagues in European football. Trouble is, it's time we don't have.

Bringing in Djuricin and Canos looks like a great (and desperately needed) move; but to me it seems like papering over some pretty enormous cracks. The defence is terrible, central midfield is awful, and we need at least one new explosive winger.

The big question mark for me is Dijkhuizen. Yes, he's been dealt a terrible hand, but disregarding that, is he up to the task? Of course he needs time to prove himself, but I have an awful feeling he simply isn't the right man for the job. Yes, he's lost Odubajo, Dallas, Pritchard, Jota, Bjelland, McEachran and Gray, but is he able to galvanize the players and get them scrapping? From what I've seen, the answer is no.

Of course, we have to give him another ten or fifteen games to work with the players and prove he's up to it. Then and only then can we judge him. But injuries and departures aside, I fear he lacks the necessary qualities (leadership, passion, knowledge of English football and the capability to rouse the squad into fighting for every single ball and every single point) to keep us up… let alone get us pushing for the playoffs.

The Championship is a formidable league and last season we had a manager who was beyond exceptional. This season we have a guy with limited experience and a squad that literally doesn't know if it's coming or going. If it were up to me, I'd give Dijkhuizen twenty games. If we stabilize, great. If we are fighting a relegation battle (or worse, are by that point cut adrift by ten points or more) I would seriously consider putting Lee Carsley in charge, with support from Kevin O'Connor. Two passionate English pros who might just be able to get the players to fight as hard as they'll need to if we are to survive this season.

Final thought: last season, brilliant as he was, many of us said that Warburton didn't have a Plan B. This season, Dijkhuizen hasn't even got a Plan A.

I agree with much of what he said however I think that Dave is being extremely harsh about Marinus Dijkhuizen who, whilst still an unknown quantity, has certainly been thrown in at the deep end and already suffered several serious and unexpected body blows. It is far, far too early, in my opinion, to make any judgement at all about his qualities and capabilities and whether he is able to cobble together and create a cohesive and effective team out of the squad that he has been given.

For me the next couple of weeks are crucial as he finally has some uninterrupted time on the training ground to work with his new squad, with the exception of Vibe who is on international duty, and can hopefully integrate the new additions, of whom more shortly, and have the breathing space to decide how he wants to play, what formation best suits the players now available to him and who is in his first choice eleven given all the departures and injuries. He desperately needs our support during this tough settling in time, rather than brickbats.

Mike Rice had also given a lot of thought to the current situation and the problems we face:

Mark Warburton's departure was a massive loss to the club not least in that he had ideas and skills derived from outside of football. Len Shackleton may have been right – and right about the current Brentford board as well – but it's not the board that has caused this mess. It's down to the owner and his view of what needed to be done to secure the club's long-term sustainability. I use the word long-term deliberately because in the long-term he's right. But it's in the short-term that we have the problem, and possibly the medium-term as well if the whole project goes pear-shaped, which on Saturday seemed highly likely.

As things stand, I think too many steps have been taken too quickly. Maybe some were out of our hands, like the long-term injuries. But other decisions have been taken by the owner. We have gone from one director of football to two, an unusual step in itself. One of them has no direct experience of football and the other leads another club, in another country, as chairman, with all that involves. That strikes me as taking novelty to ridiculous lengths.

Why not twin the statistician with somebody steeped in the English leagues and football academies, or at least a grassroots football person with good club contacts? As if intoxicated by the novelty, we've then taken it further by appointing a foreign coach with no experience of the Championship, and apparently little influence on how the other two are thinking and operating. That may not be the case, but as somebody said above, having taken such radical steps isn't it incumbent on the club's well-staffed PR machine to discuss and explain to fans the reasons behind such radical thinking and how it is intended to work?

The answers to all of the questions will become much clearer in time. It's far too early to say whether all or some of the gambles will pay off. I agree with the long-term strategy, but I have a horrible feeling that the execution in the short-term may damage the club's medium-term plans and perhaps cause the strategy to be abandoned altogether.

I said in an earlier comment that we are ill-equipped for a relegation battle and I think Saturday showed why. I desperately want the strategy to work, but I don't think that at moment it's being given a fair chance. I really want to be able to eat my words come Christmas.

Mike has eloquently expressed all the fears that many of us are experiencing at the moment and the next few weeks will be crucial and illuminating and go a long way towards determining how the season will eventually pan out.

The Transfer Window shut last night and high praise must be given where it is due, as it would seem that our recruitment and analysis department came up trumps as three new top quality players arrived who, all being well, will massively strengthen the squad and fill gaps that were previously of concern to us all.

Austrian international striker Marco Djuricin arrived on loan from Red Bull Salzburg. Yes, we have signed a young, current international striker, what is there not to like about that? He is initially here on a season-long loan deal and I suspect that we will have a chance of making the deal permanent at the end of the season if things turn out well. Marco was close to joining the Bees in January after scoring for fun at SK Sturm Graz but instead signed for Red Bull. So what can we expect from him? Ideally goals, and plenty of them, but it would seem that he is quick, an excellent predatory finisher, plays on the shoulder of the last defender and is not afraid of hard work.

Most importantly, we now have some options in attack with three strikers who all bring different and ideally complementary skills to the team. Philipp Hofmann is tall and strong and holds the ball up and Lasse Vibe can play wide or just behind the front man. Will we play with one striker or two? That is an interesting conundrum for Marinus to ponder over before our next match.

Brentford also demonstrated that the current regime retains the crucial ability to prise priceless nuggets and jewels from the grasp of the Premier League when eighteen year-old Spanish youth international attacker Sergi Canos arrived on a half-season loan from Liverpool. A highly sought after product of Barcelona's youth academy, he can play either wide or through the middle and given his age and lack of experience, I would expect that he will play, initially at least, on the wing and hopefully inject us with some much-needed pace and guile.

We need to manage our expectations about him as he will need careful nursing, and we should not expect any miracles. Hopefully he will be given far more opportunity to bed in and impress than our last loanee from Liverpool, Joao Carlos Teixeira, who despite his obvious talent, was ignored and left to wither on the vine by Uwe Rösler. Maybe in time he might be able to fill the playmaker role that we so desperately lack, but that is a massive ask of such a young player.

Brentford also beat the deadline with the rare and welcome signing of a home-grown player in Shrewsbury Town's much vaunted midfield player Ryan Woods for an undisclosed fee. The twenty-one year old has impressed over the last couple of seasons, particularly since he moved into midfield from his initial right back berth. He looked calm, composed and comfortable on the ball when we beat Shrewsbury a couple of years ago but it has to be admitted that he was partially culpable for the winning goal when he was left for dead by Kadeem Harris's step-over and instant acceleration and Marcello Trotta scored from the resulting cross.

Ryan enjoyed a wonderful season in 2014/15 when he inspired his team to promotion, was named as one of the best ten young players in the Football League by *FourFourTwo Magazine*, earned a place in the League Two PFA Team of the Season and finished second in the voting for the League Two Player of the Season.

He has been compared in both looks and style to the late, great Alan Ball, uses the ball well, tackles and presses like a demon, and he is expected to slot into the role of holding midfield player which we have struggled to fill so far this season. Ideally this will then allow Toumani Diagouraga the freedom to roam forward as he did so successfully last season, secure in the knowledge that his back has been covered as he ventures upfield.

There was more good news last night when the club announced that the unfortunate and luckless Scott Hogan has been offered and signed a new contract, extending his stay at Griffin Park for a further year until the end of the 2017/18 season. Ideally this will allow him sufficient time to recover fully from his second knee operation and return to contention for the first team. This decision was both generous and honourable and has certainly shown the club in an excellent light. Similar action was taken in previous decades when both Brian Statham and Danny Boxall, both recovering from long-term injuries, received the same treatment from the club.

So a good day for the club and one which will ideally help us on the long road to recovery, revitalise us and restore our fortunes and buy us some breathing space as everybody associated with Brentford tries to get things back on an even keel so that we can all face the challenges of the season, stronger, better prepared and in a much calmer state of mind.

International Break – 3/9/15

International breaks seem to be all the vogue at the moment, so if you can't beat them then join them.

Tomorrow I am off on my own short break and will do my utmost to try and think of things other than Brentford FC for the next week or so. In reality I suspect that the club and everything relating to it both on and off the field will cross my mind perhaps once every five minutes instead of the permanent tape loop that is my normal state of affairs.

It is a good time to go away. The maelstrom of uncertainty that seemed to envelope and overwhelm us finally seems to have dissipated and there is a clear breathing space before the next match at our old friend Uwe Rösler's Leeds United where we will also come up against Stuart Dallas and a particular favourite of mine in Tom Adeyemi, someone who I really wish that we had been able to sign on a permanent basis.

We did the double over Leeds last season and were comfortable winners in both matches against a toothless and insipid team who barely managed to lay a glove on us. With the exception of the Blackpool walkover when he could just as well have taken a book out onto the pitch with him, David Button certainly enjoyed his two most comfortable games of the season against Leeds and he was hardly called upon to dirty his knees in either match.

It will be illuminating to compare ourselves against Leeds and see if we are able to repeat our dominance over them or if the balance of power has changed.

The players are now enjoying a few days off and given the background of the majority of the squad, have probably spread themselves far and wide throughout Europe. Hopefully they will return to training next week refreshed and reinvigorated and more attuned to the challenge that awaits them.

With a now replenished squad containing three new players to integrate, Head Coach Marinus Dijkhuizen will, for the first time since his appointment, have the very real problem of who actually to leave out rather than having to worry about how to fill the substitutes' bench so that it doesn't resemble a crèche.

There is much to look forward to and the onus is now on the team management to use the break productively to hone and develop the squad into an effective and cohesive unit and hopefully demonstrate that we can both win matches and entertain at the same time. Mind you a clean sheet would not be unwelcome given our recent defensive shortcomings.

August was a truly horrible month where everything that could have gone wrong did so – and more too! September can, and hopefully will, be a lot better.

It is now time for the family, a good book or three, a sun lounger and a snorkel and for conversation to range around subjects far away from Griffin Park and its environs.

We are all feeling a bit jaded and beaten up by the traumas of the past month and I for one am really looking forward to my break.

I suspect that as the week progresses, my brain and typing fingers will start itching and twitching and I might just fall into temptation and find a subject that merits another article.

Maybe…maybe not.

If not then I look forward to seeing you all at Leeds a week on Saturday.

Give Football Managers Some Slack – They're Living On The Volcano – 7/9/15

So who would be a football manager?

The Griffin Park Grapevine fans' message board is currently awash with mocking and derogatory comments regarding former Brentford manager Terry Butcher's lack of success at his new club, Newport County, who currently languish at the foot of Division Two with a mere single point from their opening six matches. *Schadenfreude* at its malicious worst!

Yes, Butcher proved to be a dismal failure throughout his tenure in charge at Brentford eight long years ago, failing to connect with the Brentford supporters and recruiting a ragtag and bobtail of uninspiring journeymen who failed to deliver on the pitch.

It is so easy to carp and criticise but it takes far more effort to look beyond the superficial and obvious and try and analyse why things go wrong. Butcher's efforts at Griffin Park were hamstrung by a total lack of investment and he was forced to recruit in the bargain basement.

The situation at Newport is even more desperate. In the close season *EuroMillions* lottery winner Les Scadding decided to stop throwing his money into a black hole and the club found itself bereft of his investment, money that had enabled Newport to climb back into the Football League and even come close to promotion to Division One. Manager Justin Edinburgh, the architect of their onfield success, buttressed as he was by Scadding's massive financial support, quite understandably decided to jump ship and has now led his new team, Gillingham, to the top of League One.

It might be slightly exaggerating to state that Terry Butcher has inherited a club in turmoil, but it can't be by very much. The Supporters' Trust is valiantly attempting to run the club but they have had to cut their cloth accordingly and the very future of Newport County remains in doubt.

The playing budget has been cut dramatically, the better and higher paid players have left the club and their squad now contains a hodgepodge of players released by National League teams, including the unforgettably named Lenell John-Lewis, kids, rejects and bargain basement signings plus some untried young loanees including our own Josh Laurent.

Brentford supporters saw with our own eyes just how strong and talented a full strength Oxford United team was when they obliterated our young and weakened eleven a few short weeks ago. No wonder Newport County are struggling to keep their head above water given the number of recent body blows they have suffered.

Terry Butcher has previously proved at Motherwell and Inverness that he can be a successful manager if he is given a modicum of support and I am sure that his calmness and experience are now crucial as he needs to impart some confidence into his young and overmatched squad and put a metaphorical arm around their shoulders as they learn the hard way about the realities of the game at that level.

His beleaguered team is certainly playing for him and creditably fought back from an early two-goal deficit recently against promotion favourites Leyton Orient before falling to an unjust late defeat.

His squad on Saturday was down to the bare bones and included six teenagers given the recent transfer of highly rated teenager Regan Poole to Manchester United and another defender, Kevin Feely deciding to retire and return to full-time education. There is also an ever-growing injury and suspension list that further limits his options.

It never rains but it pours and Butcher is fighting against almost insurmountable odds as his team fights for survival and he tries to remain in a job.

Surely he deserves a little bit of sympathy and understanding rather than the cheap jibes he is currently being subjected to by fans and pundits alike who are totally unaware of the constraints under which he is working?

Brentford no longer have a manager but new Head Coach, Marinus Dijkhuizen has also been subjected to some second-guessing and criticism barely after he has got his feet under the table at Griffin Park.

After all, expectations have been raised to a ludicrous degree after last season's massive overachievement, the team has got off to a slow and stuttering start and also Marinus isn't Mark Warburton.

Reason enough surely for some Brentford fans to get on his back?

Rather than find fault, they should instead consider the long list of serious problems that he has inherited and has had to cope with recently at a club which has undergone a radical revolution from top to bottom over the past few months rather than the more gentle evolution that the majority of supporters would have preferred:

- Inflated expectations after reaching the playoffs last season

- The determination on the part of our opponents not to underestimate us again or take us for granted

- Enduring disappointment at the departure of Mark Warburton and David Weir

- The loss of key squad players in Craig, Odubajo, Dallas, Douglas and Gray

- Losing Bjelland, Jota and McEachran to long-term injuries

- Having to rebuild a team on the verge of the new season

- Trying to integrate a whole raft of new signings from abroad, none of whom with any experience of playing in England or an understanding of the demands of the Championship

- Being marooned in a new environment and country without the support of his family

- Inheriting a new management structure at the club where he does not have the final say on player recruitment

- Facing incessant media questioning over matters that are not under his control

- The chaos and embarrassment caused by the appalling new pitch at Griffin Park which has had to be relaid

I am quite sure that football fans would be more patient and have a better understanding of the problems and pressures that managers face every day if they took the time to read Mike Calvin's fascinating and illuminating new book, *Living On The Volcano*.

Calvin has gained a well-earned reputation over the past few years for obtaining the inside track on what goes on behind the scenes in football and he has now focused his attention on the role of football managers and how they deal with everything that is thrown at them. Calvin has followed his tried and tested method of becoming a fly on the wall and observed a variety of managers, young and old, established and new, successful and otherwise from the Premier League down to Division Two as they went about their business throughout the 2014/15 season.

The title of the book came from Arsene Wenger who compared the insecurity of his job to that of living on a volcano where any day might be your last, and the statistics substantiate his concern.

The average lifespan of a manager is seventeen months in the Football League and a mere eight in the competitive jungle of the Championship. On average it takes a sacked manager eighteen months to get a new job and fifty-eight percent of first time sacked managers never receive a second opportunity to get it right. Ian Holloway has spent nineteen years as a football manager and moved home thirty-three times throughout his long and illustrious career.

The pressure is intense and unrelenting and just as is the case in all other walks of life where one in every four of us suffers from mental health problems, some football managers also cannot cope and become ill. Martin

Ling, a chirpy, confident manager at Leyton Orient and Torquay United was so stricken with depression that he underwent an ultimately successful course of Electroconvulsive Therapy and is now making his way back into the game despite the self-proclaimed *coffee stain* on his CV and the ignorance and prejudice he has to overcome if he is to find a new post.

Despite the fact that managers are in competition against each other every week and new jobs only come about as a result of dead men's shoes, there is a real sense of family, brotherhood and fraternity between them all and a deep shared understanding of the problems they all face to a greater or lesser degree, such as lack of financial support, second guessing owners and chairmen and the ignorant vitriol spewed on fans' message boards.

Yes, there are some well-publicised feuds such as that between Neil Warnock and Stan Ternent but Ling was touched to receive many calls of support during his darkest hours from illustrious members of the League Managers Association such as Sir Alex Ferguson and Sam Allardyce.

Notts County manager Shaun Derry was visibly shocked and angered at the total lack of respect paid to Russell Slade by Leyton Orient's ignorant and bumbling new Italian ownership who totally disrespected him and cut him off at the knees by threatening him with the sack in front of his players if he did not win his next match. Nobody deserves to be treated like that, let alone a manager of Slade's stature and accomplishments.

Managers cannot show weakness or their true feelings in front of their players and Tommy Docherty once talked about his *stuck–on smile* that he wore every day at the training ground irrespective of his true feelings.

Readers also could not fail to be affected by the poignancy of Aidy Boothroyd's fourteen year-old son bursting into tears when informed of his dad's sacking by bottom of the league Northampton Town and how well his father dealt with the situation and turned it into a life lesson for his son.

Boothroyd also talks a lot of sense about picking a good chairman before you pick a new club and ensuring that football does not take over your life. He also confirms what I have long suspected, that most club chairmen have no real idea of how best to hire a new manager so Adie often has been forced to set the agenda and pose the following key questions during interviews:

- What is their strategy

- What is their structure

- Where do they want to be

- What are they trying to do

- What are they prepared to accept

- What aren't they prepared to accept

He also makes the gratifying if frankly surprising point for somebody whose job depended on results, that winning football games is not as important as how you play the game.

Gareth Ainsworth is another young manager rapidly making a name for himself at Wycombe Wanderers. He admits that this job consumes your life and eats you up. He transformed the fortunes of a club that was one match away from being relegated from the Football League. They survived by the skin of their teeth with a last day of the season victory at Torquay, a win wildly celebrated on the triumphant bus trip home. Yet in the ruthless and merciless game of football, the following week seven of those self-same players were released and in all fourteen players left the club.

Ainsworth highlights the importance of providing suitable pastoral care for the young men, often vulnerable and impressionable, who are under his care and he fully admits how painful it is to release players at the end of every season. Football manager as social worker.

He admits too that he has finally learned not to worry too much about the opposition. As a player he always felt that more attention should be given to what we would do to them rather than the other way round. A lesson here perhaps for the likes of Uwe Rösler?

The book continues in this vein as other managers such as Brendan Rogers, Mark Hughes and Garry Monk also reveal the secrets of their trade, their inspirations and the insecurities that they have to acknowledge and deal with on a daily basis. There is much for Brentford fans to identify too with former favourites Jimmy Sirrel, Micky Adams and Mark Warburton also coming under the spotlight.

I can do no more than wholeheartedly endorse and recommend a book that lifts the lid on a subject previously so shrouded in arcane mystery and secrecy. Calvin used the title *Family* when writing about Millwall FC a few years back and the same title could just as easily have been used for this book as it so perfectly describes the manner in which football managers regard each other as fellow members of a rare and talented breed.

"Living on the Volcano: The Secrets of Surviving as a Football Manager" by Michael Calvin is published by Century.

Nightmare Revisited – 9/9/15

I was idly flicking through the *Sky Sports* channels the other night looking for my football fix when perchance I came upon the highlights of our playoff final disaster against Yeovil back in 2013. I use the term *highlights* loosely, as there is absolutely nothing memorable about a game that still makes me feel quite nauseous every time I think about it – which thankfully is not very often.

In fact this was the first time I had ever watched the television coverage of the match as pretty much the first thing I did when I came home from Wembley, sick, stunned, gibbering out loud, disbelieving and fed up, was to delete my *SkyPlus* recording of the entire proceedings, still unwatched. Somehow that made me feel slightly better.

I also threw the massive match programme, a mini-book in everything else but name, still unread, into a dark corner of the lounge where it remained untouched for many months before I could bear to pick it up again and then safely dispose of it.

I was trying to expunge all memories of a quite appalling day and perhaps also endeavouring to punish myself for my stupidity and naïvety in actually allowing myself to believe that we were going to allay our playoff bogey and finally win promotion by this means at merely the seventh time of asking.

I was utterly convinced that we were going to beat Yeovil at Wembley. There was really no question about it. It was our turn. Surely God would finally and belatedly allow his countenance to shine down upon us as some sort of payback and compensation for the harrowing and ridiculous events against Doncaster and the entire Trotta *will-he – won't-he* penalty kick fiasco.

Like every other Brentford fan I was in a state of stunned, traumatic shock after the Doncaster match and couldn't bear to face yet another playoff lottery, and indeed I travelled to the first leg of the semi-final at Swindon still in a befuddled and totally disinterested state of mind.

On the journey I remember listening in a slightly distracted manner to reports of strange happenings taking place at the crucial Watford versus Leeds clash and how their automatic promotion hopes had been dashed after some goalkeeping howlers perpetrated by a callow and untried youngster forced to deputise at the last moment after a series of unlikely injuries to Watford's two other keepers.

That was my introduction to poor Jack Bonham whose career has so far been cursed by misfortune but hopefully his luck will change as he finally gains more experience.

Brentford's fortunes also received an unexpected boost deep into injury time at Swindon. Trailing deservedly to an excellently made and taken goal, and after a typically Rösler-esque performance of caution and negativity that deserved nothing better, a rare and desperate excursion into the home penalty area was rewarded when Harry Forrester, going nowhere, was tripped, the perpetrator receiving a volley of abuse from home hero, Alan McCormack, and a last gasp penalty kick was awarded.

There was never any question that Kevin O'Connor was going to take the kick after the Doncaster shenanigans and his spot kick was perfection personified as it raged into the side netting to earn us an unlikely and undeserved draw.

The second leg saw us play with vim and vigour for an hour and we should have been home and hosed and far more than the two goals ahead we found ourselves as Clayton Donaldson and Harry Forrester ran riot and Marcello Trotta went a long way towards getting back in our good books with a skilful and determined display.

As per normal we funnelled back for the last quarter attempting to sit on our lead and having given away the initiative we were punished by two scrambled goals from our proven weakness defending corner kicks.

The playoff curse had seemingly struck again but, aided and abetted by a harsh red card for our former loanee, Nathan Byrne, we dominated extra time but despite our incessant pressure the tie went to a dreaded penalty shootout.

Surely this would see the end of our season given our ghastly record from the spot, but this time we rose to the occasion and every player kept his nerve and finished unerringly. Wes Foderingham, the Swindon keeper was hampered by injury and unable to move freely and we took full advantage. Sam Saunders and Paul Hayes both found the bottom corner, Harlee Dean's kick was more central and Tony Craig smashed one into the top corner before celebrating wildly. When Simon Moore plunged to his left to paw away Miles Storey's kick it was all down to Adam Forshaw and his kick raged into the roof of the net. We all celebrated wildly and joyfully invaded the pitch.

Yeovil awaited us at Wembley, the final obstacle standing between us and a triumphant and surely fully deserved and long-awaited return to the Championship.

Despite conceding all six points and six goals to Garry Johnson's well organised and abrasive team we all felt smug and confident that it would be third time lucky against them and that we would finally allay our bogey. We should have realised that the wily old fox in Johnson more than had the measure of Uwe.

Jonathan Douglas was not felt to be fit enough to start the match and we missed his strength and influence against a strong and well drilled team that played effective percentage football aided and abetted by the predatory finishing of the clinical Paddy Madden having a season to remember.

It was he who scored early on with a fulminating volley that raged into the net when the ball fell unerringly to him on the edge of the box. This took the wind out of our sails as we collapsed like a pricked balloon and we never really recovered.

Harry Forrester was at his most infuriating worst on the left wing, dribbling into blind alleys and creating little and Marcello Trotta and Clayton Donaldson played like distant strangers with Clayton isolated and marooned on the right wing where he was never likely to become a major influence on the game.

Our defence looked rattled, the midfield created little and were totally outmuscled and apart from a Trotta header saved with an unnecessary flourish by Stech, we never threatened.

Hopes of getting into the dressing room at halftime without further damage were shattered when we conceded a horribly soft, avoidable and totally demoralising second goal just before the interval when the massive Dan Burn rose unchallenged at the far post from a left wing corner and his header trickled through a scrum of players in the six-yard box and almost apologetically crossed the line before being booted clear by Shay Logan.

I walked the concourse in a daze during the break, seeing and speaking to nobody, looking for an open door through which I could escape the nightmare I was witnessing, but to no avail.

Thankfully the second half saw Brentford finally decide to turn up with Adam Forshaw taking control of midfield and driving us forward. We needed the fillip of an early goal and got it when Harlee Dean met a Forshaw corner with a thumping header.

Yeovil retreated and simply dared us to break them down again. We did our best and struck at their heart several times but despite all our efforts we were doomed to failure.

Donaldson forced a wonderful save from Stech with a near post header and Bradley Wright-Phillips, caught on his heels rather than his toes, unaccountably failed to convert the rebound with the goal gaping. Stech earned his man of the match award with two more saves, from Forshaw when he managed to sit on the ball and block a close in effort and then a full length dive kept out a late Wright-Phillips volley.

Time ran out on us and all our hopes were dashed when another nemesis from the past Andy D'Urso blew the final whistle. Yeovil frolicked in the sunshine and we slunk away in silence.

Watching the *Sky* coverage brought all these horrid memories flooding back. I was also surprised at the lack of quality of our football on the day. We played far too many long balls which were meat and drink to the Yeovil defenders and we very rarely got the ball down and played through the opposition.

We were a decent enough team that season and boasted excellent players in Donaldson and Forshaw but we had a soft underbelly and all too often flattered only to deceive. Wembley was a prime example. We failed to do ourselves justice and in truth, the game was up at halftime. Tony Craig and Jonathan Douglas did their bit all season, but we lacked leaders as well as mental strength and toughness.

The manager also did not help build confidence amongst our ranks with his over-cautious approach and determination to concentrate on the opposition rather than focusing on our ability. We always seemed to play with the handbrake on and it was not until the arrival of Mark Warburton that pretty much the same group of players saw their shackles removed and were then given the freedom to demonstrate their full potential and obtain the promotion that had evaded them so narrowly the previous season.

In a strange way I am glad that I finally watched the Yeovil match again as it clearly demonstrated exactly where we were at that point in time in our development, and, far more importantly, just how far we have progressed over the last couple of years as we are now light years in terms of our planning and structure and, of course, the quality of the team that we fielded on that awful day at Wembley in May 2013.

Oh, and just look where Yeovil are now, marooned near to the bottom of the Football League. In retrospect promotion to the Championship was a step too far given their lack of resources.

Better…. Much Better! – 13/9/15

It was a typical long and frustrating stop-start drive back from Leeds last night along an M1 motorway littered with a seemingly interminable and never-ending series of frustrating and unnecessary fifty mile per hour speed restrictions and the *longeur* gave me time aplenty to contemplate the afternoon's entertainment at Elland Road.

To be honest I had had a lot of misgivings about our prospects given our shaky start to the season, the catalogue of players out with injury and the need to integrate so many new players into the team. Elland Road is also far from being the most welcoming of venues or the easiest introduction to the realities of Championship football with a phalanx of biased and one-eyed supporters spitting bile and hatred and harking back to past glories as well as subjecting the referee to a nonstop barrage of verbal abuse and demands for non-existent fouls.

Leeds are by no means one of the best teams in the league but they are certainly strong, determined, tough and rugged and that, combined with the immutable law of the ex with the Uwe Rösler, Stuart Dallas and Tom Adeyemi factors also to take into account made me nervous about the outcome.

I was really disappointed and frustrated on the way home but not for the reasons that I had anticipated. Instead, I could not understand quite how a Brentford team that had risen to the challenge and such a tough test of their poise and resolve had come away with only one point instead of the three that they so clearly deserved after a skilful and resilient display that should have been rewarded with a victory instead of the one – all draw that resulted.

There was much to be pleased about and the positives far outweighed the negatives.

Marinus employed a 4-3-3 formation that worked well and we looked compact and organised. For the first time this season rather than having a bunch of strangers who looked as if they had been introduced to each other in the changing room before the match, we finally looked like a team in which everyone knew their job and for the most part they completed their tasks to a very high standard.

David Button hardly had a save to make such was the quality of the defending in front of him which restricted the home team to very few chances. Harlee Dean easily won his battle against the giant, lumbering Chris Wood who took the expression *a minimum of effort* to new heights – or should that be depths?

Harlee has been a new man this season. He looks fitter, sleeker and far more composed and is finally content to let his football do the talking do him. In other words, he has grown up and matured and has developed into an excellent Championship calibre central defender who totally merits his place in the team, leads by example and is a captain in everything but name.

James Tarkowski had also had a difficult and inconsistent start to the season but yesterday saw him at his brilliant and composed best where he combined anticipation and perceptive use of the ball with some excellent defensive work. Of course we miss the presence of the long-term injured Andreas Bjelland but the Dean/Tarkowski partnership is f ourishing and they totally dominated their opponents.

Max Colin too settled down after a difficult start that saw him booked for a late challenge before he was substituted late on after a dogged performance against the tricky and direct Stuart Dallas. Jake Bidwell was calm and competent and came the closest yet to his elusive first goal when he just failed to angle his header into an empty net after Judge's cross went over the goalkeeper as he went walkabout.

If I have spent a lot of time discussing the Brentford defence then I make no apologies, as for the first time this season they looked calm, confident and competent and really deserved the reward of a still awaited first clean sheet.

Diagouraga and McCormack dovetailed well and protected their back four with a combination of tenacity and bite. Toumani looked back to near his best, which is welcome news for all Brentford fans and McCormack was tough and combative. He tested the patience of the excellent referee, Nigel Miller, but knew exactly just how far he could go and managed to avoid a booking. It is worth noting that we conceded a goal just after he had been moved to right back to replace Colin and we badly missed his influence in the middle of the field.

Konstantin Kerschbaumer is finding it hard to settle down and nothing much that he is attempting so far is coming off. Yesterday was no exception as he underhit his shot from right in front of goal in the first minute and all too often he was knocked off the ball or failed to find a man with his passes, unerringly choosing the wrong option. And yet…and yet, there is definitely something about him and I just feel that he is still coming to terms with the physicality and pace of the Championship.

Alan Judge was the source of pretty much everything good that we did. He buzzed around on the left wing and led the Leeds defence a merry dance, twisting and weaving his way through them and Sol Bamba will be having nightmares about the ease with which Judge beat him on several occasions. It was good to see him attempting so many shots even if his radar was off and it was his dribble and perfectly timed pass that gave Marco Djuricin the chance to take his time, turn inside Cooper and demonstrate his clinical finishing ability by unerringly finding the bottom corner. This was the first time that Brentford have scored first all season and it certainly felt good and you could see the confidence course back into the veins of players and fans alike.

Marco impressed on his debut, showing skill on the ball and good vision. He is not going to work tirelessly and run the channels and harass defenders, but he is undoubtedly a goal scorer, playing on the shoulder of the last defender and he will score regularly if he is given the service that he needs. He should have been celebrating a second time on his debut but after Silvestri's slack kick out he was set up perfectly by Vibe but his first time effort pinged back off the post and bounced away. On such small margins are games decided, as Leeds would never surely have recovered from a two-goal deficit.

Lasse Vibe is also finding his feet. He is quick and sharp but his control and first touch let him down when Tarkowski slid him in on goal. He is at his most dangerous when played more centrally and I do not think he is best suited to his current role wide on the right.

Ryan Woods unfortunately had a debut to forget as it was his slip in midfield which led to the equaliser. He was introduced as a late substitute but had not yet accustomed himself to the pace of the game when he was put under pressure when Button cleared the ball to him, easily dispossessed, and Leeds took full advantage when Dallas and Wood worked the ball to Antenucci who bent the ball past Button for an undeserved, if clinically taken, equaliser.

The pass was on from Button and we generally retain possession so well in our half of the field that it is harsh to carp when occasionally things go wrong, as they did here. Woods recovered from his error and looked confident on the ball and showed enough to demonstrate that he will prove to be a massive asset for us.

Philipp Hofmann came on for the tiring Djuricin soon after the hour but he had to be replaced himself near the end by Canos, our third newcomer, after incurring an injury. The kindest thing to say about Hofmann is that he is still finding his feet in his new environment. He is massive but as of yet shows no inclination to use his bulk and strength and is easily bustled off the ball. It must be a massive learning curve for him but he needs to impose himself rather than stand on the periphery of the action and contribute very little. He combines physical presence with massive ability on the ball, and once the penny finally drops he could take this division by storm – it is up to him to learn and adapt. Canos too looked good on the ball and showed he had a trick or two in him. He will certainly contribute throughout his stay, take the Championship in his stride, and will not be overwhelmed by the challenge he faces.

So one point only when we should have taken all three was a minimal reward given everything that we put into the game, however I am sure that spirits within the camp will have been raised by the performance and there were more than a few encouraging signs that the time on the training ground over the international break had been well spent.

There is still much that needs thinking about and possibly tinkering with, particularly up front. Vibe has already demonstrated that he is a high quality player but we are not using him to his best advantage marooned out on the right wing where he also finds it hard to put in a defensive shift. We lack the pace and incision that Andre Gray brought us and we could certainly do with his selfless channel running and chasing of lost causes. Neither Hofmann nor Djuricin are that type of player and we will have to adapt our play accordingly. Djuricin though, brings us something that we have lacked for a long time – a clinical and calm finisher who will probably convert so many of those close range opportunities that always seem to be ignored or go begging for us.

The team has remained up north to prepare for the Middlesbrough match on Tuesday night. Nobody needs reminding that it was Groundhog Day when they beat us four times running last season and given the positives that we saw yesterday we will travel there filled with hope that we will put on a performance and take something from the game.

Trickery from Lasse Vibe at Elland Road

Payback Time? – 15/9/15

Brentford take on the might of Middlesbrough tonight and whilst on the face of it they might appear to be on a *Mission Impossible* there is much to be optimist about and in the immortal words of Robert Louis Stevenson, *to travel hopefully is a better thing than to arrive, and the true success is to labour.*

And believe me, we will have to work hard to get anything out of tonight's match.

Last season saw Middlesbrough firmly established as our bogey team. We could barely buy a goal against them, let alone a victory and four matches, including the playoff semi-final ties saw us suffer four defeats and score only once whilst conceding ten times in all. You can't really argue with the facts, but two of the games were closely fought and there is no way that the Bees should have lost either tussle at Griffin Park.

We totally dominated proceedings in the January league match, missed chance after chance in a totally one-sided first half and yet somehow went in at the break trailing to a soft penalty kick conceded by David Button after Harlee Dean unaccountably ducked under a harmless through ball and let in the predatory Patrick Bamford. I suspect that the explanation for this apparent aberration is that Harlee received a call to *leave it* from somebody in the adjacent area and I don't believe that the person concerned was wearing a red and white striped shirt!

We created even more opportunities in the second half and Stuart Dallas could have scored four had the luck been with him but Boro were strong, professional, organised and resilient and managed to hold us at bay.

There was a similar tale to tell in the first leg of the playoff tie when after a poor first half we battered them and finally managed a goal when the predatory Andre Gray took full advantage of the keeper's error in dealing with a harmless through ball. From then on we grew in confidence, created and missed further opportunities, saw Jonathan Douglas's header force a miraculous save and then fell victim to a sucker bunch with an injury time winner from a deflected shot after a corner kick. Life is so hard and unfair sometimes.

As for the away games, there is really not much to tell. We were tentative, disorganised, defended poorly, created little and allowed ourselves to be totally outmuscled, intimidated and outplayed. In other words we totally deserved the two thrashings we received.

That though is all in the past. Now we have to look forward and go into tonight's game with a clean slate and simply learn from the errors and mistakes we made last season and have a game plan that gives us a realistic opportunity of getting something from the match. Last season we invariably played the same way. We had a Plan A where we set up in a 4-2-3-1 formation every time and we always tried to take the game to the opposition whatever the circumstances.

It also worked far more often than not as is evidenced by our final fifth place. The one exception was against Middlesbrough, who, like everybody else, knew exactly what was coming from us, but unlike most of the other Championship teams, knew how to counter us.

They sat back, took whatever we could throw at them, dominated the midfield, kicked us up in the air whenever necessary – and sometimes when it wasn't, took advantage of poor and weak refereeing and then picked us off on the break.

Unlike us, their finishing was clinical and they wasted very few goalscoring opportunities. They also exerted a stranglehold on the centre of the midfield, so often our strength, where Toumani Diagouraga and Jonathan Douglas were totally outgunned, outfought and outplayed by Leadbitter and Clayton who dominated proceedings. They were tigerish in their challenges, gave us no peace or time to settle on the ball and then invariably used the ball effectively and set up a series of attacks that threatened our goal. Albert Adomah was also a constant danger on their right wing and led Jake Bidwell a merry dance with his pace and trickery.

So what can we do to turn the tide tonight? Firstly we must forget about the so-called *Middlesbrough Hoodoo* – it no longer exists. We start again with a clean slate and have the chance to set our own agenda against a team that has been strengthened by the arrival of experienced international players in Stewart Downing and David Nugent. Adomah though has fallen out of contention after a dispute with the management.

Our team is different and several of the players who capitulated in the playoffs last season will not be involved. Odubajo, Douglas, Jota, Pritchard and Gray won't be playing for us for a variety of reasons and we have new blood aplenty who are untainted and will not go into the game burdened with negative thoughts from last season's series of poor results against Middlesbrough.

I do not expect us to be as expansive as we were last season and we are better suited to the new 4-3-3 formation preferred by Marinus Dijkhuizen. The key will be in midfield where we ceded control far too easily in all four games last season.

Alan McCormack will be crucial to our game plan tonight and ensure that we are not bullied and knocked (or should that be kicked) off the ball. He will protect our back four and support Toumani whose passing ability will be needed to ensure that we break their press and are able to move forward whenever possible.

In my opinion this is not a game for Konstantin Kerschbaumer who is still finding his feet in English football. Instead I would start with Ryan Woods who would provide a more solid and forceful approach. He is a little ferret who wins the ball effectively and then plays with his head up and rarely wastes possession.

Middlesbrough will surely dominate possession tonight but we must not turn the ball over to them cheaply, particularly in our last third of the field. We need to be patient, absorb the pressure that they will doubtless put on us but not be as open and exposed as we were last season. Our chances will come and we need then to get Alan Judge on the ball when he can ideally feed the bullets for Lasse Vibe and the predatory Marco Djuricin.

If we defend properly, as we did on Saturday, avoid doing anything stupid or *kamikaze*, then we have every chance of getting something on the night and maintaining our improvement. We have the players, we have the ability, we simply need to allow our new team to bed in and find their feet.

Elland Road was a massive challenge that we overcame, tonight is yet another one and I feel that if we stick to our game plan we can triumph and enjoy the long trip home.

Oh, and it would also be nice to wipe the smile off Adam Forshaw's face too!

There's Really Nothing We Can Do – 15/9/15

I had an evening in with *Bees Player* tonight and enjoyed listening to Billy Reeves and Chris Wickham describing Brentford's more than decent performance at The Riverside Stadium against promotion favourites Middlesbrough.

A Lasse Vibe equaliser just after half time gave us false hope that our efforts would receive some tangible reward but it wasn't to be as a strong, tough and experienced Middlesbrough team kept up the pressure and finally prevailed by three goals to one.

The match was far closer than the scoreline suggests and we certainly had our chances – and excellent ones too: Marco Djuricin disastrously missed twice from close range from opportunities that a striker of his pedigree should have snapped up, Alan Judge chipped just wide when the scores were level and Konstantin Kerschbaumer hit the keeper with the goal gaping.

That is certainly a cause for optimism but also one for frustration as you are only going to get a few chances against a team of Middlesbrough's quality and you have to take them if you are going to come away with any tangible reward. The quality of finishing was what separated the two teams on the night. Boro took their chances – we didn't.

Ultimately we can really have no complaints as the home team dominated and were ultimately just too clinical and strong for us on the night. We kept our shape, defended heroically and the midfield trio of Diagouraga, McCormack and Kerschbaumer more then held their own but we were forced backwards and were unable to cope with Middlesbrough's pace down both flanks. Harlee Dean and the debutant Yoann Barbet did their best to stem the flow but we were overrun and the goals finally came.

The defeat was disappointing but not a disaster or even a surprise when you put things into perspective. We were playing one of the promotion favourites and we certainly put on a far better performance than in either match at The Riverside Stadium last season.

As Exhibit One for the defence I give you the Brentford substitutes' bench last night:

Bonham | Smith | O'Connell | Woods | Udumaga | Canos

Yes, that only makes six in total. We were not even able to fill the bench with our full complement of seven substitutes and we were forced to include two goalkeepers in Jack Bonham and Mark Smith.

None of them had ever started a league game for Brentford either, which just highlights their inexperience and the seriousness of the situation that we currently find ourselves in.

A quite ridiculous and unique state of affairs caused by an unprecedented and ever increasing injury list that is totally sabotaging our efforts to compete this season.

Two of last Saturday's squad in James Tarkowski and Philipp Hofmann were also unfit to play at Middlesbrough and we now have a dozen players who are currently *hors de combat*:

Andreas Bjelland | Scott Hogan | Jota | Josh McEachran | Lewis Macleod | Sam Saunders | Marcos Tebar | Philipp Hofmann | Josh Clarke | Andy Gogia | James Tarkowski | Nico Yennaris

Just look at the talent that is currently in the treatment room, players of the calibre of Jota, Bjelland and McEachran.

How can you compensate for this ill fortune? The answer of course is that you can't and we are simply totally stymied at the moment.

Middlesbrough by comparison were able to bring on players of the calibre of Albert Adomah, Kike and Adam Forshaw at a time when it looked as if Brentford might just be on the verge of taking control. They are all players of massive talent and experience who changed the game in their favour.

In contrast we gave a late run out to Jermaine Udumaga a young kid being asked to do a man's job and Ryan Woods, a new signing from the lower leagues. How can you expect either of them to change the course of the game?

As for having two goalkeepers on the bench – that just shows how desperate a position we are in at present. I remember Gordon Phillips being named as a non-playing substitute at Crewe back in the bad old days of the early 70s but those were times when we had a minuscule squad and were on the breadline.

Hopefully we can begin to get some players back soon but things might yet get worse before they improve as colossus, Harlee Dean, suffered a nasty looking injury late on. He managed to play on but who knows whether he will suffer a reaction and also be forced to sit out the next few games?

So what can we do to help us through this nightmare? We could possibly enter the loan market but we need some experience and some leaders rather than callow youngsters and they are almost impossible to come by. It will be interesting to see if we do manage to bring in some reinforcements and if we do so, what type of player we are able to recruit.

I have racked my brains for a solution and quite frankly there isn't one apart from patience. We just have to keep our guard up, suck it up and take the blows that will rain down on us whilst we are on the ropes. As long as the team retains its spirit and some level of confidence then we will recover once we do manage to get a stronger team back on the field.

Margins are so narrow at this level of the game that the quality of the bench can make all the difference, as was shown tonight. We are miles away from being able to influence the results of matches by having game changing talent on the bench and we just have to accept that this is the case for the time being.

I really cannot think of a time in the recent past when we were afflicted so badly by injuries as is the case at present and it is doubly galling that this state of affairs is occurring whilst we are competing in perhaps the toughest league in Europe.

The knock-on effect of tonight is that after an exhausting schedule, a long and tiring journey home and a day off tomorrow, a weakened and tired squad will not be in the best shape to compete on Saturday in what is now looking to be a crucial and even must-win match against Preston North End.

Batten down the hatches, we are in for a tough time and there is choppy water ahead.

We need to stay positive, calm and united if our current difficult situation is not to overwhelm us.

A Star Is Born – 20/9/15

A lot of good things came out of yesterday's match against Preston North End. Most crucially, the Bees won for the first time this season at Griffin Park after coming back from a one-goal deficit having conceded a demoralising goal within the first minute of play.

We also discovered a potential star in young Liverpool loanee Sergi Canos who almost singlehandedly turned the game in Brentford's favour when he came on as a substitute on the hour with Brentford on top but still struggling to find inspiration and an equaliser.

Canos of the twinkling toes and fast, nimble feet was simply too good for the visitors. He played with his head up and saw openings quicker than anyone else in the field. He was as brave and determined as he was skilful on the ball, he was a pest as well as a talent and he made an immediate impact by taking an excellent Diagouraga through pass in his stride, cutting in from the right wing and his low cut back was comfortably converted at the near post by the predatory Lasse Vibe who scored his third goal of what promises to be a successful season for the striker.

Confidence flooded back into the team and the game turned on its head soon afterwards when Bidwell's header found Djuricin who turned his marker and under stiff challenge still managed to stride into the area and plant the ball unerringly between Jordan Pickford and his near post.

Suddenly from almost out of nowhere we have a flourishing and dangerous strike partnership with five goals between them in only four games.

From then on there was only one winner and Brentford comfortably survived a long ball barrage from a now dispirited and it has to be said, limited Preston team that had run out of ideas, without too many heart-in-mouth moments.

Sergi Canos glides over the turf

This was a must-win match if the Bees were to avert the recent slump and avoid being sucked into the relegation zone, and after the training injury suffered by Max Colin, resources were stretched even further with Josh Clarke given his first league start at right back.

He recovered well from an appalling start with Preston attacking down his flank and he was left trailing by Doyle whose centre was met by May. Button saved heroically but Daniel Johnson easily converted the rebound and the Bees were coming from behind get again – the story of this entire season so far.

The first quarter hour was shambolic as Preston found time and space as Brentford were like rabbits in headlights and they wasted several gilt-edged chances to score that crucial second goal that would surely have killed the game almost at its outset.

Alan Judge was everywhere and his influence, energy, effervescence and example allowed a shell-shocked Bees team to finally claw themselves off the floor and start to compete. From then on their superior technique came to the fore and the first half chances came and went. Kerschbaumer missed twice after finding time and space in the penalty area, Vibe had his shot blocked from close in and Pickford saved well from Bidwell and sensationally from a free header from Barbet which looked bound for the net.

Button too arched backwards to tip over a close range header from Joe Garner and prevented the striker from scoring his first goal of the season.

After halftime Brentford took control as Preston sat back to defend their lead but it was not until Canos came on and we moved Vibe from out on the right wing where his talents had been wasted, to play just behind Djuricin, that the tide fully turned and the Bees finally took advantage of their superiority.

There will be far tougher tests than Preston, starting next Saturday when Sheffield Wednesday come to town, a team we failed to score against last season, but you can do no more than beat the opponents you are facing on the day.

The defence settled down after an uncomfortable start and Barbet gave us balance and composure on the left hand side and formed a strong and effective partnership with man mountain Harlee Dean. Tarkowski should get his place back when his calf heals but the young Frenchman has impressed since he was thrown in two games ago.

Clarke too looked good going forward but less so defensively, and we were far more solid when Alan McCormack moved back from midfield to replace him and if, as looks likely, Colin is yet another long-term absentee then it will be interesting to see who gets the nod next weekend.

Canos too looked like the ultimate impact substitute but it will surely be tempting for Marinus Dijkhuizen to start him against Sheffield Wednesday in the hope that he can weave his magic from the off.

We are still short of experience and inspiration which is hardly surprising when you consider our injury list which shows few signs of diminishing – if anything it is getting even worse.

The midfield trio of Diagouraga, McCormack and Kerschbaumer competed well but lack pace and attacking flair and Ryan Woods must surely be close to his first start.

Jermaine Udumaga came on near the end but was completely outmatched and overwhelmed despite having a shot blocked after more Canos magic, and we are desperately short of cover up front.

The fixture list is relentless and unforgiving and reinforcements are still desperately needed if we are to maintain our impetus or even keep our head above water in the short term. Another striker who can spell Djuricin and Vibe and a creative spark to assist Alan Judge would be more than welcome additions next week.

This win has given us some welcome breathing space and much needed confidence but we are still fragile and punching above our weight given how stretched we are in terms of player availability.

The good news has to be that the newcomers are all learning on the job – even if it is the hard way, and they will all benefit in the long run from having to be thrown in at the deep end.

The crowd dipped below ten thousand for the first time this season, which is not totally unexpected given our shaky start to the season and the problems we have faced but the fans were patient and understanding for the most part and there is a general feeling of sympathy, support and understanding towards Dijkhuizen given his torrid introduction to the hot seat.

A good day then for the Bees after the worst of all possible starts and we all left the ground relieved and wreathed in smiles – but it could all have been so different had Preston taken their early chances and if a star had not been born. On such narrow margins are games decided. We move on re-energised and with increased hope and enthusiasm.

Blazing Meteors – Part One – 22/9/15

Young Liverpool loanee Sergi Canos's mesmerising and eye-catching home debut as a second half substitute last Saturday who turned the game on its head and inspired the Bees to victory has persuaded me to recall some other youngsters who made an immediate impact for Brentford.

I missed John Bostock's memorable debut against Millwall when he took the game by the scruff of its neck and scored twice from a clinical volley and then direct from a corner. I had a bad back, my Achilles' heel for anyone interested, and it's lucky that I was safely tucked up at home in bed as I suspect that all the excitement would have given me a relapse and put me into spasm!

Unfortunately Bostock flattered only to deceive and could not maintain his form and he soon fell out of contention and eventually drifted into obscurity in Belgium where he remains to this day.

Being a half-empty kind of guy I'm going to concentrate on some other eventual failures – players who began like world beaters and blazing meteors but for a variety of reasons soon blew themselves out and became damp squibs who never really made the impact that had at one time had looked likely or even inevitable.

So where shall we start?

How about with **Andy Woon**, a tall, powerful and raw long haired striker who arrived from non-league Bognor Regis and was soon thrown into the deep end and asked to inspire and reinvigorate a toothless Brentford team on its inevitable and irrevocable journey towards relegation. Stan Webb had already proved beyond doubt that he was not an adequate replacement for the departed John O'Mara, and Woon made history and an instant impact when he became the first Brentford player to score a hat trick on his full debut in a totally out of the blue five-goal thrashing of a listless Port Vale team.

Nobody could be expected to keep up that type of form and Woon inevitably suffered from unreasonably raised expectations. Andy hung around for a couple of seasons, even scored a few more goals but he never threatened to repeat the magic he displayed on that unforgettable afternoon in February 1973 when he looked like an absolute world beater and everything he hit went in.

Richard Poole became the second youngest ever Brentford player when he made his debut at the age of sixteen years and five months. The crowd took to him straight away, as he was a local boy who was playing for the team he had always supported and his coltish enthusiasm did much to inspire the Bees to pull away from the bottom of Division Four.

The future looked bright for the tall, rangy target man but it just never happened for him. He fell out with the new manager, John Docherty, injuries took their toll, and he disappeared from the scene. He had a short spell at Watford where he played against us in the unforgettable Paul Priddy double penalty save match before moving to France where injury sadly brought a halt to a once promising career.

Paul Walker captained the England schoolboy international team and a glittering future was predicted for the diminutive midfielder. He made his first team debut as a fifteen-year-old schoolboy but despite his obvious ability it just never happened for him.

He had great vision and passing ability and could ghost past players but he never looked fully fit or a well-honed athlete and his early promise was never fulfilled. Fred Callaghan seemed to believe in him and he scored a memorable volleyed goal at Walsall in Terry Hurlock's televised debut match but he eventually ended up playing in South Africa.

I watched sixteen-year-old striker **Gary Rolph** make a massively impressive debut in the FA Cup at Colchester where he showed a maturity well beyond his tender years and scored a coolly taken goal, but that was as good as it got for him and he soon fell away.

Willie Graham arrived as an unheralded trialist from Northampton Town but Bill Dodgin saw something in him and he slotted in perfectly in midfield alongside his namesake Jackie Graham and David Carlton as the Bees won promotion from the bottom tier. The magic only lasted a season as he was unable to cope with the demands of the higher division and he was never a major influence again.

Billy Eames was a diminutive winger who scored on his debut and was man of the match on his debut as a trialist against Lincoln City. Surely Bill Dodgin would offer him a contract, but for some reason he didn't and Eames retired and became a teacher.

Lee Frost took Griffin Park by storm as a marauding winger during a productive loan spell from Chelsea but he was a totally different player when he joined us on a permanent basis two years later. He was moved inside to partner Gary Johnson where he totally failed to impress and looked languid and lightweight and he soon left the club and the professional game.

Tony Spencer was another who lost a promising career to injury. A composed young defender who was on the verge of establishing himself in the team, he suffered a serious knee injury from which he never fully recovered and he was forced to retire before his twentieth birthday.

Tony Lynch was a speedy winger who promised far more than he ultimately delivered before Frank McLintock released him. All credit to Lynch as he fought his way back to the Football League with Barnet for whom he played against Brentford.

Robbie Carroll was an underrated striker who scored regularly when given a chance but couldn't manage to establish himself in the team. He never appeared to be particularly valued by the management and rejected the offer of a monthly contract and signed for Fareham Town.

The immortal **Steve Thorne** of eponymous fanzine fame scored a long-range thunderbolt on his debut at Gillingham and ended up scoring the winning goal in his one and only Football League appearance.

Paul Birch cost ten thousand pounds from Portsmouth and scored an excellent goal at Fulham – always a good way to make friends and influence people at Griffin Park. He looked full of promise and hard running but surprisingly retired from football when barely twenty-years-old and became a successful businessman.

Andy Driscoll made an immediate impact with a wonderful solo goal against Blackpool as an eighteen-year-old winger of immense potential. His promise was never to be fulfilled as he never recovered from a serious knee injury and he eventually became a personal trainer. This was a tragic loss as he could well have become a star.

Kelly Haag was a prolific scorer at junior level notching fifty goals in a season, but he was unable to make the step-up to senior football with Brentford but played for Fulham and Barnet with more success.

Winger **Rob Peters** is best remembered for a thunderous free kick goal at Huddersfield that helped us earn a playoff berth in 1991 but he never really made the grade.

I will try and complete this list in a day or so.

A View From A Blazing Meteor – 23/9/15

I wrote an article the other day inspired by Sergi Canos's blistering home debut, about other young players who started off like a house on fire at Griffin Park and then fizzled out for a variety of reasons and never really made their mark.

One of the players I mentioned was 70s striker Richard Poole who has some strong views on the subject:

Well Greville your list could go on and on. At the time when I was promoted into the Brentford first team I was playing in the South East Counties Under 18 League against the likes of Chelsea, QPR and Fulham and we always tried our utmost to ensure that those bigger teams knew that they had been in a game when they came up against the Bees.

As you know I came into the side as a sixteen-year-old apprentice in February 1974 and just a week later my friend Kevin Harding followed me into the first team. We were coming straight from junior football into a team that had just been relegated to the bottom division the year before and we were fighting a desperate battle to avoid the need to seek re-election.

You must remember at that time in the Fourth Division there was no automatic relegation but the bottom club had to be re-elected by its peers and although I do not know the political ins and outs and how the system worked, I still wonder to this day what would had happened to us if we had needed to seek re-election to the Football League. How would our archenemies QPR and Fulham have voted? Would they have done their best to see us kicked out of the League?

We could not take the chance of that happening so we just did our best to ensure that we finished out of the danger zone. So here we were like new born babies coming into a team that still boasted inspirational veterans like Peter Gelson and Jackie Graham. Kevin and I trained each day with our boyhood idols and we were welcomed with open arms and treated so well along with Roy Cotton, another promising player from the Under 18 team.

Having avoided the threat of re-election we all started the new season with fresh hope and enthusiasm but alas, things did not work out and John Docherty replaced Mike Everitt as manager midway through the season. So here I was with a new manager who had been my teammate when I made my first team debut and who now would sign me as a professional footballer on my eighteenth birthday.

Although I have made it clear previously that I seemed to fall out with him, it was only later on in my life that I realised certain things about that difficult time that I am still unable to put into words even to this day over forty years on.

Yes I did play a few games for him, generally in midweek at the likes of places like Tranmere and Northampton and I always tried my best but I feel even now that I was not given a proper or decent chance.

The tipping point came in April 1975 after I came on as a substitute and helped the team to a good result at Lincoln. I was delighted to be named in the team the following week against Southport but was surprised to see that both Roger Cross and Micky French were in the team too. I must confess that I thought that having three centre forwards in the starting line-up was bizarre in the extreme.

I did not see much of the ball in the first half and at half time I was replaced by Alan Nelmes – a striker replaced at home by a defender in a match that was still goalless. What did that say about my prospects at the club? No wonder I left soon afterwards! But I still treasure to this day the fact that I played in the red and white stripes of my beloved Brentford and no one can take that away from me.

Anyway before that fiasco, about half way through that season I came to a very difficult decision and asked to be put on the transfer list or even loaned to a non-league side, as I just wanted to play first team football somewhere!

We had a reserve team that year and I always gave my best when I played for them but I simply needed to stretch myself and progress. Maybe I was not good enough but I thought I could do a decent job for somebody if they gave me a chance!

Anyway John Docherty refused to let me go and said he needed me. And yet he barely played me and I was frozen out of the reckoning.

Nothing had changed at the end of the season and I was given a free transfer. We played an end of season game against Hounslow and several clubs approached me directly and said that they would come and watch me play as they knew I would be a free agent. This was an opportunity for me to put myself in the shop window and earn myself a decent move.

Little did I know what was in store for me! John Docherty announced the team just before the match and amazingly I was the only one of all the players who had been released who wasn't given a game. I wasn't even put on the bench.

I could not believe it and when I spoke to the manager afterwards and told him that there had been clubs there to watch me play all he said was "You should have told me beforehand."

To this day I do not know if he was scared that I might go to another club and do well and make him look bad, or if he thought I was not good enough to play in the Football League. Eventually I joined Watford although I was also asked to sign for SC Toulon, one of the top teams in France so I must have had something about me!

I still look back at the Brentford junior team I played in and in my opinion it contained so much ability in the year I made my first team debut but none were retained apart from me and I can tell you I was by no means the best player in that talented side.

When John Docherty arrived we were swamped by a lot of fairly decent young players who he knew from his previous club, QPR, but not many of them lasted long or made any impact at Brentford.

It is a shame that I fell out with the manager and at the time I was a starry eyed kid who was living the dream, but I think that today's young players are not as naïve as I was but despite everything I regret nothing and would not change a moment of those incredible five years I spent at Brentford as both an apprentice and as a professional footballer.

When John Docherty became manager I think he had the choice of running either a youth or a reserve side and even though I came straight into the first team from the juniors I think that not having an Under 18 team was a big mistake. Most of the time we had first team players coming back from injury, some of whom even refused to play in Reserve games.

We were in the Midweek League and going to places like Peterborough or Southend I think was not too enticing a prospect for some first team players! We also had lots of trialists as well so you never knew who was playing with you from week to week whereas we knew each other in the youth team and could develop partnerships on the pitch.

I really think that the club wasted a massive opportunity, as there were several talented youngsters who were not really given a chance to impress. Brentford and the management did not know how to bring these players into the first team.

John Docherty preferred skilful ball playing players but in the Fourth Division you needed more than that. Just look at some of the players he brought in. Some of the youngsters like Danis Salman did work out but not too many others made it.

In my first year as an apprentice with Frank Blunstone in charge the youth team felt part of something great in the making and this even continued under Mike Everitt but I think when John Docherty took charge, and do not forget he inherited quite a few players he had played with and others who were brought in by Mike Everitt too, I really think that things did not go as well as they should have done.

Trenchant views and plenty of food for thought from Richard Poole who felt totally frustrated and stifled as he was forced to leave the club he loved and where he still thought he could have made the grade had he been given a decent chance to establish himself.

I will end on a lighter note.

I was reading a programme from January 1987 today and my eyes were drawn to a letter from a certain Mr. R. P. Marsh from Ealing who could barely contain his excitement:

It made a nice change to hear that we had secured the services of David Geddis on a month's loan with a view to a permanent transfer. I have long been an admirer of Geddis and the prospect of him playing up front with Robbie Cooke is the sort of Christmas present I could really enjoy.

Here's hoping that Geddis and Cooke can give the new Brook Road stand the send-off it deserves against Middlesbrough.

Oh dear!!

Geddis was a total disaster – a damp squib rather than a blazing meteor who missed at least three sitters in that aforementioned Middlesbrough game, was dragged off at the interval and his services were swiftly dispensed with – if not quickly enough for most Brentford supporters!

A Real Dilemma! – 26/9/15

I really wasn't too sure if I wanted either team to win last night's West London derby between our two hated rivals Fulham and Queens Park Rangers.

Unfortunately Football League regulations do not yet allow for a verdict of *nul points* to be awarded so I was feeling utterly conflicted about the eventual outcome.

Perhaps I would settle for a nil-nil draw with lots of injuries – nothing too painful but certainly lingering and long-term to be suffered by the likes of star players Ross McCormack and Charlie Austin and the game to be refereed by Keith Stroud at his enigmatic best and be littered with a series of red and yellow cards which would leave the two teams seriously weakened for the challenges that lie ahead throughout the remainder of the season.

The outcome was a surprise as Fulham pulverised QPR by four goals to nil and the score could easily have been doubled had they taken more of the clear chances that they created on the night. French teenager Moussa Dembele was a towering target man who combined pace and power in abundance and proved a handful for the Rangers defence. Hopefully he will not remain for too much longer at Craven Cottage before a Premiership team snatches him away.

The aforementioned McCormack was far too clever for the visitors with his movement and scored twice and O'Hara and Pringle dovetailed beautifully in midfield. Fulham it has to be said looked like a team bursting with purpose, poise and confidence and their previously porous defence was barely tested on what turned out to be a night of shame and humiliation for the visitors.

Rangers barely mounted a challenge, ran up the white flag from the early moments when they conceded a ludicrously soft opening goal and after they eventually managed to carve open the Fulham defence with an admittedly lovely move which ended with Luongo spurning a golden chance to equalise by firing carelessly wide, their heads went down and they allowed Fulham to take total control.

Success in the Championship is obtained by a winning combination of perspiration and inspiration and you have to demonstrate both qualities if you are to prevail. On the night Fulham, to their credit, certainly did so and the entire team, apart from the totally redundant Andy Lonergan in goal sweated buckets as well as playing some beautiful one touch football, but their task was made far easier by the fact that Rangers were not prepared to press or challenge or do any of the unseen and nasty work off the ball that is necessary if you are to ensure that possession is won back after it is conceded.

Rangers never really appeared to want to break sweat on the night and their lack of commitment is highlighted by their only committing ten fouls throughout the game and barely putting in a tackle worthy of the name.

The question has to be asked if Fulham were simply unstoppable on a night when everything came off for them and they performed to their full capability, or if they were in truth made to look far better than they really are by a totally inept and craven display by QPR?

The jury is out on that matter, but last night's match certainly reinforced the fact that the overall quality of Championship players is exceptionally high and the majority of teams possess game changers – players who have the ability to take a game by the scruff of its neck and turn it in favour of their team by virtue of one moment of brilliance.

By the end of the evening QPR had degenerated into an ill-disciplined shambles exemplified by the totally inept Chery stalking straight off to the dressing room in an apparent hissy fit after being dragged off and substituted before the interval and top scorer Charlie Austin limped off on the hour with what appeared to be a hamstring injury which hopefully will be a serious one and take quite a while – ideally well over a month – to heal!

Their supporters were reduced to silence by their team's pathetic display and it is also interesting to note that there was much made of the fact that they brought 4,000 fans to Craven Cottage – over two thousand less than we took to our match there last season!

I have a rather annoying acquaintance who is as fanatical about his beloved Queens Park Rangers as I am about the Bees and he persists in sending me a series of taunting texts and tweets whenever his team wins or we loses. Interestingly enough he seems to have gone very quiet over the past few hours and disappeared from social media and I wonder if I will hear from him today? I somehow think not!

The humiliation of QPR has certainly brought about a more than decent start to the weekend, ignoring of course the necessary but unpalatable fact that as a result Fulham took the three points on offer. What would top things off perfectly would be for Brentford to do the business this afternoon against a tough and resourceful Sheffield Wednesday team that will be bursting with confidence after beating Fulham and then Newcastle United in their last two games.

They had the better of us last season with a fairly even goalless draw at Griffin Park followed by a totally self-inflicted one-nil defeat in the return match when we conspired to miss a plethora of gilt-edged chances and then set up the winning goal for our opponents on a plate after yet again overplaying at the back and losing possession in a dangerous area of the pitch.

Our confidence will have been boosted by last weekend's much needed victory over Preston North End and the defence will also be strengthened by the return of James Tarkowski who has recovered from his calf injury. There are some selection dilemmas for Marinus Dijkhuizen today in terms of whether he retains Josh Clarke at right back and whom he selects to play in midfield. Will Ryan Woods get his long awaited first start for the club? Marinus will also have to decide whether Sergi Canos merits a start or if his flair is best used as a substitute when he can come on and ideally wreak havoc against a tiring defence.

Wednesday carry a real threat up front where they combine strength and flair in abundance and today would be an ideal time for that long awaited first clean sheet of the season to arrive.

These are interesting and challenging times for a Brentford squad that remains seriously depleted in both numbers and quality. Our fighting spirit however is not in any doubt and if we can somehow find a way to overcome adversity and obtain at least four and ideally six points from today and next Tuesday's home game against a revitalised Birmingham team then the season might be on the verge of taking off.

Time For Changes – 27/9/15

Now that really hurt!

Any defeat is upsetting but some far more so than others and yesterday's loss to Sheffield Wednesday certainly came into that category.

I left Griffin Park with an awful sick feeling in the pit of my stomach and the walk back to my car was a long and depressing one.

I have long since learned to put defeats behind me very quickly if I am to retain my sanity and maintain any semblance of a normal family life, but last night it was difficult for me to do so given the circumstances of the loss.

The first half was pretty much a mirror image of every home game this season. A slow start, marked by a total lack of incision and penetration with few chances created and the midfield never getting forward to join and support the isolated Djuricin with Vibe wasted and ignored on the right wing. Judge was our only creative outlet with Toumani and McCormack both sitting deep and Kerschbaumer invisible.

The visitors finally realised that we were really not up to much, and slowly took control with Bannan elegant in midfield and the *Giant Haystacks* figure of Nuhiu their fulcrum in attack. Dean marshalled him well but when the delivery is right he is almost impossible to stop and he hit the bar with a fearsome header from a corner.

Button saved well twice as we came under the cosh whilst Westwood was totally untested at the other end. The only rays of hope for the Bees were the two fullbacks. Josh Clarke overcame a nervous start but once he settled down he gave us a real attacking outlet on the right. Jake Bidwell too did the same on the other flank and he came the nearest for the Bees when Judge picked him out with a lovely curling cross which he met with a volley which kissed the crossbar as it flew over.

When the goal came for the visitors it was really no surprise given their extra cutting edge but again, it was a soft one which highlighted our general lack of awareness. Nuhiu played a long punt from the keeper back to Bannan wide on the left. He then made a wonderful positive run into the area losing Dean as he did so. Tarkowski dozed and saw the danger too late as Bannan's perfect through ball set the striker in on goal. Tarky challenged from the wrong side and it was an obvious penalty.

Bidwell was covering behind him and might even have averted the danger had Tarkowski not committed himself. Surely a yellow card at worst, but the referee Geoff Eltringham dithered, vacillated and allowed the Wednesday players and their vociferous bench to get in his ear and after a long and interminable delay and conversation with his assistant the red card was produced and finally Nuhiu scored from the spot. A triple whammy for the Bees on the day – penalty, goal, red card, and Tarkowski will now also face a one game ban unless we are able to make a successful appeal against the decision.

We managed to get into the halftime break only one goal in arrears but in truth the game resembled nothing more than an average Championship team playing a mediocre Division One outfit. We had effort and hard tackling in abundance but we demonstrated no craft or cutting edge in what was an extremely poor and vapid first half performance.

O'Connell came on to boost the defence and it was no surprise to see Kerschbaumer sacrificed. He has started every league game so far this season so I wonder exactly what it is that the coaches and analysts are seeing in him that is being missed by pretty much every Bees supporter? He has obvious ability on the ball, can see a pass and makes decent late runs into the area but he is being patently outmuscled and overmatched at present and his influence on games is, quite frankly, utterly non-existent. The matches simply seem to pass him by and without meaning to be cruel the closest he came to an opposition player yesterday was during the pre-match greeting ceremony when he and his fellow Austrian, Nuhiu, enveloped each other in a bear hug, otherwise he was nowhere to be seen.

I appreciate that the more he plays, the quicker he will hopefully become acclimatised to the Championship but at the moment he is a total passenger and given our current plight we cannot afford to carry anyone who is not fully pulling his weight. Our midfield is unbalanced, outnumbered, outmatched and outplayed with monotonous regularity and much of that is due to the fact that McCormack and Diagouraga are occupied in their defensive duties and neither of them appears likely to open up opposition defences.

Ryan Woods came on for the final push and impressed from his first touch. He is well used to the hustle and bustle of the Football League, if not the demands of the Championship, but he looks a far, far better bet than Konstantin. He plays with his head up, pushes forward to support the attack and rarely wastes a pass. It is quite baffling why he has not been given his opportunity to date. He surely must start on Tuesday instead of Kerschbaumer but that is a decision for Dijkhuizen.

We have another home game on Tuesday and it will be instructive to see the team that Dijkhuizen selects. He is not afraid to change things when they are not working – and our current formation really isn't doing so! I would hope that he takes heed of yet another appalling first half performance at home and that we do not start with the customary ineffective 4-3-3 setup which means that Vibe is never in the game and is unable to play close enough to Djuricin who is currently living off scraps.

At the interval yesterday I reflected on the Birmingham match early last season when we lost Tony Craig in similar circumstances and were trailing deservedly at the break. I took comfort from the fact that Birmingham sat back in the second half and allowed us to seize the initiative and we were able to rescue a point. Maybe Sheffield Wednesday would become similarly complacent and feel that they had already completed the job?

My hopes and prayers were answered and with Judge moved into a more central role where he dictated play, and Vibe finally playing closer to Djuricin we took control. Wednesday were forced backwards and were rarely an attacking threat in the second half. O'Connell was a revelation, giving us balance on the left side of defence alongside the imperious Harlee Dean. He also showed an unsuspected ability to hit accurate long passes and even hit a thirty-yarder not too far wide.

We now have a welcome problem in central defence with four excellent players competing for two spots. Dean is an automatic choice and a reformed and far more mature character and we must get his new contract sorted and recognise and reward him for the progress he has undoubtedly made in recent months. Tarky was imperious at Leeds and is the best creative option we possess but he loses concentration, as was shown yesterday, and both Barbet and O'Connell are now breathing down his neck.

Who will play on Tuesday if the red card is not rescinded? Your guess is as good as mine and I would be happy with either Barbet, so impressive against Preston, or O'Connell. If I had to choose I would go with Barbet as he has far more ability on the ball than O'Connell and we need somebody at the back who can ensure that we maintain possession.

Despite our second half dominance, chances were few and far between. Djuricin met a beautiful Bidwell cross flush on his forehead and his header crashed against the bar but he had moved too soon and the flag was up. Judge's free kick from wide out on the left evaded everybody straining for the ball in a crowded six-yard box and pinged against the post, but again, more surprisingly this time, the flag was up from an assistant referee who seemed hell-bent on doing his best to frustrate our efforts.

Bidwell is surely going to break his goalscoring duck shortly and he saw the whites of Westwood's eyes before the keeper blocked his shot. We were knocking at the door but had to rely on Button making a fabulous low save from a long range effort from lithe substitute Joao which kicked up off the turf before being pushed away by the straining keeper.

Button's next contribution was equally effective as he was first to a loose ball near the halfway line and picked out Judge with a perfect fifty yard lobbed pass and Alan brought the ball under instant control and sent a sublime curling effort just inside the far post for a well-deserved equaliser.

Media staff member and Programme Editor Mark Chapman also deserves mention for his manic celebration, beautifully caught by the television cameras, which showed just how much he cares!

Now the force was with the Bees and the game seemed to turn on its head when substitute left back Helan received two crass and stupid yellow cards for fouls on the marauding Clarke and Canos. The Bees turned the screws and an unlikely winner seemed on the cards. Canos tore their left flank apart and was unstoppable. He ran and jinked but never overplayed and then the moment came. He twisted his way to the byline and pulled the ball back perfectly to the unmarked Vibe who surely had to score. He had time to think and maybe even control the ball but his instant volley raged over the bar.

On such moments are games won and lost as deep into injury time another frenetic attack broke down, a swift counter attack saw the ball played towards Joao, he miscontrolled, and the ball bounced off the helpless O'Connell's back right into the path of the marauding forward who was not to be caught. He finished impeccably and the game was lost in an instant.

A point would have felt like three given the way we had started the game and our one man disadvantage for so long a period and perhaps we chased the game too hard once we had equalised and left ourselves open and too exposed at the back. That is a mere quibble but the fact remains that we lost against a very average team and we gave ourselves an uphill task and far too much to do.

We have conceded first in all four home games, gone two down twice, and let in eight goals, or two goals per match. We have barely started any of the games until the second half when we already had a mountain to climb and reacted accordingly by changing our formation and approach. Vibe has been wasted out wide and Kerschbaumer has contributed little or nothing. These are in my view indisputable facts and for all the problems we face in terms of our current injury crisis they have to be addressed – and quickly too, if we are not to fall into the relegation zone.

We will probably more than hold our own once we get back the likes of Jota, but other injured players such as Macleod, Hofmann, Colin, Gogia and McEachran are still relatively or totally untried and unknown to us and, with the exception of Josh, are new to the English game and will need further time to settle down, reach full match fitness and find their feet. We therefore need to stay in touch and pick up points as and when we can until we manage to strengthen. This will need a change of personnel, style and formation when we play at home as we cannot keep having to come back from behind. We have trailed in every game this season bar one and it is proving to be too much of a handicap.

There is still talk around the club of maintaining the progress of last season. This is arrant nonsense and claptrap and we need to face facts. Until further notice we are in a relegation scrap, early days though it might still be. This is no time to be complacent or say that things will simply get better.

There is much that is out of our control but we still have to do far better with all the situations that we can influence. For all the good things that we did after the break, and the last second kick in the teeth, yesterday was a massively missed opportunity to pick up at least one point. Every point is crucial, even at this early stage of the season and there are immediate changes that need to be made – now.

Why Marinus Has Gone – 28/9/15

Today's news that Brentford Head Coach Marinus Dijkhuizen and his Assistant, Roy Hendriksen have both left Griffin Park frankly comes as little surprise. The official statements from the club and Chairman Cliff Crown are brief, carefully worded and they take pains not to use the *S* word. *Parted company* is the bland and anodyne expression used to explain their departure but let's make no bones about it – the two of them have been sacked.

Dijkhuizen lasted a mere one hundred and twenty days in his post. Appointed on the first of June he departed on the twenty-eighth of September having presided over a mere nine competitive matches. Whilst he was officially titled Head Coach, he was team manager in everything bar name and should therefore be compared against previous occupants of that position.

Let's get the history out of the way first. In modern times the previous shortest managerial tenure at the club was Eddie May's who lasted nineteen games in his three months in charge followed by Leroy Rosenior and Terry Butcher who were both in charge for twenty-three games and Scott Fitzgerald who managed one more match.

Eddie May potentially presents an interesting parallel for those of us who are conspiracy theorists. An unknown appointed out of left field from Dundalk with indecent haste by David Webb in August 1997 at a time when the club was in total disarray with a squad that had been decimated by the sale of players and the arrival of unknown journeymen replacements, he quite understandably struggled to get results and when the repeated promises of funds to improve the team failed to materialise he was sacked along with his assistant Clive Walker in November 1997, after just four league wins had left the club embroiled in a relegation battle which they ultimately lost on the last day of a quite dreadful season.

May was perceived as Webb's dupe, the fall guy for the previous manager who had taken over as Chief Executive with the prime intention of ensuring that funds were brought in so that the club was debt free before it was sold to Ron Noades the following year.

Are there any similarities when we come to consider the reasons and rationale for the change in management that took place today?

I have thought long and hard about matters and whilst the start we have made to the season has been horrible there have certainly been extenuating circumstances. Let's get the hard facts out of the way:

- Brentford have gained only eight points from their first eight Championship matches and find themselves in nineteenth place, only two points off the bottom of the league

- We have conceded the first goal in every match bar one and have yet to keep a clean sheet

- The Bees have won only two matches, both against teams just promoted from Division One

- We have lost two of our first four home games, could quite easily have lost all four and have trailed at half time every time

- A weakened team lost by four clear goals to Second Division Oxford United in the Capital One Cup

- Performances have been stuttering and inconsistent, we find it hard to start matches on the front foot and there is no settled pattern of play

That is the prosecution case but there is an equally strong case for the defence that more than explains away our less than impressive start to the season:

- Let's try and keep a sense of perspective and simply take stock and recognise just how far we have come in such a short space of time particularly given our lack of resources compared to the overwhelming majority of our Championship rivals

- The enforced sale and departure of five leading players from last season's squad in Andre Gray, Jonathan Douglas, Moses Odubajo, Alex Pritchard and Stuart Dallas which rendered Dijkhuizen's preseason preparations almost meaningless

- Last season's team included five potential match winners and game changers in Jota, Alan Judge, Odubajo, Pritchard and Gray – a figure currently reduced to one

- A relentless and seemingly ever-increasing long-term injury list that has rendered key players such as Jota, Andreas Bjelland, Max Colin, Philipp Hofmann, Lewis Macleod and Josh McEachran *hors de combat*

- The consequent need to blood members of the Development Squad who will certainly all benefit from the experience but for them to compete in the Championship at this stage of their career is a tough ask

- Being forced to name only six substitutes including two goalkeepers at the strongest team in the league in Middlesbrough

- The need to bed in simultaneously nearly half a team of newcomers from around Europe who have no knowledge of English conditions and The Championship and are not being buttressed by more experienced players around them

- *Pitchgate* – a total embarrassment for the club which necessitated the re-turfing of Griffin Park and the cancellation of the Birmingham City home game

- The scandalous situation at Jersey Road where the main training pitches are still unusable

Whilst there have been some rumblings and murmurings from supporters spoiled by the constant stream of success over the past three seasons and used to the wonderful attacking flair of Mark Warburton's playoff team last season, the overwhelming majority of Brentford supporters are extremely patient and fair minded and were prepared to give Marinus more time, particularly given the almost insuperable problems he faced that were totally out of his control.

That being said there were growing concerns about his commitment to an impotent and restrictive 4-3-3 formation that patently wasn't working given the limited resources he had and required constant changes on the hoof when we were chasing games that were already slipping away from us.

Lasse Vibe, a proven international striker was hamstrung from being forced to play out wide on the right wing where he has been an isolated figure, rather than more centrally where he and Marco Djuricin looked a highly potent threat when they were finally allowed to play closer together.

Konstantin Kerschbaumer was an ever present in the team despite seemingly overwhelming evidence that he was still unable to cope with the physicality of The Championship and the presence of expensive new signing Ryan Woods on the bench who has been clamouring for a start.

I have spoken to many of the key protagonists over the past few weeks and I have found absolutely no evidence that Marinus was in any way, shape or form, overruled, instructed, hamstrung, restricted or second guessed in any of his key responsibilities in terms of picking the team, training and preparing them for action and most crucially in terms of game management, tactics and substitutions. He was given an entirely free hand and the freedom to act as he best saw fit. So any comparisons to Eddie May are totally inaccurate and invidious. Marinus was no puppet and was allowed to be his own man.

He had bought into the Brentford project and was happy with the new management structure. He was consulted on all player moves both in and out and whilst he would have liked some additional loan signings to cover for the current injury crisis, Marinus was content with the quality and calibre of the new signings.

So why then did he leave if he was not being made the scapegoat for a series of poor results that were to a large degree out of his control? Now this is where I have to resort to speculation and informed guesswork as well as what I have picked up from informed contacts.

Perhaps the alarm bells were beginning to ring with the powers that be because of some of the on-field tactical and selection problems that I have previously mentioned earlier in this article as well as exploring in greater depth yesterday?

He also suffered in comparison with his predecessor. Mark Warburton was certainly a hard act to follow and his successor needed to get off to a flying start, something that was denied Marinus.

Warburton was also a workaholic control freak, in the nicest sense of the words. He arrived early at the training ground and left extremely late. Training routines were meticulously planned and organised well in advance and the players knew exactly where they stood and how they were going to spend their days.

It would appear that Marinus and Roy Hendriksen did not run such a tight ship in terms of either time keeping and preparation and a far more *laissez faire* atmosphere prevailed. This apparently did not go down well with either players or management.

This, I feel is where the real problem lay. The training programme was apparently not as organized or rigorous as what was required and I believe that today's action has been taken by Matthew Benham on the recommendation of the Co-Directors of Football in order to nip matters in the bud before they could be allowed to get out of hand and beyond control.

It cannot be denied that this is an enormous blow to the credibility of the new regime at the club and I am sure that the media will not be slow to point fingers and make fun at our expense. Such are the vicissitudes of life and we will just have to cope with this opprobrium as best we can.

Brentford pride themselves on doing things differently to other clubs, thinking out of the box and acting far smarter than their rivals. An enormous amount of due diligence was done before Marinus was hired and he interviewed exceptionally well and seemed to tick all the boxes.

However the fact remains that actions speak louder than words and apparently he has not convinced the powers that be since he arrived and drastic action has been taken sooner rather than later to avert the slump before too much damage is done.

It could reasonably be argued that this is an extremely brave move rather than a panicked knee jerk reaction and this could even be a turning point for us in what is developing into a tough season and one where consolidation is perhaps the best we can hope for rather than pushing on from last season's massive and incredible achievements. As they say – one step backwards – two steps forward!

Lee Carsley is an excellent choice to take over the mantle as Head Coach until the end of the season. Supported by Paul Williams he is a known entity who has already gained the unconditional respect of the entire squad through his efforts with the Development Squad.

He is an experienced and proven international footballer who can put his caps on the table and he has previous managerial experience at Coventry City. Most importantly he has a deep working knowledge of The Championship and he will be keen to put one over one of his old clubs, Birmingham City, at Griffin Park tomorrow night.

So, on the surface, this has not been a good day for the club, but when you drill down deeper and think matters through, then perhaps it has been a brave and correct decision to relieve Marinus and Roy of their jobs.

All will surely be revealed and become apparent over the coming weeks and months.

Marinus Dijkhuizen contemplates his fate

Nothing Ventured! – 29/9/15

After all the off the field drama of the last twenty-four hours I was hoping to write an article that concentrated solely on the football and our first match under the new Head Coach, Lee Carsley, but in truth there is very little to say about Tuesday night's drab and dismal two-nil home defeat to a distinctly average Birmingham City team, and even less if I do not want to be particularly gloomy or negative in my comments.

This was a tepid, desperately disappointing and below-par performance where we created little and there was no pace, energy, confidence, passion or spark of ingenuity and even less creativity about our game.

We played pretty passing football in our own half where the ball was sent back and forth interminably between the defenders and we got nowhere. There was no cutting edge and the entire team lacked the confidence to try and play through two banks of four Birmingham players who funnelled back and simply waited patiently for the ball to be given to them by our players, which they did with monotonous regularity.

Our possession figures approached seventy percent but this was a meaningless statistic as the overwhelming majority of our ball retention took places in areas where we were never going to hurt the opposition.

The team lined up in a 4-3-1-2 formation but as has been the case all season, the midfield was desperately disappointing with Diagouraga attempting to hold things together without much success and Kerschbaumer flitted in and out of the game. Ryan Woods finally earned his first start and the best that can be said about him was that he was neat and tidy and rarely gave the ball away but he never hurt the opposition or created an opportunity.

We desperately missed a creative dynamo playing behind the front two who could stretch the opposition and run at them and ideally make things happen.

Djuricin and Vibe played as the strike duo and the Austrian found space on a couple of occasions in the first half without getting any real power into his shots and the closest they came was when Vibe streaked clear down the left channel after the break but shot straight at the keeper with the unmarked Djuricin screaming for the ball to be squared to him in front of a gaping goal.

In truth we lacked any pace or cutting edge and looked lightweight up-front and both strikers were easily smothered out of the game. They never managed to hold the ball up although the service they received was spasmodic at best and the ball generally sailed three feet over their head rather than landing at their feet.

Button made one excellent save from a close-range header but the game seemed to be drifting ever so slowly to a nil-nil draw which in the scheme of things might not have been the worst result in the world as it would have meant that we would have earned our first clean sheet of the season, but it wasn't meant to be. As it was, all that we could celebrate on the night was for the first time all season going into the break drawing at home and not losing. Big deal!

The defence finally dozed off at a right wing corner with twenty minutes to go and Morrison easily out jumped O'Connell to score with a thumping header. Perhaps the players were distracted by an injury to McCormack just before the corner came in and we seemed to lack concentration and were punished yet again at a set piece. Alan's game went to pieces after that, hampered as he was by his injury and it was surprising that he was not replaced by Josh Clarke, unused on the bench. As it is Donaldson's theatrical collapse earned McCormack his fifth yellow card of the season and an enforced rest next Saturday.

Surely there would now be a spark and a reaction as we sought an equaliser, but instead of going hell for leather and chasing the game we went even further into our shell. Our talisman, Sergi Canos was tightly marked and was totally unable to work his magic.

As the game drifted towards its welcome close Alan Judge suddenly came alive, won a ball that was never his on the right flank, jinked inside his man and his brilliant rising left footed effort from the edge of the penalty area looked bound for the top corner, but, as is invariably the case this season, the luck was not with us and the ball hit the top of the crossbar and flew over.

To add insult to injury, Gleeson threaded the ball between our absent defenders deep into injury time and Clayton Donaldson bundled the ball home for the second goal, celebrated with silence as the hushed crowd quickly left the stadium, fed up, bemused and depressed by what they had witnessed.

The team has lost its Mojo and looked utterly drained of any confidence. I would have suspected that they would have upped their game given the appointment of the new Head Coach but if anything the performance went down a gear rather than up and Lee Carsley has much to do if the slide is to be arrested.

His staggering post-match revelation that he probably expects to leave the club at the end of the season and does not want the job on a long-term basis will also do nothing to raise spirits and expectations on what had already turned out to be a dismally disappointing evening and this massively negative announcement was the final kick in the teeth for Brentford supporters who are perhaps at their lowest ebb for quite some time.

We have, as we know, an uneven squad with far too many new overseas players of unproven quality lacking leadership and trying to bed into a new team playing in an unfamiliar league with the established stars either sold or on the injury list.

Tonight the passion, invention and joy seemed to have been squeezed out of the entire Brentford team and for the first time in perhaps three years I was bored and distracted and found my attention wandering and my eyes glancing at my watch so sparse was the entertainment value being provided by a team seemingly afraid of its own shadow and unprepared to risk making a mistake by attempting anything ambitious or unexpected. This is how badly a team can be affected when it totally loses confidence.

Perhaps the evening was best summed up by Gogia, returning from his injury break and instantly hammering the ball miles behind the goal when shooting from a ridiculously impossible angle in the final moments of the match with his team mates queuing up in the penalty area and waiting for a simple cross which never arrived.

I have deliberately avoided using the *R* word until this point but for the first time this season I have to say that relegation will be inevitable if performances of this ilk are repeated on a regular basis.

There were no redeeming features and there is absolutely nothing positive that can be said about tonight so I will end here and just hope for a massive improvement on Saturday when we need to demonstrate a completely different attitude if we are to have much chance of success at Derby County. You have to take calculated risks to win and tonight we simply played it safe and received our just reward.

Position	Team	P	W	D	L	F	A	GD	Pt	Form
1	Brighton and Hove A	9	6	3	0	13	7	6	21	W W W W D D
2	Middlesbrough	9	6	2	1	17	5	12	20	L W W W W W
3	Reading	9	4	3	2	14	7	7	15	D W W L W W
4	Hull City	9	4	3	2	12	7	5	15	L W L W D D
5	Birmingham City	9	4	3	2	14	10	4	15	W W L D L W
6	Cardiff City	9	4	3	2	13	10	3	15	W W W L L W
7	Burnley	9	4	3	2	12	10	2	15	W W W W D L
8	Ipswich Town	9	4	3	2	15	15	0	15	W L L W D D
9	Derby County	9	3	5	1	10	7	3	14	D L W W D W
10	Wolverhampton Wndrs	9	3	3	3	12	11	1	12	L W L D D W
11	Nottingham Forest	9	3	3	3	9	9	0	12	D L W W L D
12	Sheffield Wednesday	9	3	3	3	12	13	-1	12	D L L D W W
13	Queens Park Rangers	9	3	3	3	14	17	-3	12	W W L D D L
14	Fulham	9	3	2	4	15	14	1	11	D W W L W L
15	Leeds United	9	2	5	2	9	11	-2	11	D W D L W L
16	Huddersfield Town	9	2	4	3	10	11	-1	10	D L L W W D
17	Charlton Athletic	9	2	3	4	9	12	-3	9	W L D L L L
18	Blackburn Rovers	9	1	5	3	10	10	0	8	L D L D W D
19	Brentford	9	2	2	5	12	17	-5	8	L D L W L L
20	Rotherham United	9	2	2	5	11	17	-6	8	L L D L W W
21	Bolton Wanderers	9	1	5	3	6	12	-6	8	D D W D L D
22	Preston North End	9	1	4	4	6	10	-4	7	L L L D L D
23	Milton Keynes Dons	9	2	1	6	8	13	-5	7	D L L L L L
24	Bristol City	9	1	3	5	11	19	-8	6	W L L D L D

[29th September 2015]

October

What The Fans Think! – 1/10/15

This has certainly been a horrendously difficult and unsettling week for everyone involved with Brentford FC - players, management, staff and supporters alike. Head Coach Marinus Dijkhuizen and his assistant, Roy Hendriksen were both sacked on Monday and replaced until the end of the season by Lee Carsley, whose job as Development Squad Coach went to Bees stalwart and legend, Kevin O'Connor.

On the field, Saturday's narrow and frankly undeserved home defeat by Sheffield Wednesday was followed by a dreadful performance on Tuesday when a totally listless, rudderless and dispirited Brentford team limped to a two-nil defeat by Birmingham City which was immediately followed by Lee Carsley's naïve and unexpected, if totally honest post-match admission that he had no real wish or desire to become a football manager and would therefore be likely to leave the club once his spell in charge was completed. Comments that understandably, have not been well received by Bees supporters.

I can't speak for anybody else, but my head is certainly spinning and reeling trying to process and assimilate so much traumatic and negative activity in such a short period of time and I have already written at length about my own analysis and reading of the situation.

Over the last couple of days I have received many comments from readers and here is a selection of their views on the current situation:

Former player **Richard Poole** starts the ball rolling:

Well things certainly look gloomy with a newly appointed Head Coach who does not think he will be there next season and a team with no apparent motivation, something I find hard to understand.

When we were fighting against re-election in 1974 everyone wanted to do their best and the players who were pulling out of tackles or not giving their all were simply replaced by others, or even by young players like me who were maybe not good enough but who ran theirs sock off for the club.

Yes I know football has changed a lot and yes this is not the Fourth Division we are talking about, but for God's sake just give me a team of eleven players whatever their age who give their all for the club, and I cannot believe that there are not a couple of players in the Development Squad who cannot step up to the plate and help the first team. They might not be quite up to the standard required but I am sure they would give their total commitment.

As for the coaching side, maybe the owner will admit that things aren't working quite as anticipated and put his new-fangled approach on ice and appoint a real manager for the time being.

Come on you Bees, at least show us that you've got guts and will give your all. Whatever the outcome we are behind you.

Rebel Bee was more outspoken:

The team on show on Tuesday was a League One outfit at best and I think we have to admit to a lack of quality and physicality too. We seem to have signed a bunch of continental footballers who lack touch and technique – the two things that you would expect them to have whilst they adapt to the more physical side of the English game.

I'm so down on our club right now. I actually feel very emotional about it. Five years of intelligent endeavour to build something special is being wrecked before our eyes – with both things initiated by the same person.

What Matthew Benham does next will determine his legacy and our future – I doubt he'll read my words, but just in case, please Matthew come out and speak to us, and let's try to get everyone back on board before it's too late.

Mike Rice was also concerned:

Last night we were a League One quality side with three passengers: Vibe, Djuricin and Kerschbaumer. We were playing another League One side which was incredibly well organised and did all of the right things at the right time.

We are ill-equipped to fight a relegation battle, but we are certainly in one. I excused Lee Carsley last night because he probably didn't know he definitely had the gig until last Sunday. I was saying that the jury was out and maybe he was a wonder coach. He would be able to turn things around despite not having any track record at this level.

Now I learn that he expects to go at the end of the season, which sounds to me like he had his arm twisted to take the job. To say that is not encouraging is an understatement. Perhaps the owner should get in touch with Ian Holloway or Neil Warnock to hold Lee's hand?

And get in some Championship calibre players on loan as well to replace our foreign imports who will take too long to become acclimatised, as well as some of our League One standard players.

beesyellow22 was equally fatalistic:

Another excellent article and the reason why there's no point in me writing a blog myself – after all, you say very eloquently what I think most of us are thinking!

Not much to add to the excellent comments above, except to agree with many of them. Key points for me:

1. *Letting Warburton go or engineering a situation where he felt he had to go was a MASSIVE mistake by the club. As much as we owe him for getting us where we are today, the blame lies squarely at the owner's door.*

2. *The mathematical model should have been put on hold for as long as Warbs was with us. For goodness sake, we finished FIFTH IN THE CHAMPIONSHIP last season! After years of languishing in lower league obscurity! Surely Benham should have parked his new approach, kept our best manager ever and held onto Warburton for another season at least?*

3. *Dijkhuizen was a nice guy, but to coin a phrase, "nice guys finish last" or nineteenth as things currently stand. He was the wrong appointment and hopelessly out of his depth. I sit next to a Derby fan at work and we talk about the Championship all the time.*

   As he puts it, it is a relentless league. Not amazingly high quality, but you need to be on you're A-Game every single Tuesday and Saturday with the occasional Friday and Monday thrown in for good measure.

   Dijkhuizen simply did not have the experience, wherewithal, tactical nous or, I'm afraid, connection with the players to be successful. Yes, eight games (actually nine, counting the battering by Oxford) is not nearly long enough to prove yourself – but anyone who watched the Reading match or the first half versus Wednesday will know how awful we were, and I'm afraid that when it comes to preparation, team selection and tactics, the manager ultimately has to carry the can.

4. *To coin another phrase, where Bournemouth went for evolution, we went for revolution. Too much, too soon. And one area where the club really failed was in anticipating just how many of our key players from last season would want to leave after Warburton departed.*

5. *The question has already been posed, but why on earth has Ryan Woods been stuck on the bench? Yes, he made a mistake against Leeds, but when he came on against Wednesday he looked absolutely sensational – but he was only given five minutes. To me, he is the future and we should be building a team around him.*

Dijkhuizen should have shown positive intent against Wednesday, started with Woods and Canos and gone for the win from minute one. If I was Benham and had spent the best part of a million pounds on League One's most exciting young player, I wouldn't have been happy that my head coach wasn't giving him a game.

I am sad for Dijkhuizen and I am angry with the club we all love so much, but I am also excited and pleased that we now have another chance to hopefully start the season afresh from this point on. Like most Bees fans, when I go to a game I want to see passion, commitment, heart and some semblance of a plan based on intelligent attacking football that primarily involves keeping the ball on the deck.

In the games I've seen against Ipswich, Reading and Sheffield Wednesday this has simply not been the case (sadly the only home game I missed was the only game we won). I appreciate that we have shown flashes of good play here and there, but here and there is not enough – especially not at this level. For that reason Marinus had to go and I am looking forward to an English (Irish) manager who will hopefully take the passion we all feel for the club, channel that to the players and begin to turn things around on the pitch. Even with all the injuries, we still have the makings of a good team. Let's now have the confidence to show it.

He also commented again after the last home defeat, as follows:

Another great, if deeply depressing, post, Greville. Also very insightful comments by Mike and Rebel Bee. I wasn't at the game and it shows how not actually witnessing it first-hand can give you such a false impression. At nil-nil I thought it was looking okay, with possibly our first clean sheet of the season coming. But reading about what actually happened has only served to darken my mood even further.

The worst thing about all of this for me was the words coming out of Carsley's mouth. In the interview with Billy Reeves, he sounded flat, downbeat and pretty disinterested in the whole thing. In fact, he actually used the word "detached" when asked about his emotions. He also said, "I wasn't looking to be a manager" and "you just have to get on with it."

What kind of response is that? If he was so reluctant to take the role, then why on earth did he accept when it was offered? What kind of example does that set for the players – to say nothing of the fans?

Let's make no mistake; we are now in a relegation battle. We can probably expect to get battered on Saturday and should maybe write that one off right now, but come the next home game against Rotherham we need to be totally focused on the task in hand, because only a win will do.

The way I feel at the moment is confused, nervous and incredibly upset. Did Crown/Benham/Devlin/Ankersen/Giles have any idea of the way Carsley felt? You would surely have to say no, otherwise why give him the role in the first place? Did they see him as being so honest with the press? Again, you would surely have to say no. It makes us look amateur – to say nothing of the way our Championship rivals will surely seize on it to gain the initiative when they play us.

Will Carsley still be there in a month's time? I honestly don't think so. Forget all this "leaving at the end of the season / I don't want to be a manager" nonsense. We need a passionate figurehead in charge who can galvanise the players and inspire the fans. I am sorry Mr. Benham, but that person is not Lee Carsley.

What's Neil Warnock up to these days?

Gary Hennell commented as follows:

I think the decision for this sacking was constructed far earlier than this week. How many of us would succeed in a new company where your equipment is broken (pitch), your best staff dispersed to your competitors and then replaced with untried temps who are learning on the job and then, to compound it all your ace sales team all end up on long-term sick leave? The manager's fault? Hardly. I just wish Crown and Ankersen stood up and said "you know, we got this gamble wrong." I would have way more faith and respect for that, as this is the path we have publicly stated we want to follow (no harm in that) – who of us has never made a management mistake? But it was their mistake not the manager's.

Too many foreign so-called bargains, not enough Championship tried and tested players – a lesson learned concerning the right mix. As for Marinus, coming from Excelsior to the Championship was in my view a step too far, or maybe too early but he was also not given the right tools to succeed by Brentford.

Culture differences, game pace and media scrutiny make the Championship brutal and possession is pointless if you do nothing with it.

Last weekend I listened to some clever nitwit on Sky announce that the team with the highest level of possession in the entire football league was Brentford – he then followed by adding "and let's look at their league position." I did use a few unrepeatable words at the telly, which the wife overheard. The media wants us to fail at this so badly, make no mistake about that.

I do still think we are in Warburton withdrawal mode (me included). I need to get over that. Be brave – stand up and say it – we gambled on our manager and came up short and we sold off too much talent before being certain of its replacement.

Don't be so hell-bent that every purchase or decision has to be totally radical because that is what the media expect of us now.

I think the Carsley decision makes much more sense in terms of his pedigree, international experience and internal club knowledge. It really is a massive chance for Mr. Carsley, who I think stands to receive more support than his predecessor did, which seems unfair on reflection.

I suppose what I really wish is that we don't try to play bargain hunting with our managers like we do with our squad acquisitions and the Marinus appointment had that feel to it.

How badly does our team need a man manager right now?

His thoughts were equally strong after the match:

We need a determined leader/manager to drag their sorry backsides out of the sea of self-pity and get stuck in and raise the game tempo. I travelled four hours last night to see Brentford play at such a pedestrian pace that you would have thought we were the away team trying to kill a game off. Honestly, what team in this division cannot defend when provided with over five minutes to set up their defence for a corner?

What I can't understand is it was blindingly obvious last year that the Championship respects and fears pace in equal measure. The money we received for Odubajo and Gray confirms that. So when did we decide that seventy-five percent possession and zero penetration played at snail's pace will return better results?

So the thought occurred to me, the statistical models identified them as good enough – but do they play like they believe they are?

The brand of football being played right now is choking the flair and inventiveness out of the players and it is as much crushing as boring to watch, as you rightly pointed out.

I read that one of the first things that Warburton did when he arrived at Ibrox was post a big sign up in the dressing room....do you know what he had written on that sign? SEND THEM HOME HAPPY in big capital letters above the dressing room door. Hmmm, can it really be that simple?

Some fans are saying don't criticise or Matthew Benham may pull the plug, if he is truly one of our own this won't happen, he'll work his socks off to fix this and regain all of our trust and goodwill. If he does withdraw support then you'd have to ask what sort of a club would we have become anyway, and was the price of having such a benefactor worth paying?

He must have a hard and at times thankless task, but some communication and engagement now is not so much to ask for, surely?

It has been really tough going so far, the thrill of my next Brentford fix has been erased overnight. I am sad to admit that I will not be at Derby and need the international break to get over the last week. I'll never give up on my team but it kills me to see others thinking of doing so.

John Hirdle also has questions to ask about our recruitment policy:

Matthew Benham's judgement must surely come under scrutiny. He had months to scour Europe for a replacement for Warburton and came up with a guy he has got rid of after eight games and then gives the job to someone who was under his nose all the time.

I don't know how much say Dijkhuizen had in transfers but surely the mass signings of unproven foreign players with no experience of English Championship level by Benham, Giles and Ankersen was a mistake. Coupled with the departures of several key players and our horrendous injury run it is no surprise that we have struggled.

After the debacle of the Reading home game, performances since have undoubtedly improved and despite rumours of training ground unrest I have seen nothing to suggest that the players haven't been giving it their all for club and manager on the pitch.

The jury remains firmly out on the effect of the stats based system in my opinion. We remain totally ineffective and impotent on free kicks and corners despite expensively assembled specialist coaches employed in this field.

One also wonders how stats from the second division of a European League correlate with the level we are now playing at.

As always we will rally round and get behind the new manager who may well turn out to be an inspired choice, he will hopefully be helped by returning players soon.

Interesting, passionate, heartfelt and well-thought-out comments that make depressing reading at what is a pretty depressing time for us all.

Ten Games In – The Verdict! – 4/10/15

For once the M1 was kind to us and the drive to and from Derby was swift, incident free and almost pleasant. If only we could have said the same about what came between both journeys and totally spoiled the day.

To develop the travel theme a bit more, apparently Derby striker Darren Bent was caught in traffic and was left out of the squad after his late arrival, not that his team needed him on the day. As for the Brentford team – they never turned up.

The Bees were second best from the first whistle and subsided without much of a fight to a two-nil defeat by a Derby County team that despite three consecutive away victories were still searching for their first victory in front of their own supporters.

Had the Bees even tried to start the game on the front foot and put the home team under any sort of pressure then they might well have caused problems and quieted a slightly nervous and apprehensive home crowd but as it was they were forced back from the opening whistle and the only surprise was that it took almost twenty minutes for Chris Martin to score.

A second followed just before the interval from Tom Ince and with better finishing and a more measured final pass Derby might well have run up a cricket score as they found space and time on both flanks and tore us open on numerous occasions and were in total control for the overwhelming majority of the match.

David Button was his customary heroic self and Dean and Tarkowski did their level best to make up for the myriad deficiencies exhibited by those in front of them although Dean was caught ball-watching for the first goal and left marking fresh air as Martin's well-timed run gave him an easy chance to score.

Brentford were slow on the ball, timid and lethargic in their general approach, showed little or no incision and lost possession with monotonous regularity.

The lower than normal possession stat of a mere forty-six percent highlighted their main problem and weakness on the day. This really did not look like a Brentford team as we know it out there but eleven ill-matched strangers who had been cobbled together at the last minute.

As is now customary the midfield was neither fish nor fowl, providing little protection for the beleaguered defence and creating nothing of substance for the isolated Vibe and Djuricin who were forced to feed off scraps.

Vibe barely touched the ball in a performance of shocking ineptitude and apparent lack of commitment, and his only real contribution apart from shooting wastefully wide early on was to shriek in vain for a foul when cleanly tackled and dispossessed deep in home territory and twenty seconds later he was still on the ground and the ball was in the back of our net as Derby broke from defence with pace, intent and incision.

One goal down at halftime would have been tough enough for us to face, a two goal deficit meant that the game was over.

Woods worked hard and kept going to the end without much end result but he merely duplicated the efforts of Diagouraga who was submerged as we were outgunned and outfought in the middle of the field.

New arrival John Swift, on loan from Chelsea, came on for the last quarter and showed that he has skill on the ball, and can see a pass and he will be an asset to us when he settles in. He also possesses a bit of devil in him and will fight for the cause.

For the home team, Bradley Johnson and George Thorne combined size and strength with footballing ability that we could not match.

In comparison, we looked small, weak and frail and lacking in overall stamina and fitness without the skill to compensate, and our players were knocked off the ball far too easily and barely won a challenge or second ball all afternoon.

Last season we were similarly lacking in strength and brute force but it hardly mattered as you have to catch somebody before you are able to kick them up in the air and we possessed far too much pace and pure ability for most teams to bully us. Now the situation has changed as we are slow and ponderous and are being outplayed as well as outfought week after week.

Gogia and Judge started the match on the wings but were starved of possession and this was surely a day for a 4-3-3 formation as we were far too open and outnumbered in midfield.

Canos flitted in and out of the match when he replaced Gogia after the break but we only threatened – and spasmodically at that – when Hofmann replaced Vibe. He did well, held the ball up, even won the odd aerial challenge and at last gave us a target to aim at upfront. He came close twice, forcing Carson into a plunging save and seeing a late effort hacked off the line but we were well-beaten on a day when we again resembled an overmatched and outclassed lower division team.

This was a terrible, spineless and abject performance against a decent team who were made to look far better than they really are by our disorganisation, failure to get the basics right and total ineptitude.

It is only a few short months ago since we played pretty much the same Derby team off the pitch in a performance packed full of confidence and brio but we are now a mere shadow of that team and those days are sadly long since gone and show no sign of returning in the immediate future.

Ten matches in is quite long enough for us to have a fair idea of how the season is likely to turn out and there is absolutely no point in my mincing my words.

We are currently in free fall and on the evidence of the last couple of games there is every chance of us plummeting straight back to Division Two unless the slide is reversed – and quickly, before what little confidence that remains drains away.

It does not take much to pinpoint what is going wrong both on and off the pitch but it is far harder to understand how to turn things around but hopefully the international break will allow Lee Carsley the opportunity to work hard with the squad.

I have no intention of repeating the words that I have written so often over the last couple of months – words that come so easily now that they almost seem to write themselves. We all know about the ravages of Financial Fair Play, our lack of resources in comparison with the rest of the league and our utterly ridiculous injury list but despite all of these obstacles we are beginning to look a shambles of a club.

We botched the recruitment process for the Head Coach in the summer and the club has at least held its hand up and rectified the problem before it got out of control. Then came the short-term appointment of Lee Carsley and his unfortunate post-match interview on Tuesday that further put the cat amongst the pigeons.

That being said our two worst performances have come since the departure of Dijkhuizen, two defeats where we have barely looked like scoring and the body language of the players today spoke volumes.

It is trite and far too easy to say that matters will improve when we get our long-term injured players back. I am now not so sure as only Jota, who will take time to regain match fitness, and McEachran have any experience of this level of the game.

Our new foreign players resemble nothing more than rabbits caught in headlights as they have been thrown in and are currently well out of their depth and struggling to cope with the relentless mental and physical demands of the Championship. Are they good enough? Well the jury is still out and whilst Colin, Barbet, Vibe and Djuricin have all flickered into life spasmodically, far too much is being asked of them too soon and it is quite frankly unfair to expect too much of any of them.

We now have a welcome respite and a break of two weeks before what is now turning into a massively important match against Rotherham, a team that currently looks as if it will be competing with us to fill one of the three dreaded relegation spots.

So what do we do in the next fortnight or so to ensure that we arrest the slump?

Here are my suggestions, none of which are likely to make me popular with the powers that be at the club:

Look to bring in an older head to mentor and support Lee Carsley. Somebody like Steve Coppell would be ideal for the role. He would command instant respect and be able to provide a wealth of experience and football knowledge that is sadly lacking throughout the club at the moment. Steve Perryman fulfils a similar position with Paul Tisdale at Exeter City and adds massive value. In truth I would really welcome a new Head Coach from outside to provide a fresh voice, outlook and perspective but I fear and suspect that is a step too far at the moment despite it being a seemingly obvious move

I would offer our two Co-Directors of Football some external assistance too. Someone similar to Andrew Mills (now working at Millwall) who knows the English game inside out and has extensive contacts with agents, managers and coaches and can ensure that we are offered the right players and that we get the deals done for the right price without waste or extravagance. It might also be that come January we could be looking to move some players on too and we need someone experienced in handling such a difficult situation and getting players out of the door

Compromise our ideals a little bit given our current circumstances and try and find, hard though it will be, a couple of battle hardened, wizened veterans who can become teachers and leaders, things that we currently lack both on the pitch and at the training ground. I can still remember a gnarled Jimmy Gabriel coming to us back in 1974. He could barely run or move around the pitch but he inspired a young team to play above themselves and avoid the threat of re-election

Work on improving the players' fitness, which seems to be sadly lacking at the moment

More controversially, find a couple of independent non-executive directors, men of substance and experience who are not beholden to Matthew Benham, who will have the forcefulness of character and the strength of mind to make their opinions heard at Board Meetings so that the owner's wishes are not just nodded through but their implications are discussed and fully thought through before a decision is made. Sometimes the word *no* has to be heard.

I spoke at length tonight with my friend and fellow Brentford fanatic **Gary Marson** and he summed up the situation far better than I ever could and I totally concur with his wise words and opinion so eloquently expressed:

The vast majority of Bees fans recognise that Matthew Benham's philosophy is the only game in town. His approach of securing competitive advantage through innovation and risk has already secured us success beyond our wildest dreams and in the long- term is the only realistic way in which we can hope to continue to punch so far above our weight in a stale and rigid footballing hierarchy where there is normally such a stifling correlation between financial resource and performance.

The present crisis therefore need not, indeed must not, mark the end of the Benham project. But in order to preserve the long-term strategic vision, not to mention his enormous investment, he may be well advised to consider a short-term tactical retreat and re-think the approach for the remainder of the season. This means supplementing the playing squad and management team, both of which appear to be desperately naïve at the rarefied level of the English second tier, with the type of solid if unexciting domestic experience and organisational knowhow that we might have previously disregarded.

We have attempted open-heart surgery to cure a minor ailment and as a result found ourselves in intensive care. Before we can begin to think about a healthy and sustainable return to full fitness we must do everything that it takes to ensure that the patient survives.

The future can still be ours, but for now it must wait.

The Fans' Verdict – 7/10/15

With ten games gone and Brentford wallowing in the nether regions of The Championship I wrote an overview of our current situation on Sunday and made a few suggestions on how I felt matters both on and off the field might conceivably be improved.

Here is what some of you had to say in response.

Richard Poole harked back to the past and the influence that an experienced old hand could have on his younger teammates as well as the importance of the fans maintaining their support when things are going wrong:

You're right about Jimmy Gabriel. I was playing alongside him at the time. Yes, he could hardly run but he did not need to as he dominated possession and was a total inspiration to us youngsters and someone to come into the team like him now would help a lot.

Jackie Graham also played in that Brentford team and even now you could take him out of retirement and I'm sure that he could help, if not on the field at least in training, even at his advanced age. He would put grit into the team and let everyone know exactly what it means to pull on that red and white striped shirt.

I can understand the effect of so many injuries and even that some players might not be up to standard but if I am reading correctly in between the lines these players are not coming off the pitch having given everything. There's nothing you can do if they not prepared to run and you fans know who is trying and who isn't.

Yes it looks like we are going to be in a long relegation fight and I can understand the fans being disappointed after last season's showing but that's football – it turns so quickly.

We have just got to get behind our team, yes that's what supporting a club means and I know so well how much you fans have suffered over so many years but I can tell you after what I experienced as a young teenager coming in to the side THEY NEED YOU FANS more than ever.

We were nearly bottom of the fourth division but the supporters got behind us home and away. They were fantastic and we need that spirit again.

Larry Signy agreed that more independent representation was needed in the Boardroom:

Any form of dictatorship is a bad thing – so your fourth suggestion – "a couple of independent non-executive directors" – hits the nail firmly on the top of the bonce. It is, I would suggest, essential. I for one don't want a backroom that is in my opinion full of yes-men and I include the two Bees United board directors, who are outvoted in any case.

David M felt that it was simply a case of too much too soon:

Too much change too fast. We needed evolution not revolution. The new players needed time in the Development Squad building up their fitness whilst getting well acquainted with our system of play.

Meanwhile players already proven in this league should have been brought in to replace those sold on. Players that would slot in to the role they were replacing.

And yes we need someone with some football experience having some kind of say, someone who knows how to go about things in this league because at all levels we lack experience and the one thing that will get us out of this mess is someone who's dealt with it before and knows exactly how to go about repairing the team.

Rebel Bee used an extremely pejorative expression to describe what is going on – one that I do not concur or agree with:

The most positive thing I can find after ten games is that we are fifth from bottom after an awful start. This suggests that the division isn't as strong as last time and that there are plenty of other candidates for the drop. If we could find a way to finish the season in our current league position I'd bite your hand off for it right now.

Our problems are not simply coaching related, this team isn't nearly strong or balanced enough at present. The vanity project is flawed and there is a startling lack of football experience in the club to put it right.

I would love to be proved wrong but I fear the worst, and I don't want to describe how bad that looks.

Ben picked up on this point:

There is nothing wrong with vanity as it covers many things such as arrogance, pride and self-regard - traits that most successful people possess. So I find that a cheap dig at Matthew Benham's initiative.

However there are some very good thoughts on here regarding the situation even if there are not many solutions that excite me.

I have worked out that all was not well with Marinus at the training ground but I can't understand why that didn't come to light in preseason training in Portugal some three months ago. I liked Marinus and thought that he would eventually have turned things round as he seemed like a good coach and proper football man. Lee Carsley hardly excites at the moment.

Rasmus gave a good interview in the week and seemed very laid back and reassuring about Carsley's position and admitted they had got it wrong with Marinus but if we lose the next four games which is very possible, how long will he be given before he has to repeat these words? Why didn't they just say Carsley was overseeing the first team for an indefinite time and save any more embarrassment?

I would go for Karl Robinson, sort out who wants in and who wants out on the playing side and that goes for Dean, Judge, Tarks and anyone who is sulking on the pitch. I agree that this is a poor league this season and the hope is that there are a few clubs worse than us.

Rebel Bee came back as follows:

I think that analytics have some value and support Matthew Benham for looking at ways to make us more competitive. The concept has value I'm sure, but the forced pace of change culminating in Mark Warburton's departure, and the subsequent outcomes from the decisions taken, in a results based business, totally justify questions and balanced criticism.

I would have preferred Warburton's time at the club to have run its course, he wasn't at all against analytics and was the perfect man to take Benham's ideas forward. Warburton may well have left us ultimately, and then Matthew Benham could have pushed on further. So if the concept has value then I have to question its implementation, the way it has been communicated to the fans, and most of all the personnel entrusted to make it work.

So in summary I don't disagree with the project in its entirety, what I disagree with is getting beaten every week by ordinary teams, and throwing away a brilliant platform that Matthew Benham and Mark Warburton built together. The damage seems self-inflicted to me.

You defined vanity as "arrogance, pride, self-regard" and I'd include all of those words in my description of this as a "vanity project."

beesyellow22 summed it all up extremely well:

A fantastic response from Rebel Bee!

You have put it all so eloquently that I really have very little to add except for a big round of applause for what you said and the way you said it.

Unfortunately this is now the way things seem to be at Brentford. Matthew Benham has done so much for our club, that to be seen to criticise him in any way attracts criticism itself.

The forced pace of change has been horrendous and we are now seeing the evidence of that on the pitch, the table does not lie, we really have only won two games out of ten. Also, I agree that the people brought in have, so far, not exactly covered themselves in glory.

I like Ankersen and Giles as people. In interviews and at the Fans' Forum they came across very well. But again, the proof of the pudding is where we sit in the table, the lack of any clean sheets and the way in which we have played.

Yes, we have injuries, but we also have the likes of Djuricin, Vibe, Kerschbaumer and Gogia playing. Players all brought in by our new Co-Directors of Football who have patently not yet performed to the required standard.

Like Rebel Bee I too do not disagree with the project and I applaud our owner for having the vision to seek success in a brave new way. But when you have your most successful season for eighty years and then do not do everything in your power to retain the person largely responsible, then that, in my opinion, is pure folly.

To call it a vanity project might be a little harsh on Matthew Benham. However, the fact is, he did allow Warburton to leave and was seemingly implacable in his belief that the Moneyball approach was worth the sacrifice.

We all hope the international break does us good, helps the players bond with the new Head Coach, hones things on the training pitch and ultimately brings about a good win over Rotherham, which we can then build on. However, until we see a definitive turnaround on the pitch, including a bit of desire from the players, coupled with something resembling a game plan, then people will continue to question the actions of the owner and I believe they have every right to do so.

Interesting comments from everybody, some of which I feel are more balanced than others, but football is certainly a game that stirs the emotions!

It will be fascinating to see what happens over the next week as the Bees take the opportunity to recharge their batteries, concentrate on upping their fitness levels and working on team shape and will hopefully come out reinvigorated and refreshed for the tough challenges that lie ahead.

Last night saw perhaps the first chink of light at the end of the tunnel with the Bees winning yet again against the Old Enemy, Queens Park Rangers, in the Under-21 Premier League Cup. What's more Lewis Macleod started the match, played for an hour, set up the opening goal and then scored the winner with a delicately flicked header from a delicious cross from Sam Saunders, who was also making his comeback from injury.

It is early days, of course, but Lewis looked full of energy and was one of the best players on the field. What a boost it will be to see him recover full fitness and start to make the impact that was so eagerly anticipated when he arrived at the club nine long months ago.

Pure Gold Dust – Peter Lumley's Brentford Memories – 9/10/15

For the last couple of seasons I have sat in the same row in D Block in the Braemar Road stand as a wonderful hale and hearty, friendly gentleman who has entertained me with many stories of his long years supporting the Bees. Peter Lumley is a man of modesty, charm and obvious intellect and lucidity and it took quite a while before he let slip that he had for many years been a well-known and regarded local journalist who covered Brentford on his regular sports beat.

The opportunity was far too good for me to miss and I asked Peter if he would pen some of his memories of his time spent following the club as both writer and supporter, and here is what he has to say:

I am grateful to Greville for inviting me to write this article on some of my memories spanning seventy-three years as a Brentford supporter.

What are my credentials for taking on such a task?

Firstly, my ambition as a teenager was to become a sports journalist and as a stepping stone, my first job on leaving school was as a cub reporter on the Middlesex County Times at Ealing, a local paper that I believe is now more generally known as the Ealing Gazette.

For most of the 50s and early 60s I was Sports Editor of that newspaper and covered virtually every Brentford home game during that period, and many away games into the bargain. I spent many happy days in the Griffin Park Press Box and fondly recall a delightful couple in the late Bob Parkes who acted as the club's Press Steward and his wife who provided cups of tea and sandwiches for the starving hordes of journalists at half time.

I also have fond memories of the late Eric White, who was for many years the inspiration behind the Brentford programme and, of course, two iconic local newspaper colleagues in George Sands of the Middlesex Chronicle and Ernie Gifford of the Richmond and Twickenham Times.

My credentials as a player were modest to say the least. My best days were as a reasonably talented schoolboy performer with two special highlights to recall. I played against George Robb, a Spurs and England amateur and full international winger as well as on a separate occasion the great Johnny Haynes of England and Fulham fame, too.

My first introduction to Griffin Park was in 1942 at the age of ten and in my first season my Father and elder brother took me to Wembley for the London War Cup Final in which the Bees beat Portsmouth by two goals to nil with two superb goals by Leslie Smith, an England international left winger. On the right wing was Welsh international Dai Hopkins and other Brentford players from that period who I recall most vividly are goalkeeper Joe Crozier, centre half Joe James, right half Ernie Muttitt and full back Billy Gorman.

Mentioning Dai Hopkins reminds me of an extraordinary incident when the Bees met Wolves in the first full First Division season after the Second World War. Hopkins was lying prostrate on the turf on the extreme right wing touchline and he was obviously injured. Wolves centre half Stan Cullis, the England captain, ran towards the injured Hopkins and I was convinced that he was about to express his concern for a fellow professional and international player. Instead he appeared to aim a kick at the stricken winger. I may have been mistaken but I do not think so! Incidentally Brentford were relegated at the end of the season and have yet to win back a place in the top division, but I still live in hope!

That brings me onto something of a gripe about those who supported club owner Matthew Benham in his spat with Mark Warburton in February. I was repeatedly told that Mr. Benham had invested millions of pounds in the club and had been its financial saviour.

In my seventy-three years as a Brentford supporter I calculated that relative to our respective incomes I must have invested an equal proportion of my income in the purchase of season tickets, match tickets, programmes and club-related purchases for myself, my two sons and two grandsons too. Many thousands of other long-serving fans who also wanted Mark to stay as manager would've done the same, yet our voices were seemingly completely ignored.

I wrote a number of protest letters to the Chairman of the Board of Directors with copies to Mr. Warburton and others at the time. I received a delightful personal response from Mark which I will treasure for the rest of my life.

From Mr. Cliff Crown I received a stereotyped letter some months later in which he managed to address me as "Dear Mr. King" – I threw the letter away in disgust!

That is now water under the bridge but I'm sure we have not seen the last of the repercussions and the Chairman and his fellow directors may end up with considerable egg on their faces in the weeks and months ahead. I sincerely hope that this will not be the case.

Having got that grievance off my chest I will now return to the substantive task in hand. One of Greville's suggestions was for me to name the best Brentford players or team I had witnessed over all those years, or perhaps even the worst.

On further consideration I felt that this was a virtually impossible task so I've opted for a safer solution.

I will mention the players that have impressed me the most and whose names come readily to mind. I will classify them within the old-fashioned positions that I have become familiar with from the beginning of my Griffin Park journey.

So here goes:

GOALKEEPERS: *Joe Crozier | Alf Jefferies | Gerry Cakebread | Chic Brodie | Len Bond | David McKellar | Gary Phillips | Stuart Nelson | Ben Hamer | David Button*

FULLBACKS: *Billy Gorman | George Poyser | Ken Horne | Ken Coote | Billy Manuel | John Fraser | Alan Hawley | Alan Nelmes | Roger Stanislaus | Martin Grainger | Kevin O'Connor | Alan McCormack | Jake Bidwell | Moses Odubajo*

CENTRE HALVES: *Joe James | Ron Greenwood | Jack Chisholm | Mel Scott | Peter Gelson | Stewart Houston | Pat Kruse | Terry Evans | Jamie Bates | Tony Craig | Harlee Dean | James Tarkowski*

INSIDE FORWARDS: *George Wilkins | Peter Broadbent | Jimmy Bloomfield | Johnny Brooks | Jim Towers | Jackie Graham | John Dick | Bobby Ross | Chris Kamara | Alan Judge | Alex Pritchard*

CENTRE FORWARDS: *Jack Holliday | Dave McCulloch | Len Townsend | Billy Dare | Tommy Lawton | George Francis | A.H. (Jackie) Gibbons | Ian Lawther | Billy McAdams | John O'Mara | Carl Asaba | Steve Phillips | Francis Joseph | Gary Blissett | Gordon Sweetzer | Dai Ward | Nicky Forster | Roger Cross | Andy McCulloch | Robert Taylor | Andre Gray*

WINGERS: *Leslie Smith | Dai Hopkins | Dennis Heath | John Docherty | Gary Roberts | Marcus Gayle | Alex Rhodes | Stuart Dallas | Jota*

MANAGERS: *Harry Curtis | Malcolm MacDonald | Jackie Gibbons | Bill Dodgin Jr. | Tommy Lawton | Frank Blunstone | John Docherty | Phil Holder | Martin Allen | Micky Adams | Ron Noades | Steve Perryman | Uwe Rosler | Frank McLintock | Mark Warburton*

OWNERS: *Fred & Harry Davis | Jack Dunnett | Dan Tana | Martin Lange | Ron Noades | Matthew Benham*

Many thanks to Peter for his marvellous reminiscences, which are highly evocative and pure gold dust.

Hopefully I can inveigle him to write some more and tease some additional gems out of him, as he is a repository of wonderful stories about our great club's past.

How Many Points Do We Need To Get? – 10/10/15

It is just wonderful when I receive unsolicited articles from my fellow Brentford supporters. Firstly it is great for everyone else to hear other voices as I am sure that you all get a bit bored with me prattling on all the time – I know that I do, and it is healthy and thought provoking to read some different perspectives, viewpoints and opinions about the club - favourable, supportive or even at the other end of the spectrum.

Most importantly, and selfishly too, from my point of view it means that another day can go by without the necessity of me having to gird my loins and struggle to write something new and hopefully interesting myself.

Dave Washer has just sent through some fascinating comments and as an advertising copywriter, he can certainly write – as is proved by this article that analyses the current state of play on the pitch at Griffin Park and I hope you enjoy it as much as I did:

What with the gap between the last game and the next one, my thoughts have turned (inevitably?) to the games we have ahead of us this season and, specifically, how many wins and draws we potentially will require to remain a Championship club next season – surely now the summit of our ambitions.

I'm certain that if you asked officials at the club, they would still say we are looking to push on from where we left off last season; but the reality is, with all the turmoil off the pitch so far since the departure of Warburton and Weir, many (if not all) Brentford supporters would snatch your hand off right now if they were offered a finishing position of twenty-first place.

A depressing admission perhaps, but one which I think sums up the mood on the terraces (and in the seats) after a mere two wins from ten games.

Before we realised just how incredible our team actually was last season, I was working on the sixty points for survival philosophy, targeting thirty points between August and December and another thirty points between January and May.

Taking this as a basis for this season (and readjusting slightly to reflect the fact that I don't think we are capable this season of reaching sixty points) I have jotted down below the games in which I believe we will find the wherewithal to take all three points, as well as where I think we will get a draw.

Naturally we all have differing opinions about who we will be able to beat between now and May, for example, I see Rotherham at Griffin Park as an easy win, whilst others may view it as a tense six-pointer that will inevitably end in a draw or even, God forbid, a defeat, but for me the following list gives me something to cling on to as we seek to plot our course away from the wrong end of the table.

Obviously it is not definitive but I thought others might be interested in my thoughts as a conversation-starter as we count down the days until kick-off against the Millers next Saturday.

To be anywhere close to the thirty points by the end of December target, we need to take seventeen points from the next thirty-nine available. Then, to get close to a tally of sixty points (which should definitely see us stay up) we need to take thirty-four points from sixty-six between next January and next May.

Seventeen from thirty-nine actually gives us quite a lot of room for dropping points, with twenty-two points written off before a ball is kicked. That is a win ratio of less than fifty percent, surely the kind of statistic that a lower-mid table Championship side should be more than capable of achieving?

Similarly, thirty-four from sixty-six after Christmas sees a sizeable thirty-two points sacrificed by the Bees. The prediction: that we will gain just over fifty percent of the points on offer to us between January and May. Again, surely more than achievable if we are to have any pretensions of staying up?

Games we will win (in 2015): *Rotherham (H) | Nottingham Forest (H) | MK Dons (H) | Huddersfield (H)*

Games we will draw (in 2015: *QPR (H) | Bolton (A) | Fulham (A) | Brighton (H) | Reading (A)*

Games we will lose (in 2015): *Wolves (A) | Hull (H) | Blackburn (A) | Cardiff (A)*

Games we will win (in 2016): *Leeds (H) | Wolves (H) | Rotherham (A) | Charlton (H) | Blackburn (H) | Bolton (H) | Bristol City (H) | Cardiff (H) | MK Dons (A) | Fulham (H)*

Games we will draw (in 2016: *Burnley (H) | Sheff Wed (A) | Derby (H) | QPR (A)*

Games we will lose (in 2016): *Birmingham (A) | Middlesbrough (H) | Preston (A) | Brighton (A) | Hull (A) | Forest (A) | Ipswich (A) | Huddersfield (A)*

As I say, these are only my thoughts and of course there will be many who completely disagree with my predictions! Added to which, who knows what will happen with all of the currently injured players between now and the end of the season? Once we get back the likes of Jota, Colin and McEachran, we could well exceed all expectations and actually finish nearer to the playoff places than the relegation zone.

Speaking of Jota, Colin and McEachran brings me onto my next point: namely, what will the team selection be for the Rotherham game and what will our new Head Coach decide to do?

Although we were apparently awful against Derby, Lee Carsley will have had two weeks to work with the players, bond with them and mould them more into his own team.

Will he persevere with Vibe sitting behind Djuricin however? According to Greville, Vibe was pretty awful against Derby, so perhaps a change in formation is in order? Or will he think about playing Hofmann up top with Djuricin and try to batter his way through what is sure to be a resilient and defence-minded Rotherham line-up?

I was thinking about what made us so successful last season and, apart from the obvious man-management and tactical skills of Mark Warburton (ably assisted by David Weir) and a relentless brand of attacking football that simply did not allow the opposition to settle (unless they were Middlesbrough!) the one constant was an almost slavish deferral to a 4-1-4-1 system which, correct me if I'm wrong, we don't seem to have employed this campaign.

Were we to revert to 4-1-4-1 against Rotherham, my selection would be thus:

Button (Goal) | Clarke (RB) | Bidwell (LB) | Barbet (CB) | Dean (CB) | Diagouraga (HM) | Woods (AM) | Swift (AM) | Judge (LW) | Canos (RW) | Djuricin (A)

I would bring Josh Clarke back in at right back, as I simply do not think Nico Yennaris is Championship standard and I still have nightmares about the game at The Valley last season.

I would give Barbet another go at centre back as a) he looks a quality player and b) the fact that we have conceded in every single match so far this season tells me that the current de facto centre back pairing of Tarkowski and Dean is simply not working.

In front of the holding role of Diagouraga I would give youth a chance in the shape of Ryan Woods (playing the Jonathan Douglas role of bursting creative midfielder) and John Swift (filling in the attacking midfield role that has been so desperately missing since Alex Pritchard went back to White Hart Lane). I would stick with Judge on the left, as he has been outstanding all season and, for true pace, give Canos a chance on the right, until Jota is back to full fitness.

Assuming that Lewis Macleod doesn't trip over another twig between now and the Rotherham game, I would have him on the bench, waiting in the wings to burst on and add another goal or two to the tally with twenty-five minutes to go. And of course, moving forward, if Macleod carries on the way he left off against QPR the other night, he will command a starting place right at the heart of our midfield before long, hopefully leading us further and further up the table.

What will Lee Carsley decide to do? Of course it is difficult to say. But, assuming everyone is match fit, and because it is a match we simply have to win, I think he will go for a 4-1-3-2 formation, lining up like this:

Button (Goal) | McCormack (RB) | Bidwell (LB) | Tarkowski (CB) | Dean (CB) | Diagouraga (HM) | Woods (AM) | Swift (AM) | Judge (AM) | Vibe (A) | Djuricin (A)

The main thing of course is that we win – whatever the formation and however we achieve it! However, it would be monumentally encouraging were we to win playing good, confident, attacking football, which could then give us a good platform on which to build as we go on to seek that additional fourteen points between then and the end of December.

The club, the team and the fans have been through a lot this season and now we have a chance to draw a line, put in a performance of intent, desire and skill and kick on towards the next batch of ten league games – from which, we hope, we will garner a) more than a paltry two victories and b) start to shut up shop at the back and actually look a bit more difficult to score against.

If we can manage that, we might all be able to predict a far happier outcome when the final league table is published next May.

Thanks again to Dave for his predictions and team selection. I would note that Peterborough went down in 2012/13 having finished with a record high Championship points total of fifty-four so he is being very cautious with his proposed target of sixty points – or so I hope!

I do share his optimism, as I believe that we are a couple of short months away from being able to field a potent and attractive midfield comprising four – or even five out of:

Diagouraga | Woods | McEachran | Macleod | Swift (if he remains with us) | Jota | Judge | Canos

Now they might be lacking a bit in bite but you cannot tell me that we would not dominate possession, and more importantly, create chances given the talent that they all possess.

The key question for me is whether we revert to a 4-2-3-1 formation like last season or keep two men up top?

I am concerned that Djuricin cannot play the lone striker role and run the channels like Gray did, although he might prove me wrong once he regains full match fitness. Vibe is currently proving to be a bit of a damp squib and the jury is still out on Hofmann, although he impressed in his cameo at Derby.

I would prefer us to have the extra man in midfield if at all possible, as what is the point of having two strikers if there is nobody there to load the gun for them?

The defence is serviceable but for all his dominance at Leeds, Tarkowski does not totally convince me as I believe that there is always a mistake in him. Dean has become more consistent and measured in his play and I would like to see a left footer play alongside him, and I would choose Barbet because of his better distribution and the fact that he is becoming more accustomed to the rough and tumble of the Championship.

As for right back, I have no real preference between McCormack or Clarke as they both bring different skills to the party. I simply hope that Colin recovers quickly and regains his place as he showed real promise before his injury.

You have now read the views of both Dave Washer and myself.

What does everybody else think?

First Thoughts About Next Saturday – 12/10/15

There was a good response to **Dave Washer's** recent article that provided his view on how many points we need to obtain in order to ensure Championship survival.

edmundpw queried the points total that was suggested by Dave:

Where does the idea that sixty points are required come from? Can anyone find an instance of when fifty-five wasn't enough? And quite often fifty is more than adequate.

He is quite correct in what he said as the most points gained by a relegated team that I can remember was when Peterborough went down on the last day of the season in 2012/13 in heart-breaking circumstances despite having an incredible fifty-four points. A points total that I would bite your hand off for at the moment.

Rebel Bee took a gloomier view on the current situation:

A good read from Dave, but I'm a bit more pessimistic and need to see some signs of recovery before being able to contemplate safety. I expect Rotherham will be a very hard game – more typical of the division below us, and our lack of physicality worries me.

All that matters is that we find a way to win, then we can push on a little. Lose and I think we may be looking for another head coach, part of me thinks that somehow we will get out of trouble, but there is no science behind this, just hope. At least you've gone for some predictions.

A view that was also shared by **Andrew Martin**:

The number of points needed is a tough one, Saturday's game is crucial. Rotherham will have a new manager so the players will want to impress. I think it is vital for us to score first, to give the players and fans a lift, the first clean sheet this season will also be massive for the confidence of the players, fifty points is always a target to aim for, but it may need more or even slightly in a very competitive championship.

Mike Rice also advocated caution:

I hope Lee Carsley has been studying the recent Birmingham versus Rotherham game, which Rotherham won two-nil, arguably one of the more surprising results so far this season. I have a (depressing) feeling this will be nil-nil as we try to keep a clean sheet at the expense of an attacking threat.

If we lose at home to Rotherham, it will be difficult to imagine who we can beat this season, placing an awful lot of pressure on the shoulders of young players who have barely played for us, or not yet played at all.

Dave Washer took note of everything that had been said and then came back with the following riposte:

Thanks to Greville for publishing my ramblings and thanks too to everyone who has taken the time to post a comment. To be honest, nothing I wrote was based on any particular kind of watertight analysis, and to take edmundpw's point, the whole sixty-point equation was really just me looking at fifty possibly being enough for survival and then sticking an extra ten on top just to be sure!

Reading the comments from Rebel Bee and Mike, I cannot disagree with your somewhat downbeat appraisal of the situation. The article was not so much based on what I truly believe will happen in terms of us picking up points, as much as giving me a set of targets for us to hit if we are to have any chance of staying up this season.

Like Rebel Bee I also think Rotherham will be a tough game – even more so now that they have a new manager in charge – and I think anyone who rocks up at Griffin Park next Saturday expecting a guaranteed three points is living in a dream world.

We must expect that Neil Redfearn will have them fired up and well prepared for an intense battle. However, we can only hope that our reluctant manager has also imbued his Bees side with the same kind of battle-ready mentality.

This is a genuine six-pointer and whoever wins will gain a massive psychological advantage. However well Rotherham defend and whatever kind of resilience they show on the day, we have to be ready to match and exceed them in all areas across the park. Quite simply, this is the day for every single Brentford player to step up, work their socks off and get the result we so desperately need.

If, as expected, Tarkowski partners Dean at the back, they need to show a resilience that has in the main been completely absent this season. If McCormack is reinstated at right back, he has to match his unquestioned tenacity with a capacity to support and feed whoever is playing on the right side of midfield – just as Odubajo did so brilliantly last season.

And on the left, captain Bidwell needs to finally stand up and be counted, combining his defensive duties with a strong attacking performance that will inspire the rest of the team.

In midfield, Diagouraga needs to be the fulcrum that breaks up the opposition play and starts our attacks, whilst Ryan Woods and John Swift (if indeed he actually starts the match) need to be tenacious and rapier-like in their forward play, giving Marco Djuricin the kind of service that his undoubted finishing will hopefully feed off with one or possibly more goals.

As for the remaining players that will start the match, Alan Judge has just to keep doing what he has done so far over the first ten games, take the game by the scruff of the neck and exert his undoubted ability on the Rotherham back four, whilst Vibe (if selected) has to step out of the shadows, realise that we need him to have his best game yet in a Brentford shirt and hook up with Djuricin in a potent and dangerous attacking partnership.

Of course, I hope that all of that will happen. I also hope that Sergi Canos will come on and make a goal or two and that we will run out comfortable winners and send us home happy for a change.

But as I sit here writing this with just under six days to go, I can honestly say I really don't know what will happen. I can see us winning it, I can see us drawing it and, God forbid, I can also see us losing it as well!

All we can do is cheer them on from the first minute until the last, keep everything crossed and pray that these two weeks have given them a chance to regroup and discover some kind of collective spirit and common purpose.

The nightmare scenario: we lose to Rotherham, lose at Wolves and then lose to Charlton. If it's five defeats out of five from Carsley's first five games in charge, I predict that we will then be looking for our third manager since the start of the season!

What stands out a mile from all the heartfelt, pragmatic and even in some cases, pessimistic, comments expressed by everybody above, is that realism rules and nobody is under any illusions and is expecting anything against Rotherham other than a tense battle.

The gauntlet has been thrown down to Lee Carsley and his squad and the supporters expect – nay demand, a performance from them all next Saturday.

Nothing less than total commitment will do and if the players show the required level of energy and tenacity and tackle, cover and press like demons, then maybe, just maybe, our superior technique will shine through and we can obtain a morale boosting and much needed victory.

The alternative hardly bears thinking about.

Martin Lange – RIP – 14/10/15

Martin Lange, the former Brentford Chairman died on Monday after a long illness. He was only seventy-one, no age at all in the grand scheme of things and he died long before his time.

He was also a man who was ahead of his time as he was rightly recognised for his innovative and original ideas and approach throughout his long career in football. He owned the majority shareholding at the club for a sixteen-year period, between 1981 and 1997 and also served as the Third Division representative on the Football League Board.

Like our current owner, Matthew Benham, Martin Lange was no outsider as he was Brentford through and through and his father first took him to Griffin Park as a small boy.

His hobby soon became an obsession and after he became a successful property developer he was invited onto the club board at the early age of thirty-seven by the club's then chairman, Dan Tana and soon afterwards he took over the reins for what turned out to be a real rollercoaster ride.

His new position was rather a poisoned chalice as he took over a club saddled with debt and his first task was to stump up the ludicrous seventy thousand pound fee decided by the transfer tribunal for Alan Whitehead's purchase from Bury.

A salutary lesson for him about the economics of the madhouse that so often prevailed in football given how poorly the central defender was to perform and the size of the loss we incurred on him when we were finally able to offload him.

Lange wasn't afraid to take tough decisions and one of his first was to replace the loyal and long serving Denis Piggott, who had become part of the furniture at the club but was soon swept out by the new broom.

He surrounded himself with exceptional people such as Keith Loring, Christine Mathews and Polly Kates but there was never any doubt who was in charge.

Just as the Roman Emperors ensured their popularity by giving their citizens games and circuses, so too did Martin Lange guarantee his place in Brentford folklore by coming up with the idea of signing Stan Bowles, a man who became a Brentford legend and singlehandedly revived the spirits of a supporter base who had had very little to get excited about in recent years.

Brentford were a middle of the road third tier club attracting small gates, going nowhere fast, and Lange had to balance ambition with pragmatism and reality as he fought a constant and losing battle to balance the books.

Lange inherited Fred Callaghan as manager who was a terrific judge of a player and knew the lower leagues well buying players of the calibre of Terry Hurlock, Gary Roberts, Chris Kamara and David Crown and Martin also gained respect by always being approachable and he handled Terry Hurlock brilliantly as a combination of Father Figure and Dutch Uncle who ensured that the sometimes hothead always toed the line but was also persuaded to invest his money wisely in bricks and mortar rather than fritter it away.

Lange eventually decided to replace Callaghan – in retrospect a bit too quickly, as he gave in to the entreaties of the fans to make a change and his first appointment was Frank McLintock who proved to be a far better player and captain than he did a manager. John Docherty, a former Bees manager, surprisingly reversed roles and became Frank's assistant but despite an abortive trip to Wembley and a Freight Rover Trophy Final defeat to Wigan in 1985, the combination did not gel and Steve Perryman was promoted from within.

Lange had got it right this time as Perryman proved to be a success both on and off the field and together they slowly improved the playing fortunes and infrastructure of the club. The team ran out of steam in 1989 and missed out on promotion when it looked within their grasp after an incredible run to the sixth round of the FA Cup with famous victories over Manchester City and Blackburn Rovers before bowing out with pride and dignity at Anfield.

Lange and Perryman fell out spectacularly apparently over the abortive signing of Gary Elkins and it appeared that the club would go downhill again but Phil Holder seized the opportunity as caretaker, and Lange was brave and astute enough to appoint him and recognise that very little needed changing. Holder was perhaps more chirpy and streetwise than Perryman and the team responded well to his promptings and after an abortive playoff campaign (now where have we heard that before) he led the Bees to the title and promotion in 1992.

Amazingly at the time of his greatest triumph Martin Lange was not there to share in the glory. As he said in his interview in *The Big Brentford Book Of The 80s:*

The sad thing was that I had to go over to America to oversee a big, four hundred acre development – it's been well documented, but I simply had to be there, but I never actually saw Brentford get promoted!

It was Sod's Law, as a lad I'd seen Brentford in the old Second Division when my dad brought me down in the early 50s, so I knew all too well how important it was to finally escape from the third tier again, so to miss the Peterborough match was devastating. Then to add to my frustration, the only two matches I was able to see in the 1992/93 Division One season were at West Ham and Bristol City!

Without his steady hand on the tiller, Brentford imploded. Dean Holdsworth was sold badly to Wimbledon, incredibly without a sell-on clause being included in the deal – total madness and poor business practise which cost the Bees dear when he made a big money move to Bolton Wanderers.

Money was squandered on a series of poor signings – Joe Allon and Murray Jones anybody? Relegation was confirmed after a disgraceful last day of the season surrender at Bristol City and the Bees were back from whence they came.

Phil Holder – perhaps unfairly, also did not survive relegation and Lange's return to take day control of the club.

But things were never the same again and Lange admitted that *the blow of relegation was the beginning of the end as far as I was concerned I think.*

David Webb was rapturously received as the new manager and he embarked on a cost-cutting exercise, weeding out the older players and building a team in his own image that was tough, gritty and hard to beat but always had some inspiration and goals up front given the likes of Nicky Forster, Bob Taylor and Carl Asaba.

Promotion eluded the Bees cruelly in 1995 when they finished second in the one year when only the top team gained automatic promotion – *It's Brentford innit?*

And two years later they collapsed spectacularly as they neared the finishing line in a manner that almost begged a Stewards' Enquiry.

Exhausted and frustrated after the best part of twenty years in charge without being able to lead the club to the promised land, Lange decided to sell up and a consortium fronted by Webb and including Tony Swaisland and John Herting, bought fifty-one percent of his shares for the same price that he had paid for them so many years earlier.

There is no escaping the fact that Martin Lange was also responsible for pulling down the famed Royal Oak Stand and he admits to regretting his decision but he gave the following explanation:

The truth is that the back of the stand was condemned and the cost of repairing it was phenomenal. The combination of the dilapidated conditions and the club debt, plus me being a property developer, meant that redevelopment just had to be considered to clear the debts.

And once the bank was off the club's back, running the club certainly became a lot easier.

I understand passions still run high over the demolition of the Royal Oak, and in hindsight it has restricted Brentford's scope to develop Griffin Park, but it was the right decision at the time, especially as I was constantly looking for a site to build Brentford a state-of-the-art new stadium at Western International.

Even if we'd decided to pull the Royal Oak down, rebuild it just as big, but with executive boxes, the council wouldn't have let us.

Hindsight is easy but at the time, rightly or wrongly, it seemed the most sensible thing for him to do.

After selling the club Martin remained on the board until 2002 before withdrawing from the spotlight but he always remained a good friend of the club and was keen to do whatever he could to ensure its future success and he was highly supportive of Matthew Benham and his plans for Brentford.

Martin's influence within the game spread far beyond the boundaries of Griffin Park and he proposed a number of changes to tackle falling attendances and hooliganism, including introducing the end of season playoffs in 1986 as well as supporting the introduction of individual squad numbers and names on each player's shirt.

When asked to assess his time at the club, Martin Lange responded with characteristic modesty and self-effacement:

Looking back at my time as chairman, in hindsight maybe I would have done a few things differently, some people, rightly or wrongly, have suggested I could have been more adventurous and spent big trying to get Brentford to the promised land, but as a custodian I think fans can look back and say that, when I was there, there was never a survival threat, there was never any real crisis to deal with, and I was a safe, stable and genuinely caring chairman.

That is not a bad epitaph and way to be remembered even if for the time being no Brentford fan can yet look kindly upon the introduction of the dreaded playoffs.

Martin Lange though was a thoroughly decent, pleasant and talented man who achieved so much that was good during his time at the club and we should all give thanks to him for everything he did for us, celebrate his life and mourn his premature passing.

RIP.

David Carpenter's Bees Memories – 15/10/15

I am sure that David Carpenter would not mind my referring to him as a Brentford fan of deep experience and long vintage given that he has been coming to Griffin Park for over seventy years, and despite all the bad times he has witnessed he still retains his enthusiasm and optimism for the future.

He possesses a sharp eye for cant and hypocrisy and not much escapes his scrutiny and he is quick to express his sometimes trenchant opinions, but what shines through is his deep love for a football club which has played such an important part in his life. Here are his memories of supporting the Bees:

I'm pretty sure it was 1942 when I first came to Griffin Park. My Dad used to take me on the crossbar of his old Hercules bike from Chiswick and we parked in the garden of my mother's Aunt Hetty's house in New Road. Not a freebie, though. We paid our penny, or was it tuppence, like everyone else. In those days all the houses around the ground took in bikes, and there were so many, literally thousands, that if you were late you struggled to find a space. Front gardens, back yards, even hallways were full.

In those days of low footballers' wages, top players in leading teams like Brentford in those days, like Leslie Smith and Ernie Muttitt, and probably others, didn't live in mansions like today's stars. They lived in Braemar Road. Handy for the ground!

Looking back, getting there was quite an adventure. The war was on and my Dad was just too old to go back into the army. He had been in the First World War and had had a bad time. But West London was a bit of a war zone, anyway. Now and again you could be lucky enough to find a bit of prized shrapnel in the back garden. Air raids were common and later the dreaded doodlebugs – cruise missiles to younger folk – were a terrifying threat. You did not want to hear that ramjet cut out! All these years later the sound of a siren on an old film clip still has the ability to send a shiver down my spine.

Looking back, it was a bit crazy to go to Griffin Park by bike, dodging doodlebugs. But that was the draw of Brentford Football Club. Incidentally, we stopped going by bike after being stopped by a policeman. Riding on the crossbar was deemed dangerous. Never mind all the high explosives going off!

Once through those turnstiles and then onto the terrace, what excitement! Maybe a military band marching up and down, or the Dagenham Girl Pipers. And then the cheering when the players came out.

An old lawyer friend had a wonderful homily: "Recollection improves as memory fades." So it may be a case of rose-tinted spectacles, but the crowd was very good-natured in those days. The referee was fair game, of course, but the players were treated with respect. I really don't understand why some spectators feel that they have to hurl abuse even at their own players, even if they are having an off game – especially if they are having an off game. I do think it has got better just lately, but so has the football.

In those days Brentford were a top team. They were in the First Division, now Premier League, albeit interrupted by the war. We enjoyed all the greats coming to Griffin Park – Arsenal, Manchester United,

Everton, Burnley, Chelsea, Charlton, Preston, Sheffield United, and so on. Great clubs of the day, but they are not all so great today with many of them now with us in the lower leagues.

A great memory was coming early to a match to see the Busby Babes play our juniors before the senior game. It would be good to see that sort of thing again. Or perhaps our junior/development squad matches being shown on live feeds.

Another was a testimonial game when Stanley Matthews and other top stars appeared. An abiding memory from that game was to see Raich Carter, long retired, standing in the centre circle, never taking more than a gentle step or two before making a series of inch-perfect passes.

After the war and relegation to the Second Division, it was still a busy place. We could still attract crowds of seven thousand – for reserve games! And between twenty-five to thirty thousand for league games.

Who could forget days like the sixth Round FA Cup tie with Leicester City with thirty-nine thousand jammed into Griffin Park, and all us kids were passed over heads down to the railing and allowed to sit at the edge of the pitch?

That was possible in the days before the New Road stand was reduced and the old shed or Spion Kop at the Brook Road end was still large. Everywhere was standing, the only seats being in the Braemar Road stand behind the paddock. Sadly part of the Brook Road end was sold off for re-development. But for that the club might not have to be moving to Lionel Road.

While I'm not old enough to remember the glory days of the 30s, this was still a major club in the 40s and 50s. We had so many great players like Tommy Lawton, Ron Greenwood, Dai Hopkins, Jackie Gibbons and many, many more too. There is a lot about them in all the books on the club's history by Greville and others for a nice wallow in nostalgia.

You can see a lot of them on the DVD of the film, "The Great Game", also featuring the delightful Diana Dors. In that film she gets passed over heads behind the Ealing Road goal. Apparently her boyfriend tried to punch the lights out of someone who goosed her.

Later we had super players like Francis and Towers, Kenny Coote and one I will never forget, Ken Horne who sadly died very recently. He was an excellent full back and perhaps the fastest ever to bathe and dress after every game.

Once we went to the Boleyn for a memorable game with West Ham. As a kid collecting autographs, we went straight to the dressing room exit just in time to see Ken come out shiny as a new pin. He kindly took my book into the West Ham dressing room and got the whole team to sign. It was wonderful to see him at Griffin Park again before he died.

I finally got to meet George Francis too just before he died. He was a delightful man who was a hero to me. He had a wonderful technique of being able to get some part of his body between the defender and the ball. Worked a treat.

It has not all been great. There was the aborted QPR take-over. Not surprising that feelings there still go beyond local rivalry. There was the awful moment in the last game of 1947 when we were relegated, and not quite going straight back up the following year. If only...

There have been other things to forget, like two of our players I can remember being booed off by their own fans, one a thug and the other who just didn't want to be there.

Some of the highs and lows have been combined, like our appearances at Wembley (apart from 1942) and Cardiff.

I only decided once to stop going to Griffin Park and that was in the Webb era. Otherwise, it's been a pleasure from the top division to the bottom. It's been a place for heroes if not a whole lot of success.

For the future I hope we have some success. But I do hope that it does not change the character of the club too much, and that after seventy-odd years my grandson, too will feel part of Brentford FC.

When I retired (for the second time) I said that only two things would tempt me back to work. One was to work for a magazine for a long-term hobby interest, and the other, something to do with the club. My early career was as a journalist with national daily and weekly newspapers and I returned to edit my favourite magazine a year after retiring.

Later, I joined the board of Bees United at a most interesting time, the lead up to the sale of the majority share in the football club and the start of the project proper for Lionel Road.

The decision to sell to Matthew Benham was a no-brainer really. By the time of the sale he was putting in so much money (but only a fraction of the amount today) that there was no alternative. I took on the role of devil's advocate in all this, which did not always go down well!

But I was happy to leave after the sale with safeguards in place to ensure that Brentford Football Club would continue in the event of the unthinkable happening. One of the Bees United directors has recently stated that is still the case. Excellent!

It is the one thing they have to keep on top of. Especially now that all the independent directors have been moved off the main club Board.

"If history repeats itself, and the unexpected always happens, how incapable must Man be of learning from experience?"

George Bernard Shaw.

Thank you David for your wise and evocative words, which I hope that everybody enjoys as much as I have.

Relief! – 18/10/15

The overriding emotion after yesterday's narrow and hard fought two-one victory over Rotherham was simply one of relief.

Relief that we had arrested the rot of three successive defeats, relief that we had beaten a team likely to be in the relegation zone, perhaps alongside us, and relief that Lee Carsley had finally broken his duck as a Head Coach and led us to our first victory under his direction.

This was a game where, in all honesty, very little mattered beyond the result. A defeat would have seem morale and confidence amongst players and supporters alike plummet to new depths and the Bees would have dropped into the relegation zone for the first time this season.

Going into the game it hadn't helped to watch a confident and revitalised Bristol City team totally outplay and pulverise a poor and dispirited Nottingham Forest on Friday night and to see them play the ball around with such precision and accuracy and a certain *joie de vivre* just emphasised how much the Bees needed to improve in order to get their season back on track and escape from the pack stuck around the bottom of the Championship table.

The three points that we eventually won, not without a desperate struggle, were the absolute priority and I believe that given the fillip of yesterday's much needed victory, we will now improve slowly and gradually as we regain some confidence and cohesion.

It will also help if we can get some high quality reinforcements into the squad either from outside, during the January transfer window, or hopefully well in advance of then when the likes of Jota, Macleod, McEachran and Colin report back for duty as soon as they have recovered from long-term injury.

I therefore do not intend to dwell too much upon the myriad shortcomings that were exposed yet again yesterday afternoon.

We know that the players currently available to us have not proved to be of sufficient quality or experience to get us to where we want to be in the Championship and to carp and criticise them might be good for the soul but is hardly likely to be productive in the great scheme of things.

To emphasise where we are at the moment, we were out passed and out-possessed yesterday by Rotherham. Nothing really more needs to be said, as there is really very little point in doing so.

We all know that our visitors are a set of decent, honest journeymen, toiling hard at a level that is probably just a little bit beyond them and we recognise and appreciate that they do their utmost to make up for their deficiencies in terms of class and ability through the virtues of organisation, effort and sheer hard work.

Please do not think that I am trying to patronise or denigrate them or minimise their achievements as I greatly admire Rotherham as a club for more than making the most of what they have, and it is fair to say that they played as much football as we did, if not more, and probably just had the edge in terms of creating opportunities.

Brentford had forty-seven percent possession of the ball and attempted three hundred and eighty-four passes of which sixty-seven per cent found their target. Rotherham had fifty-three per cent possession and attempted fifty-two more passes than us with a slightly higher rate of accuracy.

In the corresponding match last season Brentford enjoyed sixty-six per cent possession and whilst comparisons are both pointless and invidious you can see how much things have changed in the interim period.

There is really no possible benefit in wailing, gnashing our teeth and bemoaning the fact that we have fallen so far from grace since the high points of last season and have also massively declined in terms of the quality of our squad and footballing ability – that is simply a fact that we have to accept and get beyond at the moment if we are to retain our sanity and sense of proportion.

The time for recriminations will come later on if the season ends in disaster. Now is simply a time for all hands to the pumps and for us to work together to help ensure our survival at Championship level as it would be a disaster of massive proportions if we allow our hard-won Championship status to be surrendered come next May.

Apart from the victory there were many other positives to come out of yesterday's match:

- A five-figure crowd that, whilst quiet and muted at times, got behind their team and appreciated their efforts

- A positive up-and-at-'em start culminating in a quite brilliantly taken early goal from Alan Judge

- Scoring the opening goal for the first time this season at home

- A solid defensive display with Dean and Tarkowski particularly impressing

- Nico Yennaris making the opening goal and playing his best ever game for the club

- Ryan Woods playing in a holding role alongside Alan McCormack and looking calm and composed on the ball, winning his challenges and rarely conceding possession

- Young guns Sergi Canos and John Swift justifying the faith shown in them and demonstrating their ability and youthful enthusiasm on their first start for the club

- The imperious Alan Judge, scorer of two quite beautifully taken goals, including a rare header, and running the game from start to finish

- Brentford scoring two excellently worked, constructed and taken goals

- A recognisable and effective team shape being employed in the 4-2-3-1 formation that worked so well last season

- A determination and will to win, evidenced by the Brentford players putting their body on the line and defending desperately during the six interminable minutes of injury time when Rotherham threw the kitchen sink at us

- A team selection which ignored the stuttering claims of all our fit if underperforming preseason foreign signings in Barbet, Kerschbaumer, Vibe, Hofmann and Gogia and contained seven of last season's tried and tested squad, plus Woods and recent loanees, Canos, Swift and Djuricin

I fully recognise the lack of quality on display at times yesterday, our inability to keep possession, the lack of incision, the paucity of attempts on target, the fact that Djuricin must surely have been suffering from a communicable disease, so isolated was he upfront, the languid start to the second half that cost us so dear and our appalling marking at opposition set pieces where we relied far too much upon David Button's brilliance to save the day.

I would also hope that somebody introduced Philipp Hofmann after the game to returning legend Robert Taylor as I think that they could have had a most productive conversation on centre forward play that would have greatly benefitted our new German striker who still has so much to learn about the demands of English football.

Yesterday was still an improvement on what we have seen recently and you can only beat the opposition that is facing you on the day.

We now have two tough away games in the next week at Wolves and Charlton and I will withhold any judgement until after we have played both of these matches.

I would hope and expect that we improve gradually from game to game but I have no real expectations of a massive change in our fortunes until the injured players return.

But hey – WE WON!

In The Dark – 22/10/15

We have got the builders in at home at the moment and the last few weeks have been a living hell with constant and seemingly never ending banging and crashing as they remorselessly get on with their work.

Whilst I am not looking for any sympathy, life has been pretty stressful and difficult as we have been reduced to burrowing ourselves away upstairs with access only to two rooms downstairs, and cooking is a real challenge and adventure at the moment with no kitchen and a rickety microwave doing the honours in the front room.

Disposable plates are the order of the day and we have coped as well as possible and my wife's ingenuity has been stretched to its limits given the restrictions we have faced.

Given the situation we decided to get away for part of half term week and now find ourselves ensconced in the sanctuary of Luton Hoo.

It is an absolutely beautiful old country house hotel tucked away in acres of rolling woodland and is an oasis of calm and tranquillity and traditional old-English splendour despite being a mere ten minutes away from the cosmopolitan hustle and bustle of Luton town centre.

I was under strict orders and a three line whip last night – total relaxation and absolute concentration on the matters in hand rather than thinking and commenting about affairs taking place simultaneously at Molineux.

Normally in such circumstances I speak with forked tongue and am guilty of flagrant cheating and, worst of all, I was once caught red handed and shamefaced listening to a Bees match commentary on *BBC Radio London* during a wedding ceremony in a synagogue.

Not one of my proudest moments and one that took me years to live down and the embarrassment still lingers when I recall it!

Last night was totally different as the surroundings were calm and quiet and the light muted and soothing.

We passed a lovely evening relishing the sort of pleasant and wide-ranging shorthand conversation of a long married couple who can generally read each other like a book but happily still take massive comfort, pride, enjoyment and support from each other's company.

It was also so good to be able to luxuriate and make the most of good food, wine and a great companion.

As far as the football was concerned I had willed myself in a near trancelike state of calm and tranquillity and was reconciled to the outcome, whatever it might turn out to be.

I have expressed my view many times that I believe that our improvement will be slow and gradual and I have limited expectations in the short term until we get the likes of Jota, McEachran, Colin and Macleod back in harness.

We had already achieved my minimum target of three points from our next two games by virtue of the win against Rotherham and anything gained against Wolves was therefore a bonus.

They had looked vulnerable defensively against Derby last Sunday but the partnership of Afobe and Le Fondre spelled danger for our back four.

I was fully reconciled to a defeat last night and had no expectations beyond our putting on a decent performance and remaining competitive and in the game for as long as possible.

I had recurring nightmares of our porous defence cracking and crumbling under pressure and that we might subside without much of a fight and so the prospect of an evening without going to the match, listening to the *Bees Player* commentary or even receiving any score flashes or updates, whilst alien and even unique in my recent experience, did not, in the circumstances, seem to be too much of an imposition.

And so it transpired. We enjoyed a lovely meal, my phone buzzed a couple of times but the texts remained unread and unanswered.

It was not until we had finished our post meal cup of tea that I finally cracked and checked my phone and did a double take as the unexpected good news of our comfortable victory was revealed to me.

I have now watched the highlights and spoken to some trusted and reliable sources who were present at the game and it is plainly evident that confidence is finally returning to the squad and the long awaited first clean sheet of the season will only help in this process.

We seemed far more comfortable and confident on the ball with Judge, Swift and Woods dovetailing perfectly to create the opportunities for Djuricin and, later, Hofmann.

Toumani and McCormack protected the back four who were largely untroubled throughout the entire evening.

Djuricin and Hofmann both scored excellent and well-taken opportunist goals which will do their confidence no harm either.

Kerschbaumer also put in a good shift as a late substitute, which is even more encouraging given his recent series of poor performances.

Of course we are still a long way short of where we need to be and we would be totally deluding ourselves if we felt that we are completely out of the woods yet, but let's give credit where it is due, and the situation is far, far rosier than it was five days and six points ago.

We have now gained some momentum that will hopefully be maintained over the coming weeks.

As for me, I proved that Brentford FC is not necessarily the only or most important thing in my life, although sometimes I am sure that I give the erroneous impression that that is indeed the case.

Nothing can beat family, love and a good relationship and we are looking forward to another couple of days of rest and recuperation and some more peace and quiet before we return to the madhouse that is our home at the moment.

Will I be at Charlton on Saturday though?

I certainly hope so, as a week without my Brentford fix is quite long enough!

The Good Times Are Back – 25/10/15

We shuffled into Griffin Park last Saturday with the reluctance of French aristocrats exiting the tumbrels on their way to the guillotine with the jeers of the *tricoteuses* ringing in their ears.

The season was balanced on a knife-edge and we simply did not know what to expect or how matters would turn out.

Had the international break provided new Head Coach Lee Carsley with sufficient time and opportunity to revitalise a demoralised looking squad that had disintegrated into a near-rabble and desperately lacked fitness, confidence, structure and organisation?

Eight days, three wins and nine points later we have had our answer and today the world is a far cheerier place for everyone associated with Brentford FC.

What a week it has been for us as we have in turn seen off the challenge of Rotherham, Wolves and now Charlton Athletic, scored seven times, conceded only once, kept two consecutive clean sheets and now find ourselves safely ensconced in twelfth place, in mid-table and we can now start looking up rather than down.

I arrived at Griffin Park last Saturday with minimal and limited expectations and would have been happy with a return of four points from the nine on offer over the coming week.

If truth be told, I had a recurring nightmare that we would end up with only one or two, so to end up with nine is an incredible achievement that is quite above and beyond my wildest dreams.

The amazing happenings of the past three games take me back to the same weekend last year when we were in practically the same place in the league.

A listless performance and a fully deserved defeat to a poor Bolton team led to some soul searching on the long, bleak journey home, and with Alan McCormack also lost to a serious ankle injury we next faced three seemingly insuperable hurdles within a week in the shape of Derby County, Nottingham Forest and Millwall.

We feared the worst but emerged with flying colours and came of age as a Championship team after three brilliant and unforeseen victories which saw Andre Gray establish himself as a forward of pace and deadly menace, and the impetus from our success paved the way to our eventual playoff challenge.

It is a really big ask to expect a similar outcome this season but we have certainly made a massive and praiseworthy recovery after a horrendous and appalling September when it looked as if the Bees were in free fall and looked likely to plummet into the relegation zone from where it would be extremely tough to emerge.

There were many reasons for our poor start to the season which have been well documented previously, so I will instead discuss what has brought about this recovery and, more importantly, whether it can it be sustained?

Quite simply we are looking like a totally different team than the one that struggled so desperately under Marinus Dijkhuizen last month. Lee Carsley has overseen a total sea change and the team now looks compact, organised, fit and bursting with confidence. Players know their roles and are encouraging and congratulating each other and also reminding everyone of their specific responsibilities.

If a gap emerges then there is somebody there immediately to fill it and cover his teammate. Everyone is pressing and tackling back, opponents are given no time to settle on the ball and, most crucially, we are moving and passing the ball quickly and sharply and finding gaps in our opponents' defence.

These are definitely the signs of a successful team that is enjoying itself again and the style and quality of the football being played reflects this too.

Sergi Canos started the match against Rotherham but otherwise the team has remained unchanged with a strict 4-2-3-1 formation employed. The midfield has been our real strength with Diagouraga and McCormack anchoring and supporting the back four whilst still having the freedom and flexibility to move forward when the opportunity arises.

Alan McCormack made a triumphant return to The Valley – one of his less successful stopping off points in his long and illustrious career, and he ignored the jeers of his erstwhile supporters to drive the Bees forward and he almost scored an unforgettable goal which would have guaranteed him his bragging rights, when his rasping twenty-five yarder rebounded clear off the underside of the crossbar.

Ryan Woods has found a home on the right side of midfield where he dovetailed perfectly with the ever-improving Nico Yennaris, and he is another who has helped to revitalise the team with his energy and all action style coupled with his intelligent use of the ball. There is so much more to come from him too.

John Swift has quickly become an automatic choice on the left side of midfield. He is tall, rangy and full of running, plays with his head up, glides effortlessly past opponents and is always looking for a defence splitting pass. He also relishes a good strong tackle and is no shrinking violet.

Swift is already becoming a massive influence on the team and marked an excellent performance with a well-taken headed goal from Alan Judge's perfect curling cross.

That leads us to Alan Judge who is quite simply playing the best football of his career and is totally irreplaceable as the talisman of the team.

In the last three games he has scored three times and assisted on three other goals too. He is on the verge of international recognition and his recent performances demonstrate his sheer determination to earn that elusive first cap. He is playing at a different level to his teammates and is an utter inspiration.

Yesterday he and McCormack combined perfectly before he cut inside and curled a wonderful shot just inside the far post for a goal of awesome quality and confidence.

For the third goal he seized on a loose ball just outside our own penalty area, headed the ball past an opponent, showed instant control whilst under challenge before pinging a perfect fifty yard pass directly to the feet of Lasse Vibe who cut inside and buried the ball inside Henderson's near post.

Those two goals highlighted our pace, energy and enthusiasm and demonstrated just how quickly we are now able to turn defence into attack and how we seem to have regained our speed of thought and action.

The five-man midfield has worked perfectly in the last two away games as we have dominated in terms of numbers and possession as well as in our ability to snuff out danger and launch dangerous counter attacks.

It remains to be seen whether we will retain this formation in home games when we are expected to set the tone and take the attack to the opposition rather than counter their moves as we do when we play away. Canos would be the obvious replacement for Toumani, however I would leave well alone as the current system is working so well.

Djuricin is also improving his match fitness and he worked tirelessly at Charlton. He is looking better in every game and I think that the best is yet to come from him. Hofmann and Vibe have both come on as late substitutes recently and scored well-taken and important goals and they and Kerschbaumer are benefiting from having more experienced players around them and being allowed to develop and grow into the English game at their own pace rather than being allowed to sink or swim before they are ready.

Yesterday could have ended totally differently had Charlton taken the four gilt-edged opportunities that they squandered in the opening fifteen minutes. As it was Brentford escaped unscathed from those early scares and slowly grew into the game before taking over and totally dominating proceedings. As Mark Warburton used to say, the margins between success and failure in this unforgiving division can be so narrow.

Finally it appears that the luck has changed and that things are beginning to go our way. That coupled with tons of hard work and organisation allied to the enthusiasm of youth has enabled us to arrest what appeared to be an irrevocable slump and our season has turned around.

There is so much to look forward to with the prospect of Jota, McEachran, Colin, Saunders and Macleod returning to fitness and further replenishing our once depleted squad over the next month or so.

To make the last week even better, the Development Squad also won twice with Sam Saunders scoring three times including two trademark free kicks and Lewis Macleod is also knocking at the door after two recent goals including a searing thirty-yard winner on Friday against Bristol City.

The good times are on their way back to Griffin Park and what a week lies ahead of us with Queens Park Rangers to come next Friday.

I can't wait!

The Paul Williams and Lee Carsley Brains Trust in action

Shared Thoughts – 27/10/15

It is amazing how quickly things have turned around and how our spirits have been revived. That is what three wins in a week can do for you particularly as they came at a time when it was hard to see any light at the end of a particularly dark tunnel.

My delight and excitement was shared by all my regular correspondents:

Michael Ohl was bubbling over with happiness:

I have to say the turnaround is nothing short of miraculous, how a team essentially with the same players can be so different. Clearly the talent is there, yes, the opposition as we can see is struggling as much as we were, but even so . . . and whilst things might have been different if Charlton had taken their chances, who is to say the final outcome would have been different?

We just don't know and I don't think we can take away all the credit that is due to the team. Also, Lee Carsley must take a lot of the credit.

I really am looking forward to this Friday's game.

Alan Dally was a bit perplexed and struggling to understand why things had changed so quickly:

What a strange game football is.

From a very nervy and in honesty a somewhat fortunate win against Rotherham, we seem to have grown massively in confidence. As many said at the time the result was far more important than the performance. It also had an instant positive impact on the belief of the players, as we put in a very professional performance against Wolves and ran out deserved winners. Then after a slow start at The Valley we eventually controlled the game and were comfortable winners.

I take my hat off to Lee Carsley who has obviously addressed the problem areas and we are starting to look like a decent team again. I personally don't see us being as impressive as last season, but compared to a few weeks ago, just like the players, I am also growing in confidence.

Long may it continue, especially this coming Friday, as I so dearly want to beat the rabble from Shepherd's Bush.

beesyellow22 as is his custom, tried to analyse the reasons for our success:

Same comments as above, really. What a truly miraculous turn around in a remarkably short space of time. I can do nothing other than take my hat off to Lee Carsley and the players. Brilliant stuff.

The standout things for me are as follows:

1. *The 4-2-3-1 formation, with no recognised wide players – yet Diagouraga, McCormack, Woods, Swift and Judge have all been absolutely outstanding in the last two games, providing energy, width, pace, power and outstanding attacking intent*

2. *The form of Alan Judge. Never has he more rightly deserved the moniker of the "Irish Messi"*

3. *The transformation of Nico Yennaris. Still early days and presumably Colin will be knocking at the door once fit, but again, well done to Lee Carsley for seeing something in a player many of us had written off long ago*

4. *The sudden resilience of the back four. Two clean sheets in a row – fantastic*

5. *The increased strength of the squad once Jota, Macleod, Colin, Saunders, McEachran return. Dare we even dream of the playoffs or better*

Like everyone else, I can't wait for Friday! The confidence is back, the energy levels are up and we all feel that we can beat anyone!

We don't know who our manager will be this time next year, but let's relish what's happening right now and rise to the challenge of QPR as one!

Rebel Bee had his own explanation for the improvement in our results:

An excellent summary and I agree with all the great comments too, beesyellow22 has nailed it with his five key points. We love football so much because it can do this to you like no other sport - desperation to elation in a week!

We've all had differing opinions over what has gone on at Griffin Park over the past months, it's been emotional and we've fallen out with our own at times.

Barring a few on both sides of the debates I felt a sense of healing and togetherness in the stand on Saturday – ironic that it should come at the very place where the cracks opened so nastily a few short months ago.

That's the first time I've seen us win at The Valley and it was so worth the wait. We were superb after that dodgy first few minutes. Such a good away day there, and to play well in an iconic old London stadium left me feeling drained and emotional.

Whilst Judge will deservedly get the headlines, huge credit goes to the other boys in midfield, and in particular to Alan Mac, who had possibly his finest game in a Bees shirt.

I now feel it was a brave and correct call to make the managerial change, it wasn't nice how it went down but it has potentially saved the season.

Some won't like this fact, but Lee Carsley has gone back to basics, playing a largely British team who look fitter and happier than a month back – confidence and passion abundant and the foreign boys are correctly being drip-fed into the Championship, some may turn out OK – others won't.

We have turned a corner but mustn't get carried away, we've taken three scalps at just the right time, but far bigger tests await us in the next two games at Griffin Park.

Greville could I possibly ask that you work your magic on a fitting piece ahead of the QPR game?

I was trying to explain to some of our younger fans why to many Bees they are our bitter rivals – not Fulham or others.

It needs the historical context and facts to be explained properly as so many just don't know what went down back in the 60s. You have the knowledge and the writing ability to do this justice.

No pressure then and I am girding my loins preparatory to writing something about our rivalry with QPR and why it is so deep-felt and intense.

Let me end with an enthusiastic comment from **Richard Poole** who also has some salutary words of warning for us all:

I am writing this from far away but I am so happy for my Bees and, if you remember, I commented quite a while ago about how difficult it is for foreign players to accustom themselves to our way of football and to living in a foreign land – remember Betinho last season!

I am also glad to see some youthful passion and enthusiasm in the side.

I so wish I could see Friday's match against THEM but there is no chance marooned out here in France. But all the same I will look out and hope for good news, but remember that football is a funny game so let's not get too carried away at the moment!

Brentford v QPR – The Rivalry! – 29/10/15

The tension and excitement are already building in advance of tomorrow's local derby against Queens Park Rangers.

Last season's matches against Fulham were eagerly awaited and anticipated and the celebrations went on long into the night when we completed the double over our near neighbours and joy was unconfined with Jota becoming an instant hero with his two unforgettable last second strikes.

That being said there are many Brentford supporters, in particular those of a slightly older vintage, who look upon the Fulham games as a mere taster for the main course – the clashes against QPR.

Why is that the case and how did the rivalry develop?

The first and most obvious reason is the proximity of both clubs to each other as Griffin Park is a mere four-and-a-half miles away from Loftus Road, as the crow flies.

Families in Acton, Ealing and Chiswick would grow up either as Bees or Rangers fans and there was a good-natured rivalry with some supporters attending the home matches of both teams at a time when it was less common to travel in large numbers to away games.

As the Bees fell from grace after the war and stabilised in Division Two before dropping to the third tier in 1954 the paths of the two teams crossed on a regular basis throughout the 50s until indeed the mid-60s.

Honours were fairly even and the derby matches at Griffin Park would attract massive crowds of up to eighteen thousand as the two teams competed for local bragging rights.

Transfers between the clubs were not uncommon but there was much disquiet when *The Terrible Twins*, George Francis and Jim Towers were scandalously offloaded to QPR in a blatant cost-cutting move in 1961 at a time when the Bees were desperately shedding overhead when they were staring relegation to the bottom division in the face.

It just didn't seem right to see two such Brentford stalwarts wearing blue and white hoops after such long, devoted and successful careers in a red and white shirt.

There was also a swop of wingers in which we sent the veteran George McLeod to Shepherd's Bush and received the enigmatic Mark Lazarus in return.

Initially we seemed to have got by far the better part of the bargain as the *Kosher Garrincha* was an effervescent ball of fire who rampaged down the right wing and celebrated his goals with his own individual lap of honour and then by shaking hands with members of the crowd.

He became an instant hero with the Brentford fans but apparently fell out with the club after a petty dispute over a bonus payment that he felt entitled to. As a man of principle and also not one to argue with given his membership of a famous East London boxing family, he returned in high dudgeon to Loftus Road where he helped inspire Rangers to a League Cup victory and two promotions.

The ill-feeling and antipathy were raised to a fever pitch when early in 1967 at a time when Brentford were languishing in Division Four and a Rodney Marsh inspired QPR team was scoring one hundred and three goals on its way to winning the Division Three Championship and League Cup double, news broke totally out of the blue that plans were afoot for QPR to take over Brentford and move to Griffin Park with the Bees disappearing into oblivion.

Dennis Signy was General Manager at Brentford before later joining QPR and he was a close bystander to the entire shenanigans. He was interviewed many years later for the *Vital QPR* website which I would like to thank for reproducing extracts from his interview where he reminisced about the incredible happenings of that time:

The biggest story of my career over sixty years in newspapers and football came in 1967 ... the QPR bid to take over Brentford.

The headline story went round the world yet, strangely for me, I did not write a word on the subject. I was General Manager of Brentford at the time – in fact, I started the whole saga.

It was a chance remark I made to QPR Chairman Jim Gregory that sparked off the soccer sensation of 1967. Billy Gray was my team manager at Brentford – having turned down an offer from Alec Stock to join him with Rangers – and he and I were standing in Ellerslie Road waiting for my wife to arrive for a game against Carlisle United, when we saw Jim.

The previous Saturday Bernard Joy, the famous ex-player who wrote so authoritatively over the years for the Evening Standard, had produced a feature on the old theme of ground sharing and had linked Brentford and QPR as logical clubs to tie up.

Jim asked: "How many do you think we'll get tonight" I told him: "I don't know – about eighteen thousand. If you were playing at Griffin Park you'd get thirty thousand."

From that casual remark we progressed to a discussion on Joy's ground-sharing theme and, when Jim Gregory said that he might be interested in pursuing this further I said I would mention it to my chairman, Jack Dunnett, Brentford's MP Chairman.

I did – and that started the train of events that led to the eventual take-over bid. The two chairmen went into the appeals of ground sharing but moved on to discuss the possibility of Rangers buying the Brentford ground whose capacity at the time was thirty-eight thousand.

Various ideas were thrashed around by the two wealthy chairmen, including Brentford using Griffin Park on alternate weeks as tenants of Rangers.

I remember sitting in on some of the preliminary discussions as a modestly paid journalist who had moved into football management and knew more about headlines than balance sheets. I did understand, though, that both clubs were losing money heavily.

I was fascinated hearing sums of thousands and hundreds of thousands of pounds being bandied about between the Mayfair solicitor who was my chairman and the self-made millionaire from Rangers.

It was like Monopoly – with real money. I used to smile at being asked to intervene with important decisions.

The discussions evolved into this: – Rangers were to buy Griffin Park for two hundred and twenty thousand pounds and were to sell Loftus Road to the council for three hundred and ten thousand pounds. The ninety thousand pound surplus was intended to be used to improve Griffin Park.

I was to be in publicity and fund-raising projects.

What was not known even when the story broke in the newspapers and on radio and television was that the two clubs were UNDER CONTRACT. After the breakdown of the merger talks Jim Gregory had proposed to Jack Dunnett: "We'll buy you out, shares, ground, the players, the lot."

The deal was announced with Alec Stock to be overall manager and Billy Gray and Bill Dodgin the coaches.

The Daily Mail headlined: "Fans call it a sell-out." The Daily Mirror: "Goodbye, Brentford."

The next crowd at Griffin Park was a best-of-season ten and a half thousand and the fans left us in no doubt what they thought of the idea. "Who done it? Dunnett dunnit" was the poster I remember.

To cut it short, it never went through and I resigned some weeks later and Billy Gray followed me out of Griffin Park when Dunnett handed over to new chairman Ron Blindell.

Would it have been such a bad thing? I recall Alec Stock's words: "This would be a great thing for us. If agreement is reached it will mean that we have a first-class ground for what is already a first-class team." Jim Gregory said: "Economically it was a good proposition for Rangers."

That is the whole point – it was a wonderful deal for QPR and one that would have brought about the demise of Brentford FC.

Now does everybody begin to understand why there is such antipathy felt by so many Brentford fans towards our neighbours from Shepherd's Bush who were actively plotting to kill us and put us out of business less than fifty years ago?

What is far worse is that the whole appalling idea was welcomed and encouraged by our own Chairman, Jack Dunnett, who was looking for a way out of the club after he became the Member of Parliament for Nottingham Central after the 1964 general election and his extravagant expenditure on players over the previous few years had failed to pay off with the anticipated reward of promotion to the top two divisions.

A couple of years ago Dave Lane, Mark Croxford and I interviewed Jack Dunnett who although aged ninety-one was spry and fit with a handshake like a vice and here are his detailed recollections of what happened after the news was made public:

I did consider the views of the fans and I said that I would hold some public meetings. I'd seen enough of football supporters to know that it would be seen as a very unusual move but it had a lot of economic benefits.

I did have some misgivings so I called a public meeting and around a thousand people turned up. I'd already announced what it was about and I'd made it clear what we were considering.

At the meeting, the fans wouldn't have it and in fact it got so bad that I had to tell Denis Piggott to call the police and twelve policemen came to the ground to rescue me. I really did feel threatened.

I went onto the pitch with a microphone but I wasn't really able to get my message across. It was very difficult.

With hindsight, I might have suggested that the supporters should have selected a small group of representatives to come and speak with me. I remember Peter Pond-Jones, he was a difficult man. He just didn't even want to consider the idea.

The reaction of the fans did surprise me somewhat because here I was, in good faith, trying to do something which would give the club a future. I think I was right too – how many times since 1967 have Queens Park Rangers not been in the top divisions?

Within ten years Jim was in the First Division and finished second, they were in Europe and did fantastically well. If the amalgamation had gone through, Brentford would have been swept up in that.

I didn't really care about whether QPR would have taken up more of the new club than Brentford – we'd have still been playing at Griffin Park. I wouldn't have been chairman of the new club as that would have been Jim Gregory. I'd have been a director.

My objective was to secure a future for Brentford but without me having to run up and down between Nottingham and London.

I don't recall that Brentford were losing all that much money at the time. We had a good commercial set-up but we didn't have a surplus of money that would have enabled us to buy players. We certainly weren't in danger of going out of business, there's no way I would have allowed that to have happened.

I don't think we could have sold the idea to the fans in a different sort of way. I spoke to some supporters after tempers had cooled down and it was apparent that they just didn't want to be associated with their nearest rivals. Eventually, I could understand that but the main thing for me was to be able to progress through the divisions, to get to the First Division.

The fans seemed to want to rather stay where they were, at the bottom of the Fourth Division, than amalgamate with our rivals and get into the First Division, which I couldn't understand at the time and still don't understand.

When we started discussing it, it looked to be a good deal to me.

I know that football fans are passionate about their club but to me, doing well means seeing my club go up the leagues and if it isn't ever going to happen, then what's the point? In those days, with a slice of luck and if you were well managed, a small club could go right up to the First Division. I proved that with Notts County.

I don't think I would have benefitted financially. I didn't care whether I got my investment back or not. I hadn't paid money that I couldn't afford and my business was doing well at the time.

Anyway, I was all set to carry on with things continuing as they were and then out of the blue I got a telephone call from Ron Blindell who had been chairman at Plymouth Argyle. He asked if he could see me and when I asked why, he said that he was interested in buying Brentford.

He said he thought he could do better with Brentford than he'd done with Plymouth although I'm not sure how he came to that conclusion.

I told him that it would take a good bit of money to move the club on and that he'd also have to buy me out but he said he could find the money. I'll never forget that we were having a cup of tea or coffee and I told him the figure we were talking about and he dropped his little gold pencil in surprise because the sum was much larger than he'd realised.

But he agreed and it was duly announced and he took over weeks later. As soon as the Brentford fans had made it clear they were against the amalgamation, the deal was dead as far as I was concerned.

I didn't try to push it further. Jim Gregory understood the position too. It had been a great idea though and well planned apart from agreeing the name for the club but I wouldn't have gone through with it without Brentford being mentioned in the name.

There is so much that I could write about my feelings regarding Jack Dunnett's words and how they clearly demonstrate his total lack of understanding about how supporters feel and their passion for their club and their determination for it to retain its individual identity.

We wanted a Brentford team wearing red and white stripes to be playing at Griffin Park – not some bastard child amalgam.

I will simply let his comments speak for themselves.

On Thursday the twenty-third of February 1967, Jack Dunnett resigned as Chairman and a new board, headed by Ron Blindell, assumed control of the club, with Blindell's personal financial commitment amounting to one hundred and forty-five thousand pounds.

Brentford FC had been saved, not without a massive fight and the efforts of so many unsung heroes amongst our supporters who were determined to ensure their club's survival.

Austerity though was the rule for the next few years as a huge debt had to be repaid and we were forced to operate with a skeleton playing squad.

After 1965/66 when Brentford hammered QPR by six goals to one on the first day of a season that saw the Bees relegated – *It's Brentford innit*, our paths did not cross again on the field until the early part of the current century when we played each other for three seasons.

QPR were on the upwards slope and established themselves as a top division team, we hovered in the nether regions, simply trying to stay alive.

Occasionally we would sign some of their castoffs and rejects and in return we sold them our shining star in Andy Sinton, thus sabotaging our late season playoff push in 1989.

We had a young Les Ferdinand on loan who was a mere shadow of the player he eventually became and other names such as Mark Hill and Mark Fleming will hardly be fondly remembered by Bees fans.

In 2002 we came so close to promotion but fell just short, not helped by dropping two vital points at Loftus Road in the last-but-one game of a momentous season.

Who can ever forget Mark McCammon's late header bouncing down and then over the crossbar from almost underneath it?

The final nail in the coffin of our relationship was hammered in by Martin Rowlands, for so long a crowd favourite at Griffin Park with his dynamic midfield play.

His last couple of seasons were dogged by injury and his performances suffered. He eventually left for QPR on a Bosman free transfer and when his new team narrowly defeated a severely weakened Brentford team by one goal to nil after a tough encounter at Loftus Road he marked the result by goading and taunting the long-suffering Brentford fans by parading in front of them and kissing the Rangers badge on his shirt. This went down as well as you would expect, could easily have caused a riot, and he has never been forgiven for his actions.

With the exception of two glorious matches at Griffin Park back in 1965 when the Bees scored eleven goals, games that helped ensure that I became a lifetime Brentford supporter, Brentford versus QPR matches are generally tense and tight affairs with little between the two sides.

It is now fifty years since we last beat what I hope I have clearly demonstrated is the real old enemy and victory tomorrow night would be especially sweet.

The Long Good Friday! – 31/10/15

Please excuse the late appearance of this article but Friday was a long, long day.

I left what I thought was plenty of time to get to the ground as I wanted to savour the incredible atmosphere that would be generated by a packed Griffin Park – but it wasn't to be.

The North Circular was a carpark owing to an accident at Hanger Lane and we inched forward seemingly centimetre by centimetre and were getting nowhere. Nerves were fraught and things were so bad that I even contemplated abandoning the journey and making do with the televised coverage – an appalling prospect given what this game meant to all true Brentford supporters.

Fortunately my friend Ian, a died in the wool Manchester United fan, calmed me down and he knew the back doubles and we roared through an industrial estate, eventually hit the Edgware Road and after the journey from hell we left the car at Willesden Green, took the tube and finally arrived late, tired, hot and very bothered soon before kickoff.

Matters could only improve, and they certainly did so as the Bees put on a performance which incorporated an intoxicating and unstoppable combination of grit, determination, passion and organisation, tempered with no little skill and ability and they fully deserved their reward of their first victory over the old rivals, Queens Park Rangers for fifty years.

Marco Djuricin became an instant Brentford legend when he outmuscled Clint Hill and got in front of the veteran QPR defender to score emphatically at the near post from Alan Judge's perfect near post centre. Toumani Diagouraga, so imperious throughout, also deserves massive praise for his instant turn and trickery on the ball which created the space for his trademark disguised outside of the foot pass that set Judge away down the left flank.

A beautifully created and executed goal that fully deserved to win any game.

Of course Rangers had quality in their squad, but they could not match our sense of togetherness, will to win and total commitment and determination to work hard and cover for each other.

Brentford have become a team again in every sense of the word and there was also much skill on display from us as we probed for openings.

The first half was a cagey affair with neither team prepared to take chances and risk defeat. Brentford had the lion's share of possession but were unable to beat the press and get through a congested midfield.

Judge, McCormack and Swift went close but it was the visitors who eventually showed some ambition and got the skilful Phillips and Luongo on the ball. The latter hit the junction of post and crossbar with a firm header and then the inside of the far post with a curler and had either gone in then I might well be writing a totally different account today, however fortune smiled on us and we certainly deserved the rub of the green given how hard we worked throughout the match.

The second half was a totally different story as the Bees started on the front foot and Rangers were reduced to long-ball mediocrity and the imperious Dean and Tarkowski won every aerial challenge and the midfielders were always on hand to mop up the second balls.

Bidwell was exceptional, anticipating and snuffing out any danger and he finally came out on top of his tussle with the speedy Phillips and Yennaris was never noticed, evidence indeed that he has settled into his role without fuss and he performed exceptionally well on the night. He has quite clearly demonstrated how well a player can perform when he is finally given an opportunity and feels that his manager has faith in him.

Good defending requires everyone to muck in and share the load and the Bees worked in packs to press and win the ball back. It is quite noticeable that the intensity levels have risen recently and we have gone up a gear and play far more on the front foot.

We still pass the ball around the back four, probing for gaps but we have become far more risk averse, get the ball forward quicker when it is necessary to do so and we are taking less chances of turning over the ball in potentially dangerous areas of the pitch.

The other key to our success has been reverting to a five-man midfield. This means that Djuricin is forced to fend for himself and chase scraps but he never stopped putting himself about and he worked tirelessly and made a total nuisance of himself. He also had the energy and increased fitness levels to retain his composure in front of goal when the opportunities came.

He took his goal beautifully, anticipating the centre quicker than his opponent and having the strength to ward off the physical challenge of his marker. He also came close immediately after halftime when he was left in space from McCormack's clever flick and Green brilliantly saved his instant volley.

Diagouraga and McCormack covered each other and worked hard to win the ball back and then use it effectively and Judge, Swift and Woods dovetailed well, switching positions and ensuring that we won the midfield battle and showed some composure on the ball.

Ryan Woods is quickly developing into a player of real quality. He plays with his head up, rarely gives the ball away and wins far more than his fair share of challenges.

The three substitutes Kerschbaumer, Vibe and Hofmann also provided evidence that they are all finally coming to grips with the demands of the Championship and provided fresh impetus when they came off the bench.

Most encouragingly the penny seems to have dropped with Hofmann and he used his size and strength to good effect and held the ball up well.

Alan Judge was substituted late on with a tight hamstring which might require an enforced rest but what a month the effervescent bundle of energy has enjoyed with three goals and four assists in his last four games.

Championship Player of the Month perhaps? And what about the reluctant hero, Lee Carsley? He still insists that he sees his future in coaching and that he is simply keeping the seat warm for a more experienced manager.

That might well be the case but the truth is that the players trust and respect him and have bought in totally to the methods and pattern of play that he and his coaching staff have introduced.

Remember that incredible November last year when Andre Gray won the Player of the Month Award and Mark Warburton was named as Manager of the Month? Perhaps history will repeat itself shortly with both Judge and Carsley?

Exciting times indeed and proof that two weeks is an extremely long time in football, as a mere fortnight ago we were in the depths of despair and were anticipating a horrid looking clash with relegation rivals Rotherham with apprehension and pessimism and with the abyss of the bottom three looming before us.

Now four consecutive wins and twelve glorious points later we have been catapulted into the top ten in the Championship table and are now beginning to look at the playoff places rather than the bottom three.

Proof indeed of the narrow margins in football and the massively competitive nature of the Championship.

I was a young impressionable schoolboy back in August 1965 and still remember the sense of wonder and excitement of being taken by my father to Griffin Park for the opening day of the season clash with our neighbours QPR.

I left the stadium skipping and jumping for joy after we had demolished our rivals and put six goals past the helpless Frank Smith. It has been a long, long wait for that feeling to be repeated.

The journey home last night was equally arduous and interminable but it really did not matter as I was floating on air and our long wait was finally over. Brentford had defeated Queens Park Rangers.

I have waited over fifty years to write those words. The victory meant so much to me and I know it did the same to so many other Brentford supporters.

What a wonderful evening!

Marco Djuricin becomes an instant Brentford Legend

Position	Team	P	W	D	L	F	A	GD	Pt	Form
1	Brighton and Hove A	14	8	6	0	19	11	8	30	D D W W D D
2	Hull City	14	8	4	2	21	8	13	28	D W D W W W
3	Burnley	14	8	4	2	20	13	7	28	L W W D W W
4	Middlesbrough	14	8	3	3	23	9	14	27	W L D L W W
5	Derby County	14	7	6	1	21	10	11	27	W W W D W W
6	Birmingham City	14	7	3	4	19	15	4	24	W W W W L L
7	Reading	14	6	5	3	21	13	8	23	W W W D L D
8	Sheffield Wednesday	14	6	5	3	19	16	3	23	W W D D W W
9	Cardiff City	14	5	7	2	15	11	4	22	W D D W D D
10	Fulham	14	5	5	4	26	20	6	20	L D D D W W
11	Brentford	14	6	2	6	20	20	0	20	L L W W W W
12	Queens Park Rangers	14	5	4	5	22	23	-1	19	L W L D W L
13	Wolverhampton Wndrs	14	5	3	6	20	20	0	18	W W L L L W
14	Ipswich Town	14	4	6	4	16	21	-5	18	D L D L D D
15	Blackburn Rovers	14	3	6	5	14	14	0	15	D W L D L W
16	Huddersfield Town	14	3	5	6	14	18	-4	14	D L D W L L
17	Nottingham Forest	14	3	5	6	11	15	-4	14	D L L D D L
18	Preston North End	14	2	7	5	10	13	-3	13	D L D W D D
19	Leeds United	14	2	7	5	12	19	-7	13	L L L D D L
20	Milton Keynes Dons	14	3	2	9	12	21	-9	11	L D W L L L
21	Bristol City	14	2	5	7	16	26	-10	11	D D W L D L
22	Bolton Wanderers	14	1	7	6	10	20	-10	10	D L L L D D
23	Charlton Athletic	14	2	4	8	11	24	-13	10	L D L L L L
24	Rotherham United	14	2	3	9	15	27	-12	9	W L L D L L

[31st October 2015]

November

Hull City – A Tough Nut To Crack – 2/11/15

Hull City come to Griffin Park on Tuesday night bang in form as they are unbeaten in eight games and they sit proudly in second place in the Championship table and look certain to mount a strong promotion push in an effort to regain their recently lost Premier League place.

They are certain to provide tough opposition but the Bees are none too shabby themselves at the moment given their four consecutive wins and three clean sheets on the spin. They will also be bursting with confidence after that momentous first win in fifty years over close rivals Queens Park Rangers as our supporters almost blew the roof off at Griffin Park with their celebrations on Friday night.

There is further spice to the proceedings given the early return of Moses Odubajo following his controversial three and a half million pound move to the visitors just before the start of the season and Hull also made repeated efforts to divest us of Andre Gray before being pipped at the post by Burnley.

Some Bees supporters queried why Moses and Andre would even contemplate joining a team like Hull but the reasons were pretty clear to me. Despite their relegation last season they have retained a massive squad packed with Premier League experience and, buttressed by their parachute payments, they are able to make financial offers to prospective new signings that dwarf anything that we are able to put on the table.

Anyone who thinks that we are a bigger club than Hull City is totally deluding himself and that situation cannot conceivably change until we have moved into our new stadium at Lionel Road and ideally won promotion to the Premier League.

Our prospects against them depend to a large degree on the strength of the team that we are able to field. Friday's match will have taken a lot out of us and there are sure to have been a lot of bumps and bruises that will need shaking off.

The inspirational Alan Judge, the fulcrum for so much of our recent success, was forced off late on with a tight hamstring and we will miss him desperately if he is not risked on the night. Better though perhaps that he misses only one match rather than several if he does further damage to himself. He will also be looking forward to a potential return to his old stamping ground at Blackburn on Saturday as well as the two crucial Republic of Ireland playoff matches too. Personally I very much doubt that he will play against Hull City.

The squad is getting stronger by the week and if Alan doesn't play then it will be interesting to see who replaces him with Sergi Canos and the improving Konstantin Kerschbaumer both in the frame. Canos is largely untested and unpredictable but he possesses that spark of creativity and individual genius that could make something happen for us and he would be the brave selection choice. Lasse Vibe might also have a case too depending on how Lee Carsley decides to set us up on the night.

Hull have generally had the better of things against us but there have been several memorable clashes in fairly recent times that still stir the emotions.

Surely none of the near eleven and a half thousand fans present will ever forget Brentford's rampant performance in a Football League Cup Second Round tie in September 1968? Fourth Division Bees blew their Second Division opponents away and flying winger Allan Mansley was unstoppable as he celebrated his recent twenty-first birthday with two goals in a wonderful and unexpected three – nil victory which saw the Bees defeat Hull for the first time in eighteen meetings. It was an incredible night of high drama and excitement with the supporters barely believing what they were witnessing.

Our next cup meeting in 1971 ended far less happily and in highly controversial circumstances when two late goals gave Hull an extremely fortunate FA Cup Fifth Round win over a brave and resilient Brentford team that deserved far, far better on the day. Bobby Ross put us ahead with a classic diving header from John Docherty's cross and Brian Turner's shot which would almost certainly have sealed another giant killing cruelly clanged back off the post before a Hull equaliser that came against the run of play after a poor defensive clearance. Ken Houghton's winning goal was dubious in the extreme after a dubious aerial challenge on Gordon Phillips that was surely a foul and goalkeeper Ian McKechnie taking far more than the permitted four steps before whacking his clearance downfield. The rotund keeper then piled insult onto injury by celebrating the winner with a somersault.

The local paper report lyrically summed up our feelings far better than I possibly can:

Such a sense of outrage and grievance among the stricken, silent supporters of Brentford as they gazed despairingly at a Boothferry Park arena which had been so unbelievably vindictive.

Six thousand seven hundred and ninety-three fans filed into a chilly Griffin Park in December 1979 totally unaware of the drama that was to follow. The Bees had lost their two previous games and changes were afoot, one of which saw the reintroduction of striker Bob Booker who had signed for the club a year earlier in return for a set of tracksuits and had done little or nothing since then to suggest that we had not overpaid for his signature.

Freshly returned from a confidence boosting loan spell at Barnet, he seized his opportunity and scored three times in an amazing seven – two victory over a shell-shocked Hull City team. The rest as they say is history as Bob went on to become a Brentford legend.

Our title winning team of 1991/92 was also potent in front of goal and we took Hull City apart at Griffin Park early in the season with a four-goal salvo before halftime. The best attempt didn't count after Marcus Gayle almost broke the net with an indirect free kick and needed to have the rules gently explained to him as he cavorted in glee and wondered why nobody else was joining him in his wild celebration.

Squad rotation is traditionally something that is reserved for the upper echelons of the game but Brentford rested nine of their normal team for the last league game of the season in May 2005. The opportunity presented itself as Hull had already confirmed their promotion and the Bees had earned their playoff place with a last-gasp winner at Wrexham in the preceding match.

Chris Hargreaves and Jay Tabb were joined by such luminaries as Jerrome Sobers, Charlie Ide, George Moleski and Ryan Watts and the Brentford team included no less than six debutants. Despite trailing to an early goal the young Bees ran, chased and harried and their efforts were rewarded with a headed goal from a corner by Sobers whose only Football League game this was to be. Not a bad way to both start and finish a career. Remarkably Jay Tabb won the game for the Bees with a beautifully taken late solo goal and over nine thousand fans went home happy although Sheffield Wednesday and our customary playoff oblivion lurked in waiting just around the corner!

As for Tuesday, hopefully there will be a five-figure crowd, as the Bees deserve a near full house given their recent efforts and success. Hull have the resources and strength in depth to rest players and utilise their entire squad. We have had an extra day's rest and need to take full advantage of the additional recovery time and hope that Hull are also fatigued after their second long journey in a few days after comfortably disposing of MK Dons on Saturday.

This will be a tough challenge for Brentford and I can only anticipate thrills and spills given the history of our previous encounters with The Tigers.

A Different League – 4/11/15

Sometimes you win a match but deep down you know that you were lucky and that the result was a travesty and a distortion of reality.

I can still quite clearly remember a Huddersfield team brilliantly marshalled by the gifted Chris Marsden playing us off the park at Griffin Park back in October 1990. Luckily that was at a time well before the obsession for collecting match statistics came into vogue and the possession figures remain shrouded in mystery.

Fortunate indeed for the Bees who were pushed back for the entire ninety minutes and relied on Graham Benstead and stand-in central defender Simon Ratcliffe to keep the visitors at bay. Having absorbed everything our dominant visitors could throw at us, Ratcliffe's long ball forward with six minutes to go found Eddie May who finished clinically and we had stolen all three points.

Conversely you can lose a game and still come away satisfied at a job well done and at a more than decent performance that bodes well for the future.

Last night was a case in point as Hull City finally emerged as victors by two goals to nil but only after being decidedly second best for the entire first half to a Bees team who played excellent, slick, passing football and really should have been leading at the interval.

The second half told a different tale as our highflying visitors finally creaked into gear and took total control and eventually fully deserved their victory.

There is an old expression – *never give a sucker an even break*, and quite frankly, we let Hull off the hook. We played really excellently in the first half, kept possession well and created several clear opportunities which were all spurned by Djuricin, Vibe and Woods.

McGregor made three excellent saves but he should have been left helpless on at least one occasion. Vibe too had a more than decent shout for a penalty when his shirt was tugged as he ran through but his appeal fell on deaf ears.

Djuricin also created space for himself right after the break but scuffed his shot wide and then Hull took over. They began to take control of the midfield and both full backs overlapped with menace.

We were forced back and smothered with all our out balls covered and we found it hard to get out of our own half of the field although we contributed to our own downfall by constantly giving the ball away to our opponents.

The goal finally came when the excellent Clucas combined well with Robertson and when McCormack fatally stopped his covering run, the fullback strode on unchallenged to thrash the ball past Button who was beaten at his near post.

Vibe had been replaced by Kerschbaumer to help address our problems in midfield and the substitute came so close to equalising when after Tarkowski made a rousing forward run, his beautifully taken instant volley from outside the area seemed a goal all the way but frustratingly bounced clear off the post and the rebound was skied over by Woods.

We wasted a free kick for a back pass well inside the area, which caused much merriment as Hull raged at the referee for his decision, but otherwise that was that and we were left to appreciate Hull's dominance with substitutes Huddlestone and Diamé a class above anything we could offer.

They saw the game out comfortably and deserved their second goal scored late on by Clucas after a short corner.

A short while ago there was uproar amongst some Brentford fans at the prospect of Moses Odubajo leaving us for Hull City who they considered to be a smaller club than us. Last night I am sure finally dispelled that ridiculous assertion.

Hull City took in over sixty-six million pounds last season from television rights payments and will be the recipients of sixty-four million pounds in parachute payments over the next four years following their relegation from the Premier League.

Their starting eleven cost about thirty-five million pounds in transfer fees and their three substitutes another eleven million. Every time they brought in a replacement (with the exception, of course of the clumsy Harry Maguire) they improved and went up a gear.

They simply had far too much in their armoury for us and we did so well to match them, and indeed, outplay them for half of the match.

By way of comparison, our team cost well under three and a half million pounds and I am sure that their wage bill exceeds ours by a quite laughable amount.

No wonder Moses decided to forgo the social delights of London and join them. He will quite possibly be celebrating promotion next May, his bank balance will have been swollen and he will be a part of a massively strong squad packed full of internationals. What's there not to like?

That being said there was much to be happy about last night. We more than matched one of the best teams in our division for long periods and imposed our own style of football upon them.

We have regained much of the confidence that was lost after our stuttering start to the season and there are several subtle changes to our approach that have become evident now that Lee Carsley has had time for his influence to take effect.

We press far higher up the pitch and generally show far more energy and bite in our efforts to regain possession. Our fitness levels have gone up a notch or two and we are no longer running out of steam. We still pass the ball around in our own defensive area but we are taking fewer risks and are getting the ball forward quicker with Button kicking the ball more often.

We are packing the midfield which enables us to keep possession for longer periods but McCormack, Woods and Swift are quick to get upfield in support of the lone striker, Djuricin.

In other words we are no longer a soft touch and are well able to compete within this tough division.

We achieved all this last night without our most influential player, Alan Judge, and for half the match we barely missed him. Good news indeed as it confirms just how well the entire team is playing. Of course we could have done with his industry and imagination as it might well have made the difference between us going in goalless at the interval and enjoying a confidence boosting halftime lead.

There is talk that he might be back on Saturday when I am sure that he will be keen to show everybody at Blackburn Rovers that they were wrong to let him go. He will then be off with the Republic of Ireland squad for their two crucial Euro 2016 playoff clashes. That elusive first cap is not too far away!

Like every other Bees fan, I don't like losing games, but there is a way to lose, and last night was one of those occasions when despite the final result there were so many positives to take out of the entire proceedings – a bit like after the Norwich clash at Griffin Park last season.

We lose, we learn, we move on. Such is the way of life in the Championship. Unlike last season when we kept doing the same things match after match, many of them, of course, really good, others less so, there is a real sense that we are far more flexible now and ready to change and adapt whenever necessary.

The future is looking bright at Griffin Park.

Nico Yennaris and Toumani Diagouraga taking care of the football

Double Celebration – 6/11/15

October was a really exhilarating month for everybody connected with Brentford FC and the recent run of success and indeed total revitalisation after a humdrum start to the season has been marked with today's announcement that Lee Carsley has been named as *Sky Bet* Championship Manager of the Month for October and, just to make things even better, Alan Judge has also become the *Sky Bet* Championship Player of the Month for October. A double celebration indeed!

If you had dared even suggest the possibility of either or both these awards coming to fruition to the bedraggled and dispirited mob of Bees fans as we wended our way home after the shambolic performance at Derby County five short weeks ago then you would have been laughed out of court.

Yet since that sad day there has been an amazing turnaround at Griffin Park with four consecutive victories followed by what can only be described as a glorious defeat by table toppers Hull City. The defence has more than done its job with three clean sheets in a row and there has been a return to the slick, confident one touch football of the Warburton era.

We are now safely ensconced in mid-table after a plunge into the relegation zone looked far more likely and our improvement and recovery were confirmed by last week's momentous victory over QPR.

Lee Carsley, the reluctant interim Head Coach has stepped up to the plate and after a shaky start when his first two games in charge were lost, he has transformed our fortunes and we now look – and are – a totally different team.

The players look a happier bunch too and are fitter and far more confident in everything they do.

Carsley and his sidekick Paul Williams have totally changed our training regime and we now look far more organised with everyone aware of their role.

We have reverted to last season's successful 4-2-3-1 formation, flood and dominate the midfield with players switching position at will and we also press far higher up the pitch to win the ball back. We have also stopped taking so many chances through overplaying at the back and get the ball forward a fair bit quicker then we have been accustomed to do.

Carsley appears to be calm and measured and has earned the respect of the squad as he is a talented coach and with forty international caps he also practised what he preaches.

Of course there will be setbacks and blips and even rocky roads ahead, but we are in safe hands at the moment and his success has bought us the time to make the correct management decision without being rushed into another poor appointment. Maybe Carsley might even change his mind and throw his cap into the ring and if he did his claims would have to be taken extremely seriously, but to paraphrase Margaret Thatcher, *this man is not for turning.*

Brentford have become a team worth watching again, with a firm sense of purpose, and much of the credit for this should go to Lee Carsley who has settled down so well into his new role.

Four wins and twelve points in October ensured that he received the coveted Manager of the Month Award and his achievement was recognised by George Burley the Chair of the *Sky Bet* Manager of the Month judging panel who made the following comment:

Lee took on the difficult task of trying to get Brentford back to the form of last season, which he has done successfully, winning the last four games.

The win over Queens Park Rangers showed the standard of football he is imposing on the team.

Pundit Don Goodman was also impressed:

The way that Lee has turned Brentford's fortunes around in such a short space of time is highly commendable.

When Marinus Dijkhuizen departed the role five weeks ago, few would have predicted that Brentford would be sitting comfortably in mid-table, or that his replacement would be picking up the October Manager of the Month award.

Brentford fans will all join me in saluting his achievement today and long may it continue.

If that was not quite enough then there is also the equally amazing achievement of Alan Judge to celebrate.

He scored three goals and assisted in four more as Brentford won four of their five Championship matches in October. He dominated almost every game in which he played and looked a class above most of his opponents.

The goals themselves were all brilliantly taken and comprised a controlled volley from outside the area, a darting header and a perfectly placed curler into the far corner.

Charlton could not get near him as he laid on two of our three goals and showed an unstoppable combination of pace, energy, vision, passing and dribbling ability as well as the ability to shoot on sight.

He missed Tuesday's defeat with a hamstring injury and is doubtful for tomorrow's match. He will then go away with the Republic of Ireland squad and that elusive first international cap cannot be far away as he is a class act.

He has regained the goal touch that eluded him last season and has relished the responsibility of being the main man in the absence of the likes of Jota. He is coming into his peak as a player and hopefully he will decide to remain with the club and sign an extension to his contract.

It is an interesting conundrum for him particularly as it is rumoured that some Premier League clubs are sniffing around him. Should he stay at Griffin Park or earn more money somewhere else but run the risk of playing less often given that he is a player who just loves to play football?

Lee Carsley spoke for us all when he commented:

I am really pleased for Alan to get this recognition and reward for his hard work. It is something he deserves. He has been the outstanding player in the Sky Bet Championship this month and his focus is now on winning this in November, December and every month.

We have spoken internally that if he wants to be a full international, the consistency he has shown in the last month has to be replicated for ten, eleven, twelve months. That is his target.

Don Goodman also sang his praises:

In the month when Alan welcomed a new addition to the Judge family, he also finishes as the Sky Bet Championship Player of the Month. His displays at the tip of the Brentford midfield diamond have been nothing short of outstanding and he has really come into his own since Lee Carsley took charge at Griffin Park.

Let's just bask in the reflected glory of these two highly prestigious awards to two such deserving candidates.

This is the twenty-third time that a Brentford manager has won this coveted award, and only three of them - Frank Blunstone, Phil Holder and Mark Warburton have lost their next match after the announcement of their award.

Let's just hope that Lee Carsley leads the Bees to at least a draw tomorrow so that we can justifiably claim that as far as Brentford is concerned the so-called curse of the Manager of the Month barely applies.

October was a wonderful month for the Bees, and as for November – who knows, but the auspices are good.

Normal Service Resumed – 8/11/15

It is always interesting and illuminating to read what the opposition fans have to say about us and the Blackburn supporters were in full voice both before and after yesterday's draw at Ewood Park.

There had been several patronising comments beforehand from various ignoramuses who belittled us and felt that a long-overdue home victory was assured given that they were playing what they felt was a smaller and less established team like Brentford who they still thought should be confined to the lower divisions – shades of last season when many clubs felt that they were demeaning themselves and sullying their hands by playing us and that they had a divine right to the three points on offer. *We are going to totally hammer them* summed up the general smug tone of the pre-match assessments and score predictions.

Their tone had changed when they came to review a game in which the Bees played most of the football and dominated for long stretches and were extremely unlucky not to have come away with a victory. Finally there was a grudging respect for the quality of Brentford's display coupled with tons of vitriol aimed at the home team and their manager Gary Bowyer, in particular.

Here are a cross-section of the comments that were made by some seriously fed up and disillusioned home supporters:

For me Brentford were by far the best team to visit Ewood Park this season. They reminded me of Bournemouth over the last couple of seasons.

We were second best today.

A fair point won against a decent and very much in-form Brentford side.

Brentford played us off the park.

It was probably a fair result. If anything Brentford were slightly the better team. Lee Carsley has done a good job as Brentford were well organised and very energetic.

Brentford played simple pass-and-move football and carved through our midfield at will.

Brentford harried us all over the pitch. In all reality, Brentford had the better chances and should have won.

As for Brentford, by far the best team I've seen at Ewood Park this season and they were far better than Burnley. They pass-and-move the ball really well and in the end I was pretty happy with the result.

I felt pleased and proud when I read these words as they reinforced what we already know, that we have witnessed a massive *renaissance* and change in the Bees over the past four weeks or so and that opposing supporters can also clearly recognise our quality.

We are no longer a soft touch or bear any resemblance to that fairly disorganised rabble which earlier this season played slow, predictable football and customarily ran out of steam long before the end of every match and were an easy prey for the predators who inhabit the Championship.

Lee Carsley and Paul Williams have stripped us bare, taken us back to basics and then put us back together again and we are slowly but surely regaining our touch and are going some way towards repeating our role as the surprise packet that we were for so much of last season.

We are trying to replicate what worked so well for us last season and are now pressing far higher up the pitch and playing simple and accurate pass-and-move football with the ball being moved quickly and slickly between a five man midfield who rotate their positions at will.

We are retaining possession but also looking to do something with the ball and create chances in the final third, as possession for possession's sake is a total waste of time. In that respect we are also getting the ball forward quicker than we have been accustomed to and there is also some pace in the team which helps us turn defence into attack.

We haven't got everything right yet as our lone striker is still far too isolated as we sometimes struggle to get sufficient midfielders into the box quickly enough to support him but chances are now being created far more regularly even though too many of them are being spurned.

Yesterday was a case in point as we let a poor Rovers team off the hook. Djuricin was injured early on and as of yet there is no news about his prognosis and his loss for any period of time would be a real blow as he has settled down well in the team. Vibe was moved upfield and he scored our goal and bothered the giant but clumsy and immobile home central defenders with his sharpness, pace and movement.

Swift's incisive and perceptive through ball gave him the chance to bundle the ball past Steele to open the scoring and we then took total command of the game and were never in any trouble until Lawrence's low, angled cross from way out on the left wing squirmed through a packed penalty area and somehow ended up in the corner of the net for an undeserved equaliser that came totally out of the blue with Button unsighted by the straining Harlee Dean..

Button was forced to turn a Marshall drive onto the post but Woods shot wide and McCormack almost restored our lead when Steele saved well from his effort.

Brentford dominated the second half with Diagouraga running the show in midfield but were unable to turn their possession into goals with Vibe and Kerschbaumer both missing excellent opportunities to regain the lead. Sam Saunders also made an effective cameo performance as a late substitute and his energy and excellent use of the ball auger well for the future.

Blackburn finally roused themselves out of their lethargy when Ben Marshall moved forward to support the attack and Button made a phenomenal late save to push his late rasping long range effort past the post and preserve our point.

So a point it was when three were really well within our grasp and we can also bemoan the absence of Alan Judge, still recovering from his tight hamstring, as his energy, vision and effervescence might well have made all the difference and helped us to the victory that we fully deserved.

The international break comes at a good time as we now have a fortnight in which a lot of tired bodies will have the chance to recover from their recent exertions. Carsley has relied upon the same bunch of players with changes kept to a minimum and he has been rewarded with a series of excellent and fully committed performances.

It is noticeable that our improvement in results and performance has coincided with Lee Carsley restoring the rump of our homegrown players with all but one of the foreign newcomers relegated to the substitutes' bench.

This has allowed them some breathing space in which they can gradually acclimatise themselves to the demands of the Championship, and it was illuminating to listen to Lasse Vibe's post-match interview in which he admitted that he was still coming to terms with what was required of him in what he now realised was a higher and far tougher standard of football than he had been accustomed to before he joined the club.

The spirit might well be willing, but the flesh is weak and the bruised and battered squad will benefit from a rest. Hopefully Judge and Djuricin will be fully fit in time for the Nottingham Forest match and ideally there will also be some good news about poor Lewis Macleod who suffered yet another injury setback in the Development Squad's win at Reading on Friday.

Sam Saunders can also work on his fitness and perhaps the likes of Jota, Colin and McEachran will also be inching their way closer to a return to full fitness.

It has been a rollercoaster ride for every Brentford fan but the tide seems to have turned in our favour recently as we have gone back to the future in our approach and, as is demonstrated by the comments of the Blackburn supporters, it is evident that normal service is gradually being resumed.

The Bees are currently the *Kings of West London* in the Championship as we are ahead of our deadly rivals QPR and Fulham who have both responded to the indignity and shame of the situation by sacking their manager.

Brentford are back!

Stick Or Twist? That Is The Question – 10/11/15

According to *Sky* sources Brentford are actively engaged in trying to recruit a new permanent Head Coach and might even be close to making an appointment.

Two names are supposedly in the frame with Gillingham manager Justin Edinburgh and Walsall's Dean Smith both apparently under serious consideration. There is also talk that we are considering a British-based foreign manager.

Who knows if there is any truth in these rumours and we've learned to our cost that you cannot discount what is being said as we are still smarting after poo-pooing and dismissing out of hand the article in *The Sun* suggesting that Marinus Dijkhuizen was on the way out and yet, despite our scepticism, he was sacked less than a week later when the general feeling was that he would be given more time to turn things around at Griffin Park.

On the surface it would appear an irrational decision to upset the applecart and make fundamental changes particularly at a time when things are going so well at the club.

Just to recap, we are coming off a month in which Lee Carsley won the Manager of the Month Award and Alan Judge was also named Player of the Month to complete an incredible winning double.

After losing his first two matches and presiding over two appallingly insipid performances against Birmingham and Derby County, Carsley took advantage of the opportunity provided by the international break to put his own stamp on affairs and he spent valuable time with the squad on the training ground and what has happened since is barely short of miraculous.

We have played six games since then and taken thirteen of the eighteen points on offer, beating Rotherham, Wolves, Charlton and most notably, QPR, drawing with Blackburn Rovers and losing to promotion favourites, Hull City.

The results have been sensationally good, particularly given the state of affairs when he took over when confusion reigned, results were poor and performances even worse with the team unrecognisable in terms of both personnel and style from the salad days of last season when the Bees, under the reassuring and empowering management of Mark Warburton, took the division by storm.

The recent turn around encompasses far more than a massive improvement in results as Lee Carsley, not ignoring or forgetting the contribution of his sidekick Paul Williams, can take full credit for the following changes:

- Improving the fitness levels of a squad that was visibly wilting in the final minutes of matches

- Making training sessions sharper and better organized

- Totally changing the playing style and increasing the pace and tempo of our game with players pressing far quicker and higher up the pitch

- Reintroducing the slick, quick passing game that worked so well last season

- Switching from the 4-4-2 and 4-3-3 formations favoured by Marinus to the 4-2-3-1 set up that worked so well last season

- Encouraging possession football but with an end result rather than possession for possession's sake

- Relying on the proven, Championship experienced homegrown players remaining from last season and taking the rump of the new foreign signings out of the firing line where they had generally struggled to keep their heads above water

From what I have heard the training ground is a happy place at the moment and the smiles have returned to the faces of the entire squad who totally believe in their new interim Head Coach.

Alan McCormack, a player who has particularly benefited from the influence of Carsley and is once again a mainstay of the team, has been extremely vocal in terms of confirming how much the squad would like Lee to become the permanent Head Coach.

Given all of the above it would seem that he should be a shoo-in for the post given his popularity and obvious success, but there is where the problems begin.

Lee is an honest man who has unequivocally stated on many occasions since his appointment to the job at the end of September that he has no interest in the position on a permanent basis as he wants to concentrate on his first love, coaching young players, rather than becoming a first team manager or head coach, and he has remained true to his word and not once has he changed his tune or gone back on his initial assertion that the job was not for him, stating:

I didn't ask to be a football manager and when I retired, my first thought wasn't I want to be a manager. I want to coach Under 21 and Under 18 teams, that's where my strength is.

In fact he has also gone on record as saying that the Brentford job is *far too big* for a rookie boss without any relevant experience.

Normally you would take these words with a pinch of salt and as the normal negotiating ploy of a man cynically pretending not to be interested in the job but in reality doing everything in his power to be seen to be *reluctantly* accepting the accolade.

But with Lee, what you see is what you get and barring a remarkable and totally unexpected *volte-face* I cannot see him becoming our permanent Head Coach.

So what happens now? Why upset the applecart when everything has gone so well and Lee's approach and success has bought us the time to make a measured decision about the next appointment?

That is a damn good question and one that I cannot answer apart from reminding everybody about what somebody very close to the action said to me about Matthew Benham last season.

Whereas Mark Warburton's view of life was *if it ain't broke then don't fix it,* Matthew Benham's motto is far more akin to *it might not be broken but let's keep improving it.*

Matthew Benham is dedicated to developing his beloved Brentford both on and off the pitch and if Lee Carsley has made it clear that he is not the right man for the job or if indeed Benham has independently come to the same decision, then perhaps he has decided to fill the post with the best possible candidate as soon as possible.

Maybe Carsley has also intimated that he would like to relinquish this role for his own good reasons and peace of mind well in advance of the end of the season and that a more immediate change needs to be made.

Those are the only possible interpretations as surely the Bees have learned from February's fiasco and are not merely looking to sound out potential candidates now and then bring one in at the end of the season. All that leads to is chaos for all parties when the news inevitably leaks out.

The downside is that I cannot see Lee Carsley remaining at the club once a new man takes his place and to lose a man of his ability would certainly be a sad loss to the club.

His previous job as Development Squad Manager has been filled by Kevin O'Connor who has started exceptionally well in his new post and I cannot see Carsley relegating himself to becoming the assistant to the new Head Coach as this would seem to make little sense for him and probably not suit the new man either.

Perhaps he can increase his involvement with the England set up or seek a position as Academy Director at a Premier League club?

In any case his success at Griffin Park has deservedly put him and his achievements into the spotlight.

So what happens now and who are the likely candidates under consideration? I have to say that given Carsley's popularity and success to date I fully expected him to remain in charge until the end of the season, and that, of course, might still be the case.

I also thought that Brentford would probably select somebody who would not be available until the end of the season and ideally avoid the need to pay his club any compensation.

Both Dean Smith and Justin Edinburgh have proved themselves to be astute operators in the lower divisions and Dean in particular has established an excellent reputation for playing decent football and bringing through young talent and Romaine Sawyers and Tom Bradshaw have both caught the eye this season, as has Bradley Dack at Gillingham.

Neither Smith nor Edinburgh have managed in The Championship but either would be reasonable options, although of the two I would be far happier with Smith as I believe he would be far better attuned to how we want to do things at Brentford.

Having been badly burned once with Dijkhuizen I am certain that a prerequisite for any new Head Coach will be a sound working knowledge of the Football League and I would be staggered if we bring in somebody who hasn't already had some managerial experience in England.

As *Sky* have intimated he could also be a foreigner and Jimmy Floyd Hasselbaink, for one, has gained a flood of admirers for his work at Burton Albion over the past year and he would tick many of the boxes although he would still be a calculated risk.

I have long been an admirer of Slaviša Jokanović who led Watford to promotion last season but he has taken on a new challenge at Maccabi Tel Aviv.

We have just started a fortnight's international break and this could turn out to be a crucial time for the club and whatever decision is taken will have enormous ramifications for the future success or otherwise of the club.

Having made such a poor appointment in Dijkhuizen, Brentford cannot afford to make another mistake and it might well be that the best decision is to do nothing and leave well alone, unless Lee Carsley has made it perfectly clear that he wants out as soon as possible.

Peter Lumley's Best Ever Brentford Players – 12/11/15

Last month I was both delighted and honoured to be able to publish some fascinating and evocative memories of watching the Bees from **Peter Lumley**, who has been supporting Brentford FC for more years than he cares to remember.

Peter was delighted with the many appreciative responses he received from the readers of his article and I am pleased to say that he has just sent me some follow-up information, which I am sure that you will all enjoy:

In my recent guest contribution to Greville's blog I ducked an invitation to name the best team drawn from all the Brentford players I have watched during my seventy-three years as a fan at Griffin Park.

On reflection I have decided to take on Greville's challenge but with one proviso – that I can name more than one team.

Team A will be made up of players blessed with great technical ability.

Team B will feature those more aptly described as robust or physical.

I will then take on the almost impossible task of naming a best eleven made up from both categories as Team C.

Finally I have also selected a team of eleven players – Team D who, in my opinion, were exceptionally loyal to the club over a number of years and also demonstrated great enthusiasm and commitment whilst on the pitch.

I am sure that everyone will appreciate that the selected players span seven decades and that, inevitably, there will be those who rightly point out some glaring omissions.

Also, assessing the ability of players is, by definition, highly subjective. One man's hero can be another man's Nick Proschwitz or Murray Jones!

So here we go!

TEAM A: Joe Crozier | Alan Hawley | Ken Coote | Jim McNichol | Mel Scott | Jonathan Douglas | Stan Bowles | Johnny Brooks | Dean Holdsworth | Jimmy Bloomfield | Leslie Smith | Subs: Chic Brodie, Moses Odubajo, Stewart Houston, Peter Broadbent, Neil Smillie, Roger Cross, Alex Pritchard

TEAM B: Alf Jefferies | Billy Gorman | Martin Grainger | Tom Higginson | Terry Evans | Jamie Bates | Terry Hurlock | Gary Blissett | George Francis | Jim Towers | Gary Roberts | Subs: Len Bond, George Poyser, Jack Chisholm, Ron Harris, Dai Hopkins, Andre Gray

TEAM C: Joe Crozier | Billy Gorman | Ken Coote | Jim McNichol | Mel Scott | Terry Hurlock | Stan Bowles | Jimmy Bloomfield | Dean Holdsworth | Jim Towers | Leslie Smith | Subs: Chic Brodie, George Poyser, Stewart Houston, Billy McAdams, Roger Cross, John Dick, George Francis

TEAM D: Gerry Cakebread | Kevin O'Connor | Ken Coote | Tom Higginson | Terry Evans | Keith Millen | Billy Dare | Francis Joseph | Dave McCulloch | Bobby Ross | Jackie Graham | Subs: Alan Nelmes, Alan Hawley, Joe James, Sam Saunders, Jamie Bates, Alan Judge, Robert Taylor

I am quite certain that you will all take great pleasure in pointing out lots of glaring omissions, so I will list just a few more players who, if numbers permitted, would have graced one or more of my selected teams:

Dave McKellar | Andy Sinton | Billy Scott | Ernie Muttitt | George Wilkins | Len Townsend | Clayton Donaldson | Steve Phillips | Ken Horne | Nicky Forster | Jimmy Hill | Ron Greenwood | Tony Harper | Barry Silkman |

Alan Cockram | Barry Asby | Leon Legge | Harlee Dean | Jota | Jake Bidwell | Stuart Dallas | Roger Joseph | Ben Hamer | Stuart Nelson | Richard Lee | Dai Ward | Keith Jones | Danis Salman | Wally Bragg | Barry Tucker | Gordon Phillips | Kevin Dearden | Graham Benstead | Steve Sherwood | Toumani Diagouraga | Adam Forshaw | James Tarkowski | D J Campbell | Danis Salman | Roger Joseph

I have also listed Brentford managers in a somewhat haphazard order of preference apart from the top two who in my opinion stand head and shoulders above the rest:

Harry Curtis | Mark Warburton | Steve Coppell | Martin Allen | Phil Holder | Steve Perryman | Frank Blunstone | Jimmy Sirrel | Bill Dodgin Junior | Jackie Gibbons | John Docherty | Uwe Rosler | Frank McLintock | Fred Callaghan | Malcolm MacDonald | Wally Downes | Micky Adams | Ron Noades | David Webb | Nicky Forster

I very much look forward to reading all the comments that we are certain to receive once everybody has read Peter's interesting and thought provoking list.

I will start the debate off by mentioning a name that despite my reading through Peter's note to me three times I was still unable to find – Peter Gelson.

An accidental or deliberate omission on his part?

What do you think?

Walking Wounded – 13/11/15

There was mixed news for supporters in Brentford FC Head of Medical Neil Greig's Thursday update on the current injury situation.

Let's take it from the top.

Alan Judge has thankfully fully recovered from his hamstring strain, which caused him to miss our last two matches – neither of which was won – which underlines just how valuable he is to the team.

He has now joined the Republic of Ireland squad as they prepare for their crucial European Championship playoff clashes. Let's just hope that they wrap him in cotton wool and that he returns to the club fit and well and refreshed and raring to go before next week's match against Nottingham Forest.

I doubt that he will be required to play in either of Eire's next two matches but his time will come and he is desperately close to making his full international debut, an accolade that will be fully merited given his consistently brilliant performances for us.

Josh McEachran is also back in training after recovering from his fractured foot and is currently working hard to regain full fitness having missed much of the preseason training regime. He is expected to play some part in today's behind closed doors friendly match against AFC Bournemouth and all being well, should he suffer no adverse reaction, then we might well see him in the not too distant future.

Josh is a real talent who should fit right in with the pass-and-move approach that we are currently employing and I cannot wait to see him successfully integrated back into the squad and finally make his long-awaited debut for us

Success in the Championship requires all of the old fashioned virtues of strength, organisation, tackling, pressing and fitness but the best teams also possess some game changers – players who can take a match by the scruff of its neck and singlehandedly influence its outcome with a piece of individual brilliance that brings about victory.

Last season we had a plethora of such talent in Alex Pritchard, Alan Judge, Moses Odubajo, Andre Gray, Jota and Nick Proschwitz. OK, forget the last named – I was just checking that you were all still awake!

Things have been really different this time around as for various reasons we have lost three of our former inspirations, Jota has been *hors de combat* and Alan Judge has been left pretty much on his own to make things happen, although John Swift has recently demonstrated that he too is a real talent with an eye for an opening.

Jota contributed eleven goals and so much more to the team last season with his pace, vision and dribbling ability and in April his talent was recognised when he was named as one of *FourFourTwo Magazine's* top forty Football League players of the season.

He has not featured since the opening game of the season when he came out second best after a challenge by his erstwhile teammate Jonathan Douglas and his influence has been sorely missed.

The last three months have been equally frustrating for both him and us as he has been forced to undergo ankle surgery and then kick his heels on the sidelines but he is now due to return to team training next week and all being well it is hoped that he will take part in a friendly match within a couple of weeks.

Wouldn't it be marvellous if he was fit enough to make his comeback against Fulham in the middle of next month given his two last minute goals against them last season? Perhaps that is too much of a fairy tale to come true – but who knows?

Maxime Colin is also close to recovery from his knee ligament injury and is also expected back fully fit by the middle of December. He too looked like he was going to develop into a real asset and will be welcomed back although Nico Yennaris has performed exceptionally well in his absence and will not give up his place without a fight.

Scott Hogan completed a successful reconditioning camp in Philadelphia last month and is also making encouraging progress and we can all live in hope that fortune will finally and not before time, shine down on him and that he will be able to resume his career, hopefully this season rather than next.

Record signing Andreas Bjelland is now undergoing rehabilitation after his knee surgery and is working towards his objective of returning to straight line running. He is not expected back until next season.

The major setback is to Lewis Macleod who had been progressing so well over the past two months and had impressed in a series of Development Squad matches and we were beginning to relish the thought of finally seeing our starlet in first team action.

Unfortunately he sustained a small strain to the same hamstring last Friday, albeit to a different area, which prevented him from completing the game as planned.

Whilst the injury is felt to be minor no risks will be taken with him and he will be conservatively managed. Assuming that all goes to plan (and who knows if that will be the case given his continued ill fortune) I would doubt that he will be playing again this side of Christmas. We will all just have to be even more patient but I suspect that he will be well worth waiting for.

The news about Marco Djuricin, crocked at Blackburn last week is also not great, as he has also injured his ankle ligaments. This seems to be a common injury nowadays but thankfully it appears that he does not require surgery. Even so it is doubtful whether he will be fit for at least a couple of months, and maybe even longer.

The key question is whether we can get by without him and rely upon Lasse Vibe and Philipp Hofmann to provide the goals that we need to continue our progress up the league? It might well be that we will be looking to bring in a loanee to help fill the gap as neither appears best suited to play the lone striker role.

Touch wood, everybody else is fit and well at present but I wouldn't shout too loud about that for fear of tempting fate.

Candidly, I have never known a season like this for injuries and my memory goes back quite a long way. The nadir was surely reached back in 1970 when reserve goalkeeper Gordon Phillips was forced to sit on the bench as a non-playing substitute at Crewe owing to a series of injuries which stretched our minute squad to its limits however things reached such a state at Middlesbrough earlier this season that we were forced to have two goalkeepers in Jack Bonham and Mark Smith on the bench too.

To be safely ensconced in mid-table given our seemingly never ending injury list and the need to bed in so many new players is a quite magnificent achievement and I can't wait to see us finally field a first choice injury-free eleven.

Maybe that will happen early next year and will be something well worth waiting for.

Pep Talk – 15/11/15

Talk is cheap and whilst all the rumours are still unsubstantiated, the fact remains that there is growing speculation that Brentford are closing in on their preferred choice to replace Lee Carsley as Head Coach.

Much of the chatter is on social media but the mainstream press has finally joined in the fun too with *The Daily Telegraph* yesterday naming a new candidate, and one who had not previously been openly mentioned in connection with the club.

According to journalist John Percy, the Swansea City Assistant Manager, Pep Clotet, is in serious contention to take over at Griffin Park. It would appear that any leak has come from the Swansea rather than Brentford end given that Percy is the Midlands football reporter for the *Daily* and *Sunday Telegraph* and predominantly deals with the Premier League.

Indeed only a few days ago, on the ninth of November, he wrote a detailed story about the current state of affairs at Swansea and revealed that their manager, Garry Monk, has effectively been told by the club's chairman, Huw Jenkins, to agree to changes to the overall management structure of the club or risk losing his job given Swansea's recent dire run of only one win in their past nine games.

It is alleged that Jenkins has suggested that Monk must agree to bring in an experienced coach to assist him and in that regard the name of Colin Pascoe, a Swansea legend and Brendan Rogers's former assistant at Liverpool, has been mentioned.

Now it emerges that Clotet, whose role at his current club might now be under real threat given the chairman's apparent ultimatum, could be a serious target for the Bees and has apparently been interviewed by Matthew Benham over the past few days.

Is Percy jumping to conclusions or could there be some – or even a lot, of truth in his suggestion regarding Clotet which has now been picked up by other media outlets in Wales?

Perhaps it would help if we examined Clotet's background and credentials in more detail in order to see if he might fit the criteria required for Brentford's new Head Coach.

He was born in Barcelona and is still in the first blossom of youth at only thirty-eight years of age. He had a totally undistinguished playing career before earning his coveted Pro License when only twenty-six years of age and took his first coaching role whilst still in this twenties at UE Cornellà before moving to RCD Espanyol's where he worked with their youth teams.

He then joined another local team in UE Figueres but was fired after only nine games as they were relegated from Segunda División B. He subsequently returned to his previous club, still in charge of the youths.

Not the most impressive of starts but all the time he was gaining crucial coaching experience which he then began to use to good effect at Espanyol before he was spotted by Roland Nilsson at Malmö FF, who won the 2010 the Allsvenskan championship with Pep acting as his assistant.

His first major Head Coach appointment then came at Halmstads BK but it ended in disappointment when they finished bottom of the table.

Still he kept moving on and learning and coached at Viking FK before catching the eye at Málaga CF where he began to make his name under Manuel Pellegrini by developing several young players who would shortly make an impact in the first team.

Swansea City were impressed by what they had seen and in November 2013 Clotet was appointed academy consultant at the club before being promoted to assistant manager in May last year where he has remained ever since as manager Garry Monk's main *confidant* and support.

Those are the bare facts which confirm that Pep has packed in a massive amount of coaching experience despite his tender years but we also need to put some flesh on the bones and for that I am going to Mike Calvin who profiled Garry Monk in his excellent recent book on football managers, *Living On The Volcano*.

Monk spoke extremely positively about Clotet when interviewed by Calvin. Apparently Pep was influenced greatly by the coaches at Barcelona and Johan Cruyff in particular before attending one hundred and sixty training sessions when Louis van Gaal was in charge of the club in order to analyse the way he set up his teams to maintain possession of the ball.

Clotet is also renowned for breaking down matches into five-minute segments so that he can assess thoroughly what is happening on the pitch and pass on information in real time to Monk. He is quite obviously open-minded, thorough, relentless and committed to his role and would fit in perfectly with Brentford's stats and analysis led approach.

There is talk that he came onto the Brentford radar last year when he was recommended to the club and was apparently considered for the managerial vacancy at FC Midtjylland over the Summer and given the situation at Swansea, it would appear likely that he might well be available and would perhaps not require us to pay compensation in order to acquire his services.

Like the majority of Brentford fans, I would prefer that Lee Carsley remained in post until the end of the season given the way that the squad has responded to him and the renewed sense of togetherness and organisation which has culminated in a series of much improved performances and results, however that does not seem to be an option given that it seems he is determined to leave his position as Head Coach as soon as possible given his total aversion to many elements of the job.

If that is in fact the case then we can only thank him for all his efforts on our behalf and for buying us enough time to make the right appointment to replace him. I would hope that there will still be a role for Lee at the club given his obvious ability but somehow I doubt if that will suit him and his ambitions.

Hopefully if and when the new man arrives there will be a hand over period and given his popularity with the players I would anticipate that Paul Williams will be retained as a coach which will help maintain some element of continuity.

I am sure that this coming week will reveal whether or not Pep Clotet is the man for us. He appears to tick many of the boxes for us in terms of his background, reliance on stats and the fact that he has gained a massive amount of coaching experience around Europe given his relative youth. Most importantly, he has worked in England in the Premier League, fully understands the physical demands of the English game and is working at a club that is renowned for its excellent passing and possession-based football. How players respond to him is something I am not qualified to answer.

I might be wrong – I generally am – but it would not surprise me if Pep is the man for us and that as long as he can get the players on board and convince them to buy into his methods then we might well have identified a massively impressive candidate who will become exactly the type of Head Coach that we have been seeking.

Pep – Yes Or No? – 17/11/15

The rumours about Brentford's potential interest in bringing in current Swansea Assistant Manager Pep Clotet as our new Head Coach received a fairly mixed response from many of the readers of my initial article.

Bill Benn spoke for many of us when he commented:

I hope we keep Paul Williams who has played a big part in the recent upturn of results.

Some, like **Jim Rourke** felt that his lack of managerial experience counted against him:

My comment would be is that when Pep gets the top job things have not gone well. I would suggest also his appointment as Monk's assistant coincides with the downturn at Swansea. Sorry to be so negative!

Mark Croxford took issue with this viewpoint and I feel that his rebuttal contains much sense:

How can that be true? Last year Swansea had their best ever season – and that coincided with Clotet's appointment.

Swansea are probably the nearest model to the way that Brentford operate so it seems to make a fair bit of sense to be interested in someone from there.

Whether he would be the right appointment remains to be seen, of course, and it's a big jump from being the adviser to the decision maker but with a team of coaches to share the burden, maybe it would be a good move for him?

beesyellow22 expressed his thoughts very emphatically:

The situation at Griffin Park has become like a soap opera this season – it's hard to keep on top of what's happening anymore!

Like you Greville, I would love for Carsley to stay in place until the final ball is kicked next May, but apparently the owner does not share this point of view. I understand and appreciate the desire to get the new man in place ASAP but who's to say it won't be another Marinus situation – particularly given Clotet's poor managerial record? We could then find ourselves onto our fourth head coach before we've barely gotten into 2016.

If Clotet is indeed to be the new head coach at Griffin Park, then good luck to him. But the big fear for me is that the players have already been through so much already this season, that to get a new man in now could have a real adverse effect and undo all the fantastic work that has been done since Marinus and Roy were given the bullet.

Let's see what happens, but Clotet's (admittedly youth-based) managerial record does not fill me with excitement or optimism. In fact, if the plan is to bring in a guy with predominantly youth management experience, why the hell not give the job to Mr. Brentford himself – Kevin O'Connor?

He's doing a great job with the development squad, he knows the club inside out and he is Brentford through and through. Unlike Pep Clotet.

Bill Benn seized upon the hole in this argument – the fact that any managerial change is coming at the request of Lee Carsley and not necessarily Matthew Benham and his Directors of Football:

This is nothing to do with Matthew Benham. Lee Carsley simply doesn't want to be a manager and wants to go to other pastures as soon as the new coach is in place.

I suggest you check out Lee Carsley's background in football management too as he hadn't been too impressive in the short periods he's been caretaker boss. King Kev as manager at the current time? God give me strength!

beesyellow22 was quick to come back in his own defence:

It is all very well talking about Carsley not being impressive but facts are facts. We won four on the bounce. The players now know what they are doing. The players are happy once again. The training methods are now working. The players are fitter and stronger. The players enjoy playing for Lee Carsley. Pretty much the same players who were failing under Marinus.

"Nothing to do with Matthew Benham" – this is also extremely wide of the mark! Of course it is everything to do with Benham. Benham is the driving force and the beating heart behind everything that happens behind the scenes. He is a successful and driven businessman and someone who plays to win.

Hence the (apparent) decision to now dispense with the services of the man who has a) dragged us kicking and screaming out of a relegation dogfight and b) won the Skybet Championship Manager of the Month award for October! This has EVERYTHING to do with Matthew Benham, presumably hastened by Carsley's consistent reiteration that he does not want the job.

And why the derision regarding Kevin O'Connor? How is he any less of a suggestion than Clotet? At least he is passionate about Brentford FC and his early results as Development Squad Manager would appear to be extremely encouraging, I'm interested to hear what your reaction was when Warburton was given the manager's job.

Rebel Bee then gave his opinion on the current situation:

In the main I'm with beesyellow22 on this, let's just rewind to the statements that came out of Griffin Park when Lee Carsley was put in charge until the end of the season. So that went well then didn't it, as it seems he can't get away fast enough – so why did he take it and why didn't Brentford FC just say it was going to be a very short term move?

If Clotet does join I can't see Carsley or Williams being part of the team going forward. And what has Clotet actually achieved in the game to justify our pursuit of his services?

There seems to be a fascination with overseas coaches, ironically I'd now convinced myself that Edinburgh and Smith could be decent appointments.

Here we go again.

Bill Benn stuck firmly to his guns:

bees yellow22, you said that Lee Carsley is leaving due to Matthew Benham which is complete rubbish and a slur against our owner. How many more times does Lee Carsley have to say that he doesn't want the job? In actual fact he hates it and wants to move on.

Lee Carsley has done a good job and I also would have liked him to have continued but he just doesn't want to. He wants to coach young players as he does with the England Under 19s and it gives him the flexibility for him to work on other things outside of football.

I was not dissing Lee Carsley by saying look at his CV but it's just an example of if he was on our list today as a target check out his history before joining us and you could find many negatives.

We have had an horrendous injury list this season and unfortunately picked the wrong coach in Marinus Dijkhuizen, but this can happen to the best, Manchester United for example.

You might think this season is a soap opera but I among many other fans have enjoyed some great times this season with number one beating that lot down the road as well as our performances against Charlton, Leeds, Wolves, Bristol City and Blackburn to name a few.

When the new manager comes in I expect Lee Carsley to help the transition for a week or so and Paul Williams to stay. I know the majority of our fans will get behind the new man and also expect the usual uninformed claptrap to continue on message boards.

Rebel Bee still hadn't given up and had an excellent point to make:

Bill we know you're not dissing Lee Carsley, but if he doesn't want the job and hates it so much then something has happened right? As a reminder here are the relevant quotes from our Chairman's statement when he was appointed:

"The Club has moved swiftly and decisively in order to maintain its long-term vision and philosophy. That's why Lee Carsley has been appointed as Head Coach for the remainder of the season. Lee has shown with the Under 21s that he is an outstanding leader. His work at the training ground has been hugely impressive whilst coaching the development squad and has demonstrated he understands the Club's philosophy and the ambitions of Brentford FC. We believe these qualities will help Lee settle into his new role effectively and quickly."

As to his reasons for not wanting to continue, we can only guess and speculate – I don't blame Matthew Benham for this at all, however the management team shouldn't get a pass for the Dijkhuizen disaster.

I do wonder why once again why we have managed to make a mess of this, even if it is just in the way it was communicated. As for "uninformed claptrap" – really is that your answer to anyone who sees it slightly differently? I think you can do better than that.

Bill Benn was more conciliatory in his response:

"Claptrap" wasn't aimed at you but the more extreme stuff that has been aimed at Matthew Benham on other forums and social media sites whenever there are decisions being made.

I would agree our PR has been dreadful at time over the last twelve months. Lee Carsley has never ever stated that he wanted to be manager until the end of the season although others have been quoted suggesting that for reasons I don't know, maybe wishful thinking.

It's no secret that he gives a lot of time to charity work and being in youth football gives him the time to do that. I wish him all the best and look forward to the new Head Coach taking over hopefully this week.

As was **Rebel Bee** and it is hard to argue with what he had to say:

Fair do's Bill, but there are some wide of the mark views on both sides of this. Like you I have enjoyed some great days already this season – with Charlton and QPR the standouts.

I don't expect Brentford FC to be top six or chasing promotion either. I love this league and I'd just be happy to stay in the division with a bit to spare. I'd just like to see us settle down with the coach and players pulling together and playing some decent stuff.

And I'd like the club to communicate and do its PR a bit better, so that we don't need to speculate so much.

I will end with **Peter Lumley** who had a more radical and resigned viewpoint:

Whoever is appointed it will be just another Matthew Benham gamble with little regard for the views of the Griffin Park faithful.

For my money the "dream ticket" would be Kevin O'Connor and Paul Williams.

Thanks to everybody who participated in the discussion and I think that there will be far more to say as the situation develops over the week.

For what it is worth here is where I stand:

Lee Carsley was the obvious immediate short-term appointment when the decision was made not to continue with Marinus. Who knows how hard he had to be persuaded in order to convince him to take the job and agree to take the reins until the end of the season?

If there was any doubt at the time about his willingness to remain in post until May then it was a mistake to make the statement confirming that he would do so. What I suspect is that Lee did agree to do so, however reluctantly, but soon realised that he had made a mistake and has been actively trying to relinquish his position ever since.

This is terribly disappointing given how well he has adapted to the role and the positive response that he has obtained from the squad as is reflected in our improved results and style of play.

We therefore need to make another appointment and whomever we choose will be a gamble to some extent.

Clotet is an interesting prospect for all the reasons I outlined in my previous article in terms of his obvious coaching ability and the lovely football that Swansea attempt to play.

How will he do when elevated to the Head Coach role and will the players buy into his approach?

These are imponderables that cannot be answered.

I suspect that a firm decision has yet to be made and that the situation will not be resolved quickly.

Lull Before The Storm As Bees Prepare To Return To Action – 19/11/15

Preparations are well underway for Saturday's attractive home fixture against Nottingham Forest and the Brentford squad will be full of confidence and raring to return to action after their enforced fortnight's break.

That is not to say that they have had their feet up as they were subjected to a gruelling series of training and fitness sessions before they were given a well-deserved few days off which allowed the foreign contingent to return home for a brief visit.

There was no rest for some, with Alan Judge, John Swift and Daniel O'Shaughnessy all involved with their respective international squads over the last week or so with Judge now playing for a place in the Eire squad which has qualified for next year's European Championship Finals and Swift receiving his first heady taste of England Under 21 football which has hopefully whetted his appetite for more of the same.

Judge sounded particularly bright and chirpy in his *Bees Player* interview yesterday and he fully recognises and acknowledges that he needs to maintain the form he has shown recently if he is to spend next Summer in France as he so desperately wishes to do, and that can only be good news for us in the meantime.

In that regard I cannot remember the last time that a current Brentford player appeared in the finals of a major tournament such as the World Cup or European Championship and I well suspect that if Judge is named in the final squad, assuming of course that he is still at the club and perish the thought that he is not, that he will be the first Brentford player ever to do so.

Former Bees Brian Turner and Bill Slater played for New Zealand and England in the finals of the World Cup in 1982 and 1958 respectively and Hermann Hreidarsson came very close to qualifying with Iceland whilst still a Bee. Two more ex-Bees in Stuart Dallas and Will Grigg are also in line to play for Northern Ireland this Summer.

The squad has been strengthened with the return to full fitness of the evergreen Sam Saunders and Josh McEachran played half a game in last week's friendly match against AFC Bournemouth and cannot be too far away now, with Jota and Max Colin hopefully shortly behind him.

I recently read a report that attempted to put a monetary value to the cost of player injuries in terms of wages, treatment, insurance premiums and the financial implications of fielding a weakened team. It was hardly surprising that Arsenal came out near the top of the list with their massive and ongoing injury list costing them a whopping twenty million pounds last season. The formula also highlighted that the fewer injuries you have, generally the better you perform with Premier League Champions Chelsea suffering the least number of injuries.

I therefore think that we have not paid Brentford nearly enough credit for the way that they have performed this season despite what can only be termed a crippling and seemingly never ending list of injuries that at one time affected nearly half the squad, including several star names.

We finally seem to be over the worst now, although I do not want to tempt fate but even now for every player we get back to full fitness, another one seems to be struck down. Our current healthy league position simply emphasises the quality and depth of the squad and maybe at some point fairly early in the New Year we will really have a selection problem when the majority of players return to fitness.

Talking about injuries, the news about Lewis Macleod and Marco Djuricin is not good and I would be surprised if we see either of them back in action before the New Year at the earliest. That leaves the Head Coach – and don't you worry I will come back to that complex situation very shortly – with a selection dilemma for Saturday's match.

Lasse Vibe played well as a lone striker as a late substitute at Charlton and after Djuricin's injury at Blackburn, scoring on each occasion and Philipp Hofmann did exactly the same at Wolves.

Reassuring news, indeed, but I am more concerned about how they will fare as a lone striker at home when the opposition sits deep and packs its defence unlike the situation in the away games when the opposition was chasing the game and left huge gaps in their defence for us to exploit.

I would suspect that we will keep to our successful 4-2-3-1 formation which allows us to dominate the midfield rather than allow the two strikers to play together and it will therefore be up to whoever is picked from the start, and I think it will be Vibe, to demonstrate some upper body strength, vim and vigour, make intelligent runs and hold the ball up until the midfield can get forward to support him.

They have both had several months to settle down, find full fitness and become accustomed to the demands of the Championship and it is now up to them both to seize this opportunity as the squad and supporters alike are now relying on them to produce on a regular basis.

Alan Judge has demonstrated his sharpshooting ability in front of goal, scoring six times to date, which means that he has already doubled his tally for the whole of last season but we need Swift and Ryan Woods to step up to the plate too bearing in mind that Pritchard and Jota notched double figures last season and Douglas and Dallas were not too far behind them. We really need those extra goals from midfield and ideally Jota will supply some of them once he returns to action.

As you can see, I have made no mention of the back four as I have pretty much given them up as a bad loss in terms of their goal scoring potential and prowess.

Tarkowski was deadly from six inches in the last seconds against Ipswich and Bidwell is getting a fair bit closer with some of his efforts as he still attempts to break his goalscoring duck but despite the services of our Free Kick Coach our defenders either make the wrong run or the delivery is not up to scratch. I look back at the likes of Terry Evans and Micky Droy who caused havoc in the opposition penalty areas (as well as their own from time to time) and scored far more than their fair share of goals. Where are their like when we need them so desperately now?

Pep Clotet remains the elephant in the room.

Is he our preferred choice to become our new Head Coach? If that is the case, is he likely to agree to join us and if so, when? How long is Lee Carsley prepared to remain in his current role given his oft-stated antipathy to it? Can he even now be persuaded to stay until the end of the season? If he is replaced will there still be a role for him at the club? Could the powers that be have handled things any differently and gone public about what is currently going on?

These points and many more have been debated at great length both in my articles and on social media and who knows what will transpire, and when.

I have made my views perfectly clear.

- Lee Carsley would be the ideal choice to remain as Head Coach given how well he has performed and the players' response to him, but he has made it quite clear that he wants out as soon as possible

- We are conducting a recruitment process as far under the radar as possible and the media leaks have not emanated from the Brentford end

- No statement will be made until there is any firm news

- Hopefully there will be firm news as soon as possible which will bring the current uncertainty to an end

- Pep Clotet is an exciting option who comes highly recommended by the likes of Steve Coppell and he would fit in well with the management philosophy currently employed at the club

- His appointment – as would anyone else's, would be a gamble in terms of how he deals with the players and the myriad of coaching and support staff

Who knows how long it will take before there is anything more to say rather than mere speculation, but as supporters it is our right and privilege to have an opinion and air our views – and we have certainly done so!

Maybe now is the lull before the storm. Saturday's match against an underperforming but improving Nottingham Forest team packed with big name players looms ever nearer and nothing must distract the squad and get in the way from their immediate priority, which is quite simply to win the game.

Nothing else really matters.

Hofmann – The Pinball Wizard! – 22/11/15

Football is traditionally referred to as a game of two halves but the Brentford versus Nottingham Forest match yesterday afternoon broke new ground as it is best described as a game of three thirds – a first forty-five minutes where absolutely nothing happened, a pulsating fifty-two minute-long second half packed with incident and action and then the post-match press conference where much was revealed.

The Bees had not seemed to have benefited from the international break and were flat and off the pace in the first half. There was lots of passing – mostly sideways but there was absolutely no movement, energy, vigour or penetration.

In another words this was not a typical Brentford performance and it felt almost like a practice match or shadow boxing as the ball was moved slowly and carefully from player to player with nobody able or prepared to attempt the killer pass. Our sole tactic seemed to be to give the ball to the ever-willing Alan Judge and hope that he could create something out of the blue.

Forest set up in two banks of four and stifled us and their goalkeeper Dorus de Vries must have been the coldest man at a frigid Griffin Park given his total lack of action. The visitors kept Ward and Mendes wide and they created several chances for Nelson Oliveira but thankfully David Button was sharp and alert and kept the Bees in the game with a series of saves – none out of the ordinary it has to be said, but the first half was total one way traffic and the Bees were distinctly fortunate to go into the break on level terms.

Lee Carsley apparently got into his team at half time but nothing much changed early on and Brentford were indebted to Button for a wonderful clawing save from Oliveira's header and Lansbury was allowed to run through a static midfield who waved him past before shooting a presentable opportunity over the bar.

John Swift had endured a tough day with nothing going right for the youngster but he finally put in Brentford's first on-target effort when his twenty-five yarder finally forced the frozen de Vries into action.

Carsley had already demonstrated his frustration at what he, along with the rest of us, was being forced to endure – although he at least was being paid to freeze – by belting the ball miles in the air when it fell out of play by the dugout. Finally, his patience exhausted, he made two significant changes on the hour in an effort to breathe some life into his sluggish team.

Swift and the totally anonymous Vibe were replaced by Canos and Hofmann although there were several others could also have been hooked without too much complaint.

Suddenly the tempo changed as the Bees were inspired by the effervescent and gifted young Spaniard, and just as was the case against Preston, Canos had an instant impact, scoring his first ever league goal with a close range effort in a packed six-yard box when Dean headed down a Judge cross after a McCormack corner had been half cleared.

The Bees were inspired by the substitution as Canos roared around the field pressing, passing and dribbling and Hofmann too finally provided an outlet with the size and strength and ability to hold the ball up. He is also a gifted footballer and used his sleight of foot to bamboozle his tall markers and bring others into play.

Suddenly the Bees took control. Judge shot over and a pulsating move ended with McCormack stretching but just failing to reach a deadly low Judge cross in front of an empty net.

Then the Bees self-destructed when Dean mis-controlled, overran the ball and tried to make up for his mistake with a lunging tackle which was harshly penalised by the referee. Dean heatedly disagreed, picked the ball up to remonstrate and demonstrate the legitimacy of his challenge and when Williams went to grab the ball, Dean's swinging arm apparently caught the Forest substitute who went down as if shot.

Referee Malone produced the red card with Stroud-like speed and in an instant the match was turned on its head. Villain or *Silly Sausage*, as Dean was unforgettably described by Billy Reeves after the match? Make your own mind up. Williams certainly made the most of his opportunity but Harlee was impetuous and gave the referee a decision to make, not forgetting that the whole incident was caused by his own error whilst in possession of the ball.

Whatever actually happened, and the incident was over in a flash, I cannot see an appeal succeeding and we will lose Dean for three crucial matches at a time when he and Tarkowski were playing so well together.

Jack O'Connell replaced Judge and slotted in well but the damage had been done and a Forest team which had squandered its opportunities was offered an undeserved way back into the game and they took immediate advantage when a Mills cross was criminally mis-controlled by Diagouraga on the edge of the penalty area and the predatory Lansbury took full advantage of the gift and slotted the ball low into the corner.

Brentford now had twenty long minutes to hang on, as Forest would surely go for the jugular, but the anticipated bombardment on our goal never happened. Bidwell and Yennaris were immense and the two centre halves won everything. Woods, McCormack and Diagouraga covered, chased and held the ball whenever possible and Hofmann and Canos worked hard and never allowed their defence to settle.

In short we looked like a Brentford team again and we finally began to believe that we could hold onto our hard-won point. Even better, Carsley kept waving us forward as he realised that attack was the best form of defence. Canos turned brilliantly in the box and his effort forced a wonderful save from de Vries. McCormack had impressed with his set piece delivery and Tarkowski met his perfectly placed free kick but his header bounced clear off the post.

Forest had shot their bolt and we waited for the six long minutes of injury time to expire but the Bees had different ideas. Diagouraga slid a perfect through ball to Woods who roared through the defence, fought off his marker and hammered an angled shot which was parried by de Vries straight to Hofmann, and his instant effort from the edge of the area caught not one, not two, but three defections off Vaughan, de Vries and then Lichaj on the line and ended up in the corner of the net.

Philipp Hofmann was *The Pinball Wizard,* as his effort had won the game for us

Cue tumultuous celebrations and yet another in a catalogue of late winners by a team that never knows when it is beaten.

The rollercoaster ride of a second half had ended with three glorious and unexpected points when at one time one or even none had appeared more likely. What can ever beat the excitement of a ninety-sixth minute winner?

Let's just hope that it was simply a case of blowing the cobwebs out of our system after what was a lacklustre first half non-performance. Canos and Hofmann provided the catalyst for our recovery and we were much improved in the last half hour.

Alan McCormack – definitely a Pitbull!

If that was not enough there was far more to come when Lee Carsley was interviewed by Billy Reeves after the match and made it perfectly clear that this had probably been his last match in charge with a new man expected to be appointed early next week.

Lee then stated that he would be remaining at the club to support the new Head Coach and would also return to his development role. Paul Williams would also remain in post. Good news indeed!

There is a lot there to assimilate and I think I will let the dust settle before I attempt to do so. I assume that Pep Clotet will be the new man in charge with Carsley staying around to assist in the handover and Williams remaining as a first team coach. Whether Lee then returns to his former position as Development Squad Manager and, if so, what that might mean for Kevin O'Connor are questions that remain unanswered at the present time.

At this point I am sure that all Brentford fans would like to join me in giving thanks to Lee Carsley who has won five out of his nine matches in charge and been responsible, along with Paul Williams, for a total sea-change in our approach and performances.

Brentford always break the mould and do things differently and I am sure that never in the history of the game has an interim Head Coach had such a run of success, won the Manager of the Month Award and then voluntarily given up his post despite the entreaties of the club, because it is not what he wants to do at this juncture of his career.

Only at Brentford…

Thanks Lee for everything you have done and I am delighted that his talent and influence will not immediately be lost to us. What a day and I am sure that there will be more exciting news unfolding within the next forty-eight hours. What I can say without a shadow of doubt is that it is never dull being a Brentford fan!

Blazing Meteors – Part Two – 24/11/15

A couple of months ago I began to tell the story of some of the Brentford players who began their career at the club so well but merely flattered to deceive and who all fizzled out for a variety of reasons without fulfilling their seemingly once abundant promise.

I ended the last article in the early 90s and will pick up the narrative with **Lee Luscombe**. He joined the club from Southampton and in fact cost us a fee of up to fifteen thousand pounds predicated totally on appearances. He was clumsy and ungainly but when he occasionally managed to get every part of his body working in unison he could be devastating and he scored some incredible goals including a soaring header in a vital promotion clash against Stoke City and a wonderful angled volley against Charlton. He was plagued by inconsistency and was released after our relegation in 1993 and soon faded out of the game which was a real waste of an excellent talent.

Mickey Bennett was a makeweight in the Dean Holdsworth deal but for a short while it looking like we had signed a gem as he initially showed directness on the right wing and an eye for goal, but his impact was to be short-lived and he was slowed down by a chronic injury. He missed a crucial penalty at Bristol Rovers when his weak shot was saved easily by a goalkeeper in Brian Parkin who should never have been on the pitch after rugby tackling Bennett in front of a gaping goal and escaping with a yellow card when a red seemed inevitable.

David Webb played him as a striker but with little effect and his Brentford career ended in ignominy after Joe Allen was left with a broken jaw after a notorious training ground incident.

Grant Chalmers should have been a star and I still do not understand why he did not have a long and successful career in the Football League. He made an immediate impact as a ball playing midfielder on his arrival from Guernsey and made a massively impressive debut at Peterborough where he ran the entire game before being one of the best players on the pitch against Spurs in the Coca-Cola Cup. He scored a well-taken goal in the five-one romp against Bristol City but soon faded out of contention.

Famously he was dragged out of the club bar just before the kick off against Derby County on Boxing Day when Chris Hughton was injured in the warm-up but he was himself substituted after apparently suffering from the effects of a now unwanted pre-match pie! Phil Holder, ironically a skilful midfielder himself, never seemed to trust Chalmers and he lost confidence, drifted away and out of the game before returning to Guernsey.

Craig Ravenscroft was another homegrown player who started well with a goal at Huddersfield but he could never quite overcome the handicap of his lack of height and strength and soon dropped into Non League.

Scott Canham looked a world-beater throughout his loan spell from West Ham in 1996 and he was massively influential in leading us to safety when a relegation battle looked far more likely. He was small and compact but played with his head up, put his foot in and showed vision in his passing.

He returned to Upton Park but unexpectedly signed for the Bees at the beginning of the following season for twenty-five thousand pounds. I had tried to get my client Ericsson, the club sponsor, to help underwrite the move but their assistance wasn't necessary.

He looked a totally different player on his return and failed to secure a regular place in the first team before joining Orient where he also struggled to establish himself.

Allan Glover, Lee Frost and **Pim Balkestein** are three other players who similarly enjoyed wonderful loan spells at the club but singularly failed to impress when signed on a permanent basis. I am sure that we will never be able to fathom out the reason why!

Kevin Rapley was asked to shoulder too much responsibility too soon and I believe that this hindered his future development. He scored eleven goals in his first full season when he was our main striker and one of the few successes in an awful season that ended up in relegation. Who can ever forget his brilliant last minute winner against Burnley from a dramatic scissors kick and the wild celebration that followed with his manic run half the length of the pitch triumphantly waving his shirt above his head?

The following season he fell out of favour with Ron Noades and was loaned to Southend before leaving for Notts County for whom he scored on his return to Griffin Park in the game made infamous by the exploits of Gary Owers. For a striker of his quality and potential to score a mere thirty-three goals in his entire career was a major surprise and disappointment given how well he had started.

Tony Folan should now be enjoying his retirement after a glittering career and at least one hundred Republic of Ireland caps under his belt, such was his outrageous ability. As it was a constant stream of niggling injuries beset his career and he was never able to make the impact that he promised after his series of outstanding displays when he joined the Bees from Crystal Palace in 1998.

I can still picture that mesmerising dribble and goal against Peterborough and the *Folan From The Halfway Line* effort against Cambridge United. He had so much time on the ball and he possessed elegance and grace and opponents just could not get close enough to tackle him.

Unfortunately he was unable to overcome the injury jinx as well as off-field problems and his career simply petered out far too soon and well short of what he could and should have achieved had he been granted a modicum of good fortune.

Mark Williams was another local boy who almost made good and for a time it looked as if he might establish himself as a speedy winger but he became typecast as a *Super Sub* and set a new club record for substitute appearances with seventy-one in total.

Striker **Mark Peters** arrived at the club with a great fanfare and a glowing reputation from Southampton. He soon proved his ability in front of goal and he scored twenty-one times in thirty-two reserve team matches. He even scored for the first team against QPR, a sure fire way to gain instant hero status, but it never happened for him with stories of off-field and attitude problems.

Martin Allen soon cancelled his contract and he then played for a plethora of local teams without ever making the impact he should have done in the Football League. Football is not just about ability but also about hard work and dedication.

A nodding mention here to **Alex Rhodes**, of whom I have already written elsewhere at great length. It was a real tragedy that his career was blighted by injury and misfortune as he was such a promising talent and will always be remembered for scoring the solo goal against AFC Bournemouth that secured *The Great Escape* from relegation in 1994.

Karleigh Osborne has made a decent career for himself and is still playing well for AFC Wimbledon but somehow you feel that it might have gone even better for him given his ability. Perhaps he was promoted to the first team a bit too quickly and I remember Andy Booth giving him a fearful bashing but he persevered and established himself in the team as a powerful and pacy central defender who surprisingly failed to flourish at either Millwall and Bristol City.

Remarkably, **Charlie Ide** is still only twenty-seven years of age and is playing at a level of the game far below his true ability. He started off so well for the Bees and shone in that dreadful relegation season of 2006/07 as well as scoring some valuable goals. He never appeared to show the dedication necessary to make the grade and his career disappeared as rapidly as it had burst into life.

Sam Tillen established himself in the first team as an exciting attacking left back and scored a great equalising goal at Leyton Orient with a perfect angled volley. He was even selected for a Football League Under 21 match against Italy but he went backwards rather than developing and he was released by Andy Scott and is still playing in Iceland.

Ross Montague had his embryonic career wrecked by a stress fracture in his back and a torn cruciate knee ligament otherwise he might still be our current first team centre forward, so talented did he appear to be when he broke into the team as an eighteen year old.

Gary Smith looked like he was the answer to our midfield problems after he joined in 2007 and he blossomed under Andy Scott but the injury jinx hit and he was never the same player again.

I am not sure if **Nathan Elder** deserves to be mentioned in this context given the tragic nature of his injury at Rotherham but until that terrible collision with Pablo Mills which I can still clearly recall with horror and which left him with a double fracture of the cheekbone, fractured jaw, triple fracture of the nose and impaired vision, he was a bustling centre forward and a clear crowd favourite.

He had been sent off twice that season, at Gillingham when he defended Marvin Williams and far more contentiously by Stuart Attwell against Notts County and he was totally devoid of luck and good fortune. He never played for the Bees again and his career never recovered. A tragic loss.

Thinking about some of these players and how fate conspired against them has deeply saddened me, others have nobody else to blame but themselves for not making the most of their ability.

Let's just hope that there are not many names to add to this list in the near future and that our players all fully realise their potential.

Damned If You Do… – 28/11/15

The airwaves and social media channels alike have been red-hot with activity and comment, most of it negative, exasperated, mocking and even vituperative in tone, in response to Brentford Co-Director of Football Phil Giles's statement last night updating the supporters on the current state of play regarding the head coaching position at the club.

This is what he had to say:

In Lee's last post-match press conference, he discussed the possibility that the Nottingham Forest game would be his last in charge. This was the expectation of both Rasmus Ankersen and myself. Lee's comments were made in good faith based on the conversations we held last week.

Circumstances this week have meant that we haven't been able to make the change as originally anticipated. We will continue with our process to find the right long-term Head Coach for Brentford, rather than make a hasty appointment.

Lee has done a superb job since taking charge in September and we look forward to our game with Bolton on Monday evening.

This has been enough to rouse much of the fan base to fury.

Now before everyone starts with the accusation that I am merely a mouthpiece, shill, or an apologist for the club I will make the point that the purpose of these articles is simply for me to spout off and give my opinion about anything and everything that is happening in and around Brentford FC both on and off the pitch.

I try to avoid unnecessary knee-jerk reactions and, unlike Keith Stroud and Brendan Malone, allow myself time to think before making a final decision. I try as hard as I can to avoid factual errors by taking soundings from friends and contacts in and around – and sometimes well outside – the club and I always endeavour to check my sources before rushing into print. I also take the law of libel very seriously indeed.

Of course I am probably proved wrong as often – or even more so, than I am correct in my musings, but that is just the luck of the draw. I welcome, publish and respond to any and all feedback and comments to what I write and I am quite used and inured to readers telling me that I am deluded in what I have to say.

I have also not held back in heavily criticising the club over its actions whenever I feel that it is justified. Just to give a couple of examples: I felt that certain individuals were naïve in the extreme not to anticipate that ongoing behind closed doors negotiations with potential replacements for Mark Warburton would not leak out into the media and cause the horrendous destabilisation that threatened to jeopardise our promotion push last February. I also felt strongly that the club's initial crisis management was inept and poorly executed in the extreme.

The appointment of Marinus Dijkhuizen was also totally bungled and we do not know yet how much its impact will eventually influence the outcome of this season given that we have been forced onto the back foot ever since.

I have given a great deal of thought to the current managerial or head coaching hiatus and as far as I am concerned the club cannot and should not be criticised in any way, shape or form for how it has managed and continues to deal with a difficult and complex situation.

Here is my reading of affairs and how they have developed since the end of September and the sacking of Marinus. I fully expect however that much of what I set down is not totally accurate but it is as close to the truth that I can get:

1. An interim Head Coach is needed at short notice and Lee Carsley is the obvious immediate candidate given his previous, albeit limited, managerial experience and the respect he has gained from the entire squad since his arrival last season

2. Lee is persuaded to sign on for the rest of the season despite his misgivings, possible concerns about the necessary commitment owing to his family situation and preference to remain as a development coach but he is assuaged by the knowledge that the club will be looking for a permanent replacement from the outset

3. After two initial defeats, Lee Carsley, aided by the invaluable Paul Williams and Flemming Pedersen is able to put his stamp on affairs and the seemingly terminal decline is arrested and reversed. Not only that, the dramatic improvement in results leads to Lee winning a fully deserved Manager of the Month Award for October

4. Lee remains entirely consistent and honest in all his public statements reiterating his preference for youth coaching and that he feels that he is not ready for a job of this magnitude which requires a far more experienced pair of hands

5. Efforts are being made behind the scenes to identify and verify potential candidates for the permanent role but Carsley's success means that he has bought us sufficient time to ensure that a panic or rushed appointment does not have to be made and that the optimum candidate can be sourced and ideally hired

6. Given his success I would expect that efforts were made to persuade Lee to change his mind and take on the role on a permanent basis. Maybe he even prevaricated and considered the option too, but the end result remains the same. He does not want to continue in his post any longer than is strictly necessary

7. A short list is being considered and soundings taken and three names appear in the media: Pep Clotet, Dean Smith and Justin Edinburgh

8. There is no smoke without fire and it soon becomes evident that Clotet is the preferred candidate. He has limited managerial experience but is an acclaimed coach with an excellent track record, particularly for a man of his relative youth, and Swansea, where he is currently employed, would appear to be a benchmark and exemplar for how Matthew Benham wants his club to set up and play in terms of the quality and style of its football

9. The situation at Swansea, however is complex, confused and ever changing. Will the manager stay or will he be sacked? Is he being pressurised to make changes in his coaching staff? Will the *status quo* finally prevail? Is the Chairman willing to allow Clotet to leave or does he want him to stay? Is he looking to obtain compensation for him? To a large degree these questions remain unanswered and I am certain that there have been shifting sands over the past couple of weeks

10. Assuming that Clotet is the man and that he has passed our due diligence and it is of course entirely possible that we have changed our mind too, then it must be a difficult, longwinded and frustrating challenge to firstly persuade him to leave the Premier League and take up the job at Griffin Park and then extract him from his current situation

11. It would appear that last weekend Brentford believed that this interminable process was near to completion and that we were on the verge of announcing an appointment

12. Lee Carsley was obviously kept fully updated on the progress of all negotiations and therefore quite reasonably made it clear in his post-match interview that he fully expected that the Nottingham Forest match would be his last match in charge

13. Unfortunately the goalposts changed and what we thought was almost a done deal is no longer the case. Has the change of heart come from Clotet? Has his club decided to hang onto him? Are agents muddying the water? Does his family prefer to stay put rather than move to London? Can we afford his wage demands and keep all compensation and salary costs down to a manageable level and still remain within our budgetary constraints?

14. The bottom line is that what we thought and honestly believed would happen has not yet taken place. Maybe the Clotet deal is dead. Perhaps there will, even now, be a change of heart from whoever is holding things up and he will still be appointed. Highly doubtful, in my opinion

15. More likely we are on to our next preferred candidate who apparently is the Walsall manager, Dean Smith, and hopefully we will have better luck with him

16. Second choice does not mean second best. I fully expect that we have identified at least two excellent and ideal candidates for the job either of whom the club would be happy to appoint. For my part I would have liked Clotet for the reasons previously expressed and feel that Smith also has the experience at the coalface to do well and has a football philosophy in line with our own

17. The only consideration is to get things right this time. We cannot afford another poor appointment if the club is to continue to progress as we fully intend. Thankfully we do not have to make an appointment simply for the sake of doing so and can within reason, take whatever time is necessary

18. As long, of course, as Lee Carsley continues to play ball and is prepared to hold the fort until the new man is in place. I have no idea if he has set a deadline or if he is willing to remain in charge for an indefinite period as necessary. My gut feeling regarding Lee's state of mind is that the sooner we are in a position to appoint a new Head Coach the better

19. I would also add that we are only one of three attractive managerial/head coaching vacancies in West London and it does not appear that either Fulham or Queens Park Rangers are having any more success in getting a deal over the line than we are

I feel that the club has acted entirely responsibly in this entire process and does not deserve the flack that it is receiving from all quarters. Hiring a new manager or head coach is an extremely complex and crucial undertaking. There are so many variables that can change or go wrong.

You are dealing with a plethora of individuals, from the candidates themselves, to their agents and representatives. You then have to negotiate with the club and cope with family interests as well. In other words there is a lot of juggling that needs to be done and so much is totally out of your own hands.

I am happy and content that Lee Carsley will remain in charge on Monday and know that he will be fully focused on the task ahead. I also know that the massive amount of work being conducted by the club behind the scenes and under the radar will continue until we are ready to announce the identity of our new Head Coach and I am fully confident that this time it will be the right choice.

Second Time Lucky? – 30/11/15

So *The Chosen One* is now the Walsall manager Dean Smith as Brentford supporters wait agog for confirmation that he will hopefully become the new Head Coach at the club.

Whilst Pep Clotet was apparently the first choice for the job, that deal could not be consummated for a variety of reasons perhaps not unconnected with the current uncertainty at Swansea as well as the total cost of the package required to bring him to Griffin Park.

It is important to say up front that *second choice* does not mean *second best,* as I understand that the club would have been more than delighted with either candidate accepting the position.

So whilst we wait for the situation to be resolved and I am sure that the cameras tonight at Bolton will be panning the stands in the *Macron* in the hope of seeing Smith lurking in the background or skulking in the shadows, I thought that it might be helpful if we examined his career in greater detail and looked at his background and achievements.

Smith is still relatively young in managerial terms at forty-four years of age and had a long and distinguished playing career as a no-nonsense centre half who played well over five hundred Football League games for the likes of Walsall, Hereford, Leyton Orient and Sheffield Wednesday.

He will fit in perfectly with Brentford as he played in four unsuccessful playoff campaigns for Walsall, Hereford and Leyton Orient and fully understands and has experienced the heartache of falling short at the final hurdle!

His best friend would not have described him a cultured defender but he read the game well, was tough and effective and he almost broke the heart of every Brentford fan back in 2004 when he equalised for Sheffield Wednesday in Martin Allen's *Great Escape* season seemingly long after James Alexander Gordon had begun to recite the final scores after the referee, George Cain, had lost all sense of time and played on until the home team scored.

After retirement, Smith became Youth Team Coach and Assistant Manager at Leyton Orient and remained there until 2009 when he was named as Head of Youth at Walsall before taking over as manager in January 2011, making him the fourth longest serving manager in the game, behind only Arsène Wenger, Paul Tisdale and our old friend Karl Robinson with an incredible tenure, given the vulnerability of any manager's position, of four years and three hundred and twenty-nine days.

I am sure that all Brentford fans, desperate for a speedy resolution to the current situation, sincerely hope that he does not make it much beyond that impressive figure!

He is a well-qualified and respected coach who possesses his UEFA Pro License and he encourages his teams to play positive, passing and attacking football and to play the ball to feet, as we have learned to our cost in previous meetings between the two clubs.

His time at Walsall has been highly successful given their relative lack of resources, and he took them to Wembley for the first time in their history last season in the final of the Football League Trophy and he has established them in the top half of the table with the promise of a promotion challenge this season as they hover around the top six in League One.

He has an encyclopaedic knowledge of the lower divisions and youth football at all levels and has brought through or purchased many young players of exceptional ability such as Will Grigg, Florent Cuvelier, Sam Mantom, Romaine Sawyers, Tom Bradshaw and Rico Henry.

Brentford have never found Walsall a pushover in recent years and I well remember a hard-fought draw at The Bescot Stadium in January 2014 when The Saddlers ended our run of eight consecutive victories and could easily have won the game late on.

Mark Warburton's verdict on the home team that day: *It was a tough game and Walsall worked hard and moved the ball well*, perfectly sums up the approach of a typical Dean Smith team.

From what I can tell Dean Smith fits the bill as far as Brentford is concerned. He has nearly five years' worth of managerial experience and has gained a deserved reputation as an excellent coach who more than makes the most of what he is given. He develops and encourages young talent and allows them to flourish within a positive environment and I am told that he is good at man-management.

Smith is a great friend of Martin Ling, so cruelly afflicted by depression in recent years and he has now amended his approach to the job now given the potential risks to his health:

What Martin went through made me realise how important it is to appreciate that there is an outside world, away from football. The support network of your family, friends and staff is integral.

I have always seen myself as a positive person and you come to realise that you are dealing with the natural sensitivities of human beings. That's why I don't go into the dressing room after games. It is too emotional a time. I would rather wait, and speak to the players rationally on Monday morning.

Thanks to Mike Calvin and *Living On The Volcano* for that quote which emphasises just how thoughtful, decent and well rounded a character is Dean Smith.

It is quite obvious that his team respects and plays for him and he has also done a good job of managing upwards to a tough Chairman in Jeff Bonser who does not attend home matches because of his unpopularity with the Walsall supporters.

Bonser admires Smith and his achievements at the club:

His philosophy is to play good football and, regardless of the results, I think that's how we play. We've stuck to the philosophy and we're going to continue to stick to it, because it's bringing us some success.

I can totally see why Brentford want Smith and let us just hope that the feeling is reciprocated. Bonser will probably be a hard nut to crack in terms of compensation and he refused his manager permission to talk to Rotherham when they came calling a few months ago.

Hopefully Smith will want to take up the challenge at Griffin Park and make it obvious to his Chairman that this time he wishes to leave.

Smith was fairly disparaging towards Brentford at the time when we signed his star striker Will Grigg, whom he felt should have joined a bigger club, rather than another League One outfit, however I will take that as a simple case of sour grapes as all is fair in love and war – and football too!

I am sure that nothing is finalised at the present time and that this, just like the Clotet deal, could still go either way. There are no guarantees as there are so many intangibles and potential obstacles that can arise as well as a plethora of different parties involved in any deal including agents and family members.

We also have to keep within our budget and ensure that the entire recruitment package is realistic and affordable.

There will also be the need to decide if he brings any of his staff with him, ideally Richard O'Kelly, another gifted and experienced coach.

Bonser might have something to say about that, as might Matthew Benham given the continued presence of Paul Williams who would surely expect and fully deserve a coaching role in any new set up. Lee Carsley's role will also need to be clarified if it is not already decided.

As you can see, there is much to ponder on and a lot that needs to be settled before we can breathe easily. Walsall have a crucial match against local rivals Shrewsbury Town on Tuesday night and I am certain that all parties would like to know where they stand before then so I expect a speedy decision one way or the other within the next twenty-four hours.

Let's all keep our fingers crossed!

Position	Team	P	W	D	L	F	A	GD	Pt	Form
1	Brighton and Hove A	18	10	8	0	24	14	10	38	D D D W D W
2	Middlesbrough	18	11	3	4	27	12	15	36	W W W L W W
3	Derby County	18	10	6	2	26	11	15	36	W W W L W W
4	Hull City	18	10	5	3	27	11	16	35	W W W W D L
5	Burnley	18	9	7	2	26	17	9	34	W W W D D D
6	Birmingham City	18	8	4	6	25	20	5	28	L L D W L L
7	Ipswich Town	18	7	7	4	28	25	3	28	D D W W D W
8	Sheffield Wednesday	18	7	7	4	25	22	3	28	W W D L W D
9	Reading	18	7	6	5	26	21	5	27	L D D L W L
10	Cardiff City	18	6	8	4	19	16	3	26	D D L W L D
11	Brentford	18	7	4	7	24	25	-1	25	W W L D W D
12	Queens Park Rangers	18	6	5	7	23	25	-2	23	W L L D L W
13	Fulham	18	5	7	6	31	30	1	22	W W L L D D
14	Blackburn Rovers	18	4	9	5	19	18	1	21	L W D D W D
15	Wolverhampton Wndrs	18	5	6	7	22	23	-1	21	L W L D D D
16	Nottingham Forest	18	5	5	8	16	19	-3	20	D L L W L W
17	Leeds United	18	4	7	7	16	21	-5	19	D L W W L L
18	Preston North End	18	3	9	6	13	16	-3	18	D D W D L D
19	Milton Keynes Dons	18	4	4	10	15	24	-9	16	L L W L D D
20	Bristol City	18	3	7	8	18	30	-12	16	D L W D D L
21	Charlton Athletic	18	4	4	10	15	29	-14	16	L L L W W L
22	Huddersfield Town	18	3	6	9	17	28	-11	15	L L D L L L
23	Rotherham United	18	4	3	11	21	33	-12	15	L L L L W W
24	Bolton Wanderers	18	1	9	8	12	25	-13	12	D D L D L D

[30ᵗʰ November 2015]

December

A Good Day – And Almost A Perfect One – 1/12/15

A day jam-packed with action and activity has left every Brentford supporter exhausted and exhilarated and extremely excited about the future prospects for the club.

As expected, Walsall manager Dean Smith was named as our new Head Coach after a compensation deal was agreed with his former club, whom he served with distinction for almost five years.

His assistant, Richard O'Kelly, will join him, which as far as I am concerned is almost as good news as the appointment of Smith as they work hand in glove and O'Kelly has gained a justified reputation as a gifted and innovative coach.

Lee Carsley will remain until the end of the year to help in the transition process, however it is expected that he will then leave the club with our thanks and gratitude ringing in his ears for a difficult job wonderfully well done.

Just to recap, when he took over as interim Head Coach the Bees were languishing in nineteenth place and were on the road to nowhere. Impeccably assisted by the popular Paul Williams, they worked in tandem to turn the situation around and his back to basics approach worked a treat and restored belief to what was a faltering squad and his achievements were deservedly recognised with the award of the coveted Manager of the Month Trophy for October.

He was in charge for ten games which produced a total of five wins and seventeen points and he relinquishes control with Brentford a mere three points shy of the playoffs and looking firmly upwards rather than down.

Dean Smith and Richard O'Kelly were amongst the crowd at Bolton last night but they will take charge today and they both must be delighted with the quality of the material they have been left to work with and further develop.

Paul Williams is away on England duty at the present time and ideally his future will also be decided shortly and we all hope that there will be a role for him at the club within the new management structure given his popularity with the players and the beneficial affect he has had on them.

Brentford came away from the *Macron* with one point when three really beckoned had good chances not been squandered by Lasse Vibe on two occasions and John Swift. Jake Bidwell too came within inches of scoring that long awaited and elusive first goal when his header drifted just wide after he was found quite brilliantly by Alan Judge, as usual the best and most inventive player on the pitch.

In truth this was a frustrating game for the Bees who interspersed some breathtaking one touch football which had the commentators on *Sky Sports* purring with appreciation, with a lot of careless passing and squandering of possession which allowed a limited but forceful and committed Bolton team back into a match which the Bees should have put firmly beyond them. We really let them off the hook and have only ourselves to blame.

As is customary, some of the defending was casual in the extreme with Tarkowski doing his best to gift Bolton another goal from a short back pass with barely a minute on the clock. He and O'Connell defended manfully but this was a match for the suspended Harlee Dean, and the home team outmuscled us at set pieces and always looked dangerous when the ball was in the air and won far too many second balls with Woods, in particular being regularly muscled off the ball.

The equaliser was soft with a cross half cleared by Woods and returned with interest by Danns with a bouncing volley through a crowd of players from just outside the penalty area which squeezed in off the post.

John Swift scored with a Premier League quality curling effort from long range after he and Judge had combined beautifully and he was booked for diving on the stroke of halftime when a penalty kick could just as easily have been given – another major turning point.

Pretty much every fifty-fifty decision went the way of Bolton but they also had more possession than us, a measure of how careless we were with the ball, with possession conceded with monotonous regularity.

And yet from time to time we got it right and tore holes in a porous home defence as we broke with pace and menace. Vibe worked hard but missed his two chances. He had too much time when sent clear before the break by Bidwell and Amos stretched out a long leg to save, and then, near the end, after some scintillating one touch play had torn the defence wide open, Vibe could not beat the keeper who saved well at full stretch.

Button too made a crucial point blank save from the lurking Ameobi when a loose ball fell his way and a game that we could have won comfortably had we scored that elusive second goal ended all square.

We are so close to being an exceptionally good team as our vision and skill on the ball is often of Premier League class. Judge and Swift were always on the same wavelength and worked well together and Diagouraga won every loose ball and also survived a horror challenge from Mark Davies that surely merited a red card from a benign referee who totally shirked his duty.

Yes of course we have weaknesses and shortcomings. We are susceptible to high balls and set pieces and teams that try and overpower us, but try and play football with us and we are likely to come out on top.

We are also profligate in front of goal and miss far too many chances and let teams off the hook. We are lacking in quality up front until Djuricin returns and rely far too much on our midfield to score goals.

That being said McEachran, Colin and Jota are close to returning to fitness and might be followed soon after by Djuricin and even Lewis Macleod so we are going to get even stronger as the months progress.

A mere two months ago we were looking down the barrel of a gun with the bottom three beckoning and the locals muttering and beginning to fear the worst. Changes were needed and they were made and the team now is fitter, far more solid and confident, moves the ball from back to front far quicker and is much better equipped for the demands of the Championship.

Maybe another playoff campaign is going to be a step too far this season, but who knows?

Welcome to Richard O'Kelly and Dean Smith

Dean Smith will be sure to want to make his mark and put his own stamp on things, but I suspect that he will not make too many fundamental changes as the way that we set up and play totally suits the players that we currently possess, as is evidenced by the quality of our football, the results that we are achieving and the fact that this is patently a happy camp at the present time.

Three points tonight would have made this a perfect day but despite the two dropped points, things are going remarkably well at the moment and I fully believe that they will be getting even better quite soon once Messrs. Smith and O'Kelly get to work.

Dear Dean – An Open Letter 2/12/15

Dear Dean,

I am writing on behalf of every Brentford supporter to welcome you and Richard O'Kelly to Brentford and to give you a fan's view of what you will find there once you both get your feet under the table.

Brentford are a series of contradictions – small but ambitious and punching well above its weight, possessing traditional values but also very ambitious and forward seeking, community focused but also looking to broaden and develop its footprint and fan base.

The club is unrecognisable from what it was a mere few years ago before Matthew Benham took control and is now an exemplar and poster child for innovation, originality and breaking the mould, and also as Phil Giles highlighted in his note yesterday, gambling and taking calculated risks.

On the field we used to play either 4-4-2 or 4-3-3, knocked it up to a big man up front, worked off scraps and we could be pretty agricultural at times.

Now things have totally changed and as I am sure you have discovered, we have the highest ball possession percentage in the Championship and, under Mark Warburton, we developed a patient style of football which concentrated on passing the ball along the back four, keeping possession and patiently probing and searching for gaps before breaking forward quickly and striking with deadly speed and effect. We are small and skilful and at our best can run rings around larger and less mobile opponents.

The system depends upon every player, including (and particularly) the goalkeeper, being comfortable on the ball, taking risks (which sometimes do not come off, with cataclysmic effects), having a five-man midfield in which every player rotates position and takes responsibility and has the ability to find a man quickly and accurately as well as getting forward to support the attack.

The lone forward has a difficult and thankless role as he needs to make selfless runs, hold onto the ball and bring others into the game as they advance to support him and also have the energy and prowess to take his chances in front of goal when they eventually come along.

We rely on a combination of inspiration and perspiration and a team ethos as everyone has to work hard, press and cover and there are no real stars, rather a combination of gifted, young and enthusiastic professionals who are all looking to improve and eventually better themselves.

That leads to another problem as we have become a victim of our own success with players like Moses Odubajo and Andre Gray attracting interest from larger and better funded predators higher up the food chain which has resulted in an influx of new players this season to replace our outgoing heroes.

Many who came from abroad and lacked experience of English conditions and the demands of the Championship are only now beginning to find their feet and have required time to settle in. You will need to find the best blend of homegrown and foreign players if we are to progress.

Hopefully your arrival and influence will also help persuade some of our players who are coming towards the end of their contract, such as Harlee Dean, David Button and Alan Judge, to decide that they can fulfil their ambition at Brentford and agree terms to stay with the club.

The most important thing to say is that we possess a treasure trove of talent in almost all positions and it should be an absolute pleasure for you to work with such a bunch of talented and enthusiastic players who are all eager to learn and improve.

Footballers are also footballers but we do our utmost to avoid signing self-obsessed or difficult players and *prima donnas* and you will find a bunch of good pros that will work hard for you and a total absence of cliques.

I am sure that you are well aware that we do things differently here and there are a phalanx of advisers, analysts and support staff at the club – far more than you are used to in your previous job. You will have to face the challenge of how you manage upwards as well as down and create a positive working environment where all these innovative tools are used effectively and help us maintain a competitive advantage.

Similarly you will need to develop a positive and effective working relationship with the Owner, Chairman and Co-Directors of Football who will all be determined to support you and ensure that you are working in tandem and towards a common goal.

We play good, attacking, positive football, just as you did at Walsall. Maybe you will want to tinker with things and put your own stamp on the way we set up but I suspect that you will find that there is not too much that needs changing – merely refining.

Perhaps you will tighten us up a bit at the back as we are not the biggest and strongest of teams and sometimes our midfield stands around admiring opponents rather than pressing, covering or getting stuck in. We also find it hard to get bodies in the box to support our lone striker and do not make sufficient goal attempts from within the penalty area.

I believe that you are used to playing with only one man up front so I doubt if you will be looking to change our 4-2-3-1 formation which has served us so well.

We have a set piece coach but our scoring record from free kicks and corners is abysmal and given our speed on the break we generally look more dangerous from opposition corners than our own. You might well have your own thoughts on how best to deal with this knotty problem!

The elephant in the room is our recruitment strategy and whilst you might not have the final word on who comes in I am sure that you will make your influence felt as you and Richard O'Kelly will be responsible for getting the most out of the squad you are given and the buck will stop with you, so hopefully you will get the type of players that you want and feel most comfortable with.

Pre-Benham we brought in whoever we could and had a squad packed with journeyman players generally way past their best. Now the emphasis is on young burgeoning talent.

A year ago we had great success with signing players from the lower divisions but the emphasis shifted last summer to a hotchpotch of fairly unknown foreign players as we sought to make our money go further. As mentioned earlier, the jury is still out on most of them as they were all thrown into the team far too quickly owing to our injury crisis and generally sank rather than swam.

The signing of Ryan Woods demonstrated a welcome reversion to the policy of finding homegrown nuggets and it will be interesting to see what your preference is given that we are coming closer to the January transfer window.

I do not think that we need many additions at all as we are if anything slightly overloaded in the midfield department once the likes of Jota, Macleod and McEachran return from injury, but you might have a few thoughts about the forward line as we always seem to be struggling to have sufficient strikers at the club and have not yet been able to replace Andre Gray with an affordable player possessing similar assets of pace and power.

We have also been really successful with our loan policy with players such as Alex Pritchard, Chris Long and now John Swift and Sergi Canos sparkling and adding massive value to the squad. We already have a structure in place as well as excellent relationships where it matters but ideally you will also have your own valuable contacts which will help ensure that we will be able to continue our success in this area and obtain the temporary services of more emerging stars.

There is a root and branch review going on of the Academy and given your background in youth development it will be fascinating to see how you attempt to raise standards in that area, eliminate wastage and also attempt to integrate our best youngsters into the first team arena.

We made a massive error of judgement in throwing four inexperienced youngsters to the wolves when we inexplicably played them all together in a Capital One Cup disaster against Oxford United and that mistake must not be repeated, however it would be wonderful if we could get to a point soon when the eighteen players named in every first team squad always include at least one locally developed young player from the Academy.

Dean, I am sure that you will find many similarities between Walsall and Brentford in terms of the passion and enthusiasm and determination to play positive attacking football but here there is a real sense of ambition, and a determination to question traditional ways of doing things, take risks and to invest and progress in a controlled manner, ideally to the Premier League.

There is a plethora of talent at the club, both on and off the pitch and I am sure that you will find it a positive, refreshing and also challenging environment in which to work where everything possible will be done to support you and your endeavours.

As for the fans – the majority of us are still in dreamland and are happy just to be in the Championship. We rejoice in the quality of the players that we are privileged to watch out on the pitch and are more than happy with our lot. We simply crave good attacking football combined with passion, enthusiasm and a real rather than contrived or simulated pride in wearing the shirt. We do not tolerate dilettantes or egomaniacs; they are not welcome at Griffin Park.

Yes, you might need to manage a few expectations as some fans have got a bit above themselves and have forgotten from whence we have come and how far we have progressed in so short a time, but if you are able to give us a team of hardworking and skilful players who play attacking football and demonstrate their commitment every week, and engage in regular and open and honest dialogue with the supporters as you did so well and thoughtfully in your *Bees Player* interview today then we will have very little to complain about and you will receive our full and undivided support.

I will end by wishing you both every good fortune in what I fully expect will turn out to be a magnificent platform and opportunity for you to shine and be the catalyst for further improvement and development at this great club of ours.

Good luck to you both!

Strength In Depth – 6/12/15

In truth, yesterday saw the Bees stroll to a comfortable victory over a poor and overmatched Milton Keynes Dons team and the two goal margin should have been doubled, if not even tripled, given the fact that the Bees controlled the game totally once the impressive Lasse Vibe scored with what was our first attempt on target after twenty minutes.

From then on the floodgates should have opened and a four-goal lead at the interval would have by no means flattered Brentford who created and then frittered away chances with the generosity of potentates distributing largesse – they knew there was more to come and could afford to be so profligate.

The second half continued in the same vein with the Bees in total control but for us long-suffering supporters, we could never relax despite the sumptuous quality of some of our football.

It was almost torture at times as the chances kept coming without consummation, and gilt-edged opportunities too, and a sense of frustration and concern prevailed as we waited with resignation for the careless error, the quick breakaway or set piece that might enable our outplayed visitors to get out of jail and steal away from Griffin Park with an ill-deserved point.

But this is *New Brentford* and despite our profligacy up front, we kept the back door tightly bolted and eventually the second goal came and we could finally breathe more easily.

MK Dons were always a benchmark for us in Division One as they used to set the standard for ball possession and the quality of their passing, and looking at yesterday's stats, they pretty much matched us for possession and pass numbers, but we have now left them far behind us and trailing in our wake as we were so much more incisive than our visitors who went backwards and sideways with mind-numbing regularity and Maynard and Bowditch were lightweight upfront and were never able to cause the imperious Tarkowski and the improving O'Connell any problems that they were unable to deal with.

The speedy Murphy put the afterburners on and beat Yennaris once early on, but never again, as Nico smothered his threat and was also lively and impressive when supporting the attack. As for Jake Bidwell, he set a captain's example, had his usual long range shot fly high, wide and not too handsome and put a perfect curling cross right onto the head of the straining Lasse Vibe who converted the chance with *élan*.

The strong wind played tricks with the ball blowing back towards Ealing Road but we kept the ball on the deck and coped easily with the elements, as well as being turned round to play towards our supporters in the first half by the wily Karl Robinson who is well aware of our preference to attack Ealing Road after the break.

Our visitors' most effective players were our goal frames as Alan Judge, who has been named as Man of the Match more times than any other Championship player this season, struck the top of the post with a wonderful curling thirty-yard free kick which sailed over three walls – two of which were set by us, before bouncing clear with the excellent David Martin totally helpless in this instance and merely waving it past and hoping for the best.

Sergi Canos was left with a clear run in on goal by Vibe's persistence and hassling of the central defenders and hammered the ball onto the crossbar when a little less impetuosity and more control would surely have seen him scoring and, early in the second half, Vibe turned inside after some lovely interplay, and hammered the ball onto the crossbar.

Alan Judge also missed carelessly when sent clean through by Kerschbaumer's brave header but he hit Martin's head as the keeper spread himself when the goal was gaping. Kerschbaumer then saw his poke cleared off the line, Vibe had a clinically taken effort disallowed for offside but also shot horribly over when he saw the whites of the keeper's eyes after Button's brilliantly placed and weighted half volley sent him streaking away down the right wing.

The litany of misses continued in the second half with Judge firing over from close range after a corner was flicked on by a defender and Woods was also denied right in front of an empty net before the clincher finally came and settled our nerves.

We are not the most dangerous of teams from corners, let alone short corners, but this time we hit the jackpot, aided and abetted by some lumbering and inept defending. The ball was played to Sam Saunders whose raking cross was headed almost out of his keeper's hands by Kay and Alan Judge sent the ball back towards goal, rather than shot, where it eluded a bunch of straining defenders and slowly trickled past the unsighted Martin and settled into the corner of the net.

It was ironic indeed given the quality of some of our earlier play which cut our visitors apart that the match clinching goal came from a lucky break, but one that was long overdue and well-deserved given the earlier happenings of the afternoon.

This was a wonderful start for the new management duo of Dean Smith and Richard O'Kelly who must both be jumping for joy at the obvious quality, and more importantly, depth of the squad that they have inherited.

Yesterday we were without the suspended Harlee Dean and his return to the team cannot now be guaranteed given how well the new partnership of Tarkowski and O'Connell has settled down. They look comfortable and well matched together and Tarks is a far better and happier player on his more natural right hand side of defence.

The acid test of our new central defensive pairing will come next Saturday when they will have to deal with the massive threat of McCormack, Dembele and Smith at Craven Cottage but we have an embarrassment of riches in this position given the talent of the emerging Barbet who is patiently learning about the English game and waiting for his chance to arrive.

Nico Yennaris had his best ever game for us yesterday and will not relinquish his shirt to Max Colin without a fight. We certainly have two high quality right backs.

Yesterday we were without the injured John Swift, and Alan McCormack also tweaked his groin in the warm-up, yet we shrugged off their loss, never missed either of them, and totally dominated the midfield.

Toumani Diagouraga was imperious, comfortable on the ball, showed vision and commitment and drove us forward. Ryan Woods was finally moved to his favoured central spot and was the glue that held us together. You never really notice him until he isn't there, as was the case after his late substitution when we lost our way for the final few moments. He is fast becoming an indispensable part of the team.

Konstantin Kerschbaumer also justified his selection with a hard running display which demonstrated his quality and good use of the ball. He has been slow to settle and I do not see him as a first choice when everyone is fit but he is fast improving.

Sergi Canos stepped in at the last moment and excited and frustrated in equal measures but he is a massive talent and has now proved that he is fully capable of starting – rather than just finishing – games. He led Dean Lewington a merry dance and will be a massive asset to us as the season progresses.

Alan Judge was simply energy personified and was unstoppable at times and he is the fulcrum of the entire team. Sam Saunders also showed that he is fully restored to fitness and put in a good shift off the bench.

If that is not enough, yesterday saw the return of Jota and our first sight of Josh McEachran. Jota was given a short run out and looked as good as ever as he glided over the turf and also put in a couple of enthusiastic challenges. Welcome back to *The King* after so long and frustrating a break. We must not expect too much too soon from him but his return is an enticing prospect. Josh too will add immeasurably to our strength in depth. Oh and maybe Lewis Macleod will also be challenging for a place one day in the not too distant future.

I cannot remember when we last, or ever, boasted so much strength in depth, talent and quality in midfield.

Lasse Vibe, or *our Jamie Vardy*, as Dean Smith so memorably referred to him, was energy personified and never gave his opponents a moment's rest. He held the ball up well, looked sharp, brought others into the game and looked dangerous in front of goal. Maybe we will be fine with just him and Philipp Hofmann as our only available strikers for the next month?

I have left the best to last. Yes, we were excellent on the ball and at times resembled last season's team in terms of our quality, pace and incision but what stood out yesterday was how hard we worked without the ball. We pressed and challenged as a team and were tireless and relentless in our efforts to win the ball back.

Perspiration and inspiration in equal quantities – surely the sign of a good team?

Dean Smith's era has started off with a bang and there is much to look forward to as he begins to impose his influence on what, with key players finally returning from injury, is starting to look a high quality squad with excellent options in every position.

Craven Cottage awaits!

Alan Judge mesmerising the MK Dons defence

It's FA Cup Time Once More – 8/12/15

The draw for the third round of the FA Cup is traditionally one of the more anticipated and truly magical moments of every season as it is the time when dreams can come true and David gets the rare chance to put Goliath firmly in his place.

A favourable draw can help put a minnow on the map and even mean the difference between surviving for another season or even falling into the ravages of administration.

Just put yourself in the place of Whitehawk's manager Steve King whose team fully deserved their last gasp equaliser at Dagenham & Redbridge yesterday. They are now just a replay win away in a game that seems certain to attract live television coverage from a money-spinning tie at Premier League Everton, one that will offer an outside chance of glory, put their players in the shop window and probably earn the club more in an afternoon than in an entire season in the confines of the National League South.

Given the occasion, I made a special effort and rushed home from work last night in order to catch the draw which was apparently set for seven o'clock. In retrospect I really needn't have done so, as like every other sap who was imbued with romantic memories of sepia-lit FA Cup ties in the dim and distant past and who had done the same as me, I had to sit through fifteen interminable minutes of boring and sterile filler material – a series of totally unnecessary interviews and highlights intended to set the scene and build the atmosphere and sense of theatre before the numbered balls were drawn out of – not the traditional velvet bag – but a soulless Perspex container. Where had the magic gone?

There was one snippet of previous action that I did enjoy watching over the weekend, Scott Hogan soaring in the air to score a perfect header for Rochdale against Leeds United. We can but hope that we will be seeing him in similar goalscoring action for the Bees in the not too distant future.

Apparently I am now a supporter of one of England's so-called elite clubs given our fairly new-found Championship status and somehow that also makes things feel rather different given that we now enter the competition at the Third Round stage and have not had to fight our way through two previous ties to get to this point.

So what was I looking for from the draw, once it finally began? A matchup against a Premier League big boy and the chance to test ourselves on national television? A lower league team at Griffin Park? An away game at a minnow? Death or glory?

What we actually received highlighted the wonder and the unpredictability of the competition. A home tie against either Chesterfield or Walsall, Division One opposition who should both surely be beatable at Griffin Park. Or so you would have thought as you can take nothing for granted when it comes to predicting the outcome of cup matches and as we know to our cost the Bees have been the victims of giant killings themselves. Does anyone else remember Guildford City turning us over in 1968 and the likes of Barrow and Wrexham too in more recent times?

Chesterfield earned a replay with a late scrambled equaliser on Saturday and should they come out on top next week then that would set up the first ever FA Cup meeting between the two teams.

Walsall are a far more enticing prospect given the recent arrival of their former manager Dean Smith as the new Head Coach at Griffin Park. Their supporters would doubtless relish the opportunity to obtain some quick revenge against the team that enticed him away from The Banks's Stadium.

Since his move was first mooted the airwaves and social media have been buzzing with harsh, ribald and ill thought through comments from diehard Walsall fans on the one hand damning their former manager and his achievements on their behalf with faint praise and also suggesting that he has barely bettered himself by moving to Brentford. Fighting talk indeed and Brentford supporters will also be looking for the chance to refute their assertions.

Walsall currently boast several of the lower divisions' finest young prospects within their ranks and the Bees will welcome the chance to view the likes of Tom Bradshaw, Rico Henry and Romaine Sawyers at close quarters particularly at a time when the Transfer Window will have recently opened. It would be an enticing prospect if one or more of them ended up using this match as an audition before a move to us – we can but dream!

Should Walsall earn the right to play us next month then it would be the fourth time that the two teams had been drawn against each other in the past forty-five years and the Bees have come out on top on every occasion to date. Hopefully another good omen.

The Bees defeated Walsall in the Second Round in 1970/71 when we reached the last sixteen of the competition and eventually went out with full honours to Hull City. The match against Walsall was closely fought and after Gordon Phillips had foiled the evergreen Colin Taylor with a series of excellent saves, Roger Cross finished off a carefully choreographed move from a free kick to settle the match.

It was a similar situation in 1988/89 when we reached the Sixth Round before losing at Anfield. Walsall were higher division opponents and a Keith Jones goal earned a draw at Fellows Park before the replay was settled by Allan Cockram who gleefully scored from close range after Fred Barber had parried an effort from Kevin Godfrey.

Our most recent meeting was in 2009/10 when newcomer Leon Legge gave an all action display, winning the match with a typical towering header from a corner and saving it with a perfectly timed and executed sliding tackle to rob Walsall striker Steve Jones who had a clear run in on goal.

Unfortunately we were not destined to have a long FA Cup run that season as we went out in the next round to Doncaster Rovers.

Whoever we play it will be certain to be a tough and closely fought match against a team determined to bring its so called better down a peg or two.

We now have three home games in a ridiculously short six-day period and with promotion challengers Middlesbrough and Burnley due to visit Griffin Park immediately after the cup tie neither League game can be termed a gimme.

The management has always spoken of the need to build up a large squad with excellent cover in every position and our depth will surely be tested as changes will need to be made over this period to ensure that the players are well rested. Lee Carsley certainly picked practically the same team for every match but squad rotation will be a must over this packed period of activity and thankfully, with our stars returning from injury we will be able to cope with the challenge.

It is now almost three years since we last had a decent FA Cup run and I still find it hard to believe that we did not beat Chelsea in that epic Fourth Round clash at Griffin Park but that is a story for another day.

After a slow and difficult start, this season is finally gaining momentum and promises much excitement as Christmas approaches. An FA Cup run would simply be the cherry on top.

They Played For Brentford And Fulham – 10/12/15

The sense of anticipation and sheer excitement is mounting as we start to count down the days, hours and even minutes until Saturday's massive clash at Craven Cottage where local bragging rights are once again up for grabs.

It is notoriously hard, if not impossible, to predict the outcome of local derbies as form so often seems to go out of the window and matches can be decided on one incident, a referee's whim or a lucky bounce so I shan't even try to do so at this juncture.

Instead I shall try my hardest to alleviate some of the tension that we are all surely beginning to feel by reminiscing about some of the footballers who have played for both the Bees and Fulham over the years.

Starting way back in the mists of time with a remarkable man in **Tom Wilson** who was hardly an archetypical footballer as he was also a qualified surveyor who played with distinction for both clubs throughout the 50s as a sturdy and reliable right back.

After retirement he returned to Fulham as a director of the club where he worked closely with his former teammate **Jimmy Hill** to negotiate the purchase of Craven Cottage from the Bank of England, which saved the club from being merged with Queens Park Rangers and Craven Cottage from being sold for development. Jimmy Hill is worth an article on his own given his lengthy lists of achievements both on and off the pitch and his amazing career began at Griffin Park where he was a member of the acclaimed half back line with Tony Harper and Ron Greenwood.

John Richardson is a name that should have become well known throughout the football world as he seemed certain to become a star, but it somehow didn't happen for him and his career never reached the heights that at one time seemed likely. He followed his Uncle, Billy Gray, from Millwall to Brentford as a seventeen year-old and soon broke into the first team at a time when the Bees were concentrating on youth as they could not afford to pay older and more expensive players.

Some, like Eddie Reeve, Phil Basey and Mike Ogburn soon fell by the wayside but Richardson was an exciting prospect who, despite his youth, dominated games from his berth at inside left until he broke his ankle in three places soon after scoring at Port Vale. He recovered, but was never really the same and was moved to a more defensive role and the fans were not the most patient with him either. He was sold to Fulham when still only twenty but his career fizzled out at Aldershot after a spell playing in America.

I have written so many times about the late, great, **Allan Mansley** and I mourn him still as watching him sprint down the left wing leaving a trail of beaten opponents in his wake was one of the wonders and delights of my youth. Injury cruelly halted his career in its tracks when greatness beckoned and he had a brief and unsuccessful loan spell at Craven Cottage, playing once in a heavy defeat at Swansea before his career ended so sadly and prematurely.

Roger Cross is another who is pretty high up on my list of boyhood heroes. He of the flowing locks, white boots, long throw and howitzer left foot shot. He oozed elegance and class amongst the dross that surrounded him after his move from West Ham United and it was no surprise when after scoring fourteen times in his first full season he moved on to Fulham for a thirty thousand pound fee when the directors kept their word to allow him to return to a higher level if the opportunity ever arose.

He looked a different and lesser player in the Second Division, more cumbersome and less prone to take a match by the scruff of its neck and he soon returned to his natural home where he sparkled for another four years before making a surprise move to Millwall which never worked out for him. He is still involved with the game as a scout at Charlton and has enjoyed a long and illustrious career.

Barry Salvage forged an excellent career for himself as a quick winger with an eye for goal. He never left London and played for four local clubs, starting with a brief spell at Fulham before moving to Millwall and Queens Park Rangers. He enjoyed a productive stay at Brentford, often cutting in for a shot and I remember his winning goal after a mere twenty-four seconds against Charlton. He had a second spell at The Den and then moved to play in America and Norway before tragically dying very young.

Dave Metchick was a small and skilful ball playing midfielder whose career never quite took off. He started off at Fulham but failed to establish himself in the First Division and drifted from club to club before making a surprise move to Arsenal where he never played in the first team. He joined the Bees in 1973 on his return from playing in the North American Soccer League and made an immediate impact, pulling the strings in midfield and using the ball neatly and effectively. He was a really good player for us who shone in a mediocre team.

John Fraser joined the Bees after a decent spell at Fulham which included him playing in the 1975 FA Cup Final out of position at left back when Les Strong, also to play for Brentford later in his career, was forced to pull out through injury. He transformed himself from a fullback into an excellent ball winning midfielder who was a mainstay of the team until, like several others, he apparently fell out with a former Fulham colleague in Brentford Manager Fred Callaghan, and ended up as a taxi driver.

Dave Carlton was a bargain signing by Bill Dodgin – another ex-Fulham stalwart – who gave us excellent service for four years. He had a wonderful eye for a pass and often switched the point of attack. He created many goals but could sometimes lose his head on the pitch and incur the wrath of referees. Fulham left him go as a youngster but Carlton established himself at Northampton Town before a mere three thousand pound transfer fee brought him to Griffin Park.

Steve Scrivens is another footballer who bemuses me to this day. A lithe and quick left-winger who played a few games for Fulham as a teenager, he joined Brentford on loan in December 1976 and impressed everyone with his ability. Despite all our efforts, Fulham would not allow us to sign him on permanent basis and he returned to Craven Cottage – and never played for them, or any other Football League club again. Can anybody please explain why, as it appeared to be a total waste of an exceptionally talented young player?

Paul Shrubb is quite simply one of the bravest men it has been my honour and privilege to meet. Rejected by Fulham after one measly appearance, he made a name for himself in South Africa before joining Brentford where he sparkled for five seasons and played nearly two hundred games for us in a variety of positions. He was consistent, honest, versatile and skilful whether he played as a central defender, midfielder, striker or even as an emergency goalkeeper.

He gave everything to the team and was a wonderful clubman. He then gave equally good service to Aldershot where he also became a local hero and to this day he continues to be an inspiration to everyone as he fights Motor Neurone Disease. Shrubby, every Brentford supporter salutes you.

Barry Lloyd is one of the rare players who had spells at all three West London clubs as he started at Chelsea before making over two hundred and fifty appearances for Fulham and was on the bench for the 1975 FA Cup Final. He also captained the club and is best remembered for a superlative volleyed FA Cup goal against Leicester City's Peter Shilton which wowed the *Match of the Day* viewers. For some reason he never captured the hearts and minds of Brentford fans and was subjected to some unpleasant barracking. He did a decent enough job in midfield and contributed to our promotion push but his stay was short and he moved to America before beginning a long and successful career as a manager and scout.

Most goalkeepers count the number of clean sheets but for **Trevor Porter** it was clean windows. He was Peter Mellor's understudy at Fulham and did a good, unassuming, reliable and unspectacular job when he signed for Brentford after Len Bond's injuries sustained in a car crash. He remained at the club for a couple of seasons combining the role of reserve goalkeeper with his window cleaning.

Terry Hurlock is best remembered for his swashbuckling and rambunctious performances for Brentford. A terrifying and unforgettable sight with his long flowing hair, beard and gold earring twinkling in the sunshine, he combined aggressive tackles with an unexpected range of more subtle skills and enjoyed a long and illustrious career which was finished off with a short spell at Craven Cottage where at the age of thirty-seven he retired after he suffered a broken leg after a tackle by Martin Grainger, ironically enough in a friendly match against the Bees.

Francis Joseph is another near-legend at Brentford who played a few games for Fulham in his swansong. He promised so much but never fully recovered from a badly broken leg, lost his greatest asset in his pace and was never the same player again. What a terrible waste of an exceptional talent who could and should have reached the top.

His partner during his golden spell at Griffin Park was **Tony Mahoney**. Fulham discarded him like an unwanted old sock after his early promise evaporated but he was revitalised after Fred Callaghan signed him for the Bees. He proved to be an exceptional target man who scored fifteen goals in only twenty-eight games before tragedy struck and he suffered a broken leg on an icy pitch against Swindon Town. And that was pretty much that for him as he never fully recovered form or fitness.

Left back **Les Strong** was a Fulham stalwart for many years and is best remembered for missing the 1975 FA Cup Final through injury. He had a brief loan spell at Brentford near the end of his career but retired soon afterwards.

Terry Bullivant was another Barry Lloyd in that he did well at Craven Cottage as a midfield player who earned a big money move to Aston Villa but he never really impressed at Griffin Park where his over-aggressive style and inconsistent form ensured that his stay was short. He later returned to Griffin Park more successfully as part of Ron Noades's coaching team and later became Assistant Manager to Andy Scott.

Tony Parks also had a loan spell at Fulham after he lost his place in goal at Brentford to Graham Benstead and he eventually joined Fulham on a permanent basis but he only played twice for them.

Striker **Tony Sealy** had two loan spells at Fulham before joining them on a permanent basis and was a regular goalscorer. Small, nippy and sharp, he made his debut for Brentford at Anfield in the FA Cup before scoring memorably after just thirteen seconds against Bristol City.

Striker **Kelly Haag** scored prolifically in the reserves and youth team but he found the step up to first team football a bit too steep and never managed a league goal for the Bees but scored a few times for both Fulham and Barnet.

Tony Finnigan was another player who never really settled down anywhere after leaving Crystal Palace and had brief spells at both Brentford and Fulham without much effect.

Gerry Peyton was a Fulham goalkeeping legend who played nearly four hundred games for the club. Despite being thirty-six years of age he was wonderfully calm and consistent when he had two spells at Griffin Park in our ill-fated relegation season of 1992/93 and was one of our few bright spots in a disastrous season.

Gus Hurdle never managed a first team appearance at Fulham but he was rescued from a career on the buses when he walked in unannounced to the Brentford training ground and had a decent career as an attacking fullback.

Glenn Cockerill joined the Bees from Fulham as Micky Adams's assistant manager but he played an important role on the field as a solid defensive midfield player despite being nearly forty years of age. He had enjoyed an illustrious career but still had something left in the tank.

Bees manager, **Micky Adams**, a former Fulham player and manager himself, made one forgettable appearance for the club as a substitute in the Auto Windscreens Shield match at Luton but thankfully concentrated more on his thankless task of attempting to save the club from relegation to the bottom division in 1997/98.

He brought in several of his old boys to assist him and **Paul Watson** was one of his more successful imports. A right footed left back who excelled in swinging in dangerous curling corners and free kicks, he soon became a fan favourite but he was replaced by the quicker Ijah Anderson and left for a successful stay at Brighton.

Danny Cullip was a no-nonsense bullet-headed centre half who took no prisoners but he lost his place after damaging his knee and, like Watson, moved on to help Brighton to promotion.

Darren Freeman of the long curly mane was an effective if inconsistent winger or striker who was surprisingly released by Fulham and had a free scoring start to his Brentford career under Ron Noades before joining the exodus to Brighton.

Steve Sidwell proved to be one of Brentford's most effective loan signings. Despite his youth and total inexperience, Arsenal entrusted him into the care of Steve Coppell and he quickly flourished into a wonderfully skilful midfielder with an eye for goal and the ability to open up a defence with a single pass. He was far too good to join us on a permanent basis, particularly when we failed to gain promotion in 2002 and he eventually made his mark in the Premier League with the likes of Reading and Aston Villa before providing excellent service to Fulham too.

John Salako made his name as a two-footed winger with electric pace at Crystal Palace and later enjoyed a short spell at Fulham under Kevin Keegan. He was thirty-five when Martin Allen signed him but he found a new lease of life and produced some excellent spells on the left wing and some less good ones as an emergency left back. He was deadly from the penalty spot too – except when it mattered in front of the television cameras at Hinckley.

Michael Turner was a wonderfully strong and elegant centre half for the Bees and gave us wonderful service for two seasons before being spirited away by Hull City. He became a Premier League regular and last season he played against the Bees for both Norwich City and Fulham.

Darren Pratley continues in his career as combative midfielder who caused us many problems a week or so back when playing for Bolton Wanderers. He began his career at Fulham but made only a single appearance for them as a substitute before he had two successful loan spells at Griffin Park under Martin Allen before joining Swansea. He was hard running and strong with an excellent shot on him and did well for us until he fell out with some of the supporters after a mad and chaotic night at Gillingham in 2006.

Paul Brooker deserves an article all to himself! He was a tricky winger who was predominantly a super sub at Craven Cottage before establishing himself at Brighton. He joined the Bees on a free transfer but despite his obvious talent he never produced or did his ability justice on a regular basis despite scoring a solo goal of utter world class at Swindon and his spell at the club ended in acrimony after he fell out with supporters and management alike.

Junior Lewis drifted from club to club after making his debut for Fulham before making his mark at Gillingham. He joined the Bees as a non-contract player in 2005 and played an immense part in a Boxing Day victory over promotion rivals Swansea City when he totally controlled the midfield. A true on-field leader, he has since become a coach and manager.

Calum Willock was a total waste of over fifty thousand pounds when he signed from Peterborough as the last-gasp replacement for DJ Campbell. It is really hard to understand quite why he was so inept given his previous track record as a regular goalscorer for Posh, whom he joined after unsuccessful spells at Fulham, QPR and Bristol Rovers. He scored a mere three goals for the Bees and never looked likely to become the player that was required to spearhead our promotion push. The one abiding memory of him was his farcical and appalling air shot against Barnsley that a naïve referee embarrassingly interpreted as having been caused by an opponent's trip and he awarded us the softest penalty kick imaginable.

Jamie Smith had a good spell as an attacking fullback at Crystal Palace and enjoyed a loan spell at Craven Cottage. He joined the Bees on loan from Bristol City in 2006 but never really impressed and missed a very presentable goalscoring opportunity in the playoff defeat by Swansea.

Robert Milson was a young red headed midfielder who along with his colleague **Wayne Brown**, a small but tricky right-winger, joined the Bees on loan in 2008. Milson could certainly play and split the Accrington defence with a perfect through pass for Alan Connell to score an excellent goal and Brown too played an effective role in an improving team before they both returned from when they had come.

Richard Lee was an all-time Brentford favourite for his ability in goal allied to his sunny temperament and I have already written many times about him. He had fallen out of contention at Griffin Park initially through injury and made a surprise loan move to Fulham as injury cover late last season but never played a game. Despite that we still remember him with great fondness!

Pacy fullback or winger, **Ryan Fredericks** had a spell at Griffin Park on loan from Spurs but barely played a game. He is now at Fulham after a short stay at Bristol City.

We will end, appropriately enough, with **Marcello Trotta** who is written indelibly in Brentford's history for what transpired deep into injury time against Doncaster back in April 2013. He was brave and confident enough in his own ability to venture back to the club for a second loan spell from Fulham and he helped lead us to promotion and more than vindicated himself. He is now making a great success of his career back in his native Italy.

There are so many close links between the two clubs, so many shared hero and villains, and we have not even taken into account the careers of Brentford managers such as **Bill Dodgin, Fred Callaghan, Micky Adams** and **Leroy Rosenior** who all cut their teeth at Craven Cottage.

Roll on Saturday!

Sitting With The Enemy – 13/12/15

Phil Mison used to do the commentaries on the Brentford match video back in the days of Gary Blissett, Terry Evans and Keith Millen. He did a fine job but for all his on-air enthusiasm for the Bees he managed to conceal a deadly secret – he is and always has been a rabid Fulham fan – a revelation that might have seen him drummed out of Griffin Park had it become more widely known.

We have always stayed in touch over the years and he invited me to accompany him to yesterday's match which I watched from the Hammersmith End, a solitary Bee in amongst a horde of Fulham supporters.

It was both interesting and illuminating to watch the game through their eyes and also observe the Brentford supporters – all five thousand of them – packed behind the opposite goal.

There is a feeling of muted anger, disappointment but also acceptance amongst the Fulham fans. They know that their team has massively underperformed over the last couple of years, that they have been landed with a series of managers who have been unable to turn things around and with the money expended upon the squad and the massive amount of talent within it they should at the very least be up and around the top of the Championship table and not languishing down amongst the also-rans.

But nobody seemed to get too worked up about it, they gently seethed in the wind and rain and politely put up with the multitude of inadequacies that they were forced to observe throughout the afternoon without overly criticising or subjecting any of their players to much vitriol or abuse.

Their supporters finally came alive when they scored and near the end of the match when the dangerous McCormack and Dembele were combining dangerously and looked as if they might earn their team an unlikely and totally undeserved victory.

There was no real feeling of emotion or anticipation or that we were at a West London derby match being played against a deadly rival where bragging rights were at stake and that the result really mattered and a defeat would cause the remainder of the weekend to be spent in a fog of despair.

The Brentford team and fans were barely abused, noticed or even referred to, we were simply another in a long line of teams outplaying their heroes on their own home turf and the only time the Fulham fans became really animated was to jeer when the Bees supporters celebrated in vain when Jota's late effort was controversially disallowed.

This was in massive contrast to the Brentford supporters who could be heard quite clearly from the other end of the pitch as they provided their team with non-stop encouragement and vocal support for the entire game.

That is the difference between the two clubs. We are on the way up and are revelling in the excitement of our journey and rejoice in the anticipation of even more triumphs and glories to come.

Fulham are merely faded glory and look likely to drift rudderless and fall even further until somebody eventually gets tight control over them and an inspirational and competent manager succeeds in clearing out the plethora of deadwood and getting the rest of their overpaid and underperforming former stars to put in a shift every week and, more importantly, learn how to defend.

Brentford looked a compact, well-organised and talented team and in truth should have come away with all three points but they shot themselves in the foot by conceding a daft equalising goal close to halftime and then missing three golden opportunities to retake the lead early in the second half when they were totally dominating the game.

Fulham scored a well-taken second goal totally against the run of play but, miracle of miracles, the Bees equalised almost immediately from a beautifully worked corner before seeing their celebrations stifled when Jota's close range header seemed to have regained the lead but was adjudged to have been narrowly offside.

Diagouraga and Woods worked tirelessly to win possession back from a talented but immobile Fulham midfield which out-passed but never out-worked Brentford.

Judge buzzed around as normal providing energy and inspiration in equal doses, Canos burst into life spasmodically before being booked for an unnecessary and overzealous tackle and praise is due to Kerschbaumer who finally looked comfortable and not out of place in the first team and produced a hardworking display in which he used the ball effectively and could also have broken his goalscoring duck had his first half effort not been blocked and the keeper not got down well to save his close-range poke after the break.

McCormack and Dembele are without doubt the two best strikers in this division and they were a real handful, particularly when Woodrow and Smith joined them late on and Fulham fielded a four-pronged attack which stretched our defence to its limits.

We coped well with Bidwell immense and inspirational, twice blocking seemingly goal bound efforts when Fulham threatened late on.

O'Connell and Tarkowski stood up well to the tough challenge they faced, but Tarky lost concentration twice and his errors were extremely costly as he headed a McCormack cross almost out of Button's hands into his own net and he then allowed Dembele to run off him onto McCormack's subtle flick and he was outpaced and was unable to get in a tackle before the ball was dispatched past Button for a goal of brilliant simplicity.

Yennaris was as efficient and competent as normal and Button made one stupendous save from a rasping McCormack free kick.

Brentford took time to grow into the game but took the lead when a poorly timed tackle by Richards ended Bidwell's run into the area after a sweeping move. The Fulham fans belatedly emerged from their torpor and bemoaned the decision. *Never a foul* and *outside the area* was their one-eyed verdict but the television evidence was damning and Judge took responsibility for converting our long-overdue first spot kick of the season and scored calmly and confidently.

Fulham had a lot of the ball but did little with it as we pressed them relentlessly and Parker and O'Hara never looked a convincing or effective pairing for our hosts and but for Tarkowski's aberration we would have been in front at the interval.

Bidwell almost won a second penalty straight after the break but this time Fredericks timed his tackle perfectly. Woods frustratingly scuffed his shot when well placed and Lonergan saved well from Kerschbaumer and quite brilliantly from Vibe before Fulham scored with their first effort on target in the second half.

We responded quickly when Bidwell's perfectly placed corner was flicked on by Tarkowski at the near post and converted jubilantly by Jack O'Connell for his first goal for the club.

Swift and Jota made a real impact as substitutes and it was Swift's centre that Jota flicked home with his head for what we all felt was the likely winner, but the assistant referee thought differently and all available evidence would suggest that he got the decision hopelessly wrong.

The last quarter of the match was frenetic with non-stop action and the game ended with Fulham pressing hard, but the Bees held out and the honours were even.

Brentford are now a competent and above average Championship team with aspirations to progress far higher than that.

The foundations have been laid, there are yet more talented players to come back from injury and suspension and challenge for a place on the bench – let alone the starting eleven, and we look likely to get even stronger as the New Year approaches.

I enjoyed my afternoon sitting with the enemy and greatly appreciated that I was allowed to walk directly towards Hammersmith after the match rather than being sent on the same circuitous detour endured by every other Brentford fan, but I know which one of the two clubs is going somewhere fast – and it certainly isn't Fulham.

Bees Top Fan – Barr-None? – 15/12/15

Brentford supporter Peter Lumley's literary contributions have previously graced this column and today I am proud and delighted to say that he wants to pay tribute to a dear friend of his who is a fellow Brentford fanatic and someone that he believes is also the top Bees fan, Barr-none!

During my seventy-three years as a Brentford supporter I have naturally chosen my heroes from the scores of talented players, managers and now coaches. But I do not want to overlook the thousands of supporters I have met on the terraces and in the stands over the years. So I have chosen one who, for me, has a record of support that is second to none and which epitomises the loyalty of a legion of fans.

He is John Barr, known by his friends as head of a clan calling themselves the "Barr Boys."

Before going any further I should declare an interest. John and I have led parallel lives that were described in the Brentford programme some months ago.

First things first:

1. *We were both born in the month of September; me in 1932, and John a year later.*

2. *We both went to primary schools in Heston about the same time.*

3. *We both served two years of National Service with the RAF in the early 1950s.*

4. *We both embarked on careers in local newspaper journalism, firstly in Ealing, Southall and Hayes areas where we first met reporting on inquests at the West Middlesex Coroners' Court at Ealing Town Hall.*

5. *We then both worked eventually for the pharmaceutical company, Glaxo (now GSK at Brentford) in the Press and Public Relations Department. John remained with the expanding global company for the rest of his working life while I moved to the industry's trade association on which Glaxo was the leading British-owned company.*

6. *We both share a love of golf as a recreation, but our enthusiasm for the game outshines our competence.*

7. *And for the past fifty years or so we have, for much of the time, occupied adjoining season ticket seats in D Block, immediately in front of the Press Box.*

I have encouraged my two sons, Nick and Mike, and two of my five grandsons, James and Matthew, to become Bees fans. Mike is a season ticket holder and the two grandsons have, in turn, been Junior Season Ticket holders.

But that family achievement pales into insignificance when compared to John's family record of memberships.

So here it is:

1. *Three brothers, Dennis, Brian and Cliff, of whom Dennis and Brian are sadly no long with us;*

2. *Two grandsons, John and Peter;*

3. *Two great-grandsons, Joshua, aged 7 and an established Junior Season Ticket holder, and Jasper (just five months at Christmas) has recently been enlisted in the Babees.*

Brother Cliff, retired journalist and ex-Middlesex Chronicle reporter in the era of legendary Bees scribe George Sands, has lived in Florida for many years but on his rare visits to the UK insists on seeing every game possible and otherwise maintains an active interest in the team's performances through the internet and televised games.

John was one of the founder members of the Brentford Lifeline initiative some 30 years ago, a member of Bees United, a holder of the fund-raising Loan Bond a subscriber to the lottery and, with his clan has sponsored home kits for many players including, most recently, Stuart Dallas and Alan McCormack. He has also been a regular at end-of-season dinners and other social events, usually with family and friends.

It was his late older brother, Dennis, who introduced him to Griffin Park in the 1946/47 season and one of his early memories was seeing Bees beat Wolves by four goals to one in the old First Division. Sadly, the Bees were relegated soon after, and not for the first time!

Dennis had a son, David, who coincidentally was a friend of another David, the son of the late Eric White, the Bees press officer for many years and a pioneer of match day programmes.

Over the past sixty-eight years, John has missed only a handful of home games and, at the age of eighty-two, still travels to all points of the UK to watch as many away games as possible.

He is invariably accompanied by his fire officer grandson, also John Barr and affectionately known as "Little John"- a nickname bestowed on him when he first came to Griffin Park at the age of eight. "Little John" is now over six feet tall. And has already been a season ticket holder for about twenty years.

There was a period of time in the 1960s when John worked for a newspaper group in North London and was forced to report on teams such as Arsenal at Highbury, and semi-pros like Enfield. He recalls that one of the consolations at Arsenal were the half-time refreshments and being in the press box with the famous Compton brothers, Denis and Leslie. But he claims that most of the time he was thinking about how Brentford were performing.

These days, and for many decades, John has been sitting outside the press box at Griffin Park immediately in front of Bees Player commentator Mark Burridge. And John can often be overheard on match commentaries urging the Bees to get forward or for goalkeeper David Button to release the ball earlier.

He is not a great fan of the disciplined, but somewhat overdone, strategy of defenders passing the ball across the face of goal and then back to the keeper. In our days of schoolboy football and immediate post-war soccer, passing the ball across the face of goal was regarded as a cardinal sin!

How times have changed.

John moved to the Thames-side village of Laleham from his family home in Heston some 21 years ago to find that one of his near neighbours was the iconic Peter Gelson who he sees regularly at football or shops and has a quick chat. (What they find to talk about I cannot possibly hazard a guess!)

When not able to follow Brentford away, John's passion for football is met by visits to Staines Town who in recent times have been managed by Marcus Gayle and currently Nicky Forster. Their fixtures, and other non-league matches, often provide John with glimpses of former young Bees players.

We have discussed Brentford performances ad infinitum over the years, but I can recall only one real difference of opinion and that was over the club's shock decision to part with the services of manager Mark Warburton.

As former journalists and professional PR advisors, we agreed that the Board's initial statement, responding to media leaks, was a communications disaster.

But on the decision itself I was a severe critic, but John's deep loyalty to the club led him to taking a much more conciliatory approach. So we had to agree to differ on that one.

I have to note that in recent weeks the club's top management team has displayed a vast improvement in terms of PR/Communications, but not before time.

Finally, like me, one of John's remaining ambitions is to see Brentford playing Premier League football at the new Lionel Road stadium.

If that ambition is fulfilled it is nothing less that John (and so many loyal fans) deserves for his dedication to the sporting love of his life.

Thank you, Peter for this wonderful tribute to a very special man who I am also privileged to have met.

I wrote about Bob Spicer last year, the much missed veteran Brentford supporter whom I confess I still think about to this day and I am sure that there are many others out there like the two of them.

I would love to hear from anyone who would like to write about other similar long-serving and loyal Brentford supporters as I am sure that they all have a great story to tell.

Over to all of you!

Far Too Much Christmas Generosity from The Bees! – 16/12/15

I fully appreciate that Christmas is the time for giving but over the past two matches Brentford have shown far too much holiday spirit and conceded five ridiculously soft goals.

Away games at Fulham and Cardiff City are tough enough obstacles to overcome without giving the opposition a leg-up and a serious helping hand and after two glaring defensive errors at Craven Cottage last Saturday which cost the Bees victory, Cardiff were not made to work very hard to score three times last night and earn a last gasp win.

The winning goal deep into stoppage time was a bitter blow to take given that Brentford had fought back to equalise after deservedly trailing by two goals at the interval after a quite dreadful and listless first half display which bore much similarity to the spineless surrender against Derby County.

Brentford had lots of possession but did absolutely nothing with it and also defended like statues as they all stood back and admired firstly Tony Watt and then the ever-dangerous Kenwyne Jones as they were both allowed the time and space to score simple goals.

Yennaris was the fall guy for the first when the Bees failed to clear a long throw and the ball eventually bounced off the hapless defender straight to Watt and, for the second goal, Swift dwelt on the ball in midfield and was dispossessed before Cardiff capitalised on a two-on-two situation with O'Connell and Tarkowski both drawn out of possession and the fullbacks marooned upfield.

Nothing much changed in the early part of the second half until Dean Smith took off the invisible Kerschbaumer and also Diagouraga, who had had one of his more frustrating evenings where little had gone right and he was never able to influence matters. The tireless Alan Judge had been trying to create and finish chances on his own, so insipid and off the pace had been the overall team performance, but Jota and McEachran made an immediate impression as Brentford were finally able to raise the tempo, show some penetration, create chances and threaten a nervous looking home team which had conceded two goal leads in both of their previous two home games.

Lightning struck for the third time as firstly Jake Bidwell with a header from a perfectly flighted Judge corner and then John Swift, following up a half save from Marshall after a Judge effort who had been set up well by Hofmann, brought the Bees level and with the home crowd nervously and angrily baying its disapproval, an unlikely win even appeared to be a possibility before disaster struck right out of the blue with the Bees unforgivably losing concentration and caught napping and ball watching from another throw in with Fabio allowed to make a dangerous run unchecked and his left wing cross was allowed to reach the predatory Jones who scored easily to deny the Bees any reward.

Three horrible and scruffy goals, all down to a series of individual and team errors and all three easily avoidable if players had been doing their job properly and had seen their task through to the bitter end.

Not good enough and further proof that we are still the *nearly* team.

Cardiff are by no means a good team, far too reliant upon the long ball, and yet Brentford allowed them to bully them and boss proceedings for much of the game and the Bees eventually left themselves with too much of a mountain to climb, close though they came.

Dean Smith kept faith with the Tarkowski/O'Connell partnership but might now have to reconsider his decision given the number and type of goals conceded in the last two games and suddenly Harlee Dean is looking a good option once again after being left to stew on the bench on a night when all three goals were scored by the Cardiff twin strikers.

It is so easy to use hindsight and say that Dean would perhaps have been a better bet against the height and strength of Jones, but O'Connell had done nothing wrong – and much that was right, over the past three games.

The most surprising news of the night was that Jake Bidwell finally broke his goalscoring duck at the one hundred and eighty-sixth time of asking. He had, it is fair to say, been getting closer and closer to opening his Brentford account over the past few games – and, if it had been me, I would also have done my utmost to claim what eventually turned out to be credited as an own goal by a Wolves defender last Christmas, but now he has finally scored maybe he will get the taste and become a far more potent threat in the opposition penalty area?

The substitutions changed the game with Josh McEachran making a superb cameo appearance on his long-awaited and much-delayed debut for the club. He quite simply oozed Premier League class, was always available to receive the ball and probed ceaselessly in order to create opportunities for his teammates.

I cannot wait to see him, Judge, Jota, Swift and Canos combine to tear opposition defences apart, as they most surely will as soon as Josh and Jota are fully up to speed in terms of their match fitness. Alan Judge in particular, is a man on a mission and last night he added two more assists to his ever-growing tally.

Last season we were able to rely on the skill and guile of the likes of Odubajo, Judge, Pritchard, Jota and Gray in order to turn the screw on our opponents but our current five-some will, perhaps by the New Year, go a long way towards providing us with a similar goal threat.

Hofmann replaced the ineffective Vibe who had missed gruesomely from a gilt-edged one-on-one opportunity and the substitute held the ball up well and was also involved in the equalising goal but I believe that we remain well short in the striking department and something will need to be done in January to help rectify this problem if we are to even threaten the playoff positions.

A tally of only one point from the last two games is well under expectations and what was hoped for, particularly given the fact that we scored four times in the two matches, including, interestingly enough, three goals from set pieces, something that augurs well for the future.

The Championship is tough and unforgiving and any mistakes and shortcomings are punished mercilessly as the Bees have really found out to their cost over the past two games.

Dean Smith has now had three matches to run his eye over his squad and come to some initial decisions about the makeup of his best team and I suspect that there will be some changes made for the next game.

We have options in pretty much every position and Harlee Dean and maybe even Max Colin might well be looking at Saturday's team sheet with some level of hope and expectation given the porous nature of our defence in the past couple of games.

The forbidding and quite frankly, scary, presence of Alan McCormack last night might well have galvanised some of his teammates into more strenuous action, particularly in the first half, but for all his passion, bite, drive and positive dressing room influence, I feel that his time as a first team regular has perhaps come and gone as we are now looking to play a more patient, technical and cerebral brand of football in which the likes of McEachran will play an integral part.

The last two matches have provided us with a real learning curve and the harsh lessons need to be taken on board extremely quickly.

I believe that a top ten finish is most likely the summit of our ambitions and expectations for the remainder of the season, and that would be a massive achievement, but unless we are able to eliminate the quantity and type of defensive errors and shortcomings to which we have become far too prone lately, then we will fall short of that target.

Get it right and also become less profligate up front, then, who knows, we might yet even challenge for a playoff spot.

We are so nearly a very good team. When we are on song we are capable of an exceptional brand of exciting, one-touch, imaginative and incisive football that just lacks the final touch.

We have some quite exceptional midfield players and McEachran last night demonstrated that we now have an abundance of riches in that department. Our sole problem will be in identifying the optimum blend and ensuring that we have round pegs in round holes.

Last night was ultimately a massive disappointment, but at halftime we looked as if we were going to be beaten out of sight and whilst to lose in the manner that we did is utterly frustrating and infuriating, at least we roused ourselves from our torpor, came alive after the interval and so nearly recovered from a seemingly impossible situation – even if it had been one that was mainly of our own making.

Christmas is a time for giving but we have been more than generous enough already and it is now time for us to start resembling Scrooge rather than Santa Claus.

Season On A Knife Edge – 18/12/15

Almost exactly a year ago Brentford won by three goals to two at Cardiff City. The Bees put on a sparkling first half performance, perhaps their best of the season, which saw us sprint into a three-goal lead.

Alex Pritchard pulled all the strings in midfield and scored early on with a peach of a drive, placed precisely low into the corner from twenty yards. His perfect chip then sent Andre Gray clean away behind a defence caught hopelessly square, for the predatory striker, in the midst of a hot streak, to lob the ball over Marshall, with the ball dropping in a perfect parabola into the roof of the net. Jota then scored a goal of breathtaking brilliance from the far corner of the penalty area after a quick breakaway that left the Cardiff defence chasing shadows.

With the boos of their supporters ringing in their ears which were still burning after a halftime tongue lashing from manager Russell Slade, Cardiff attempted to regain some lost pride and launched an aerial bombardment at a Brentford team that sat back, evidently feeling that the job was done.

Lacking the massive influence of the injured Jonathan Douglas, our defence was exposed and could not deal with the threat of Kenwyne Jones and conceded twice. The last few minutes were hairy and nervous in the extreme but Brentford eventually held on for a well-deserved victory in a game that saw them both at their imperious best and frustratingly sloppy worst.

Cardiff extracted some element of revenge by reversing the scoreline when the two teams met again on Tuesday night.

This time it was the home team that took control early on and Cardiff were deservedly two goals ahead at the break.

Their cause was helped enormously by a limp performance from the Bees who dozed through the first half, created very little and conceded two soft goals.

Brentford recovered their poise in the second half and took the game by the scruff of its neck. The home fans were then forced to endure some of the free flowing football that the Bees have made their trademark, and after totally dominating possession, Brentford scored a late equalising goal which would surely earn them a point which was perhaps the least they deserved after the quality of their comeback.

But it wasn't to be and there would be a sting in the tail as Cardiff showed sufficient character to sneak a totally unexpected last gasp winner which yet again owed much to some disorganised defending and tired minds and bodies.

It is illuminating to compare the makeup of the team that Brentford fielded in each of these matches.

Last season Brentford lined up as follows:

Button | Odubajo | Dean | Craig | Bidwell | Diagouraga | Douglas | Jota | Pritchard | Judge | Gray | Substitutes: Bonham, Tarkowski, Saunders, Toral, Dallas, Smith, Proschwitz

Last Tuesday the team was:

Button | Yennaris | Tarkowski | O'Connell | Bidwell | Woods | Diagouraga | Kerschbaumer | Judge | Swift | Vibe | Substitutes: Bonham, Colin, Dean, Saunders, McEachran, Hofmann, Jota

There have in fact been far more changes in the past twelve months than I initially thought had been the case.

Only four players; Button, Bidwell, Diagouraga and Judge, started both games, although nine players were named in both squads.

In the meantime we have lost the services of Odubajo, Craig, Douglas, Pritchard, Gray, Toral, Dallas, Smith and Proschwitz.

They in turn have been replaced by Yennaris, O'Connell, Woods, Kerschbaumer, Swift, Vibe, Colin, McEachran and Hofmann.

I have previously written at length about the reason and rationale behind so many of the enforced changes in the makeup of the Brentford squad and given the quality that we have lost, the injuries that we have suffered and the need to assimilate so many new players, not forgetting the management hiatus and change, we have done remarkably well to recover from our stuttering start to hold a top ten position in the Championship table and to be in a position to challenge for a playoff spot.

I think it is entirely fair and reasonable to call us *Brentford Lite* this season as we are trying to play the same way as last season but also make bricks without sufficient straw as, unsurprisingly given the calibre of player that we have lost, we lack the overall quality in key positions that we possessed last year.

Last season we spread our goals across the midfield and we have certainly missed the goal threat of Pritchard, Jota and Douglas, however the efforts of Judge and to a lesser degree, Swift, mean that have not suffered too badly in comparison.

Similarly, the cumulative total of goals scored by Djuricin, Vibe and Hofmann surpass the efforts of Gray – and of course, Proschwitz, at this stage of last season.

The return of Jota and Judge's continued excellence in front of goal should also mean that our goal tally from midfield increases and that we will be able to overcome the fact that neither Diagouraga nor Woods appear able to hit a barn door with their efforts. McEachran also does not have a track record that inspires me with any confidence regarding his prowess in this area.

What worries me more are our defensive frailties and the number of unforced errors we are making resulting in so many soft goals being conceded.

The excellent David Button has only managed four clean sheets to date which is hardly surprising given some of the defensive aberrations being committed in front of him.

In fact it is quite hard to recall any goal since Rotherham's long-range screamer that could properly be described as unstoppable, and even that only came about after Bidwell carelessly gave the ball away.

Fulham's second goal arrived as a result of some really excellent interplay between two highly gifted strikers in McCormack and Dembele but we could still have defended it far better.

The goals we conceded against Blackburn, Nottingham Forest, Bolton, the first against Fulham and all three against Cardiff were without exception down to avoidable individual errors.

It is almost impossible to win matches away from home if you need to score two or even three goals simply to draw.

The way that we play leaves us vulnerable at the back given that our central defenders split as soon as Button gets hold of the ball and the two fullbacks bomb forward at every opportunity.

The second goal at Cardiff illustrates the problem as Swift dwelt on the ball and was dispossessed in midfield and the fullbacks were nowhere to be seen as Cardiff immediately turned defence into attack.

We are now in an interesting period with players returning from injury and a series of tough matches compressed into a tight timeframe over Christmas and the New Year.

Dean Smith must surely rotate the squad and spread the load but at the same time work even harder on our defending which has been pretty laughable at times lately.

Tenth is about right at the moment but we can now go in either direction.

Integrate the new and now fit players into the team, lose no stars and perhaps even strengthen slightly in January, then a charge towards the playoffs is a real possibility.

Continue to donate goals as if we are a charitable foundation and we will struggle to remain in the top half of the table.

The weather and pitches will start to deteriorate in the New Year and we are always going to rely upon out-footballing rather than out-battling the opposition as that is what is ingrained in our DNA.

I fully expect us to eradicate some of our defensive frailties and go on to greater things over the next few months but the season, for me is now poised on a knife edge.

Thank God For Brentford! – 19/12/15

I slept extremely well last night, particularly between the hours of seven forty-five until nine forty-five pm as I kept nodding off throughout the *Sky TV* coverage of the Birmingham City versus Cardiff City clash.

What an appalling match between two teams who exemplified everything that is wrong with the game of football today as they both hoofed the ball forward at every opportunity and gave it away with monotonous regularity on the rare occasions when they attempted to play football.

Quite frankly the match was almost unwatchable as both teams cancelled each other out and seemed to be trying to outdo each other in terms of the number of unforced errors they both committed.

Perspiration, certainly, but so little inspiration and it was quite fitting and appropriate that the eventual result was decided by an appalling refereeing error.

There was plenty of effort, sweat, energy, passion, running, defensive organisation, covering and tackling but a total lack of imagination, guile or skill on the ball – and both these teams are ahead of Brentford in the Championship table!

How can this be the case? What can we learn from these teams?

Well, simply that success in football is evidently not obtained by possessing the most talented and pure footballers. Other attributes are required and we quite plainly lack some of them.

I would not for one moment change our style or the manner in which we play. Our football can be exhilarating and breathtaking at times and provides us with so much enjoyment and pride as a club renowned – or maybe the better word is perhaps *notorious*, in previous decades, for being massive proponents of the long ball game has now found the faith and metamorphosed into becoming one of the best footballing teams in the country.

I do not want to be too picky, and yet… and yet, there is still something missing from our game. We have become much more diligent and remorseless in our pressing and efforts to win the ball back higher up the field and we maintain a quick tempo in our game which can be impossible for opponents to cope with, but we continue to struggle against the larger, tougher, stronger, more Neanderthal teams.

Both Birmingham and Cardiff have beaten us twice running and I well remember today's opponents, Huddersfield Town bullying us off the ball, aided and abetted by a benign referee who did nothing to protect us, and then defeating us in our encounter last December.

I do not believe it is a case of our working less hard than these teams but more that we can at times be knocked out of our stride and put off our game.

That being said when we are really on song it doesn't really matter how large our opponents are.

I remember watching the Leeds United team emerge from the tunnel at Griffin Park last season and remarking that they looked more like the Land of the Giants and tag-team wrestlers rather than footballers, but we ran rings around them and played them off the pitch and they could not get anywhere near us on the day. We were simply too good and too quick for them to catch up with us and they could not kick us even if that had been their intention.

Earlier this season under Marinus Dijkhuizen, we slowed down our tempo and became far more predictable and teams were able to catch us and cope with us far easier and we found ourselves knocked off the ball and unable to dominate matches as we had done so often last season.

Thankfully things have changed and we have now recovered our mojo and reverted to a style that suits us far betterm

In my view we must accept things for how they are. We will always be a bit vulnerable given the expansiveness of our play and the way our defenders play out from the back and support the attackers, and quite simply that is the price we have to pay, and for me it is a totally acceptable one.

What is less acceptable to me is when we shoot ourselves in the foot and contribute to our own downfall. This has been the case far too often recently when we have conceded a series of totally avoidable goals that have come about from our own stupid and unforced errors and lack of concentration. I am still replaying Tuesday's defensive horror show back in my mind as I write these words.

I hope and expect that Dean Smith and Richard O'Kelly are already working hard on improving our defensive shape and that we will soon begin to eliminate these expensive errors from our play as we cannot afford to donate any gifts to the opposition given how narrow are the margins between victory and defeat in the Championship.

I am so grateful for the way that we play the game and watching the dross on television last night simply emphasised how fortunate we are to be able to enjoy a team as gifted and easy on the eye as Brentford. Moreover, we have proved categorically that such a positive style of play can and does bring about success too.

As I keep saying, we are so close to becoming a really excellent team and with just a bit more care in defence we will become even more formidable opponents for the rest of the league and perhaps challenge for a coveted playoff spot.

I have not seen anybody at our level of the game play football with the verve and brio that we do and long may that remain the case.

Jekyll And Hyde – 20/12/15

Brentford's performance against Huddersfield yesterday touched the heights but also, at times, plumbed the depths.

For forty-five minutes the Bees were totally unstoppable and tore the visitors apart. Everything Brentford attempted came off and their combination of accurate passing, interchanging of positions, vision, dribbling and, just as importantly, hard work and relentless pressing, ensured that we fully merited our three goal lead at the interval – and it could easily have been a lot more.

After a minute's silence impeccably observed in memory of the late, great Jimmy Hill, a wonderful visionary, Huddersfield chased shadows as Alan Judge pulled all the strings in midfield. Sergio Canos was almost unstoppable on the right wing and Lasse Vibe's movement was far too much for the lumbering Hudson and Lynch at the centre of the Huddersfield defence.

Dean Smith took note of the potential effects of having played on such an energy-sapping pitch at Cardiff on Tuesday evening and rotated his squad. There were recalls for Max Colin, Harlee Dean and Canos in place of Yennaris, O'Connell and Kerschbaumer and Alan McCormack returned to the bench.

The fact that there was no space for Yennaris and Kerschbaumer in the eighteen simply highlights just how strong our squad is becoming.

Any nerves or self-doubt as a result of our late and cruel defeat at Cardiff evaporated when we scored early on when Vibe found Swift who played a one-two off a hapless defender before slipping Canos through and the youngster turned Holmes, who was far too tight on him, and placed his shot precisely into the far corner for a goal which emphasised his class and massive potential.

Huddersfield's confidence was shot to pieces and they funnelled back and allowed us all the space we needed to rip them to shreds. Diagouraga and Woods were given the room, time and freedom required to drive us up the pitch and it came as no surprise when Tarkowski strode forward imperiously, picked out Vibe's run and chipped the ball into space and Vibe was set free behind a faltering defence and he took the ball on unchallenged before thundering a shot high into the roof of the net from a tight angle.

Whenever our hapless visitors did manage to string together a few passes – mainly backwards or sideways, the Bees swarmed around them, never gave them a moment's peace and regained possession with ease.

This was a footballing masterclass and whilst a Huddersfield team, lacking it must be said most of its first choice midfield through injury, were totally inept, it is impossible to overstate just how well we played. We were awesome and it was a performance as good as, if not better, than anything we have seen on this ground in living memory.

Our third goal came when Hudson was reduced to a tactical handball as the only way to stop Vibe bursting past him and Judge's free kick from way out on the left wing was driven in towards goal and evaded everybody, friend and foe alike, before nestling perfectly in the far corner of the net.

The score could really have been almost anything at halftime given Brentford's total dominance and the brilliance of their play and whilst the applause rang out from three sides of the ground, our visitors left the field to a torrent of boos from their supporters.

Unfortunately football matches last ninety minutes rather than forty-five, and what had appeared to be a stroll in the park became a far more even and competitive match. David Wagner could have substituted any of his players at the break but he hit the jackpot when he brought on Nahki Wells and Kyle Dempsey who revitalised his faltering team.

They went up a couple of gears and caught us cold with a well-worked goal within a minute of the restart when Wells found Lolley who scored emphatically from close range.

Suddenly the game changed as our visitors, who had absolutely nothing to lose and with lost pride to regain, went for the jugular with Dempsey, playing behind the front two, causing us problems as he ran at our suddenly exposed back four.

Dean and Tarkowski, totally unemployed defensively in the first half when they had the lumbering Miller in their pocket, now found themselves under pressure and found it hard to deal with small tricky opponents who ran at them unchallenged from midfield.

We creaked ominously and a second goal might well have turned the game on its head, but the Bees are never more dangerous than when breaking away at pace, and Judge gained possession on the halfway line from a Huddersfield corner and his run was ended by a bodycheck from Chilwell. A penalty it was and Alan converted emphatically to reach double figures in goals – a quite remarkable achievement for a midfielder at this point of the season.

Wells, Lolley and Dempsey continued to cause us problems and several efforts whistled narrowly wide of our goal as the game flowed from end to end.

Colin made an impressive return to the team, strong in defence and quick to support the attack and he won a ball that he should not have been allowed to do, before shooting narrowly over the bar. A raking move ended with Vibe missing the ball when unmarked right in front of a gaping goal and substitute Jota was far too casual and languid when sent clear on goal and his lame effort was easily saved before Vibe, challenging for the rebound, was taken out for what appeared to be a far clearer penalty kick than the one that had previously been awarded, but this time Mr. Gibbs kept his whistle to his lips without pointing to the spot.

There was a further bit of nonsense when Diagouraga tripped and fell on the ball deep into injury time and Paterson was able to streak away and his shot was parried by Button into the path of Dempsey who scored a goal that was totally deserved given the quality of his, and his team's second half performance.

It is strange to come away from a two-goal victory feeling slightly frustrated and flat but the difference between Brentford's display in the first and second half was immense. As Huddersfield went up several gears, we changed down, thought that the job had been done, and were punished accordingly.

It just goes to show that you cannot take anything for granted in the Championship.

Without carping too much given how good we were before the break, what changed in the second half is quite simply that we were for once outworked by the opposition and we stopped pressing and challenging, allowing skilful opponents to have the space to run at pace at our suddenly exposed defence.

That is a lesson that we must learn, and learn quickly. There is no substitute for hard work and we fell short in the second half yesterday.

Brentford are now the second highest scorers in the league behind Fulham and, on average, there are three goals scored in every Brentford game.

Thrills, spills, skill and excitement are all guaranteed when you come to Griffin Park!

The recipe for success is to continue doing what we did in the first half yesterday, ideally eliminating the casual and unforced errors and remembering that a match lasts for ninety minutes or more.

Do that and we could become unstoppable.

The Reasons Why I Love Brentford FC – 23/12/15

1. The indestructible Peter Gilham's banshee cries of encouragement as the Brentford players take to the field

2. Meeting up and *kibitzing* with my football friends at every home game and the sense of continuity it provides

3. Having a pre-match drink in *The Griffin* or a meal in *The Weir*

4. The long post-match telephone calls to friends and fellow supporters where we dissect and analyse every kick

5. Endeavouring to guess the identity of players who we will sign

6. Seeing the Griffin Park floodlights for the first time when I am driving down Ealing Road never fails to excite and re-energise me

7. Griffin Park. It is old and obsolete but it makes my heart sing every time I go through the Braemar Road turnstiles

8. Having my favourite secret hideaways where I know that I can still park my car before matches

9. The imminent prospect of Lionel Road and knowing that it will also have style, class and a sense of identity and not just be another faceless cookie-cutter stadium

10. The red and white striped home shirt that symbolises perfectly who we are and what we stand for

11. Bumping into Brentford legends like Peter Gelson in the Braemar Road forecourt and knowing that they are still part of the club and will always be made welcome

12. Seeing so many new faces at every home game and realising that the secret is out – Brentford are on the rise and are a team well worth watching

13. Watching us play away from home. All united in a common purpose

14. Hearing the cries of appreciation mingled with lingering feelings of disbelief at the quality of the football we now play

15. Knowing that the heritage and tradition of the club is recognised, appreciated and respected by everybody involved with Brentford FC

16. The sense of innovation, originality and ambition that permeates our thinking and everything that we do

17. The intoxicating prospect of being a supporter at a time when we are potentially writing a new chapter in the club's history

18. The reassurance of knowing that the club is in safe hands and is owned and run by people have its best interests at heart

19. The fact that the supporters are close to the pitch, feel part of the game and create a supportive yet intimidating atmosphere at every game which is second to none

20. Evening matches under the floodlights at Griffin Park – pure magic

21. The Ealing Road Terrace – a wonderful anachronism

22. Serenading opposition goalkeepers with resounding choruses of *It's All Your Fault*! And hoping that they will shrivel under the verbal pressure

23. Worrying before every Championship game that we will get hammered and totally outclassed but being reassured by realising just how good we are

24. The sense of freedom, positivity and adventure with which we play and running rings around teams packed with lumbering giants

25. Knowing that you will almost never see a poor game of football at Griffin Park and that the entertainment levels will be extremely high

26. The look of amazement on the face of smug Premier League supporting fans who I bring to matches and are without exception stunned at the incredible quality of the football we play

27. The sense of community that is engendered particularly thanks to the efforts of the Community Sports Trust team. We are all in this together and the involvement of the local people really matters

28. The friendliness and efficiency of the management, marketing and media teams who are never too busy to have a chat or reply to an email

29. The fact that our players are without exception decent and talented young men who are committed to the cause and give everything both on and off the pitch – there are no *prima donnas* here

30. The massive increase in the quality of our squad and the intoxicating blend of foreign talent and promising youngsters from the lower leagues

31. Having an ever increasing number of current international footballers in our squad

32. Seeing more and more young Academy players being encouraged and nurtured and getting closer to the First Team squad

33. Watching the Development and Academy teams play the same brand of skilful, attacking football as the First Team as our philosophy is embraced throughout the club at all levels

34. That I can now proudly state in wider company that I am a Brentford fan and no longer receive a barrage of smug, pitying and patronising looks and comments – the worm has turned. It is *our* time now

35. Historians and authors like David Lane, Mark Croxford and Paul Briers who have a massive respect for the club's heritage and are determined to preserve it for future generations

36. The Hall of Fame which will ensure that the exploits of past club heroes will never be forgotten

37. The Brentford Programme Shop, hidden under the Braemar Road stand, the best kept secret in the ground and packed full of wonderful memories

38. Seeing more and more of the media's big names, like the immortal Brian Glanville at Griffin Park and the professionalism and friendliness of Dave and Ian in the Press Lounge

39. Mark Burridge and his wonderful *Bees Player* team who provide so much comfort and joy

40. The enthusiasm, passion and erudition of Billy Reeves and the glorious word pictures that he paints when describing his favourite club

41. The match programme and fanzines – more high quality publications disseminating the Brentford message

Brentford FC & Boxing Day – 24/12/15

The prospect of playing promotion challengers Brighton & Hove Albion on Boxing Day is an exciting and enticing one as the Bees will have the opportunity to test their mettle and their own playoff credentials against one of the Championship's best teams, and one that has only just lost its undefeated record at the twenty-second time of asking.

A quite remarkable achievement and we will need to be at our absolute best in order to come out of the match with any reward.

As we await Saturday's match with a mixture of relish and impatience I thought I would attempt to take our mind off the match by looking back at some of the more memorable Boxing Day tussles we have enjoyed – or not as the case might be – over the past few decades.

Our first Boxing Day clash of the 70s was away at Scunthorpe, hardly a local derby or crowd pleaser over the festive season! A more than healthy crowd of just under five thousand saw a late Roger Cross goal give us an undeserved equaliser.

The following season a bumper crowd of over eighteen thousand crammed into Griffin Park in the anticipation of seeing top of the table Brentford pulverise perennial strugglers Crewe Alexandra but the plucky visitors hadn't read the script and the Bees squeaked home with a trademark header from John O'Mara.

Our 1972 Boxing Day defeat at Bournemouth was remarkable for us scoring twice away from home for the first time in that horrible relegation season – our hosts, of course, scored three times, but also for Jackie Graham actually scoring with our well-rehearsed pantomime season free kick where two players pretended to argue with each other before a third took a shot at goal.

The 1973 match against Newport County was the one-thousandth consecutive match covered by the *Middlesex Chronicle*'s George Sands and also the last game played for us by Stewart Houston before he departed gratefully to Manchester United.

I wonder just how many loyal and bleary-eyed Brentford supporters caught the coach at eight o'clock on Boxing Day 1975 and were eventually forced to endure a goalless draw away at Exeter City? At least they must have been able to catch up with their sleep, before, after and probably during the game!

Boxing Day 1977 was appropriately named as it will always be remembered for the fisticuffs between Andy McCulloch and Aldershot's behemoth of a defender Joe Jopling, which resulted in the Brentford striker seeing red in more ways than one. Not a happy day all round as our promotion push was dented by a narrow defeat after an error by Len Bond and I sulked all the way home.

The following year saw Barry Silkman give a sumptuous display for Plymouth Argyle but two late Dean Smith goals saw the Bees come out on top.

1983 saw Brentford host Wimbledon on Christmas Eve, the last time a Football League match has been staged on that day, and the visitors won a seven goal thriller.

1984 saw a real Boxing Day dampener when a totally lethargic Brentford team never turned up and were hammered by three clear goals by a Bristol Rovers team who strolled to an easy victory.

Arsenal loanee Graham Rix lit up our easy three-nil win over a hapless Aldershot in 1987 and gave a performance that simply oozed class.

A goalkeeping error by Tony Parks led to a narrow defeat at Reading in 1989 and made me question the sanity of my decision to drive from Devon that morning to attend the game.

Our brief stay in Division One saw a memorable Boxing Day win over big spenders Derby County. Goals from Joe Allon and a perfectly placed own goal from Richard Goulooze ensured a much needed victory for the Bees.

Next season we won a ridiculous and farcical match at Dean Court which saw Bournemouth keeper Vince Bartram slice a simple back pass comically into his own net and then scream abuse at his blameless defender – pure slapstick – and Steve Cotterill then missed two penalty kicks for the home team as we strolled to a three-goal victory. Denny Mundee's also used his inimitable shuffle to good effect against his old team that day.

Orient were equally appalling the following season and after conceding three first half goals to a rampant Brentford, their entire team was sent back onto the pitch with a flea in their ear by their furious manager, John Sitton well before the end of the halftime break.

Brighton last came to Griffin Park on Boxing Day in 1995 for a match that surely should never have started given the frozen pitch and icy conditions. They certainly didn't suit Dean Martin who was cruelly lambasted for his tentative performance by the Brentford faithful and appropriately enough the game was settled by a mishit cross by Dean Wilkins which floated into the far corner over the head of Kevin Dearden.

In 1996 we were forced to make the ridiculous journey to Plymouth but came back with a four-one win marked by a rare goal from Joe Omigie.

Brighton again came out on top the following season, this time at the Priestfield Stadium, and we beat Bristol City in 1999 in a match which saw Peter Beadle blatantly knock the ball out of Andy Woodman's hands but the goal was allowed to stand.

Leon Constantine, who never scored a single goal for us, made a triumphant return in 2004 with a well-taken second half hat trick which gave his new team, Torquay United a surprise win at Griffin Park.

The following year Brentford leapfrogged Swansea City and went to the top of the table after beating our rivals in a thrilling contest in which the unlikely duo of Eddie Hutchinson and Junior Lewis dominated the midfield and reduced Lee Trundle to a mere spectator.

Adam Griffiths gave Millwall a Boxing Day gift after twenty-three seconds in 2006 when he completely misjudged a backpass to Clark Masters and the game went further downhill from there as we were hammered by our near neighbours.

Not too many of our recent Boxing Day encounters have been very memorable, bar an excellent victory at Colchester in 2012 and the exciting three-two win over Swindon in 2013 marked by Sam Saunders falling flat on his face when about to take a free kick and after dusting himself off, he recovered and put his next attempt into the roof of the net totally silencing the jeering Swindon fans in front of whom he celebrated with a theatrical dive.

The least said about last season's catastrophic Boxing Day collapse to Ipswich Town the better and I am sure that it is still fresh in the memory of most Brentford supporters.

Thankfully we seem to have a pretty decent record in matches played on Boxing Day and it is also good to note that more and more of these games are played against reasonably local opposition and we are no longer forced to endure endless treks to the other end of the country.

As for the likely result of this year's clash with Brighton, who knows, and hopefully it will be as exciting a match as last season's five-goal thriller.

We come into the match in excellent form and Dean Smith will have some difficult decisions to make before finalising his squad.

I can't wait!

Patience Is A Virtue – 27/12/15

One should always strive for continuous improvement whatever your endeavour, hobby or line of work and I greatly admire people who set themselves challenges and push themselves as much as they possibly can.

Sometimes however a dose of realism is called for and I think that now is the time to look back calmly, objectively and rationally on Brentford's nil-nil draw with Brighton yesterday.

Our visitors came into the match boasting a quite amazing record of only suffering one defeat in their opening twenty-two matches and whilst last season was an aberration for them as they were down amongst the dead men clustered around the bottom of the Championship table, there were good reasons for their temporary fall from grace and the current campaign sees them in their customary position of challenging for promotion, either automatically or through the playoffs.

Led by the astute and understated Chris Hughton, Brighton fielded a team jam-packed with Championship experience or even higher with the likes of Stockdale, Zamora, Bruno, Greer, Dunk, Stephens and Calderon as well as the massive emerging talent of Manchester United's Jamie Wilson, currently on loan at the club.

Owned by another betting magnate in Tony Bloom, there are definitely similarities between the two clubs but, buttressed by their magnificent new stadium and near capacity attendances, as well as this being their fifth season in the Championship, it should be recognised and accepted that Brighton are well ahead of us at this point in time on their potential journey to the top.

Brentford, on the other hand are still learning and inexperienced at this level. Last season our wonderful brand of passing football, movement and high pressing took everybody by surprise and we came so close to making the seemingly impossible dream come true.

I might be alone in my opinion, but quite frankly I consider our current achievement this season of reaching the halfway stage of the season established in the top ten and within touching distance of the top six to be far more meritorious.

Consider the circumstances: for a variety of reasons we lost the backbone of our squad when the likes of Odubajo, Douglas, Dallas, Pritchard and Gray left the club and our recruitment in terms of both management and players left a lot to be desired with far too many foreign players untested in the Championship, and understandably struggling initially to come to terms with its relentlessness and its physical and mental challenges.

The appointment of Marinus Dijkhuizen as Head Coach also proved to be an abject failure.

We suffered a quite ridiculous number of injuries, and not just the normal run of the mill knocks and bruises but serious problems that affected players such as Bjelland, Colin, McEachran, Macleod, Jota and Djuricin who were expected to become mainstays of the team. Only now are we getting close to welcoming the majority of these players back to full fitness.

There have been massive changes behind the scenes with two new Co-Directors of Football and the players have had to listen to a variety of different voices and approaches in terms of their training and coaching given that we are now onto our third management team of the season.

There was also the fiasco of the Griffin Park pitch which caused more early season problems, hiatus and embarrassment.

No wonder we got off to a slow start as we were basically competing with one hand tied behind our back. Thanks to Lee Carsley and Paul Williams who reverted to basics and what had worked so well last season, benched many of the newcomers and established a settled team and pattern of play, we arrested what was looking like it might become an irreversible slide and fall from grace and turned the season around.

Carsley turned down the opportunity of taking the Head Coach position on a permanent basis which caused more uncertainty and upheaval, but his success bought us the time to make a measured appointment and the new duo of Dean Smith and Richard O'Kelly has settled down quickly and made an immediate impact.

I am sure that we have made an exceptional appointment in Smith and I was even more reassured when I read these comments from one of his former players at Walsall, Romaine Sawyers:

He created a great environment to work in. Everybody seemed to learn. Everybody has the right to an opinion. He'd speak to every single player, before and after training.

I'd say his greatest feature was his honesty. He'd never tell you something you wanted to hear or say something just to provoke a response. He was straight down the line and I'm sure that the Brentford players will love him.

I hope that makes you all feel as good as it did me when I read it.

We are continuing to improve and progress and have established a fully deserved reputation for being one of the best and most attractive footballing teams in the division.

Given the level of backing we receive from Matthew Benham and our justified reputation for off-field innovation and excellence, it is a good bet, if not a sure fire certainty, that within a short period of time, maybe even before we move into Lionel Road, that we will be knocking at the door of the Premier League.

Our last two home performances against MK Dons and Huddersfield were both excellent and we blew both teams away, scored six times and could quite easily have doubled that total.

The mood was therefore optimistic with real hope and maybe even a sense of expectation that we could also defeat Brighton.

In the end we didn't but we should have done so, as but for three exceptional saves from Stockdale, from Judge twice and then a phenomenal full length dive to push away a header from Tarkowski that looked a certain goal, a poor late miss from Hofmann and a lack of penetration in the final third where the final pass too often went astray, we would have scored the goal that would have settled the game which instead ended up as an exciting nil-nil draw.

As I left the ground and when I read the comments on social media from other Bees supporters I felt that far too many fans were feeling not just slightly disappointed at what they saw as the Bees dropping two points but also even a bit let down.

Remember, this is Brighton we are talking about, not Championship lightweights like MK Dons or Huddersfield. We have no divine right to beat teams of that calibre and in my opinion given all the problems that we have had to overcome this season we are still punching way above our weight.

That is not to say that I do not feel that we can make a challenge for the final playoff position should we maintain our form, not lose key players in January and maybe even strengthen the squad, particularly up front where we are not yet firing on all cylinders.

We cannot yet compete on an even playing field with the big boys in this league although given time, a new stadium and more experience at this level there is no reason why this situation cannot change but at present we should simply take pride and pleasure from the quality of our displays and the effervescent football that we play realising that we still cannot match many other teams in terms of resources and size and experience of squad.

That being said we possess so many real footballers who are so comfortable on the ball and provide us with so much pleasure and excitement.

We dominated proceedings yesterday, with fifty-nine per cent possession, twenty shots at goal and ten corners and out-passed our visitors, who pride themselves on maintaining possession for long spells by a vast margin – five hundred and fifty seven to three hundred and ninety.

Perhaps the most telling comment about our quality and the journey that we have come on came from Brighton manager Chris Hughton – a former Bee, after his team had clung on for a barely deserved point:

There are lots of exciting games at Brentford at the moment. They play a brand of football which revolves around a lot of sharp players good on the ball, and they will test any opposition.

As a team we had to dig deep because Brentford are a good team.

There is so much to take pride and pleasure in at Griffin Park, and as I keep saying, we are so nearly a really excellent team – and there is still plenty of room for a massive improvement far beyond the levels that we have reached now, which are way above what I ever really believed I would be watching from a Brentford team.

I am just tickled pink and more than content with the fact that we will end 2015 as the best placed West London team in the Championship in our private but deadly battle with Fulham and Queens Park Rangers!

I know that there is far more to come but that will do me nicely for now.

I would simply urge a little bit more patience and understanding about the situation we currently find ourselves in. We are well on the road to success, it might just take slightly longer than some supporters expect.

Something Special Times Two – 29/12/15

For most fans, watching your football team play can sometimes seem like a prison sentence without hope of parole, a hard and endless slog or even running through treacle in gumboots. Lots of hard work and running, effort, energy, but so little entertainment, reward or quality.

Perspiration but so little inspiration. It is a habit that is easy to get into but so hard to get out of once the routine has been established.

These words would sum up much of my experience of watching Brentford over the past fifty years or so. Of course there are seasons and matches that stand out and are irrevocably engrained in my memory banks but in real terms they are few and far between and interspersed with so much that, looking back, can only and best be described as drab, boring, inept and instantly forgettable.

Over that period there have been many memorable goals that are totally unforgettable, an instant example would be Gary Blissett's strike against Peterborough, but more for what they meant to the team, club and us supporters rather than for the actual quality of the goal.

Off the top of my head probably the best goal that I have ever seen Brentford score was Paul Brooker's effort at Swindon in 2006 when he slalomed his way three quarters of the length of the pitch leaving seemingly half the Swindon team trailing helplessly in his wake. In that moment he was totally unstoppable and an amalgam of Messi and Maradona and it stood out even more given the customary functional and plebeian style of football employed by Martin Allen's team at that time.

All that changed yesterday afternoon when the Bees came away with a desperately hard-won and narrow victory at Reading.

The performance was decent and organised if not inspired and for once Dame Fortune smiled down on us as we won a match that could quite easily have gone the other way had Reading made more of their possession.

A lot of credit for that must go down to the Bees who refused to be beaten and absorbed the pressure exerted on us by a home team that looked quick and innovative in midfield if insipid and wasteful up front.

We defended well and restricted Reading to very few clear chances and only conceded once when substitutes Vydra and McCleary combined beautifully with a series of one-twos to tear us open and create the space for the latter to score easily.

In truth Button was forced into only one decent save and much of the credit is due to the back four of Colin, Dean, Tarkowski and Bidwell who simply rolled their sleeves up and presented an almost impassable barrier.

The midfield did not gel with Diagouraga and McEachran never really dominating or getting to grips with their task and sometimes chasing shadows with Toumani's influence blunted by an early booking by Keith Stroud, a ticking time bomb of a referee who was, as ever, far too quick with his cards.

I wish he would adopt the following statement as his mantra: *a foul is not necessarily a yellow card offence*, but Stroud seems programmed to blow his whistle and brandish a yellow card almost simultaneously without ever giving himself time to think and his looming presence cast a shadow over the entire proceedings with Button, Dean and Tarkowski also falling foul of the eccentric official.

Judge too was strangely muted and Swift drifted in and out of the match stranded as he was out on the left flank.

For once we created very little with Vibe's threat snuffed out but now I am coming to the real point of this article as we scored what were quite comfortably the best two goals that I have ever seen Brentford score in one match over all the years that I can remember.

For the first, which came at a time when Reading were well on top and looking likely to score at almost any time, Tarky strode imperiously out of defence, sold a perfect dummy and slid the ball to Swift in midfield. He laid the ball off to Woods just inside the home half of the field and he made towards the Reading goal.

On and on he dribbled as the defenders backed off complacent and secure in the knowledge that they were dealing with a man who is hardly prolific in front of goal as his record of only scoring one career goal in over one hundred and twenty games surely attests. Now he has doubled his tally!

With Vibe making a decoy run to the right and Swift trying to make a late run into the penalty area, there were few passing options available so Ryan let fly from twenty-five yards and the ball screamed towards the goal and was still rising as it hit the roof of the net with Bond a helpless bystander.

I am old enough to remember Bobby Charlton's long range Exocet against Mexico in the 1966 World Cup and I can only say that Ryan's goal yesterday was in the same class.

It was a phenomenal effort that knocked the stuffing out of the home team and we were able to retain our lead until the interval largely untroubled.

Reading regrouped and dominated the early part of the second half, missed an open goal straight away and fully deserved their excellently worked and taken equaliser and looked by far the more likely team to earn the victory.

All that changed after seventy minutes when Judge found Woods who had now switched to a more central position where he was far more effective.

His perfectly placed forty yard pass out to the right wing cleared the straining Quinn and found the ever-willing substitute Sergi Canos who now produced seven seconds of pure magic as his first touch took the ball over his marker, Quinn, his second left Hector helpless as he moved into the penalty area and his third was a rasping and unstoppable left foot volley into the far corner of the net.

The youngster celebrated wildly in front of nearly three thousand adoring Brentford fans, as well he might, as this was a goal of true international class, executed instinctively and without fuss by a young player who has the football world at his feet.

What a way to celebrate his loan extension and his post-match *Bees Player* interview clearly demonstrates just how committed he is to the Brentford cause.

We are fortunate and, indeed, blessed to have a young player with his ability, but just as crucially, his wonderfully positive and bubbly attitude, playing for us. He is a total breath of fresh air and a joy to watch and yesterday's effort will never be forgotten by anybody who was privileged enough to witness it.

Reading huffed and puffed for the remainder of the match but their spirit had been broken by Sergi's wonder goal and if anything Brentford looked the more likely to score a third than they were to equalise.

The clumsy Hector saw red for a second yellow card after a pathetic and embarrassing dive and his side's fortune plummeted with his unsolicited fall and we saw the game out with some degree of comfort.

2015 has seen Brentford play football of a standard unsurpassed in living memory and what a fitting way to see the old year out with two of the best goals that you could ever wish or hope to see. This has been a quite wonderful year for the Bees and who knows what riches 2016 will bring?

What is quite certain is that the goals scored yesterday by Woods and Canos have whetted our appetite for what is to come.

Sergi Canos celebrating the goal of the season at Reading

Stats And Stuff – 30/12/15

It is quite staggering just how much statistical information about football teams and individual players is now freely available within the public domain.

Statistical analysis is now an accepted and growing part of the game and given the quality and depth of the data that I was able to unearth free of charge on the internet I can only wonder at the level of information that is gathered and provided privately to the clubs themselves.

I generally go to a wonderful website, *WhoScored.com* which provides a treasure trove of easily accessible data that can be understood even by a mathematical dunce like me.

What I find so fascinating about using the data before I write anything about Brentford FC is that it makes me question my judgement about pretty much anything that I have seen unfurl on the pitch in front of me when I watch the team play.

Watching Brentford play can be a veritable rollercoaster ride with so many highs and lows as your spirits and emotions are taken to the heights and then plummet to the depths all within the course of a ninety-minute match.

Judgements can be clouded by what you think that you have seen rather than what actually took place out on the pitch.

We also all have prejudices and preconceived views about every player.

For example if you spoke to a Brentford supporter today and asked for an opinion on John Swift, our talented midfield player currently on loan from Chelsea, there would probably be some purring comments of appreciation about his quality on the ball, eye for a pass, ability to glide sinuously and effortlessly past opponents and also make late runs into the penalty area but these would probably be interspersed with some grudging mention of his supposed defensive weaknesses, as to the naked eye he does not always appear to track back, press and support his defenders as much as you would like or is needed.

Is John Swift a defensive liability and a luxury player? Fact or fiction? Does his offensive contribution more than make up for his supposed defensive shortcomings?

In order to come to some sort of conclusion I consulted the oracle and Stats God at *WhoScored.com* and here are the stark, objective facts, untainted by any bias or rose tinted spectacles.

I looked first at his defensive statistics and they were telling. Swift makes 0.9 tackles per game, comfortably the least of any first team regular, apart from Lasse Vibe. Yennaris and Colin make the most (2.5) and all of his midfield colleagues attempt more tackles than Swift. He also makes less interceptions than any of his teammates and he has yet to block a shot.

These stats would therefore appear to bear out the suggestion that defending is not yet a strong part of Swift's game. Tellingly in a description and profile of his overall game *WhoScored.com* rates his defensive contribution as *weak*.

Where things begin to look much better for him however is when you look at his offensive statistics. John has scored three goals and made four assists in his fourteen appearances to date. He also takes 1.3 shots on goal every game and makes 1.4 key passes per game, more than anybody else in the team apart from Alan Judge. He also attempts more dribbles than all his teammates apart from Max Colin.

I could break his game down even more, but hopefully the message is coming through loud and clear that John Swift is making an exceptionally effective offensive contribution to the team that more than justifies his starting position, even if he needs to pay more attention to the defensive side of his game, as it is what you do without the ball that can often be just as important as being a *Fancy Dan* when in possession.

I thought it might be interesting to delve a bit deeper into the Brentford team analysis on *WhoScored.com* and see if there were any trends emerging after the first half of the season.

According to the figures our style of play is typified by the following:

- Possession football
- Attacking down the right
- Play with width
- Short passes
- Playing in their own half
- Opponents play aggressively against them
- Aggressive
- Consistent first eleven

Our strengths are:
- Counter attacks
- Finishing scoring chances

- Shooting from direct free kicks
- Creating chances using through balls
- Creating chances through individual skill
- Coming back from losing positions

Whereas we are deemed to be weak at the following:

- Defending against attacks down the wings
- Aerial duels
- Defending counter attacks
- Defending set pieces
- Stopping opponents from creating chances
- Avoiding fouling in dangerous areas

These all look pretty much spot on to me and it is reassuring that the figures in this instance back up and totally substantiate the subjective opinion I had already come to after watching the overwhelming majority of our twenty-four Championship games to date.

Our top six performing players given an analysis of all aspects of their game have been Alan Judge, James Tarkowski, John Swift, Harlee Dean, Jake Bidwell and Nico Yennaris, again, no surprises there, and interestingly enough, of the regular players, Toumani Diagouraga and Konstantin Kerschbaumer rate the lowest.

Judge and Tarkowski are also rated as the top and fourth best player in the entire Championship to date – a wonderful achievement by the pair of them.

According to *WhoScored.com* the best eleven players in the Championship over the entire first half of the season were as follows:

Martinez (Wolves) | Onuoha (QPR) | Duffy (Blackburn) | Tarkowski (Brentford) | Friend (Middlesbrough) | Gallagher (Preston) | Norwood (Reading) | Stephens (Brighton) | Judge (Brentford) | Forestieri (Sheffield Wednesday) | McCormack (Fulham)

Not too many surprises there either, in my opinion.

Of our thirty-six goals to date, one of the highest totals in the league, an eye-opening nine have come from set pieces, including two penalty kicks and two have come from counterattacks. That is a massive improvement on last season.

We attempt just under five hundred passes per game with a seventy-seven per cent accuracy rate. Eighty per cent of our passes are short, but we also hit nineteen crosses every match.

In that respect I only wish we could find out the average number of attacking players we had in the opposition penalty area every time we hit a cross as I am pretty sure that is an area where improvement is still needed.

I suspect that our analysis department might have a few words to say if they saw this article and would draw my attention to all sorts of facts and figures that have escaped my attention or that I have misinterpreted, and I am sure that I have barely scratched the surface of what is a fascinating subject that will become more and more important as the years progress.

Statistics have certainly changed the way that I look at matches and I have found them an invaluable tool in terms of helping me write more sensibly, rationally and objectively about players and matches and avoid going off on an unsubstantiated and ignorant rant.

Most importantly, what they show quite clearly is just how well we are performing as a team and also on an individual basis too, as well as where improvement is required.

Position	Team	P	W	D	L	F	A	GD	Pt	Form
1	Middlesbrough	23	15	4	4	34	12	22	49	W W D W W W
2	Derby County	24	13	9	2	37	15	22	48	D D W W W D
3	Hull City	24	13	5	6	34	17	17	44	L W W L W L
4	Brighton and Hove A	24	11	11	2	31	24	7	44	W D D L D L
5	Burnley	24	11	8	5	34	23	11	41	L D L W L W
6	Ipswich Town	24	11	7	6	34	30	4	40	L W W L W W
7	Sheffield Wednesday	24	9	9	6	35	28	7	36	D D L W W L
8	Brentford	24	10	6	8	36	33	3	36	W D L W D W
9	Birmingham City	24	10	6	8	28	26	2	36	L D D W L W
10	Cardiff City	24	8	10	6	29	26	3	34	W D W L L D
11	Wolverhampton Wndrs	24	8	7	9	31	32	-1	31	W D L L W W
12	Leeds United	24	7	10	7	25	27	-2	31	W D W W D D
13	Reading	24	8	6	10	29	28	1	30	L L L W L L
14	Nottingham Forest	24	7	9	8	24	23	1	30	W D D W D D
15	Queens Park Rangers	24	7	9	8	29	31	-2	30	W D D D L D
16	Blackburn Rovers	23	6	10	7	22	20	2	28	D W W D L L
17	Preston North End	24	6	10	8	19	21	-2	28	W W D L L W
18	Fulham	24	6	9	9	40	42	-2	27	L D L D L W
19	Huddersfield Town	24	6	7	11	28	36	-8	25	W L W L W D
20	Milton Keynes Dons	24	6	4	14	20	32	-12	22	L L W L W L
21	Rotherham United	24	6	3	15	29	42	-13	21	L L L W W L
22	Bristol City	24	4	9	11	22	43	-21	21	L W L D D L
23	Charlton Athletic	24	4	7	13	20	41	-21	19	L D D L D L
24	Bolton Wanderers	24	2	11	11	19	37	-18	17	L L D D L W

[29th December 2015]

186

January

Brentford's Top Eighty Goals – 1/1/16

Firstly I would like to wish everybody a very happy and healthy New Year and today I am going to set you all a poser as you gaze weary and bleary-eyed at the page and do your best to recover from an evening of excess and a lack of sleep.

We were graced with two goals of pure brilliance from Ryan Woods and Sergi Canos at Reading on Monday afternoon and I am therefore going to ask you all to nominate the best goals you have ever seen Brentford score.

The one ground rule to remember is that we are **only** talking about quality here and **not** the importance of the occasion so, for example, a certain Gary Blissett strike at Peterborough in 1992 might not necessarily qualify despite what the goal actually meant for the club.

Given my rapidly failing memory I have only gone back to 1970 so apologies to my older readers although I am happy to consider any nominations for goals scored before that date.

So here we go and the goals are all in date order rather than being ranked in terms of actual quality as that would be a mammoth task that is totally beyond me, I am afraid!

1. **John O'Mara's** second goal v **Darlington** in 1971/72 when he finished off a wonderful flowing move by smashing home a long-range effort from a cross from Paul Bence.

2. **Paul Bence's** thirty yard screamer at home to **Rotherham** in September 1974

3. An acrobatic overhead kick by **Micky French** against **Barnsley** on his debut in February 1975

4. **Bob Booker** curling the ball into the **Gillingham** net from twenty yards in April 1980

5. **Paul Walker** scoring from a well-worked short corner routine at **Walsall** in August 1980

6. **David Crown's** second goal against **Oxford United** in November 1980 when he beat three defenders before scoring

7. **Chris Kamara's** looping twenty yard header at **Swindon** in November 1981

8. An unstoppable curling free kick by **Stan Bowles** against **Wimbledon** in April 1982

9. **Gary Roberts's** thunderous goal against **Swansea** in the Milk Cup in October 1983

10. **Robbie Cooke's** turn and shot at **Bournemouth** in the Freight Rover trophy in April 1985

11. **Andy Sinton's** winner against **Port Vale** in October 1987 when he beat two men, cut in from the left and buried the ball into the top corner

12. **Roger Stanislaus** running from the halfway line and scoring from thirty yards (not fifty as popular legend has it) at **Fulham** in the Littlewoods Cup in August 1988

13. **Roger Stanislaus** against **Northampton** in January 1989 when he combined brilliantly with Andy Sinton and Kevin Godfrey before scoring emphatically

14. **Dean Holdsworth** turning on the edge of the box and rifling home an unstoppable drive into the roof of the **Walsall** net in January 1990

15. **Neil Smillie's** solo goal against **Shrewsbury** in March 1990 when he ran from inside his own half, jinked past a defender and hit a thirty-yarder into the roof of the net

16. **Dean Holdsworth** finishing off a slick four man move with a fantastic volley against **Bolton Wanderers** in September 1990

17. **Marcus Gayle's** first senior goal with a turn and long range thunderbolt into the roof of the **Reading** net in October 1990

18. **Marcus Gayle** almost breaking the **Bradford City** net in March 1991 with a thirty yard Exocet after a powerful run

19. **Lee Luscombe's** debut goal against **Barnet** in the Autoglass Trophy in December 1991 after a slick move which went from one end of the pitch to the other

20. **Lee Luscombe's** solo run and finish at **Leyton Orient** in December 1991

21. **Lee Luscombe's** outrageous swerving volley from way out on the left wing against **Charlton Athletic** in November 1992

22. **Gary Blissett's** curler at **Derby County** in the Anglo-Italian Cup in February 1993

23. **Denny Mundee's** hat trick goal against **Bristol Rovers** in January 1994 when he hammered home from an acute angle after a mazy run

24. **Robert Taylor's** perfect long-range lob against **Cambridge United** in January 1995

25. **Paul Abrahams** running from the halfway line and lobbing the **Gillingham** keeper from twenty yards in August 1996

26. **Carl Asaba's** winner at **Gillingham** in March 1997 when he picked the ball up on the left touchline, knocked it over a defender's head and allowed it to bounce before unleashing a rocket from a tight angle into the roof of the net

27. **Tony Folan's** solo goal at **Peterborough** in October 1998 when he went on a mazy run, cut in from the wing, left several defenders with twisted blood as he dribbled past them before floating a perfect chip over the keeper

28. **Tony Folan** from the halfway line in December 1998 after he picked the ball up on the edge of his own penalty area before lobbing the **Cambridge United** keeper from fully forty-five yards

29. A **Paul Evans** thirty yard angled screamer against **Swansea City** in May 1999

30. **Martin Rowlands's** solo goal at **Bury** in August 1999 when he ran forty yards and beat several defenders before scoring emphatically

31. **Paul Evans** scoring straight from our kick-off from sixty-two yards, still inside the Brentford half, in September 1999 against **Preston North End** with the ball travelling like a shell and still rising as it hit the net

32. **Paul Evans** scoring two games later in October 1999 at **Burnley** from a mere forty yards, taking his effort on the run

33. **Martin Rowlands** scoring against **Bristol City** in December 1999 when he ran thirty yards, beat three players before curling home an exquisite shot

34. **Gavin Mahon's** thirty-five yard rocket at **Bristol City** in December 2000

35. **Paul Evans's** chipped *Panenka* penalty kick against **Oldham Athletic** in September 2001 – pure class

36. The **Ben Burgess** swivel and volley from the edge of the area against **Brighton** in January 2002

37. **Lloyd Owusu's** spectacular volley at **Blackpool** in March 2002

38. **Steve Sidwell's** perfectly placed lob from thirty-five yards against **Stoke City** in March 2002

39. **Stephen Hunt's** weaving run and curler against **Northampton Town** in March 2003

40. **Jay Tabb's** fifty yard solo run at **Barnsley** in April 2004

41. The **Alex Rhodes** solo effort against **Bournemouth** in May 2004

42. A searing volley from **Kevin O'Connor** against **Wrexham** in August 2004

43. **Deon Burton's** flick over a defender and wonderful finish against **Luton Town** in December 2004

44. **Deon Burton's** cool finish at **Sheffield Wednesday** in December 2004 after Alex Rhodes's solo run

45. **Isaiah Rankin's** thunderous twenty yard hooked volley at **Bournemouth** in January 2005

46. **Deon Burton's** thirty yard volley against **Sheffield Wednesday** in February 2005

47. **Michael Turner's** spectacular long range effort against **Tranmere Rovers** in April 2005

48. **Jay Tabb's** solo run and shot against **Hull City** in May 2005

49. **Isaiah Rankin's** curling effort at **Chesterfield** in August 2005

50. Sam Sodje's defence splitting pass to **Kevin O'Connor** who scored against **Chesterfield** in December 2005

51. **DJ Campbell's** superlative flick up and volley at **Southend United** in January 2006

52. **Paul Brooker's** outrageous solo goal at **Swindon** in April 2006 when he ran seventy yards before scoring

53. **Jo Kuffour's** scissor kick against **Bradford City** in September 2006

54. **Glenn Poole's** swerving volley at **Rochdale** in October 2007

55. **Glenn Poole's** fantastic volley from a Ryan Dickson corner against **Wycombe Wanderers** in December 2007

56. A three man breakaway against **Macclesfield** in October 2008 which led to a **Charlie MacDonald** goal

57. **Ryan Dickson's** trickery on the ball before scoring against **Accrington Stanley** in April 2009

58. **Cleveland Taylor's** headed goal at **Southampton** in August 2009 after a beautiful dribble and cross by Ryan Dickson

59. **Charlie MacDonald's** midair volley at **Oldham Athletic** in March 2009

60. **Clayton Donaldson's** goal against **Colchester United** in September 2011 when he was set free by Myles Weston and scored clinically

61. **Clayton Donaldson's** thirty yard volley at **Notts County** in October 2011

62. **Saido Berahino's** unstoppable curling effort against **Carlisle United** in February 2012

63. **Clayton Donaldson's** solo effort against **MK Dons** in March 2012

64. **Clayton Donaldson's** left foot volley at **Swindon** from Paul Hayes's flick on in November 2012

65. **Harry Forrester's** solo run and long-ranger against **Sheffield United** in November 2012

66. **Bradley Wright-Phillips's** header at **Crewe Alexandra** in April 2013 after a lovely flowing four man move

67. **Shay Logan's** cut inside and long-range left footed curler at **Port Vale** in August 2013

68. **The Sam Saunders** *falling over* free kick routine against **Swindon Town** in December 2013

69. **Adam Forshaw's** instant no-back-lift thirty-five yarder at **Crewe Alexandra** in February 2014

70. **Moses Odubajo's** goal against **Brighton** in September 2014 after a perfect Alan Judge through pass

71. **Andre Gray's** powerful run and clinical finish against **Wolverhampton Wanderers** in November 2014

72. **Jota's** unstoppable angled effort at **Cardiff City** in December 2014

73. **Jota's** breakaway goal at **Norwich City** in January 2015

74. **Jota's** pitch length run at **Blackburn Rovers** in March 2015

75. **Stuart Dallas's** fulminating thirty yarder at **Fulham** in April 2015

76. **Alex Pritchard's** clinical curling finish at **Derby County** after a wonderful breakaway move in April 2015

77. David Button's perfect assist for **Alan Judge** to score with an angled shot against **Sheffield Wednesday** in September 2015

78. **Alan Judge's** breakaway goal at **Charlton Athletic** in October 2015

79. **Ryan Woods's** long range screamer at **Reading** in December 2015

80. **Sergi Canos's** trickery and sheer brilliance at **Reading** in December 2015

Frustration! – 3/1/16

I am going to pose a deep and hopefully interesting and relevant philosophical question to all of you this morning.

What would you prefer to watch, a team that plays with freedom and attacking abandon and entertains and frustrates in almost equal measures, or one that sits back and simply grinds its way to victory?

I suppose it depends if you are a Cavalier or Roundhead in your approach to the game or whether you support Brentford or Birmingham City?

I know exactly where I stand and I will nail my colours to the mast without any delay or prevarication.

It would drive me quite mad to have to watch Birmingham play every week, and that is not to denigrate or decry what they do and how they go about things.

They are supremely well-organised and have been perfectly set up by their talented manager Gary Rowett to draw the sting of the opposition, absorb their pressure like a moving sheet of blotting paper and then rely on set pieces, mistakes and the odd fast breakaway to snatch the points.

This they did to perfection yesterday and you have to respect and admire them for the thoroughness, skill and single-mindedness with which they executed their manager's game plan.

It worked a treat and Brentford just could not find a way to break through two solid banks of four players determined that nothing should pass them by.

Brentford dominated totally in terms of possession and successful passes but never really got in behind the home defence or created much in front of goal and they subsided to a defeat that does little for their playoff chances.

In many ways the match was a carbon copy of last season's dreary encounter with the Bees having the lion's share of possession but doing nothing with it, constantly running into blind alleys, being crowded out and, fatally committing to attack, getting picked off on the break.

Birmingham will look back at a job well done and can also point to a run of three consecutive home wins against Cardiff City, MK Dons and now Brentford so their approach is certainly successful and bears fruit, but would I cross the road to watch them?

Personally, I would draw the curtains if they were playing in my back garden and to me, Birmingham City represent everything that is bad about the game, they are the epitome of anti-football who squeeze all the joy and excitement out of the game and concentrate on boring and frustrating their opponents into submission. They are total parasites and drones who feed upon mistakes and bring very little to the party except solidity and organisation and an ability to carry out their manager's instructions to the letter.

There is certainly talent within their squad and I suspect that if the shackles were taken off they would still thrive and win their fair share of matches but as things stand I cannot believe that any but the most rabid Blues supporter can honestly say that they enjoy the fare that is being put in front of them.

Maybe I am being naïve and results are indeed the total be all and end all, but I suspect that the majority of Brentford fans would share the view of the late, great Danny Blanchflower of Spurs fame in that *the great fallacy is that the game is first and foremost about winning. It's nothing of the kind. The game is about glory. It's about doing things in style, with a flourish, about going out and beating the other lot, not waiting for them to die of boredom.*

These forty-four words, in my opinion totally summarise the Brentford philosophy of football, for better and for worse.

There have been many games over the last couple of unforgettable years when we have snatched victory out of almost certain defeat and *vice versa* and not allowed games to drift into boring draws, but you have to take the rough with the smooth and yesterday was certainly a perfect example of where we sacrificed an almost certain point and lost at the death when chasing an elusive victory.

In that respect it was almost a replica of the Cardiff match where we fought our way back to equality but refused to settle for a draw and lost sickeningly and frustratingly through a soft goal in the last minute.

Of course we need to defend better and avoid daft and stupid errors and total giveaway goals but otherwise we adopt a policy of risk and reward and it is easy to forget the many times when our positivity has paid off particularly at time like this morning when we are left sulking and licking our wounds.

We were drawn into Birmingham's spider's web and were unable to set ourselves free and did not manage a shot on target until late on when we equalised Maghoma's well-worked and well-taken goal when he was set free by a clever pass from Toral, was allowed to make an unchecked run into the area with Diagouraga not tracking his run and his instant angled shot beat the previously untested Button at his near post.

190

Toral should not even have been on the field after his potentially leg-breaking assault on Bidwell right on halftime was punished with an extremely lenient yellow card when his red mist should have been punished with a card of the same colour.

The pattern of the match remained unchanged with Brentford unable to create opportunities or gain a foothold in the final third of the field until Hofmann's arrival in place of the invisible Vibe helped us get up the pitch and gain momentum and cracks finally began to appear in the home team's previously impassable defence.

Judge was set free on the halfway line and ran unchallenged towards goal with the defenders trailing in his wake. Surely this would be the equaliser, but, shades of MK Dons a few weeks ago and Sheffield Wednesday last season, he missed horribly and unforgivably, blazing over the crossbar with the goal gaping.

That surely was that and I was reconciled to the game drifting towards what seemed an inevitable conclusion until Colin fed Judge and his well hit shot from long range was surely meat and drink for the previously untroubled Kuszczak but he unaccountably fumbled the ball straight to the feet of Hofmann, following in like all good strikers and he couldn't miss.

Under Uwe Rösler the game would have been closed out and we would have gone away content with a draw, but Brentford do not settle for one point when three are still on the table and we pushed on and fell to a sucker punch when Dean advanced into the final third but telegraphed his pass which was easily intercepted and the home team broke away down our deserted right flank and Vaughan's cross shot was turned in by Kieftenbeld who had made a positive supporting run, and he beat McEachran to the ball to score a late and totally undeserved and sickening winner.

So what have we learned from yesterday's defeat, and here I am going to be totally objective and I apologise for any perceived negativity:

- We lack pace throughout the team and are vulnerable to quick breakaways

- We do not track runners and have conceded several avoidable goals recently by allowing players to run into the area unchallenged

- Defenders are caught upfield and we lack cover and numbers at the back when the opposition breaks quickly at us

- We lack bite, height and doggedness in midfield and rarely win a tackle or second ball or impose ourselves upon the game or opposition

- There is nobody prepared to fight and scrap and fight fire with fire

- We do not have a box-to-box midfielder who can replicate what Douglas did for us when he was in his pomp. Kerschbaumer is the nearest we have but he is patently not yet ready

- We are too well behaved and polite. There is an acceptable middle ground but Birmingham got into the ear of the referee at every opportunity and benefited from his decisions. We stand around like choirboys

- We lack strength up front and the ability to win the ball, hold it up, run the channels and are not at all clinical in front of goal

I make no mention of our approach in terms of never settling for anything other than a win as, firstly, I totally agree with this philosophy as long as we do not go too *kamikaze* when chasing the win, and secondly, this is how Matthew Benham insists that we play, and nothing will change this, whatever I or any other pundit says.

I fully appreciate that we are nowhere near the finished article and we are limited by our resources but I wonder whether any of the weaknesses noted above will be addressed and rectified in the transfer window?

We are still a soft touch to teams like Birmingham and seem unable to deal with them as this was the third time in a row that they have defeated us and we have to learn some lessons from this as Bolton and Cardiff City were other teams that recently have succeeded in knocking us out of our stride and I am sure that Middlesbrough will not be shrinking violets either when we meet them again in the very near future.

Brentford play beautiful one touch football, but we can come unstuck when the pitches are bad or when the opposition simply set up to frustrate or kick us out of our stride. It is all very well being known as the Arsenal of the Championship but we have a soft underbelly and unless rectified this will prevent us reaching the heights that we aspire to.

Should We Change Our Approach? The Fans Speak – 5/1/16

I gave some grudging praise, as well as some deserved brickbats to Birmingham City after their late and extremely fortunate victory against us on Saturday and suggested that I would even draw the curtains if Birmingham were playing in my back garden so boring, negative and lacking in adventure and attacking ideas were our opponents.

I wanted to gauge the views of fellow Brentford supporters in terms of how they feel about our approach which is always to chase the win and never to settle for a draw even if we risk losing by doing so, as in fact has been the case in two of our last three away games when we have conceded late and crucial goals after fighting our way back to equality.

Should we always go hell for leather for the three points on offer or are there times when it would be more sensible and prudent to settle for one?

Michael Ohl was happy overall with our playing philosophy but pointed out some of our shortcomings:

I agree with you Greville about not settling for a draw – watching The Bees these days is not for the faint-hearted. Also, it is a team game, so although Harlee made the original mistake, it was in their half – so where was the cover?

I think we could do with a couple of good defensive midfielders who also have a bit of flair. Clone McCormack? We ARE lightweight in that area.

For this season I am content to watch The Bees play entertaining football, knowing that our ambitions are to be in the Premier League. And when we get there I want us to stay there. That means a team with depth, experience and skill.

Unfortunately, players like the ones he mentioned – a Bradley Johnson, for example are few and far between at our level and also totally unaffordable given our current limited resources.

Peter Lumley was far more resigned and fatalistic about Saturday's defeat:

Any long-term supporters of Brentford could have forecast the inevitable defeat almost from the kick-off knowing Birmingham's game plan. That is what sets us apart from the fans of the likes of Middlesbrough, Derby and Hull!

Rebel Bee also pointed to a weakness in midfield as well as the problems we face with three tough home games looming up over an intense six-day period:

Birmingham certainly have the drop on us and that is a hugely disappointing fact, and whilst I agree with your sentiments regarding our playing style versus theirs, this feeling won't last indefinitely.

Three interesting games over the Christmas period, and a four point return felt just about right, although our best performance was at home to Brighton.

What is weird for me is that our gifted midfield has been a bit of a mess over the last games and that as more players become available Dean Smith needs to find his best combination from the array of options we have. And perhaps make some additions and changes.

Some of us crave a midfield enforcer, or to see more of Alan Mac (the only squad player of this type) but sadly I've accepted the reality that we just won't sign such players in the future, they are not part of our philosophy.

We are only after ball players and try to pass around sides and play a slightly more industrial version of Barca's wonderful football from a few years back.

We are patently some way off being promotion or playoff contenders, so for me the task now is to carefully secure and assemble a side that can really challenge next term.

Finishing as strongly as possible of course, also try to go a few rounds in the FA Cup. We must try to avoid the huge churn of players seen last summer – that work starts now.

We have three really tough games to come, in six days and all at Griffin Park – whilst the spectre of the transfer window looms over us. It's a real test for Dean Smith and the boys, but one that they need for us to see what we really have.

Former Brentford striker **Richard Poole** reminded us all of a much loved and feared Brentford midfield dynamo and enforcer from long ago and the influence that he had on friend and foe alike and how we could do with someone like him now:

All this is food for thought but it comes down for me that for the past two years we have needed a grafter in our side just like Brentford had in the seventies. Jackie Graham was the man and, yes, he was a talented footballer with an eye for a pass who could play football as well as anyone else in the team but on top of that he could also destroy the opposition's midfield. He was a winner even without the football and totally controlled the midfield area.

Look at the best teams around today. Even Arsenal who pride themselves upon maintaining possession feel the need for Flamini or Coquelin to protect their more delicate ball players. This is something that I feel Brentford are missing.

I totally agree with Richard and yearn for a Jackie Graham, Terry Hurlock or even Jonathan Douglas-type figure who could fill that gap for us.

Mike Rice had to suffer in silence on Saturday:

A few points Greville, having experienced superb hospitality with my Blues-supporting in-laws. Interestingly, all of them were convinced that the referee was on our side, given the number of free kicks he gave us, particularly in the second half.

They were getting quite incensed, but naturally I agreed with almost all of his decisions, except when he gave us a free kick from a breakaway, instead of playing an advantage. He couldn't wait to brandish yet another yellow card!

I agree with all of your comments about Birmingham, good and bad, but want to add some context. The owner is in jail and the current manager inherited League One quality players (e.g. Donaldson and Cotterill) signed by Lee Clark, and some talented juniors and a few loanees such as Toral who couldn't get a regular game with us. He has done a superb job organising them into a team challenging for the playoffs.

We played the first half with all of the possession, but in front of their two banks of four. In the second half, they were told to close us down and give us less time on the ball and perhaps shake us up, which duly worked very well.

They played like an away side and were very negative, but I would contend that Gary Rowett has little choice with the players at his disposal. They certainly know how to execute his game plan.

And as for watching Birmingham every week, you should have experienced the delight all around me when they scored their second goal. It may be about the glory, but winning when you know you're second best (and the ref's supposedly against you) can be very, very satisfying! There were a lot of smiling faces after the game.

I said after the game that I would not swap a single Birmingham player for a Brentford player with a view to improving our team. Birmingham are far more than the sum of their parts, but I do wonder with Financial Fair Play if our owner's playing style aspirations currently far overreach our ability to achieve them successfully.

Roll on Lionel Road!

Mike Lumley also has a reasonable point to make:

I agree with most of your comments and observations on what the Birmingham game (and others like them) tell us.

However, I am a bit perplexed by the implied assumption that we either have to be a devil-may-care collection of death or glory heroes or a bunch of faceless defensive drones.

The difference between the class of 2014/15 and our current squad is that last season's group combined the best of both worlds – with the aggression and clatter of Dougie and Toums complemented perfectly by the flair and panache of Jota and Pritchard.

I also believe that despite his alleged negativity and outspokenness, Dougie would still be a regular starter this season if he had not fallen out with the owner and opened his mouth once too often.

We are where we are – and despite my earlier views – I may have to accept that Alan McCormack may be a better option (at least pro tem) alongside Toums and Ryan Woods than Josh McEachran who still seems to be struggling with the intensity and hurly-burly of Championship football.

I also believe that with the current set up – a playoff berth is already beyond us this season but add in a genuine box-to-box replacement for Douglas and additional cover for Djuricin/Hogan either now or in the summer and we will be major contenders next season.

I will let **Rebel Bee** have the last word:

The choice isn't about going for a win or parking the bus, it's about sensible risk versus reward which doesn't mean that you have to give soft goals away.

Bees fans I know assume that Josh McEachran will step into the side and be all the things we want him to be, for me he still has plenty to do and prove in order to be a starter at this level – maybe he's one to come good next season?

And that is where we came in!

The Facts Of Life – 6/1/16

The silly season has just begun and the predators are apparently already bashing our door down and lining up to pluck our best assets away from our clutches at Griffin Park.

Yes it is that time of the year again and our collective blood pressure is sure to rise on a daily basis until relief arrives with the closing of the January Transfer Window.

In the not too distant past we did not contemplate January with dread or a sense of foreboding simply because nobody really coveted any of our players enough to pay the panic premium that seems to be charged at a time when the heart often seems to rule the head and nonsensical fees are paid by clubs looking for that final player who will help them ensure promotion or avoid the drop.

Now things are different and we boast at least three star players in Alan Judge, James Tarkowski and Jota who, according to the rumour mill, are all on the verge of leaving the club.

It is still early in the month and nobody knows for sure if any or even all of them will move on but there was identical speculation this time last year about the likes of Andre Gray and Moses Odubajo and despite all the rumours, both players saw the season out at Griffin Park.

To put it bluntly, we are simply the victims of our own success. Through a combination in recent years of enlightened ownership, inspired management, for the most part superb player analysis and recruitment and a determination and commitment to play a unique brand of positive, attacking football the Bees have totally over performed and punched way over their weight.

Despite having one of the lowest average attendance and turnover figures in the Championship, Brentford have established themselves as one of the best footballing teams in the division and built up a squad that contains many valuable assets who are coveted far and wide.

We pay more than decent wages but our budget is dwarfed by the larger and more established clubs within the division, some of whom spend reckless and unjustifiable amounts and ignore the dictates of Financial Fair Play given their determination to join the Premier League gravy train and others are buttressed by a series of enormous parachute payments that give them a ridiculously unfair financial advantage.

We are not competing on an even playing field and for us to have reached the playoffs last season and to have a realistic chance of repeating that feat at the end of the current campaign is an incredible achievement which highlights just how well we are managed and run and the quality of the players we have managed to identity, attract, recruit and develop.

That last verb perfectly sums up where we are as a club at the moment. Brentford, in my opinion can best be described as a stepping-stone club where young players of potential know they will be given a showcase where they will be able to hone, demonstrate and improve their skills in a positive and nurturing environment.

Being situated in London is a double-edged sword with the attractions of a big capital city offset by the price of housing and cost of living but we are a more than attractive proposition for well advised young players who want to progress.

In other words Brentford puts them in the shop window and there are many clubs out there who are happy to let us do all the hard graft in terms of player recruitment and development and then swoop in to pluck them away from us and benefit from all the hard work we have done with them.

Unfortunately given the disparity in our size, income and wage bill we are still at a stage of our development when we are totally unable to prevent this asset stripping as it is pointless to keep a disaffected footballer, and all we can do is grin and bear it, ensure that we receive top dollar for our players, replace them more than adequately with more diamonds in the rough and wait for the time to come when it is our turn to be in the catbird seat.

The situation will only change once we move to Lionel Road and start to benefit from the additional income streams that it will offer or actually get to the Premier League ourselves. Then we will be able to call the tune and hang onto our best players until we decide it is time to move them on.

Players are tapped up as a matter of course and have agents and other intermediaries in their ear all the time telling them of the riches on offer elsewhere and our current crop will be well aware how much the likes of Moses Odubajo and Andre Gray are currently earning. Can you imagine the sort of tales that Alan Judge hears when on international duty with Eire?

There is talk that Sheffield Wednesday are currently offering to triple Alan Judge's wages and as a family man entering the prime of his career he cannot fail to be attracted by such an offer than we cannot hope to match and nor would it be a sensible decision for us to do so given our financial constraints.

Players have to look after their own interests as the average professional playing career lasts for less than eight years and injury can strike at any moment.

I do not blame the like of Simon Moore, Harry Forrester, Adam Forshaw, Clayton Donaldson, Stuart Dallas, Odubajo and Gray deciding to move on for reasons that in several cases appear to have been more financially driven rather than a way of improving their career prospects.

Moore, Forrester and Forshaw have faded into the background and their once promising careers seem to have withered on the vine.

Whilst they can all point to inflated bank balances they might also reflect upon the fact that they could conceivably have actually earned more by staying at Brentford and benefiting from the massive bonus payments that were made last season for reaching the playoffs!

I have written previously about the parallels between Brentford and Southampton and our approach is pretty much identical.

- We do not need to sell anyone and want to keep our best players

- We will only sell them if they decide irrevocably that they wish to leave

- They will only leave on our terms and not theirs – in other words the buying club will have to meet our asking price

- All departing players will be replaced by someone who either already is, or is expected to become, an even better and more valuable player

If a player wants to go and we don't want him to go, as appears to be the case currently with Tarkowski and Judge, then the club's response is simply to say that they are not for sale unless our valuation is met and if that is not the case then they will remain at Brentford FC.

It is rare that players have been allowed to leave on their terms or to run their contracts down. It happened with Clayton Donaldson and the same situation might be repeated with Harlee Dean but more often than not the club manages difficult situations exceptionally well.

Looking back at previous deals, I think it is more than fair to say that selling Moses and Andre was fantastic business for the club as we will earn up to thirteen million pounds for the pair of them plus a hefty sell-on percentage if and when they move on again. This is money that will be reinvested in new players.

We are, after all a business and must take advantage when such a deal is on the table, as long, of course, as we replace the players with new ones that could turn out to be even better and more valuable.

It would be hard to deny that Max Colin is as good as Moses and he is probably a better defender than his predecessor and whilst it is fair to say that there is no current individual player at the club who can be said to have replaced Andre Gray and what he brought to the team, the facts speak for themselves.

At this point last season Andre had scored nine Championship goals whereas the trio of Lasse Vibe, Marco Djuricin and Philipp Hofmann have contributed fifteen Championship goals between them.

Like all other Brentford fans, I do not want either Tarky or Judge to go, however if they decide that that is what they want to do and our valuation is reached, then I retain full confidence in the club replacing them more than adequately whether it be now or at the end of the season.

The time to worry is if players leave and nobody arrives of a suitable calibre and so far, despite some narrow squeaks in the last close season where some of the newcomers have yet to fully prove themselves for a variety of reasons, we are still well ahead of the game,

As for Jota, who knows what the situation is and whether or why he has become unsettled. The talk of a swift loan move back to Spain can surely only be explained by a pressing personal or family problem that needs to be sorted, rather than footballing reasons.

I hope that this is just scuttlebutt and unfounded social media rumour as he is a footballer who is touched by genius and we have all been waiting for his return with a combination of expectation, anticipation and bated breath.

It would be cruel if the cup is dashed from our lips and he also decides for whatever reason that he needs to leave the club, however Jota, for all his undoubted quality, is also a replaceable asset even if it is hard for us to accept that fact.

Our current squad is immeasurably stronger than it was three years ago and I am certain that it will become even stronger in three years' time. Players come and players go, that is the way of the world, and we just have to trust in the club to manage our affairs properly as has undoubtedly been the case up until now.

We are growing and evolving rapidly as it is. Four seasons ago we were a reasonable Third Division team, now we are looking realistically at getting to the Premier League.

That is a massive jump and we have to accept that we are competing in a different arena now and have to play by a different set of rules.

With the welcome loan extensions for Canos and Swift we have actually started the window well by ensuring that two excellent young players will remain at the club for the rest of the season.

There is a lot of water to flow under the bridge between now and the end of January and there are certain to be some highs and lows for us supporters to endure and even enjoy, however I would, suggest that by the beginning of February we will have a playing squad that is as strong, if not stronger than the one we currently possess.

Time will tell.

Why Peter Lumley Loves The Bees – 8/1/16

Peter Lumley has already provided some wonderful memories of his many years watching the Bees and I am delighted to say that he was written another wonderful and evocative article that explains and expands upon his passion for the club.

I hope that you all enjoy it as much as I did:

Watching Gary Blissett receive his Hall of Fame accolade on the pitch ahead of the Boxing Day game against Brighton reminded me of one of my previous communications in which I named a Brentford team compromised solely of players with a surname beginning with **B***.*

The players spanned the seventy-three years since 1942 when I first paid a visit to Griffin Park.

My Dream Team selection was as follows:

Chic Brodie | Paul Bence | Jake Bidwell | Jamie Bates | Wally Bragg | Bob Booker | Stan Bowles | Jimmy Bloomfield | Johnny Brooks | Gary Blissett | Peter Broadbent

I challenge anyone to name a more talented team compromising players sharing the same first letter from the remainder of the alphabet.

I am appending a brief note about each of my selections:

Chic Brodie: *Perhaps the most reliable goalkeeper to don a Brentford green jersey. His all too short career was blighted by a bizarre incident at Colchester when a stray dog ran on to the pitch and in a one-on-one situation almost broke the keeper's leg above the kneecap.*

It left him with an injury that had a detrimental effect on the remainder of his career. His selection was marginal due to the excellence of three other contenders, Len Bond, Graham Benstead and David Button, who now has the potential to reach the very top.

Paul Bence: *Loyal, versatile and reliable defender who was equally at home in the old fashioned right back or right half positions and you could count his off-days on one hand. A true Griffin Park servant and a wonderful example to aspiring young players at the time.*

Jake Bidwell: *There is nothing I can write about Jake that current Brentford fans do not already know. As the captain of the team he leads by example and his charges down the left with the resultant crosses into the box are* a feature of virtually every Brentford performance. And now he has broken his duck as a goal scorer, let us hope there are many more to come.

Jamie Bates: Another long serving Griffin Park favourite and a natural successor to the iconic Terry Evans in the Bees defence. Like Terry, a great header of the ball both in attack and defence. Few strikers got the better of him in fifty-fifty situations but he was always resolutely strong but fair in a tackle. A possible candidate for future Hall of Fame recognition.

Wally Bragg: One of a long line of outstanding centre halves and in the same league as, for example, Joe James, Ron Greenwood, Jack Chisholm, Mel Scott, Stewart Houston, Pat Kruse, Peter Gelson and Leon Legge.

Bob Booker: There is nothing I can write about Bob that has not already attracted the attention of those with far mightier pens than mine. One of my all-time favourites.

Stan Bowles: Another outstanding performer who came to Griffin Park quite late in his illustrious career but was an absolute joy to watch. Falls into that category of players who could be regarded as the most talented of all time.

Jimmy Bloomfield: I can remember a very young Jimmy coming to Griffin Park as an extremely talented inside forward who possessed exquisite skills on the ball. His play was as smooth as silk and I was desperately sorry when he left us for pastures new and subsequently I was saddened to learn of his death at a relatively young age.

Johnny Brooks: Came to Brentford after an illustrious career with Tottenham and England. In many ways he was an older version of the aforementioned Jimmy Bloomfield. His skill on the ball had to be seen to be believed and he possessed one of the most powerful shots in the game. A pity he did not join Brentford some seasons earlier.

Gary Blissett: Yet again another player to fall into that category where it is difficult to find words to add to those already written about him. Arguably the best out and out striker Brentford have ever had, certainly in the modern era.

My own personal highlight was to see him scoring the winning goal in that never to be forgotten promotion-clinching win at Peterborough. With members of the family I had to drive, somewhat hastily, back to Griffin Park to greet the team as they arrived back to a very noisy reception in Braemar Road.

As mentioned earlier, Gary's recognition as a newcomer to the Hall of Fame was the event that encouraged me to write this particular article.

Peter Broadbent: As the then Sports Editor of the local newspaper, now known as the Ealing Gazette, I struck up a friendship with Peter shortly following his debut as a Brentford player.

In fact I recall that the two of us as young unattached lads, going to Saturday night dances at Ealing Town Hall after a game on a number of occasions.

Again I was extremely sorry to see him move on to Wolverhampton Wanderers where he subsequently won a number of caps with the England team.

Another of my all-time favourites who I was privileged to know as a friend.

Other Brentford players who fell into the same category were Ken Horne, Tom Higginson, Jim Towers and George Francis.

My substitutes in this team would be a selection of seven from the following candidates:

Goalkeepers: Len Bond, Graham Benstead and David Button

Defenders: Billy Brown, Danny Boxall, John Buttigieg, George Bristow and Paul Brooker.

Forwards: Mickey Bennett, Mike Block, Micky Ball, Deon Burton and Willy Brown.

Quite apart from the players, I wish to extend the "B" theme to include other Griffin Park heroes.

This is my list for starters:

Chairmen: Ron Blindell and Matthew Benham.

Managers: Jimmy Bain, Frank Blunstone and reluctantly, Terry Butcher.

Supporters: John Barr and his fire officer grandson, also named John Barr or "Little John" as we nicknamed him when he first visited Griffin Park as an eight year old.

Last, but by no means least, I nominate the incomparable Mark Burridge as my favourite Bees Player commentator.

Mentioning Len Bond earlier leads me into a postscript to this communication. My wife has a habit of waking up in the unearthly hours of five or six most mornings. She then trawls through the various early morning TV channels to ensure that I wake up at about the same time.

But one morning over the Christmas holiday, I could not believe my ears, or my eyes, when I heard the names of Len Bond, Danis Salman, Barry Tucker Jim McNichol, Paul Shrubb, Dean Smith and Steve Phillips beaming out from the TV set.

Quite by chance my wife had hit upon an ITV4 program entitled "Big Match Revisited". The featured match was a 1970's Third Division clash at Griffin Park between Brentford and Watford. The result was a thrilling 3-3 draw with Dean Smith and Steve Phillips scoring for the Bees, his second goal from the penalty spot to earn a point.

Thank you Peter and I hope some of you will rise to his challenge and name your own favourite teams comprising players with a surname beginning with the same letter.

So Who's Leaving Brentford This Transfer Window? – 9/1/16

I wanted to write some original and perceptive comments about what Brentford should be looking to achieve in the current Transfer Window but we seem to be on ever shifting sands with the situation seemingly changing every day and what I write now might well be totally out of date by the time that you read it.

All my conversations and soundings over the last week or so seemed to reinforce the view that this would be a quiet month for the Bees with a minimum of activity. In other words we would be reactive rather than proactive, not seeking to strengthen or change the squad too much, or even at all, unless our hand was forced by enemy action with players leaving the building.

Now things are completely different with rumours abounding about the likes of Alan Judge, James Tarkowski, Jota, Harlee Dean and Toumani Diagouraga and the prospect of some or all of them finding new homes before the end of the month.

As Phil Giles stated in his excellent recent interview with *Beesotted*, we would certainly struggle to cope with all of them going at the same time but he felt that it is very unlikely that they would all be on the move.

I have already written about our philosophy and how, whilst we are not looking to sell our best players, everybody has his price and if we receive an acceptable offer and can replace the player properly then we will do so assuming that the player wishes to leave the club.

I do not intend to bore you by repeating why in my opinion we are for the time being a stepping stone club, vulnerable to approaches by our richer rivals, but the fact remains that contracts are often not worth the paper they are written on and if a footballer becomes disaffected and decides for whatever reason that the grass is greener elsewhere then it is almost invariably the best policy to allow him to leave as long as it is on our terms rather than his.

Adam Forshaw is a perfect example of this policy as he was made to kick his heels on gardening leave until Wigan finally and belatedly coughed up a high enough fee to persuade us to sell a player who had made it perfectly clear that he wanted to leave.

Footballers are well aware from the grapevine and the bush telegraph just how much other clubs are paying in terms of salaries and given the uncertain nature of their career which can end at any time and is highly unlikely to last for more than eight years, they cannot be blamed for chasing the money and seeking to maximise their earnings.

Sometimes you feel that money is the overriding priority and that ambition and career development can take a back seat.

Only Andre Gray and Moses Odubajo of our recent departures can really be said to have bettered themselves as they are both currently starring in teams challenging for promotion to the Premier League as well as earning sums that they could only have dreamed about at Brentford.

Adam Forshaw has criminally allowed a burgeoning career to at least temporarily wither on the vine as he sits gathering splinters on the Middlesbrough bench instead of playing every week and proving himself as one of the best midfielders in the Championship.

Stuart Dallas has had an in and out season for a massively unpredictable and inconsistent team in Leeds United, Clayton Donaldson plies a lonely furrow as Birmingham's lone striker and Simon Moore has disappeared almost without trace as he waits patiently for David Marshall to leave Cardiff City. Harry Forrester has had a couple of years in the wasteland at Doncaster – what an appalling career decision he made when he decided to jump ship, and might now finally be on the road to resurrection at Glasgow Rangers.

The point I am making is that sometimes chasing the money does not bring guaranteed career progress and success, a message that some of our current squad might benefit from taking into consideration.

What happens next is to a large degree out of our own hands and we simply have to wait and see if any of the clubs rumoured to be interested in our players step up to the plate and meet our asking price.

Even should that be the case the player will need to decide if he wishes to remain within the positive and nurturing environment at Griffin Park where everybody mucks in and there are no cliques or rampant troublemakers amongst what is a young and dedicated squad.

Looking at the situation with each of the five Brentford players who are rumoured to be attracting external interest, my view is as follows:

Alan Judge has quite simply been the best player in the Championship throughout the first half of the season as his highly impressive tally of goals and assists clearly testifies. No wonder there is serious interest in him from the likes of Sheffield Wednesday who are rumoured to have offered to triple his wages. I also wonder if a Premier League team might yet come in for him.

On the one hand Alan is the man at Griffin Park, everything revolves around him and he is the catalyst and fulcrum for most of the good things that we do. He is the conductor who sets the tempo and the rest dance around him feeding off his magic and inspiration.

He is in an ideal situation to show off his talent and earn a place in the Eire squad for the European Championship tournament this summer.

But, money talks, and at twenty-seven, he is not getting any younger and might never again recapture his current form. Maybe he should strike while the iron is hot and take the money that will surely be on offer before the end of January?

He needs to play every week and as long as he does not become a bit part player and fall out of the spotlight then I could understand him deciding to move to a bigger club, even in the Championship, despite the fact that he and his family seem settled and happy – such is the nature of football.

Opportunities do not come along very often and need to be carefully considered and not spurned whenever they do.

The situation from Brentford's perspective is also very interesting. Ideally he will either sign an improved contract, something that I feel is highly unlikely to happen, or we will keep hold of him unless our valuation, and I hear figures of between six to eight million pounds being bandied around, is reached.

As for Sheffield Wednesday, they seem to be bidding for all number of players so who knows how serious they are about signing Judge.

We are obviously a far better team with Judge than without him but I can also understand the viewpoint that he is at the absolute peak of his game and is unlikely to improve much or any more and perhaps we should take the money if it is on offer, particularly bearing in mind that promotion is far less likely a prospect this season than it was last, his contract expires at the end of next season and he will soon become a depreciating asset.

Personally I hope that he remains at least until the end of the season as it would be wonderful to see a Brentford player competing at Euro 2016 but I think that we will probably have a difficult decision to make about him in the next few weeks.

James Tarkowski is a different kettle of fish as at twenty-three he is still improving and is nowhere near the finished article and given hard work, dedication, good coaching and the right attitude, he could turn out to be pretty much anything he wants to be. He really has the potential to be that good and if he progresses as I hope then I see him developing into a Premier League regular at the very least.

There was talk of interest from Fulham in the last Transfer Window and now Burnley are reputed to be making overtures for him with a fee of around four to five million pounds being mooted on social media.

Tarky can be infuriatingly casual and inconsistent and make schoolboy howlers in defence, but he also has games when he resembles a reincarnation of Alan Hansen, winning the ball, selling an impudent dummy and striding imperiously into the opposition half.

Of all the players in the current squad I believe that Tarky could go the furthest given his youth and relative inexperience.

I would go so far as to say that given the choice of keeping Tarkowski or Judge then I would choose to sell Alan Judge – as long as Tarky is not allowed anywhere near penalty taking duties at any time in the future.

The Jota situation is totally unexpected and has come as a bolt out of the blue. Unfortunately it appears that he has a serious personal family issue which makes it almost impossible for him to remain in this country if he is to maintain a family unit. This will almost certainly result in his being loaned back to a club in *La Liga*, perhaps Eibar, where he had a massively successful loan spell a couple of years ago.

This would enable us to keep Jota prominently in the shop window and give us the best chance of making a decent return on him should his situation not change and we are eventually forced to sell him. This is doubly frustrating for us given that we have waited so patiently and with such a sense of anticipation and expectation for Jota to recover from his long-term injury and we were all looking forward so much to watching him play every week and entertain us with his genius and magic wand of a left foot.

We will simply have to wait and see what happens over the coming months but if we are forced to sell him to a Spanish club, given the financial constraints of all but a minority of teams, it is very unlikely that we will be able to obtain anywhere near the level of fee for him that at one time looked likely. That is just how it is and we simply have to accept a difficult situation and wish him and his family all the best.

As for Harlee Dean, I feel that there is definitely some brinksmanship being played on both sides. Will the club make him a contract renewal offer that the player deems acceptable or will Harlee allow his existing deal to expire so that he can leave on a Bosman free at the end of the season?

Are the club happy to allow him to leave for nothing or will they even try and sell him in the current Transfer Window and get some sort of return for him?

It is almost impossible to answer any of these questions with any degree of certainty and Harlee's future could also be tied in with whatever happens to James Tarkowski as I cannot see the club allowing both of them to leave this month.

Harlee presents a bit of a conundrum, as he is a complete enigma. There are times when he is able to add concentration and discipline to his total commitment and he looks the real deal – a polished mid to high-level Championship calibre central defender. At others he lets himself down both on and off the pitch with a combination of sloppy play and thinking and he looks out of his depth.

He is a valued member of the old guard and continuity is precious but I think there also comes a time when every player has had his day and in my heart of hearts I do not believe that Harlee is good enough to help us progress much further than where we currently find ourselves.

The same could be said for Toumani Diagouraga, a veteran of over two hundred games for the club. His play last season was truly astonishing as he raised his game several notches and dominated the midfield. This season has been different and more difficult for him and I think that he has missed the presence of the combative Jonathan Douglas alongside him as he has been forced to forage for the ball, and tackling is not one of his strong points.

Toumani has been no better than average this season and has not really stamped his presence on games as was the case throughout last year, and with Ryan Woods and Josh McEachran breathing down his neck and challenging for his position in the team I would not be too surprised if Mark Warburton or, indeed, another manager, perhaps based in Yorkshire, succeeds in prising him away from Griffin Park either this month or perhaps at the end of the season.

Toumani has been a loyal servant of the club and is quite deservedly a massive fan favourite but I believe that he has jumped the shark and at twenty-eight it is time for him to be rewarded by earning another payday elsewhere at a level where he can shine and become a greater influence on proceedings.

Bill Shankly and Arsène Wenger are both managers renowned for knowing exactly when to sell a player by identifying before any opposition scouts and managers that he is just slightly past his best and I think that Toumani might well fit into this category and that his time might have come.

Hopefully other major influences on the team such as David Button and Jake Bidwell will remain well under the radar and not be subject to any unwelcome bids.

As it is I am feeling a bit conflicted as I am both concerned and yet pretty sanguine about matters at the moment and I would urge others to do the same.

As I stated right at the beginning of this article, things change on a regular basis and I might well be setting off a false alarm, and most importantly, I have learned a couple of things from observing affairs at Brentford since the start of the Benham regime, firstly that nobody is irreplaceable and finally, whoever does leave the club will be replaced, and replaced by somebody who is just as good if not even better.

A Bad Start To A Tough Week – 10/1/16

Yesterday's disappointing and frustrating defeat to Walsall in the Third Round of the FA Cup left a slightly sour taste in the mouth, so insipid and uninspiring was Brentford's overall performance, and given that fact that this was the first leg of what is certain to be a tough and arduous week that also sees us play two of the promotion favourites in the shape of our nemesis, Middlesbrough and Burnley I intend to be sensible and conserve some of my energy and ration my words in order to ensure that there is something left in the tank for me to cover the next two matches!

To be honest there really isn't too much to be said as Dean Smith rolled the dice, understandably rotated the team given the need to rest some tired legs and ensure that the squad can cope with the demands of three matches in a hectic six day period and unfortunately his gamble didn't pay off.

Colin, Tarkowski, Diagouraga, Judge and Vibe were all rested with recalls for Yennaris, O'Connell, McCormack, McEachran and Hofmann.

Conspiracy theorists will point to the absence from the starting lineup of possible transfer targets Tarky, Diagouraga and Judge but I would prefer to believe that they were all being saved for the hectic week that lies ahead.

I have no problems at all in those changes being made as the squad should be strong and deep enough to cope with them but where I do have concerns is in how we sleepwalked through the first half and showed no real interest in competing.

Brentford have built their recent success on pressing, passing and movement and maintaining a high tempo, all of which were sadly lacking in our play throughout a first half which ranks with the worst seen in recent memory at Griffin Park.

Why should this be the case as the manager was well aware of the threat that his former team presented and their decent and highly committed performance cannot have come as a surprise to him?

So lacking in pace, imagination, tempo and dare I say effort and energy was Brentford's first half performance that Judge had to be brought on after the break and his skill, pace and enthusiasm revitalised Brentford who dominated the second half and would have drawn or maybe even won an unlikely victory but for a combination of exceptional goalkeeping and profligate finishing.

Dean Smith's former team played their role as party poopers to perfection. They were neat and tidy on the ball, aided and abetted as they were by a lethargic Brentford team which sat off them, stayed deep, never pressed and allowed Walsall to maintain possession for long periods without benefit of any challenge.

Hofmann was totally isolated up front and a strange team selection which featured three holding midfielders ensured that he lacked any support from midfield runners and we created very little in that appalling first half.

It came as no surprise when Sam Mantom was allowed to run unchallenged from deep whilst we ignored the danger and simply watched, backed off and admired him and his perfectly placed curling long range effort gave Walsall a totally deserved lead.

Harlee Dean showing off his ball skills

McEachran looked yards off the pace and the game totally passed him by. McCormack ran down blind alleys and only Woods made any impact through the centre but was too easily snuffed out. The formation for once did not work, or perhaps it would be more accurate to say that the personnel selected did not gel and merely replicated each other's style of play.

Swift and Canos flitted in and out of the game and Hofmann showed some clever touches but one soft McCormack shot on target in the entire first half tells its own sad story and left the Bees with much to do.

It gives me no pleasure to say that FC Midtjylland appeared to expend more energy in their languid halftime saunter and stroll around the pitch than the Bees did throughout the first half.

After the break Brentford seized the initiative, mainly thanks to the tireless efforts of Judge, who demonstrated just how hard it would be to replace him should he leave in the Transfer Window.

We huffed and puffed and efforts from Judge, Hofmann, Swift and Canos were well saved by Etheridge and Dean missed horribly from a free header.

There was more good news with the return from injury of Djuricin who had a late run out off the bench. He found good positions but understandably lacked sharpness and missed two excellent late opportunities to save the day.

Walsall massed in defence and presented an impassable barrier and always broke quickly with Sawyers prominent and but for a brilliant save from Button and a late header from a well-worked corner kick routine which hit the post, the margin of their victory would have been greater, and we could not really have argued.

My memory of the FA Cup goes back over fifty years when I was taken by my Liverpool supporting Dad to the 1965 Cup Final where his heroes defeated Leeds United, much to his delight.

The following year I also saw Everton's narrow victory over Sheffield Wednesday in a five-goal thriller that left me breathless with excitement and my Dad a bit less impressed.

I am well aware of the magic of the cup and the mystic hold it has over supporters of a certain vintage and am saddened that this no longer seems to be the case.

I can also remember some of our wonderful days out against the likes of Cardiff, Chelsea, Southampton and Sunderland as well as the embarrassment of suffering giant killings at the hands of Guildford City and Telford amongst others.

Yesterday was therefore important to me and I resented the fact that it didn't appear to matter too much that we were knocked out of this famous and august competition at the first opportunity.

I well appreciate the juggling act that we faced given the two tough matches that lie ahead next week and have no problem with our utilising other squad members, as that is what they are there for, although the side selected could have been better balanced.

What rankled and upset me more is that certainly before the break the match and occasion really did not seem to matter to the players, so uncommitted, languid and unacceptable was their display which reminded me of the way we strolled through a recent FA Cup tie against Wrexham which also ended in another defeat by lower league opposition.

The proof of the pudding will be in the eating and should we gain four points or more from our next two matches – a really tough ask, then yesterday's debacle will be forgotten, at least until Fourth Round day when we will be left kicking our heels and without a match.

I hope we come out fighting against Middlesbrough as we will certainly need to do so. Losing can also kill confidence and I now have a horrible, nagging and negative thought running through my mind about the horrendous prospect of three home defeats in a week should we play as badly against Middlesbrough and Burnley as we did against Walsall. Surely that will not be the case!

I am just left feeling rather sad and empty that our most famous cup competition has been so devalued and is now seen as a necessary evil rather than something to look forward to with relish and anticipation.

Is this simply the price of progress and if so, is it an acceptable one?

The Fans Aren't Too Happy – 11/1/16

There was a lot of muttering after Saturday's defeat by Walsall regarding the team rotation and selection, the apparently cavalier way it appeared that some of the players treated the FA Cup given the lack of zip and intensity of our overall performance, particularly in the first half, plus concerns about whether we are likely to recover for the two tough matches that lie ahead this week as well as even the half time parade around the pitch by the FC Midtjylland squad.

In fact I think I shall just let everybody vent and offload today given how fed up most of you sounded.

John Hirdle can start us off and I agree with every word he said:

Our first half performance was as insipid and as uninspiring as I have seen in a long time. Dean Smith's pre-match words regarding picking a team to respect the competition and to win the game seemed very hollow indeed.

I felt sorry for Hofmann. He is no solo striker and had no support whatsoever from midfield. A baffling tactical line-up given Smith's inside knowledge of the opposition.

As you rightly say all will be forgotten quickly if we can get things right both on Tuesday and Friday, and we return to the tempo and energetic game we know we are capable of to prosper in this league.

It does seem that the club and the players these days don't seem to give a toss about the Cup competitions.

Even with reduced admission prices, the inevitable outcome is that the fans will eventually vote with their feet and just give these games a miss in the knowledge that the club has no desire to progress in them. I find this very sad indeed.

Clive Longhurst had lots of questions and absolutely no answers but his comments certainly concentrate the mind!

Great article, as always. My worries are: will this be an Arsenal week, when, in a few days our season effectively ends? How did our philosophy of attacking, pressing football dissipate so quickly?

The "if Judge goes we're sunk" theorists seemed to include the rest of the team yesterday! How much strength in depth do we actually have?

If Saturday's team wasn't good enough to beat a team we could be facing in the league next season, which players are pressurising our first team for their places? We have people, but do we have sufficient strength in depth?

Is it a mere coincidence that all the players who have been transfer targets over the summer and January all came from British clubs? Are our European signings still struggling to become acclimatised to British football?

I overheard our Chairman (at a certain book signing in the club shop) say he didn't think we would do much business in the January window. Does that mean the bids for our players have come as a surprise and, if they prove successful, do we have replacements in our sights or will we be forced into more team selections like the one we saw yesterday?

Will a parade of a more successful football team at half time yesterday be an inspiration to our team or fill them with feelings of being the poor relation?

I hate posing questions and not offering solutions but I just don't know. My optimism and confidence in the club and its management have been dented. I hope my worries will be reduced in seven days and forgotten by the end of January but, It's Brentford innit!

Former player **Richard Poole** puts things into context as he reminds us of a time when players just got on with things and rotation had not yet been invented:

I was not there on Saturday but Brentford, like all the other teams rest their players and don't bother with the cup competitions.

Of course I realise that football is much harder physically than when I played. At that time we had only a sixteen-man squad as well as two youngsters.

I remember at Easter time on the Friday we played at Colchester, on Saturday we went to Chester, two matches in two days, plus all the travelling, then we hosted Colchester, the team at the top of the table, at Griffin Park on Tuesday evening. On the following Saturday we had Bradford City at home and at the age of sixteen I played in all of them and just missed the first half at Chester.

Today's players are, or should be, in top condition. We had poor training facilities and did not even have the use of a gym. Our supporters have to get up every day and go to work and most footballers will tell you that they would prefer to play games rather than just train.

All this talk about tired legs makes me smile. I know that many of our players have been out injured and I would like to know how many games each player has played since the start of the season.

In other words footballers today are totally mollycoddled.

Peter Lumley also wasn't very happy:

Everyone, however competent, has the odd bad day at the office and I am afraid Dean Smith had one such day on Saturday. I had no problem with the team selection. What bemused me was the way the Bees played so deep in the first half. It was as though they were relying on breakaways without trying to make any! Dean Smith has to take some responsibility. He cannot just blame the players for the unbelievably bad performance.

Tim Ward echoed his sentiments:

That was really frustrating. I, like you, love the FA Cup and had been looking forward to this game. I knew Walsall would be a good side and provide tough opposition but had assumed that we'd be prepared and up for it.

I'm not sure what you think but I really hoped that when we needed to make changes we could have taken the game to them by replacing Macca with Marco and playing two up front. I thought Hofmann actually played quite well and has the ability to bring other players into the game but was so isolated up there on his own – I felt sorry for him.

Interestingly I thought we really missed Tarky and Toums – not so much defensively but in the way they bring the ball out and start the counter attack. The replacements just don't seem to be the same type of players. Early days maybe but the team did look unbalanced and predictable.

One last point, I wish that more players would take responsibility for shooting. I know that Dean said he wanted more shots (and how good was Woods's effort at Reading) but too many times they seem to be trying to craft the perfect goal.

As I said, I feel frustrated!

I quite agree with Tim's comments and think that a Plan B should be considered where necessary and playing two up front for the last fifteen minutes might have been a good idea unless Hofmann had run himself out.

Michael Ohl also did not enjoy what he saw:

The FA Cup matters to me as well Greville. That it appears to not matter to players makes me sad.

I think we should give some credit to Walsall. They were keener, quite attractive to watch and should they go up I think they should do just fine. They can only play what is up against them and yes Brentford were that bad and if would have been unfair to them if we had sneaked past them and won the game.

There was a lot of negativity from the Ealing Road end, and some pretty vitriolic comments made about Hofmann, unfairly I think.

I hope the saving of players for the week ahead is justified, but I have a gnawing feeling that it won't be a good week.

I hope I am wrong.

Rebel Bee found fault with pretty much everything and I cannot argue with a lot of what he said:

A very good selection of comments.

Richard Poole's reminiscences on squad size and fixture congestion back in the day are something that our staff should read.

I've been around the block with Brentford FC like you all, and the great moments have to be savoured, whilst the hits are taken on the chin. But we follow a club where everything is analysed, and by many measures we aren't where we wanted to be in terms of squad strength, depth and our transfer dealings.

Four home cup defeats since promotion is no accident and who can blame fans for not turning out on the evidence seen – six and a half thousand Bees showed up yesterday for a game versus a League One side – not bad was it?

I didn't think there was much in the game in truth, but they shaded it I guess. Worryingly until Alan Judge's entrance our only creative spark came from Swift and Canos – two loanees – not good.

We won't score many with Hoff or Vibe as the lone front man and Djuricin is a finisher, he can't head the ball or hold the ball up, so for me he needs to play with Hofmann in a two-man front line.

Most of the injured players are now back on the scene, and it seems that we overestimated the bounce this would give us.

Early days I know, but I feel but Dean Smith needs a decent week on and off the pitch, otherwise we could slump and we are not safe yet.

As for the FC Midtjylland halftime parade – frankly it was ill judged and a bit embarrassing.

I cannot see us changing from 4-2-3-1 as it has worked so well for us, but as I said above, we should show some flexibility when necessary. I think that the more accurate way of looking at it is to realise that none of our three strikers really suit the way that we play and we have yet replace Andre Gray with a player of similar style.

The parade didn't bother me at all and I think that it just did not help that it came on a day when we so patently underperformed and fans were simply looking for things to criticise.

beesyellow22 provides some sort of perspective:

Another great post, Greville and I agree with many of the comments above.

It was a very curious performance from Brentford. As has been discussed, we backed off them throughout the first half and gave them far too much time on the ball. We weren't really on it in any department and failed to create anything of any real note.

It was strange, because when I saw the lineup before the kick off I actually felt quite excited. All the changes made seemed entirely acceptable and it looked like a great opportunity to give good players who have been warming the bench in recent weeks a decent run out.

To me, our starting eleven didn't look particularly terrible and I wouldn't have said that we were either disrespecting Walsall or failing to take the competition seriously. Unfortunately what transpired over the course of that first forty-five minutes proved otherwise.

A weak, insipid, tired, uninspiring performance from a side which displayed none of our usual exciting cut and thrust and devil-may-care free-flowing football. Lots of huff and puff from the Hoff (or should that be Hoff and puff) but no incision and one solitary shot on goal. Canos was completely nullified by Walsall's left-back who was superb throughout and the team from League One were superior in every department.

Second half we looked sharper, but Walsall never looked like getting beaten and, but for the post, would have wound up winning by even more.

I am reluctant to criticise either the manager or the players but we really did seem curiously subdued yesterday.

If anything, it reminded me of watching Dijkhuizen's Brentford – no sense of common purpose and a general lack of any discernible game plan.

This is obviously disappointing, because the FA Cup is still a massive competition and, as an exciting, high tempo, free-scoring Championship side, I was hopeful that this season we might be capable of a decent cup run.

I thought the manager was right to rest Judge, Tarkowski and Toums because I believed that the players coming in would seize their chance with relish. Yes, I knew the dangers Walsall would pose and I also realised how desperate they would be to have some kind of revenge over Dean Smith.

However, I was confident that we would have both the strength in depth and high intensity kind of football to edge it on the day.

How wrong I was.

We now move onto two massive, potentially season-defining games in four days. It doesn't get any tougher than playing Boro and it will be fascinating to see how we play on Tuesday night. I was genuinely depressed about how easily we got beaten on Saturday and how little fight many of the players appeared to have, with the exception of Judge and also Swift, who I thought had a great game personally.

I still have faith in our new manager and hopefully finally breaking the Middlesbrough hoodoo will go some way to erasing the memories of the Walsall game. But it was a curious one and I, like the rest of us, am still scratching my head as to why we were so awful.

I will end with those comments, which are an excellent summation of where we are.

This is a crucial week for the Bees and at the end of it we will know far more about where we are going this season. Saturday left us all feeling flat and we desperately need a spark and some good news given all the uncertainty currently surrounding the future of a few of our best players.

Jota's loss is also an unexpected and bitter blow that we will just have to deal with and it also did not help how well Kemar Roofe performed yesterday. There have been rumours on social media that we have been looking at Oxford United's exciting young player and his brilliant two-goal performance against Swansea and Oxford's victory might make it far more difficult, if not impossible for us to sign him if those rumours were in fact correct, given the hype that will now surround him.

I am excited and, I confess, a little bit worried too about how this week will pan out but I expect that we will recover from Saturday and put in two committed and excellent performances – you cannot really ask for more than that.

Jim Levack's View – 12/1/16

I was putting off writing something today for a long as I could, as if at all possible I really wanted to avoid yet another superficially positive and cheery match preview of Brentford's massive game against Middlesbrough at Griffin Park tonight.

It just felt like Groundhog Day as I think I have written five similar or pretty much identical articles since the beginning of last season all suggesting with rather more hope than conviction that this might finally be the time when we get our act together, change our approach, allay the ghost and break the seemingly irreversible hold and hoodoo that our visitors appear to have over us.

Let's get the sad and unpalatable facts out of the way first:

- Brentford have lost their past eight league and playoff matches against Middlesbrough.

- Middlesbrough have kept eight clean sheets in a row – the current longest run in the top four tiers of English football.

- Boro have conceded just twelve goals so far this season – a league-low total.

- The last time we beat Middlesbrough in any competition was in an FA Cup Third Round tie in 1964.

- Our last league victory over them was way back in December 1938 when we won a First Division match by two goals to one..

When you take all of the above into consideration it makes it pretty hard to put a positive spin on things and I was definitely not looking forward to trying to do so yet again.

Middlesbrough seem to be able to beat us at will and have a simple but highly effective game plan that we are as yet totally unable to counter that comprises softening us up by kicking us off the pitch early on under the gaze of a supine and benign referee, totally outmuscling us in midfield, absorbing our futile pressure and then picking us off on the break.

It has worked a treat every time.

Last season it just appeared that we played the same match four times against them with the self-same inevitable outcome on every occasion. We never seemed to learn or change or adapt our approach.

We frittered away more than enough chances to win three matches in our Championship encounter at Griffin Park this time last year before frustratingly losing to a sloppily conceded penalty kick and, surprisingly enough given how poorly we had been playing, we gave them an extremely hard game earlier this season when but for a couple of appalling misses from Marco Djuricin we might easily have come back with a point.

Anyway, just as I thought that there was no escape and I had no option but to try and find yet another new way of saying the same old thing, salvation arrived quite unexpectedly in the nick of time and totally out of the blue in the form of an unsolicited email which slithered into my inbox just when all looked lost.

Jim Levack, one of the best informed and most knowledgeable, sensible, clear minded and objective Brentford supporters around had unexpectedly sent me his take on what is happening in and around the club at the moment as well as his opinion on all the problems that we are currently facing.

His article is well-written, open and honest and very hard-hitting and I am printing it just as he wrote it as I also believe very strongly that my blog should offer a platform for all Brentford fans and it is good to hear from a selection of alternative voices rather than always just from me.

Here is what he had to say:

Within seconds of the FA Cup draw being made I was tweeted by a former colleague who warned me his Walsall side would be a tough nut to crack.

It read "Walsall and Brentford are not that much different. Don't be fooled by the hype."

I disagreed and insisted that as a club we were now operating on a different level to the Saddlers but after Saturday's showing I'm not so sure.

The FA Cup exit, on the heels of a similar no show at Birmingham, has raised many questions in my mind and got me thinking that maybe it's time to recalibrate exactly where we are.

So here, in no particular order other than how they came to me on my morning run, is the way I'm currently seeing things.

I might indeed be completely wrong on many as they are purely my personal opinions so apologies for that, but here goes:

- *We are not as good as we think we are – Sure we've bought some cracking technically gifted players, but football is about far more than pure technical ability. In fact the mental side of the game is probably more important for technically gifted players because it is what separates the good from the great. We signed Konstantin Kerschbaumer who will clearly be a great acquisition once he acclimatises, but currently I'm not sure he'd get in the Walsall side and he would surely benefit from a season on loan in League One.*

- *We can't pass our way around more rugged sides who are up for a scrap – I've heard it said time and again this season by fellow fans that we don't need a Jonathan Douglas type character to boss the midfield. What absolute rubbish! Every side needs a player who the opposition look at in the tunnel and think "I don't fancy this." It's the first part of the battle won before a ball is even kicked. Ideally I'd agree with the purists that the best solution is a take no prisoners type of midfielder – a Bradley Johnson for instance, who is also technically talented but they do not come cheap.*

- *Our Academy is not producing anything yet – despite the excellent work by Kevin O'Connor and previously Lee Carsley, we've yet to see a single player come through to the first team and earn a regular starting place, a staggering fact when we should be getting all the teenage talent not wanted by Chelsea and the like. I appreciate that there is currently a review going on of our entire Academy structure and also appreciate that we have some massive talent at all the younger age groups so perhaps we just have to be patient.*

- *We don't take the Cup competitions seriously – whilst Saturday was tricky due to the upcoming Boro and Burnley games, Brentford looked like a side missing its spine – which it was. I'm all for trying to get six points in the league and accept it's arguably more important to reach the playoffs, but if we struggle to beat the limited resources of Walsall, it suggests that…*

- **We don't have any real strength in depth** – again, throwing on Marco Djuricin after weeks out injured and Kerschbaumer to try to rescue the situation spotlighted the paucity of options for Dean Smith, whose former side – on the upside – showed what he can create given time.

- **The rumour mill is affecting our approach** – I've heard repeatedly that promotion isn't realistically on the cards this season, certainly automatically, and the playoffs, whilst still a more than viable target are at best an outside bet. If that is the case then perhaps we are really building for next season and, as a result, we shouldn't expect much incoming transfer activity in this window.

  If that's the case and is not simply pub talk then it's staggering and a massive kick in the gut for Brentford's players, whose attitude could – and I stress the word could – be affected by it. I lost count of the number of heavy first touches and quick corners Brentford's leaden-footed players failed to close down yesterday, the display was lethargic and lacking any real desire. Could that be because they felt, even subliminally, that the FA Cup wasn't a priority? If I am correct then I fear many fans may not see it as a priority next season either and vote with their feet. It's already happened with the Capital One Cup and the FA Cup seems certain to follow. The fact is every season Brentford should be looking to win promotion because it breeds a positive mentality rather than a laid back one which potentially helps lead to more lacklustre performances.

- **Some players don't want to be here** – I've heard that a couple of players whose careers have either been resurrected or given a springboard to progress don't want to stay and are hoping to talk to other clubs, though mercifully not Alan Judge. One or two of the same players haven't exactly set the world on fire this season and have been prone to mistakes born out of carelessness, so perhaps it's best if we get the best money for them and bring players in who do want to be here.

- **I'm very pleased for FC Midtjylland** – but I don't particularly want to see them walking round the Griffin Park pitch when my side are losing and I don't have any real interest in them either way. That will be shot down as not supporting Matthew Benham... not so. It's just that I only have eyes for Brentford and am not convinced that it's easy to split your loyalties between two teams. Anyone who suggests otherwise doesn't really understand football, again in my opinion. A total PR flop.

- **We are far better than last season** – again, I'd beg to differ here. We are much more of a work in progress, largely because we haven't brought in any tried and tested players at this level. Potential is all very good and yes next season we may well storm the league, but to help the unproven players gel I believe you need a quality, wise, and old experienced head or two.

- **A personal one this** – I'm sick of hearing how less technically gifted sides like Birmingham who sit back and let us attack them are paying us a great compliment. The fact is that we struggle to break sides down who do that and due to a lack of concentration at the back this season, seem to get picked off on the break far too easily as was the case at Cardiff and Birmingham recently.

- **We don't need a prolific goalscoring centre forward because we're among the league's top scorers** – someone is missing the point here. Every side needs a proven goalscorer because it eases the pressure on the midfield to score. Yes, we've done well this season but in games where the midfield don't chip in, we have been shown to be sadly lacking in potency in the final third. Our first shot on target against Walsall at home was in the forty-third minute – from a midfielder. Enough said. It's not all doom and gloom because we have come an incredibly long way, but I do think the last two games against Blues and Walsall should lead to a return to factory settings and a rather more humble approach and a recognition and acceptance that maybe there's still a lot of work to be done.

Button Fingers! – 13/1/16

We seem to manage to find ever more creative, original and quite frankly daft and utterly ridiculous ways of losing to our bogey team Middlesbrough and last night took the biscuit as we totally surpassed ourselves in terms of the unbelievable way we conceded the winning goal.

The previously underemployed David Button flapped at a harmless left wing corner from Leadbitter that was caught in the swirling wind and he managed the remarkable and seemingly impossible feat of punching the ball backwards into his own net despite being under little challenge.

This totally undeserved goal on the hour took the wind out of our sails and despite a late and frenetic rally Middlesbrough held out comfortably for their sixth victory over the Bees in the last two seasons in the course of which they kept an incredible ninth consecutive clean sheet.

Middlesbrough are the epitome of a likely promotion winning team in that they are incredibly well organised, totally committed to the cause and give you absolutely nothing. We, on the other hand possess flair and ability in abundance but are profligate where it matters the most – in both penalty areas.

Middlesbrough were dull, boring, negative and cynical in the extreme and also did a wonderfully professional job of managing the hapless referee, Gavin Ward, who was mere putty in their hands and allowed them to get away with all their excesses whenever we threatened to get behind them. Grant Leadbitter was in the official's ear at every opportunity and helped ensure that every marginal decision went their way.

The Bees needed to put on a performance and to regain some confidence and self-respect after Saturday's insipid display against Walsall and they certainly succeeded in doing so.

Their football was fluent, sharp and creative, the pace and intensity so sadly lacking against Walsall was back and every player looked more than comfortable on the ball. They dominated possession and forced Middlesbrough backwards with Woods outshining the combative Clayton and Leadbitter and Colin rampaging forward at every opportunity.

Quite simply we let our illustrious opponents off the hook by squandering two early and glorious opportunities that were both created by Lasse Vibe skipping past the lumbering Ayala.

First he set up Alan Judge who tried to pass the ball into the corner of the net from the edge of the area but his effort went just wide, and then, when given a clear run in on goal, Vibe delayed his shot fatally and could only hit Konstantopoulos as the keeper flung himself at his feet.

That really should have been the opening goal and despite minor flurries at the other end, particularly when Diagouraga's poor back pass almost gifted a goal to Nugent, the Bees totally dominated the first half with Woods, Judge, Swift, Colin and Bidwell combining beautifully to find pockets of space and gaps in the visitors' defence.

For all our possession, relentless pressing and probing, the final pass was not quite there. Dean headed wide and Judge forced another excellent save from the keeper who pushed the ball onto the post (shades of Stuart Dallas in the same match last season) but far too often our threat petered out in the final third where Vibe, after his opening burst, was lightweight and easily brushed off the ball and never looked capable of holding the ball up long enough to allow our midfielders to flood forward in support of him and our threat was snuffed out.

Saunders had a long range floating free kick turned over the bar but the half ended all square when Brentford's wonderful display deserved far more.

The second half started off where the first had ended and some glorious one touch pass-and-move football ended with Colin's powerful effort being turned aside by a goalkeeper who was coming under increasing amounts of pressure.

A goal looked likely to come but when it did it was Brentford who gifted the lead to a team which took full advantage and then choked the life out of the game as they sat on their lead and dared Brentford to break them down.

For all our possession we rarely threatened to do so despite three attacking substitutions which saw Canos, Hofmann and Djuricin augment our attack and we even tried the previously elusive 4-4-2 formation but the die was cast, and after some late and cynical thuggery by Clayton who took one for the team after he cut Judge down when he was in full flight, all our efforts came to naught and Middlesbrough had stolen the points.

Last night provided a clear demonstration of all our strengths and weaknesses.

Lasse Vibe's costly early miss against Middlesbrough

I brought my Watford supporting friend to the match who left purring with pleasure at the entertainment we provided but he hit the nail on the head when he stated that for all our pretty football and the delicate patterns that we weaved we had very little upfront and our attacks too often fizzled out given Vibe's inability to act as a target man and bring his midfield into play. *Get the ball into the mixer* was his advice and one worth listening to at times.

We would have gleaned many style points for the intricacy of our play but there was no bite at either end of the field.

Unfortunately I read the game correctly when, pessimist that I am, I predicted that we would create and spurn several chances and then self-destruct at the other end and that is exactly what happened on the night.

It is time to manage expectations and look at us as a work in progress. What happens in the remainder of the transfer window is key. Will we weaken or will we continue to develop?

There are still massive question marks about the future of the likes of Judge and Tarky who are two of our shining lights. If they go they must be replaced with players from home or abroad with the potential to be even better than the ones leaving the club.

Even if they don't another new face or two would not go amiss. Colin and Woods are both exceptional young players who have slotted seamlessly into the team and we will need another few gems like them if we are to continue on our upwards path.

The loss of Jota is a terrible blow and his ingenuity and pace might have unlocked the Middlesbrough defence. A replacement has to be found as Canos is a raw and impetuous talent, a young colt who will understandably thrill and frustrate in equal measures.

The playoffs this season remain a possibility but are highly unlikely given how brittle we are in both penalty areas. We always look like conceding a soft goal.

Yesterday the culprit was Button and his error cost us dear as we were well on top when it occurred. Goalkeepers are fallible and human and in David we have an exceptionally talented one who was long overdue such a *faux pas.*

Toumani also almost gave our visitors a gift and the overwhelming majority of the goals we concede are down to lack of concentration and individual error.

Vibe, Hofmann and Djuricin all have their strengths but none of them are really what we need given the way that we play. Can something be done about that situation? Probably not until the end of the season or until Scott Hogan is fit enough to return but yesterday highlighted our shortcomings.

Frankly Middlesbrough showed us we need to toughen up, take more responsibility and do a bit more of the dirty work. We are too quiet, nice and soft where it really matters.

Leadbitter was a constant presence, screaming at, encouraging and cajoling his teammates and setting a wonderful personal example. He would not allow them to be beaten and we lack somebody like him as well as leaders on the pitch.

There is so much to admire about us and we should take all the positives out of last night's performance, but we should also recognise what we are, a very decent Championship team that is establishing ourselves in the league and one that is totally easy on the eye and full of young talent.

That is pretty good and more than enough for the moment as long as we continue to improve and progress.

Middlesbrough join Birmingham City on my personal hate list but we have much to learn from them about professionalism and game management and hopefully we can ponder on the key lesson from last night which is *never give a sucker an even break*. We had them on the ropes but let them escape to fight another day.

Last night was a reality check and we cannot afford to be so naïve, wasteful and generous in the future.

Looking Back And Forward – 14/1/16

I was really pleased to see that the general reaction to Tuesday's nights frustrating and totally undeserved defeat by Championship leaders Middlesbrough was an extremely positive one and that the overwhelming majority of Brentford supporters recognised how good certain aspects of our performance really were.

Like everyone else immediately after the end of the game, I was angry and disappointed at how capriciously we had been treated by the fates, however in the cold light of day now that I am feeling calmer and more objective, I realise that there was so much to be pleased and proud about in terms of how we performed against perhaps the best team in the league as well of course as a further reminder and confirmation of all the areas which we need to improve and work on.

I will wait until after the Burnley match tomorrow night before trying to assess what is likely to be in store for us for the remainder of the season and what we have to look forward to.

In the meantime I thought that it might be enlightening to look back at how some other supporters assessed our performance against the league leaders.

Rebel Bee was as outspoken as normal, and long may he remain so:

I agree with your match summary so I just add honest comments and apologise in advance if they are too blunt for some.

- *New signings stepping up. Woods and Colin both outstanding – and had their best games in the stripes.*

- *Vibe, looked dangerous for 15 minutes and had them worried, he then totally vanished – why?*

- *Saunders and Swift were both passengers, we carried them both until they were hooked. Swift has real talent but doesn't seem to want it enough and is too flicky at times. Sam's dead balls were really poor, and he is possibly coming to the end of his time at Griffin Park.*

- *It was great to see Toums and Tarks starting and both put in a very good shift. Judge didn't quite hit his best but was decent throughout. We will struggle badly without any of these at present.*

- *We played well, yet lack the things Boro have in spades (nous), we are so naïve at this level, and remain error prone.*

- *If I see Boro again it'll be far too soon. I hope they go up and then get smashed every week playing like they do. Give me a Watford, Bournemouth or Norwich any day over this lot.*

- *Forshaw may be better off financially but he'd have been far better off starting for us last night as our star man, instead he's picking up splinters in his backside and moving down the pecking order with them. Total madness.*

- *Our season's ambition is now safety – that's all.*

- *Where do they find these referees – he was conned by them all night.*

I guess I should elaborate a bit on my take on Swift. I think he has a lot of talent and disproves the theory that we don't produce technically gifted footballers in England. And he is still young. I think he is unfortunate in that he has to date mostly played development football, and needs to acquire the hunger and a little of the physicality that you see from those that have worked their way up the divisions.

To be fair it was a tough test against very streetwise opponents yesterday, and he is one to watch, and I am glad we have him.

Peter Lumley also bemoaned our fate:

Walking away from Griffin Park last night I could not recall feeling so dismayed at the outcome of a game we could and should have won. We totally dominated possession and had eleven corners to their five.

But more importantly, Middlesbrough committed twice as many fouls as us.

Their defence has won many plaudits for its strength and organisation but few have spotlighted the cynical fouls and faked injuries that must be condoned by their manager.

If they want to gain promotion by playing the way they do then good luck to them. I can only hope that Brentford are never tempted to follow their example! Yes the Bees did contribute to their own downfall by wasting two great scoring chances in the opening minutes. But once again the run of the ball went against us when David Button made a split second decision to push the ball away from a corner taken in a swirling wind.

Also I cannot recall a half season when so many controversial refereeing decisions have gone against us. Many say that these decisions even out over a whole season.

Let us hope that they do!

beesyellow22 has also made some extremely sensible and well thought through comments:

Good article, Greville. Good comments too. I do not totally agree with Rebel Bee (who always writes with great insight I must say) with regards to Swift.

I thought he was actually pretty good last night and linked up well on the left with Bidders, Woods and

Vibe. I do agree that he is "flicky" though!

Sadly, I also agree that Saunders is more representative of the past than the future. Last season saw him and Yennaris do great things on loan at Wycombe and, surely if we are to be serious about pushing for promotion next season, we have to put sentimentality to one side and accept that it's time to look for new attacking options and let Sam leave?

At League One or Two level he could still make a real difference but at Championship level I think he's too much of a passenger.

I thought that Tarky and Toums played pretty well but I also felt that perhaps Tarky might have had his mind elsewhere at times. Perhaps that's inevitable when you know that another team wants you and will pay you far more and take you back up north to where your roots are.

Overall I thought we were great last night and against a lesser side we would have surely won.

You can't blame Button for his error – he has been brilliant for us all season and made some excellent saves last night too and his header out at full stretch in the first half was superb.

Yes, we know how Middlesbrough play and last night they didn't disappoint. I actually didn't think they were as cynical as they were last season, mainly because we played such excellent stuff in the first half. They never had the ball!

The key points for me are two-fold: first, we desperately need a Jonathan Douglas type player to put a bit of steel in the side, galvanise the team and bite the legs of the opposition, and secondly we obviously need a long-term replacement for Andre Gray. Vibe does his best and I like him a lot but as has been said many times, he can't hold the ball up and bring the midfield into play like Andre did last season.

I like Djuricin a lot and am really looking forward to seeing what he can do between now and May. I hope he starts on Friday, as he always looks really dangerous and capable of sticking it in the back of the net – if he has the service.

I'm trying to remain upbeat about things but it is difficult when you play so well and lose yet again!

Dean Smith's interview with Billy Reeves was really positive and I'm looking forward to seeing what happens next season when he has spent a sustained period with the squad and hopefully brought in a few players of his own that will see Brentford start to take the shape of what can justifiably be called a Dean Smith team.

Michael Ohl was also pleased with what he had seen and was optimistic about the future:

It's not nice losing to teams like Middlesbrough for the reasons already stated. No real flair, cynical, tough, badgering the referee etc.

Do we want to be like that, and be top or play the Brentford way with all the ups and downs that that entails?

There has to be a middle way or more accurately we have to stop making so many unforced errors.

Although we had a lot of chances, the last half hour was total frustration. We just couldn't find a way to break them down, and I really couldn't see us scoring. If we had taken our chances at the start . . . would we have won? Or would we have given it away?

I don't know if I am alone, but I am always expecting now to see some sloppy pass to which the opposition say thanks very much and then capitalises upon. In this respect Toumani is the one I most expect it from, with Tarkowski and Dean closely behind.

I try not to be too critical about our players, but, Reading notwithstanding, the last few games have been just so frustrating. Surely the players must feel the same?

Watching Brentford these days is not for the faint hearted.

Let's see what Friday brings.

Player Power – 16/1/16

I was doing some research in the early hours of this morning and chanced upon the wording of a standard professional footballer's contract which I found particularly fascinating reading given the remarkable and unprecedented happenings at Griffin Park over the last twenty-four hours.

I have highlighted a couple of relevant clauses:

Duties and Obligations of the Player

The Player agrees: when directed by an authorised official of the Club

1. To attend matches in which the Club is engaged in

2. To participate in any matches in which he is selected to play for the Club

3. To play to the best of his skill and ability at all times

4. To undertake such other duties and to participate in such other activities as are consistent with the performance of his duties and as are reasonably required of the Player

Well it would appear that Brentford defender James Tarkowski must be suffering from amnesia or a reading disorder given his recent behaviour when he informed his Head Coach, Dean Smith that he did not wish to play against Burnley in last night's match and declared himself unavailable for the fixture despite being selected in the starting line-up.

The net result of his action was to bring about unspecified disciplinary action from the club but also to wreak havoc on team morale and organisation which surely played a major part in explaining Brentford's spineless first half surrender to a rampant Burnley team which took full advantage of the home team's ineptitude and total lack of fight, spirit, organisation or apparent ability to win any challenges for first and second balls.

It is all very well partially excusing the player for his actions by claiming that he was poorly advised and was perhaps misguidedly following his agent's instructions, but for me that does not wash.

He is not a child but a twenty-three year old man who has shown a total lack of judgement and should surely know better and be able to know his own mind and make more reasoned and sensible decisions. As it is he has painted himself into a corner and made himself a total pariah in the eyes of all Brentford supporters who were previously great admirers of his on-field ability.

Apart from breaking the terms of his contract, Tarkowski's strategy is incredibly dumb and ill-thought through and will have totally the opposite effect to the one desired by him as all it will do is harden attitudes towards him from club officials and make them even more determined that he will not succeed in his effort to leave on his terms.

He has made it patently clear that he wishes to leave the club and ideally return nearer to his roots in the North West of England with last night's opponents, Burnley, rumoured to be his preferred destination. He would also surely have noted the seriously enhanced wages that his former teammates are now earning higher up the food chain.

Well every player has his price, a statement that is particularly apposite and appropriate at Griffin Park where it has always been made quite clear that we cannot compete with the budgets and deeper pockets of our better-heeled competitors and will sell our players should they wish to leave and if, and only if, our valuation is met in full by the potential buying club.

An offer of around four million pounds plus lucrative add-ons from Fulham was apparently turned down for the player right at the end of the August Transfer Window, more I suspect because the club did not want to be seen to be selling yet another major asset at a time when the likes of Moses Odubajo and Andre Gray had already left the club rather than because the sum offered was unacceptable.

That has set the benchmark for him and it is understood that Burnley's recent offer for Tarkowski is for far less than half that sum and is therefore nowhere near the figure that is being sought by the club.

By refusing to play he is now trying to force Brentford's hand and stampede them into accepting a lowball offer for his services rather than wait for full market value to be offered by either Burnley or another of several clubs also rumoured to be sniffing around him.

His approach is totally doomed to failure as it is patently obvious that he has neither really thought matters through nor has he properly considered who he is dealing with. In a game of poker I would not expect Matthew Benham or his Co-Directors of Football to be the first to blink.

I fully expect that Tarkowski has bitten off far more than he can chew and that he is certain to follow the fate of Adam Forshaw who also made it clear at the beginning of last season that he wanted to leave the club and was promptly put on gardening leave and not selected again, and crucially was not allowed to leave the club until Wigan finally came up with the goods and offered us what we were looking for in terms of his value.

A similar fate is surely certain to befall Tarkowski as he has totally burned his bridges and it is now quite impossible for him to play for the club again as the fans would not countenance his doing so, and to allow him to win and force a bargain basement transfer would be scandalous and demonstrate that the players rule the roost and that by behaving badly and unconscionably they can force the issue.

Brentford are far stronger and more resolute than that and Tarkowski will now be left to kick his heels, ideally train on his own and, at best, play in the Development Squad until Brentford receive an offer that reflects his full value – however long it takes.

His agent would now be far better employed in drumming up further interest for his client, ideally at a fee level that will be acceptable to Brentford FC.

The current situation, which has been brought about totally by the player's actions (or perhaps inaction might be a better description) is frankly of no benefit or use to anyone and the sooner it can be resolved the better it will be for all parties, but there is only one way out of this impasse which is for the club to be offered an acceptable amount for him, and hopefully that is what will happen within the next fortnight.

Tarkowski's character is now stained and blemished indelibly and he follows the likes of Gary Alexander into our personal Rogues Gallery and Hall of Shame for his pathetic and unacceptable behaviour.

What he should have done is quite simply follow the example of Alan Judge. He too is rumoured to be the target for several clubs in the Transfer Window, so what did he do and how did he respond?

Well rather than behave in the same puerile, selfish and blinkered manner as Tarkowski, he simply played his heart out and used the televised match against Burnley as a national showcase for his talent and total dedication to the cause.

He was Brentford's best player by a mile, scored a good goal and spearheaded a second half revival that at least regained a semblance of pride for a team that had been totally overrun before the interval and could easily have been trailing by five or six goals rather than just three.

Any managers and scouts watching the match cannot fail to have been impressed by his performance and attitude and we can only hope that he remains at the club until at least the end of the season.

That is how to do it and Alan Judge went up in the estimation of every Brentford supporter for the way he handled the situation last night.

As for the match itself, well there really is not too much to say as Brentford came up against an excellent team that smelled blood, went for our jugular from the first whistle and we were never allowed to settle down into our normal rhythm. Brentford chased shadows and made football seem like a non-contact sport given the time and space they granted their visitors who were allowed to show off their ability and run rings around us in the first half.

The second half was a different affair and had the excellent Sam Saunders scored with an unlikely header or Maxime Colin's shot have brushed the net on the inside rather than the outside of the post then who knows what might have happened as the comeback would really have been on, but, in truth, Burnley were streets ahead of us and fully deserved their comfortable victory.

We have now lost four games in a row and three home matches in less than a week. There is much work to be done as we have performed for only around half of each of our last three games and scored only once.

How we should go about that is for another day.

For now I just hope that James Tarkowski is reflecting upon his behaviour and has already realised that he has totally let his teammates, the Brentford staff and supporters and of course, himself, down by his selfish and inappropriate behaviour – and more importantly, that it will not succeed or get him the result that he desires.

Brickbats & Bouquets – 17/1/16

Just as my article yesterday castigated James Tarkowski for his utter stupidity and selfishness, it is only right and proper that I give praise too whenever and wherever it is justified.

So will the Brentford Media Department please stand up and take a bow – yes that is you, Chris Wickham, and you too, Mark Chapman, to whom I am referring.

The club's statement regarding Tarkowski was a perfect example of less is more as it provided a clear but brief and unemotional description of his behaviour and its natural consequence without labouring the fact, elaborating on matters or going into unnecessary detail.

Yesterday they surpassed themselves when the club announced the sad departure of Jota on loan to Eibar on loan until the Summer of 2017 after agreeing an option to extend his Brentford contract for a further season and gave a full and frank explanation for his having no option but to leave the club *while he works through some personal issues that require him to be in Spain rather than West London.*

There is a crumb of hope and comfort for us as we are told that we have the option to recall the Spanish maestro during the next two Transfer Windows – this Summer and in January 2017 although quite frankly, I am not holding my breath.

In PR circles there are two schools of thought regarding the announcement and dissemination of bad news: you either bury it in and amongst other less contentious announcements and hope that you get away with it without the public noticing or cottoning on, something that is particularly prevalent in government circles, or, as Brentford have done, you provide full disclosure as well as a detailed and compelling explanation of the facts.

In my view, honesty is always the best policy and now every Brentford supporter is totally aware of what has been going on and should understand why, given the circumstances, the club had absolutely no option but to act in the way that they did and allow him to return home in order to sort out his personal life.

The club should be congratulated for acting in such an honourable and farsighted manner.

Jota too earned full marks by releasing a statement to the Brentford fans which made it abundantly clear just how difficult the last few months have been for him and how happy and content he has been at the club and if it had not been for his difficult personal circumstances he would not have been going anywhere.

His words are heartfelt, open, honest and emotional and he memorably and evocatively states that *my children will grow up listening to Jota in the last minute which I have saved forever in my heart as well as constantly in my head.*

He ends by simply stating, *I won't say goodbye, just see you soon,* so all we can do is wish him well and wait and see how things turn out for him and his family.

In the meantime we have to make do with our abundant memories of the little genius and keep ourselves warm on cold nights by thinking about his twinkling toes and mesmerising dribbling and the incredible goals he scored against the likes of Leeds, Cardiff and Blackburn.

In truth it has been an horrendous week for the Bees and a real eye-opener and possibly reality check for all of us supporters. I cannot recall the last time we ever lost three home games in a six day period and maybe Mark Croxford or Paul Briers or somebody else better informed than I can tell us if this sad state of affairs has ever happened before?

Losing to Middlesbrough and Burnley was bad enough if not totally unexpected, and whilst I realise that we had to husband our limited resources and rest players, in retrospect the FA Cup defeat to Walsall was just as damaging. Given where we are in the league a cup run would have ensured that we remained in the public eye and provided a real boost and fillip to our supporters in a season that now looks unlikely to end in a charge for the playoffs.

The Tarkowski and Jota situations just piled further upset and frustration on everybody and we now have to reassess where we are and what happens for the remainder of the season.

It is important to keep a sense of proportion and recognise that a position in the upper mid-table of the Championship given everything that has happened to date this season both on and off the field is no mean achievement.

We were spoiled by last season's top five finish and some senior representatives of the club were perhaps misguided in allowing us to think or expect that further progress and improvement was anticipated.

Frankly you are only as good as the players you are able to put out onto the pitch and we have been hamstrung by our massive and long-lasting injury list as well as the loss of so many talented players mainly for reasons well out of our control.

The damage might not yet be over as we face losing more players before the end of the Transfer Window. Tarkowski moving on is surely a given and Toumani might well follow him out of the door, this time with our heartfelt thanks and best wishes.

The Alan Judge situation remains totally open and up in the air and we just have to hope that no other club meets our valuation of the player.

There is also wide speculation that Sam Saunders will have his contract cancelled and leave for Tampa Bay Rowdies in the NASL. Should that be the case we cannot begrudge him his opportunity given his loyal service to the club and we can only wish him well. He has returned to the first team reckoning recently given the quality of his displays in training, but also because of our lack of resources and other options.

The loss of Jota is particularly damaging as he would have given Judge additional support and taken some of the pressure off him and also revitalised our midfield.

Sergi Canos and John Swift have also shown that they have the potential to more than contribute at Championship level, however I have felt in recent games that they have both hit the wall and need to be taken out of the firing line for a while given their youth and relative inexperience. Swift too is learning how to play a new position and adjust to a role out wide on the left hand side of midfield.

This means that reinforcements are urgently needed and there was talk yesterday that George Evans was on the verge of joining us but that he had decided to join Reading instead. This is potentially disappointing news, given that he is a very talented young player, well known to Dean Smith from his recent loan spell at Walsall who would have been an ideal replacement for Toumani as a box-to-box midfielder. Evans also has an eye for goal, something that is lacking with Toumani and it appears that we will now have to look elsewhere.

It is hard to argue with the view that so far many of our summer recruits have failed to step up to the plate and contribute to the level anticipated and even expected. Gogia has suffered from niggling injuries and not established himself and Kerschbaumer has not been able to cope yet with the pace and physicality of the Championship.

Williams has disappeared without trace, but he was simply a project anyway. Bjelland, a man of whom we had such high hopes, has barely kicked a ball due to long-term injury and Barbet has shown great promise but is probably seen as a player for next year rather than this.

As for the three strikers, if you could combine all of their best assets you would have a fantastic player indeed but none of them have totally convinced or demonstrated that they are the real answer to our problem.

Andre Gray was certainly a hard act to follow and it is probably unfair to expect a foreign player to step in and find his feet at once but neither Vibe, Hofmann or Djuricin look like they enjoy or are best suited to playing as a lone striker and perhaps they should simply be congratulated for having done as well as they have given that they have scored fifteen goals between them, far more than Gray had managed at this stage of last season.

I cannot see this situation changing at the moment and we will simply have to get on with things as best we can until the close season when we can reassess matters.

McEachran is still regaining form and fitness and of the newcomers only Colin and Woods can be said to have been total successes at the present time although hopefully that situation will change.

I would be more than happy if we remain where we are in the league and start building for the future. What is certain is that we will remain easy on the eye and play exciting and vibrant attacking football whilst retaining a slightly soft underbelly.

I hope that we are able to bring in some new permanent rather than loan players either from abroad or the lower divisions who will be part of our future rather than just short-term solutions brought in to plug up some immediate holes.

We now have a week to recover and take stock and hopefully we will not overreact to the setbacks of the last week, after all, Reading lost six games out of seven recently but have recovered, as will we.

Don't Panic! – 19/1/16

The last week or so has been pretty hard to take for most Brentford fans given the worrying combination of bad results and even worse news relating to off-field matters.

It is hard to keep smiling and your spirits up when you lose three home games in that short span of time, scoring only one goal in the process, see your most skilful and charismatic player return home to Spain out of the blue with his future shrouded in doubt owing to serious non-football related personal problems and then have to suffer the final indignity of watching one of your best and most promising players publicly announce that he no longer wants to play for the club.

There is also the continued uncertainty regarding the future of the likes of Alan Judge, Toumani Diagouraga and Sam Saunders whose loss before the end of the Transfer Window would leave the squad seriously weakened and bereft of quality and depth.

As of yet there is no solid news of any incoming transfers apart from the suggestion that an apparent target in George Evans has apparently spurned us in favour of joining Reading.

Quite rightly, Brentford make a point of conducting their transfer dealings and negotiations behind closed doors so who knows what other plates are currently spinning in the air and whether we are close to augmenting the squad or simply waiting until we know for certain which players are leaving this month and may then need replacing.

We also do not know if a decision has yet been made in terms of our recruitment strategy for January and if so whether it is an ever changing feast and one that we have to reassess on the basis of whether acceptable offers are made for any of our players.

Maybe we would also prefer to make do with what we have rather than look for permanent acquisitions who we can also bed in for next season, or even bring in short-term loan signings who can plug any immediate gaps, as required.

The key point is that we remain competitive on the pitch for the remainder of the season and maintain our comfortable position in the league.

More upsettingly we have also been subjected to some negative and in my view, ignorant and provocative comments from the likes of Martin Samuel and Adrian Durham in the *Daily Mail* and *Shock Jock* Durham has today written a bilious column packed full of innuendo and half-truths and supported James Tarkowski in the face of all logic for his refusal to play for us on Friday.

In my opinion it is provocative, inflammatory and nonsensical drivel written by a man with an agenda who is employed predominantly to polarise his audience and seek a reaction as well as being someone who has previous with Brentford, or *Loanford*, as he ridiculously and disparagingly dubbed us when squealing about the manner in which the Bees gained promotion in 2014 and finished above his beloved Peterborough United.

I well remember writing an article poking gentle fun at Steve Evans this time last year by forensically analysing and dissecting his post-match press conference after Rotherham's defeat at Griffin Park and pointing out all of his inconsistencies, half-truths and *non sequiturs* and I am sorely tempted to do the same for Adrian Durham but I will not rise to the bait and respond, as that is exactly what he would like everybody to do and his article does not deserve to be either read or taken in the slightest bit seriously.

You can all find it quite easily if you want to take a look at it and come to your own conclusion.

I am quite certain that all right-minded and informed Brentford supporters will see articles such as these for what they really are – drivel and pure rabble rousing.

But it is still unpleasant and annoying to see the club you love, its owner and his far-sighted and innovative approach and way of doing things, subjected to ridicule and unjustified, unfounded, ignorant and scathing criticism from the outside, and unfortunately there are more than enough impressionable readers out there who are unaware of the truth of the matter and will take senseless and smug attacks on us such as these at face value and as pure gospel.

The media dislikes and is suspicious of whatever it does not understand and they really have yet to get their heads around what is going on at Griffin Park, just how well we have done bearing in mind our status in the football food chain, and where we are going in the near future.

This is a time when we just need to keep our nerve, trust in the wisdom and perspicacity of the people running the club and follow the sage advice of Corporal Jones and *don't panic*!

Change is always difficult to cope with and it is hard to accept that there will be players leaving of their own volition who prefer to go elsewhere, as well as others who we feel have reached their full potential with us and need to be moved on as well.

As long as we recruit well and cleverly we will continue to thrive and progress and I firmly believe that there are lessons to be learned for the future from our recruitment strategy in the summer which has not yet paid as many dividends as might have been anticipated, but it is still early days.

It is now a question of balance as we have over a third of the season still to play and it would be both dangerous and wrong to merely write it off and declare that we are just building for next season.

Supporters expect entertainment and results and Brentford fans have enjoyed a lot of both in recent seasons and I would hope and expect that the Bees continue to provide a combination of exhilarating and successful football which will keep the fans both happy and engaged.

We have had a bad patch both on and off the field and neither Preston nor Leeds will be easy marks for us.

Who knows if there will be ins or outs before the weekend but I am as certain as I can be that we will put an end to our poor recent run and the smiles will shortly be back on all of our faces.

Happy Birthday To Bees United – 21/1/16

It is all too easy looking down from our exalted perch in the Championship with the financial future of the club secure under the benign ownership of Matthew Benham and with the new stadium at Lionel Road on the horizon to forget just how far we have come in so very short a time and to realise just how close Brentford FC came to foundering on the rocks.

Cast your mind back a decade or more and remember how we were lurching from crisis to crisis:

- The best players leaving in droves after owner Ron Noades lost interest

- An ever-mounting debt

- Running on a shoestring

- Averting the threat of a move to Woking that would surely have choked the life out of us

- Watching a series of cheap journeymen and overmatched kids floundering on the pitch

- Heroic supporters rattling their collecting boxes to help stave off disaster for another week

The club was simply not sustainable and it was death by one thousand cuts – slow, painful but inexorable and in our hearts we feared dropping like a stone and even losing our cherished Football League status.

Even when Martin Allen arrived and by sheer will and force of personality stabilised us and restored some semblance of pride on the pitch by making bricks without straw, his efforts were hindered by the financial realities that we faced.

The cup was dashed from our lips and the gloss taken off our achievement when star man DJ Campbell was sold for relative peanuts to the dreaded Birmingham City in order to stave off the threat of administration immediately after his goals had seen us defeat Premier League Sunderland in the FA Cup on an afternoon of glory and triumph at Griffin Park.

The club was on a financial precipice and the only way was down, and that was the situation that Bees United faced a mere ten years ago on the twentieth of January 2006 when the Supporters Trust took the massive and brave step of taking control of the club by purchasing the majority of shares in the football club with Greg Dyke taking over as Chairman and Ron Noades finally departing.

Things got worse before they got better with another player exodus leading to a pathetic season of capitulation when an appallingly weak, hapless and overmatched squad put together on a shoestring budget plummeted into the bottom division in 2007.

Under the aegis of BU things began to stabilise off the pitch and a semblance of financial control was established which resulted in our fortunes on the pitch recovering under Andy Scott.

Promotion back to the third tier was gloriously achieved in 2009 and the last five years have seen continued progress and success culminating in the Bees celebrating their best season since the Second World War in 2015 when we came within a whisker of reaching the Premier League.

The catalyst for this success has obviously been the arrival on the scene of lifelong fan Matthew Benham and it was Bees United who structured an initial partnership with him and then sounded out the views of the supporter base before deciding to sell their shareholding to Benham and ceding control of the club to him in 2012.

One of the secrets of success is to know when to let go and the timing of that deal was perfect and it has proved to be the springboard for our current success.

I will let David Merritt, the current Chair of Bees United and a Director of Brentford Football Club summarise precisely how things have developed since that memorable day a mere ten years ago when BU took the momentous decision to take control:

The ten years since BU took majority ownership of Brentford FC have been immense for the Club.

It was Brian Burgess, Chris Gammon and the Bees United Board that created that historic moment for the Club, and it has been Matthew Benham who has enabled the Club to be so successful since.

We started the decade in crisis – we finished it with the most successful season since World War Two, and we head in to this anniversary year for Bees United more positive than ever.

What an incredible decade!

I will declare an interest as I have been a Bees United board member for the past few years and I am proud and honoured to be a tiny cog in a wonderful organisation that has played such a crucial role in ensuring the very survival of Brentford FC.

BU remains totally relevant and still has a crucial role to play today even though we are now in far calmer waters.

We remain as a watchdog and a safeguard, observing and contributing to the running of the club and we are determined to protect the interests and long-term future of Brentford FC should the need ever arise in the future.

BU continues to have two representatives on the Brentford FC Board and one on the Lionel Road Board, we also nominate the independent adjudicator under the Club ticketing charter, and most crucially we still retain the critically important Golden Share that prevents the inappropriate sale of Griffin Park.

Everything is now stable and secure at Brentford FC but you only have to take a look around us at some of our less fortunate brethren, shudder with relief, and realise just what a close-run thing it was and how easily affairs could have turned out completely differently for our beloved Brentford.

It is also imperative that thanks, recognition and eternal gratitude are given to every Bees supporter who shook a bucket, helped fill one or joined BU, bought a Loan Note and gave their support at a time when the club was in crisis and turmoil. Your contribution will never be forgotten and can never be overstated.

Bees United continues to protect the long-term future of Brentford FC and it is still vital that we all continue to support this incredible organisation without which we would not be celebrating so much success both on and off the field today.

Happy birthday to Bees United and I will celebrate and raise a glass tonight to everybody who has supported or joined it since its inauguration.

It Is What It Is – 23/1/16

The realities of life are being made quite apparent at the moment to all Brentford fans, and the truth, to be quite honest, is pretty chilling and unpalatable.

Recent events and the possibility of future player departures have only gone to further highlight how much we are punching above our weight in maintaining a comfortable place in the Championship and also just how vulnerable we are.

We treat our players very well, pay them as much as we can afford, offer an extremely generous and lucrative bonus scheme and have created a positive and empowering environment where players receive excellent coaching, are encouraged to express themselves and even take risks and to play an exciting brand of attacking football with nary a long ball in sight.

The truth of the matter is that we are still, and will remain for the foreseeable future, a stepping-stone club where we identify young emerging and talented players from at home and abroad, mould and develop them, put them in the shop window and on the conveyor belt to riches and success and then inevitably lose them when the bigger fish come calling dangling open chequebooks.

It is annoying and frustrating particularly when pretty much all the players who have left us such as Gray, Douglas, Odubajo, Dallas and now Toumani Diagouraga have joined clubs who are currently competing at the same level as the Bees.

If players were leaving for the priceless and rare opportunity to play in the Premier League then our supporters would doubtless accept the fact that they are bettering themselves. It is when they join clubs who competitively are on a par with, or only slightly better than us, that we find matters far harder and more difficult to accept.

That is however a totally misleading fact as Burnley, Hull, Ipswich and Leeds are either benefiting from the iniquitous Parachute Payments, are larger and better established clubs with far greater income potential than us or perhaps are not as fiscally responsible as we are.

They are all able and willing to offer our best players wages far in excess of what we can afford and you cannot blame them for chasing the money.

I can only pray for the day to arrive when we are in a position to hang onto our best players, send all the predators packing and reject any offers, no matter how attractive. Unfortunately that will not happen until we finally move to Lionel Road and attract far larger attendances and have the opportunity to earn much more from off-field and commercial activities.

The key will be for Brentford to remain in the Championship until we reach that point. That is by no means a given and would be a truly massive achievement given our current size and income levels.

To a degree our whole attitude and indeed, expectations and judgement, have been clouded by the incredible season we enjoyed last season which might well turn out to have been a one-off and a statistical anomaly.

It also did not help to have senior club officials publicly state and assert that we would be looking to build upon the achievements of last season and ideally finish even higher up in the table.

Whilst every football team starts each season aiming to improve and to push for promotion, sometimes you are simply paying lip service to reality.

It is no use raising expectations unrealistically and given the forced sales of so many of last season's stars, the loss of the talismanic Pritchard, the ever increasing injury list and the need to bed in a new Head Coach as well as a host of players with no experience of English conditions, let alone the demands of the Championship, it was surely foolhardy to talk about anything other than consolidation.

Mid-table mediocrity, however meritorious, does not sell season tickets however and I feel that our prospects were overhyped and expectations were unreasonably raised. And more fool us for listening and believing!

The club might reasonably point out that the departing players have all wanted to leave rather than being pushed out of the door and have invariably been replaced by new arrivals who are cheaper and possess the potential to be even better, and a close examination of the facts does go a long way towards backing up this assertion.

In addition, we did for once refuse a massive offer for Tarkowski in August, one that far exceeded our own valuation of him, as we perhaps felt that we had sold more than enough players already that month and one more might well be seen as a tipping point.

Perhaps in retrospect the club should have remained true to itself and in fact made a massive error in not going through with the deal as we are now in the midst of an awkward and difficult situation where the player has refused to play for us and we are currently unable to offload him at anywhere near our valuation for him.

I can only imagine that if no club makes a reasonable and acceptable bid for him in the last week of the Transfer Window then Tarkowski will have to be seen to make a suitably contrite if ambiguous apology, perhaps on *Bees Player*, as I cannot imagine any independent journalist being allowed anywhere near him, and he will then be welcomed back into the fold for the time being before leaving at the end of the season.

This will not go down well with many fans and will only serve to divide the supporter base.

I am worried that all the talk is of players leaving and very little is of new arrivals and I am also concerned that there are fundamental flaws in our overall recruitment strategy.

Last season saw a level and quality of recruitment far beyond our wildest dreams and one that made the football world stand up, open its eyes and finally pay attention to us. It also set a standard and benchmark that quite naturally is proving impossible for us to surpass or even match.

I still do not understand how we managed to get deals for the likes of Gray, Pritchard, Odubajo and Hogan over the line as they were the cream of the crop in terms of emerging young British talent and the arrival of Jota represented the stats based foreign recruitment policy at its best.

Not only had no Brentford supporter ever heard of him, I can quite honestly say that from all my research I am totally unaware of his appearing on any other club's radar either.

Now we are hoist by our own petard. Other clubs watch us closely and we are never again going to have a free run at any worthwhile player as was proved recently with George Evans.

Given our progress we are also quite naturally looking to bring in better players and perhaps take fewer gambles on unknown and untested foreign players.

Players of the calibre we are seeking will all have lots of other options and that is where our problems start. A Gogia or a Kerschbaumer might bite our hand off at our offer but a George Evans won't – and didn't.

Evans signing for Reading was a particular disappointment and indeed, eye-opener for us. He ticked all of the boxes – young, elegant, strong, talented, a box-to-box player who could put his foot in and also score goals.

He would have been a proper *New Brentford* signing and likely become a potentially massive upgrade on Toumani Diagouraga, and given that he had played for Dean Smith at Walsall he was surely bound for us when we made our interest known until we were pipped seemingly at the post by Reading.

Perhaps they blew us out of the water with their financial offer to the player or maybe it was the better facilities and infrastructure available and on offer to him at a club that also has recent Premier League experience? Who knows, but not signing him was a real blow and another warning sign.

We are now faced with the task of replacing Diagouraga and unless Kerschbaumer or McEachran step up to the plate, sooner or later we will need to look outside the club.

Maybe it is a fanciful suggestion but how about a return to Griffin Park, even on a short term basis, for Tom Adeyemi, a powerful box-to-box midfielder currently on loan at Leeds from Cardiff City and surely surplus to requirements at both clubs?

Toumani gave us six years of excellent and committed service and last season he reached heights that were beyond everybody's dreams as, touched by genius as if he had made a Mephistophelian pact with the Devil, and, protected by the menacing presence of Jonathan Douglas, he totally dominated the midfield and acted as the perfect linkman and foil for the likes of Judge, Jota, Pritchard and Gray.

This season he has returned to normal after his *annus mirabilis* and it makes sense for Brentford to cash in at the top of the market given that a fee of over half a million pounds has been suggested in the Leeds-based local media (remember also that at one time, not too long ago, it looked as if he might join Coventry City potentially on a free transfer) and from Toumani's point of view he might well feel that he has not been on as lucrative a contract as some of his team mates and is looking to secure his future with one last big payday.

He goes with our gratitude and best wishes and hopefully he will not hammer the ball into the roof of our net from twenty-five yards when the two teams meet next Tuesday – *The Immutable Law of the Ex* combined with *Sod's Law* might well suggest that he breaks the habit of a lifetime and does so!

I have done some rough calculations on the back of the proverbial fag pack and also taken into account the figures that Paul Briers kindly posted on the *Griffin Park Grapevine* yesterday and if you take the fees that we have received for the likes of Forshaw, Grigg, Dallas, Gray, Odubajo and now Diagouraga over the past eighteen months then there is the potential for us to receive around seventeen million pounds, less any sell-on payments that we have to make to their former clubs.

Who knows, we might yet receive even more money should either Tarkowski or Judge be sold before the end of the Transfer Window.

Looking in turn at the eighteen players we have brought in: Judge, Gray, Tebar, Odubajo, Williams, Hogan, Jota, Macleod, O'Connell, Gogia, Kerschbaumer, Hofmann, Barbet, Bjelland, Vibe, Colin, Woods and McEachran it is fair to say that we have paid around fourteen million pounds, not taking into account signing-on fees, loyalty bonuses and wages.

So the lion's share of monies received for players has in fact been reinvested on new faces. I have also not included Nick Proschwitz but I suspect that his *free transfer* was not so free after all when his entire remuneration package was taken into account.

How much of it has been wisely invested is a moot point and one that is sure to cause much debate amongst all Brentford fans but the truth is that the club has certainly more than kept its word.

The main problem is to be able to maintain the conveyor belt of promising, young and ideally underpriced talent and, as I intimated, this will get harder and harder as other clubs get smarter and we run the risk of losing our edge.

So what happens now? Do we need to buy new players this month?

Yes and no.

Perhaps we should keep our powder dry and wait until the summer when prices will not be so ridiculous and more of our potential targets will be available? Romaine Sawyers is certainly one that has caught our eye, according to scuttlebutt and rumour, and will then be available on a Bosman free transfer – but after the Evans situation, will he decide to go elsewhere even if we are in for him?

Jota might well be irreplaceable in the short-term but we are desperately short of width and pace and I hope that Gogia will be given the chance to step up to the plate. We are fine for central defenders should Tarkowski leave and perhaps the Harlee Dean situation might even be re-evaluated before his departure becomes irrevocable.

I am not desperately happy with any of our three strikers but up until the turn of the year we had been scoring freely although the goals seem to have dried up lately, and I cannot see us changing things up front in the short term. Maybe Scott Hogan will also be fit enough to make a return to action before the end of the season?

Oxford United's Kemar Roofe is the nearest that I have seen to an Alan Judge replacement but I suspect that that ship has sailed given his recent form and enhanced profile and hopefully we will not have to worry about that problem until the end of the season, and, in the event that Judge does go this month, I really cannot see how we can replace him at all adequately in the short term.

I do not want signings just for the sake of it and spending money without proper thought and consideration does nothing except jeopardise our position regarding Financial Fair Play.

Given our lack of income we have to ensure that all monies spent are invested wisely and not wasted purely to appease the fans.

Matthew Benham might well also have looked at the form guide and decided that we are going nowhere this season, up or down, and perhaps he would be better advised to wait until the summer before we bring in any new recruits.

I can therefore understand if nobody arrives this month, bar perhaps a young untested loanee, however even looking back at the muddled situation last January we still managed to bring in three promising young players for the future in Josh Laurent, Lewis Macleod and Jack O'Connell.

Leaving aside how they have all fared up until now, I would feel reassured if we managed to bring in a couple of exceptional young prospects next week who would challenge for a first team place next season. This might well be pie in the sky, however.

Results have also been poor so far this year and that simply makes us all feel even more anxious and uneasy.

Hopefully we will get back into the swing of things and put some points on the board over the next four days.

Brentford are in a strange situation and one that needs careful managing if we are not to fall over a precipice either from spending too much, too unwisely or even not enough.

Resilience! – 24/1/16

I tried to tell it just as it is in my article yesterday and I stand by every word that I wrote about the problems that we currently face in order to progress, but I also made it totally clear that for Brentford to maintain a top ten place in the Championship is a truly fantastic achievement given the fact that we are competing against far better funded teams pretty much with one hand tied behind our back.

Yesterday was a time for all the talking to stop and for actions to speak louder than words and the Bees stepped up to the plate and turned the form book on its head by ending a run of four consecutive defeats with an exceptional performance leading to a fully deserved three – one victory at Preston.

Had we lost then the knives would have been out and confidence would have further drained away but a week is a long time in football and we can now forget about the last week or so from hell and concentrate on what lies ahead – firstly a mouth-watering home clash with Leeds United and then the end of the Transfer Window, which cannot close quickly enough for our liking.

There was further scandalous muckraking journalism on the *Sky Sports* website last night claiming how angry and upset Alan Judge was at our apparent reluctance to offer our star player a new contract commensurate with the eight million pound transfer value we have apparently put on his head. This drivel has surely emanated from an agent desperate to stir up some late interest in his client before the window clangs shut.

I suspect the truth might lie in the fact that Judge's representative has apparently insisted on a ludicrously low buy out figure being inserted into any new contract offered by the club, thus making it impossible for a new extended deal to be agreed.

This one will run and run until the beginning of February and Judge's wonderfully taken goal at Preston will obviously make scouts and managers take further note of his quite obvious class but I remain hopeful that we will not receive an offer that meets our valuation of him and Alan will remain a Bee until the end of the season and that we will enjoy the rare and wondrous sight of a Brentford player competing at Euro 2016 this Summer.

The Bees made four team changes at Preston with Barbet, McEachran, Saunders and Vibe replacing O'Connell, the soon to be departed Diagouraga, Canos and Djuricin, and Lewis Macleod was named in the travelling squad for the first time this season but did not make the final cut.

Brentford controlled long periods of the game and their slick, accurate pass-and-move style of play made Preston look clumsy and agricultural in comparison. The Bees comfortably out-possessed and outpassed the home team and scored with all three of their shots on target.

Preston somehow managed to retain a full complement of eleven players for the entire match despite the ghastly Garner and Gallagher giving the referee every opportunity to send them both off but what can you expect when the official is called David Webb?

Our performance was controlled, disciplined and resilient with Colin the best player on the field and never losing his composure despite receiving a ridiculously soft booking. Barbet too more than justified his promotion and his wonderful long diagonal pass from left to right led to Judge's instant control and incisive run inside from the wing, leaving his marker trailing behind him in his wake like a constipated camel before he finished clinically for our second goal.

Bidwell had given us the lead with a perfect angled free kick from the edge of the box which took a slight deflection but is surely his goal despite it currently being deemed an own goal, but we squandered our advantage immediately afterwards when a typical Neanderthal long up-and-under was not dealt with by Dean, who had been forced to turn, and the loose ball was eventually poked in by Reach.

We recovered from that self-inflicted setback with Woods and the immaculate McEachran seizing control of the midfield, Saunders playing his role as senior pro to perfection and Swift's energy and trickery on the ball were also far too much for Preston to cope with and they were unable to catch him, even to kick him, as they chased shadows.

We fully earned our halftime lead which was almost stretched by Woods and Bidwell just before the break but the second half was a far less comfortable affair as we were pushed back and after Doyle and Vibe had both missed early chances at either end of the pitch, Preston took control and for fifteen minutes the home team laid siege to our goal.

Huntington's header hit the bar, Garner had a goal disallowed for offside and Button made a stupendous save when Garner deflected a Johnson shot and the big keeper somehow changed direction in mid-air to turn the ball onto the crossbar for a match-winning save that totally beggared belief. His aberration against Middlesbrough is now totally forgotten and firmly put behind him!

Just when an equaliser seemed inevitable, the tide turned and we found our second wind. Kerschbaumer made a valuable contribution with his energy and running after replacing the exhausted McEachran and Canos, the destroyer of Preston at Griffin Park earlier this season, made a similar impact when his immaculate and audacious flick enabled Colin to run through a challenge into space and cross low for Swift to finish Preston off with a clinically taken low shot which also took a helpful deflection and beat the helpless goalkeeper.

Brentford fully deserved that slight stroke of good fortune and this was a performance to be proud of as the players simply rolled up their sleeves, worked hard, silenced a vociferous crowd, ignored the intimidation they faced on the pitch, as well as a weak and inept referee, and played Preston off the park for large portions of the match with some eye-catching football.

Suddenly the world seems a far happier place and now let's hope that we can put our recent poor spell of results behind us and that this victory will give us the impetus and confidence to maintain a challenge for the playoffs.

And why not?

Despite the unavoidable loss of some leading players, yesterday clearly demonstrated that there is still so much talent and ability in the squad and that they are certainly playing for each other and the team.

Colin is a star in the making and Barbet also made a positive impression. Josh McEachran faced a tough task in proving that he is fit, robust and resilient enough to play in the key holding role alongside Ryan Woods, particularly at a tough and unwelcoming bleak Northern outpost and he came through with flying colours.

There is also the imminent prospect of Lewis Macleod finally being given the opportunity to show us what he can do.

There is an old and wise saying that *patience is a virtue* and yesterday showed that there is so much for us all to be proud about and that those in charge of our club understand far better than us supporters exactly what needs to be done in order to ensure that we maintain our progress and development as an established Championship club.

We need to trust them more whilst still retaining the right to question where necessary.

We also have to repeat the mantra that margins are so narrow in this incredibly tight division. We could quite easily have lost at Reading and also picked up points against Birmingham and Middlesbrough. Such is the way of life in the Championship. Yesterday too, for all our dominance, turned on one piece of magic from Button.

This was a good day for the club and everybody associated with it and we should all simply enjoy the moment, take a deep breath and look forward to the future with renewed vigour and confidence.

Tarky's Tale – 26/1/15

James Tarkowski finally broke radio silence yesterday when he issued a personal statement intended to explain his actions last week when he refused to play against Burnley.

Here is what he had to say:

I wanted to share a message with the fans following last week's events. My plans were to do this sooner but I agreed with the club that it was better to do so once I'd returned to training.

I have always enjoyed giving one hundred per cent playing for Brentford and am always proud to wear the shirt.

As a team, and with your support, we've had two years of great progress. From the promotion to the Championship through to last season where we reached the playoffs, I have so many special memories of this club and of the backing we've had from you, the fans.

I have always had a strong bond with my teammates and the fans. I also have a very close relationship with my family who, like you and my teammates, have been there and supported me throughout my career.

Unfortunately my mum has a serious, incurable illness and her condition has been getting steadily worse. I live a good four hours away from her and during the Autumn, it became clear to me that I needed to get closer to home to support both her and my dad.

I was open and up front about this with the club, who were sympathetic and said they'd work with me and my agent to try to reach a solution which worked well for the club whilst giving me the possibility to move to closer to my mum.

We decided to keep this matter confidential in the best interests of everyone. I decided not to put in a transfer request as we agreed it would be better to work together on this.

In the run up to the match against Burnley, I felt completely frazzled and unable to concentrate properly. I felt that to play in the match in this frame of mind may actually do more harm than good. I thought that my distraction may result in an error that would let my teammates and the fans down.

After much thought and consultation with the gaffer, my family and my teammates, I felt unable to guarantee my usual standard of performance and said as much to the gaffer.

I would like to apologise to my teammates, the gaffer and the fans. I hope that you can understand the pressure I was under and that no offence or insult was intended to anyone associated with the club. I have taken the sanction given to me by the club with good grace.

I would also like to thank everyone who has offered me support over the last ten days, and thank the club for continuing to understand my situation at home.

I am still under contract at Brentford and am committed to giving my best for the club, the team and the fans, as I always do when wearing the shirt.

James Tarkowski

When I last looked earlier this morning there were already pages and pages of comments on social media endlessly and forensically examining the runes and entrails and taking every single word apart in an attempt to analyse the exact meaning and nuances of what Tarkowski had said, contrasting it with the contents of the club's own statement from last week, and in many cases comparing his situation with that of Jota who was pretty much given compassionate leave recently as a result of his own personal problems.

Please feel free to wade through them all if you have the time, energy, interest and desire to do so and the general tenet of the comments ranges from a continued and unchanged feeling of anger at his original behaviour, to a sense of understanding that the seriousness of the situation relating to his mother's illness had led him to behave irrationally and unacceptably.

I have no intention of giving an opinion on the matter as quite frankly I don't really think that it matters one iota or jot what I think. What is more important is where this now leaves us.

Frankly the club is betting each way and covering the bases as nothing has really changed. Tarkowski still wishes to leave the club and Brentford will still only sell him if they are offered an acceptable sum for his transfer. Everything else is pure gloss and window dressing.

It would be to everybody's advantage if a club does come in for the player before the end of the Transfer Window and offers a sum in excess of three million pounds. Should that be the case then I would fully expect that Tarkowski will be on his way.

The key question is whether clubs will now be looking to take advantage of the unedifying situation and offer us well below market rate?

Given what he had to say yesterday it will be particularly interesting to see how he copes with the dilemma should a club south of the Watford Gap attempt to sign him given his stated intention to return to the North of England.

What the statement did, given that it included an apology to all parties, is open the door to the possibility of Tarkowski playing for us again should his move not come to fruition, and that is where the problems arise.

There is absolutely no point in leaving the player in purdah for the remainder of the season, thus further eroding his transfer value and turning him into damaged and shop-soiled goods.

Tarkowski is finished at Brentford, that is quite obvious to me. A parting of the ways is inevitable and it is just a question of whether he leaves in the next week or at the end of the season.

As for his playing for us again should he still be at the club after the Transfer Window shuts, I would hope fervently that the form of Dean, Barbet and O'Connell makes his presence on the pitch unnecessary and superfluous, not because I feel any personal vitriol or animosity towards him, but simply because his presence would be turned into a sideshow which would take attention away and distract everybody from the only thing that matters to us – winning football matches.

The Tarkowski situation and how we should handle it has totally divided and polarised the supporter base and is just one more unsettling episode in what has been a season that in so many ways has resembled a soap opera in terms of some of the off-field happenings.

I have no way of knowing what will happen between now and the end of the month however I believe it would be in the best interests of everybody if James Tarkowski, talented player that he undoubtedly is, finds a new home as soon as possible.

A Missed Opportunity – 27/1/16

Let's just get things into context for a moment. I am sure that most Brentford supporters left Griffin Park last night frustrated and not a little fed up after Jake Bidwell's calamitous and most untypical error gifted Leeds United a late and totally unmerited equaliser that cost Brentford two crucial points as we attempt to stay on the coat-tails of the playoff chasing pack.

This morning I have had some time to think more carefully and rationally about the events of last night and now my overriding view is quite simply how far we have come as both a team and a football club when we are moaning and gnashing our teeth at our failure to defeat one of the country's biggest and most established teams – tarnished and faded glory that they undoubtedly are.

I well remember our inferiority complex when we played Leeds in 2009 after a gap of several decades and our sheer incredulity that the minnows of Brentford were actually being allowed to share a pitch with the giants of Elland Road.

Oh, and by the way, how times have changed.

Leeds have not beaten us on any of the six occasions that we have played them since then and there was only one team trying to play football out there last night.

It was also Groundhog Day as there was a similar sense of frustration earlier in the season when we totally dominated proceedings at Elland Road, squandered chance after chance to score what would undoubtedly have been a match-clinching second goal and then succumbed to a late equaliser after an unforced error when Ryan Woods was caught in possession.

Last night saw us play some quality football particularly in the first half when we totally dominated but failed to make our possession count – a failing that came back to haunt us after the break when we put the handbrake on and created very little.

Had we held on, as we should have done, and emerged with a confidence boosting and much-needed and long-overdue home win, as well as the first clean sheet of the year, then we would today be congratulating the team for a solid, competent and professional performance.

The fact that we were unable to see the game through was certainly galling and provided further proof, if any was needed, that we are still a work in progress and nowhere near the finished article, but there was also much to take pride and pleasure in.

Sam Saunders was a bundle of energy and effervescence and he frolicked around with the enthusiasm of a new born lamb. He scored a beautifully taken goal when he ran at the heart of the Leeds defence from the halfway line and distracted as they were by the excellent decoy runs of Judge and Vibe, they criminally backed off him and Sam picked his spot perfectly into the corner of the net from the edge of the area before deservedly milking the applause from the Ealing Road faithful.

Sam is rumoured to be on his way shortly to Tampa Bay but given the sheer professionalism and excellence of his performance last night there is surely still a place for him in and around the first team at Griffin Park.

Given the current uncertainty over James Tarkowski, Yoann Barbet needed to step up to the plate last night and he more than met expectations, winning all of his aerial challenges, showing strength and pace as well as demonstrating his skill on the ball and ability to pick out a pass.

He is a real find and there is now a refreshing French feel and Gallic flamboyance in our defence with Barbet and Max Colin both looking as if they are in the team to stay and I prophesy that it will not be too long before they attract serious attention from other interested parties.

There has been some recent criticism, both veiled and overt, regarding the quality of our recruitment since the end of last season so it is also important and only fair to give praise and recognise the achievements of our Co-Directors of Football whenever it is justified, and in Colin, Barbet, and, of course, Ryan Woods, we have struck gold and made potentially exceptional signings.

We might well be talking about another one very shortly if Josh McEachran continues in the same vein as last night.

Toumani Diagouraga, watching for most of the match from the Leeds dugout where he must have recoiled from the non-stop verbal onslaught from his uncouth new managerial team, must surely have appreciated the sheer quality of his likely successor's performance as Josh combined some welcome and unexpected grit, pressing and tackling with the eerie ability to find time and space in a congested midfield as well as the vision to invariably find a team mate with his pass.

McEachran clearly demonstrated that given full fitness he will become a massive asset for the club and his burgeoning partnership with the bustling Ryan Woods, lightweights that they both are, augers well for the future and will ideally prove that brain overcomes brawn.

John Swift and Alan Judge too often dribbled into blind alleys and their final ball was often lacking, but we never stopped probing for openings and perhaps the key moment came soon after we had scored when Swift found Judge who turned inside his marker, switched the ball onto his left foot and curled his shot inches over the bar with Silvestri helpless.

A second goal then would surely have put the game well beyond Leeds but we rarely threatened after the break and Leeds finally took advantage when the normally reliable Jake Bidwell shanked his clearance when under no real pressure and Carayol took full advantage with a well-placed curling shot just out of the reach of the straining David Button.

So, a curate's egg of a performance that reconfirmed many of our strengths and weaknesses.

We do not make the most of our possession and let teams off the hook and I would hate to count up the number of giveaway goals we have gifted the opposition this season.

The formation we play requires our midfield to flood forward far quicker in support of our lone striker and I am afraid to say that in my opinion we need far better up front than the three strikers we currently possess, as none of them have really convinced that they are the solution to the problem.

We are not using Lasse Vibe to the best of his ability and his minimal threat was easily snuffed out last night, which meant that the ball rarely stuck in the final third, and the pace and bubbly enthusiasm of the injured Sergi Canos was also badly missed.

However the good easily outweighed the bad and we now move on.

Who knows what might happen in the next few days before the end of the Transfer Window?

Will we escape unscathed or suffer further losses and depredations, and if so who might come in to augment our depleted squad?

That though is a reflection for another day.

Sam Saunders celebrates

The Clock Is Ticking – 31/1/16

Tick, tick, tick…

Time marches inexorably on, but yet ever so slowly and interminably as all Brentford supporters count off the days, hours, minutes and even seconds until eleven o'clock on Monday evening when the Transfer Window slams shut and then, and only then, we can all breathe a sigh of relief.

The wait is both agonising and tortuous as the longer time passes by with no bad news the more the sense of fear and foreboding that something disastrous and horrible is bound to come and bite us up the backside perhaps even at the last possible moment.

Hopefully that is just my natural sense of pessimism talking rather than a real and justifiable concern of the worst happening.

What makes the situation even less tolerable is that we have no real sense or idea of what may be happening behind the scenes and whether behind closed doors the Brentford High Command is currently engaged in actively fending off predators determined to prise away our most valuable assets, negotiating the arrival of some fresh blood or even doing very little except simply hoping that the phone doesn't ring, the fax doesn't chatter into life and that the broadband goes down.

So now it is time for me to consult my crystal ball and predict what I think is likely to happen between now and Monday evening, and I fully understand that I am sticking my neck out and laying myself open to ridicule should, as is extremely likely, I get things totally and completely wrong.

Let's first review where we are at the time of writing: we have lost three players and gained two, with Toumani Diagouraga, Jota and Daniel O'Shaughnessy leaving and young defenders Nathan Fox and Emmanuel Onariase both arriving at Griffin Park from Cray Wanderers and West Ham United respectively. Sergi Canos and John Swift have also extended their loans until the end of the season.

Toumani's departure after six years of solid and committed service came as little surprise, and given that a fee of around half a million pounds was paid, we have certainly sold at the top of the market and at a time when his transfer value was more than likely to decline over the coming months and years.

The magic and sparkle had left his game and his most recent appearances showed quite clearly that he had lost his touch and even his enthusiasm and that he no longer really merited a place in the team.

He wanted and needed a change of scene and a fresh stimulus and challenge and fully deserved the lucrative and extended contract that he was offered by his new club.

Whether or not he will flourish at Leeds and respond to the unique management style of the inimitable and unspeakable Steve Evans is an intriguing question, but Brentford should be congratulated at sucking the last ounce of value out of a player whose best days have perhaps gone and then extracting top dollar for him.

Toumani marked his first full appearance for his new club by quite amazingly scoring his first goal for nearly three years in the FA Cup tie at Bolton Wanderers yesterday so perhaps he will yet have the last laugh.

And no, nobody invaded the pitch to help celebrate his goal! Thank you, Toumani, for all your loyal service to the club.

I watched Jota come on as a second half substitute for Eibar last Sunday with a sense of resignation coupled with sadness that circumstances have forced us to allow him to return to his homeland, at least for the time being.

Who knows if we will ever see the Spanish wizard in a Brentford shirt again, perhaps his family situation will eventually allow him to return to us, but, if not, he leaves us with a plethora of wonderful memories as one of the most gifted players in our recent history, and given that he has extended his contract we should eventually at least receive a reasonable fee for him, if not as much as might have been expected if he had moved onto a Premier League team, as had at one time seemed likely.

Daniel O'Shaughnessy simply needs the chance to play first team football in order that we can find out whether he is good enough to play in the Football League, and I am sure that he will receive his opportunity during his loan spell at our sister club FC Midtjylland whom he has joined for the remainder of the season.

He has recently made his full international debut for Finland so he must possess ability even if he has never yet threatened to break into the Brentford first team since his arrival on a two-year contract in 2014.

His move does beg the question about the relative standard of the Championship compared to the Danish *Superliga* and how someone not considered good enough to play for us can hope to feature for the current Danish champions.

Hopefully we will all get the chance to see how he gets on should he be selected to play against Manchester United in the *Europa League* next month.

It is possible that there will not be any additional departures from the club before the end of the Transfer Window but I will not feel certain about that until eleven o'clock tomorrow night given that there are still two players who might well be in play.

James Tarkowski in my opinion totally burned his boats by his behaviour when he refused to play against Burnley the other week and despite attempts to rectify the situation and put a sticking plaster over a gaping wound, his continued presence at the club still casts a pall over affairs at Griffin Park and polarises opinions amongst supporters.

His recent statement, however carefully crafted, reeked of tergiversation and in my opinion begged more questions than it provided answers and I firmly believe that it would be better for all parties should he leave the club as soon as possible.

Whether that happens now totally depends if anyone comes in with an acceptable offer, which rumours suggest would need to be in excess of three million pounds plus add ons.

Any interested parties are sure to smell weakness and try and take advantage of the situation over the next couple of days however in Matthew Benham they will find an opponent who will simply refuse to blink first or accept anything under the price that he has set.

Michael Keane has not left Burnley so it remains to be seen if they remain in the frame or whether a new club will come to the negotiating table. My money would be on Burnley coming back for another attempt to sign him.

If a move does not come about then we will simply have to get on with things as we cannot allow such a valuable asset to wither away and Tarkowski, having made an apology and provided an explanation of sorts, will doubtless be available for selection should the need arises.

Dean Smith has already made it clear that he will be welcomed back into the fold and he was totally correct in doing so, however Tarky has now fallen behind Harlee Dean and Yoann Barbet in the pecking order, has lost match fitness and will simply have to wait for his opportunity to arrive should injury or loss of form strike the current first choices.

Alan Judge, with twelve goals and seven assists has quite simply been the best and most exciting and effective player in the Championship this season and he is a man on a mission and is determined to force his way into the Eire squad for the European Championships in the summer.

There has quite naturally been serious interest in him, and all Brentford fans, fearing the worst, would have been reassured by press comments yesterday, attributed to the player, confirming that he will remain at the club for the rest of the season.

Judge is a talismanic figure to us all and is our leader, conductor and inspiration on the pitch as most of our positive play and goal threat emanates from him.

It is hard to see how we can replace him, particularly in the short term given the additional loss of Jota, and hopefully we will not have to deal with that situation until the end of the season.

And yet... and yet, it would not surprise me in the slightest if one of the myriad clubs seeking promotion to the promised land of the Premier League, or even indeed a club at the lower end of the Premier League itself does not come in at the last minute and attempt to prise him out our grasp. It seems a real no-brainer as Judge would improve any team whose presence he graces and the fee would be chump change for most of them.

Will we stand fast and resist any potential suitors? Who knows? It all depends upon the sum that we are offered and any figure in excess of five million pounds would merit serious consideration.

As for Judge, despite his acknowledged happiness at the club both on and off the pitch, more money would obviously be welcome as well as the chance to play in a team likely to challenge for honours, but he also has to consider that at Brentford he is guaranteed to start every match and within reason is afforded a free role which entirely suits his game and keeps him in the spotlight, and he might not be so prominent elsewhere.

There is a lot for him to ponder upon and we will simply have to wait and see what happens over the next day or so.

Sam Saunders will also have a decision to make shortly, and perhaps the prospect of Tampa Bay is slightly less alluring now that he seems to be back in favour and in and around the starting eleven.

Alan McCormack might also have been considering his position but for the niggling injuries that have hindered him recently.

There might also be moves, temporary or permanent, or maybe even contracts being cancelled, for the likes of Montell Moore, Josh Clarke, Ryan Williams and Josh Laurent who all currently appear to be surplus to requirements at Griffin Park.

There are no rumours of interest in any other of our players although I am sure that the likes of David Button and Jake Bidwell have their suitors and admirers.

What is more important is that we succeed in persuading them to sign contract extensions as they are the backbone of the team and I am sure that every effort will be made to do so, and that ideally neither player will be allowed to enter the last year of their contract next season.

Given the uncertainty surrounding Tarkowski and the fact that Dean Smith appears to be a fan, perhaps there will also be a change of heart regarding Harlee Dean and a way might be found to keep him at the club for next season and beyond?

That is a move which would again polarise the supporters but Harlee appears to have matured both on and off the pitch (the Nottingham Forest nonsense excepted) and could well develop into the right-sided centre half that we need.

What is far more intriguing and exciting for all supporters is the prospect of new players arriving, and here I think I need to dampen expectations as I do not anticipate any permanent incomings or transfer fees to be paid unless we lose additional players from the squad.

In those circumstances I would suspect that there are contingency plans in place should either Tarkowski or Judge leave the club before tomorrow evening.

Apart from what I stated above, why do I not expect any other permanent signings given that we have already lost the likes of Toumani and Jota?

Quite simply because the players we want are either not available or will cost prohibitive sums in January, a time when fees are generally inflated and might well be available on Bosman free transfers at the end of the season.

I would hazard a guess that there is also a view in and around the club that whilst the playoffs remain a possibility it would perhaps make better sense to keep our powder dry for the time being and make whatever changes are necessary in the close season.

There is also the omnipresent spectre of Financial Fair Play looming over us. We are now allowed to lose a maximum of thirteen million pounds per season and we remain hamstrung given our lack of income and resources.

Our expenditure needs to be carefully managed and controlled and perhaps it is felt that now is not the best time to go into the transfer market given the likelihood that we will finish in a comfortable position in the league and further consolidate within the Championship with our existing squad.

There could well be some major changes in the Summer as we look carefully at who has adjusted to the demands of the Championship and who has not settled down or has been found wanting.

In addition, given that we will lose Sergi Canos and John Swift, leaving aside what happens to Alan Judge, it is pretty obvious that we will need to bring in some creative midfielders for next season and maybe we will be looking seriously at the likes of Romaine Sawyers as has already been suggested on social media.

There are rumours that high quality targets are already being lined up for the summer which is encouraging news and that would also give us time and breathing space to replace Alan Judge should he decide to leave the club either now, or as anticipated, in the summer.

Jamie Paterson, currently at loan at Huddersfield from Nottingham Forest, and a player well known to Dean Smith from his Walsall days, has been mooted as a potential arrival and perhaps that might happen either in the close season or even as a loanee next month.

I would expect that a winger will be brought in on loan next month given our lack of options in that area and maybe a defensive midfielder as well, although Josh McEachran will be given every opportunity to settle into the team and we also have the enticing prospect of the long-overdue appearance of Lewis Macleod.

Will Scott Hogan also regain sufficient fitness to be given an opportunity to boost our flagging strike force before the end of the season? That would certainly be something to look forward to, although we should not hold out too much hope of it coming to pass or harbour any sense of expectation.

The arrival of the two young central defenders initially for the Development Squad is also very interesting and is evidence that we are looking to strengthen our resources in that area of the pitch and that perhaps we will be looking to sign more youngsters who have not quite made it at a higher level elsewhere in order to boost our talent pool given that we are still waiting for some payback from the expenditure lavished on the Academy, where I am led to believe that the majority of our Crown Jewels are still a few years away from consideration for the first team squad.

I have not tried to paint a gloomy picture, but have simply attempted to take an objective look at the situation that the club is facing as we go into the last crucial days, hours, minutes and seconds of the Transfer Window and provide my own viewpoint of what might possibly transpire.

I am fully prepared to eat humble pie on Monday evening should I be proved wildly inaccurate in my predictions.

Position	Team	P	W	D	L	F	A	GD	Pt	Form
1	Hull City	28	17	5	6	45	18	27	56	W L W W W W
2	Middlesbrough	27	17	4	6	37	14	23	55	W W W W L L
3	Burnley	28	14	9	5	46	25	21	51	L W D W W W
4	Brighton and Hove A	28	13	11	4	34	28	6	50	D L L L W W
5	Derby County	28	13	10	5	39	25	14	49	W D L D L L
6	Birmingham City	29	13	8	8	37	28	9	47	W W D W W D
7	Sheffield Wednesday	28	12	10	6	42	31	11	46	W L W W W D
8	Ipswich Town	28	12	9	7	37	35	2	45	W W D W D L
9	Cardiff City	29	11	11	7	38	33	5	44	D W L W D W
10	Brentford	29	11	7	11	42	41	1	40	W L L L W D
11	Nottingham Forest	29	9	12	8	30	25	5	39	D D D W W D
12	Wolverhampton Wndrs	28	10	8	10	37	38	-1	38	W W W W L D
13	Queens Park Rangers	29	8	12	9	35	35	0	36	D L D W D D
14	Leeds United	29	8	12	9	29	33	-4	36	D D L L W D
15	Reading	28	9	8	11	32	31	1	35	L L W D L D
16	Preston North End	28	8	11	9	25	27	-2	35	L W W W D L
17	Huddersfield Town	29	8	8	13	39	42	-3	32	D W W D L L
18	Blackburn Rovers	27	6	12	9	24	24	0	30	L L L D L D
19	Fulham	28	6	10	12	43	48	-5	28	L W L L D L
20	Milton Keynes Dons	28	7	5	16	23	41	-18	26	W L D L W L
21	Rotherham United	29	7	4	18	35	53	-18	25	L L W L D L
22	Bristol City	29	5	10	14	24	47	-23	25	L L L W L D
23	Charlton Athletic	29	5	9	15	26	55	-29	24	L D L L D W
24	Bolton Wanderers	28	3	11	14	24	46	-22	20	L W L L L W

[30th January 2016]

231

February

So What Happens Now? – 4/2/16

I thought I would allow things to settle down for a couple of days or so before I made any comment about Brentford's activity, or lack of it, in the Transfer Window, its ramifications, and where it has left us in terms of the remainder of the season and beyond.

Given that we lost three valuable members of our first team squad and brought in no immediate replacements I fully expected that there would be a tirade of vituperation from those Brentford supporters who still do not understand how our club is being run or, even worse, do not want to do so.

There were indeed quite a few comments on social media which accused the club of treading water at best or even going backwards, demonstrating a total lack of ambition by not splashing the cash as well as claims that we were now holed below the waterline and had given up on the remainder of the season which we now faced with a weakened and diminished squad.

To my surprise and pleasure, of the vocal minority who made their voice heard, a far greater number supported the club's stance and welcomed the fact that even more transfer income had been received, our limited funds had been conserved and we could now build up a war chest for the summer when more quality players would be available for far less exorbitant sums than is the case in January when desperation is the rule of the game and clubs will only allow their best players to leave if they are offered far more than their real market value.

We are a case in point as Brentford placed an extremely, and perhaps artificially, high value on our star player and talisman, Alan Judge, in what turned out to be a successful attempt to ward off potential suitors, as we made it absolutely clear that only an enormous offer would persuade us to allow him to leave the club in January.

Our tough stance worked a treat and Judge will remain at Griffin Park at least until the end of the season and, given his single-minded ambition and focus on making the Eire squad for the European Championships, it is an absolute given that he will be putting everything into his performances over the next three months in order to catch the eye of Martin O'Neill.

I fully expect that Judge will be gone before the beginning of next season but we really cannot lose out as we will have benefited greatly from his service, receive a transfer fee in excess of ten times what we paid Blackburn Rovers for him and should he make the Eire squad and shine on the pitch during the Tournament then who knows how much we might be offered for him?

In the meantime we should just be grateful that he will be with us for the remainder of the season and continue to act as our spark plug and inspiration.

In passing there was an interesting debate on the pages of *The Griffin Park Grapevine* a few days ago regarding the identity of the last non-striker to score twenty goals in a season for the club as Alan, with twelve to his name to date, is perhaps within striking distance and has a realistic possibility of achieving that momentous feat.

Nobody immediately sprung to mind with the exception of Johnny Brooks who scored twenty-two times way back in 1962/63. He was a classic inside forward who played alongside John Dick and Billy McAdams in a team that scored ninety-eight goals whilst on its way to winning the Fourth Division title. We all send him our continued best wishes given that news broke last season of his ill-health.

Other midfielders or wingers who in recent times have got anywhere near the hallowed twenty-goal mark in a season are Bobby Ross with fifteen in 1970/71, Glen Poole, Paul Evans and Allan Mansley with fourteen, John Docherty with thirteen and Gary Roberts with twelve goals.

If I have forgotten any other candidates then please let me know.

Please excuse me for that brief but enjoyable diversion and now, back to the present day.

I will simply say that we have already made a massive profit on James Tarkowski which will be increased significantly should Burnley get promoted, and we enjoyed six years of excellent service from Toumani Diagouraga and also obtained a three hundred per cent profit on what we paid Peterborough for him.

Thankfully Co-Director of Football, Phil Giles, has given a long and illuminating interview on the official club website which explains far better than I can the rationale behind our entire Transfer Window strategy, why we divested ourselves of Toumani Diagouraga, Jota and James Tarkowski, what efforts were made to bring in fresh blood and, most importantly, where we are going from here.

If you have not read it, then I commend it to you as it is clear, open and honest and, at least to me, he makes perfect sense in what he has said.

Words, however wise and well meant, are cheap, and actions certainly speak louder, and we now all have to wait and see what transpires during the remainder of this season and, even more importantly, in the close season, before we can finally pass judgement on the success or otherwise of the most recent Transfer Window.

If the departing players are replaced wisely, as I fully expect, and further tweaks are also made to the squad, then all will be well.

In the meantime I have made a list of all the things that I hope and expect to see take place over the course of the next few months, which ideally will go a long way towards proving that we remain on track and that further progress will be made:

1. We retain our focus and remember that there is still over a third of the season to play and that performances and points remain crucial and an absolute priority, as is reaching the recognised safety mark of fifty-one points as soon as possible

2. A realisation that the season is most certainly not over, as has been claimed elsewhere, and that matters cannot be allowed to drift

3. Beating both Queens Park Rangers and Fulham and proving that we are the top dog in the Championship in West London. *Kings of West London* has a nice ring to it

4. Experimentation in terms of lineups and even formations as we need to assess what works best for us and which players are up to the challenge and can remain with us and contribute fully to our journey and who is not quite good enough

5. Giving Philipp Hofmann, Konstantin Kerschbaumer and Andy Gogia a run of games to see if they are good enough to thrive at Championship level

6. Likewise with Marco Djuricin as he was looking good before his unfortunate injury at Blackburn in early November and a decision will need to be made as to whether he becomes a permanent signing at the end of the season

7. Giving Lasse Vibe a breather from time to time given the amount of games he has played over the past year without benefit of an end of season break

8. Seeing if Vibe, Hofmann and Djuricin, or any combination of two of them can play together in a front two

9. Easing Lewis Macleod into the team and allowing him the chance to sample Championship football when his fitness levels allow. A place on the bench tomorrow night at Brighton would be a good start

10. Identifying a suitable backup for Jake Bidwell who could also be groomed into becoming his successor should Jake not extend his current contract with the club

11. Demonstrating to crucial mainstays of the team such as David Button and Jake Bidwell that our ambitions remain unchanged and convincing them to buy into our vision by extending their contracts with the club beyond 2017

12. Coming to a suitable agreement with Harlee Dean that allows both sides to feel content about him signing a new contract. With the departure of Tarkowski, Dean is now the only senior right-sided centre half at the club and hopefully he will thrive on the responsibility as well as the opportunity it affords him

13. Persuading Sam Saunders to put his *American Dream* on hold and coming up with a new deal that allows him to combine playing with perhaps developing a new career as a coach

14. Nursing Scott Hogan through the final stages of his recovery period and getting him back onto the field with renewed fitness and confidence in his ability

15. Giving Josh McEachran the opportunity to develop an effective partnership with Ryan Woods as our defensive midfielders and hoping he regains sufficient fitness to make some forward runs too

16. Deciding upon the future of Alan McCormack and ensuring that he has a dignified exit if that is the way things go

17. Encouraging Ryan Woods to get into the opposition penalty area whenever possible and to try shooting more often

18. Doing everything possible to persuade John Swift that his permanent future lies at Griffin Park and that next season he will be allowed to play in the centre of midfield rather than out on the left wing

19. Integrating the impressive Yoann Barbet into the team whilst still convincing Jack O'Connell that he has a future at the club

20. Keeping in constant contact with Jota and doing everything within our power to persuade him to return with his batteries recharged and spirits revived as and when it is possible for him to do so

21. Trying to persuade Nico Yennaris to sign a new contract at the club given his value as a squad member and giving him an opportunity to demonstrate if he can also play in midfield

22. Encouraging Sergi Canos to try the spectacular when appropriate but not to take on too much responsibility on the pitch

23. Ensuring that a limited number of loan players are brought in to fill the gaps that currently exist on the wing and perhaps at centre half and ideally they are on the *try before you buy* basis which has worked so well previously

24. To continue our root and branch review of the Academy and decide if it is worth the current investment given the paucity of its return

25. To bring in more promising players from outside for the Development Squad and hope that the influence of Flemming Pedersen produces a winning mentality and helps bring some emerging young players through to the first team squad

26. Finding appropriate loan moves for Josh Clarke and Jermaine Udumaga so that we can find out just how good they are

27. To identify and initiate appropriate levels of contact with potential new signings for next season from both at home and abroad and ideally formalise agreements with them for next season and beyond

So there is certainly much for us to look forward to between now and the end of the season and hopefully many of the points I have mentioned above will be actioned by the club.

I would love to hear from other supporters regarding their own wish list for the next three months, as I am sure that I have left a lot out.

A Night To Forget! – 6/2/16

I am really not quite sure what upset me more, watching our listless and inept display at Brighton last night or listening to the so called experts on *Sky Sports* line up to put the boot in on Brentford and how badly they think the club has been run over the last year.

Let's start with the performance which highlighted all our weaknesses and exemplified everything bad about us and the way that we play when things do not work out as planned:

- Tons of possession, sixty-five percent, to be accurate but with absolutely no end result

- Barely a shot on target in the whole match

- Nearly six hundred passes of which less than a third were forward in direction

- No real tempo or pace on and off the ball

- Being careless in possession and turning the ball over with monotonous regularity as soon as we got into Brighton territory

- No incision in the final third of the pitch

- The lone striker, firstly Vibe and then Djuricin, being totally starved of possession and support

- Neither striker showing any real appetite for the fray and Vibe showing a lack of anticipation when an excellent chance eventually came his way

- A total reluctance to shoot when the opportunity arose

- Never getting sufficient players into the penalty areas to threaten a tough and organised home defence

- A distinct lack of bite in the tackle as we stood off and admired our opponents as they ran through us unchallenged

- No pressing or defending from the front or committed effort made to win back possession

- Dean and Barbet being left totally exposed when the two fullbacks were far too often left marooned upfield when our attacking moves broke down and the home team taking full advantage of Dean's lack of pace

- John Swift looking like a little boy lost as the game totally passed him by

- Sam Saunders having one of those nights when nothing went right for him

- Alan Judge reduced to impotence by the incompetence around him

- Josh McEachran hardly putting himself forward for an *Ironman* Award as he gave in and succumbed to a hip injury after an evening punctuated by a series of sideways and backwards passes and an inability and disinclination to get stuck in

- Our players being shrugged off the ball with embarrassing ease as we were outplayed, outmuscled and outfought

- We were too soft, small and lightweight, the heads went down as we ran up the white flag, and there was no evidence of leadership either on or off the pitch

I am trying very hard to find anything positive to say about any of our players but I am really struggling to come up with anything beyond the fact that Ryan Woods never gave up or let his head go down and performed excellently both on and off the ball and Lewis Macleod finally made his debut for the club as a late substitute and hopefully there is much to look forward to from him.

Brighton knew exactly how to manage the game. They allowed us to keep possession for seemingly minutes at a time, happy and content in the knowledge that we did not have the wit, imagination, guile, strength or numbers in support to break them down.

They waited for our moves to break down, mainly through our own over-elaboration or careless errors and then picked us off on the break with fast, incisive attacks that tore massive holes in our defence, which had the consistency and solidity of a sieve.

What was most noticeable was how quickly they got forward and how many players they had in and around our penalty area to support their attacks.

There was danger every time they attacked and their strikers, with the exception of the lumbering Zamora, were far too quick and strong for us and we could never match their movement off the ball.

All three goals were well-taken but giveaways from our point of view. We started the game quicker than Brighton but after Judge forced an excellent save from Stockdale with what turned out to be our only serious effort of the match, Brighton grew into the game but their first goal should easily have been prevented.

Saunders gave the ball away and was brushed off like an irritating fly when he attempted to win it back. Colin was slow to anticipate a long diagonal pass that looked as if it was drifting out of play before the excellent Murphy chased a seemingly lost cause and set up Anthony Knockaert, the best player on the pitch, who brought the ball instantly under control and left our defenders with twisted blood before he finished emphatically.

The second goal, coming as it did just before halftime, ended the game as a contest. A quick free kick was played to Kayal who was waved past by McEachran whose abysmal apology for a challenge was a total embarrassment, and his perfect cross was headed in by an unmarked Hemed. Amateur hour at the back by the Bees.

The third goal came just before the final whistle at a time when the long-suffering Brentford supporters were almost past caring and we were caught by yet another breakaway with vast swathes of space on our right flank and Murphy was left to run in totally unmarked and unchallenged to score easily and set the seal on a night of misery for the club.

What highlights our lack of bite even more clearly is that we never gave Keith Stroud any reason or excuse to put his own indelible and inimitable stamp upon proceedings.

What made matters even worse and poured salt on an already gaping wound was the seemingly biased, inept and ignorant coverage on *Sky Sports*, which amounted to a total Brighton love-in.

We were a mere afterthought, the lambs to the slaughter, apart from a brief Alan Judge puff piece before kick-off. That would have been bad enough but worse was to come as the commentators and analysts alike, Ian Holloway, Peter Beagrie and Don Goodman, took pot-shots at us in turn and lost no opportunity to sneer and jeer at our apparent decline and fall from the heights of Mark Warburton's regime of last season.

Every transfer out of the club was examined with a metaphorical shake of the head and remarked upon with the overwhelming and unanimous verdict that we had weakened the squad for no apparent reason and had no strategy, plan or ambition for the future and were a headless chicken club and a laughing stock surely destined to fall further from grace.

Not for one minute was there an ounce of introspection or analysis of why we had in many cases been forced to take the action that we did and sell players who we could not afford to keep once their head had been turned by clubs with far greater resources than ours. No mention too of the dreaded words, *Financial Fair Play*.

So where do we go from here? That is the million-dollar question that needs careful consideration.

The other day I wrote a long list of everything that we had to look forward to for the remainder of the season.

Without doubt, the most important consideration was that we kept our focus and concentrated on winning football matches, something that we seemed totally to forget last night.

There was a vast chasm between the two teams both on and off the pitch last night. Brighton's well-appointed new stadium is a cash cow and their off-field income and an attendance last night, two-and-a-half times higher than that of Brentford, means that we are totally unable to compete with them in terms of income, and that was reflected on the field where an experienced and expensively assembled squad boasting players we can only dream about, was totally superior to ours.

Let's also try and keep some sense of perspective as we had taken four points from our last two matches and good players do not necessarily become bad overnight. But it has to be said that the blend did not work last night and we were far below our best and fell far short of what is required to compete at this level.

I will not resort to a knee-jerk reaction and pull everything and everybody apart but I am sure that last night was a wake-up call that will not be ignored by the powers that be at the club.

Our strategy for the remainder of the season seems to be quite simply to hunker down, retreat into our bunker, make do with what we are left with and simply count off the days and get through the season before readdressing matters in the summer and hopefully coming again next season.

Maybe the shortcomings that were highlighted last night will bring about some rethinking?

The Fans Have Their Say – 9/2/16

There is a lot of muttering and murmuring at the moment from some Brentford fans, the majority of whom I suspect are fairly wet behind the ears in terms of the length of their support and never lived through the bad old days of the likes of Stan Webb, Murray Jones and Eddie Hutchinson and many others of that ilk - players whose second touch was generally a tackle and who could also be relied upon to send the majority of their shots into orbit.

These fans have understandably become spoiled by the success of the incredible last three years which have seen Brentford finally climb out of the depths of the third tier of English football and rise to the Championship for the first time in over twenty years and then come within a hairsbreadth of reaching the unforeseen heights of the Premier League by playing a wonderful brand of effervescent, attacking football.

They are expecting our progress to be maintained and for the squad to be enhanced.

Spend, Spend, Spend is their mantra as if they were reincarnations of Viv Nicholson of pools win fame from 1961 and there is a feeling of deep frustration and even anger at the recent sales of so many talented players and their not being immediately replaced, and utterly no understanding of the realities of the situation that we face.

I always try to look at both sides of any story or subject concerning Brentford FC and then attempt to provide a measured opinion ideally based on analysis and research as well as sounding out the views of others rather than just relying on simple emotion and gut feeling.

In this instance I am fully prepared to nail my colours to the mast and in response to all the criticism I would simply refer you all to the words of the then Prime Minister, Harold Macmillan, when in 1957 he asserted that the people *have never had it so good.*

Here is what I think about our current situation:

1. We are punching way above our weight in what is only our second season in the Championship

2. The dictates of Financial Fair Play mean that we cannot just throw money that we don't have at improving the squad and have had to sell to remain compliant with its requirements

3. Even if we could, why should Matthew Benham spend more than he has budgeted, a sum which is already generous in the extreme

4. Last year was a massive overachievement due to brilliant young players, a team ethos, good management and coaching, a lot of good fortune regarding injuries and first year syndrome and the time to take an educated gamble was last January, but the opportunity was lost

5. Our best players have been snatched away because they were all more than good enough to progress higher, and were offered wages in some cases two to three times what they earned at Brentford by clubs awash in revenue due to the benefits of larger stadia and Parachute Payments

6. Players chase the money – that is a given as theirs is a short and risky career and they must strike whilst the iron is hot, and unlike in previous years when we took what we could get, we are now recruiting far better players who all have other options and they and their agent can generally call the tune

7. Given our lack of revenue, which is in the bottom four of the Championship, we could not afford to keep them or risk a divided dressing room so we made sure we got top dollar for all of them, something we have never achieved before in our history

8. This money has and will continue to be invested in new players, but not until the end of the season when we can extract maximum value rather than in January when it is a sellers' market

9. We are now hamstrung by massive over-expectations caused by a dangerous and intoxicating combination of excitement, impatience and ignorance

10. We are looking to progress but cannot do so at the pace we set last season – nobody could – and it is quite impossible to replicate or even build upon our success given the financial realities of our situation and the fact that many other clubs are now trying to replicate our recruitment model and use analytical scouting techniques

11. Yes there were some daft, ill-thought and unrealistic comments earlier this season from people high up at the club which raised expectations and should not have been made which are now coming back to haunt them – and rightly so

12. This is how it is going to be until we get to Lionel Road and with enhanced revenues we will then have a bigger budget to play with

13. How it is going to be is still pretty damn good in my opinion given our post war history as we should remain a mid-table Championship team playing good football until we can afford to invest more in the squad

14. We already have some wonderful young players in Colin, Barbet, Hogan, Bidwell, Woods and McEachran and the foundations are in place both on and off the pitch

15. All will be well as long as we continue to recruit properly. In 2014 we recruited brilliantly, in 2015 half the signings have come off and half have yet to do so and we could also do with some long-overdue luck with injuries

16. Everything hinges on who leaves and who comes in this summer. This is the key, we have to continue to bring in young, promising and undervalued players from both at home and abroad who we can develop and improve – some will come off and be successful and others won't

17. The time to worry will be if we do not make serious efforts to rebuild the squad in the close season. How we attempt to replace Alan Judge should he leave, as I expect him to do, will be very illuminating

18. The remainder of this season is about consolidation and experimentation – no more – no less

19. Be careful what you wish for and remember where we have come from if you continue to criticise Matthew Benham and tell him to get his chequebook out

It is only fair that I now publish the comments and opinion of some of the readers of my column in order that everybody can read all of the differing points of view and then come to their own conclusion about the current situation.

Bill Benn was very emphatic in his support of our strategy:

Why take notice of television pundits slagging off our club and owner? Just ask yourself why aren't they managing a football team?

These are the same people who slated Ranieri at the start of the season. Let's be fair, management is hardly an easy job as Gary Neville is finding out.

We are a club that is very much in a state of transition. I think at times like this the fans should just get behind the side and support what the club is trying to achieve.

Players don't want to play for little clubs with small crowds when big clubs with big wages come calling. We can't control that and all we can do is get the correct money for them, something we have never done in the past.

We lost a game at Brighton – so what? We were great in our last away game at Preston, now we are rubbish!

Let's keep things in proportion.

Cris Glascow was not feeling as bullish or positive:

The club's hierarchy shouldn't be surprised if a number of newer fans retreat into their own bunkers rather than wasting money watching some of the impotent performances that have been served up recently.

I hope they think seriously about how the playing side is being run at the moment.

It's all very well saying we are safe (we aren't yet) but a run of poor performances to the end of the season will just encourage our few remaining talented players to leave, thinking that the club has no real ambition.

Cutting your cloth according to your budget is one thing. Showing a lack of direction or momentum is quite another.

Russell Hawes was not happy with the way we lined up on Friday and wonders if the favoured 4-2-3-1 formation best suits the players we currently have:

My thoughts on the performance – neither Vibe, Djuricin nor Hofmann suit the lone striker role. The five-man midfield is fine, with attacking flair, but not with Sam, Woods, Josh and Swift. It is just never going to work. Judge is dropping deeper and deeper to get in the game and our striker is barely getting a touch.

We need to play to our strengths. Barbet and Woods are great passers so use their ability to play longer passes to create more opportunites.

Vibe or Djuricin need a partner up front and I would play Hoff and Vibe, sit Judge behind and use Canos, Swift/ Gogia down the wings with a holding player, Woods or Josh. The back four would remain as they are but concentrate on defending!

Rebel Bee is also worried about our current thinking and what lies ahead of us:

A very bad night and it was unfortunate that it was live on television, when it really needed burying amidst a busy midweek schedule. Yes it's open season on us with the media at present, much of the criticism is unjust but we aren't helping ourselves are we?

Do we have problems in the camp again, do we have enough to get through to the end of the season, and is Dean Smith going to be up to this job? I'm asking myself these questions today.

I'm also concerned by the now seemingly huge task of putting a new side together in the summer.

Whilst I totally understand that our resources are not at the level of many other clubs in the division, please let's not use this "little Brentford, we can't compete" stuff as a comfort blanket for some of the things that patently aren't working as hoped.

I've just watched Leicester win well at Manchester City, they top the Premier League and are real contenders – if we blindly follow the resources argument then this just shouldn't be happening.

So why is it? I'd say they have a great coach, excellent recruitment here and abroad, and a real team ethos. Leicester have a strong spine, tight defence and a real outlet up front – and he came from Fleetwood! This is totally relevant to us and where the real debate should be directed right now.

Worryingly, most of our divisional rivals have strengthened whilst we haven't, some of the sides below us will now fancy their games to come against us.

The season has been a mess and without Lee Carsley we'd be in real trouble.

Sorry to those that don't like my views, I love our club as deeply as you all do. I'll be at Hillsborough next week, but I go both in hope and fear in equal measure.

Rob O also expressed his concerns:

I'm at a loss about what I feel and think is going on at the club at the moment. I was at Preston the other week and we did play well and it was an enjoyable day out. I watched pretty much the same players at Brighton and they were completely out of sorts and not far off humiliated.

Tempo, drive and positivity seem to be the difference in the two performances. I think perhaps we should fine the players if they pass backwards or sideways, at least when quick forward movement is on.

Everything was so slow and laboured – tentative would be the word I'd use. The players seemed to be intimidated. Maybe we just don't like playing on Friday nights!

I fully appreciate the rational arguments about our relative size, Matthew Benham's dedication and huge sums of money he's invested and the amount of work going on in all areas of the club.

But supporters are generally not rational when it comes to football and we seem to be losing the emotional argument – the feel good factor.

The Bees are not an easy sell at the moment. My son and his friend are thirteen and I must admit I struggle to put into words for them what's happening (in a positive sense), though intellectually I know things are far better than they were only a few years ago.

Ray Bailey got it in one, in my opinion:

Being a pessimist by nature, I still look to see how far we are off relegation rather than looking up the table before we reach fifty-one points!

I believe some people need to get a reality check on our current position in the league.

Yes, last season was brilliant and I couldn't believe some of the football we were playing, but since winning promotion I'd certainly take our current position any day.

I'm afraid I do still worry about Dean Smith being the right man but he needs to be given time to get his style across and build his own team and then we'll see.

The pundits were doing my head in as well, especially as they were trying to portray that we were willingly selling all our best players, just because somebody bid for them rather than the players wanted away, as was the case!

So what sort of ambition have we got? Well, with crowds of ten thousand what do they expect us to do?

I'm sure Rotherham and Bristol City fans would give their right arm to swap with us!

Once we get into Lionel Road and hopefully get bigger crowds, then I will start to dream that one day we might reach the giddy heights of the premiership, but it's going to be a massive struggle, just look at Nottingham Forest and Leeds and how many years they've been trying and that's with far bigger crowds than we are going to get!

So, come on everybody, let us smell the roses and enjoy the current ride rather than expect overnight success!

Paul Fletcher also remains to be convinced:

I would hope the two Co-Directors of Football realise that the latest exodus of experienced Championship proven players cannot be balanced by the signing of two untried kids and an extended contract given to a player who is anything but a Championship regular.

I honestly feel sorry for Dean Smith and sincerely hope he is given the opportunity to show us what he can do.

I am less enamoured by the performance of Messrs. Ankersen and Giles however, who having failed with the recruitment of Marinus as Head Coach have not inspired with the majority of players they have brought to the club. Certainly only Woods and Colin have been close to the quality of signing we made prior to their appointment.

We are at a bit of a crossroads, I believe, and decisions need to be made that convince players we value and supporters alike that we are building a better squad in the long-term.

Gordonbankole feels that mistakes have been made and lessons need to be learned:

A club in transition? No problem with transition – just depends on whether it's rough or smooth, and I'd suggest the last twelve months have been pretty rough after three years when we pretty much got everything right.

It was very important that the Head Coach appointment after Warburton was right, and sadly we got it wrong. Do we have a better gaffer than Warbs now? I'd say not.

Do I have faith in the Co-Directors of Football?

I didn't like Giles to start with, but in fairness he has become the mouthpiece and has been open and forthright. As for Rasmus? Sorry, but no. We need someone working with Giles who has deep knowledge of and significant contacts within English football.

The team? Very poor recruitment in the summer, especially up front. But not just up front. We are a lot weaker now in all areas other than goalkeeper.

I understand how those ridiculous Parachute Payments have hindered us, but not all the departures were forced.

The Danish effect? I'm really not sure it's helped us, and in fact I'd argue things have gone downhill since attention was divided. Half-and-half scarves? Burn the bloody things.

Matthew Benham? Still a legend without whom we would be unsustainable, a brilliant owner for the club but someone who needs to learn from a number of mistakes over the last year.

I guess we were extremely lucky to have such a fantastic last few years when he was literally beyond reproach, but this doesn't mean he is beyond criticism now. We are so lucky to have a fan as owner, but the whole hierarchy will need to look at this season and think about how they could have done things better.

Lee Carsley? Thanks a million. The form either side of your tenure has been relegation standard. With you it was promotion standard. I hear the season is over already. Sorry, but until we have fifty-two points on the board it isn't. I still remember 1993.

On current form over the last ten games suggests we will only hit this in games forty-one or forty-two.

Graham wrote from America and perhaps distance lends perspective:

Greville – I've been following your blog for many months now and really appreciate your articles and the discussions they provoke.

They allow long-range fans like me to stay connected to all of the ins and outs of following the Bees, so thanks for your tireless efforts!

I did want to comment on the current topic of where the club is headed as, being an exiled Bees supporter (in the US for over twenty years) it seems that from a distance the current season is proving be much more of a rollercoaster than last year which was wonderfully documented in your book.

Other than a couple of weeks in February last year when Warburton's exit was made public, it seemed there was generally a good vibe around the club.

After all, most of us long-suffering fans expected last year to be a battle for survival in the second tier. Once the first few victories were achieved it just felt like a positive continuation of the promotion season with an unimaginable appearance in the playoffs.

This term by contrast started with the preseason excitement of all the new signings, followed by the rapid exit of four key players, ridiculous injuries, Pitchgate, the Marinus debacle etc.

Then it was up again on the back of the Carsley revival, combined with confusion over the Head Coach position. And most recently, the hit-and-miss start to the Smith era and the loss of even more first teamers, if you include Pritchard's loan ending, we have now lost seven of last season's first eleven. With the Tarky strike added for good measure, it's been a pretty draining campaign this year.

So, as many have previously stated, being a long-term Bees supporter, I'll take mid-table in our second season in the Championship in a heartbeat.

Keep in mind of the six clubs promoted in the last two seasons – Brentford are the highest placed (albeit now tied with Wolves) and Rotherham, MK Dons and Bristol City are all in a dogfight at the bottom.

And look at how Doncaster and Yeovil have fared since they both stole promotion from us in 2013.

Establishing a multi-season presence in this league would be a great achievement and a platform to push on from once the new ground is built.

That all said, we definitely need those three extra wins to put any lingering concerns to bed. Then we can enjoy the rest of the season and play the role of spoiler – defeating Fulham in the penultimate game of the season to send them down! We can always dream, right?

Peter Lumley would also like some answers from the club:

We are fast approaching the first anniversary of one of the most controversial days in the club's long history.

It was the day we were told that if Brentford were to successfully compete in future with bigger and wealthier clubs it would have to replace the weaknesses of human judgement and experience with the virtues of statistical analyses.

Unsurprisingly, the consequences of that fateful decision are still with us today. One is that a large segment of the UK's football community is under the impression that Brentford is a club that is at war with itself.

Please can someone at the club put a hand on his heart and tell me that I have got it all wrong? Also that supporters have a good chance of seeing their team reach the Promised Land of Premier League football at Lionel Road by the end of this decade.

Would it be too much to ask the club's owner to give a considered response to the thrust of the comments made by so many loyal and passionate fans?

Spanish Bee had a few points to make:

Being criticised by pundits on Sky TV should be seen as a badge of honour. If you don't believe me ask any fan of Valencia, I can't print what my mates there would say. We should adopt a Millwall attitude, "nobody loves us and we don't care."

The manager is very limited in his options because we don't have a variety of ingredients, as people here have clearly identified, nobody capable of the lone striker role, no ball-winning midfielders and no pace. This would suggest to me that we have a recruitment problem, ironic, no?

If Matthew Benham planned major changes this time last year, how much more important is this year? If we don't get the summer signings right, next season could be very difficult. So who is responsible for recruitment?

Rebel Bee tried to sum everything up:

The huge response to this blog is telling, and whilst there are differing viewpoints there is a lot of consensus too.

Nobody has a bad word to say about Matthew Benham, nobody is unhappy at our mid-table position. Where we all seem to find consensus is exactly where fair questions and debate are needed.

beesyellow22 also saw the bigger picture:

I've stayed out of this until now because pretty much everything's been said. But I guess I'll provide my opinion. Rather boringly, I think I'm probably something of a fence sitter.

I, like all of us, was blown away by what happened last season. Having said that, I was not such a Warburton fan that I wasn't occasionally left frustrated by his apparent lack of a Plan B.

This season promised much and I was quite excited when Marinus was appointed, along with the summer signings.

Marinus went; Carsley came in, things looked good. Then Carsley went (then came back, then went again), then Smith came in.

Thirteen games later, we've won four drawn three and lost six.

Admittedly not a great return, but some slack does need to be cut, as we were extremely unlucky not to beat Fulham, lost to a last minute goal at Cardiff, were again unlucky to lose to Birmingham, played well against lucky Boro, and should have beaten a lacklustre Leeds.

Had those results worked out as a win, a draw, another draw, a win and another win, then Smith's record would read, won seven drawn four and lost only twice, which would have given us all considerably more heart and reasons to be cheerful.

Whilst I fully understand the frustration felt by many Bees supporters at the moment, I am rather uncharacteristically erring on the side of optimism.

I think it is understandable to feel somewhat dejected and perhaps even disillusioned by much of what has transpired this season – particularly when compared to the miracle of 2014/15.

But I do think we still have to put it all into some kind of context. Yes, this season hasn't worked out the way we hoped it would. But surely when we achieved promotion to the promised land when we beat Preston two years ago, most of us would have been extremely delighted were we to then consolidate and become a recognised, established Championship team for three or four seasons, before making a serious and sustained push for the Premiership – ideally in our new stadium.

Of course last season raised expectations – including my own. But memories of 1992/93 remain pretty vivid, and surviving in this massively competitive division for several seasons should not be seen as failure!

Yes, it's been a disappointing season in terms of players that have left, and maybe we as fans should have been better prepared for the exodus in the wake of Warburton parting company with the club.

To lose the outstanding quality of the likes of Odubajo, Gray, Dallas and Tarkowski has been tough to take – but footballers are a fickle bunch and none of the above love the club as we do.

Pritchard was always only going to be with us for one season and Douglas was never going to keep his mouth shut once the writing was on the wall for Warburton.

Losing Jota has been a particular blow, but bad things happens as they say and who knows, perhaps once things settle down for him all will be better and our Spanish maestro will become a Bee once again?

As for players that have come in, Colin looks excellent, Barbet has great potential and Woods is outstanding. Yes, the likes of Gogia, Kerschbaumer, Hofmann, Djuricin and Vibe have question marks hanging over them, but they continue to gain more Championship experience with every game they play and who knows how much better they could all be next season?

It is deeply depressing when we get dismantled the way we did on Friday and even more so when compared to what we did last season.

But the fact is, that was then and this is now. We are in a state of massive transition and we need to be realistic about our goals for this campaign. Will we get into the playoffs? No. Will we get relegated? Probably not. Do we have to stick together as a club and support the team for these final, vital sixteen games? Yes – because we certainly aren't safe yet and we need to carve out four or five more wins to make sure.

Are we allowed to voice our frustration and disapproval about what has happened over the last twelve months? Absolutely. But let's not lose sight of everything we've achieved – and where we all hope we'll be by 2021 – in a fantastic new stadium in the Premiership.

If we achieve that, the disappointments of this season will suddenly seem less disappointing.

David Meyer raised an interesting point too:

I remember seeing the first few league matches under Marinus and thinking, why are we moving so ponderously, where is the speed and movement we had last season?

Then Lee Carsley took over and it was all back. Now we are slowing down again. Our movement off the ball last season and under Carsley threw other teams into confusion, it undermined their tactical plans.

Often they ended up not knowing quite what to do or where we were. Now our every pass is to a player accompanied by a marker, no one is in clear space, stronger players can just edge us off the ball.

Everything is too static. I really hope at some point Dean Smith catches on to this or with the type of players we have, we are going to start sliding.

Let's Wait Until The Summer – 11/2/16

There have been so many comments sent to me over the past few days by Brentford fans eager to give their opinion on the current *stasis* at Griffin Park and thankfully there is a great deal of consensus in terms of an overall sense of understanding about the current lack of transfer activity and the need for the club to husband its limited resources very carefully.

Our supporters are fully prepared to give the Co-Directors of Football the benefit of the doubt and wait until the Summer for the necessary recruitment to take place, however the proof of the pudding will be in the eating, and what the club does or, indeed, doesn't do in the close season in terms of replacing the star players who have already left, and any more who are about to follow in their wake, will speak volumes about the reality of our ambitions and how we are likely to perform in the short term.

That is for the future and in the meantime I am simply going to repeat the words of Phil Giles from his interview last week when he set the scene for what we can expect to see happen in the summer:

We have identified players that we would like to bring in during the summer. Having signed none this window we will look to do more business in the summer.

Some of the players that we would like to bring in are the better players at teams near the top of their divisions. It would be hard for clubs who are currently in promotion battles to countenance selling their best players and we would be the same.

In order for a club to sell in January the value would have to be very high and we are not in a position where we can spend huge money on players. A better strategy is to wait for the summer where better value will be available.

Let's leave it at that for the time being and we will doubtless return to this topic and his words in the light of what actually transpires in the close season.

Garry Smith is a supporter who has been watching the Bees for even longer than I have and he sent me his thoughts on where he believes we are and the journey we are on, and I commend his words to you all.

I don't agree with all of his conclusions but he has certainly written passionately and from the heart about his beloved Brentford and he deserves our attention and respect for doing so:

Thanks for providing this forum. This is a first time contribution to any media site for me and sorry if it is a bit long.

I both agree and disagree with everything I have read!

Maybe I am long in the tooth as my first Bees game was in 1963. Younger as well as an increased number of fans are desperately needed by the club given its fairly recent success and the club's efforts and initiatives and exciting play have been great for an increased fan base.

I sincerely appreciate the enthusiasm of youth and accept that social media is their forum of today. Because of this I fully understand their instantly voiced displeasure when standards dip, however these same fans have not experienced the pain of older supporters who not surprisingly voice their opinions by means of more historical detail. The answer is surely a balance between the enthusiasm of youth and the obvious reality.

Absolutely, I am delighted with our current standing and absolutely; I would have died for this for the last fifty plus years.

Additionally, I do agree that recruitment has been poor this year and yes the worse the season goes, the less that young and more talented players will find us an attractive proposition.

However I would like to give a heartfelt thanks to Matthew Benham, no one in my lifetime has given us more other than possibly the exception of those who saved the club from extinction back in the sixties as well as Bees United.

I truly thank Matthew Benham in the same way that I did Martin Allen when he single-handedly dragged us up from the depths of absolute despair!

This is our unique club, incomparable fans - who else remembers the nonstop singing and support the night we lost in the playoffs to Sheffield Wednesday in 2005? But we are all naturally negative after years of disappointment, occasionally dragged up into positivity and then seeing our hopes so often dashed.

My views on the topics that seem high on the agenda of most of your respondents are as follows:

Mark Warburton and the best players from last year were never going to stay, even if it happened a season later than it did. Last year was a freak and raised all expectation of our rise to fame, far too early. Remember that at the beginning of the season we were all talking about survival. Again I feel that recently recruited, younger supporters were spoiled too soon and are also the most active on social media.

For my money Dougie's leadership is something we have not replaced and because of that, all the responsibility has fallen on Alan Judge, he has always been an exciting player but should not be the fulcrum upon which we totally rely, as teams will try to negate him and it is far too much to ask of one player.

Last season, in a team of great ball players, he was not regarded as our most important player, although I for one thought our form dipped when he got injured. This year, despite a series of magnificent performances from him, we should have had more creative options to support him and thank God he hasn't got injured because then the threat of relegation would have been a reality.

I am actually disappointed in how much we are congratulating ourselves on merely keeping him as he will go at the end of the season and we really should have been recruiting to augment and then even replace his contribution, also we should have been preparing for what will happen next season although I for one am hopeful that Lewis Macleod may help here.

Dean Smith has been in a thankless situation, his record shows he can make the most of what he has, given time. I think he took the job knowing he was moving from one small budget club to another but at a higher level.

Again, post Marinus, younger supporters expected an instant improvement (not helped by the run of fixtures and players willing to try harder for Lee Carsley when he took over) but this was never going to happen with the players available and can I add here I am in no way underestimating Lee Carsley's contribution, what a great job he did with the hand he was dealt, and Dean Smith was never going to be able to carry this on to another season of pressing on for the Premier League.

I couldn't agree more that what happens this close season will be vital to us consolidating a Championship position, but what concerns me a lot more is the perception that getting to Lionel Road is going to be the answer to everything, I truly hope that Matthew Benham and the rest of the management team are not thinking likewise.

I shouldn't need to list the teams like Wigan, Bolton, Reading, MK Dons, Huddersfield, Brighton to prove that newer, bigger, better stadiums don't necessarily ensure better performances, bigger crowds or promotion.

I agree from a perception perspective that the new ground will help our profile and unlike the other teams cited, it could mean higher crowds, increased revenue and better players, however I have been at Griffin Park on so many occasions when it wasn't full with its then available capacity.

I must indulge in a quick bit of nostalgia here though for us oldies, remembering a really happy memory, queueing for an hour and not being able to move in the ground in the one-nil Boxing Day victory over Crewe in the old Fourth Division – "Go Big John" – audaciously described by the club as an eighteen thousand crowd!

Yes, playing with a good team against famous teams will help, but this needs player investment and a consistent competitive league position attained before the anticipated return will follow.

I am going to join the positive crowd here and put my faith in Matthew Benham, but this was a disappointing transfer window, although I think we, whilst missing him for the remainder of the season, made a good call in getting some cash for Toumani.

Also against the weight of opinion I have not been a Tarkowski fan, good on the ball, yes, defensively prone to errors though, mainly through over-adventurousness and an excess of confidence – definitely a problem alongside a player I like, but who is also prone to mistakes in Harlee. This partnership has been a mystery to me for some time now, they are right for a team that wants to play out from the back, but also a definite problem for a team that wants to play with its full backs way up the pitch as I believe that we need fast, intelligent central defenders, who react quickly and know when to use the long ball or hit Row Z if exposed to danger.

I am convinced that Matthew Benham thinks that we have enough points and good enough players to stay in the Championship this season, he has a potentially good Head Coach, some returning players, and good amount in the war chest without wasting it on overpriced players in the January Transfer Window.

Sadly and hopefully there will be a good transfer fee coming for Alan Judge and we all hope that there will be plenty of time and cash to allow us to build for the start of next season.

Let's hope we make a bold but balanced impression in the transfer and loan market next season like we did last season.

To finish on this subject it would have been nice to have seen a mid-season punt on a Sam Winnall or Nahki Wells, fox-in-the-box type player to get on the end of the numerous crosses we keep sending into the area with nobody near them. Here's hoping for next season.

A View From Afar – 13/2/16

It is always wonderful to hear from a member of the Brentford family who lives far away from Griffin Park and Graham Tyrrell certainly qualifies as he has spent the last twenty years ensconced in the United States of America.

Distance certainly seems to lend a sense of perspective and detachment and from what he has written below it is quite obvious that Graham is an astute, perceptive and knowledgeable supporter who maintains his love and passion for the club despite the thousands of miles that separate him from TW8.

Here are his memories of being a Brentford supporter for the last thirty years, and given that I found myself marooned in New York for three years in the mid-80s, far away from my beloved Brentford FC, I can quite empathise with the problems Graham also faced in doing his utmost to keep in touch with everything that was going on at the club as I shared the identical frustrations in those pre-internet days of trying to work with all manner of obsolete technology that was patently not yet up to the job:

I've been a Bees supporter since the mid-80s.

One of my first games was the Freight Rover Trophy final against Wigan – a precursor to three decades of Wembley misery.

I moved to the US permanently in 1994. So that makes it one decade of living and breathing Brentford FC at close hand and two decades of following their ups and downs from afar.

During this time I can safely say my loyalty to the club hasn't wavered once. But it definitely requires a different type of loyalty compared to that exhibited by the amazing fans who spend serious amounts of time and money going to games home and away every week.

To begin with, following a club like Brentford required creativity and patience. In 1994, the internet barely existed and was certainly not the endless wealth of information it has become today. This meant that the primary sources of any Brentford news were the BBC World Service (on the elusive long wave) and Richmond & Twickenham Times clippings sent by my Mum generally arriving about ten days after the games.

Over time the options to stay in touch with the Bees have grown massively. Initially, the internet at least provided live score updates of sorts but that was basically like watching Teletext.

Eventually, once the BBC started putting all of their radio content online – I soon realized I could happily listen to BBC Radio London and the wonderful Billy Reeves. At first this entailed lugging my laptop around the house and hoping the Wi-Fi wouldn't cut out just as the panic-inducing words "there's been a goal at Griffin Park" were announced.

Today, by contrast, I can get the whole thing on my phone whilst walking the dogs or cleaning the car, you name it. Then there's BFC Talk, Beesotted and YouTube highlights providing a great insight into how the team are performing and what the fans are thinking.

The personal emotional rollercoaster is much the same. Standing in stunned silence in my dining room after Trotta's penalty miss unable to comprehend what just happened or showing up to a business meeting with a huge grin after the demolition of Fulham last year, being just a couple of examples.

Last season of course elevated the Bees to the second tier and this made explaining which team I support a whole lot easier. "We're in the league below the Premier League – you know, like Bournemouth were last year and Aston Villa will be next year."

They're also occasionally on TV – the Boro playoff games for example. So to me, as an exiled fan, this higher profile and media coverage is just another important element of having Brentford in the Championship and is a bit like skipping the first two FA Cup rounds. And for that, hearty thanks are due to Matthew Benham and Mark Warburton for getting us there.

As for debate on whether we are moving in the right direction this term, I would say, looking at it from distance, yes, given the highly competitive environment.

It's an oddity in some ways that US sports leagues tend to be almost controlled economies with salary caps and drafts of new talent, whereas English football is capitalism at its finest – with one significant perversion.

The Premier League now pays off the losers who are relegated. As we all know, this means the teams dropping down have a huge financial advantage and can cherry-pick players from the competition. Given that environment and the fact Mr. Benham is wealthy but not an oligarch or a sovereign wealth fund I feel the Bees are doing very well to compete with the big boys.

As has been stated in your blog, last year the stars aligned. In my mind Warburton deserves a huge portion of credit for this. He clearly has great man-management skills and works well with David Weir to get the best out of players. I think his background in business, as well as football, has given him a unique skill set and perhaps a model for others to follow?

However, in retrospect, it does seem that other teams figured us out after half a season and those with the cash started circling our best players, an issue Warburton would have faced also. A big disappointment is that they have all gone to other Championship clubs – but again that's the harsh reality.

One thing that I didn't see too much mention of is the fact that we have (potentially) two big players to come in next season before we ever spend a pound of the incoming transfer funds in Bjelland and Hogan. Admittedly both are unproven in this league and both had ACLs, which can sometimes never truly be recovered from, but let's hope both guys prove to be great new signings next season along with the ever-elusive Mr. Macleod.

So here's hoping for a strong start to next year in the Championship of course!

Naturally, the single biggest challenge of being an overseas supporter is not being able see a live game and it's too bad that I'll probably never see Jota ply his trade in a Brentford shirt or a Dallas screamer.

I'm really hoping I can make it back for one more game at Griffin Park before it is torn down. And assuming I do, I know the other fans will welcome a guy with a funny Anglo-American accent – because it's always been a great and friendly club with pubs on the corners.

Plus I'll be wearing my 1985 Freight Rover Final scarf, so I must be legit!

Thank you Graham for your excellent contribution which I hope that everyone enjoys as much as I did.

A View From The Swimming Pool – 14/2/16

Well it all started so well, as I managed to grab a sun lounger right by the side of the pool and listened with relish to QPR's humiliation at the hands of their near neighbours, Fulham.

If truth be told I was slightly conflicted about that one but felt on reflection that Fulham's victory was probably the best possible result overall given that the rules didn't allow both teams to lose.

Now it was Brentford's turn and everything was going like clockwork as Mark Burridge's dulcet tones on *Bees Player* came over loud and clear and I looked forward to listening to a description of an improved display after the capitulation at Brighton.

I couldn't really question the team selection. Hofmann deserved his opportunity after neither Vibe nor Djuricin had fully convinced lately and Yennaris and Canos would ideally provide us with legs and enthusiasm and some support for a striker who is not the most mobile.

It all started well with early chances for Yennaris, one that he should surely have taken, and Judge, before disaster struck after a mere five minutes with a long ball over the top being chased by Hooper with Barbet trailing in his wake.

The ball ran through harmlessly to Button but the coming together of Hooper and Barbet on the edge of the area was instantly adjudged a red card offence by a referee still in the Brentford half with no apparent clear view of the incident and who made an instantaneous and game-changing decision without feeling the need to consult his assistant who was up with play and had not signalled for a foul.

A red card it was and as Barbet reluctantly dragged himself off the pitch, Dean Smith's carefully worked game plan was in tatters almost before the game had started.

The Bees switched to a 4-4-1 formation, which in cruel reality meant 4-4-0 as Hofmann, isolated and outnumbered, disappeared from sight and left us without any real attacking outlet. More crucially, Brentford no longer had an out-ball or anyone capable of holding the ball up and giving a beleaguered defence some respite or any much needed time to reorganise or take a breather.

In retrospect I wonder if it would have been better had we withdrawn Hofmann rather than the unfortunate Kerschbaumer and concentrated on packing the midfield?

Sheffield Wednesday smelled blood and attacked relentlessly and it was now simply a question of whether a revamped Brentford back four with substitute Jack O'Connell now partnering Harlee Dean, could defend properly and keep them at bay.

Well the spirit was willing but the flesh was weak as it quickly became obvious that it was a merely a matter of how soon and how many.

Brentford shipped three soft goals before halftime and they all owed as much to muddled and inept defending as they did to attacking brilliance.

The second half was a damp squib as we concentrated upon damage limitation and the Bees avoided further embarrassment until the last minute when David Button conceded a fourth goal from an eminently saveable effort.

Our Man of the Match was Mark Burridge who played an absolute blinder. He succeeded in describing the shambles on the pitch without either gilding the lily or indulging in destructive criticism. He simply told it as it was and did an expert and professional job.

What is quite apparent is that this is now a team increasingly bereft of confidence, shorn of some of its best players, that is simply trying to limp through the remainder of the season unscathed until major squad surgery can be scheduled in the summer.

I have already written at length about the rationale for such a reactive and seemingly unambitious strategy and I am not about to change my tune and criticise it as I well understand and accept why we are now in this position.

What I find of more concern is whether the players that currently remain available to us are fully capable of achieving what I feel are the two minimum requirements for the remainder of the season of keeping us competitive and maintaining interest and excitement amongst an increasingly concerned, demanding and critical fan base.

I am firmly of the view that sometimes it is necessary to take a backwards step in order to progress and now is certainly a case in point.

Our future progress is predicated totally on a combination of how well we clean the stables and how effectively we recruit fresh blood in the close season.

The last third of the current campaign is far too long to stand still and simply tread water and ideally we should be using the time to test out new formations, discover more about the players that remain and whether we should maintain faith in them, and ideally concentrate on improving them and eradicating some of the careless errors that punctuate our play from week to week.

All that in conjunction with winning some matches and keeping the fans interested, entertained and involved rather than counting off the days until the end of the season and looking over our shoulder at the teams below us.

It is unfair to read too much into a match where the luck was against us and we went a key man down so early on and it is not so long ago that we comprehensively outplayed Preston on their own patch, so it is premature to panic but it cannot be denied that there are some worrying signs and that the warning bells are beginning to jangle.

What is particularly concerning is that the same worrying traits reoccur with monotonous regularity week after week and we don't seem to learn from our mistakes or show many signs of improvement.

We have now conceded nine goals in the last four games and it would be hard to credit our opponents for any of them as they were all caused to a greater or lesser extent by avoidable individual errors.

We are a soft touch at the back and have not kept a clean sheet since Boxing Day and have never really looked like doing so. We lack pace in central defence and are horribly vulnerable to long balls over the top as was clearly demonstrated by the horror show of a second goal yesterday which came from a long, straight goal kick which was criminally allowed to bounce before Hooper showed great skill and anticipation to score with an instant volley.

I would have thought that defensive solidity would have been a coaching priority in training and I'm sure that it is, but our efforts do not seem to be having much effect where it matters, out on the pitch.

There seems to be a lack of cohesion and we do not have mini partnerships developing on the pitch similar to the one, for example, between Odubajo and Jota last season and it would be so helpful if Colin and Bidwell could develop a similar relationship with a wide midfielder as it all looks so disjointed at the moment.

Dean Smith is beginning to take on a haunted look and I feel sorry for him as he can only work with what he has got.

Maxime Colin - brilliant all season

Hopefully he can entice some pace, tempo and brio from a midfield quintet that looks slow, weak, small and overmatched although Yennaris looked more than comfortable in his new role.

Personally I believe that much of the problem stems from a lack of confidence that will only be restored by a win or two.

I am not so sure though if we can either rehabilitate or get much more out of our three ailing strikers, none of whom has contributed a jot since the turn of the year.

Leaving aside the screamingly obvious fact that our favoured 4-2-3-1 formation suits none of them, Vibe is shattered after a year of nonstop activity, Djuricin has shown nothing since his return from injury and Hofmann has much to do to prove himself after a performance of appalling sloth and ineptitude yesterday.

Unless Dean Smith or Richard O'Kelly are miracle workers I honestly have no idea how we can squeeze some performances, let alone goals, out of any of them.

Maybe the answer is to attempt to shake things up by bringing in a couple of short-term loanees who can ideally plug a few gaps and provide a fresh impetus or something different?

Perhaps Alan McCormack will return shortly from injury and add some much-needed steel and competitive edge?

Forgive me for even mentioning this but I also feel that we are too naïve and nice. Every team we play seems to make a habit of committing strategic fouls which frustratingly nip our threat in the bud. Alan Judge has been a particular victim of this practice recently, and perhaps we need to follow suit where necessary.

As you all can see, all I have are questions and concerns and no real answers, and maybe we simply have to accept the situation for what it is and just do our best to be patient and fight our way out of it and wait for our luck to change, as it most assuredly will.

I have been supporting Brentford long enough to be more than grateful for our place in the Championship and am happy for us to consolidate slowly and gradually.

What does worry me is if we are not competitive.

We now have two eminently winnable home games coming up against a Derby County team in free fall and Wolves.

Let's see where we are after these two matches before we get too concerned.

Two good performances and a minimum of four points gained would go a long way towards restoring our faith as well as a sense of calm, trust and patience.

Good News! – 17/2/16

Good news has been scarce, sparse and rather thin on the ground lately given Brentford's patchy start to the New Year, so let's shout it from the rooftops – Harlee Dean and Nico Yennaris have both joined Sam Saunders in extending their contract with the club, Harlee for two years and Nico until 2019.

Given the recent departure for a variety of reasons of Jota, Toumani Diagouraga and James Tarkowski and the accompanying uncertainty surrounding other squad members, it is encouraging to say the least to learn that two established players have decided to buy into the club's stated determination to rebuild and strengthen the squad at the end of the season and thus remain part of the Brentford project.

We certainly needed to hear something positive this week following the avalanche of unanswered goals rippling our net recently and for differing reasons we should be absolutely delighted that both Harlee and Nico have staked their immediate future with the club.

Up until very recently I suspect that you could have obtained long odds on Dean making the decision to stay, as he and the football club appeared to have fallen out of love with each other and a parting of the ways seemed inevitable.

Harlee perhaps felt that he didn't receive the respect that he deserved as well as maybe coveting the salaries received by several other Brentford *alumni* elsewhere. He had also oft-bemoaned the fact that felt that he was the scapegoat and the one generally to be blamed and dropped when things went awry.

On the other side of the fence Harlee's tendency to shoot from the hip and give vent to his feelings about all sorts of matters pertaining to the club, sometimes before apparently engaging his brain, did not apparently go down too well in some rarefied circles and there appeared to be a Mexican standoff with the club not seeming to be making serious efforts to re-sign him and the player stating that he would be leaving at the end of the current season when his contract expired, although he was hoping that something could still be worked out.

What was never in any doubt was the fact that Harlee would continue to give his all on the pitch and he has certainly done his utmost to put his finger in the dyke and try and stem the flood of goals that we have conceded.

Harlee wears his heart on his sleeve on the pitch (and off it too) and he has jumped, headed, tackled and covered to the best of his ability and has visibly improved as a footballer over the last couple of years and at twenty-four still has the potential to progress even further. He also looks far leaner and fitter than was the case previously.

He seems to have learned from his impetuous reaction that saw him punished with a daft and totally avoidable and unacceptable red card against Nottingham Forest and has become a calming influence and a leader to those around him. He also reads the game far better which enables him to use and exemplify the old adage that *the first yard is in the head* and cover up his lack of pace.

He is now a proven and accomplished Championship central defender who anticipates and snuffs out much of the danger that threatens us and he has also gained confidence in the attacking system he has been asked to play in and has become an accurate long and short passer of the ball.

Thankfully he is yet to attempt Tarkowski-esque dummies and feints as he brings the ball out of defence and he is a footballer who is equally aware of his strengths and limitations.

So what happened to bring about this *volte-face?*

On the one hand the club needed a quick triumph this week to reassure supporters given the setbacks of the past month or so, and Harlee re-signing has provided a statement of intent given that a senior, well-established player who is also a firm fans' favourite has not followed the general exodus out of Brentford FC but has seen and heard enough about our future plans and aspirations to decide to stay.

This decision also demonstrates that the opinions and wishes of Dean Smith are being listened to as he had made it clear that he wanted to have Harlee on board for next season and beyond.

The sale of Tarkowski meant that Harlee was the only senior right-sided centre half at the club and therefore an even more valuable property than had been the case previously.

Despite his all-round improvement Harlee might not have been seen as a player good enough to help take us to the heights of the Premier League and perhaps his continued stay at the club reflects that our ambitions have to some degree been put on hold or made more realistic until the move to Lionel Road comes to fruition.

I now wonder if we will attempt to bring in another defender to compete with him, such as Gillingham's John Egan, whose name has been bandied about, or whether Harlee will be seen as the undisputed first choice next season?

Hopefully Andreas Bjelland will be fit enough to play alongside him and Harlee will benefit from having an experienced partner, as he did when Tony Craig was there to support, encourage and prompt him.

Harlee excites and frustrates me in equal proportions, but I respect him for his passion and commitment and I am pleased that one of the few remaining members of the old guard will still be with us next season.

He really gets what Brentford is all about, he knows how much beating Fulham and QPR means to us all and he is a fighter and a warrior. We need more like him in the squad.

Let's just hope that he finally becomes more of a danger to the opposition at our set pieces. That Wembley header seems a long time ago now but his Fulham thunderbolt will live long in the memory.

The announcement that Nico Yennaris will remain for a further three years was not greeted as effusively by many Brentford supporters but I really can't see what they have to complain about.

Nico arrived a couple of years ago from Arsenal and given his Premier League pedigree, expectations were high but he was a damp squib, unable to displace Alan McCormack after Shay Logan's departure and he fell into the shadows where he remained until Max Colin suffered a long-term injury earlier this season.

He had also enjoyed a successful loan spell last season at Wycombe Wanderers alongside Sam Saunders and played in their losing Playoff Final against Southend United. Some were even surprised that he wasn't unloaded permanently but he returned to Brentford patiently waiting his turn.

When it came he more than seized his opportunity and Colin was hardly missed as Nico put in a series of eye-opening and dominating displays where he showed pace, strength and tenacity and he was more than unfortunate to lose his place when the Frenchman returned.

He remains in and around the team and filled in last Saturday in central midfield and came close to opening his goal account and I have a suspicion that Dean Smith will try him out more often in that role over the next few weeks as he continues to seek a winning blend in midfield.

He has certainly demonstrated that he is quite good enough a player to cope with the demands of the Championship although fans expressed a view that signing Nico to a new contract shows a sign of lack of ambition.

To that I would respond that every successful team requires a player who can slot in well in a variety of positions without fuss or complaint whenever necessary and Nico fits that bill perfectly.

He is still very young at twenty-two and is visibly improving as he gains in confidence and might yet develop into a first team regular.

At present I see him as a versatile water carrier and do not expect to see him as a regular first choice but rather as a squad player *deluxe* who will do a fine job whenever and wherever he is called upon and having him breathing down their neck will help ensure that everybody else maintains their standard.

So, some good news at last for all Brentford supporters which will hopefully go some way towards allaying our slight concerns at our current situation.

All we need now is three points on Saturday as well as the likes of David Button and Jake Bidwell to follow in the footsteps of Harlee and Nico – surely that is not too much to ask for?

Benham's Gamble – 21/2/16

Three weeks ago, as soon as the Transfer Window closed with us three first team players down and the squad weakened and diminished, I described Brentford's likely approach for the last three months of the season as follows:

Our strategy for the remainder of the season seems to be quite simply to hunker down, retreat into our bunker, make do with what we are left with and simply count off the days and get through the season before readdressing matters in the summer and hopefully coming again next season.

I thought very carefully before I gave such a damning judgement and even did my best to verify my words and opinion before I committed them to paper and, indeed, I was assured by a very senior club contact that my assessment was entirely correct.

At the time I fully understood the rationale behind such an apparently negative and craven policy given our financial constraints and the fact that our transfer targets in January had all eluded us and we were quite simply not prepared to pay over the odds.

I realised that the majority of the supporters would not be happy, but I made the point that as long as we remained competitive on the pitch and continued to play our customary brand of exciting attacking football and won more than we lost, then perhaps we would be able to muddle through without getting holed below the waterline.

So what has happened since? Has the gamble paid off?

We have faced (I hesitate the use the word *played*) three of the leading Championship teams in Brighton, Sheffield Wednesday and Derby County and have emerged with our tails firmly between our legs after three heavy defeats with only one goal scored and a massive ten conceded.

It could be argued that, given our weakened and parlous state, all of these defeats should have been anticipated and we simply have to revise and lower our expectations and just accept that for the time being we are unable to match teams of that calibre.

If you take this line of thinking further then it would also be entirely fair to say that we should be patient, and delay further judgement until the fifth of March by which time we will have played against three more teams in Wolverhampton Wanderers, who are on the same amount of points as the Bees, Rotherham and Charlton whom we have all beaten already this season and in the case of the last two are engaged in a desperate fight to avoid relegation.

Five points or more from these games would perhaps confirm that we will be able to bumble along for the rest of the season and continue to hold our own and still finish in a reasonable position in the Championship table.

That is all for the near future and we will certainly know far more about our short-term prospects in a fortnight's time but the prospect, however unlikely, of losing the next three games against teams whom we would normally expect to beat is both worrying and frightening as our last three defeats have highlighted and confirmed that without mincing words, we are in a sorry and shambolic state at the moment.

Yesterday's three-one defeat against Derby was a case in point. Afterwards, manager Dean Smith argued about narrow margins, and the fact that the game had turned on a couple of key incidents and that the final score could quite easily have been different.

Superficially and on a cursory glance, he is, indeed, quite correct in what he said. Had the officials penalised Tom Ince for handball when the ball crashed against him before bouncing unerringly to the unmarked Hendrick who equalised with ten minutes to go and if Bidwell's last gasp header had not been stopped by a combination of the swooping Scott Carson and Jacob Butterfield on the goal line then we would have come away with at least a draw and Chris Martin's three-on-one breakaway goal with the last kick of the match would surely never have happened.

I am afraid that I will not buy or accept that explanation or reading of the match, neither, I suspect will the overwhelming majority of Brentford fans. We were absolutely battered in the first half where we played more like the away team, and a poor one at that.

We adopted a negative 4-1-4-1 formation with Yennaris sweeping up in front of the back four which featured O'Connell for the suspended Barbet. Woods moved to the right side of midfield with McEachran and Judge in the middle and the ineffable Kerschbaumer on the left, and Vibe replaced Hofmann up front.

We were playing a Derby County team packed with expensive talent but also totally devoid of confidence after collecting a mere three points in their first six games of 2016.

Surely we should have had a go at them, given that we also desperately needed a win and were playing at home, but instead we set up in total damage limitation mode with no width or visible attacking intention? Yes, we certainly needed to tighten up after conceding so many soft goals recently, but surely not at all costs, as seemed the case yesterday where it appeared that a goalless draw was the summit of our ambitions.

We did threaten three times before the break, ironically all from set pieces, which worked extremely well yesterday, a rare positive to take out of the game.

Yennaris was unable to get any power on a free header and then a beautifully worked and inventive corner kick routine (poached from the AFC Bournemouth playbook, I believe) saw the ball cut back hard and low towards the edge of the box, Kerschbaumer jumped over the ball and Judge had the time and space for a firm and well-placed effort that forced Carson into a decent save.

Our best opportunity came when O'Connell stole in at the back post behind the straining Derby defence, and with Bradley Johnson hanging off him, could only head Judge's clever free kick back across goal and narrowly wide of the far post.

Otherwise it was a procession towards the home goal as Derby ran rings around us, quick to outmuscle us and pick up the second balls, winning the majority of the challenges and playing around and through us with a series of incisive one-twos.

Poor Lasse Vibe must have had a contagious disease, so isolated was he and we were barely able to get the ball out of our own half of the pitch.

Derby would have been out of sight and home and hosed had it not been for David Button who played Derby County on his own and made five exceptional first half saves, including keeping out Bidwell's involuntary close range poke towards his own goal. He also thwarted Hendrick twice in close succession, Bent, and most memorably, Russell when the keeper somehow kept out a perfectly placed effort arrowing towards the far corner.

Quite frankly, we got out of jail and could and should have slunk off the field three goals down at the interval so weak and inept had been our performance.

To give Dean Smith his due, he changed our approach after the break and tried to get the team to play more in the Derby half and stretch the two lumbering central defenders who had enjoyed a totally untroubled game to date.

Our efforts were rewarded after fifty-two minutes when Alan Judge scored a goal entirely of his making when he robbed Hanson in midfield and roared down the right flank. He could not be caught and although forced wide he hit a brilliantly angled shot that screamed past Carson for a goal of total and utter brilliance.

The game had turned in an instant and surely the Bees would take full advantage as confidence suddenly flowed through hesitant limbs and Derby heads went down?

Well, yes and no as we kept the visitors away from Button who was able to take a well-earned breather, but we never seemed to have the self-belief or incision to go for the jugular and seek the second goal that would surely have cemented victory.

Substitutions also played a crucial part in the outcome of the match. Given the depth of their squad, Derby were able to bring on players of the calibre of Martin, Ince and Blackman whereas we were restricted to the likes of the be-gloved Swift, Djuricin and Canos.

Slowly and inexorably we dropped twenty yards and retreated deeper and deeper into our shell and this seemed a self-inflicted move entirely of our own making rather than being caused by the sheer force of Derby pressure.

Where was the manager at this crucial point of the proceedings to encourage and exhort us to move up the field?

From a winning position, however unexpected and undeserved, we unforgivably conceded the initiative and invited Derby onto us, and the inevitable occurred with two quick goals turning the game, once again, on its head.

Job seemingly done, Derby now made a similar error of judgement, sat back, ceded us the initiative and we dominated the last five minutes and should have scored four times.

Djuricin has lacked fitness and sharpness but he surely had to convert one of the two glaring chances that came his way, but he ballooned a snap shot high over and then criminally put his close range near post diving header over the goal with the net beckoning.

Keogh almost deflected a cross into his own net and then Bidwell's header from a Judge corner seemed to be arrowing its way in before being hacked off the line before Martin stole away to thrust the final dagger in our heart and seal the victory.

On the one hand we could have been looking at a thrashing had Button not performed his heroics but we were then unable to seize the opportunity to win the match when it unexpectedly presented itself to us.

This was not a Brentford performance as we have become accustomed to see and enjoy and we seem to have totally lost our way.

The defence is nervous and porous. The midfield where only Woods and Yennaris make any apparent effort to cover and tackle, does not protect the back four and lacks width and pace.

McEachran is a luxury that we cannot afford as for all his skill on the ball he is a totally one-dimensional player who contributes nothing to our defensive efforts and Kerschbaumer flitted in and out of the match to little apparent effect as well as carelessly losing his man when Christie scored the crucial second goal.

We have completely lost our pace, brio and incision. There was one isolated incident in the second half when we combined quickly down the left and almost tore the opposition wide apart before the move broke down on the edge of the penalty area but that was a rare exception to our plodding mediocrity.

Vibe improved after the break when he received some limited service and used his pace to stretch the Derby back four, but we were slow and stilted in our play, and perish the thought, more resembled a mid-table Division One team than a Championship squad renowned for its invention and skill on the ball.

It surely cannot be denied that the team which won promotion in 2014 was far stronger in both midfield and attack, boasting as it did the likes of Forshaw, Saville, Douglas, Judge, Donaldson and Trotta, than is our current motley crew.

The Brentford that we know and love, cocking a snook, outplaying, out-working and out-pressing our so-called betters has disappeared without trace for the time being at least and Ian Holloway, so often an admirer of our approach, has also noticed and remarked upon the difference in our recent play:

Brentford don't look the same this season. They have lost their midfield security after selling Toumani Diagouraga. This time last year they had Jonathan Douglas and Diagouraga and now they have Josh McEachran from Chelsea and he doesn't provide the same protection. They have started to leak goals, which is not good.

Salutary words that we would do well to take notice of and act upon.

Three statistics merely confirm our current malaise. Yesterday we only had a possession rate of forty-two per cent and, more worryingly, we only played one hundred and sixty-two passes, less than half our normal number, and our pass completion percentage was a pathetic sixty-one, which implies that we played far more hit and hope long balls than normal.

As I said, that is not the Brentford that we want or expect to see.

Leaving aside some of the extremists on social media who have a totally unrealistic sense of expectation, there were far more worrying mutterings in my earshot coming from some of the hard core supporters both at halftime and as they left the ground feeling flat and deflated.

Most were bemused at how far and how quickly we have fallen and there was a sense of despondency and in some cases a reluctance to return to Griffin Park for the time being. This is worrying in the extreme.

Let's face facts, we have taken a gamble, an educated guess that we already have enough points on the board and just about enough left in our tank to get us over the line, crawling if necessary, without sliding inexorably into relegation trouble, or indeed, perish the thought, the dreaded bottom three.

Everything Matthew Benham does is calculated and the fact that you can still get odds of two hundred and fifty to one against the Bees going down suggests that he has got it right yet again but this is a bet that he cannot afford to lose and even if it comes off what will have been its overall cost?

Our supporters rightly pay good money to watch a team compete and play a brand of football that stirs the soul and warms the heart. That is not happening at the moment and quite frankly seems a long way away for the time being.

I am not sure what else can be done now. We are stuck with a weak and unbalanced squad that currently appears unable to play the Brentford way. The decision has been taken not to go into either the transfer or now the loan market and even should we change our mind and attempt to bolster the squad I have serious doubts as to whether we could at this late stage obtain short-term recruits who could provide the quality, steel, impact and experience that we need.

We are now hoist with our own petard and will simply have to see how matters turn out and if Dean Smith is capable of organising and motivating his limited squad and getting them to put on performances of the necessary quality.

It is harsh and totally unfair to criticise a manager who has not been given the opportunity to build or put his own stamp on his squad but I would like to see far more from him in terms of how he selects his team and sets them up.

We need to toughen up and become less of an easy touch but also maintain a sense of invention and positivity.

Not an easy task at the moment and I am sure that much will be revealed and become apparent over the next fortnight.

Pitbulls Or Chihuahuas? The Midfield Dilemma – 23/2/16

I could barely take my eyes off Bradley Johnson on Saturday as he rampaged unchallenged across the Griffin Park turf, and woe betide anyone, friend or foe, who got in his way. A massively built man, he totally dominated the entire midfield area with an unstoppable combination of brain and brawn.

If he could not beat you with his subtlety and skill, and undoubtedly, he is a massively talented footballer with a howitzer of a shot who can really play the game, he would simply run through you and leave you dazed, beaten, bruised and helpless.

He is a veritable behemoth of a man who reminds me of the description of the Norman leader Bohemond:

The sight of him inspired admiration, the mention of his name terror.

His stature was such that he towered almost a full cubit over the tallest men.

There was a hard, savage quality in his whole aspect, even his laugh sounded like a threat to others.

That's what you get for a mere six million pounds – a colossus who bestrides the entire midfield and stops the opposition from playing as well as scoring and making goals for his own team.

He it was who almost single-handedly rallied his Derby team mates when their heads went down after we scored and by the sheer force of his personality, raised them off the floor and inspired them to their late victory.

Watching him, I was green with envy as he exemplified exactly what it is we are missing from our squad – a leader who by force of personal example will make things happen and grab his team mates literally and figuratively by the scruff of their neck and inspire, cajole, or even terrify them and make them play to the very best of their ability – and even beyond.

Our team of lightweights and midgets tried their hardest and did their best but simply bounced off him and the likes of Josh McEachran and Konstantin Kerschbaumer wisely gave him a wide berth and kept their distance as they were all totally outmatched, outclassed and outmuscled – it looked more like men against boys than a competitive and even midfield battle.

With Alan McCormack currently sidelined with a lingering and frustrating calf injury we have nobody capable of fighting fire with fire and for all his vim, growl, tough tackling, energy and ability to manage the referee, Alan is not in the same class as Johnson, and nor should he be expected to be, but he is easily the best that we have, and his example is sadly missed as we currently find ourselves on a run of demoralising defeats and badly lack the type of leadership and inspiration on the pitch that Alan can provide.

Jonathan Douglas performed a similar role exceptionally well for four years. He is unfairly described on *Wikipedia* as a *tenacious midfielder, whose strengths are focused on energy and aggression rather than technical skill*, as in my opinion he greatly improved as a footballer last season, developing a subtle and imaginative touch with his passing as well as the ability to ghost late and unseen into the penalty area, and he scored a career high of eight goals in a season.

Douglas it was who fought and won the majority of the midfield battles and his menacing presence enabled the likes of Pritchard, Jota and Judge to weave their magic safe in the knowledge that there was somebody around to protect them and exact retribution should an opponent take it upon himself to attempt to stop them playing by fair means or foul.

Even more importantly, Douglas, along with Toumani Diagouraga, acted as a shield and protector to the back four and helped keep opponents at a safe distance from our goal.

In order to describe how much we currently miss his influence I will simply provide the following shocking statistic – no Championship side has faced more shots on target this season than Brentford - one hundred and sixty-eight in all.

Proof indeed that as a team, we are not doing nearly a good enough job of defending from the front, pressing properly, winning the ball back and, of course, preventing the opposition from getting within shooting range.

Jonathan Douglas was an exceptional on-pitch leader who led by example and only slowed up and became tired and less influential when he was overplayed by Mark Warburton and only once rested last season when he was fit or available for selection. Not the most sensible policy for a player in his early thirties who would have benefited from the odd day off.

For reasons probably linked to his influence within the dressing room, Douglas outstayed his welcome at Brentford, his face didn't fit and he became toxic and *persona non grata* and was released in the preseason, and it has come as little surprise that he has since flourished at Ipswich Town where he has played an important part in their efforts to reach the playoffs again at the end of the season.

It would seem that our current manager and Co-Directors of Football have not recognised the urgent, and to us fans, patently obvious, need to replace him with a similar type of player and we have certainly seen the results of that totally misguided policy in terms of the sheer number of goals and shots conceded at one end allied to the lack of creativity at the other.

To be fair to them, it might well be that they believe that such a player able to compete at Championship level and combine skill with strength would cost far more than we are able to afford and there is no point in buying a second rate bruiser who will only give the ball away once he has won it.

George Evans might have done the job had we managed to get his transfer over the line but we seem to hold the naïve belief that pure football will always win the day and appear to disregard the indisputable fact that sometimes you have first to battle in order to win the right to play.

Ryan Woods is certainly an excellent box-to-box footballer but is not a ball winner and he is currently paired with Josh McEachran who, for all his skill on the ball, vision and passing ability, is a non-tackler and does not pay anywhere near sufficient attention to the defensive side of his game. A total recipe for disaster.

This season we have lacked a focal point, an on-field leader and inspiration, and someone with the ability to drive us forward and pick us up when things are going badly.

The time was, not so long ago, when we scored late goals as if by rote and never knew when we were beaten. Now the boot is on the other foot and it is rare that we recover from going a goal down and we have now conceded late goals in each of our last four matches.

Tony Cascarino hit the nail on the head the other day when he discussed the Championship and what you need to come out on top in that division, and remarked:

It's dog-eat-dog in that league and you need a few pitbulls.

Players like Grant Leadbitter and Adam Clayton at Middlesbrough who ride roughshod over us whenever we come up against them, Darren Pratley, Hope Akpan, Dale Stephens, Joey Barton, Jacob Butterfield, George Thorne, Henri Lansbury and Kevin McDonald all combine the qualities that we so sadly lack and so desperately need.

Unfortunately all we have at the moment, apart of course from Alan McCormack, are Chihuahuas.

A Good Night – 24/2/16

What a difference a few days make. On Saturday Brentford were clearly second best to Derby County but still managed to throw away an unexpected opportunity to win the game and we left the ground morose and concerned.

Last night I floated on air to my car, my face wreathed with smiles, both from pleasure and also, it has to be said, a fair bit of relief after the Bees totally outplayed Wolverhampton Wanderers and coasted to a three-goal victory, our first at home this year.

Make no mistake about it, Brentford were very, very good on the night and ran rings round a Wolves team that was totally unable to cope with our pace, poise, invention and attacking incision.

Wolves, it must be said were totally inept and wandered round the pitch in a trance, as if mesmerised by the sheer quality of our performance.

I well remember a slovenly Walsall team similarly going through the motions at Griffin Park way back in January 2006 when it was patently obvious that they were not playing for their then manager, Paul Merson, who was swiftly jettisoned, and quite frankly I fear for the future of the esteemed Kenny Jackett if last night is anything to go by, as his team appeared uninterested, disorganised and disinclined to sweat or even get out of first gear.

Brentford scented blood and started out on the front foot and soon forced their opponents back.

Dean Smith had learned his lesson from Saturday and chose a far more balanced and attacking team with Judge, Swift and Canos all given license to get forward and down the flanks to run at a slow and porous defence that was swiftly overrun.

The visitors had chances on the break and Button made two early, but comfortable saves but it was predominantly one-way traffic with Swift gliding past opponents at will and Canos destroying them with his pace. A young colt brimming with energy and enthusiasm, he roamed both flanks and was a constant source of danger, heading just over and twice forcing saves from Ikeme.

Unlike Derby, who pressed us relentlessly and never gave us a moment's peace on the ball, Wolves gave us the room, space and time to play, and without having to deal with massive opponents right in their face, Woods and McEachran took full advantage and pulled all the strings in midfield, driving us forward relentlessly.

Woods was a terrier, snapping at the ankles of his opponents and demonstrating his entire range of passes, both long and short.

Josh too showed that when given room he is a match winner and he both sees and finds passes that are totally beyond the wit, vision and imagination of most players at this level of the game.

The first goal was crucial as you felt that our jaunty confidence was only skin deep and would quickly evaporate if we fell behind particularly after playing so well.

Chances came and went with Judge cracking a shot onto the outside of the post, Swift forcing a flying save from Ikeme and Djuricin finding a perplexing and frustrating variety of ways to miss the target, but our fears were unfounded as Wolves finally capitulated.

Brentford have only had the merest nodding acquaintance with good fortune lately but finally the Gods smiled down upon us, and not before time.

Judge put on the afterburners and roared into the area where he seemed to have been brought down but the ball fell perfectly for Swift right in front of a yawning goal. His instant shot was blocked by Ikeme but rebounded straight back to him, bounced off some part of his anatomy and dribbled into the corner of the net.

Not a goal to live long in the memory, but priceless nevertheless, as it was no more than Brentford deserved.

Button made a crucial save early in the second half, spooning McDonald's effort around the post but Wolves soon returned to their torpor and the one-way traffic resumed with the Bees totally on top and their dominance was duly rewarded by two quite excellently worked and taken goals.

McEachran spotted Bidwell's run and threaded the ball to him through the eye of a needle. Judge returned the instant cross to Canos who controlled the ball and almost in the same movement thrashed it into the corner of the net.

Canos was a man inspired and shortly afterwards he twisted past two defenders at pace before his low cross gave Swift a tap in.

It was now a question of how many, as a rampant Brentford team with the shackles off played with a confidence and freedom seldom seen since the halcyon days of last season.

It was time for party tricks and Dean, a hero all night, rampaged down the middle like a modern day Nat Lofthouse before finally being caught and overpowered on the edge of the area.

Vibe set up Bidwell whose effort was blocked by the overworked Ikeme who saved his best to the last when he somehow tipped O'Connell's header away when a fourth goal seemed certain.

Brentford's display ticked all the boxes last night:

- The first home win of the year

- Three goals scored, and it could quite easily have been six

- A confident, pacy and vibrant performance

- Our trademark short passing game returned with a vengeance

- A much-needed and long-awaited clean sheet

John Swift celebrates after his first goal against Wolves

The match statistics confirmed just how good a performance this was as Brentford dominated with fifty-eight per cent possession, had twenty shots on goal and attempted over five hundred passes, a much more Brentford-like figure, with a meritorious seventy-six per cent success rate.

Even more encouragingly, Josh McEachran, much maligned for his supposed defensive inadequacies, made seven tackles, more than anyone else on the pitch.

Everyone played their part in what was a real team victory, but Swift, Canos, Woods, Dean and Yennaris were particularly impressive and the injured Colin was barely missed.

Only Marco Djuricin was slightly off the pace but he still managed six efforts on goal and there is surely far better to come from him as he slowly regains fitness and sharpness.

Neutral observers were also greatly impressed by Brentford's performance.

BBC reporter Jacqui Oatley commented:

Brentford lovely to watch. Passing and moving with pace, always an option. Teamwork, cohesion. Hope Alan Judge gets his chance with Ireland.

Nectar to our ears and some totally merited and deserved praise given the overall quality of our display.

Dean Smith also deserves great credit for his bravery in the way he set us up as well as for his positive team selection.

The team responded perfectly and will now be full of confidence before two tough matches against Rotherham and Charlton, teams both fighting for their life at the bottom of the table.

Brentford are unlikely to be given as much space and time as they were last night but have the strength of character and sufficient skill on the ball to prevail.

Isn't life beautiful when your team wins and plays well?

The Inside Track – Football & The Media – 26/2/16

Peter Lumley has been a regular contributor to this column recently and his razor-sharp reminiscences from over seventy years of watching the Bees are always welcome and of great interest.

Today he has used the knowledge gained from his professional experience of being a local journalist covering the club and then a public relations practitioner to provide his viewpoint on Brentford's current PR stance and approach.

Peter, as always, holds strong opinions and trenchant views, and it is perfectly obvious that there is much that has happened at the club over the last twelve traumatic months that has certainly not been to his liking and which has left him feeling angry, concerned and confused:

There has been much debate recently regarding Brentford's expertise (or lack of it) in communicating with various media outlets – newspapers, radio, television and social media in general. It is a subject that is close to my heart in that I have had the privilege of working on both sides of the fence, so to speak.

My first job on leaving school at the age of sixteen was to join the Middlesex County Times at Ealing as a trainee cub reporter with a special interest in sport. At that age I had already been a Griffin Park regular for six years since my first visit in 1942.

I should point out that the newspaper had a weekly circulation of over fifty thousand copies and covered an area embracing Ealing, West Ealing, Hanwell, Greenford and Northolt – a very fertile catchment area for Brentford fans at a time when the club encountered so many severe financial problems.

One of my primary objectives was to help the club by trying to expand the coverage and gain greater support. I also wrote a weekly column covering a range of local sports activities – similar to a blog in modern parlance. One regular feature of that column was references to Brentford of which at least ninety percent could fairly be described as more than favourable or positive.

Among my many sources of information were a number of players with whom I formed a friendship and who were always interested in what I had written about their performances and those of their teammates. And I can honestly claim that I never betrayed a confidence nor did I compromise their relationship with Griffin Park officials.

For all these reasons I looked forward to establishing a close working relationship with senior club officials to share in a common cause. But subsequent events proved otherwise. There were two local newspaper rivals at that time. One was the iconic George Sands, of the Middlesex Chronicle, a lifelong bachelor who devoted much of his life to Brentford and covered every Bees game, home and away for season after season. The other was Ernie Gifford, of the Brentford and Chiswick Times. Both gave the impression that they watched Brentford through red-and-white tinted spectacles.

This quite naturally endeared them to the Brentford management, particularly the club's Secretary, the late Denis Piggott, and it was this fact that led me into my first confrontation with club officialdom.

Regularly on Thursday mornings I phoned Mr. Piggott to try and glean any information of potential interest to my readers before going to press later on in the day. Invariably Mr. Piggott was less than enthusiastic about giving any information away even though he was well aware that my intention was to try and whip up interest among potential supporters for the next match.

Mr. Piggott seemed much more interested in complaining about any criticisms I had levelled against Brentford performances in the previous week's edition. The fact that I had significantly extended the coverage of Brentford games went utterly unappreciated.

On one very memorable occasion, when I had written an article that club officials took particular exception to, I walked across the Braemar Road forecourt to be confronted by the then manager, Malcolm MacDonald, who threatened to punch me on the nose if I ever repeated the perceived offence.

And my alleged criticism that caused so much consternation would look like praise compared to some of Greville's critiques of recent Brentford performances, particularly the one at Brighton!

But one Brentford official who did appreciate the extra coverage given to the Bees, warts and all, was the late, great, Eric White who for a number of years acted as the club's Press Officer. We became firm friends right up until his sudden and untimely death.

Another was no less than Mr. Jack Dunnett, who as Chairman invited me and other journalists to his luxury home for a pre-Christmas party for players and club officials. Mr. Dunnett was later to become a villain among Griffin Park fans as he prepared to sanction a takeover by West London arch-rivals, Queens Park Rangers.

Fortunately another wealthy benefactor, Mr. Ron Blindell who succeeded Mr. Dunnett as Chairman, saved the club from extinction. Mr. Dunnett later moved to Nottingham on becoming their Member of Parliament.

My years covering Brentford games spanned the years 1948-64. It was a period that produced an exciting but nerve-racking rollercoaster of a ride but was also dramatically newsworthy for a young local journalist.

1) *There were two relegations from the Second Division to the Fourth and promotion back to the Third.*

2) *The retirement of that great manager, Mr. Harry Curtis, who in the pre-war days took Brentford from the Third Division to the First.*

3) *England international Leslie Smith, hero of Brentford's two-nil victory over Portsmouth in the London War Cup Final at Wembley in 1942, returned to Griffin Park for a short spell on being released by Aston Villa.*

4) *Perhaps my favourite player of all time, Ken Coote, completed more than 500 appearances for the club.*

5) *The defection of two of the stars of that wonderful half-back line of Tony Harper, Ron Greenwood and Jimmy Hill.*

6) *The great Tommy Lawton was Player/Manager for a brief period.*

7) *The skill and artistry of wonderful players like Johnny Brooks, Peter McKennan, Johnny Rainford, Dai Ward and John Dick.*

8) *Starlets Peter Broadbent and Jimmy Bloomfield, plus the Terrible Twins Jim Towers and George Francis, who were both so deadly in front of goal were all transferred, much to the dismay of every Griffin Park fan. How we could do with two strikers of their calibre today?*

All these events – good and bad – were the subject of detailed analyses in my reports and personal weekly column. But it was my reporting of the various setbacks that befell the club that caused me the greatest heartache in terms of my relationship with the club's management who appeared to perceive any criticism in a local paper as an act of disloyalty.

As an aside, it was my experience as a journalist that led me to encourage a school friend of one of my stepsons to follow his dream of becoming a sports journalist. He is none other than Neil Ashton, the Daily Mail's brilliant award winning soccer correspondent, who also has his own regular Sunday morning slot on Sky TV.

Back to the debate on how the club should handle criticism from the Press.

A number of contributors urge the club to hire the services of a professional PR practitioner with the specific responsibility to improve the image of Brentford among the various media outlets and to the UK football community at large.

I take a contrary view based on my experience spanning some twenty years of working for an organisation that represented multi-national companies in an industry that has been regularly been under the media spotlight and has been the target of much criticism – the pharmaceutical industry.

I make these points to put into some sort of perspective the demands placed on such organisations to represent themselves to the press in the same way that football clubs, in general and Brentford in particular seek to influence media and public opinion.

My experiences convinced me that while PR practitioners have a role to play in routine press relations activities, organisations should always seek to rely on a chief or senior executive to step up to the plate and appear on television or radio to put the case on behalf of their club or company. They will always command more authority and credibility than is possible with a slick smooth-talking PR man or woman.

A good example of this was when Brentford's Co-Director of Football, Phil Giles, gave an interview to explain the club's position on bringing in new players (or not) during the recent January Transfer Window.

Unsurprisingly, not everyone agreed with me, but, on balance, I believe his contribution was appreciated by a majority of those who saw it.

In conclusion, I would like to mention a particular hobbyhorse of mine. I fully appreciate that benevolent club owner, Matthew Benham, has always pursued a policy of staying out of the limelight so far as his role is concerned. And, of course, no one should criticise him for that. It is clearly his right to do so.

But I sincerely believe that the departure of Mark Warburton was so controversial that it demanded a much more forthright explanation than was offered at the time by the chairman on behalf of the owner.

And who better to give that explanation to the media, and to thousands of loyal but baffled supporters, like myself, than the man who was the driving force behind the intended change of direction?

With the benefit of hindsight I hope he might be persuaded to give an update on what he believes has been achieved in the last twelve months towards the stated aim of improving the recruitment of better players and coaches.

Another Fans' Forum could certainly provide an appropriate platform!

Thank you, Peter, for your fascinating insight into the paternalistic way in which football clubs viewed their local paper and the cosy relationship that existed far too often between them.

As for his suggestion and exhortation for better, more open and regular communication between club and supporters, I really do not see how anybody can disagree with him.

From my perspective I always feel that it is fascinating and instructive to hear it from the horse's mouth from club officials as well as the players, past and present when they are contributing to *Bees Player*, and it is always illuminating to be made privy to the inside track on what is really going on in and around the club and to how footballers think.

Weak, Wet, Lily-Livered & Spineless – 28/2/16

Football is an emotional game and being a fervent supporter of almost any club means that you have to experience both the highs and the lows on a regular basis.

It is therefore so easy to over react and quickly lose sight of your sense of perspective so I make it a firm rule never to comment on a game when emotions are still running high immediately after the final whistle at a time when initial superficial and knee-jerk reactions can so easily dominate and overrule common sense and clear judgement.

More often than not once everything has calmed down, you have taken a few deep breaths and sufficient time has passed to reflect on what occurred in a more measured manner, things can look a lot different to how they initially appeared the previous day.

It is also pointless to change your mind repeatedly about a team from match to match simply depending upon the result as many other factors come into play. In other words, because they lost last week they are all useless, but they won the next game, so they have become heroes again.

I think we are all running the risk of falling into this trap at the moment when we consider what we are currently watching on the pitch at Brentford.

The knives were out recently when we lost three games in a row to the likes of Brighton, Sheffield Wednesday and Derby County and barely laid a glove on any of them, and many supporters felt that we were in free fall.

We desperately needed some points on the board against Wolves in midweek in order to boost our flagging confidence and help ensure that we kept a safe distance between us and the stragglers at the foot of the Championship table.

We were fortunate indeed to come across a team as inept as we had been in our previous few matches just at the right time and we easily beat quite the worst team I have seen this season, and one that made the donkeys of MK Dons appear like Real Madrid in comparison.

One swallow does not make a summer and yet many rabid and one-eyed fans on social media and the message boards alike saw this win as a massive turning point and perhaps even as the precursor to a late run on the outside towards the playoffs rather than recognising it for what it really was, simply a much-needed and long-awaited opportunity for us to fill our boots against another average team like us on a bad run and having a particularly awful evening.

Credit to the Bees, they did not look a gift horse in the mouth and took full advantage and were not flattered by the margin of their victory.

But did it change anything? In my opinion, not a jot or iota.

I certainly thought that we would have more chance of winning points against the likes of Wolves, Rotherham and Charlton than had been the case against the top teams, but as yesterday's abject, weak, and dispirited show against relegation favourites Rotherham clearly demonstrated, we are and will likely remain a soft touch and a poor or average team at best for the remainder of the season.

I was desperately praying and hoping that yesterday would show a new side of the Bees and that we would use the confidence gained from Thursday's victory to show some fire in our belly, fight fire with fire, stand up to the long ball barrage and onslaught of a typical Neil Warnock team desperate for the three points, and scrap and win the right for us to play our football and eventually let our undoubted skill do the talking.

Fat chance!

That was not the case as despite dominating possession we did little with it, allowed ourselves to be pushed back and then wilted under the unrelenting pressure and conceded two utterly avoidable goals both totally down to appalling defending firstly by O'Connell and then by Canos.

But let's face it; Rotherham could have scored five if they had taken the majority of their chances.

Judge benefited from a soft and bizarre penalty decision to score from the rebound after Camp saved his weak spot kick, but the unexpected fillip of an equaliser right on half time was frittered away and did not give us the impetus to take the game to a home team that came out after the break still seething from the perceived injustice of the award.

Instead we allowed Rotherham to take the initiative, pin us deep in our own half and their pressure finally told, aided and abetted by a referee who had stood firm before the break but finally wilted under the pressure of a vociferous home crowd and who gave us absolutely nothing in the second half as the ball kept coming back into our half and we were never able to impose our preferred style of play upon the game.

What was particularly worrying was the number of aerial duels that we lost in our own penalty area as we were totally outmuscled, and also how infrequently we won the crucial second ball.

Brentford allowed themselves to be drawn into a battle, a fight to the death with a team desperate for the points and one that was always going to overpower us as we gently subsided to defeat and proved, yet again, that this team is totally incapable of scrapping for a result.

Swift and Hofmann between them ludicrously missed a glaring opportunity to equalise straight after we went behind and the game drifted away from us as the home team held on for a fully deserved victory and we rarely threatened to pull a late rabbit out of the hat until Vibe missed two last-gasp chances to salvage something from the mess.

Everything that we already know about this current squad was reinforced yesterday.

- We are rarely able to keep a clean sheet

- We defend set pieces appallingly

- An overworked back four receives little cover and support from the midfield

- You have to win the second balls – and we don't

- There is barely a tackle in any of our midfield and we have a soft underbelly, and as I said last week, far too many Chihuahuas and barely a Pitbull in the team

- We miss the influence of Alan McCormack terribly – that in itself is an indictment of just how weak we are

- When the going gets tough, too many players simply disappear and we are so easily bullied out of a game and are vulnerable to any team that attempts to out-battle us

- We pretty much depend upon one man, Alan Judge, to both create and score goals

- We do not currently have a fit striker worthy of the name

- We have forgotten how to score late goals

- For all our possession we create so very little and are powder-puff in attack

- It is rare that we press as a team to win the ball back in key areas of the pitch

- Our ratio of goals to shots on target is poor in the extreme

- Despite the odd glimmer recently we rarely threaten or score from set pieces

- Without Tarkowski, or perhaps Barbet, we lack the ability to move or pass the ball out incisively from the back and beat the opposition press

- We need to show some patience as the squad is packed full of young, callow and inexperienced players still finding their way in this division but the best two, in Swift and Canos might well be playing elsewhere next season

In sum, nothing has really changed since the dog days of January. We still have a weak and overmatched squad largely lacking in pace, goals, experience, strength, determination, invention, desire and quite frankly, although it pains me to say this – balls.

All that is different is that thankfully we do not have too many of the promotion challengers left to play. What remains to be seen is how we stand up to the teams fighting for their life down at the bottom of the table.

From the evidence of yesterday, we might well capitulate to anybody who really wants to win and does not allow us any time to settle on the ball, and despite how appalling they are, I fear for us next weekend if Charlton employ the same tactics as Rotherham.

Charlton have also come up with a gem in the loan market with the pacy and talented Yaya Sanogo from Arsenal and he could well lead us a merry dance next weekend if we are not careful.

I am pretty certain though that we will play enough uninterested teams merely, like us, going through the motions to ensure that we finish the season safe and sound in lower mid-table mediocrity.

We desperately need to rebuild and examine carefully some of the blatant errors in recruitment that have been made this season and at some point soon I will go through the entire squad and give you my opinion on who will or should remain and who is likely to depart.

That, and the key question regarding how well we are likely to recruit fresh blood this Summer, is for the future though, and the squad now has a week to reflect upon their myriad inadequacies and shortcomings and then prepare to put on a performance next Saturday in what will be a tough and keenly contested local derby against an equally desperate Charlton team.

Are we up for the fight and this time, can we impose our style of football upon yet another team mired in a relegation battle?

I hope that the players' ears are burning from the tongue-lashing that I expect they will receive after the Rotherham disappointment and every Brentford supporter can simply hope that we will put on an acceptable performance next Saturday.

Position	Team	P	W	D	L	F	A	GD	Pt	Form
1	Burnley	34	18	11	5	53	27	26	65	D W D W W W
2	Hull City	33	19	7	7	48	19	29	64	W L W D W D
3	Middlesbrough	32	19	7	6	44	17	27	64	L D D D W W
4	Brighton and Hove A	34	17	12	5	49	34	15	63	W W D L W W
5	Derby County	34	15	12	7	45	30	15	57	D D L W W L
6	Sheffield Wednesday	34	14	13	7	50	35	15	55	D W W L D D
7	Cardiff City	34	13	13	8	45	38	7	52	W D D W L W
8	Birmingham City	33	14	9	10	39	32	7	51	W D L D W L
9	Ipswich Town	33	14	9	10	41	40	1	51	L W L L L W
10	Preston North End	34	12	12	10	33	32	1	48	D W W W W L
11	Queens Park Rangers	34	10	14	10	41	40	1	44	D W L D D W
12	Reading	33	11	10	12	38	36	2	43	D L D D W W
13	Wolverhampton Wndrs	34	11	10	13	42	47	-5	43	D D L L L W
14	Brentford	34	12	7	15	47	53	-6	43	D L L L W L
15	Nottingham Forest	33	10	12	11	32	30	2	42	W D W L L L
16	Huddersfield Town	34	10	9	15	44	46	-2	39	L L W W D L
17	Leeds United	33	8	14	11	30	39	-9	38	W D L D D L
18	Blackburn Rovers	32	8	13	11	31	30	1	37	D D L W L W
19	Bristol City	34	9	10	15	31	53	-22	37	D W W W L W
20	Fulham	34	8	12	14	51	56	-5	36	D W L W D L
21	Milton Keynes Dons	34	8	8	18	28	48	-20	32	D D W L D L
22	Rotherham United	34	8	5	21	38	59	-21	29	L L D L L W
23	Bolton Wanderers	34	4	13	17	32	56	-24	25	D W L D L L
24	Charlton Athletic	34	5	10	19	30	65	-35	25	W L D L L L

[29th February 2016]

March

Dean Smith – Thumbs Up Or Down? – 1/3/16

Given the indisputable fact that the Bees are currently in the midst of an appalling run of results since the New Year with only two wins and a solitary draw to set against seven Championship defeats, plus of course suffering a painful FA Cup giant killing at the hands of Walsall, it is hardly surprising, given the fickle nature and impatience of football supporters, that there have been murmurings and rumblings, and some questions and concerns have already been raised about the new Brentford Head Coach, Dean Smith and whether he is up to the job.

The criticisms levelled against him can best be summarised as follows:

- He is not getting the best out of the squad and is out of his depth
- We are porous in defence and concede too many goals
- We no longer come back and recover after going behind in a match
- The quality of our football is declining and we no longer play the Brentford way
- He is unable to attract new players to come and play for the club
- His substitutions are ill-thought through and generally make things worse
- He is not animated enough on the bench and appears to allow things to drift
- He sometimes refrains from acknowledging the Brentford supporters
- He is not Mark Warburton or Lee Carsley – delete where applicable

How fair are these accusations? Are some of them totally ridiculous? Have we hired another dud or, in the interests of fairness, do we need to make allowances for circumstances totally beyond his control that have made the manager's job difficult if not impossible for the time being?

I wanted to get an informed, objective and detached view about Dean Smith so I asked former Chronicle journalist and now *PA Match Day* reporter Jim Levack to give his own measured opinion on a man, who, given his Midlands base, he already knew extremely well from his successful spell in charge at Walsall.

Here is what Jim had to say, and it certainly makes interesting reading:

When the constant stress of the football season ends in May, chances are you will find Dean Smith settling back to take in a rather more sedate sport.

As an ardent cricket fan he's adept at playing the longer, more tactical game.

He did so to impressive effect at Walsall, where he repeatedly contended with an annual summer break-up of his squad only to return the following season even stronger.

That his squads were repeatedly torn apart by predatory clubs looking to pick up exciting young talent speaks volumes for his gift of spotting promising youngsters, developing them and then selling them for a profit.

Presumably that is what brought him to the attention of Matthew Benham, who I'm sure – unless he is foolish – will listen very closely to Smith's end of season shopping list.

The jury is out on the club's Co-Directors of Football, whose track record, at Brentford anyway, has so far been patchy in the extreme.

The signing of Konstantin Kerschbaumer is symptomatic of a system that, in my view, will only work with strong input from a footballing man with great knowledge of the English game.

That man is Smith, a bloke who will stand by his footballing principles come what may and who is, most importantly of all, a good man who has been plunged into a difficult situation.

Comments on websites – this one included – suggesting he is "not the man for the job" or "out of his depth" are, quite frankly, totally laughable.

Kerschbaumer, contrary to some of the unkind comments being levelled at him, will be a decent player given his bags of energy, good engine and an eye for an incisive pass, but not for another season or so when he has bulked up and shaken off his lightweight tag.

The fact that he is still playing and has not been sent out on loan to a League One side says more about the paucity of the squad and limited options available to Smith. Well I hope that's the case anyway and nothing more sinister. Smith has inherited a squad bereft of its quality players who have all moved on for a profit that the club couldn't say no to. And that will be the way of things until we move to Lionel Road.

The loss of defensive lynchpin Tarkowski and midfield protector Diagouraga since he took the job has turned Brentford into a side that, without the presence of Alan Judge, does not look consistently competitive in a league that demands that, at the very least.

We have a soft underbelly and as has been chronicled elsewhere, there doesn't appear to be the same fight and desire that the Griffin Park crowd has always demanded as a bare minimum.

I posted recently on another site the list of players who have left and – in my opinion – not been replaced on a like-for-like or quality basis. It was met with the inevitable responses of "yawn" or "stop being negative." Not negative. Just realistic.

Smith, like a footballing Mike Brearley, is playing a tactical game and deploys an impressive dead bat forward defensive shot every time he is questioned about personnel… or the lack of it.

He has clearly been told plans are afoot for the summer, which is good news. I've heard some deals are close to completion already and other quality signings are on the radar.

Great news, and a cause for optimism if Messrs. Ankersen and Giles find the right people this time round and the existing signings finally come good after a bedding-in season.

But here's the rub. When my son and others like him stumped up the increased season ticket price – student rates were scrapped in favour of a young person's card – they did so on the premise of a Big New Ambitions advertising slogan.

The club's failure to remain properly competitive after January will make him and others think twice in future. After all two hundred and thirty pounds is a lot to a teenager doing an apprenticeship.

Should the ad blurb have read – "Big New Ambitions until we decide to call it a day and watch the season peter out midway through the season?"

I think we'll be safe – Charlton will be a big game – but I do hope that next season's season ticket prices reflect the wasted four or five months of this.

One thing is certain though. Dean Smith is the right man for the job and once he's allowed to put his mark on a depleted squad, any doubts currently held will evaporate leaving the cynics to turn their attention to something or someone else… probably me after this.

Just to sum up, Dean Smith's treatment – so far at least – has been like asking a journalist to knock out a back page or web lead without a laptop, Mac, notebook or recording device.

Smith is quite simply working with one hand tied behind his back given the lack of numbers and quality in his squad.

Smith is no fool, is the best man for the job, is a great fit for our club and will have us challenging and competitive next season – of that I have no doubt.

I just hope we're not being too cocky thinking that safety is guaranteed because at the moment it certainly is not a sure thing.

I am sure that many supporters reading Jim's words will have much to say about the sentiments expressed in them and I look forward to the debate which is certain to ensue.

Where do I stand on this issue?

I feel that Dean Smith is an excellent match for our specific needs and requirements as he understands our approach and buys into it. He is an eminently intelligent, pragmatic and sensible man who motivates and inspires footballers and he can also manage upwards as well as down.

I also suspect that given his knowledge and experience of the lower divisions we have moderated our *modus operandi* and Smith will be intrinsically involved in all decisions regarding recruitment and it would not surprise me if we bring in several promising young players already well-known to the manager.

It would be very interesting to know what his terms of reference are for the remainder of the season. Probably no more than remaining as competitive as possible, picking up enough points to remain well clear of the scrum in and around the bottom of the league, playing high-tempo attacking football and continuing to integrate and involve the foreign signings from last Summer so that we are in a position to make informed decisions on their future and as to whether they are able to cope with the demands of the Championship.

That means a hopefully temporary scaling down of our lofty ambitions and frankly we are currently struggling to achieve even these limited aspirations given the recent run of results and disappointing performances.

In his defence, there have been some excellent spells of football but a total lack of consistency, Smith has seen the loss of three quality first team players in January without any hint of replacements, good fortune has not been on our side with a succession of contentious refereeing decisions and injuries continue to bite deep into our limited resources.

Perhaps yesterday's welcome and long-awaited return of Scott Hogan who came back with a bang with a poacher's goal and a spirited sixty-minute run out in the Development Squad match against Crystal Palace will provide a much needed boost and hopefully Alan McCormack will also be in line for a much needed return against Charlton on Saturday.

In truth, I was disappointed with the negative and pusillanimous way he set the team up against Derby County, which totally ceded the initiative to a team also struggling for confidence and in my opinion, contributed to our eventual defeat in a match where we never attempted to play our customary style of football.

It is also very easy to look back with hindsight, however I wonder if he now regrets throwing away the chance of a morale boosting FA Cup run by fielding a weakened team against Walsall particularly given our subsequent defeats by Middlesbrough and Burnley in what turned out to be a totally dispiriting and demoralising week?

To lambast the manager given the obstacles he currently faces is patently unfair, unrealistic and absurd and he needs and deserves our total support.

The time to judge him will be next season assuming that, as expected, he is given the necessary tools to work with and the opportunity to rebuild the squad in conjunction with the Co-Directors of Football and we recruit players with the required level of ability and experience.

Lumley's Lament! – 3/3/16

I am always keen to give loyal readers of this column the right of reply and to publish articles that they submit to me either spontaneously or sometimes at my request. After all, we share one thing in common, we are all fervent, if not rabid Brentford supporters who only want the best for our beloved club and we all have our own opinion and take on everything that has been happening at Brentford FC.

I might not always succeed, but I always attempt to provide a calm, considered and objective view and opinion on the way that the club is run and what is happening both on and off the field.

Sometimes I feel that I am a little bit too cold blooded, detached and rational and that occasionally it does no harm to vent a bit and let those emotions out and today is going to be one of those days, even if the words that you are about to read are not my own and perhaps they also go too far!

Peter Lumley is quite evidently not a happy man and he appears to be feeling a combination of anger, sadness, frustration and disappointment at most of the events of the past year and he has just sent me the article that I enclose below which succinctly sums up his current state of mind.

Some of you might well agree with every word of what he says, I certainly do not share his opinion on most of the matters that he criticises and have already rebutted his arguments many times in previous articles, others might see it as an impassioned or maybe even ill-founded rant or, more charitably, simply as a dedicated, loyal and long-suffering supporter offloading because of what he perceives as an opportunity lost and that we are now a club that is drifting and suffering from the mistakes made in our overall strategy over the past year.

Whilst I accept that you can generally only predict the future by examining the past, and that there are certainly several things that I would certainly have done differently, I have made it clear over the course of well over half a million words that I have written since I started putting together articles in June 2014 that I am fundamentally massively supportive and appreciative of the way that Matthew Benham, Cliff Crown and the rest of the senior staff have constantly tried to innovate and think outside the box in order to catapult Brentford way up the football pyramid so that we are competing on an even keel with clubs far richer and larger than us and teams that we would barely have dreamed that we would be playing against, let alone defeating.

That being said, nobody is above criticism as long as it is fair, constructive and carefully thought through.

I have given chapter and verse on countless occasions exactly why I feel that we have gone backwards this season, but only after we began from a ridiculously high base line that could never in reality have been sustained given our circumstances.

Mistakes have certainly been made and we are currently in a bad patch, but we have also been the victims of bad luck and poor fortune on a massive scale as well as, it has to be acknowledged, poor judgement and we have suffered grievously at the hands of rapacious and far better-heeled teams with the power to divest us of our better players. Such is life and we simply have to get used to it, keep planning for the future and simply wait for our luck to change.

As for the future, again, I have made it clear just how crucial this summer will be and I await what transpires with interest as well as the expectation that the right moves will be made, not just from blind faith, but also from my soundings regarding the way in which we intend to operate.

Perhaps I will be proved wrong, but somehow I doubt it, and I firmly believe that we will retrench and come again next season.

In the meantime, here is what Peter has to say, which is hard hitting in the extreme.

I decided to write this item in the hope that it represents the views of dozens or hundreds of other Brentford supporters like me. From the outset I should state that I was just one of the ninety-eight percent of fans who, according to a social media poll at the time, were opposed to the announcement by the Board of Directors, on the eleventh of February last year, that the club intended to dispense with the services of Mark Warburton as Manager at the end of the season, come what may.

At the time I wrote at least four letters to the club chairman, Mr. Cliff Crown, expressing fears that this decision would, almost inevitably, lead to a destabilisation of the club with a consequent loss of morale among a very successful squad of talented players who had treated fans to a quality of football they had not seen at Griffin Park for years.

Not surprisingly, my fears fell on deaf ears. It took at least two to three months for the Chairman to even acknowledge my letters. When his response did eventually arrive it was not worth the paper it was written on – quite apart from the fact that I was addressed as "Dear Mr. King" rather than by my correct name. Many may say that this was a trivial offence. But to me it was symptomatic of the club's attitude towards its loyal fans.

Perhaps I should recap, briefly, on the events that led up to the controversial decision and the subsequent fallout from that fateful day last February.

That morning an exclusive leaked story appeared in The Times newspaper announcing that Mark Warburton's rolling contract would not be renewed at the end of the season even if the club was promoted to the Premier League.

In a panicky response the club issued an interim statement that was an utter disgrace and an insult to anyone with a scrap of intelligence. To the press and the UK football community, it made the club a laughing stock from which, in my opinion, it has never really recovered.

In an attempt to make amends, the club subsequently issued a more considered response, the gist of which read as follows, using, of course my own words and interpretation:

The club believes that if it is to sustain the progress achieved over the past three seasons and is to compete successfully against bigger and wealthier clubs in the future, it must rid itself of the hazards of human judgement and experience and replace them with a greater use of statistical analyses.

Particularly as an aid to the recruitment of better players and coaches. Then, and only then, will we be able to reach the Promised Land of Premier League football at the proposed new stadium at Lionel Road.

Again, briefly, I went through all the emotions of shock, anger, bemusement, but I eventually came to terms with the decision and decided, in the interests of sanity and loyalty, to give the new direction a chance to succeed. And although I rated Mark Warburton as a great and highly popular manager, there were those who took the view:

That he possibly overplayed Jonathan Douglas, when he was not getting any younger and his box-to-box style of play demanded an enormous amount of energy.

There was a reluctance to recruit a second striker to take the pressure off Andre Gray.

But to me he was the perfect manager and a great asset to the club.

Now I want to fast forward to the present day. There are a growing number of fans who believe they are owed an explanation for what appears to have gone wrong with the current approach and a prediction of what they can expect in the immediate future. This should come from the club Chairman or a representative of the senior management team and should take the form of a progress report.

If I were to be asked to ghost write a statement on his behalf it would probably read as follows:

Hello, all you grateful and loyal Brentford fans. We very much regret that many of you are suffering from a severe bout of nostalgia at this very trying time. We are confident, however, that this problem will soon pass and you can look forward to some quality football again shortly!

Quite naturally, our esteemed club owner is very reluctant to admit that, possibly, he has made a ghastly mistake and that, as yet, his massive gamble does not seem to be paying off. By nature he is a very shy and private person who wishes to remain incognito for as long as it takes. He believes he has a right to remain silent and no one should criticise him for that. Fair enough.

He also believes that fans should understand that money talks (or doesn't talk!) to the tune of ninety million pounds! He is confident that his much-cherished direction will soon seem like music to the ears of many of you – and he will come up smelling of red and white roses.

Finally, he would just like to point out that foresight is a wonderful thing and he hopes you will now be prepared to show a little more patience!

We also have to admit that we have lost far too many good players to our rivals in the Championship and have been unable to recruit adequate replacements except with two possible exceptions. We would like to point out, once again that foresight is a wonderful thing…

We also admit that we cannot claim that our recruitment of new and better coaches has been wholly successful but we would like to point out…

Our club chairman has agreed that the fears expressed that he was putting the club's stability at risk were, with the benefit of hindsight, possibly well-founded. But he asks us to point out…

Yes, we are conceding far too many goals and missing far too many scoring chances but would like to point out…

At least one of our Co-Directors of Football has other fish to fry (possibly Danish) and cannot possibly be expected to devote more time and energy to the interest of Brentford. But he does ask fans to show a little more patience and a lot more loyalty to the club!

We ask fans and potential fans to show a lot more patience, loyalty and optimism in the future. Because that is the only way that we will achieve our common goal (strikers permitting) of a place in the Premier League.

We also admit that the recruitment of better coaches has not really improved the performances of our youth and development teams in recent weeks. Due to unforeseen circumstances we lost the services of, arguably, the best Development Squad coach in the land. We then appointed the ultra-loyal Kevin O'Connor as lead Development Squad coach but quickly replaced him in what some describe as undue haste.

Patience has, however, never been one of our strong points. In fact there are some among us who hardly know the meaning of the word! Regretfully, Kevin's replacement has not met with much success but we would like to point out…

Finally, we pledge to give our very loyal fans regular and forthright updates, based on our very latest statistical analyses of the progress being achieved, we will then not have to rely on that young upstart, Peter Lumley, to do the job for us.

Time For Some Answers! – 6/3/16

Normally articles seem to write themselves. I just sit down at the computer and the words generally flow without too much effort but today was totally different as I pondered and vacillated endlessly over the most suitable subject matter and how best to express my feelings.

My first reaction after Brentford's inept, shambolic, disjointed and passionless performance as they stumbled to an appalling defeat against an equally poor Charlton team was to assert that since the entire Brentford team seemed to have gone on holiday a couple of months too early then perhaps I should do the same writing-wise, and that therefore I would make as much effort as the team had done yesterday and simply refrain from making any comment at all.

I then thought about giving vent to my feelings and forensically dissecting each player's myriad shortcomings, but that was far too depressing a prospect and quite frankly I would simply be repeating so much of what I have already written after previous unacceptable performances.

I finally decided to confine myself to giving a brief summary of Saturday's non-event and then highlight some of the broader issues that now face us, before attempting to find some solutions.

Facing a relegation-haunted team sorely lacking in confidence we all hoped for a precious early goal that would ideally settle our nerves both on and off the pitch and that is exactly what happened and our prayers were seemingly answered as the ball hit the net less than twenty seconds after the opening whistle – unfortunately at the wrong end, as a Brentford team which still looked as though it was in its pre-match huddle got into a mess at the back as a left wing cross was allowed to reach the unmarked Harriott who found space in a packed penalty area and easily slotted home.

Dean Smith said that our game plan had gone out of the window after such an appalling start, but surely we still had well over ninety minutes to put things right and address matters?

The Bees eventually clawed their way back into the match and played some reasonable football for the majority of the first half without showing much spark or invention.

Swift and Canos shone spasmodically and the Chelsea youngster headed a glaring chance well wide of a gaping goal from a similar opportunity to the one he scored from at The Valley before declining to fall down when clearly clipped and a penalty kick seemed inevitable.

Frankly it is unfair and unrealistic to put so much pressure on two such talented but inexperienced teenagers and expect them to pull a rabbit out of the hat more than occasionally.

As has happened far too often, Judge was left to forage alone and cut in from the wing to force a brilliant plunging save from Pope. Canos then slipped Djuricin clean through a square defence as the applause rang out in the twenty-fourth minute for the sadly departed Dean Langford, but he showed his total lack of confidence and sharpness by allowing the keeper to block his shot when a goal seemed inevitable before Barbet marked a memorable God-given minute by heading home Judge's corner kick when left totally unmarked and he scored his first ever goal for the club.

Surely the Bees would now take control, but we never found that extra gear nor succeeded in putting a wilting defence under any real pressure.

Early in the second half Canos was sent away by McEachran's exquisite pass but from an identical position from where he rippled the net against Wolves, he could only shoot wide of the post and, quite frankly, that was that as we barely created another chance for the remainder of the match, and that miss was to come back and haunt us when Charlton realised just how poor we were and finally awoke from their torpor, broke away down their left flank, and the totally unemployed Button could only paw a cross straight to Harriott who made a difficult chance look easy. A ghastly error from a goalkeeper playing against his former team.

The game drifted away from us as we gently subsided to defeat without making much apparent effort to recover as we lacked any shape, invention, confidence or frankly, passion.

As has happened far too often lately our three substitutions seemed only to weaken us even more. Saunders replaced Canos who seemed to be our main threat although perhaps the fact that he had been booked and subsequently warned for a dive helped make Dean Smith's mind up for him. Sam barely touched the ball and never played a dangerous pass or cross into the penalty area.

Djuricin gave perhaps the worst and most spineless and inept performance I have seen from a Brentford striker since the days when the likes of Joe Omigie and Neil Shipperley provided a non-existent goal threat and his replacement, Vibe, who at least gave the impression of breaking sweat, was easily smothered by the Charlton defence. Hofmann came on near the end for McEachran and lumbered around without noticeable effect and it was quite impossible to detect our formation as we degenerated into a hapless and shapeless rabble and we were fortunate not to concede a third as we were cut open repeatedly on the break.

Not for the first time this season the patience of the Brentford supporters was sorely tested and they made their displeasure known at the final whistle.

Charlton came expecting to be defeated but they were let off the hook as they out-battled and outfought a Brentford team that was in reality anything but and they fully deserved their ultimate victory.

Quite frankly we played with one hand tied behind our back given the lack of incision from our midfield where Woods and McEachran duplicated each other and never gelled as a partnership and Judge provided our only consistent threat but cannot always be expected to do everything on his own.

As has been the case for several months now, we do not possess a forward worthy of the name and the Charlton penalty area resembled a *cordon sanitaire* so seldom did we get players into it.

This sad and sorry state of affairs cannot be allowed to continue, nor can the remainder of the season be allowed to drift away. Not only is this situation patently unfair and unacceptable to supporters who pay good money and quite reasonably expect some level of entertainment and effort in return, and are now justifiably feeling short-changed, we are also beginning to look at the clubs below us with apprehensive looks.

When we lost last month to the likes of Brighton, Sheffield Wednesday and Derby, the exhortation was for patience until we played Wolves, Rotherham and Charlton and then the points and performances would follow. Well those games have now come and gone and bar one bright spark when we hammered a Wolves team which played as if it was tranquillised, we have now lost comfortably and deservedly to two of the relegation favourites without putting up much of a fight. I fully realize that we have no divine right to succeed but this is not how we expect a Brentford team to perform.

What happens now and where do we go from here? We all deserve some answers. Not because we are spoiled and have massive expectations but quite simply because the squad is patently far too weak and thin and with injuries again biting is now struggling to hold its head above water.

We all know and mostly accept the reasons why the squad has been diminished and denuded without any reinforcements, but we expected the remaining players at least to be competitive and to provide a reasonable and realistic level of competence, entertainment, effort and results for the remainder of the season before the necessary squad strengthening can take place, not too much to ask for, surely, but the wheels have now come off with a vengeance and Dean Smith is, perhaps unfairly, coming under growing pressure from supporters who are now losing patience and looking for a scapegoat.

That being said he appeared to be a man in despair in his post-match interview and one who was struggling to find the answers to the multitude of problems that currently face him.

Rather than play the blame game I would rather be constructive and look for answers, explanations and firm promises for the immediate and mid-term future as I am extremely concerned at the moment.

I have therefore contacted the Brentford Co-Director of Football, Phil Giles, who responded quickly and courteously and has agreed to meet me next week when I hope to get the answers to some of the questions that we would all like to ask him.

In that regard I have already sent him a comprehensive and voluminous list of question, not that I expect the answers to all of them given the limitations of time and the dictates of commercial confidentiality, but I shall report back on what I am told at our meeting and Phil has also agreed to provide some written answers which will be published as an article as soon as I receive it.

Here are the questions that I have posed and please let me know if there is anything else that you would like me to put to him when we meet:

- How did a Maths and Stats graduate and a PhD from the University of Newcastle end up as Co-Director of Football at Brentford FC?

- How much of your time is spent working with the club as opposed to Smartodds?

- What is the division of roles between yourself and Rasmus Ankersen?

- Roughly what proportion of his time is spent working for Brentford FC?

- The role of the new breed of executive versus the traditional *football man* – discuss

- Dealing with agents and rapacious clubs – are Brentford considered a soft touch or worthy adversaries?

- How much contact do you have with your peers at other clubs?

- How does the rest of the football world now regard the club?

- *We look to be stronger after every Transfer Window* – please discuss with reference to the January 2016 Transfer Window?

- How do you manage expectations amongst supporters who were told that any finish below fifth would be a comedown from last season?

- What would be realistic expectations for the club until we move to Lionel Road?

- In retrospect was 2015 an *annus mirabilis* or a massive missed opportunity?

- How can we possibly hold onto our prime assets when they are offered more money elsewhere or persuade the likes of Button and Bidwell to buy into us and re-sign?

- Try before you buy *à la* Bidwell & Forshaw. Why have we stopped using this successful policy re loanees?

- What is our relationship like with the top Premier League clubs?

- What is your strategy for recruitment for the summer (within reason!)?

- How much say will Dean Smith and Richard O'Kelly have in player recruitment both in terms of identifying targets and deciding to sign them?

- Who has the final say?

- FFP and its effect on us

- How can a team with our financial constraints find and afford flair players who can make and/or score goals?

- Please discuss our three strikers and how they fit into the current style of play?

- Jota – discuss

- How much of a gamble is it signing players from lower divisions at home and abroad e.g. Woods & Gogia?

- How attractive a proposition is Brentford FC for young players from lower divisions, experienced Championship players and players from the EEC and beyond?

- What are the minimum expectations and KPIs for you and the club for the remainder of the season?

    1. Win as many matches as you lose
    2. Remain competitive
    3. Stay out of the relegation dog fight
    4. Continue to play the Brentford Way
    5. Bed in the new signings from abroad
    6. Persuade Button and Bidwell to resign
    7. Complete a recruitment list for next season

- How would you respond to supporters who are feeling let down, confused and disappointed at the moment and will soon be asked to buy season tickets for next season?

- Getting transfers over the line – discuss

- Undisclosed fees. I understand why you favour them but they are the bane of our lives – discuss

- What will it take to bring about a change in policy and for you to bring in loanees this month?

- Where can you find loan players now who can add value to the team?

- I appreciate that there is a review being conducted, but why has the Academy so far failed to produce a home-grown first team squad player?

- Has the loss of some well-regarded Academy coaches had a detrimental effect?

- Why do non-playing first team squad players rarely play in Development Squad fixtures?

- Can you talk us through the process from acknowledging a need to signing a player i.e. how did we go from knowing we would lose Odubajo to signing Colin?

- How advanced and complex is the proprietorial analytical data we use to identify and recruit players compared to the likes of *Wyscout* & *Opta* etc?

- In reality how much does our approach really differ from most other clubs nowadays?

- Can you explain the process by which we combine analytical and physical scouting?

- Matthew Benham has stated that a player should be watched one hundred times. How often do we watch potential players as opposed to watching DVDs and film clips?

- What sort of physical scouting network do we possess or plug into?

- How many analysts support yourself and Rasmus?

- How do you evaluate players in terms of their character and likelihood to settle in the UK?

- Do we have a constantly updated list of potential and VIABLE prospects from around the world?

- How far down the pyramid do we analyse players and teams?

- How happy are you with the 2015 batch of signings in terms of their current performance levels and were some thrown in prematurely?

- Is it getting more difficult every year to recruit well?

- What signing and sale have given you the most satisfaction?

- What lessons were learned from the Marinus recruitment process when it came to appoint Dean Smith?

- What qualities does Dean Smith possess that make him the ideal manager for Brentford FC?

- What are the benefits to Brentford of the association with FC Midtjylland?

- We have sent them Moore and O'Shaugnessy, when will we receive one of their players on loan or a permanent basis?

- Why so many injuries this season – coincidence or happenstance?

- Scott Hogan – what can or should we expect or hope for?

- When will we take the Cup competitions more seriously?

- Is a box-to-box player with footballing and tackling ability on the agenda for next season?

More Questions And Concerns – 8/3/16

The airwaves have been buzzing with activity since I wrote an article the other day suggesting that it was now *Time For Some Answers* from senior staff at Brentford FC given the current run of poor results and performances and the resulting uncertainty and concern at how matters have been deteriorating on the pitch since the turn of the year and a Transfer Window which saw the club further weaken its squad without bringing in any reinforcements.

I fully understand and totally buy into the financial and practical reasons why the club has taken some of the decisions that it has but did not expect that they would result in quite such a massive and immediate deterioration both in results and, just as crucially, the quality of our performances.

Losing at home to the bottom team in the Championship on Saturday certainly did not help improve matters and some supporters are also beginning to lose patience regarding what is going on and, as our slump continues, are now openly questioning our strategy as well as the impact that manager Dean Smith is having on the team.

I will continue to support the club in all its actions and for its current business model as I quite frankly can see no alternative way forward for us given our financial constraints and our need to compete on an uneven playing field with teams whose resources totally dwarf our own, and buttressed by income levels we can only dream about and massive Parachute Payments, can spend millions of pounds on strengthening their squad and seemingly with a mere snap of their fingers can also entice our best players to leave us, even though they now have to pay us handsomely for the privilege.

Last season massively raised expectations and I still feel that a huge opportunity was lost when we did not strengthen a squad in January that looked as if it might continue on its triumphant and seemingly unstoppable path to the Premier League.

Had things turned out differently in January, who knows, maybe even the schism and eventual divorce between Matthew Benham and Mark Warburton might have been avoided although I suspect that I am clutching at straws as it would appear that there might well have already been a breakdown in trust as well as fundamental differences between them that would inevitably lead to a parting of the ways.

It is pointless now to look backwards although last season plainly showed what is possible, even against all the odds, for the club in terms of results, performances, style of play, quality of recruitment and overall sense of togetherness and we can only aspire to what was achieved and do our utmost to replicate and even surpass it in the future.

This season has seen us facing an ongoing and relentless series of obstacles, barriers, setbacks and problems, some of them of our own making, others largely unforeseen and unfortunate and should we finish the season somewhere around halfway up the Championship then I for one would see this as a successful season given all the circumstances and such a final placing would be something that I could barely have dreamed about only a couple of years ago.

The problem is managing supporter expectations that quite frankly have been raised unrealistically by some ill-judged comments from within the club as well as a natural sense of optimism and anticipation, if not entitlement amongst supporters, created by the triumphs of last season.

I also revealed that I am meeting Phil Giles later this week when he has agreed to answer some of our supporters' current concerns and I am hoping for reassurances regarding the way forward and how we expect to plan for next season and beyond.

A busy close season culminating in the club retrenching and recruiting cleverly, creatively and effectively from both home and abroad would certainly help to turn things around and bring about a renewed sense of optimism.

In the meantime I have been overwhelmed by the response to my article which included a list of the questions that I have sent to Mr. Giles, and I have heard from many Bees supporters who share my love and support for the club as well as varying degrees of concern about the current situation.

Former player **Richard Poole** is worried that our slide could continue until we go into free fall:

Great questions Greville, I just hope they provide the answers as the fans have a right to know. I was not there on Saturday but the players should at least try in respect of the shirt and the fans too as relegation could creep up on us more quickly than we think.

Red Rose Bee also helped to put matters into context in terms of fan satisfaction:

I am a season ticket holder living in Lancashire. Every home match is a five hundred mile round journey and costs me around ninety pounds. I first went in September 1961 and have been through all the many bad times as well as the few good. I was at Birmingham, Rotherham and Sheffield Wednesday recently.

I made the decision not to go on Saturday because watching this team is so depressing at the moment. If the players cannot be bothered, why should I? I predicted that we would lose to Charlton. Like many others who watch us play I am not a football expert but every week we see the same players make the same mistakes as well as the lack of urgency and pride.

I don't blame Dean Smith for this as he has been handed a very difficult situation, it is the Co-Directors of Football who must answer the questions. I cannot imagine that Matthew Benham is happy with what is happening now. Without him we have no future though.

I just hope that Saturday will focus minds and will represent the lowest point of a forgettable season, if not, and if we carry on like this, we are definitely in a relegation scrap.

Rob is concerned about the current makeup of the squad:

Another great incisive article, Greville – and I look forward to some of the questions you have asked getting answered honestly and fully. Yes, last season was a brilliant one for us, and I fully accept after fifty-two years of supporting the Bees that we cannot have it like that every year. However, there is still the expectation that life will not always be going from high peaks to low troughs. A few weeks ago I thought that we had enough points to stay safe for this year but after Saturday's performance, I'm not quite so confident.

It is not just the persistence in playing the lone striker that concerns me; there is the lack of an effective midfield. Whilst I was never the biggest fan of Douglas, and obviously he is approaching the twilight of his career, he has not been replaced.

Equally, Toumani's departure has left a gap in the defensive midfield and it was interesting to hear comments in the stand about how much we miss him coming from people who were often vociferous critics of him in the past – you don't know how good someone is until they go. I fully appreciate that players will come and players will go, but I feel that far too many have gone without adequate replacement – and that is one of my biggest concerns.

Rebel Bee gave his analysis of the current situation:

Something is very wrong at Brentford, and without taking any pleasure in it; some of us have felt this for a long while now. An air of complacency set in at the turn of the year, leaving the squad short in strength, character, and quality in this unforgiving division – which is relentless right up to the last game. We could yet pay a very heavy price for this complacency – our predicament is that serious.

You'd have to write a book to pick over that performance on Saturday – it was that bad – Smith's pre match "start on the front foot" quote in tatters after twenty seconds. Even our superb keeper has got the yips, gifting their winner with a soft punch – we are unable to dig in and take a few scruffy draws and that is what alarms me most in this bad run. A glaring problem for us is the lack of pace in the squad – it's a big part of why we lost yesterday.

My questions to Phil Giles would be all about the balance of the squad and the rationale behind the signings made this season. Why sign three forwards who are unable to play in our lone striker role? Why have we lost and not replaced our powerful, pacy players? We have no width or an outlet up front, something that even hapless Charlton possessed. I'd also ask how the summer recruitment process will be handled, assuming we stay up, is Dean Smith being given more input and say on this than Marinus was?

Saturday was the day that even some of the most positive people I know are starting to accept that we've made a real mess of things, and wonder where our next point will come from. It's backs against the wall time – all we can do is to get to QPR and try to do our bit, all of the staff need to respond this week and man up a bit.

I fear something has seriously gone awry at Brentford, complete supposition on my part but all is not well and it goes far deeper than the on-pitch issues. Clearly the frustrating delays to the Lionel Road project are part of this, maybe a bigger part than I imagined.

Within reason the senior figures at the club need to come out and communicate – tell the truth and try to pull everyone together – otherwise our golden moment getting to and competing in the Championship will be a fleeting memory.

Iain is also looking forward to hearing some answers:

Thanks for another good article, Greville. Quite a list of questions! If these will be properly dealt with, then you'll have a fairly lengthy meeting.

Clearly Saturday was as bad as it can get right now. You can do no worse in a league game than lose at home to the team occupying bottom place. Not a specific question but one troubling observation which you might be able to build into your discussion. Did you look at the players before kick off yesterday? My friend remarked that their body language was all wrong and that they didn't look like they were up for the challenge. You know, he was right, it was definitely visible. The contrast with the Charlton players was there for all to see.

Surely the players should at least come out looking like they can't wait for the game to start? You can have the worst group of players, with a bad owner but still come onto the field highly energised.

So the events of the first minute only seemed to verify all was absolutely not well in how the players were prepared.

I am still very reluctant to become too critical of our Head Coach – but when this is coupled with the obviously ineffective substitutions and too many long balls, which we invariably lose, there are more serious concerns now.

None of us wants to see much more of this. We have no divine right to win but we expect the team to come out, champing at the bit to go and players to know how the team is expected to play and how they are meant to be a part of that.

Maybe what we need to get things going again is a local derby against a team which fires everyone up? Perhaps we have one of those coming up very soon?

John Hirdle would prefer a public forum:

Good luck in trying to get some answers from Giles. It is long overdue for him and Ankersen to break their wall of silence and front up with some explanations on the current state we find the club in and their proposed actions to improve things both short term and long-term.

I can't help feeling though that instead of a private meeting with yourself they should be addressing these concerns to all of us publicly at a Fans' Forum. I have little confidence in either of them to be honest.

dwp26 added a few extra questions:

Excellent post. I always come here to get a more balanced view, and I often find that it helps me realise things are not as bad as the post-match trauma would suggest.

Some questions to pass on:

Is the overall target of Premier League football in five years still feasible?

Why should I and many others renew season tickets for next season, given that the football we play currently resembles nothing like last season's quality?

Will we see that exciting brand of high intensity attacking football again at Brentford, or are we now condemned to sideways passing and long balls to players who have a poor first touch and can't head it?

275

Chris White wants better and more frequent communication from the club:

Regular communication from the powers that be acknowledging the good and what needs to be improved and what the club intends to do about it would be a good start. I think this would be good for the standing of the club as there are many within the game who because of what happened last February, really want us to fail. We need to acknowledge this and re-emphasise that we have to do things differently if we want to be successful with our resources. But the silence has become deafening.

Lastly, we're all in despair because we were actually given that most precious thing – hope. We hoped that we could be successful and last year we saw that it could be done, which has given us belief. There's no way we can allow that to disappear now – it's already rooted and mediocrity is only making matters worse. The fact that the mediocrity is now within a Championship setting show how far we have come but also what our current expectations now are.

Good luck with the meeting, Greville, and I can't wait for the feedback.

Let's end with the thoughts of **Jim Levack** who, as normal, succinctly summed things up:

Greville, your article and questions are absolutely on the button. It has spawned some intelligent and reasoned responses too.

Just one thought though – Should it not be Matthew Benham answering those questions as he hired both Giles and Ankersen? It is not really fair on Giles to take the flak alone, just as it's unfair for people to judge Dean Smith on a side that he has had no say in developing.

To those who say Carsley got more out of the same players, that is selective thinking. Carsley had a quality centre back in Tarkowski and an effective, gangly pain-in-the-backside play-breaker in Diagouraga.

I'm not going to rant on, but to my mind failing to sign any replacements in January has created a destructive mindset at the club. If you tell your office profits don't matter until the next financial year, the team will cruise.

Interesting thoughts from all of them and many others too. It is good to offload as well as express your concerns.

Let's just wait for some of the answers and hope that I am not fobbed off with platitudes and that they allay our worries and help reunite us all.

Bragging Rights – 9/3/16

I am fortunate enough to live in a pretty, leafy and quiet road tucked away in a beautiful backwater in North London where the days go by calmly and peacefully without us being assailed by the constant irritating noise of passing traffic as thankfully it is neither a main road nor a cut-through or rabbit run.

Neighbours nod politely to each other as they pass each other on the street whilst walking to the nearby shops and tube station and always find the time to stop for a brief moment to enquire about the health of their respective offspring and how they are doing at school or university.

The odd creaking and arthritic labrador or relative bent with age is gently walked up and down the road to get some fresh air and exercise. Nobody pries or attempts to invade each other's privacy and the nearest we have come to united action was when there was a dispute with the local council over rubbish collections and which of two neighbouring boroughs different parts of the road were situated in.

The residents are an eclectic bunch encompassing a variety of races, ages, backgrounds, creeds and religions, they keep themselves mostly to themselves and rarely reveal anything private or personal. Imagine my amazement then when the peace was disturbed late in the afternoon of Saturday twenty-fourth of May 2014, a date now indelibly fixed in my fading memory.

I had been watching the Championship Playoff Final between Derby County and Queens Park Rangers and was left reeling from the shock of Bobby Zamora's last gasp goal with the only shot on target that they managed all afternoon which somehow took the R's to the Premier League on an afternoon where the Gods most certainly favoured them, as they had been totally outplayed and the result was an aberration which quite frankly beggared belief.

The Bees had already secured their place in the Championship and whilst I knew that Fulham awaited us in 2014/15, the real prize was QPR and I was devastated that our prey had escaped us and had been snatched from our grasp in so unfortunate and unfair a manner and that the fates had yet again laughed in our face.

I needed to go for a walk around the block in order to calm down, get over my disappointment and settle my shattered nerves and as I passed a house no more than fifty yards from mine I saw something that still haunts me to this day.

Occasionally some of the local residents celebrate Christmas or Chanukah with a few muted and tasteful external decorations but this was different as the entire outside of this house was covered and daubed from roof to basement with Queens Park Rangers banners, scarves, posters and blue and white bunting. Lights flashed and music blared, breaking the customary sepulchral calm and quiet of the neighbourhood and the drive was filled with cars full of raucous QPR supporters celebrating their unlikely achievement.

I had no idea that our street housed a rabid QPR supporter given that we are situated so far away from their heartland and whilst I am by nature a calm and totally law-abiding individual my hackles rose and it was all that I could do to restrain myself from giving vent to my frustration and tearing down the decorations which so offended me.

Worse still, they remained in place, although thankfully fading, throughout that long hot Summer and it was not until the season began and it became obvious that Queens Park Rangers were in over their head and totally overmatched in the Premier League, and were certain to return shortly from whence they came that they were dismantled, at which point I calmed down and finally refrained from thinking poisonous and murderous thoughts every time that I walked past that house on my way home.

I wrote at great length about the longstanding rivalry and history between Brentford and QPR and the reason for the *animus* between both clubs before our first meeting last October and I was so delighted and proud to be present at what was our first victory over our bitter rivals for fifty years on an evening packed full of pride, effort, energy and passion – all of which was expended by the team wearing red and white stripes.

The entire Brentford team raised its game, as every player was well aware of just how much the game meant to the home supporters. Beating QPR was everything to us all and the throaty roar of triumph at the final whistle almost raised the Ealing Road roof.

We outplayed and outworked our opponents who strolled through the match and gave a limp and pallid display which seemed to imply that they felt that it was rather beneath them to be forced to sully their hands and share a pitch with a team and a club that was not on their radar and that they thought so little of, and that aristocrats like themselves had no need to sweat.

Much has changed for the Bees in the months since that momentous victory. We were then in the midst of a brief but highly successful spell under Lee Carsley when the team seemed well organised, confident and extremely hard to beat. Everybody seemed to understand their role and there was a sense of togetherness with every player working hard to cover his teammates.

QPR rarely looked like scoring bar for two efforts from Luongo just before the break and once Marco Djuricin became an instant Bees legend by timing his run to perfection to convert Alan Judge's incisive near post cross, our eventual victory barely seemed in doubt as we played out the remainder of the game with total confidence and determination.

This year has seen the Bees crumble and disintegrate and a weakened squad lacking so many of its best players and bereft of confidence and the apparent ability to either score goals or keep them out, is crawling and limping towards the finish line, praying that the games run out before they can be caught up and overtaken by the bottom three.

Despite their victory at Griffin Park last Saturday, Charlton Athletic as well as Bolton Wanderers appear to be beyond salvation but a resurgent Rotherham team, responding brilliantly to the management style of the inimitable Neil Warnock has now won three on the trot and we are beginning to look anxiously in our rear view mirror.

However insipid have been the team's recent performances, the fans also need to do their bit, particularly on Saturday when just under three thousand Bees will face a hostile home crowd at Loftus Road. It was noticeable just how loud and intimidating the atmosphere was when we played at Rotherham recently as the home supporters provided unconditional support, forgave their heroes for all their mistakes and bayed for free kicks, real and imaginary. Brentford and, of course, the referee wilted under the relentless pressure as we eventually caved in for what could well turn out to be a damaging defeat.

Griffin Park has been like a morgue recently with the crowd seemingly stupefied and reduced to silence or at best groans of anger and disappointment given the horrendous lack of quality of so many of our recent performances.

We are now facing a drama which we can help become a crisis if we continue in the same vein. Of course the team needs to do its bit and at least show some effort, organisation, energy, bite, aggression and determination on Saturday – and some quality too would also not come amiss!

We supporters also have a job to do and we need to take on board the marvellous example of those long-suffering Rotherham fans just the other week. We have to provide a nonstop cauldron and cacophony of noise and simply exhort and encourage our team totally and unconditionally and for the entire duration of the game.

That is something that is well within our gift, everything else is out of our control and we can only hope and expect that Dean Smith selects the right team and game plan and that the players remember just how important this game is and perform accordingly both with and without the ball.

To beat QPR twice in a season, do the double over them and win for the first time at Loftus Road since the ninth of October 1964 would go quite some way towards ensuring that this season is remembered for far more than our recent fall from grace and nosedive towards the nether regions of the Championship table.

Saturday is a quite massive game for a variety of reasons, not least because I want to maintain and extend the bragging rights within my road and make sure that my misguided neighbour knows exactly who is the best Championship team in West London.

Meeting Phil Giles – 11/3/16

Good communication with your customers is paramount in any successful organisation and is something that should be a given in today's world of social media and instant access to news and information and the near impossibility of keeping matters under wraps.

Unfortunately many football clubs have lagged far behind the times, seemingly taking the unquestioned loyalty of their fans for granted, smug and complacent in the knowledge that unlike consumers in practically any other sphere of business activity, real supporters are wedded to their team for life and would never contemplate changing their allegiance to a rival however much they are tempted to do so.

Brentford have always made a point of bucking the trend and in recent years there has been a succession of managers, chairmen, owners and chief executives willing to put their head over the parapet and engage with the supporters at a series of Fans' Forums which have generally resulted in an exchange of views and in fans being kept in the loop.

Given the fact that the services of former Head Coach Marinus Dijkhuizen were disposed of immediately after the last such event when all had been made to appear in public to be sweetness and light between him and senior club management, there has been an urgent need to rebuild some bridges particularly given the rising concern over recent results as well as the sale of key players without the squad being replenished.

With the exception of an interview ten years ago and a quite brilliant and totally bizarre and left-field online Q&A last season, both held on *The Griffin Park Grapevine,* plus a few carefully crafted and placed articles within the national media, owner Matthew Benham has kept out of the spotlight and refrained from communicating with the Brentford fanbase given that to do so is not within his nature or something that he feels comfortable about doing.

That all changed the other day when he met with the crew at *Beesotted* and gave them a fascinating in-depth interview which I commend to you all and urge you to read if you have not already done so. He answered many key questions about the current situation and how he sees the future developing and his commitment and ambition thankfully cannot be doubted.

I therefore thought that it would, in tandem, be useful, interesting and illuminating to seek out the views of Co-Director of Football Phil Giles and he was kind enough to spare me the time to meet yesterday as well as answer many of the questions that Brentford supporters would hopefully like to ask him in order for him to clarify his role and how he operates.

Ideally his responses below should be read in conjunction with Matthew Benham's *Beesotted* interview as hopefully the two complement each other and viewed together provide a thorough and contemporaneous insight into the thinking, approach and aspirations of the people who are running our club.

Here is what Phil had to say and I hope you find his answers as illuminating as I did:

Introduction

Greville, many thanks for inviting me to contribute to your blog. I've tried to address as many of your questions as possible – and it was quite a long list of questions!

Rather than answer each individually, I've broken down the questions into sections and written about each one in turn. Hopefully this gives a bit more insight into what we're doing.

This Season And The Summer

I understand the current frustrations among our fans. Many of them made their feelings known at the end of the Charlton game. There have been lots of changes at the club in the last year, and we, collectively as a club, haven't consistently reached the same levels of performance as last season. The league table will tell you as much.

However, there are still eleven games to go this season and here is what we want to achieve between now and the end of the season:

We want to finish the season as strongly as possible.

We have a young team – three of our four defenders against Charlton are twenty-two years old. Harlee is only twenty-four. The midfield that started against Charlton are twenty-three, twenty, twenty-two, nineteen and twenty-seven (Judge). Djuricin is twenty-three.

The experience the players gain over the coming weeks will serve us well next season. With experience will come consistency – we were very good against Wolves, but not so good four days later at Rotherham.

We will bring in a loan player if we feel we can improve the team and our long-term prospects.

We are already planning our summer recruitment. We didn't add anyone in January because the players we wanted were overpriced. As Matthew also said this week, we intend to add good players in the Summer.

We want to finish with some good performances by playing the Brentford way, and would like everyone associated with the club to be united in a positive outlook ahead of the summer.

Longer Term Ambitions For The Club

If we ranked all Championship clubs by revenue we'd be right at the bottom of the league. The new stadium is an important step to allowing us to compete on a more level playing field.

The long-term ambition is to build a financially sustainable club that plays at the highest level possible. The quickest route to sustainability is to earn promotion. That is our ultimate target, but we're not in a position to do what other clubs have done recently by investing huge sums in the team. We'll have to find a different way of doing it and take a few risks along the way. Some of those risks will work, and some won't, that is the nature of taking chances. It's important that we learn from what works and what does not along the way – and we will do.

Football Staff – Roles And Responsibilities

I'll try to set out the specific roles that Rasmus and I play at the Club here.

Let me begin by saying that whenever one of us gives and interview or makes a statement, we do so on behalf of both of us.

I have spent one hundred percent of my time on Brentford since I started in the job. Ras spends half of his time with Brentford and half with FC Midtjylland. We aren't always visible but we are working hard to help build a long-term sustainable and successful club.

Ras and I have different strengths so we dovetail quite well I think. He tends to focus on the big picture and thinks about things in the longer term. For example, he has been reviewing our Academy and considering how it can compete with every other club that wants to basically do exactly the same as us.

I am more focused on the details and making things work in practice on a day-to-day basis. We have put in place several management processes to improve the way we operate – it's the sort of stuff that shouldn't be noticed if it's working properly.

For example, I was keen to make sure that the football department gives every support needed to the Brentford Community Sports Trust, and we've reviewed the process to ensure that we are fulfilling our obligations in that respect.

I manage the recruitment process and negotiate the contracts, but I tend not to get too involved in watching or evaluating players. It's important to realise your strengths and weaknesses, and I'm certainly not a qualified coach or scout. My strengths are more on the management and organisational side – making sure we build a club with strong foundations for the future.

There's room for all types of backgrounds in football I think. Accountants and lawyers are prevalent in football and involved in all transfers, although their work tends to be in the background.

Part of my job is making sure that the relevant skills are brought into play at the right stage of the recruitment and negotiation process.

The "football man" is essential in identifying a player and creating a development plan for that player, but the "executives" are needed to make sure that any deal makes legal and financial sense for the club, and that proper process and protocols are followed.

We set out the qualities that Dean Smith brings to the role of Head Coach when he joined us – he is experienced, has good leadership skills, wants to play in the Brentford way and has an excellent track record of developing young players.

He has had to deal with both the Jota and Tarky situations, and we weren't able to add players in January which was the first opportunity he had to influence our transfer policy. We are working very closely together both on current projects and longer term planning, including our recruitment plans for the summer.

Relationships With Other Clubs.

I'd like to think that our relationships with other clubs are very good, in particular with some of the top Premier League clubs. That is a continuation of some of the efforts put in during previous seasons which allowed us to bring in on loan Pritchard and Toral last year, and Swift and Canos this season.

We tend to spread the load of building relationships with other clubs across several of the staff, rather than relying on one or two people to be solely responsible, since if those one or two people leave then the club can't build and grow optimally in the long-term. For example, Dean has pre-existing contacts which we've made use of, as does Ras, Rob Rowan and others including myself.

In terms of the rest of the football world, I'd like to think most people see Brentford as a well-regarded Championship club that goes about things in the right way. I think we look after our players very well. We've had some good meetings with other clubs about how we do things and whether there are some mutually beneficial things that we can work on together.

If there is an opportunity to sign a loan player permanently then we will consider taking that opportunity – the policy hasn't changed from that which brought Bidwell and Forshaw to the club.

Players And Recruitment

I will try to set out the general process by which we identify and sign players.

Ras and I have regular meetings with the coaching staff. At those meetings we will go through the squad and discuss our key requirements. That information will be passed to the scouting team, along with profiles of the type of players we're looking for. The scouting team will use every available resource to identify players – they watch games, they speak to contacts and agents, and they use data where appropriate. We will do as much research into the character and personality of each player as possible. A selection of potential targets will be fed back to the coaches, who will review the options and prioritise targets.

From there we will decide on which players to target, approach the clubs and finally speak to the players. This is predominantly my responsibility, as described above. Dean and Richard have a huge input into the type of players we want to target, and who we eventually try to sign or sell. Their input is the most important part of the whole process.

In my experience there hasn't been a single occasion where we've not been able to reach a collective agreement on a transfer. Sometimes we all need to compromise a bit to get things done, but that is a normal part of the management process as far as I'm concerned.

I suspect that this process isn't too different from other clubs, although perhaps we place greater emphasis on certain elements than others. It is essential that we do this however, since we aren't in a position to employ a large team of scouts who can be at every game. This goes back to the idea that we need to take some risks in order to compete with clubs that have greater income. If we scout in exactly the same way as other teams, then most likely our results will be defined by our budget in the long-term.

The data that we have access to isn't too different to many other clubs, but it's what you do with it that's the important thing. I think that the background of some of the management team allows us to do some interesting and sometimes complicated proprietorial stuff with that data.

Statistics and data analysis is my background although I don't do so much of it these days. In reality it's only one of the tools we have, complementing the more traditional approaches where it makes sense.

Sometimes we fail to sign players that we target. I think it's healthy to sometimes miss out on players – if we always signed every player that we targeted then it probably means that we're either overpaying or that no other clubs want to sign our targets. We always have an up to date list of other potential and viable targets so there is always a next player on the list.

Disclosing transfer fees and alerting other clubs to how much we can afford to pay for players, or how much income we receive from sales, doesn't offer us any competitive advantage over those teams, which is why the terms are normally undisclosed.

Were we in a stronger position on the pitch after January 2016? As I said in an interview for the club website in February, it is impossible for me to state that the squad was stronger having sold two players and Jota having left on loan. However, we took all those decisions with the long-term interests of the club at heart.

I understand that this is frustrating for fans, especially in the light of recent results. However, I am absolutely determined that we'll be in a stronger position in the long-term for having taken the difficult decisions now regarding players who, ultimately, didn't see themselves as a long-term part of Brentford's plans.

The strategy for the summer is simple – we'll try to sign good players who improve the squad and who ultimately win us football matches and move us up the table. We've signed good players in the past, and we'll do so in the future.

Miscellaneous

Here is one example of how we've found the link with FC Midtjylland useful. They played Manchester United twice recently. It was a perfect opportunity for people associated with both Brentford and FC Midtjylland to meet the key Manchester United staff and continue the process of developing relationships, which as I discussed earlier is an important part of what we do.

I think we've been very unlucky this season with injuries but we don't think that is anything other than bad luck. Some of the injuries have been quite freakish. Hopefully we'll get more luck next season.

With regards to the cup competitions, we underestimated the strength of Oxford in the League Cup. In the FA Cup, we had three games in six days and the Walsall game was the first of those. We fielded a team that we believed should be able to beat Walsall, but didn't. It was a match worth winning in hindsight. We don't ever field a team not intending to win the match, and we'll continue to look to win every cup game that we play.

I enjoyed the couple of hours that I spent with Phil and found him to be pleasant, bright, thoughtful, open-minded and good company. He takes his time and thinks before he speaks and his words are clipped and carefully chosen. He was certainly polite and endlessly patient given the voluminous number of questions that I had posed him in advance but he shirked no issue, he neither prevaricated nor refrained from answering anything that I asked him although some matters were only discussed on an off the record basis which I have respected given his reasonable concerns about commercial confidentiality and the disclosure of proprietary information.

That being said his answers were controlled, carefully composed and organised and I am quite certain that he revealed nothing to me other than what he had originally intended to do – and why, indeed, should he to a total stranger who he knew was intending to go public with what he had heard?

Pleasingly, he is also a true soccer *aficionado* and finally came alive when discussing the fortunes of his beloved Newcastle United and he exhibited an encyclopaedic knowledge of their marvellously exciting squad of the mid to late 90s and could see the clear parallel with the Brentford of last season when I described them as everybody's favourite second team.

Phil is well aware of his strengths and weaknesses, what he has yet to learn and the need to be part of a team ethos where between everybody all necessary skills and expertise are provided.

He is a highly impressive young man thankfully devoid of arrogance with a bright and enquiring mind who will push boundaries, innovate and explore new options.

We are in good hands.

Good Hunting! – 13/3/16

Over three thousand Brentford supporters went to Loftus Road yesterday afternoon, perhaps more in hope than in expectation and for half an hour or so the team, and we will come back to its composition shortly, was well in the game with Canos twice and Judge going close before conceding a brilliantly taken but eminently avoidable opening goal which was totally demoralising after we had given as good as we had got.

Even after such a sickening blow we showed some fight and resilience and came so close to an immediate equaliser when Ryan Woods took a short free kick in his stride and drilled a long-ranger against the post. The second half was a different story as after Judge curled narrowly but wastefully over we created next to nothing and the ball became a hot potato as we conceded possession with monotonous regularity and our final ball was invariably overhit or poorly directed.

We conceded two quite appalling goals after schoolboy errors firstly when Woods was dispossessed and then after Swift played a careless and suicidal pass across the midfield, each time leaving us with a yawning chasm down the middle. QPR took full advantage of both gifts, that horrible celebratory *Pigbag* tune blared out and assailed our senses and eardrums and yet another game had slipped away without any reward.

We collapsed like a pricked balloon as the fight and confidence drained out of us and the last twenty minutes was more notable for a mass exit as Brentford supporters left in droves, shocked, horrified, confused, infuriated and let down by what they had seen and, sadly, many of those who were left turned upon each other and the players too who were subjected to vitriol and insults as the game dragged on to its by now inevitable conclusion.

Such is the reaction, however unacceptable and unattractive, when a team loses for the ninth time in its last twelve Championship matches and subsides to a comprehensive and embarrassing defeat to its local rivals who quite frankly barely had to break sweat to beat us, so eager were we to help them given that all three goals came gift wrapped with a bow on top.

Effort and passion there most undoubtedly was – at least for the first three quarters of the match, but we played exactly like the team we have become over the horror show of the past couple of months, one that is desperately lacking in quality, imagination, creativity, pace, craft, strength in midfield, defensive organisation and most importantly, confidence.

Dean Smith took the brave if highly unusual step of leaving both of his two remaining fit, if pallid strikers, Djuricin and Vibe on the bench and playing Alan Judge up front on his own in a new 4-1-4-1 formation. The main thinking behind this move was to encourage the nimble Judge to run at the man-mountain Clint Hill in the home defence.

Perhaps Smith also intended a coded message and that this move, which quite frankly smacked of desperation, was also a cry for help to the two Co-Directors of Football and an acknowledgement that we currently do not possess a striker worthy of the name and that none of them merit a first team spot.

Jake Bidwell - consistently excellent and never noticed until he is is absent

Judge did his best but was a fish out of water and he was never really able to hold onto the ball in order to create things and give his defence some respite particularly when far too many passes aimed at him were fired at his head rather than directed to his feet. His influence was sorely missed elsewhere as our main creator of goal chances and it has to be said that the experiment did not work and contributed to our defeat although Vibe was typically weak, anonymous and infuriating when he was finally introduced as a second half substitute.

Alan McCormack made a welcome return in front of the back four and helped shore us up and for a time appear more solid but he must accept some of the blame for the crucial opening goal when the dangerous Hoilett picked the ball up on halfway and was allowed to drift towards our goal as we simply backed off him. McCormack belatedly thought about making a challenge but criminally pulled out and allowed Hoilett to pass unscathed and, left in splendid isolation, the winger had the ability to curl a sublime effort into the top corner of the net. If you give a good player time and space he will punish you.

The game turned on this moment as the home team was energised and reinvigorated by a moment of sheer quality and noticeably went up a gear and after that near miss from Woods our heads went down and our challenge faded.

Dean Smith now appears to be simply rearranging the deckchairs and desperately trying to find some semblance of a structure or shape from the same small, ever-diminishing and underperforming squad of players. We are quickly disintegrating into a rabble and are quite frankly in free fall and his face is taking on an increasingly haunted look as he seeks some answers and solutions which continue to elude him.

Whether the manager deserves criticism for not managing his limited resources better and ensuring that we at least put in a decent shift and make the most of what little we have is open to question. Comparisons at this stage with Lee Carsley are both pointless and invidious.

There is no appetite within the ownership of the club to make another change at this juncture of the season and such a move would be totally unjust, reek of panic and make us a laughing stock given that Smith has not been able to introduce a single new face while losing three key members of his squad as well as seeing the injury bug begin to bite deep again. Luck has certainly not been on his side.

That being said the current state of affairs cannot be allowed to continue given that even with Bolton and Charlton seemingly doomed there is still a third relegation place left to avoid as Rotherham's revival continues unabated.

The thought persists, indeed it is a raging certainty, that we should not have allowed ourselves to get into this situation with an ever-worsening spiral of defeats but recriminations and analysis are for later, now we simply have to concentrate on the task in hand and do whatever it takes to ensure that we start next season in the Championship. Given our plans and ambitions, relegation is utterly unthinkable but it is looming up on the blindside and could still yet overtake us if we do not take strong and immediate remedial action.

My recent meeting with Phil Giles left me excited and reassured about the mid to long-term future of the club but I was also extremely concerned about the here and now as it is no use having ambitious plans about squad strengthening in the Summer if we end up having to start next season in League One. The chances of this happening are admittedly still low but increasing by the week and at present it is hard to see where the two wins we need are going to come from.

I understand why we sold players and did not strengthen the squad in January given the exorbitant prices we were quoted for some of our targets but perhaps if you sell high as we most certainly did, occasionally there is the need to buy high too in order to maintain the *status quo*.

I believe that the speed and extent of our current fall from grace has taken the senior management totally by surprise and caught them with their pants down and they are struggling to cope with the situation.

Fortune has certainly not favoured us but it is hard to look back at the horror show that has been the story of this year and identify many matches where we were unlucky not to take points. We should not have lost at Birmingham or been beaten by Middlesbrough or even dropped two stupid late points at home to Leeds, otherwise we have very little to complain about and the results and performances speak for themselves.

So what can we do? Is there any potential salvation from within our current resources? I do not expect to see Macleod again this season and have no expectations of Hofmann once he recovers from injury. The only potential ray of hope is Scott Hogan, which shows just how desperate we are, as untested and half fit though he undoubtedly is, I would hope that he is given a place on the bench next weekend for what is now a crucial clash against Blackburn Rovers.

Perhaps his return would give us all a boost and fillip although it would be patently unfair on him to see him as our potential saviour. He is, however, enthusiastic and hard running and a clinical finisher who would provide us with an injection of energy- and he is also untainted by the cloud and gloom that surrounds the team at present.

We need fresh faces and belatedly I am now certain that stringent efforts are being made to bring in short-term reinforcements in time for next Saturday. We will need to take a deep breath and temporarily at least ignore our principles and accepted *modus operandi.*

Think about the likes of Bidwell, Schlupp, Berahino, Forshaw, Harris, Trotta, Pritchard, Toral, Swift, Long and Canos and they all had something in common being young, promising and inexperienced. What we need now are a couple of players who have been around the block a few times, battlers who know and fully understand the demands of the Championship and can lead and inspire our faltering squad as well as provide a spark in front of goal.

It will be difficult both practically and philosophically for us to do so as well as cost us a lot of money currently earmarked for other purposes. I fully expect that some of the war chest ideally being pigeonholed and conserved for next season will now need to be used in order to pay for players who will probably be earning far more than our current squad. Such is life and we will need to be adaptable and flexible as our salvation is paramount.

Other clubs in and around us have found such players recently and have been able and prepared to pay the necessary wages in an attempt to ensure Championship survival. Blackburn sold their prime asset in Jordan Rhodes but have brought in high quality short term replacements in Jordi Gomez, Tony Watt and Danny Graham, who we will all face next week. Charlton signed Yaya Sanogo from Arsenal, suspended now but a striker who led us a merry dance last week. There is an unsubstantiated rumour going around that we were offered him first but turned him down. MK Dons brought in Alex Revell, Nottingham Forest, Federico Macheda, Huddersfield have just signed Rajiv van La Parra and most noticeably Bristol City have splurged out on Lee Tomlin and Peter Odemwingie.

I am sure that most of these names will understandably make our Co-Directors of Football come out in hives and not all of them quite frankly, fill me with much too enthusiasm, but much as it pains us to do so, we will need to follow suit with someone of that ilk next week if we want to do absolutely everything within our power to ensure that our precious Championship status is preserved.

I wish our two Co-Directors of Football all good fortune in their quest.

When Does Banter Become Abuse? – 15/3/16

There was so much that I didn't enjoy about Saturday's visit to Loftus Road. Firstly let's get the obvious out of the way. Losing by three clear goals to your closest rivals after a performance that started well and deteriorated the longer the game went on made for a pretty gloomy and depressing afternoon's viewing.

The fact that QPR were really no great shakes themselves and simply cashed in on our plethora of mistakes and inadequacies simply made matters worse and left me with a feeling of total frustration as well as one of impending doom unless serious steps are taken immediately to reverse our slide before it becomes terminal and irreversible.

The day started well when I found a free parking space ideally situated just a short hike from the ground but it was all downhill from there.

What struck me forcibly as soon as I took my seat half an hour before kickoff was the dark, aggressive and ugly mood amongst so many of the Brentford supporters. Rather than looking forward with relish and anticipation to the chance of completing a rare double over the old enemy, the packed School End was a cauldron of hate with far too many supporters totally out of control and resembling a baying mob of howling banshees.

Their songs and chants were inflammatory and obscene as well as boringly repetitive and unimaginative and the language foul in the extreme as quite appalling words and sentiments that could very easily see you facing a serious Public Order charge in different circumstances repeatedly poured out of the mouths of supporters of all ages, most of whom were quite old enough to know far better.

I am all for poking some gentle fun at our opponents and for making Griffin Park a fortress and an intimidating place to visit, but this went far beyond the pale as QPR, their players, supporters and anything and everything connected with that club were subjected to a fusillade of nonstop abuse and woe betide anybody who made any attempt, however futile to make our supporters behave themselves with some small element of decorum.

What is even worse is that as the game began to turn against the Bees, moods darkened even more, the wind changed and now it was the turn of our own players to become the whipping boys and the targets for abuse. They were assailed with moronic and vitriolic comments and insults both singularly and collectively, with poor, hapless John Swift a particular target. Fans also turned against fellow fans as any supporter who continued to cheer on his team also risked becoming a target. Just as had been the case against Charlton, the previous week, the final whistle saw more boos, catcalls and derogatory comments as the team slunk off.

I had a similarly unpleasant afternoon earlier this season at Derby when a large group of intimidating so-called Brentford supporters unfortunately seated right by me spent the entire match eyeballing rival home fans and singling them out for a nonstop torrent of vehement abuse. What happened on the pitch – nothing much if truth be told – was totally immaterial to them and I doubt if many of them could have told you the final score given that they had watched so little of the game. Again this sickened and quite frankly, frightened me and fortunately I managed to move to a slightly more salubrious spot at halftime but it ruined my afternoon and I could not wait to leave. The difference though was that the mindless abuse was aimed solely at the opposition supporters whereas now it is the Brentford team and management that is more often than not being targeted.

Perhaps the solution is simple and a couple of good wins would end this nasty trend that seems to be becoming more and more prevalent but it is something that is making my visits to football less and less pleasant and I am sure that I am not alone in feeling this way.

I suspect that we have also picked up quite a few floating, fair-weather and glory hunting supporters attracted by our success of last season who have no sense or even interest in the history and tradition of the club and what it stands for, and now, when results are going against us they are quick to criticise or worse without any understanding of the reasons why matters have deteriorated so quickly.

Just look at the Rotherham fans who have become their team's twelfth man and have contributed so volubly to their recent success. Their sheer passion and nonstop roars of encouragement have helped to turn games in their favour and influence referees, as we learned to our cost. That is what we should be aiming for, a team and band of supporters united as one and working towards a common goal.

I can't say that I am too thrilled either by a lot of the rubbish that is currently being spouted on social media sites where supporters seem to feel that it is open season on owners, players and managers alike who are subjected without a second thought to torrents of filthy abuse with Dean Smith, Matthew Benham and the Co-Directors of Football being particular recent victims.

Again, there seems to be no sense of tolerance or decency and boundaries of reasonable behaviour seem to have been ignored and overturned. Anyone appears to be fair game for an ever-increasing phalanx of mindless keyboard warriors who feel that they have an inalienable right to make their opinions and feelings known however stridently or abusively they wish to express them.

Any criticism of them regarding the way in which they form their arguments and the actual words they have used is either ignored or more commonly results in a further tirade of splenetic abuse and strident claims that they are fully entitled to have their say however they choose to do so. So often they excuse their excesses by claiming that their comments are simply harmless banter but that explanation does not wash for me as anything said or written that is wounding, demeaning and insulting is totally inexcusable and they quite evidently do not know the real meaning of the word.

And that is where the problem lies, as many people do not understand just how far they can go and where acceptable behaviour ends. I totally accept that nobody, however exalted, should be above criticism but in my opinion it is how that criticism is couched that makes all the difference. Why should anybody read, take in, assimilate or even respond to torrents of crude and foulmouthed abuse? A more reasoned comment, opinion or argument might well generate some sort of answer but I suspect that the intent is generally to shock and mock and promote a sense of self rather than encourage a proper debate.

I am not going to run the risk of being called an old fogey by calling for the return of National Service or the stocks as I am a massive supporter of social media and instant access to the news agenda. Properly used it allows for an immediacy and an honesty, clarity and openness of communication that cannot be matched elsewhere. I just hate it when mindless oafs who know no better and just spoil things for everyone else, abuse its powers.

Let's Get Behind The Team! – 17/3/16

I wrote an article just the other day about my growing concerns about the increasing amount of foulmouthed abuse that the team and individual players and indeed the Brentford management are increasingly being subjected to both at matches as well as on social media.

It is a subject that I feel extremely strongly about as I fully support the right of all people to express their opinion but only if it is done in a reasonable manner, and I think that most sane and sensible people fully understand and realise when the line between acceptable and unacceptable behaviour has been crossed.

I also fully accept that football is a passionate game that stirs the emotions and fans can quite easily lose momentary control in the heat of the moment particularly when, as is the case at the moment, the team is neither playing well nor winning games.

Frustration, fear, confusion, disappointment and anger are an intoxicating brew indeed and can well lead to behaviour that in the cold light of day would be deemed well out of character.

That though is not to excuse it and some of the aggression and comments that I have either witnessed or read recently are, in my opinion, totally beyond the pale and serve only to further break the crucial bond between the team and the fans, and indeed create divisions between different factions of supporter at a time when we all desperately need to be pulling together.

The time for inquests is surely at the end of the season, or when our fate is finally sealed, and not now at a key point in the season when we need to be united and act in concert to support the team unconditionally and do whatever we can to help ensure that we get over the line unscathed by obtaining the points required to ensure our Championship survival.

I was not sure what reaction my initial comments would receive and whether I would simply be seen as out of touch and a dinosaur but the article seems to have touched a chord amongst many Brentford supporters, young and old who all contributed their views on this difficult and emotive subject.

Edward Coleman also had an upsetting experience at Loftus Road last Saturday:

I was sitting in the lower stand with my fifteen-year-old daughter and was appalled. When I have been at previous way games it has been noisy but with an element of humour. This was just nasty. It was reminiscent of an English Defence League rally and I am not saying this flippantly as I was caught up in one several years ago.

I live in South Ealing where Fulham and QPR fans are mixed in with Bees and I do not hate my neighbours. Whilst I am a newish fan (I got back into football because my daughter is football mad) I am not some sort of prude. I have worked in nightshelters and used to work in adult mental health. We sit at home in Braemar Road because both of us enjoy the adult repartee. I met another local fan who was at the match with her daughter and she also found it very frightening.

Steve was far more succinct and forthright in his comments:

Well said Greville. Keep this blog as a beacon of sense as elsewhere there is madness.

Regarding the insults, seeing men in their forties screaming abuse at teenagers playing football does make me wince. How do they think it is either acceptable or likely to help the players?

More of the same from **Lew:**

You've touched upon something that's been aggravating me for a while but I've not fully been able to vocalise it. As a group we've been split into two rough groups for ages: keep the faith or go back to how things were, we've stopped getting behind the team and started looking for excuses. But that lack of unity in the stands is just as important a factor as the lack of consistency on the pitch. It would be excellent if everybody modified their opinions and just cheered as one on Saturday.

Wise words indeed and I totally endorse his analysis of the situation.

Simon Pitt took a different stance:

Last season we finished fifth and were told by Matthew Benham that the club needs to be taken in a different direction to make us more competitive with big clubs with more resources in the championship. Finishing fifth to me suggests we are going in the right direction and so (if it ain't broke don't fix it) why the need for change? If we finished in the bottom half or survived a relegation battle then fair enough.

Every player and athletes in general strive to reach the top of their sport and those players of last season must have known how close they were to achieving their goal of playing in the Premier League.

Matthew Benham's vision should have been put on hold and encouraged the players and manager to give us one more year. I fully respect Matthew Benham and understand his philosophy, but he got the timing wrong. Mark Warburton obviously had huge respect from the players and I'm sure that if he had stayed so too would have the players. A couple more signings and I'm sure we could have done it this year. This is why the fans are so angry, frustrated and mystified as to what has been going on and so normal placid fans are making their feelings known.

When I asked Simon if he felt that the manner and way in which disappointed and disgruntled supporters are currently making their views known is acceptable, and if he agreed that it was just making things far worse rather than helping as the extreme negativity being expressed so unpleasantly is driving us all further apart and polarising us rather than bringing us all together, he replied:

No I don't think it's acceptable but it goes on at most grounds up and down the country and will never change and there is very little that can be done about it. If people are offended then stop going and choose a different sport to follow.

I understand his frustration but cannot accept that the end justifies the means and that we should simply ignore the problem, put our head in the sand or simply stop attending matches and let the idiots win.

Rob also shared my view:

Greville, great blog as always and I totally agree one hundred percent. Although we qualified for tickets quite early in the process we as a family passed up on the QPR game. My eleven-year-old hates football at the best of times but surrounded by a Bees-mad Father, Mother and elder brother he has to put up with it. However various away games this season (and last) really have put him off away games. The vile verbal abuse seems the best we can resort to rather than creative singing and chanting to try and raise the team.

I recently attended the Brighton versus Sheffield Wednesday game, midweek, rubbish weather and to be honest very poor football. But over fifteen hundred Wednesday fans, no matter how poorly they were playing, not only stood as one throughout, but sang their hearts out in encouragement – even when the simplest and most basics of mistakes were being made by their team.

Compare that, and I do understand we are at the other end of the table, to the abuse dished out not just at away but also home games to individuals in our team.

For thirty-nine years I have watched good and bad performances and players (more bad than good I'm afraid) but never feel it is either our right, or correct that players should be abused or booed.

The trouble it would seem is with the relative success over the last few years or so, those thirteen to fifteen year olds who started with their fathers as supporters are now sixteen to eighteen year olds who believe in a culture where they feel through social media it is their right to verbally abuse and insult not just the players, but management, coaches and owners.

They spout off regarding team selections, who should be sold and who should be sacked all in the strongest terms and yet then in the next sentence complain how tough their A Level homework is! They have no experience of life and yet feel they know all there is to know about running a football club (and much more) and engage their brains without any due consideration to the impact of where they are saying.

The next best thing in their mind is launch into vile, personal and disgusting abuse. Those older should know better, but they are role models for those younger who without any consideration to their actions don't really care about much else than themselves.

It is not my intention to point the finger at all within their age bracket, but the same bunch that demand immediate gratification and believe it is our God given right to win promotion season after season are the same ones who sometimes make me ashamed to be a Bees fan.

John Hirdle has also seen and heard more than enough:

An excellent article as ever and something that I think has been waiting to be said by somebody for a while now. It is the way of the world these days though and sadly I don't see it changing any time soon. I am old school like yourself and do find some of the vitriolic stuff rather distasteful I must say. We are all frustrated and angry at what has happened over the last year and our current spectacular nosedive.

None of us, including myself, are exempt from letting our frustrations boil over from time to time, but there is a fine line between momentary passion-led shows of disappointment and personal targeted vile abuse which gets us all nowhere.

I used to love standing amongst the younger lads at away games and having a good singsong. But in recent seasons I must say I deliberately make sure I book seats well clear of the back of the stands and most of the smoke bomb idiots. It was the main reason I chose the Upper Tier at Loftus Road on Saturday as I knew I would be amongst more reasoned people.

I don't by any means label all of our younger lads with the same tag as I personally know many and they are good guys, and indeed some of my own generation and older are just as culpable of foulmouthed and offensive behaviour. Maybe it is just bigger crowds brought about by the success of recent seasons and you notice it more, but I, like you, have become more aware of the less than savoury minority element of support we now have both at games and across social media. Or maybe I am just getting old?

Rebel Bee was characteristically hard-hitting and forceful in his comments:

Some of the stuff that took place on Saturday really wasn't good and it is completely right and fair to raise it in your fine blog. But with huge respect to you and other posters I am going to try to offer some mitigation and push back a touch. Rangers fans were dishing it out to us all day and it wound a few Bees up before and during the game – getting spanked by them brings out the worst in people, and I too had to walk out before the end to avoid losing the plot. Is it right – no, but we are watching football not rugby – football and its culture is different – warts and all.

As to aggression between Bees fans, I've seen this a few times and it is sad to see, trust me it is coming from both sides of the argument over the club's deteriorating fortunes. People have invested in our big new ambitions massively, many are confused, anxious and angry at the way this season has been conducted.

By the way this part of a far wider football issue than you may think, I've heard of Arsenal fans turning on each other recently – and the same at many other clubs. We invest more than ever in support of our team and I don't just mean in monetary terms.

You reference Rotherham – sure, but they are as mean and hostile a bunch of fans as you'll find on their day, this has been lacking at Griffin Park this season because we don't have a unified cause or purpose and aren't pulling together – but they are not a group of librarians – trust me.

Where I strongly agree is the use/misuse of social media. It is easy to be really offensive when you are anonymous or don't face your victim. It is a societal problem though, often football fans get blamed for things that go on and are worse in wider society – it's always been that way since I've been around. We all used to go to the pub to let off steam and say what we needed to say in a confined space. Now people jump on to Twitter and most regret if afterwards.

Whilst it may not be ideal, football fans come from all backgrounds and types of upbringing, some are more articulate than others. It doesn't mean that really bad behaviour should be blindly tolerated, but it should also not be forgotten that it has always been the game of the working class. Fan culture and tribalism are aspects of all that we love, sometimes it boils over and is ugly.

Finally there is a risk that we allow the narrative to shift over our club's failings this season, and move the root cause so that it becomes the fans' fault for being so negative. I see this happening already, those that have backed all the big decisions said we'd be fine, and they aren't so sure now, fair enough but please let's not put this on our brilliant fans – regardless of their point of view on the big topics. Football fans are always such an easy target.

Saturday was a bad day all round – we move on and hopefully can pull together to get the wins we need to all be able to leave this season behind us – united again.

Spanish Bee agrees with him:

I think Rebel Bee is making a very valid point here. There is no justification for the behaviour you criticise and from a practical point of view, it doesn't help the team, so it is self-defeating or to put it another way just stupid. However, changing everything so radically when we had had our most successful season for decades was a very risky thing to do and it has not turned out well. Without going into details, Brentford Football Club has significantly raised expectations and then has fallen very short. We should not blame the fans for this.

Red Rose Bee blames matters on our new batch of so-called supporters:

Empty vessels make the most noise and drunken empty vessels desperate to impress their equally empty-headed mates make a great deal of noise.

One of the problems of our great success of the past five years is that we have attracted some idiots who have jumped onto the bandwagon and who lack the intelligence and maturity to realise that supporting a team like Brentford will inevitably have more downs than ups.

I never saw these characters at places like Scunthorpe, Rochdale, Macclesfield and Morecambe in the very recent past.

The only bright side to our present plight and possible relegation is that they will take themselves elsewhere and go and pollute a different club.

Lawrence Bending also puts the blame on raised expectations and the presence of glory hunters:

The sort of bilious hatred on view by some supporters leaves a sour taste regardless of the outcome of the match. I first watched the Bees regularly in 1967 so QPR will never be favourites of mine – but funnily enough – their fans and players are just other human beings. The atmosphere has changed recently due to our relative success, and probably huge disappointment at seemingly throwing this away, has contributed I believe to most of these excesses – it is ironic that if God forbid we are relegated it will largely disappear. For goodness sake let's pull together and concentrate on supporting the team and not abusing the opposition.

beesyellow22 tried to take a balanced view:

I'm sure we would all like for us to beat Blackburn and come together as supporters and a club. Unfortunately I don't think it will be as easy as that. Yes, a win on Saturday will help, but until survival is guaranteed and there is something positive to look towards next season I think that many will continue to share the philosophy of Simon Pitt (one I don't completely disagree with myself) and question where the club is actually going and why Matthew was so happy to dispense with the services of our greatest manager in the modern era.

Of course it does not excuse the kind of behaviour that Greville is talking about – but at the same time there is an enormous amount of frustration amongst supporters, surely borne out of a perception that so much of what we have witnessed this season has been self-inflicted.

Yes, it is up to the fans to continue to get behind the team and the manager – but it is also up to the powers that be to give the fans a reason to keep believing. Is blind faith the answer? Sometimes – particularly when you love your club. However, blind faith after ten defeats out of the last thirteen games is a hard thing to muster.

Jim Levack is also fed up with the type of behaviour he has witnessed:

I totally agree with Greville's take on the unfortunate civil war that seems to be enveloping the club and its supporters.

I have had, at times, quite heated disagreements with some close Brentford supporting friends since Mark Warburton left the club so I know how easy it is to become embroiled in an exchange of views.

The common theme among these rows is passion, we are all passionate about our club and passionate about how we feel the current slide can be arrested.

Last week against Charlton I watched Sergi Canos chase a lost cause. He didn't win the ball but was roundly applauded. If Brentford fans see total effort they respond. If they don't they won't.

We want the people running the club to be as passionate as we are, but currently the lack of action in strengthening the squad gives the impression – most likely a false one – that they don't share our passion. To my mind they have forty-eight hours to allay fears by bringing in at least two loan players to freshen things up and give Dean Smith a fighting chance of putting his mark on the side. If they don't their actions could be considered as bordering on negligent.

Whatever happens though, in-fighting – however satisfying it might be in the short term – will do more harm than good to our chances of staying up.

Bernard Quackenbush made a pithy comment:

One of the things I hate about the modern game is this practice of abusing others quite mindlessly and then trying to excuse it by referring to it as banter.

Finally, **Garry Smith** gave his measured view from afar:

I have been moved to contribute by the current situation and the very raw tones of all your contributors of late, dare I say many of them in panic at the potential loss of a league status that all but the most recent of supporter recruits have yearned for, for a long period of time.

I will re-iterate my previous assertion that whilst used by many generations, social media is the younger person's preferred (if not only) avenue of communication and that a fair amount of these critics are the very same recently attracted supporters that only know the successful Brentford, we need these young blood supporters as they are the future, but we must understand they are trying to compete with their peers who support Premier League teams who they can support via television and the internet and therefore these supporters are far more frustrated with their first period of hardship than us who have seen it all before.

I am not sure what the driving force behind the older generation of critics is, maybe they have always been critics (and maybe always had poor performances as a reason to be) or maybe they too are recent recruits. Maybe the in-fighting is an attempt by the hardened critics (who are really loyal supporters) not liking the attitude of recent critics, I don't get it anyway, because a supporter is allowed to moan but should never be in a big enough minority to actually affect everybody else!

Here is the nub of why I wanted to contribute again, I am sure that a conscious decision was made by senior management (once the Marinus experiment failed) to bring in a proven English-style manager (who likes to play a passing game) with a view of building for next season, it was felt that enough points (no small thanks to Lee Carsley) and enough good players had been accumulated for us to survive and at the same time gain premium prices for players we were never going to find it easy to hold onto, so we could hoard our resources for a real go again next season.

I have always been fully behind this approach, this is the first time we have been in the second flight for two successive seasons in all my fifty-three years of supporting and I KNOW we have Matthew Benham to thank for this, I am sure recent supporter recruits will not fully understand this for the reasons given above.

Unfortunately it has probably been underestimated how quickly and vehemently the fans would turn on senior management, coaches and players. This is contributing to an undermining of confidence in players and coaches alike, which cannot fail to translate itself onto the pitch. Yes I know our current squad has nowhere near as much skill and quality as last season, but I am sure they are a lot better than they are appearing at present.

This is where I would like to make my big plea, please can all supporters reading this, or being influenced by fans reading this, realise we will be in serious trouble if we do not all pull together very soon. I will harp back to Martin Allen again, whose contribution I will never forget, One man pulled everybody together by being positive. We can only pull this around by being together – the negativity, in-fighting, criticism of players, coaching staff and management, can only harm our chance of remaining in this division until we strengthen our squad.

Please, please, all pull together and encourage the players, staff and each other, even (or maybe especially) when we don't always do things well, this is real and it is now. We have enough winnable games left if we all get together and pull in the same direction.

Go On You Bees!

I cannot end this article on a better note than with Garry's rousing rallying call.

It's Time For Our Luck To Change! – 18/3/16

Mark Warburton was always one to say that matches in the Championship were invariably closely fought, tightly contested and generally turned on a mistake, a moment of genius or the whim of a referee's decision.

In other words the result hinged on a hairsbreadth and narrow margins prevailed.

Who can recall the home game against Norwich last season, which to a disinterested observer appeared to end in a conclusive and comprehensive three-goal victory for the visitors?

Brentford fans knew far better, as a contest totally dominated by the Bees was decided by a series of outstanding saves by the unbeatable John Ruddy, a momentary loss of concentration by James Tarkowski which led to the crucial opening goal and the referee's incomprehensible decision not to award a seemingly stonewall penalty when Alex Pritchard was clearly sawn off at the knees a few moments later.

Brentford go into tomorrow's match after a run of three demoralising defeats to Rotherham, Charlton and, most upsettingly, local rivals Queens Park Rangers.

On the face of it, losing to three teams who can hardly be described as Championship powerhouses is worrying and does not bode well for the immediate future.

Confidence both on the pitch and the terraces is quite naturally at a low ebb at the moment and the season is now poised on a knife-edge.

Will the team belatedly recover its poise and with one bound be free of the looming threat of a relegation dog fight or will we all be in for an exhausting, stressful and nerve shattering last ten games of the season?

A closer examination of the key moments in each of the last three games should provide some crumbs of comfort for supporters whose nails are bitten to the quick, whose nerves are clanging and who are quick now to remonstrate and express disapproval when things go wrong on and off the pitch.

John Swift and Philipp Hofmann both missed glaring chances to equalise late on at Rotherham when scoring seemed by far the easiest option.

Who knows how the home team would have responded to such a mortal blow so soon after they had gone ahead in the match for the second time?

Maybe heads would have gone down and a revitalised and re-energised Brentford team would have gone onto an unlikely victory?

Having recovered from conceding a daft goal within the opening twenty seconds Brentford were dominating proceedings against Charlton and having deservedly equalised were pressing hard for the go ahead goal.

The opportunity came early in the second half when Josh McEachran saw a gap in the leaden-footed Charlton defence and his perfectly weighted pass sent Sergi Canos streaking through on goal but unfortunately he pulled his effort narrowly wide and the chance had gone.

A goal then, and the Bees would probably have scored at least once more afterwards and gained a morale boosting victory.

Even at Loftus Road last weekend there was a massive turning point almost immediately after QPR had taken the lead when Ryan Woods pinged a twenty-five yard effort off the post and it bounced out instead of in. An equaliser right before the break would surely have deflated the home team and then, who knows what might have happened?

Narrow margins indeed and maybe it is finally time for the fickle finger of fate to point in our direction and for the ball to start running in our favour after so long a period when we have been totally starved of good fortune?

There has already been some very good news this week which hopefully we can build upon with the long overdue signing of a new loan striker in Uruguayan forward Leandro Rodríguez from Everton.

He is largely untried in this country but comes with a good reputation and a decent goal scoring record for River Plate and at twenty-three he is hopefully mature enough to take this opportunity in his stride and if he is as successful as our previous loanees from Everton we will have nothing to complain about.

Scott Hogan also came through another Development Squad outing on Monday and clearly demonstrated his disappointment when taken off near the end. Perhaps a good sign and maybe he will be considered fit enough to take his place on the bench tomorrow?

Given the lack of bite and incision this year from any of our three strikers and their overall impotence, the arrival of Rodríguez and the possible presence of Hogan will give us a huge boost as we face a massive and tough tackling Blackburn defence which takes no prisoners, as Marco Djuricin can surely attest given the serious injury he suffered after a horror-show challenge in the first meeting between the two teams.

Encouragingly, Max Colin is also back in training and contention for selection and will hopefully come through the match without breaking down, as his steadiness and attacking forays have been sorely missed and his return will provide us with an additional potent weapon in our armoury.

Alan Judge will certainly return to his best position behind the striker after last week's failed experiment at Loftus Road and he will want to impress against his former team as well as try to catch the eye of the Eire team management, given that he hopes to make his full international debut in the next couple of weeks.

News also broke yesterday of a players-only behind closed doors meeting which was held earlier this week when some home truths were undoubtedly spoken and individuals reminded of their respective responsibilities and how much is currently at stake.

A similar such inquest after the Stevenage debacle in 2013 had a massively beneficial effect as the Bees immediately went on a long and uninterrupted run of victories.

Would that there is an identical reaction starting tomorrow afternoon!

Our recent record against our visitors is excellent with two wins and a draw in our last three meetings.

We scored six times in our two encounters last season, marked by Jota's magnificent solo effort at Ewood Park and given that our goals were scored by Jota twice, Gray twice, Douglas and Long someone else will need to step up to the plate tomorrow.

It doesn't necessarily take much to change a seemingly never ending run of poor results and performances and tomorrow would certainly be a perfect time for the Gods to smile down upon us.

All we can do as fans is unite as one and provide loud and unconditional support throughout the entire game.

Beyond that matters are totally out of our hands, but let's keep our fingers crossed!

Not Good Enough And Where Do We Go from Here? – 20/3/16

It would be all too easy and also perhaps satisfying and even cathartic to have a real go at the Brentford team which was unable to beat ten men and fell to a potentially disastrous defeat to a Blackburn Rovers team that on the day was never more than big, tough, well-organised and hard to break down.

But what's the point of doing so as all fourteen players patently gave everything that they had and were unflagging in all their efforts to end Brentford's appalling run which has seen them nosedive from a position of midfield serenity to the throes of a relegation battle that they seem totally ill-equipped to cope with and which appears to have taken them completely by surprise.

I am also not going to criticise hapless manager Dean Smith as he can only use the tools that he has been provided with and once the players cross the white lines what happens then is totally down to them.

The plain truth of the matter as we thankfully go into an international break which will allow us some respite and the time to take stock and fully prepare for a massive nine match mini-season which will decide our season and immediate future, is that the current squad is playing far below its potential and at some point the question has to be asked if they are good enough to compete in the Championship and if not, why not? That again is not going to be a productive, beneficial or helpful conversation at the present time given the severity of the situation that we face.

Yesterday was both deflating and demoralising as the Bees totally dominated proceedings and had sixty-six percent possession but did absolutely nothing with it as the ball was shuffled backwards and sideways with monotonous regularity with nobody able or prepared to take responsibility, try something ambitious or attempt an incisive pass.

Dean Smith admitted afterwards that the team had been set up to ensure that we were more solid with the intention of avoiding more of the giveaway goals that have been a frustrating feature of our recent matches. To a degree he achieved these objectives as our visitors barely threatened apart from at set pieces where as expected they dominated given their height and strength. What he patently failed to address was our lack of attacking potency.

Button was forced to save comfortably from Gomez and brilliantly from Akpan's close range header when he was left criminally unmarked from a free kick. Our soft underbelly was left exposed and the longer we went on without scoring the more the nagging thought remained that we would fall to yet another sucker punch, and our worst nightmare finally came true when close to the end of an eminently forgettable match our defensive fallibility came back to haunt us and poor defending from a simple free kick which arrowed into the box from out wide saw a misplaced header from McCormack fall to the feet of Watt who cleverly set up Duffy for a fulminating close range finish which raged into the roof of the net.

For all our possession it is hard to recall more than a handful of times when we actually looked like scoring. Steele dived to paw away Barbet's curling free kick which circumnavigated Brentford's two walls as well as our visitors' but in truth the save was fairly routine.

Even when a rugged and agricultural Blackburn team was reduced to ten men on the hour when Hanley walked for his second yellow card after a deliberate handball, unforgivably we never managed to trouble the keeper who was well protected by a massive wall of blue and white which funnelled together in the centre and comfortably smothered what little danger we provided.

Brentford were allowed to keep unchallenged possession out wide and positively encouraged to swing in any number of crosses which were meat and drink to the phalanx of huge defenders waiting eagerly to deal with them. Leandro Rodríguez, making his full league debut must have wondered what he had let himself in for as he was left totally isolated in the area and rarely had the benefit of players running beyond him in support. He was treated as a punch bag and given no protection by yet another weak referee who also ignored a blatant handball in the area. There is real hope for the future as Leonardo looked energetic, keen and clever on the ball but he was never given a clear sight of goal.

Scott Hogan also made his long-awaited return from his injury nightmare and will provide a boost to our striking resources.

Alan Judge tried too hard to impress against his former club and had a game to forget. The responsibility of being both our only real goal threat as well as the architect of most of our chances now seems to be weighing down heavily upon him and he will welcome the respite and boost to his confidence which will come from some time away from the club with the Eire squad.

Judge selfishly and myopically squandered the opportunity to set Canos clear away on goal when deciding instead to shoot and had a succession of wasteful efforts which went nowhere near before he finally got his bearings correct deep into injury time when his curling effort extended the keeper who was forced to concede a corner from which Harlee Dean's last gasp effort threatened the departing supporters already outside the ground on Ealing Road rather than the Blackburn goal.

That really sums up our goalscoring efforts for the entire match and highlights the extent that nerves and loss of confidence have rendered our team impotent.

In the glory days of last season we played a vibrant and positive brand of attacking football where five skilful midfielders were encouraged to rotate positions and all get forward in turn to support a strong and quick forward who ran the channels, and they all got into the area and never gave the opposition a moment of peace.

Jota, Pritchard, Douglas, Dallas and Toral all provided a real goal threat and scored over forty times between them, and Judge, who only managed to score three times, helped pull all the strings. We played through the opposition and were able to create space and a seemingly nonstop series of openings through our sheer ability and ingenuity as well as the relentlessness of our attacking approach.

I make these points not in anger or sadness but to highlight how greatly the situation has changed from those halcyon days when we had the players that suited the 4-2-3-1 formation that we employed. Now we have lost the pace, positivity and I am afraid to say, much of the talent, that made us so effective.

We are slow, ponderous and predictable and only Judge, Swift (absent yesterday after his *Instagram* indiscretion) and Canos have any clue in front of goal whilst the likes of Woods, McCormack, McEachran and Kerschbaumer have scored only once between them all season.

Our lone striker remains isolated and without support and we never seem to get players in and around him on the edge of, and inside the penalty area. No wonder Blackburn were happy for us to send cross after cross into the box where we never threatened any danger.

McEachran should have come into his own after the sending off as the stage was set for him to take control of the match and make something happen for us. It was an ideal situation for him as he was able to pick the ball up unchallenged deep in our half from Button or a defender and move menacingly into the Blackburn half. This he did on countless occasions but absolutely nothing came of his efforts as he never attempted a pass that threatened to cut the opposition open. He always took the easy and safe option and we literally went around in circles and got nowhere – very, very slowly.

So where do we go from here? The situation now looks extremely serious and increasingly dire as Rotherham continue to come up with an unlikely series of results, winning yesterday at Ipswich. We are now seemingly playing only to avoid the last relegation place and all our efforts now need to be totally focused on that objective.

Our whole short-term future depends upon us remaining in the Championship as I cannot begin to imagine the consequences for the club should we get relegated.

My suggestion is for us all to have a day or so of mourning, anger and offloading and allow all the frustration to come out and then we have to gird our loins, put our disappointment behind us and work in unison to try and get ourselves out of this mess, which in my view is entirely of our own making.

The time for inquests and recriminations is for later and definitely not now. Hopefully we will be able to breathe a deep sigh of relief in early May and then, and only then, dissect this disappointment of a season and do whatever it takes to ensure that the multitude of mistakes that have been made by all parties are learned from and never repeated.

It might well mean that our structure needs to be examined extremely closely and that individuals are forced to take responsibility for their actions. We might also need to change the fundamentals of how we operate. Who knows? But all that is for later and not for now.

Hard though it will be to do so, we quite simply need to keep calm and the fans more than ever have to get behind the team, as indeed they did yesterday.

Most crucially we need to throw away our current default formation and adopt a system that suits the players we have. 4-4-2 with two strikers playing up top would be my choice given the current and obvious lack of incision and support from midfield.

We need to score some goals and win at least a couple of matches and currently we barely look like scoring and are creating little. Scott Hogan made a more than welcome return yesterday and he and Rodríguez must be allowed to develop a partnership and attempt to provide some goal threat.

The easy option for Dean Smith will be to try and make us even more defensive but this must be avoided at all costs. I do not mean that we become naïvely open and attack at will, simply that we defend properly, something that we have not done all year, but also concentrate on asking some questions of the opposition and getting a couple of players into their penalty area would be a good start.

As we have seen, our lack of confidence has drained our energy and imagination away and helped make our legs leaden and apart from Judge nobody will take any responsibility. Yesterday the players appeared to be paralysed by nerves and indecision. McCormack is now doing his best to offer some leadership and fill this void but we desperately need width and pace down the wings.

Money is tight and I doubt if there are many options out there available at a price that we can afford but I would hope that one more fresh face comes in this week, either a winger or a midfielder with bite and presence.

The next two weeks require a mixture of rest, recuperation, self-examination and hard work. We have eight matches to play in April, a month that will decide our future and a combination of fresh legs and fresh minds and a fresh approach are needed from management, squad and supporters alike.

We have to start again after the international break with a clean slate. Let's look on the bright side, there is still a long way to go and we aren't in the bottom three and our fate lies entirely in our own hands.

The season starts now!

Pointing The Finger! – 22/3/16

Immediately after the disappointment of the Blackburn Rovers defeat on Saturday I gave my suggestions concerning what we should do next and how the team and management should use the international break productively in order to both rest up and also prepare for the next crucial batch of eight matches in April which will decide our immediate fate.

I also suggested that a change of formation as well as approach would probably serve us well as if the way we are playing at the moment continually fails to provide results, as has been the case, then you need to change it or risk more failure.

Rightly or wrongly it has always been my stated policy to provide Brentford supporters of all persuasions with the platform within this column to express their own opinions. Sometimes I agree with them to a greater or lesser extent, more often I do not, but despite our differences we all share a passion for the Bees and are in awe of what Matthew Benham has done to revitalise our club, and it also provides a catalyst for other supporters to respond and have their say.

Lately emotions and tempers have been rising and patience and tolerance are in short supply, hardly surprising given the events since the turn of the year and I can well understand why people feel the way that they do.

By sharing conflicting opinions on the club I am not trying to be a rabble-rouser, neither am I aiming to cause mischief or gain attention for myself and I have urged us supporters many times to unite and get behind our team at such a crucial time when perhaps our ambitious plans for the immediate future are at risk should we return to the lower divisions. Inquests and recriminations can wait until later.

I fully intend to continue as I have done and today welcome back **Jim Levack** who has been a regular contributor to this column and he now shares his opinion about what is happening at the club, how we have allowed ourselves to get into this mess and what can be done to improve matters and I concur with some, but not all of what he has to say:

In almost half a century of watching Brentford I can't recall a time when the club has been more riven by division than now. Fans fighting fans, terrace arguments, acrimonious and frequently personal internet battles, the current situation is sad beyond belief.

Not even during the dark days of Webb and Noades were the fans so divided over the right way to take the club forward. I have my own personal view of where the blame lies for this rift but it's an opinion far too unpopular and incendiary to ever share.

Irrespective of what I think, one message board has almost four thousand posts on the subject of Dean Smith and a relatively low thirteen hundred on the subject of the Co-Directors of Football.

And that, in a nutshell, is the problem.

Because Phil Giles and Rasmus Ankersen are Matthew Benham's right hand men, they have inexplicably escaped much of the criticism for the current slide towards the trapdoor.

Why? Their job is, as the club widely and foolishly proclaimed last season, to identify undiscovered talent with potential to avoid paying the ludicrous transfer fees and wages that make other clubs financially unstable.

I say foolishly because the second we did so and effectively got rid of Mark Warburton – no, he wasn't sacked but we made his position untenable – the whole football world turned against us to the extent that if we now move for a player it sets alarm bells ringing.

No problem with the concept though. The strategy makes perfect sense for a club with limited revenue streams like Brentford. But why did we feel the need to shout about it?

Strip the whole thing down and the players we've brought in – Woods and Colin being notable exceptions – are patently not ready to play in a thriving Championship side, let alone one fighting for survival.

Last season's side had a great balance, strong competition for places and a ruthless edge.

If Pritchard got knocked about, Douglas was there to drag him to his feet and snarl at the bloke who did it.

Diagouraga, if the ball did get past the midfield, mopped up the bits and pieces and passed it simply and accurately, a fulcrum if you like.

Tarkowski and Dean were a generally peerless combination, Gray was powerful, quick and usually clinical, the likes of McCormack couldn't get a start.

When Pritchard wasn't doing it we had Jota, Dallas, Toral or even Odubajo bombing on as well as Judge, all capable of producing a moment of magic.

We effectively had a four-pronged attack as well as creative, vibrant, skilful, quick options on the bench who could change a game that was drifting away from us.

Saunders and Yennaris were plying their trade in League Two. Now they are pivotal to our survival.

Don't think for a second I'm denigrating the current squad in any way. They are, mostly, technically strong with huge potential, but are being asked to do the job of seasoned professionals with several years knowledge of the Championship.

That's not fair or sensible.

Josh McEachran is a case in point. We were told that he was the Douglas replacement. Don't make me laugh!

Skilful yes, intelligent occasionally, but a ball winner? I'm sorry. The sooner he casts off the Chelsea starlet tag and starts bossing games as his talent suggests he surely can, the better. He was given the opportunity when Blackburn went down to ten men and singularly failed to take it.

Now we have a midfield lacking steel and stature that is overrun on a weekly basis.

McEachran and Woods are so similar it's painful to watch, Judge has drifted into an I'll play where I want thanks mentality to the side's detriment, and Canos and Swift are young lads with huge potential who would benefit from a protector alongside them.

The best football teams are combinations of different characters, personalities and types of players, but if I had to pick one word to describe the current Brentford side, it would be lightweight.

"Dean Smith must go" posts and worse have littered social media whilst Rasmus and Phil have got off relatively lightly.

Grossly unfair in my view as they have effectively assembled this squad for Smith whose use of the word "finally" on bringing in Leandro last week was perhaps the first public hint of his frustration.

It's far too easy to go to the other extreme and actually blame the Co-Directors of Football for everything too, as I'm sure they are moving heaven and earth to bring in loanees. Their reputations are, after all, on the line here.

I know that several quality players have been lined up for the Summer, but I'm guessing they won't want to play in League One so we need to sort out this mess soon or I fear for our immediate future.

As Greville confirmed in his interview recently, Phil Giles comes across as a likeable, thoughtful and decent bloke doing his best and I'm sure he's crunching the numbers to get it right, but sometimes football is – as I said at the time of Warburton's exit – about far more than numbers.

As far Rasmus, I'm not entirely sure what his role is or the extent of his involvement at Brentford so it's probably unfair to comment. Suffice to say that I'm sure he's feeling the pain the same as Giles.

What I will say though is that the signings of Gogia – remember him? – and Kerschbaumer epitomise the malaise surrounding our new system.

I've watched Kerschbaumer closely when he's played and although he may well become a decent player in the future, his positional awareness is poor. The best players have an unerring ability to be in the right place at the right time and if I'm honest it's an innate ability and not one easily learned.

The ball never breaks to him because he's constantly out of position. When it does, he's brushed off it far too easily at the moment.

Now, after all the carefully placed pro-pieces in the media surrounding our strategy, whenever we approach a club or agent they think one of three things:

- *This lad must be better than we think if Brentford are in for him*

- *We can get more money for him if Brentford think he's good*

- *If Brentford want him and see something in him, then bigger clubs will too so I can get him more money in wages*

Last season I read somewhere that Matthew Benham's theory meant that a side near the bottom wasn't necessarily bad because over the course of a campaign things even themselves out as luck plays its part. Right now though I'm reminded of the saying "you make your own luck in this game."

The bottom line is that most Brentford fans with a brain have seen for many months that we lack steel, guile, bottle, balls, size, strength or whatever you want to call it. So why couldn't Giles and Ankersen when the window was open?

If it's because we don't want to play that way and won't abandon our principles then that's arrant nonsense and, I hate to say it, arrogant in the extreme.

We also lack quality where it matters, but I accept that only comes at a price and, if rumours of a sudden cash squeeze are to be believed, it's one we're not prepared to pay whatever the outcome.

However, and here's the stark truth, we are now staring trips to Northampton and Oxford in the face unless the squad is strengthened fast or the approach or pattern of play changes.

My fear is that a refusal to stray from the principles of finding young fringe Premier League players – unless they are exceptional talents – will not help our cause at a time when we currently need people with knowledge of this league.

To bleat on about Smith not being able to motivate the same side Lee Carsley had at his disposal is a red herring.

Carsley had Tarkowski and Diagouraga, two key players who both, in differing ways, played their part in ensuring the back four didn't look vulnerable.

Importantly he was also given a short-term brief by Matthew Benham to steady the ship, stop the rot and stabilise by whatever means possible after the Dijkhuizen departure.

By contrast Smith has been told to work towards a longer-term project with far less quality to call on. I might be wrong but I'd put a few bob on the fact that in confidential company he isn't happy at having his reputation put on the line by the club's lack of activity in January, however valid the reasons for doing so.

That same lack of activity and dare I say it Big New Ambitions will, I hope, be reflected in season ticket prices for next season when people will adopt a once bitten, twice shy approach.

So what is the solution? To stick or to twist? It's a dilemma that Matthew Benham, as a gambling man, may well be relishing but I for one am not.

It's fairly obvious to me – bring in a quick, pacy young winger on the fringes of a Premier League start and a mid-twenties defensive midfielder with a bit of bite and Championship know-how because a youngster in that role simply won't do given our current predicament.

Maybe easier said than done at this stage of the campaign given our cash constraints, but the financial ramifications of relegation will be far more damaging than a few extra quid shelled out now.

I'll leave the final word to this probably over long ramble to Jeff Stelling, whose stunning on-screen analysis of Aston Villa's season and predicament made me sit up with a start.

Without detriment to our new signings – some of whom may well go on to be real assets to the club IN TIME – or our scapegoat manager, there are clear parallels to be drawn.

If you haven't seen it take a look at https://www.youtube.com/watch?v=oL_zCdeIyQ8

I'm Tired – 23/3/16

- I'm tired of all the infighting between Brentford fans – something that is tearing our great club apart

- I'm tired of the lack of tolerance and manners being shown by some of our supporters

- I'm tired of genuine supporters being bullied, abused and denigrated because others disagree with their opinion
- I'm tired of the toxic atmosphere that seems to pervade everything and everyone in and around the club at the moment
- I'm tired of reading page after page of endless negativity, arguments, insults and vituperation on all of the message boards
- I'm tired of reading the sick and appalling comments regarding Dean Smith recently on *Twitter*, some of them potentially actionable in my opinion
- I'm tired of having to referee disputes between readers of my own blog site – not something that I ever expected to happen
- I'm tired of reading comments accusing our best player of selfishness and of not caring about the club
- I'm tired of being accused of being self-serving and encouraging negativity on *BFC Talk* when entirely the opposite is true
- I'm tired of trolls who seek only to cement discord by spreading their poisonous bile
- I'm tired of the attacks on Matthew Benham without whom…
- I'm tired of the ceaseless blame culture which is helping to wreck our season
- I'm tired of my own sour grapes
- I'm tired of the inquests which should all be delayed until the end of the season when I am certain that lessons will be learned and changes will be made
- I'm tired of the massive over promising from the club which has led to unrealistically raised expectations
- I'm tired of self-proclaimed experts spouting off and pontificating
- I'm tired of know-it-alls who seem to be taking a positive delight and glorying in our current misfortune
- I'm tired of not enjoying anything at the moment regarding Brentford FC both on and off the pitch
- I'm tired of not being able to persuade any of my friends to come and watch us play this year
- I'm tired of watching a vibrant, brilliant and exciting team that played without fear become boring, slow, pedestrian and mediocre
- I'm tired of having to make excuses when in reality we are totally underperforming
- I'm tired of watching players who are simply not up to scratch do their best to compete in the harsh world of the Championship
- I'm tired of an obsession becoming a chore
- I'm tired of going to sleep worrying about the Bees and waking up doing exactly the same
- I'm tired of this season
- I'm tired of going to away games recently expecting nothing
- I'm tired of going to home games recently expecting nothing
- I'm tired of losing games week after week
- I'm tired of counting off the games until the end of the season
- I'm tired of praying that there will be three Championship teams even more inept than us
- I'm tired of bemoaning just how far we have fallen so quickly and how easily it might have been avoided
- I'm tired of waiting for a striker to score a goal for us
- I'm tired of waiting for Harlee Dean to score for us
- I'm tired of waiting for us to get more players into the opposition penalty area
- I'm tired of waiting for us to show bravery and attempt positive passes rather than go backwards and sideways

- I'm tired of the disgusting behaviour of some of our supporters at away games

- I'm tired of the barracking of some of our players during and after recent matches

- I'm tired of waiting in vain for a referee to do his job and send an opponent off after he has tried to cut one of our players in two

- I'm tired of horrid abuse being laughed off and excused as mere banter

- I'm tired of our never ending injury jinx

- I'm tired of excuses

- I'm tired of feeling disappointed and conflicted about us struggling in the Championship when I would have given my eye teeth to have merely got there a few years ago

- I'm tired of rumours and innuendos that are never backed up or substantiated

- I'm tired of our inflexibility in our approach towards transfers

- I'm tired of waiting for Championship-tested players to arrive in order to reinforce our beleaguered squad

- I'm tired of thinking about the furore there will be if tomorrow ends without another loan signing

- I'm tired of asking kids to do a man's job

- I'm tired of pointless comparisons between Lee Carsley and Dean Smith

- I'm tired of people failing to recognise that we have a Head Coach and not a Manager

- I'm tired of supporters not accepting that Dean Smith plays a key role in player identification and recruitment

- I'm tired of nonstop and ignorant criticism of Dean Smith which does not take into account the problems he is facing

- I'm tired of continual references to Mark Warburton and how he was *fired*

- I'm tired of fans bemoaning the lack of news and PR from the club and then complaining when the likes of Matthew Benham and Phil Giles are interviewed by supporters

- I'm tired of the mainstream football media treating us like a laughing stock and just hoping and waiting for us to implode

- I'm tired of Adrian Durham and his mindless shock jock jeering

- I'm tired of *Pitchgate*

- I'm tired of waiting for our luck to change

- I'm tired of us shooting ourselves in the foot

- I'm tired of the thought of the supporters of other relegation haunted clubs like Rotherham, MK Dons and Fulham taking comfort from the obvious dissension in our ranks

- I'm tired of waiting for the Lionel Road CPO decision to be announced

- I'm tired of counting off the days, months and years until we arrive at Lionel Road and just hoping that we can survive in the Championship until then

- I'm tired of being patronised and laughed at by my Watford and Queens Park Rangers supporting friends

- I'm tired of all the moaning about our association with FC Midtjylland

- I'm tired of all the pointless match day parking restrictions around Griffin Park

- I'm tired of all the ignorant criticism about our set pieces which are greatly improved this season

- I'm tired of living in fear of being hit by the damn ball in Ealing Road

- I'm tired of conspiracy theorists spouting nonsense about Matthew Benham's plans for us

- I'm tired of waiting for our Academy to develop some worthwhile prospects

- I'm tired of our slavish devotion to a 4-2-3-1 formation when we do not possess the players to suit it

- I'm tired of reading about Jota's accomplishments in Spain when I want him back with us

- I'm tired of poor Lewis Macleod's never ending bad luck and injury traumas and feel so sorry for him

- I'm tired of having to remind people that we need to remain united if we are to survive this season unscathed

- I'm tired of waiting for next season when hopefully we can repair some of the damage that has been inflicted this season

- I'm tired of writing these articles

Dunne It The Hard Way – 25/3/16

The average length of a professional footballer's career is no more than eight years according to figures provided by the PFA and for those who go on to play for longer than that there is generally a very good reason for their not falling by the wayside much sooner.

For the favoured few it is simply a case of their outstanding and overwhelming talent, but even then that can sometimes not be enough.

Back in the early 60s Barry Fry was considered to be one of the most promising *Busby Babes* coming through the ranks at Manchester United but despite his huge talent and self-evident confidence in his own ability, his lack of off the field discipline and application, in addition to a series of recurring injuries condemned him to a frustratingly short career that comprised less than twenty Football League matches at far less glamorous outposts of the game such as Bolton, Luton and Leyton Orient rather than the heady heights of Old Trafford that at one time seemed certain.

Talent alone cannot guarantee that a fledgling footballer makes the grade, what matters just as much is good fortune in avoiding chronic or career ending injury, having the luck to play for a manager who believes in you and the attributes that you can bring to the party as well as showing a combination of total commitment and dedication to the cause.

Millwall is a club that seems to attract players of a certain type who are totally in keeping with the gritty and tough nature of the local area. It is not a place for fancy dan ball players and they, as well as men who shirk challenges and lack moral fibre generally do not remain at the club for very long. It is hardly surprising that the three players who have made the most appearances for the club were all tough and uncompromising defenders in Barry Kitchener, Keith Stevens and Harry Cripps. No shrinking violets there, and any tricky forward attempting to go past any of them was liable to experience the delights of cinder rash.

Interestingly enough, there have already been a couple of outstanding books about Millwall. Eamon Dunphy's *Only a Game? Diary of a Professional Footballer,* remains a classic of the genre over forty years after it was written and clearly demonstrates how a midfield player skilful enough to earn twenty-three caps for Eire was forced to modify and simplify his game and cut out all the frills in order to fit in and gain acceptance from the Millwall faithful.

Journalist Michael Calvin's more recent account of a promotion winning season, *Family: Life, Death and Football*, provided a brilliant insider's view of life at the sharp end of the football pyramid as well as the importance of the club to its local community and *vice versa.*

Now there is a worthy new addition to the Millwall library with the publication of long-serving defender Alan Dunne's recollections of a fine career, which saw him play almost four hundred times during his twenty-three years at the club.

Dunne is a passionate and impetuous character who had to learn the hard way how to control his temper and ensure that his behaviour both on and off the pitch remained within bounds, and his book is full of stories of his scrapes and escapades which on many occasions threatened to cut short what eventually became a long and meritorious career.

Make no mistake about it, Dunne is a talented defender who at his peak came close to full international honours with Eire, but what really set him apart from many former teammates was his total determination to succeed and his ceaseless will to win. He was not going to let anything come between him and his heartfelt ambition to become a professional footballer and woe betide anybody that got in his way.

There is much here of interest to Millwall supporters. Dunne speaks of his massive hurt and disappointment at missing out on a starting place in the 2004 FA Cup Final team despite an apparent promise that he would play some part in the game. The numbing feeling he felt after being released by his former teammate Neil Harris. How he missed an opportunity to prolong his stay at the club when he should have pressed for a new contract and struck when the iron was hot at the start of the 2014/15 season soon after he had just spearheaded Millwall's great escape from relegation from the Championship.

He gives full, frank and honest opinions on a plethora of Millwall managers and teammates good, bad and indifferent as well as writing honestly about his sense of insecurity after being released and his struggle to find a new club.

He also paints a vivid picture of what it means to play for a club like Millwall and how the players feed off the fans and *vice versa*. Some footballers shrivel under the relentless pressure and are never accepted by a crowd that demands total passion and commitment at all times, others revel in the need to demonstrate their grit and determination and are quickly accepted and become part of the family as well as local heroes. Dunne certainly belonged to that last category and he writes lucidly and with pride about his strong relationship with a marvellous bunch of supporters.

The book is honest in the extreme and Dunne provides frank and graphic descriptions of all eleven red cards that he has been shown to date and how the red mist sometimes came down and he even acknowledges that perhaps three or four of them were in fact the correct decision.

Brentford fans will be interested to note that Dunne's favourite goal was his equaliser at The Den last season in a match where Millwall were wearing a special camouflage kit to commemorate the hundredth anniversary of World War One. Dunne's shot squeezed through the legs of Brentford defender Tony Craig on its way into the net and Dunne is also full of praise for Craig, his ability, temperament and dressing room influence. Another excellent professional who has fully deserved his success.

Dunne almost came to blows with giant striker Mark McCammon in the lead-up to the Cup Final when tension was building and let's just say that he probably shares the same opinion about McCammon's footballing ability as most Bees supporters!

This is not just a book for Millwall fans and there is much that will be relished and enjoyed by supporters of all teams. Dunne clearly represents *Everyman*, and the archetypical lower division footballer. He has made the most of what he has and has overcome the vicissitudes of fate, injury, personal shortcomings and the whims of his managers as well as referees!

He has enjoyed a wonderful career and one that he has fully deserved given what he has always put back into the game and he is a shining example of what hard work and commitment can bring.

This is an excellent book, which is highly recommended.

"Dunne It The Hard Way" by Alan Dunne with Chris Davies, published by Pitch Publishing.

Mind Games – 29/3/16

It's been a really strange and frustrating Easter weekend as, like I am sure so many others, I have been feeling lost and bereft without my customary football fix. I am sure that I will soon be corrected but I cannot for the life of me remember any other Easter in recent years which has coincided with yet another international break and resulted in my having to find other ways to amuse myself.

I can still vividly remember Good Friday and Easter Monday last year which saw the nonstop excitement and adrenalin rush of those two unforgettable clashes against Fulham and Nottingham Forest. Hammering Fulham on their own turf will naturally go down as one of my best ever Brentford matches and I can still easily summon up all four of our goals on my personal memory bank and mental tape loop of great Brentford moments, but our late recovery from a seemingly insurmountable two-goal deficit against Forest was perhaps just as massive an achievement as it simply exemplified everything good about us at that time and highlighted our relentlessness, never-say-die attitude and total refusal to give any game up for lost as Andre Gray's clever turn and instant shot put us right back in the game and then deep into injury time Tommy Smith stood his cross up just above the straining hands of Karl Darlow where it was met by the bouffant hairstyle of Jota for a wildly celebrated equaliser.

Where has that spirit gone now, as we appear to have had the stuffing knocked out of us by a seemingly never ending series of body blows, some coming from out of the blue, others quite frankly self-inflicted, that have punctuated a season which promised so much but has ended up being such a cruel reality check to all of us, management, players and supporters alike?

This season has been death by a thousand cuts and is still delicately poised and can go one of two ways as we now face a crucial nine match mini-season which will have so many repercussions for the club depending upon where we finish up after our final game at Huddersfield in less than six weeks' time.

In that respect perhaps we all desperately needed and will greatly benefit from a two-week break which ideally will enable us all to catch our breath, recover our poise and get ourselves ready for the struggle and potential torments or even triumphs that lie ahead as the Bees prepare to fight for their very Championship life.

We should all take some degree of comfort by recalling that we went into the international break in early October in total disarray on the back of three consecutive defeats, the loss of a Head Coach, the shocking and demoralising foot-in-mouth announcement by Lee Carsley that he had no desire to become the permanent replacement as well as sinking like a stone into a sorry twentieth place in the league table.

We only looked like going in one direction but Carsley apparently put his squad through a mini preseason boot camp which addressed our lack of fitness and sharpness and we came out of the traps recharged and re-energised, a totally different team in every way, shape and form which won its next four games and went on to take twenty-eight points from fourteen games and ended the year in eighth place just outside the playoff positions. Promotion form indeed, and an amazing turnaround which unfortunately has not been maintained since the New Year began.

So we know that we can do it and let's face it, depending on the results of the other strugglers, our minimum requirement for safety is probably a mere seven points from nine matches. Surely not too much to ask for? Given the run that we have been on since early January even that paltry target might seem a tough ask but hopefully Dean Smith will have used the time afforded him by the international break productively and his ministrations and perhaps tweaking of his resources will hopefully produce the same effect as Carsley had in October.

There must be much for him to ponder on. Does he keep things as they were and hope that our luck will turn and we recover some form or will he freshen things up by changing the way that we play? He will also have to cope with an injury list that now has the names of Josh McEachran and John Swift added to it and we are all waiting anxiously for news about their potential availability for the run in. Given a likely shortage of midfielders will he decide to gamble by naming two forwards, not a formation that he has utilised previously either at Brentford or Walsall?

Hopefully we'll be able to glean some information as the week develops but we might have to wait until just before kickoff next Saturday before his intentions are finally revealed.

Our squad has looked mentally and physically exhausted and slowed down by a total loss of confidence, which is hardly surprising as defeats beget more defeats and with every loss the pressure increases and self-belief withers on the vine.

Players stop acting instinctively and instead start thinking about what once came naturally and they become afraid of taking chances and running the risk of making mistakes and having the crowd get on their back. As was clearly seen against Blackburn this results in a pallid and listless performance with the safe option taken at every opportunity and the ball being passed endlessly sideways and backwards with nobody prepared to put his head over the parapet and use his undoubted ability to try and make something happen for fear of failure.

There is one positive to consider in that Alan Judge and Lasse Vibe will both hopefully return to the club on a high and full of beans from their full international appearances for Eire and Denmark respectively over the past few days and that they might help raise the spirits of their team mates.

Reading the above which I believe succinctly sums up our current situation, perhaps the most important person at the club throughout this international break is not Dean Smith but instead, Tom Bates. Who is he I hear some of you ask, did we manage to make a last minute loan signing before the loan window shut last week that has somehow remained unremarked upon?

Unfortunately that is not the case, but that is another story given the injuries suffered in the last few days by Josh McEachran and John Swift which might yet rob us of their valuable services and reduce our selection options even further.

No, Tom Bates is a Performance Psychologist at the club who over the past ten years has worked with youth and senior domestic international athletes, coaches, managers and teams helping them to perform under pressure and be at their best when it matters the most. In his own words, Tom specialises in *enhancing athletes' mental and emotional performance states through creating, sustaining and improving supreme optimistic spirit and self-belief.*

That might all sound like gobbledygook, jargon and management speak but he has an excellent track record and if he can help revive the spirits of a dispirited squad that doesn't seem to know where its next win is coming from then we will all owe him a massive debt.

Most Premier League footballers use sports psychology as a matter of course as it can help players to maintain or rebuild confidence, deal with anxiety or anger and keep their focus. Players are encouraged to try positive self-talk and convert their negative thoughts and fears into more positive ones. There is a sound scientific basis behind this as ideally thinking positively releases dopamine into the bloodstream which is linked to feelings of certainty and confidence and helps reduce cortisol levels, a hormone linked to stress and physiological reactions related to potentially harmful feelings and sensations of fight and flight.

Visualisation is another technique commonly used whereby players are encouraged to imagine and picture themselves succeeding in their specific tasks such as scoring from free kicks or saving penalty kicks and focusing on positive memories and recollections of doing the same on previous occasions.

Players might also be encouraged to repeat key words or phrases to themselves in an attempt to help regain focus when things go wrong or if the red mist comes down during a game.

I am barely scratching the surface as this is now a sophisticated science that has progressed way past early attempts in this field which included the notorious *Romark*, or Ronald Markham, to give him his real name, a hypnotist who was used by Malcolm Allison to assist Third Division Crystal Palace on their unlikely run to the 1975/76 FA Cup semi-final.

Unfortunately it all ended in tears when he claimed that he had not been paid for his services and promptly put a curse on the club which apparently remains in force to this day.

Hopefully Tom Bates will be more successful in his efforts on our behalf. In the meantime I just have one question for him, can he please suggest something that will help keep all us fans calm, measured, united, supportive, positive, patient and stress free?

Position	Team	P	W	D	L	F	A	GD	Pt	Form
1	Burnley	38	21	12	5	61	31	30	75	W W W W W D
2	Brighton and Hove A	38	19	14	5	52	35	17	71	W W D D W W
3	Middlesbrough	37	21	7	9	48	23	25	70	W L W L L W
4	Hull City	37	19	9	9	50	23	27	66	W D L D D L
5	Derby County	38	17	13	8	51	35	16	64	W L W L D W
6	Sheffield Wednesday	38	16	14	8	56	36	20	62	D D L D W W
7	Cardiff City	38	15	14	9	49	41	8	59	L W W L W D
8	Ipswich Town	38	16	10	12	46	44	2	58	W W D L W L
9	Birmingham City	37	15	11	11	41	35	6	56	W L W L D D
10	Preston North End	38	13	14	11	36	35	1	53	W L D L W D
11	Queens Park Rangers	38	12	15	11	47	43	4	51	D W L W W D
12	Wolverhampton Wndrs	38	12	12	14	46	51	-5	48	L W L W D D
13	Leeds United	37	11	14	12	37	45	-8	47	D L W W W L
14	Blackburn Rovers	38	11	13	14	37	36	1	46	W L W L L W
15	Nottingham Forest	38	11	13	14	34	36	-2	46	L L W L D L
16	Huddersfield Town	38	12	9	17	52	53	-1	45	D L L W L W
17	Reading	37	11	12	14	42	43	-1	45	W W D L L D
18	Brentford	37	12	7	18	48	59	-11	43	L W L L L L
19	Bristol City	38	11	10	17	40	58	-18	43	L W L L W W
20	Rotherham United	38	11	6	21	44	62	-18	39	L W W W D W
21	Fulham	38	8	14	16	57	64	-7	38	D L D L L D
22	Milton Keynes Dons	38	9	10	19	32	51	-19	37	D L W D D L
23	Charlton Athletic	38	7	11	20	34	69	-35	32	L L W D W L
24	Bolton Wanderers	38	4	14	20	36	68	-32	26	L L L D L L

[19th March 2016]

302

A Golden Day – 3/4/16

I have been a massive John Mellencamp fan for many years now and there is a lyric from one of his songs that seems totally apposite to describe the events of yesterday:

Sometimes you're golden, man that's all I got to say.

Yesterday turned out to be a golden day for almost everybody connected with Brentford FC, directors, players, management and supporters alike as we ended a depressing run of four consecutive defeats and celebrated only our third victory of the year.

Unfortunately for some, like rabid Bees supporter, Paul Briers, the day didn't start out too golden when he made the unremarkable discovery that pouring diesel into a fuel tank designed to receive unleaded petrol is not conducive to an effortless and trouble-free journey. Similarly, Chairman Cliff Crown, and I am sure many others, were caught up in a massive M1 tailback around Luton and didn't get there to share in the celebrations.

Minor quibbles, as otherwise yesterday was a total triumph and provided some much needed respite for a team that had been in free fall and appeared to be dropping like a stone towards the bottom three.

Now everyone's face is wreathed in smiles again, there is an overall feeling of relief and some much needed confidence has been restored as we go into Tuesday's home match against bottom of the table Bolton Wanderers a much healthier nine points, and a far superior goal difference clear of the hated MK Dons, marooned in the final relegation place.

Nottingham Forest, to be quite frank, were a shambolic disgrace on the day and ambled around in the Spring sunshine without any sense of purpose or menace and their defensive aberrations contributed greatly to all three of our goals, but all you can do is beat whoever is opposing you on the day and Brentford, for once, took full advantage of the opportunities that were put on a plate for them.

The experienced Kevin Wilson whose dithering led to Lasse Vibe scoring the crucial opening goal was subjected to incessant and totally unnecessary booing and vituperative abuse after his error and the apathetic and demoralised home crowd streamed away in droves as soon as the second goal went in. The European Cup-winning glory days seem a lifetime away now for a once great club that appears to be rudderless and to be going nowhere fast, and their supporters certainly did not appreciate their team losing twice in a season to the minnows of Brentford.

Dean Smith had sensibly concentrated on working on defensive organisation during the international break, perhaps because most of his midfielders and strikers were either injured or away on international duty. His efforts were rewarded with a passionate and energetic display in which the back four played like a well-drilled unit, covered for each other and, most importantly, eradicated the daft errors and lack of concentration that had cost us so dear recently.

Forest, frankly did not get a sniff of goal and barely created a chance worthy of the name all afternoon and David Button enjoyed one of his easiest games of the season.

Dean and Barbet are finally developing a real understanding and are fast becoming a cohesive partnership and once the Frenchman stops passing the ball to the opposition in dangerous positions he will be a formidable player. Max Colin made a triumphant return to the team, almost scored and defended with his life before, worryingly, limping off late on and Jake Bidwell was back to his unobtrusive best.

Our first clean sheet away from home for over five months was testimony to the efforts of the entire team as we defended from the front. McCormack, Woods and Yennaris ran, covered, pressed and harried and never gave the lethargic home team time to settle on the ball and when one of our elaborate free kick routines backfired and set Forest away on a five-on-one breakaway reminiscent of Tony Craig against Oldham in 2013, it was Alan Judge who showed energy and total commitment to the cause by chasing back eighty yards and putting in a crucial last ditch tackle to save the day when all seemed lost.

Nico Yennaris covered every blade of grass, used the ball well and gave his best ever display in a Brentford shirt and was deservedly rewarded with his first goal for the club. A few repeat performances and he runs the risk of moving beyond grudging acceptance and becoming a firm fan favourite.

The first half was almost devoid of action and goal chances were at a premium, and given the recent poor record of both teams the first goal was always going to be crucial. The injury bug bit yet again when Leandro Rodríguez damaged his hamstring and as he disappeared down the tunnel we wondered if we would ever see the Everton loanee again in a Brentford shirt. He now joins the likes of McEachran, Macleod, Swift, Hofmann and Hogan on the injured list where he might well be joined by Colin, Button, Judge and Yennaris who all suffered knocks yesterday and the selection process for Tuesday's match might well be a formality as we are rapidly running out of fit players.

Someone's injury, however, is another's opportunity and Lasse Vibe, so lacking in strength, bite and verve recently, took full advantage. He ran around like a scalded cat, his confidence restored by his recent appearance for Denmark and the time he spent training with his high quality international teammates. He scored for the first time since mid-December when he got in behind Wilson and poked home Alan Judge's perfectly placed lofted through ball which held up and needed to be dealt with by either defender or goalkeeper and when they left it for each other Vibe nipped in and scored a predator's goal.

Brentford visibly grew in confidence as Forest wilted in the sunshine and it soon became obvious that the only team that could deny Brentford the coveted three points was themselves and as long as we avoided a similar giveaway then a much-needed victory was well in our sights.

The second goal came from an unexpected source when Bidwell's right wing corner was somehow missed by Dean, in total isolation on the near post, and as he was still remonstrating with himself, the ball caromed off a defender and dropped perfectly for Yennaris who just beat the straining Vibe to hammer the ball into the corner of the net. Cue wild celebrations with the travelling hordes tucked away in the corner of the pitch.

Inspired by his goal, Vibe ran the channels selflessly and when he got in behind Lichaj the hapless defender dragged him back and saw red. Victory was assured when Forest surrendered the ball in midfield and Vibe sent his pass into the now yawning gap on Forest's right flank and Sergi Canos took the chance perfectly and angled his instant shot into the far corner. Game over!

Three goals, three points and a clean sheet. What more can you ask for? A few less injuries perhaps, but this was a day when everybody came together again and the entire club united. The fans fed off the team and the players responded to the massive support that they received.

This victory has hopefully arrested our slump but this is not a time for complacency as our last win, also by three clear goals over Wolves, was followed by a demoralising run of four consecutive defeats and we need to keep our foot on the gas and not feel that the job has been done. We still need at least one more victory to assure ourselves of Championship football again next season and the long-suffering supporters are also long overdue some victories at Griffin Park. There is still much to play for and the season must not be allowed to peter out with a whimper.

Hopefully yesterday, golden though it was, was a turning point rather than a one-off.

It's Time For Us To Beat Our Bogey Team – 5/4/16

No visiting team ever enjoyed playing at Burnden Park, home of Bolton Wanderers in the late 50s as they knew exactly what they were about to receive. Nat Lofthouse, *The Lion Of Vienna,* would be ever ready and willing to chase lost causes upfront and as Manchester United's Harry Gregg would attest in the 1958 FA Cup Final, no goalkeeper was immune from the threat of a solid shoulder charge, a challenge that would bring about an assault charge today but which remained legal in those far off days, and one that left a dazed goalkeeper and ball together in the back of the net for the goal that clinched victory.

Things were not much better at the other end of the pitch where the likes of Roy *Chopper* Hartle and Tommy Banks awaited.

Hartle was half of one of the most terrifying fullback combinations to grace the top flight of English football in the last century. He lined up on the right flank and was partnered by the equally pugnacious Tommy Banks on the left. There was no respite or escape for any tricky winger.

Play on the right then he faced the awesome strength of Banks, switch flanks and the tender mercies of Hartle awaited him. Legend has it that most teams were beaten even before the game began, particularly when they heard Hartle shouting to Banks, *Hey Tommy, when you've finished knocking the living daylights out of that fella, chip him over here and let me have a go!*

Bolton have maintained a reputation for being hard and tough to play against and even in the Sam Allardyce glory days when for several years they performed way above expectations and cocked a snoot at the Premier League big boys they were certainly no shrinking violets.

Brentford have had real problems coping with Bolton since we were promoted to the Championship and have yet to find the answer. The Bees were physically second best in every department in their first clash last season. The giant Mills and Ream towered over Andre Gray who barely touched the ball all afternoon and we were never afforded any time or room to play our own style of football – or given any protection by an indulgent referee. Bolton received six bookings to our none, a fact which tells its own story and we subsided gently to a richly deserved defeat as we never looked up to the physical challenge we faced.

We never really got started in the return match late on last season at Griffin Park. Playoff nerves were jangling and perhaps got the better of us and we were unable to find any rhythm. Even then we dominated possession and would surely have won but for that incredible and unforgettable aberration when a combination of Button, Diagouraga and Tarkowski unerringly managed to turn a short goal kick for us into a daft equalising goal for our visitors.

We played Bolton for the third time without managing a win back in November when, again, for all our domination and pretty football we were unable to make our possession count and squandered chance after chance of making the game safe after John Swift's excellent opening goal. We were really not helped by a ludicrous booking for an alleged dive by Swift when he was clearly taken out in the area and Mark Davies also escaped with a yellow card for a horrific lunge on Diagouraga. We were always vulnerable to crosses and set pieces and finally conceded a scrappy equaliser and could even have ended up losing a game which we should surely have won.

Tonight provides us with our fourth opportunity in the last two seasons to win a match against what is always a tough and obdurate Bolton team. Given that they remain marooned at the bottom of the league, are doomed to relegation, have yet to win away all season and are currently without a manager after the departure of Neil Lennon you would think that the dice are finally stacked heavily in Brentford's favour.

Hopefully that will turn out to be the case although we have struggled far too often this season against the tougher and more rugged teams such as Birmingham, Rotherham and Blackburn who have taken full advantage of our physical shortcomings and inability to battle on every occasion when it is necessary.

Last season we possessed sufficient pace, guile and sheer ability throughout the team to outplay the majority of teams that wished to engage in a battle with us but unfortunately our more limited resources at the present time mean that we have found it far more difficult to prevail in this situation given that we are quite unable to fight fire with fire and without the likes of Gray, Jota, Pritchard and Odubajo we can no longer outclass the opposition.

On Saturday we put on a disciplined performance in which the defence appeared far more organised and the midfield quintet worked extremely hard in terms of their pressing and challenging. Lasse Vibe too made a massive difference when he came on as a substitute as he worked the channels tirelessly and eventually we were able to find sufficient space to allow our footballing skills to come to the fore.

Tonight we will have to repeat that winning combination and outwork Bolton in all areas of the pitch. Should we do that then there is still sufficient quality remaining within our team to ensure that we create and hopefully take our chances in front of goal.

We will also have to wait anxiously until just before kickoff until we know who is fit enough to play. We were without McEachran, Swift, Hogan and Hofmann on Saturday and Colin, Judge, Yennaris, Rodríguez and Button all picked up knocks during the match. They have not had too long in which to recover and I am sure that the treatment room has been full to overflowing with our medical staff working overtime.

We are really down to the bare bones and Josh Clarke made his first appearance off the bench for over six months on Saturday when he replaced the limping Colin. He slotted in perfectly although the match had long since been won before his late arrival. I still think that there is a footballer in Josh and I hope that he is given another opportunity to prove that he deserves a new contract for next season.

Leandro Rodríguez hobbled off with a damaged hamstring just before halftime and unfortunately that might well be the last that we see of the young loan striker. We therefore need at least one of Hofmann, Djuricin or Hogan to have recovered sufficiently from injury or illness to take his place in the squad tonight as five fit strikers have rapidly been reduced to one.

A win tonight would pretty much guarantee our Championship place for next season as well as help to restore some confidence and a general sense of well being amongst our supporters. A victory over Bolton is also long overdue as it was way back in April 1992 when we last came out on top against them.

It is now time for us to allay our bogey and I am pretty sure that we will.

Job Done? – Not Quite – 6/4/16

The league table is looking a lot more cheerful than was the case a mere four days ago as two wins, six goals and six points have taken the Bees up to the giddy heights of fourteenth place in the Championship, twelve points ahead of MK Dons who fill the final relegation position and I really cannot see them making up that gap, plus our massively superior goal difference, in the six games that remain to them.

Whilst we are now looking comfortable with forty-nine points safely stored in our locker and our supporters breathing far more easily there is still much to play for.

Dean Smith, understandably a much more cheerful figure of late, rightly insists that a top ten finish remains the target and that would be a massive achievement given the topsy-turvy nature of the season as a whole.

We are currently seven points behind Preston who are in tenth place and we also have a game in hand so the target is tough but viable.

We now also trail Queens Park Rangers by three points and lead Fulham by five in the West London mini-league that is so important to our fans in terms of local bragging rights.

If you think that I am clutching at straws then perhaps you are correct, as I am not used to Brentford reaching the business end of the season without having much to play for. The last four years have seen us challenging for promotion each time and it is strange to be in a situation in which we need to set our own goals in order to keep us interested and motivated, so hopefully the season will not be allowed to fizzle out and we will at least ensure that our safety margin is maintained if not even increased.

The recent international break seems to have done the trick as the team appears to have been re-energised and is rapidly increasing in confidence. The victory at Nottingham Forest, added to the three goals scored and clean sheet achieved had left the players with an extra spring in their step and Bolton Wanderers were on the receiving end in the first half last night.

Granted, the opposition, as good as doomed to relegation, were not up to much but that is not to take anything away from a resurgent Brentford team which purred into top gear with a magnificent first half display.

The football played was crisp, neat and incisive, players wanted the ball and made positive runs and three goals were scant reward for our domination and invention.

McCormack and Yennaris hoovered up every loose ball, rendering the combative Darren Pratley totally ineffective and Nico is fast developing into a Coquelin-like thoroughbred.

He scored for the first time at home, poking home from close range after an excellent four-man move and more was to follow soon afterwards. Woods played Vibe through and Lasse fought off the challenge of his marker and crossed low and hard towards Judge and when the ball rebounded back to him off a defender he took his time, waited patiently for the keeper to commit himself and rolled the ball home for a goal redolent of confidence, if not arrogance.

Soon it was three when a flowing move saw Yennaris play the ball to Judge, who had earlier hit the bar with a cross, and this time his first time centre was perfectly placed for Vibe to glance the ball home with his head.

What a transformation there has been in Vibe with his three goals in the last game and a half taking him to a creditable ten goal tally for the season with hopefully even more to come.

It wouldn't be Brentford if we didn't do our best to self-destruct and we gifted Bolton three massive first half opportunities through our own carelessness and lack of concentration that a better team would surely have taken full advantage off.

As it was the closest they came to scoring was when Vela hit the outside of the post and shortly afterwards the impressive Clough could not benefit from Button over-elaborating on the ball – not for the first time this season.

That being said the back four looked mean and confident and also used the ball well. Colin is nursing an injury and appears to be playing well within himself but Barbet is improving with every game.

Bolton went for damage limitation after the break and tightened up with the introduction of the experienced Wheater and Danns. Poor Alex Finney, a tall, young defender making his full debut was removed to save him from further embarrassment after a ghastly first half display haunted by nerves and as Bolton improved, the Bees went down a couple of gears and apart from a hooked volley from the impressive Sam Saunders which went narrowly over the bar and a McCormack thunderbolt from nearly forty yards out which required an exceptional save from Amos, the Ealing Road faithful had little to cheer about.

David Button in total command of his six-yard box

We played the ball around but lacked our earlier pace and urgency and it came as no surprise when McCormack's clumsy and unnecessary tackle was correctly punished with the award of a penalty kick that Clough easily converted.

The game drifted to its inevitable conclusion with Canos, Hogan and Clarke given brief run outs.

Given how far we have come in the last few days it is tough to carp and criticise but the second half inertia clearly demonstrated that there is still much work that needs to be done and that we are still nowhere near the finished article.

The match clearly resembled the one back in December when we put Huddersfield to the sword with a rampant first half display which could not be matched after the break when the visitors roused themselves and fought their way back into the game.

That being said there was much to be optimistic about, not least the commitment shown by the entire team and their determination to ensure that they would pick up the points on offer, as well as give their supporters something to cheer about.

We will shortly be facing tougher opposition in the shape of Ipswich Town and we will need to be at our best and most determined in order to cope with the massive physical challenge that they will provide.

Brentford have been feast or famine since the New Year began and we can only hope that they maintain the impetus from the past two matches and go into the Ipswich game full of confidence, as indeed they should.

I look forward with relish to the clash between Alan McCormack and Jonathan Douglas, which might well go a long way towards settling the outcome.

More Good News! – 7/4/16

This has been a week that has just kept giving!

Some supporters might say that they fully deserve some good news after all the ups and downs that we have been subjected to over the past nine months whereas I feel that given all the obstacles that we have had to overcome both on and off the pitch we have done amazingly well to be in a position where our Championship future has pretty much been secured and given a fair wind we could yet finish in the top half of the table.

Despite the warm glow of satisfaction that we must all be feeling after two such comprehensive wins in a marvellous four-day period – and believe me I had pretty much forgotten how wonderful it felt after back-to-back victories, there are some things, believe it or not, that are even more important than the football.

In that regard there were two massive announcements from the club yesterday that in the medium to long-term dwarf everything else that has happened recently.

Firstly we finally received the long and anxiously awaited announcement that the Secretary of State, Greg Clark, had on April the first approved the Compulsory Purchase Order (CPO) for the land required for the new Brentford Community Stadium project.

This CPO included the Capital Court site, currently occupied by a disused and derelict office block, together with other small parcels of land that will complete the development site.

Chairman Cliff Crown was understandably euphoric and stated that *achieving the approval for the Compulsory Purchase Order is another step forward in our development plans. This approval marks the start of further important legal steps that the club and the London Borough of Hounslow now need to follow. We look forward to being able to make further progress over the coming months.*

Lionel Road is now even closer to becoming a reality and one that will mark a turning point in the club's long and chequered history.

A move to a twenty thousand capacity all-seater stadium will enable us to compete on a more even keel with the remainder of the Championship teams who currently dwarf us in terms of their average attendances, facilities and overall earning potential.

We are currently competing at a massive disadvantage and given that our average attendance is in the bottom three in the division with the resultant financial shortcomings, and that we are also subject to the dictates and restrictions of Financial Fair Play no wonder we have struggled to match teams who are ready, willing and able to pay players up to three times what we can afford.

As we have already seen to our cost we are unable to repel the approaches of better-heeled clubs for our best players and can only ensure, as we have done, that we receive full value for them.

This has certainly been the case in respect of Gray, Odubajo, Dallas, Diagouraga and Tarkowski and it is likely that Judge and maybe even Button and Bidwell will also follow them out of the door at the end of the season.

For the time being we will need to recognise and accept, even if we do not like to admit it, that we might face the need to replace up to half a team every season. We are simply victim of our own success.

That is of course as long as we can continue to recruit sufficient numbers of fresh, young and emerging talent, polish and develop them and then see them depart when the time and money is right.

The likes of Max Colin and Ryan Woods will undoubtedly have already gained admirers at clubs higher up the food chain than Brentford and we need to ensure that our recruitment strategy is more successful than it has so far proved to be in the last close season if we are going to maintain, or even better, improve our position over the next couple of years.

This is an unsatisfactory and frustrating way of having to operate, but quite frankly we have no alternative as long as our income levels remain as they are. That is why Lionel Road is so important to us as it represents a much-needed and long-awaited beacon of hope for the club.

If we are able to attract crowds of around fifteen thousand at Lionel Road, not an unreasonable expectation in my opinion given that we are averaging over ten thousand at present, and will also be able to fit in far more away fans as well as the extra Brentford supporters and floaters who will be attracted by a new stadium, then our income levels will increase exponentially, particularly when you take into account the certain rise in commercial and hospitality revenue.

Hopefully we will find out shortly just how soon it will be before work will begin on the site and when our dreams of a new stadium will be realised.

We simply need to hang on until then, depend upon the largesse of Matthew Benham to help us remain afloat, continue to punch above our weight, play our football and sell players as necessary in order to keep the wolf from the door whilst ideally replacing them with cheaper alternatives who will in turn ideally become the stars of the future. Not too much to ask for I am sure!

Nothing in that regard will change for the immediate future until we have moved to Lionel Road and we are better able to bring in sufficient income to ensure that we can keep hold of our best players and establish ourselves as a Championship powerhouse.

There was also the welcome announcement from the club that season and match ticket prices have been frozen for next year. It would have been hard to justify an increase given the season that we are having when supporters have so far only seen the team win eight times in the Championship at Griffin Park but the club is to be congratulated for its common sense approach and hopefully next season will see a massive improvement in our home form.

I suspect that we will lose some of the new season ticket holders who were attracted by the success we enjoyed last season but hopefully we can entice most of them back should we finish the season strongly and be in a position to strengthen the team in the summer to the degree and quality suggested by Phil Giles recently.

Brentford FC is synonymous with, and has an important part to play in, the morale and well-being of the community that it serves and yesterday's announcements can only help in those endeavours.

The past few months have in truth been pretty bleak but now Brentford supporters can start to walk around with a smile on their face again.

We are a Championship team on the field and that is also matched by all our endeavours off it too.

Mixed Blessings – 10/4/16

On the surface this has probably been the best week of the season for Brentford with three consecutive wins over former Premier League teams, nine points gained that have seen us shoot up the table into thirteenth position, our Championship place as good as guaranteed for next season, and nine goals scored, five of them by Lasse Vibe who has suddenly and not before time emerged as the prolific and deadly marksman we thought we were buying, and who has now scored a more than creditable twelve goals this season.

Ipswich Town became our latest victims and lambs to the slaughter as a determined and well-organized Brentford team which broke forward with purpose and menace comfortably took the points and thus gained their first ever victory at Portman Road.

Every silver lining has a cloud and the gloss was taken off the victory and totally overshadowed by the awful injury sustained by Alan Judge who has suffered a broken leg after a horrendous challenge by Luke Hyam.

There is much that I want to say about the circumstances relating to this injury as well as its ramifications for the player and his current club.

My blood is also boiling at the crass, one-eyed and indefensible comments expressed immediately after the match by the Ipswich manager Mick McCarthy, a man whom I had up until now held in high esteem, but no longer do so. Given how spitting mad, upset and concerned I am feeling, along I am sure with every Brentford supporter I am delighted that **Stephen Burke** had already kindly offered to provide me with a match report from yesterday's game, just as he did for the same match last season.

He did a fine job then and I hope you share my opinion that he has surpassed himself today. By publishing his excellent work now it also allows me a day or so in which to cool off and gather my thoughts about the Alan Judge situation on which I will write very shortly, hopefully in a calmer, more objective and less emotional frame of mind, as if I put pen to paper today I believe that the libel lawyers might well be combing through my words and that they would find much to interest them.

Here is what Stephen had to say and many thanks to him yet again for his perceptive contribution:

It was quite a remarkable afternoon at Ipswich for Brentford FC.

It was our third victory in a row in just a week, with nine goals scored and Lasse Vibe responsible for five of them, after fans despaired about our lack of a striker. Our future in the Championship was also secured for another season.

It was our first ever victory at Portman Road against Ipswich – and our first win against The Tractor Boys since 1955.

And the three-one victory looked a very distant dream just couple of minutes into the game when Alan Judge lay on the ground in excruciating pain after an awful tackle. With our best player taken out and replaced by Konstantin Kerschbaumer, who has consistently disappointed, it seemed like Brentford would be in for a long and difficult afternoon.

But the nine-minute break as Judge was treated and then carried from the pitch in obvious distress seemed to motivate and unify Brentford and shock Ipswich.

The home team had started on the front foot, pushing high up the pitch and causing jitters around several hurried clearances by David Button.

Then came the terrible tackle on Judge which surely merited a red not yellow card for Luke Hyam.

But the Bees regrouped and started pressing themselves, forcing mistakes from a vulnerable Ipswich defence. Brentford looked much more like scoring, which was not surprising given that Ipswich had not scored in their last three matches. Their hopes of a playoff place this season were hanging by a thread. But they failed to compete with a buzzing and clearly angry Brentford.

The home crowd were nervous too. Apart from the Bees fans, Portman Road was near silent. "Is this a library?" sang the Bees fans, who booed Hyam mercilessly every time he touched the ball.

Vibe had already forced errors in the home defence and Kerschbaumer also missed a chance before he redeemed himself by winning possession from Skuse, who claimed a foul, driving towards the byline and pulling the ball back to Sam Saunders. His neat and instant curling finish put the Bees a goal up just before the half hour.

The Bees kept pushing forward and could have had a second goal. Instead just before the end of the first half, Hyam tangled with Ryan Woods and was given a second yellow card for retaliation and dismissed – belated justice had been served but far too late.

This seemed to spur Ipswich on. They forced a couple of corners and Button saved well as added time amounted to nine minutes for the Judge injury.

Ipswich made two changes at half-time. On came Jonathan Douglas, the former Bees skipper, and veteran striker, David McGoldrick, as Ipswich tried to regain the initiative.

Douglas's appearance was one of a number of sub-plots in the afternoon. It was odd that he hadn't started the match but perhaps he had paid the price for missing a clear chance in the previous Ipswich home game. Douglas was on the front cover of the programme which featured an interview with the Irishman. The Brentford fans jeered him whenever he got the ball and he looked a shadow of the player we saw at Griffin Park last season. Douglas has now earned a contract extension for next season given the appearances he has made in the current campaign but he looks like a player way past his best.

There was also no sign of two other former Bees, Jay Tabb and Tommy Smith.

Ipswich started the second half on the front foot but after twenty minutes Brentford took control against the ten men. The second goal on sixty-four minutes was exceptionally well worked. Ryan Woods, who had a good afternoon in the heart of midfield, played an excellent ball through to Colin, wide on the right. His perfect cross was headed deftly in by Vibe who perfectly concertinaed his body shape to meet a ball that appeared to be behind him. Just four minutes later Vibe dispossessed Berra from a home throw-in and raced towards goal before placing the ball past the Ipswich keeper with a perfect outside of the right foot finish.

When was the last time a Brentford player scored a brace in two consecutive games and five in a week? Vibe seems like a player transformed since the international break. His confidence is high and he ran all over the pitch, making life very difficult for Ipswich's defence. He has now scored twelve goals this season, a more than decent tally.

At three-nil it was job done for the Bees. It could have been more, not least when Sergi Canos capped a good game with a stunning, dipping, deflected shot that hit the bar.

Inevitably it was a mistake – by Alan McCormack – that allowed Ipswich in for a late consolation goal. Until then, every time an Ipswich player had sight of goal in the second half, they shot over or wide, clearly lacking in confidence. Dean and Barbet had been immense in defence, snuffing out any opportunities.

Make no mistake, Ipswich were very poor. They didn't look like a team on the edge of the playoffs. They relied too often on the long ball and were weak defensively, particularly down the Brentford right.

What a difference a year makes. Just over twelve months ago, Ipswich and Brentford played out a hard-fought draw as they competed for what seemed then like the last playoff place.

A year on, the future looks far brighter for Brentford. A top ten place is again a real possibility for the Bees, with Kerschbaumer, Gogia and Hogan getting a chance to show what they can do.

Ipswich are simply a Neanderthal team led by a dinosaur of a manager, full of experienced players well past their best playing a horrible, outmoded and dated brand of football.

All of which is remarkable given the injuries that Brentford have endured this season. Let's hope Alan Judge recovers as quickly as possible. A fully fit and functioning squad would make 2016/17 very exciting indeed.

Bring on Aston Villa – and Ipswich!

Judgement Day – 12/4/16

Ipswich Town used to be justifiably acclaimed and renowned throughout the football world for the dignified and principled way that they went about their business. Unfortunately things seem to have changed and men of real integrity and class like Bobby Robson and former chairman John Cobbold would doubtless be turning in their grave if they had still been alive to witness the straits that their once great club was reduced to last Saturday.

Not content with crippling Brentford's star player Alan Judge with a tackle from out of the dark ages Ipswich piled insult onto injury by their blinkered reaction to Luke Hyam's uncontrolled and dangerous lunge.

There was not a hint of remorse, an apology or even any awareness or an acknowledgement of the seriousness of the situation and the unacceptability of his player's behaviour from beleaguered manager Mick McCarthy who truly beggared belief when he instead turned matters on their head and attempted to deflect attention away from the incident by bemoaning *his* club's apparent misfortune on the day.

Anything that could go wrong, did go wrong, whined McCarthy and he reacted with incredulity to Brentford manager Dean Smith's remarkably restrained reaction to Hyam's early challenge (if you can dignify it with that word) which he described as being merely *a bit naughty* and *deserving of a straight red card*.

McCarthy replied: *I'm disappointed if he's said that. I think he's won the ball. I've actually complained to the referee as to why it's a booking if he's won the ball. I don't think it's naughty at all.*

I really do not think that his words require further comment from me or, indeed, any reasonable or objective observer and a cursory look at the match footage renders his claims laughable.

I appreciate that managers are expected to protect their players in public but you cannot defend the indefensible and retain your credibility and McCarthy would have been far better advised to have refrained from saying anything at all if he found it impossible to make the unreserved apology that was without doubt called for.

I have now lost all respect for a man who I had previously considered a decent and intelligent individual – it is amazing what pressure and the disappointment at dropping away from contention for the playoffs does to somebody's judgement.

His players simply followed their manager's appalling example. Luke Varney, himself the perpetrator of a two-footed tackle from behind on Ryan Woods after the interval that rivalled Hyam's earlier attempt for its maliciousness, premeditation and spite gave his teammate the benefit of some quite considerable doubt:

There was no malice in it at all, we all know Luke, he gets stuck in and we'd never stop him doing that. If I thought there was any malice in it I'd know. I've had a couple of those tackles off him in training in the last week; he's that sort of player.

Yes, we do all know Luke and he certainly *is* that kind of player as his disciplinary record attests.

Hyam himself eventually made a mealy-mouthed, carefully drafted and weaselly attempt at an apology which was as badly timed and directed as his tackle which broke Alan Judge's leg, in which he asserted that *there was nothing malicious in the tackle and I hope Alan recovers quickly.*

In other words whilst he regrets the result of his challenge he saw nothing wrong in what he actually did. Incredible!

Players have a duty of care towards their fellow professionals and Hyam totally abrogated his responsibility on Saturday.

We Brentford supporters are still too angry and distraught to give an impartial view so I will let the final words on this subject go to a totally objective observer in former Eire international fullback Paddy Mulligan who certainly did not sit on the fence when asked to comment on what he had seen:

It's not football as far as I'm concerned. It was a horrible, horrible tackle. It was an over-the-top tackle. It was two-footed and there was absolutely no excuse. The referee didn't even send the player off. It's quite incredible really. It was a really nasty tackle.

There really is nothing more to say after that and I only wish that the referee, the hapless Phil Gibbs, had seen the incident in the same light as Mulligan and taken the appropriate action.

The real losers in this situation are Alan Judge, Eire, Brentford FC and our supporters.

Judge has suffered a serious injury as well as the cruel and totally unfair blow of being denied his perhaps once in a lifetime opportunity of playing on a world stage at the forthcoming Euro 2016 tournament, a prize that he had more than deserved after his series of incredible, consistent performances all season where he had been the shining light in the Brentford team and scored fourteen goals and assisted on eleven more. At twenty-seven years of age he is fast approaching his peak and had just made his full international debut with the promise of many more caps to come.

It is hoped that this is a clean break without complications and that he will return to action speedily and without any permanent damage or handicap. At this stage there can be no guarantee that this will be the case and given that Judge is a player who relies upon his acceleration, change of pace and ability to turn quickly to wreak havoc upon the opposition, who knows if he will return as the player he was and who he was still developing into?

Hard though it is to speculate, it is even possible that this injury will be a terminal blow to his career and we will all have to live with the uncertainty for several months to come. Even if he makes a full recovery he will lose perhaps the best part of a year from what is inevitably a short career as a footballer.

Judge will also lose the opportunity of making a lucrative move in the summer as it seemed inevitable that he would leave the club, perhaps for a team in the Premier League.

Given his quality, commitment and the length of his service to us, no Brentford fan would have begrudged him that move, one that now appears likely to be denied him, at least in the short term.

He would likely have been playing at a higher level than the Bees next season and he fully deserved that opportunity as well as the massively increased salary that he would have earned. Footballers live under the permanent shadow of a career ending injury at any time and cannot be blamed for chasing the money when it is on offer.

There is also a knock-on effect as Brentford too would have been banking on receiving a fee of at least four million pounds which might well have comprised the greater part of our transfer kitty for the close season. That money will now not be coming into the club and that loss means that we now all have even more reason to figuratively pull on a Burnley shirt and will them onto promotion given the three-and-a-half million pounds that we will receive in bonus payments should they go up to the Premier League.

As for Judge, who knows what happens next? The nightmare scenario is for him to require all or the majority of next season to make a full recovery, play not at all, or at best very little for us, and then, having been paid by us all season, leave the club next July on a free transfer when his contract expires. Surely that cannot be allowed to happen but the situation might well be out of our control?

Perhaps we will now offer him a new contract which could be considered more carefully by Judge and his agent given the changing circumstances?

Maybe he will be fully fit and playing again before Christmas, which will enable us to sell him in the January Transfer Window? That would be the best option in my opinion should Judge still be determined to seek a new challenge elsewhere.

So many questions and imponderables and no immediate answers. As always appears to be the case with Brentford, bad luck seems to strike when all is otherwise going so well.

Whatever happens over the coming months we shall just have to get on with things and make the best out of a difficult situation.

No player, however talented, is irreplaceable and if Alan does leave, or is out of action for a long period then I am sure that moves are already afoot to replace him although we might now be scrambling around to find the necessary funds. Kemar Roofe is the nearest that I have seen to a like-for-like replacement but he might now be well out of our price range.

I will end on a positive and simply thank Alan Judge for all the pleasure, enjoyment and success he has given us and I can clearly picture some of the amazing goals he has scored for us this season like the curler at Charlton, the screamer against Rotherham followed by a rare header, and the solo effort against Derby. I can also afford to cast a veil over some of his more interesting efforts from the penalty spot!

He is a crowd pleaser and a player full of effervescence and tricks who has been a privilege and delight to watch. Without him we would probably now be reconciled to visiting the likes of AFC Wimbledon next season, so we should simply give thanks for what we have already received from him, perhaps even hope for more and wait for the future to sort itself out as it will inevitably do.

Brentford's Injury Hoodoo – 14/4/16

I have never known a season in which Brentford have suffered so many injuries, and not just common or garden knocks, sprains, pulls and bruises, but a constant stream of chronic, long-term, recurring and serious injuries that can threaten careers, take vast chunks out of a player's season and require months to heal.

The success of the last couple of years has gone a very long way towards rebutting and helping us forget that hoary old expression that we long-term Brentford supporters know all so well – *It's Brentford innit* but our continuing and worsening misfortune with injuries might well begin to make us think again.

Given the massive changes that we had to face and cope with last Summer in terms of a new way of doing things behind the scenes, the loss of a manager, the arrival of a new head coach, the departure of so many of the squad that had performed so well last season and the arrival of a clutch of new players mainly from abroad who were all totally wet behind the ears in terms of their previous exposure to the Championship, we really needed some time and breathing space to allow everybody to bed in and settle down.

But this was not to be the case as almost from the outset we were assailed by a seemingly non-stop series of injuries which affected many of the more influential members of our squad, new and old. Given this handicap and the consequent need to throw in the majority of our newcomers rather than allow them the necessary time to acclimatise, it is hardly surprising that most of them sank without trace as we got off to such a slow and uncertain start and it was not until Lee Carsley replaced Marinus Dijkhuizen and was able to bring back the solid homegrown core that remained to us and take the likes of Gogia and Kerschbaumer out of the firing line, that our season began to take shape.

At one point late last year it even appeared that there was light at the end of the tunnel and that the injury situation was improving dramatically with the likes of McEachran, Macleod and Jota returning to the fold, but unfortunately that proved to be a false dawn and we then suffered further setbacks which have continued even up until the current time with the loss of Alan Judge to a broken leg at Ipswich last Saturday being the latest body blow that we have suffered.

It might be a salutary experience to look at the entire squad in more detail and outline the number of games that players have missed through injury and how our season has been ravaged by our injury curse.

It is also worth noting that the excellence of our medical team has enabled some players to return to action far earlier than expected and helped ensure that the situation did not get even worse than it did.

Full back Maxime Colin only joined the club in late August as a replacement for Moses Odubajo and immediately made an excellent impression but he only played four times before suffering a knee injury in training which resulted in him missing fourteen games before he returned in mid-December.

He then played regularly until mid-February before suffering a groin and abdominal injury that cost him another four games and it is still possible that he will require surgery at the end of the season, although he has now returned to the team and is currently showing some sparkling form. In all however, injury has meant that we have been without his services for nineteen games, or almost half a season.

Lewis Macleod has unfortunately become the poster boy for ill fortune as he has made only one brief first team appearance as a late substitute at Brighton in February since he joined the club well over a year ago. He fought his way back from a series of long-term hamstring injuries and the effects of apparently tripping over a twig at the training ground and caused some excitement with his performances at the back end of last year in the Development Squad including scoring a wonderful long-range winning goal against Bristol City. Unfortunately the injury bug has since bitten again with fresh groin and knee problems but there might yet be light at the end of the tunnel as Dean Smith remarked almost lyrically just the other day:

He got out on the grass to run after the course of injections he had. Hopefully this will have done the trick. Hopefully this is the end of it. The light that was just a candle is glowing brighter.

Maybe we will see him out on the pitch again before the end of this season but I suspect that we will do our utmost to get him back fighting fit and in contention for the start of the next campaign. He is a real talent and we have barely had the opportunity to see him in action.

Andreas Bjelland was our marquee signing and cost a club record fee from FC Twente. He was expected to solidify our defence and become our on-field leader but the Danish international suffered a season-ending cruciate ligament injury in his first competitive start for the club in the fairly meaningless Capital One Cup thrashing by Oxford United when, ironically, he was one of the very few first team players risked on a night when we fielded a totally makeshift team, as he was recovering from a minor groin injury suffered in a preseason win over Stoke City. He has missed the entire season, a crushing blow for the team and whilst he is now back in training he will not be risked until next season.

Sam Saunders has suffered terrible luck with injuries since the beginning of 2014 when he suffered a serious knee injury at a time when he was displaying his best ever form for the club. He missed months of action until he was eventually sent out on loan to Wycombe late last season but incredibly, he tore his calf muscle just three seconds into the Wembley Playoff Final against Southend United and he missed much of the first three months of this season and is now trying to make up for lost time as he has finally regained full match fitness.

Don't listen to people who tell you that footballers enjoy an easy life given their constant fear of injury and the hard and thankless work necessary behind the scenes in order to recover from serious injury

Marco Djuricin looked set to become a Brentford legend when he scored the goal which gave the Bees their first victory over Queens Park Rangers for fifty years but just over a week later the striker learned that football is not just about the glory when he was the victim of a nasty tackle against Blackburn Rovers and suffered serious ankle ligament damage. He missed nine games before returning in mid-January but he has recovered neither form nor fitness, has barely looked sharp or like scoring since and his very future at the club remains in doubt. He was beginning to look the part before his injury and had grown into the unfamiliar role of a lone striker but everything changed and this is further evidence of the precarious nature of a footballer's existence.

Thankfully there is a happier tale to tell about Scott Hogan who was expected to be out for the entire season with his second serious cruciate injury since joining the club, but he made a triumphant return with a goal against Crystal Palace in a Development Squad match in late February. He has understandably suffered from a tight hamstring since but is being carefully nursed and has recovered enough to return to the first team as a substitute, which is a massive boost for both the player and the club and it is hoped and expected that he will be a potent weapon for us next season.

There was great excitement when news broke about the signing of former Chelsea starlet Josh McEachran and he was brought in to be the box-to-box midfielder we were looking for to replace the departed Jonathan Douglas. He also frustratingly succumbed to injury during preseason training after he broke his foot in a training ground collision with Toumani Diagouraga which cost him the first twenty games of the season.

He eventually made his debut at Cardiff in December but found himself struggling to attain full match fitness and make an effective contribution, hardly surprising after so long an absence. He managed to play fifteen matches with varying degrees of success before lightning struck twice and he broke his foot for the second time, again at the training ground, and he will miss the rest of the season and might require surgery which could yet mean that next season is also truncated for him.

Jota was another to require surgery to repair ankle ligaments injured in a clash with former teammate Jonathan Douglas in the opening game of the season. We therefore lost our star player for over three months and just after we welcomed him back, his influence and sheer genius having been much missed, personal problems necessitated his return to Spain. How can any team be expected to flourish when it loses players of his class?

James Tarkowski was another player to miss matches early in the season with a calf injury and also suffered a badly broken nose after an aerial clash that really should have seen Bristol City reduced to nine men at Ashton Gate.

Our final broken bone was suffered by the prolific Alan Judge who had his leg broken by Luke Hyam last Saturday, the second of our players to be crocked this season when playing against Ipswich. What do the conspiracy theorists have to say about that, I wonder? Judge also missed a couple of games earlier in the season with a tight hamstring, a problem also shared by Josh Clarke and Marcos Tebar.

Andy Gogia has not seen much first team action but has also had brief spells when he was unavailable through niggly injuries. Philipp Hofmann has also found it hard to settle down and has not been helped by missing a few weeks in September with a stomach injury and he is currently incapacitated with a bad back.

Alan McCormack's influence was also badly missed when he missed three months of action through a calf injury that took time to heal and the Bees slumped alarmingly during his absence.

Nico Yennaris has benefited enormously from the opportunities granted him by Colin's absences but also missed a month through a dead leg incurred in August against Oxford United.

John Swift is also still out with a cut Achilles tendon as a result of a bad tackle received whilst on England Under 21 duty and recent loanee Leandro Rodríguez barely made an impact because of a hamstring injury which necessitated his early return to Everton

Thankfully Brentford have had some Ironmen in David Button, Harlee Dean, Yoann Barbet, Jake Bidwell, Jack O'Connell, Ryan Woods, Konstantin Kerschbaumer and Lasse Vibe who, so far at least, have managed to get through the season to date relatively unscathed but perhaps I should keep quiet about them as I do not want to tempt fate!

Given all these problems and the upheaval that these injuries have caused in terms of team selection and the fact that we have found it hard to fill the substitutes' bench from time to time, Brentford's current mid-table placing in the league is even more meritorious than it appears and should we finally manage to get the likes of Bjelland, Macleod and Hogan fit and available for selection next season then there is much to look forward to, particularly as we surely cannot be so unlucky again.

Don't Miss This Book – 16/4/16

Some books are hard to get into but are eventually worth the struggle, others make my eyes glaze over almost from the opening pages and bring about an irresistible urge to fall asleep, but just sometimes you hit the jackpot and pick up a book which engages and delights you from the opening paragraph and you find yourself totally captivated and nodding in agreement with the author's comments as well as totally identifying with everything that he says.

Apologies for the radio silence over the past couple of days but I have just been indulging myself and was totally engrossed in a wonderful new book mysteriously and enigmatically titled *Gus Honeybun, Your Boys Took One Hell Of A Beating* by **Simon Carter**.

So what on earth is this all about and who or what is Gus Honeybun? Quite simply, Simon Carter is a journalist who has enjoyed a love affair with Exeter City for the past thirty-seven years and the book is almost four hundred pages worth of an intoxicating mixture of ecstasy, joy, pride, shock, horror, resignation and shattered expectations as he recounts his memories of following a mediocre lower league football club in their fight for survival against almost insurmountable odds.

As for Gus, *he was a Janner, a nickname for all those unlucky enough to be born and (in)bred in Plymouth*. He was a popular rabbit puppet who appeared on local television for almost thirty years and helped celebrate children's birthdays by doing a series of on-air bunny hops and winks. That all sounds pretty harmless and uncontentious to me but unfortunately Gus was also a rabid Plymouth Argyle supporter and would appear on-screen proudly wearing a green and white Argyle scarf whenever they had a whiff of success – pure provocation and something that used to infuriate young Simon as a dyed in the wool Exeter fan who took particular delight in his club's rare victories over their local rivals.

Fans of every other Football League team will identify with the exploits and adventures recounted in this book. Taking a total of ten supporters to midweek games up North in the depths of winter, travelling away with no hint of expectation, when actually scoring a goal, or at least winning a corner, was the most one could hope for. Losing miserably and spinelessly to the like of Warrington in the FA Cup with the further embarrassment of seeing your team's myriad shortcomings transmitted to the entire nation through the live television coverage on *BBC*. The sense of utter frustration when you just know that your team will let you down whenever it really matters, but, never mind, you will still be there for the next game or the following season with the slate wiped clean knowing full well that further embarrassments and disappointments await you.

Carter writes well and concisely with short, sharp, staccato, tight sentences and he has a keen eye for a headline and an article that grabs our attention in the opening paragraph, draws you in and then never lets go. He is a fanatic without being an anorak or statto and non-Exeter City fans will be able to stay with the book without too much trouble as it deals with a multitude of themes and subjects that will resonate with every football fan without going into mind numbing detail of obscure games, players and events from long ago which would have far more limited appeal.

Carter does celebrate local heroes such as Tony Kellow, a squat goalhanger who, back in the day, often put Brentford to the sword, the late and much lamented Adam Stansfield, goal machine Darran Rowbotham and Peter Hatch, still living in Exeter thirty-five years after spearheading a massive four-goal giant killing of Newcastle United, who Carter interviews and then writes about with much poignancy and pride. Sometimes it is good to actually meet your heroes when they turn out to be even better men in the flesh than in the imagination of a young boy.

Supporting a no-hoper is all about patience and tolerance and being able to take pleasure in small mercies and then relishing and celebrating the rare triumphs and achievements when they do come along, and there is much here about the glory of winning the Fourth Division Championship in 1990 and gaining promotion back to the Football League in 2008 through the dreaded playoffs. Who can begrudge him the opportunity to play the likes of Manchester United and Liverpool in the FA Cup and achieve meritorious draws against both Premier League giants as well as earning enough money from the ties to help keep the club afloat?

Brentford fans will enjoy his account of the quite ridiculous 1982/83 season which saw Exeter barely escape relegation despite scoring eighty-one goals – generally enough to ensure a promotion bid, but Exeter also inconceivably found a way to concede a staggering one hundred and four times and their forty-six matches saw an incredible one hundred and eighty-five goals scored, or four goals in every match.

Eight of those goals came in that unforgettable game which Brentford won by seven goals to one. Carter witnessed this humiliation yet he was back, undaunted, bright eyed and bushy tailed for the next game which saw a massive improvement as his heroes only lost by five goals to one to Orient!

Football is also about friends and companionship and there are many amusing tales of derring-do as Simon and his mates travel the country more in hope than expectation and somehow manage to get back unscathed to their South Western outpost. Bizarrely he also comes across the likes of Brad Pitt, Freddie Starr and Uri Geller in the course of his adventures.

There is gallows humour in abundance and the book is an easy, fulfilling and amusing read but Simon's account of his unrequited passion and love affair also has the power to stir the emotions and move you at the same time.

This is a book that should not be missed and it is highly recommended for supporters of any football club from Aldershot to Yeovil – apart, of course, from Plymouth Argyle.

"Gus Honeybun, Your Boys Took One Hell Of A Beating" by Simon Carter, published by Pitch Publishing.

A Good Ending – 17/4/16

There was a real end of term atmosphere at Griffin Park on Saturday as the normal pre-match tension was missing given that the Bees had as good as guaranteed their Championship survival with their recent run of three consecutive victories. We could therefore afford to relax and hopefully just enjoy a good performance without being afflicted by the normal relentless pressure.

The Bees responded and played with freedom and on the one hand were unfortunate not to come away with all three points against Bristol City but on the other were more than relieved to earn a draw thanks to an injury time equaliser – and how long is it since we scored a last minute goal, something that used to be a Brentford trademark?

The performance was for the most part confident and positive and the crowd responded with gusto to the team's attempts to play a measured and incisive short passing game.

Brentford are back on the right track and are now beginning to resemble exactly what they are at the moment, a more than decent Championship outfit which has regained its self-belief and really should have had far too much in their locker for a game but limited Bristol City team still not totally free of relegation fears.

Brentford started brightly and repeatedly carved the visitors open, sometimes with their unwitting assistance through casual defending, without making them pay and quite simply we let them off the hook.

Lasse Vibe spurned three decent chances to maintain his recent goal scoring spurt, Canos had a venomous volley blocked by a lunging defender and Yennaris was twice too high from presentable opportunities on the edge of the area and there was also a decent penalty shout for an apparent handball in the area which the referee ignored.

The ball was passed around quickly and with accuracy as we probed for openings.

McCormack was the quarterback ably assisted by Woods, Yennaris and Saunders. Bidwell and Colin rampaged forwards and Barbet's radar was spot on with a series of accurate crossfield passes.

And yet for all our dominance the goal would not come and were fortunate not to concede twice on the break when the dangerous Kodjia used his electric pace to burst clear. Barbet stopped him on both occasions but they were close-run things indeed as on another day he might well have been penalised firstly for a professional foul and then a trip.

Lee Tomlin had been a peripheral influence on proceedings but right on the interval he finally roused himself from his apparent torpor, left Woods trailing in his wake, found some space where none seemed to exist and his perfectly placed effort unerringly found the bottom corner for a goal of quite stupendous class and quality. Quite rightly he milked the applause and threw our taunts back in our face.

The goal was a body blow but the Bees kept their nerve and if not as fluent in their passing and movement as they had been before the break, they still took the game to the opposition and came close through headers from McCormack and Vibe which both forced exceptional saves from O'Donnell.

A defeat would have been hard to take after all the quality and effort on display and Dean Smith's substitutions were right on the money as Hogan, Kerschbaumer and Clarke all made a crucial late contribution that saved the day for the Bees.

KK played a wonderful long pass that split the defence and the backspin held it up long enough for Hogan to rampage through and fall under Baker's challenge.

A penalty it was and in the absence of Alan Judge there was no dispute as to who would take it and Hogan looked set to score his first goal for the club after nearly two seasons' worth of injury torment.

Anguish as Scott Hogan's late penalty kick is brilliantly saved

Unfortunately Richard O'Donnell, Dean Smith's former first choice keeper at Walsall was the party pooper as he plunged to his right to save Scott's well-hit effort.

More frustration for us all to endure, but there was to be one last twist in the tail when, well into stoppage time, Josh Clarke hit a deep cross which Bidwell headed back and Hogan demonstrated his poaching ability by anticipating the chance, reacting far quicker than the defenders and diving forward in the six-yard box to head the ball into the corner for a fully merited equaliser.

Scott Hogan has worked so hard and without any complaint to come back from not one, but two potentially career ending injuries and he fully deserved his late reward.

Brentford have lacked a striker with the instincts to score those scruffy but crucial close-in chances since the days of Bradley Wright-Phillips and Charlie MacDonald, and Hogan looks sharp, hungry, keen and eager and quite determined to make the most of his opportunity and he will prove to be a massive asset next season.

It was fascinating to compare and contrast the approach of the two teams yesterday. Brentford were ravaged by injury and could barely fill the substitutes' bench but the entire team played with commitment, energy and confidence. They all knew and kept to their role and were a team in every meaning of the word.

A few weeks ago I advocated a move to a 4-4-2 formation, but I was completely wrong. Our well-established 4-2-3-1 setup suits us and the players we currently have and they are comfortable with the system. I would also like to praise Dean Smith as he has managed to revitalise a drastically weakened squad and get the most out of his limited resources.

There are probably at least four members of yesterday's starting eleven who most supporters would not feel are of sufficient quality to play in a team seeking to establish themselves in the top half of the Championship but you would never have realised it as they all played out of their skin and demonstrated that we are all about the strength of the team as a group bonding together rather than a series of individuals.

That is what we have to do given the reality of the situation and the financial restrictions we face. Bristol City also have a wealthy owner and possess a large and well-appointed stadium and have gone in a different direction. They were overambitious in the preseason, craved a marquee signing and made ambitious but doomed bids for players like Andre Gray and Dwight Gayle who were never going to join them. They therefore bungled their recruitment through overreaching themselves and have instead got by with a raft of expensive loan signings.

Bristol City have brought in twelve loanees this season in Callum Robinson, Ben Hamer, Liam Moore, Nathan Baker, Elliott Bennett, Simon Cox, Richard O'Donnell, Ben Gladwin, Alex Pearce, Lee Tomlin, Adam Matthews and Peter Odemwingie.

Without them I am certain that they would have been marooned at the bottom of the table and contemplating a return to the third tier but what they have done has worked and bought them some time, and Tomlin in particular clearly demonstrated his Premier League ability, so it is hard to criticise their strategy, but I cannot begin to guess how much they have spent on bringing them all to the club.

Clearly theirs is a policy that we cannot afford to follow even if we wanted to do so, and yesterday demonstrated that with a little bit of tinkering and a few clever additions we will be a force to be reckoned with next season.

What Might Have Been – 19/4/15

Just imagine how Brentford supporters would have felt way back in August last year if they had been able to look into a crystal ball and read the three names nominated last week on the shortlist for the 2016 Championship Player of the Year award.

Judge, Gray and McCormack were the three names announced and whilst few of us would have been surprised to see the first two on the list, McCormack's would have been an entirely different matter and surely nobody would have anticipated Alan having a career year that enabled him to scale such heights of achievement!

Doubtless, we would also have felt that retaining the services of Andre Gray and his mounting goal threat, watching live wire and spark plug Alan Judge taking the league by storm and seeing Alan McCormack play his role to perfection as the minder and protector of the more skilful and less physical members of the team, meant that Brentford would have succeeded in building upon the success of last season when they reached the playoffs and perhaps come even closer to achieving their seemingly impossible dream of reaching the Premier League.

Taking that thought just a step further, I wonder just how far last season's team could have progressed in the highly unlikely circumstances that we had been able to ignore the dictates of Financial Fair Play, the hungry predators waiting to pounce and the economic realities of our situation and managed to keep them all together for another year?

Who knows what the answer would be but that side contained so much burgeoning talent and it is a fair bet that with a couple of additions the team would have threatened to take the division by storm.

Let us now take a brief look at how the players who have left us have fared and examine whether they have furthered their career by leaving Griffin Park for pastures anew, and also how we have coped with their loss.

Moses Odubajo's departure left a slightly bad taste in the mouth as we had no option but to comply with his release clause which totally undervalued him given the massive progress he had made since moving to fullback after Alan McCormack's injury at Bolton. It is easy to complain though with the benefit of hindsight!

Moses impressed when playing for England Under 20s last summer and there is every chance that he will have an international future ahead of him.

He has established himself in a Hull City team that looks as if it is playoff bound and has had a consistent season if not quite matching the heights of last year.

You always miss players of his calibre but Max Colin has proved to be an exceptional replacement who can defend and attack with equal dexterity and Nico Yennaris has also taken his opportunity well at fullback. We are more than covered for his loss.

James Tarkowski left under a cloud in January and is currently waiting patiently for his chance in a Burnley team that is on the verge of returning to the Premier League.

Any judgement on him is still clouded by the unpleasant and unprofessional way that he helped engineer his transfer through his controversial refusal to play against Burnley and the problems that it caused us in its wake.

He remains a genius in embryo, a frustrating combination of superlatives and pratfalls where he is just as likely to glide past three opponents as he is to overreach himself through overconfidence and lack of concentration and set up a soft goal for the opposition.

Yoann Barbet has settled down well as his replacement and is rapidly learning on the job. He has the ability to hit accurate long passes as Preston and Bristol City found out to their cost but shares his predecessor's penchant for overplaying at times. Tarky is currently a better bet given his extra experience but Barbet is fast improving, is a star in the making, and we have certainly looked more balanced playing a left footer on his natural side.

There is not much more to write about Jonathan Douglas than has already been remarked about at great length here and elsewhere. He had a massively impressive first half of last season but his performances gradually tailed off as Mark Warburton grossly overplayed him. Even so he was highly influential and provided a shield for the back four as well as making effective late runs in to the area and scoring a career-high eight goals.

He has done enough at Ipswich this season to earn a contract extension but his overall influence is waning and I believe that we are missing a similar type of player rather than the man himself and I have no regrets at his having left. Konstantin Kerschbaumer and Josh McEachran have both attempted to take over the mantle of being the all action box-to-box midfielder we crave but neither has really fitted the bill and there is a yawning chasm still waiting to be filled, perhaps by Yennaris. The biggest influence Douglas has had on our season was in injuring the majestic Jota, an action which cost us his services for the first four months of the season.

Toumani Diagouraga is another whose departure has hurt us more in the short term given his obvious ability and more unexpectedly his newfound goal-scoring prowess that has emerged since he joined Leeds! Nico Yennaris has emerged as an unexpected hidden talent now that he has been given his belated opportunity to cement his place in midfield but I expect at least one new face to arrive in the summer who will challenge for a place as a covering midfielder. As for Toumani, it was the right decision to allow an unhappy player to leave the club for a more than realistic transfer fee.

Stuart Dallas might possibly have jumped ship a bit early as he would surely have been a near automatic choice for us this season had he remained. He might well retort that he is now earning more money playing for a bigger club than Brentford, but with a mere four goals and five assists he has not really pulled up any trees at Elland Road and I am not convinced that their style of play really suits him. We have lacked a goalscoring winger all season and his directness and readiness to shoot on sight have been sorely missed. He has been a real loss.

Alex Pritchard's brilliance in the second half of last season made it a total certainty that he would not be returning to Brentford and indeed, he was expected to be challenging for a place in the Spurs team of all stars however a serious ankle injury sustained when playing for the England Under 21 team has ensured that a season that promised so much has instead become a total write-off as he has barely featured for either Spurs or West Brom.

Alan Judge took over his mantle as playmaker at Brentford and succeeded beyond our wildest dreams with a massive return of fourteen goals and eleven assists but we have come nowhere near replacing the skill, effervescence and goal threat of last season's midfield. How could we?

John Swift has enjoyed a tough baptism of fire but has shown signs of developing into a real talent and his tally of six goals is highly impressive for one so inexperienced. He, Judge, McCormack, Saunders, McEachran, Kerschbaumer, Yennaris and the highly promising Ryan Woods and Sergi Canos have all ensured that our midfield remains the strongest part of the current squad but in Jota, Pritchard, Judge, Douglas, Diagouraga, backed up by Dallas and Toral we possessed perhaps the finest midfield at the club in living memory.

At first sight, Andre Gray has been perhaps our biggest loss given the twenty-two goals he has added to the two he scored for the Bees right at the start of the season. He has developed into the most dangerous striker in the division and there are no limits to the heights that he can achieve given his improvement this season since he joined Burnley.

Of course we have missed his eager running and predatory instincts in front of goal but between them Vibe, Hofmann, Djuricin and Hogan have almost matched him as they have scored twenty-one times between the four of them – a really impressive total, and proof that we have managed pretty well without Gray even if none of our current strikers can compare with him in terms of individual quality.

That is a trend that in my view has been repeated throughout the squad. We have without doubt lost the services of a large number of exceptionally talented players who blended together so well to form last season's wonderful team, but when you look more closely you can quite clearly see that whilst some have been missed more than others, most of their replacements have stepped up to the mark and have been hits rather than misses and they are all still improving as they gradually acclimatise to a new situation.

The overall success of last season has not, of course, been matched and perhaps never could be given our current resources but the reality of our performances this season on both a team and individual basis is far more impressive than the myth.

Finally my apologies for my really puerile and obvious Alan McCormack joke at the beginning of this article and many congratulations to Andre Gray, the Championship Player of the Year as well as to the runners up, Alan Judge and of course ROSS McCormack of Fulham!

A Lot To Play For – 21/4/16

There was much to celebrate after Brentford's victory over Cardiff City at Griffin Park on Tuesday night.

We can take great satisfaction at cocking a snook at our old friend Russell Slade and yet again tweaking his tail and his forlorn and dejected manner at the end of the game was a source of great joy to us all and highlighted that he fully realised that defeat to the Bees had pretty much scuppered Cardiff's rapidly diminishing chances of making the playoffs.

Frankly, Cardiff were a very mediocre outfit, big and strong certainly but totally unimaginative in their approach and sadly lacking in incision and creativity. They mainly threatened from set pieces and long balls and for a team so limited to finish in the playoff zone would be a travesty and I suspect that there will be some bloodletting and many changes afoot in South Wales at the end of the season.

As for Brentford, the season just keeps getting better and it's a real shame that there are only four games remaining given how exceptional our form has been over the past five matches.

The thirteen points that we have gleaned over that period has made a top half finish a real possibility, something that few of us would have thought possible a mere few weeks ago and that would be a fitting reward for a team that continues to overperform and show total commitment despite being down to the bare bones and running on empty.

Team selection was a formality last night as we played pretty much everyone who was still fit. Colin could not be risked after his long-term injury problems and might well require an operation but there was a silver lining to this cloud as this meant a rare start for Josh Clarke and the youngster more than fulfilled his manager's expectations with a solid performance in which he defended impeccably and maintained his concentration but also provided an exciting attacking outlet.

He is developing into a real player and his use of the ball was excellent. He is playing for his future and I suspect that last night went a long way towards ensuring that he is offered a new contract.

Alan McCormack has also reached his appearance target for a new contract and will now remain with us next season, an achievement that will be generally welcomed. He has been a massive influence on his teammates both on and off the field and the likes of him and Sam Saunders are worth their weight in gold as they act as teachers, mentors and exemplars to what is predominantly a young and inexperienced dressing room.

He knows how to manage the game as well as the referee and poor Stuart Attwell appeared at times to be in thrall to Macca and looking to him for approval before blowing his whistle.

We are not the biggest or strongest of teams and victories over the likes of Bolton, Ipswich and Cardiff auger well for the future as these are the types of team that have so often bullied and knocked us out of our stride but no longer is that the case as with the likes of McCormack and Harlee Dean in our team we are no longer a soft touch.

On paper you could look at perhaps half of the Brentford starting eleven last night and wonder if they were all good enough to play in a team that aspires towards the upper reaches of the Championship but the sum of the whole is far greater than that of the individual parts and we have become a team in every meaning of the word.

The first half was accurately described as *dismal* by Dean Smith as the visitors dominated possession but did very little with it apart from Pilkington heading wide from close range from a corner. Brentford ran, pressed and covered but there was little quality on view and apart from a Clarke cross which fizzed narrowly past a static Vibe in front of goal and a Woods effort high, wide and not very handsome we were chasing shadows and were more than happy with a blank scoreline at halftime.

Dean Smith's words at the break ensured that the intensity levels were raised and with McCormack, Woods and Yennaris becoming more influential the chances began to arrive. Marshall saved well from Macca,

Kerschbaumer shot over and Vibe missed horribly when he could see the whites of Marshall's eyes after he and Woods were set free on a two-on-one breakaway after a Cardiff corner was cleared.

The game closely resembled the home match against Nottingham Forest last year when a listless first half was followed by a far more dynamic performance after the break and the common denominator was Sergi Canos, a real live wire who injected some much needed pace and directness into our play. His wonderful back flick played in Bidwell who shot wide and we improved even more after the arrival of Scott Hogan which led to Vibe dropping back into a more withdrawn role.

Cardiff seemed to have shot their bolt and Button was untroubled except for a smart stop from Pilkington and our pressure finally told with seven minutes to go when Bidwell's left wing corner was flicked towards goal by Yennaris on the near post and Barbet seized upon a ricochet off a defender to smash a close range shot onto the bar and Hogan, *Johnny-on-the-spot*, again reacted quickest to slot home the rebound.

As if one goal wasn't enough, along came another straight away when Yennaris won a midfield challenge and set Vibe away down the middle and he timed his pass perfectly to Hogan who swept the ball past Marshall from a tight angle. Another perfect finish from a striker rapidly recovering both confidence and sharpness.

It wouldn't be Brentford if we didn't make a drama out of a crisis and we did our level best to self-destruct when Cardiff mounted a late long-ball barrage aimed at the massive substitutes Zohore and Ameobi. The former scored when Dean got caught underneath a hoof down the middle and there were two more narrow escapes before Stuart Attwell thankfully brought proceedings to a halt.

Four games remain and all that is left for us is to attempt to go through April and May undefeated, finish the season in the top ten, give Fulham a good hiding and win the West London Championship mini-league.

Not much to look forward to is there?

Narrow Margins – 24/4/16

The Brentford bandwagon gathered further momentum yesterday afternoon when we won yet again this time away at MK Dons, relegating them in the process and the highlights of our amazing recent run can briefly be summarised as follows:

- We have gained a massive sixteen points through winning five and drawing one of our last six games

- Brentford are equal top alongside promotion challengers Brighton, in the form chart over that period

- Dean Smith has gone from zero to hero in the mind of some of our more demanding supporters and he could well be in line for the April Manager of the Month Award

- We have comfortably beaten hard, tough and physical teams in Bolton, Ipswich and Cardiff who have overpowered us in previous meetings

- We have scored sixteen goals in those six games, second only to Brighton

- We have conceded only five goals, a record bettered by only three teams

- This is our most successful run since we returned to the Championship

- Lasse Vibe has scored six goals in his last six games and finally looks more like the international striker he is

- Scott Hogan has returned to the squad with a bang, scoring three goals in just over an hour's worth of football and his return from long-term injury gives us much to look forward to next season

- We have won our last three away games, having previously only won once away since the beginning of the year

- We have scored thirty-four times in twenty-one away games to date, the best record in the Championship

- We have achieved this success despite suffering even more injuries to crucial members of the squad and being barely being able to name seven substitutes at times

- Unlikely heroes have emerged with the likes of Nico Yennaris and Yoann Barbet excelling in recent games

- Brentford now sit proudly in tenth place in the Championship and we are ahead of our West London rivals, Queens Park Rangers and Fulham

That is all that springs to mind at the moment, but I hope you all agree that it is a really impressive list of achievements and one that would have appeared scarcely credible given how disappointed, worried and concerned we all felt as we shuffled nervously out of Griffin Park after our abject defeat to a poor Blackburn Rovers team a mere five weeks ago, our fourth loss in a row and one that left us looking apprehensively over our shoulder at the bottom three.

Now a top ten finish looks a real possibility as well as our being crowned *Kings of West London* should we maintain our form until the end of the season and ideally put Fulham to the sword next Saturday.

Following Brentford this season has been a real rollercoaster ride and never have Mark Warburton's oft repeated words about games being decided by narrow margins appeared more wise and apposite.

We went into the first international break in October in deep despond in twentieth place with eight points and six defeats in our first ten games. The situation appeared dire but Lee Carsley and Paul Williams then inspired us to a run of four consecutive victories and by the time Dean Smith took over at the beginning of December we had risen to eleventh place with only one defeat in eight games.

Our last game of the year saw us win memorably at Reading after wonder goals by Ryan Woods and Sergi Canos and Dean Smith had led us to eighth place after three wins and only one loss in his first six matches.

The playoffs looked a possibility at the turn of the year but that is when everything went pear shaped as our next thirteen matches saw a massive decline in results with a mind-blowing ten defeats barely offset by a measly two wins and a draw.

That saw perhaps the nadir of our season as we went into the last international break in mid-March in eighteenth place with nervous thoughts crossing our mind about the possibility of dropping like a stone into the bottom three.

Our current run has seen all such negativity fade away and now we are looking upwards again and we find ourselves safely ensconced back in the top half of the table.

How do you explain a season in which our changes of fortune and constant ups and downs have resembled a game of Snakes And Ladders? Of course there is much that can be said about our massive and ongoing injury list which has seen so many key players missing large chunks of the season, the need to bed in a raft of new players, many of whom had no experience of the Championship or English conditions, as well as the squad having to cope with the differing approaches of three Head Coaches.

That is all very well and true, but I also feel that luck and good fortune – and the lack of them, have had a massive influence on our results. Dean Smith made an interesting comment recently when he stated that we are not playing much differently or better now than when we lost to the likes of Charlton and Blackburn in March. In other words games have been decided by a moment of genius, a piece of good or bad luck or the whim of a referee's decision.

Being as objective as possible, four of the ten defeats in our last poor run could just as easily have ended in Brentford victories as Birmingham, Middlesbrough, Charlton and Blackburn Rovers were distinctly fortunate to beat us and we should also have beaten Leeds United when they escaped with a late draw at Griffin Park.

Now it is quite simply our turn to have fortune favour us and that has resulted in a massive rise in confidence and I also believe that the better players feel about themselves and their teammates the more luck they will enjoy, in other words you can help make your own luck.

If you look back at our victory at Nottingham Forest which saw the beginning of our recent run of success, the first half was sterile with very little action as two teams on a bad run cancelled each other out and the opening goal was always going to be crucial.

The game turned on a massive and horrific defensive error that saw Lasse Vibe gifted with an open goal. Suddenly the game appeared easier for our players, confidence flooded back into their veins and they began to take chances rather than play the easy and safe pass. Vibe in particular, a player who had not scored since mid-December has suddenly been transformed into a goal machine and has gone on a prolific scoring run.

I shudder to think about what might have happened had Nottingham Forest scored first – not that they ever looked like doing so. Nobody can say for certain, but I doubt if we would now be feeling so serene and confident – narrow margins indeed.

As for yesterday, we had far too much in our locker for a poor MK Dons team which needed a victory to keep alive their slim chance of avoiding relegation. They were boosted by an early goal by Maynard who converted easily at the far post when the tricky Murphy skipped past Colin and set the goal up on a plate for the striker.

We had started the game slowly and looked slovenly and lacking in sharpness, concentration and commitment but the goal roused us out of our torpor and Canos equalised soon afterwards with a brilliant effort from outside the box which curled in a perfect parabola over the straining Cropper into the top corner of the net.

Button saved us soon afterwards after Murphy skinned Colin yet again and the keeper brilliantly blocked Maynard's close range effort.

After that escape we slowly took control and Vibe almost turned in a shot from Kerschbaumer which was dropped by an inept goalkeeper who also did his best to gift Vibe a goal when he delayed his clearance interminably and allowed it to be blocked by the alert striker.

One all at halftime was probably just about right but we bossed the second half with Woods moving into the centre of midfield and dominating proceedings and he dovetailed well with the excellent McCormack and Yennaris.

Cropper had injured his shoulder and was replaced in goal by the young Burns who was afforded little cover and appeared well out of his depth at this level of football. Soon after the restart Vibe was sent away by a Barbet clearance and took his shot early before the keeper was able to set himself and his effort was perfectly placed into the corner for a well-taken goal redolent of a player full of confidence.

Even then we did our best to allow a poor team back into the game and dozed off in the sunshine but Barbet picked Maynard's pocket as he raced clear on goal and Revell missed horribly from point blank range. Murphy's danger was minimised when Clarke replaced Colin whose attacking flamboyance did not compensate for his defensive shortcomings on the day.

Djuricin came on for Vibe and hit the top of the bar with a flicked header and he helped set up Woods for a rasping drive for the nerve-settling and match-clinching third goal which also followed a flowing move.

Now it was just a question of how many and Bidwell obliged with a fourth when his free kick from way out on the right touchline drifted past all the straining bodies in the penalty area and ended up in the far corner of the net. Gogia who had a brief run-out as a substitute then came close to a fifth and the match ended with Brentford in total command.

A comfortable win indeed but one that could quite easily have gone the other way had MK Dons not been so wasteful with the opportunities that we so generously gifted them throughout the match.

Narrow margins yet again!

A Match Too Far – 27/4/16

This was the game that nobody really wanted to play. Brentford's visit to Hull City had been put off for a seemingly interminable period of time owing to the apparent difficulties in scheduling the home team's FA Cup replay with Arsenal what seems a lifetime ago.

Having played only three times in March this was to be Brentford's seventh game of a ridiculously packed April schedule, a situation that should never have been allowed to occur and one that was to prove a match too far for a thin, exhausted and beleaguered squad.

Hull City had already safely secured their position in the top six and all they had to play for last night was to help ensure that they finish up in fourth place and therefore get to play their forthcoming playoff semi-final second-leg tie at home.

As for the Bees, it was simply a case of trying to continue their recent unbeaten run and ideally get through the match unscathed before Saturday's massive and much anticipated local derby against Fulham.

Hull City are the moneybags of the Championship, a situation that I have previously written about with great envy when I outlined the eye-watering sums they received throughout their stay in the Premier League, figures that are now being boosted even more by an ongoing series of Parachute Payments following their recent relegation to the Championship.

Given their riches, resources and overall opulence which totally dwarf the likes of Brentford and are beyond our wildest dream, it would not be unreasonable to say that Hull have an unfair advantage over the rest of the division and in essence have totally underperformed this season as they really should have run away with the league title.

As it is, owing to their inconsistency and lack of goal threat their hopes of automatic promotion have long since disappeared and they will be forced to rely upon the lottery of the playoffs if they are to fulfil expectations by returning to the Premier League.

Steve Bruce was afforded the luxury, unheard of for Dean Smith, of making seven team changes last night whilst still being able to put out a starting eleven bristling with ability and experience, and as for his substitutes' bench – words fail me and I am green with envy!

Just take a moment to examine the wealth of talent that Bruce could call on should the need arise:

Allan McGregor | Curtis Davies | Shaun Maloney | Ryan Taylor | Robert Snodgrass | Tom Huddlestone | Chuba Akpom

Seven players, four of them full internationals, worth millions of pounds and probably earning between them a sum close to Brentford's entire playing budget.

That's just the way it is in a league composed of the haves and have-nots and where there is a vast chasm between the top six teams and the remaining also-rans who are pretty much of a muchness in terms of the overall depth and quality of their squad.

Brentford had already learned to their cost about the strength and depth of the Hull squad in the previous meeting between the two clubs last year at Griffin Park when after the Bees had totally dominated the first half without reward and were still well in the game after the break, the visitors simply went to their bench and brought on two massively talented replacement players in Huddlestone and Diamé. They turned the game on its head and a brave and committed Brentford team which had finally run out of steam and imagination was unable to cope with their fresh legs and minds as Hull effortlessly went up a gear, and we were left trailing in their wake and subsided to an unfortunate defeat.

David versus Goliath with us facing their atomic weapons with peashooters.

Last night the Bees were again short of options and named in their squad pretty much every player who was anywhere near match fitness although given that this was their seventh game in less than four weeks they were running on empty with many of the players patched up, half fit and in desperate need of respite.

Colin, Kerschbaumer and Vibe were rested from Saturday's team with Clarke, Swift, recovered from injury, and Djuricin starting in their place.

That is quite simply the way of the world when a small and overworked squad has been ravaged by a nonstop series of injuries throughout the entire season. Fixtures have to be fulfilled even though we are nowhere near being on an even playing field.

Despite these drawbacks Brentford had put together an amazing run of five wins in their last six games and had risen from the depths of the league to a highly commendable tenth place and shown grit, skill, organisation and determination in abundance but last night was simply a match too far and the Bees had nothing left in the tank and gently subsided to a two goal defeat.

Brentford played their normal neat brand of short passing football but shorn of Vibe's pace and hard running and with Djuricin easily snuffed out by Maguire there was very little goal threat and Hull eventually seized control and were rewarded with two close-range goals after the Bees failed to prevent crosses coming in from either flank.

Harlee Dean, otherwise so impressive on the night, was aware of the threat behind him and stretched in vain to clear, but could only find the roof of his own net and Diamé bundled in the second right on halftime which totally ended the game as a contest.

In between Diomande missed a penalty which was most generously awarded by a referee in Darren Bond who barely gave the visitors a decision all night, not that Hull really needed his assistance.

The excellent David Button got down quickly and well to make the save but that was a rare high point for an outmatched and exhausted Brentford team who struggled to cope with Hull's pace and power on the break.

The second half was played at exhibition pace and we were saved any more embarrassment and could even have scored when the impressive Josh Clarke was brought down a fraction outside the box according the referee – I wonder if he would have been as hawk-eyed if the incident had occurred down the other end, and Sam Saunders also curled a late free kick inches past the post.

Josh Clarke took his chance well towards the end of the season

Otherwise the sole entertainment was in watching home substitute Chuba Akpom doing his level best to keep a wide berth and stay as far away as possible from the belligerent Alan McCormack who would have just loved to have been given the opportunity to teach the young upstart a much-needed lesson in manners after allegations about his behaviour during his unimpressive loan spell at Griffin Park back in 2014.

Worryingly, indestructible skipper Jake Bidwell limped off with a hamstring strain late on, thus ending his bid to play every minute of the season and hopefully both he and Vibe will be passed fit to face the challenge of local rivals Fulham on Saturday.

I am sure that given the magnitude of the occasion, tired bodies and minds will have recovered in time for the weekend and Scott Hogan will also be ready to be unleashed upon our unsuspecting neighbours.

Last night was an irrelevance and we move on.

Position	Team	P	W	D	L	F	A	GD	Pt	Form
1	Middlesbrough	45	26	10	9	62	30	32	88	W W W D D D
2	Burnley	44	24	15	5	68	35	33	87	D D W W D W
3	Brighton and Hove A	44	24	15	5	70	40	30	87	D W W W W W
4	Hull City	45	23	11	11	64	34	30	80	D W W D W L
5	Derby County	44	21	14	9	65	41	24	77	L W W W W D
6	Sheffield Wednesday	45	19	17	9	65	43	22	74	W L D D D W
7	Cardiff City	45	17	16	12	55	50	5	67	D L D L W L
8	Ipswich Town	45	17	15	13	52	51	1	66	D L D D D W
9	Birmingham City	45	16	14	15	52	48	4	62	W L L D D D
10	Brentford	45	18	8	19	67	66	1	62	W D W W L W
11	Preston North End	45	15	16	14	44	44	0	61	L L D D L W
12	Leeds United	45	14	16	15	49	57	-8	58	L W W W D L
13	Queens Park Rangers	44	13	18	13	53	53	0	57	L D W D L D
14	Wolverhampton Wndrs	45	13	16	16	51	57	-6	55	W D L L D D
15	Blackburn Rovers	45	12	16	17	43	45	-2	52	L D L D D W
16	Reading	45	13	13	19	51	56	-5	52	L L L L D L
17	Nottingham Forest	45	12	16	17	41	46	-5	52	L L D D W D
18	Bristol City	45	13	13	19	54	70	-16	52	D W D L D W
19	Huddersfield Town	45	13	12	20	58	65	-7	51	L D W D D L
20	Rotherham United	45	13	10	22	52	66	-14	49	D W D D D L
21	Fulham	45	11	15	19	65	79	-14	48	W W L D L L
22	Charlton Athletic	45	9	13	23	40	77	-37	40	D L L D L W
23	Milton Keynes Dons	45	9	12	24	38	67	-29	39	L L D D L L
24	Bolton Wanderers	45	5	15	25	41	80	-39	30	L L L D L W

[30th April 2016]

Easy Pickings! – 1/5/16

I took my Fulham-supporting friend, Phil Mison, to the local derby at Griffin Park yesterday afternoon and warned him not to make an exhibition of himself when seated in the Braemar Road stand, wear black and white, or do anything else that might out him and reveal his true allegiance. If truth be told, the only time he became animated during what turned out to be a long and trying afternoon for him was when he heard his fellow Fulham fans jeering their team with an heartfelt and scornful chorus of *you're not fit to wear the shirt* and it was only with difficulty that he managed to restrain himself from joining in, and I honestly could not have blamed him if he had.

I am reliably informed that, back in the day, the Fulham programme used to include a prominently placed advertisement for *The Samaritans* and given their abject surrender and total lack of fight I suspect that it will not be too long before it reappears, and I can certainly think of one angry and sadly disillusioned supporter who might well decide to avail himself of their services.

Fulham were a total disgrace on the day, lacking drive, positivity and commitment; they gave no appearance of really wanting to be there and were not at all up for the fight. The fact that it was supposed to be a keenly contested local derby with West London bragging rights up for grabs barely seemed to have registered with them and they ran up the white flag and surrendered from the moment that Brentford hit them hard and early and scored two goals within the first seven minutes of the game.

Their highly paid team of mercenaries capitulated without a struggle or a whimper and for all their possession and neat football they barely threatened, and apart from Ross McCormack who drifted in and out of the game but struck the woodwork twice and forced David Button into his only action of what was perhaps one of his easiest afternoons of the season, Brentford were the only team who looked as if they had any interest in either competing or scoring goals.

The Bees, by contrast were fully aware of how much this match meant to their supporters and how poorly they had played at QPR recently and put in a massive shift in order to ensure that we all went home happy and smiling.

The quality of their performance was all the more praiseworthy and meritorious given how ludicrously stretched were their resources and the eighteen-man squad included two Academy products in Reece Cole, who spent the match on the bench, and young left back Tom Field who made a remarkably composed and assured debut when surprisingly given the nod to replace the injured Jake Bidwell, who missed his first match of the season.

Lasse Vibe, Marco Djuricin and Alan McCormack were also late injury absentees and our selection problems for this match simply mirrored what has invariably been the case pretty much every week since last August, as there has been a non-stop and seemingly ever-growing procession of players who have missed large chunks of the season, and yesterday was no different with the likes of Macleod, Bjelland, McEachran and Judge joining the aforementioned Bidwell, Vibe, Djuricin and McCormack on the injured list.

Hopefully we have now used up all our bad luck and next season will see us have a near full strength squad from which to choose. Scott Hogan, as last man standing, made his first ever Championship start for the Bees and Sam Saunders joined Woods, Yennaris, Canos and Kerschbaumer in a small but mobile midfield quintet.

Any nerves were settled within the opening seven minutes which saw the Bees take the game to their opponents who could not cope with their energy, drive, pressing, direct running and movement off the ball.

The appalling Ashley Richards, a total liability at right back where he proved to be a one-man fifth column before his merciful substitution at the interval, was forced back towards his own goal by Field and was robbed of the ball on halfway by Canos, perhaps illegally, but Mr. Haywood who let the game flow admirably all afternoon, saw no evil and Sam Saunders made a lung-bursting break from his own half and was criminally allowed to run opposed towards the edge of the Fulham penalty area. Canos picked him out perfectly and Sam's finish was audacious, instantaneous and immaculate as he flicked the ball perfectly over the advancing Bettinelli with his first touch.

Fulham resorted to bickering amongst themselves and Parker and Ince gave their hapless teammate a real mouthful, and the game was won and lost in that instant. Even better was to come when Yennaris and Woods combined to win the ball back in midfield, and Kerschbaumer played a perfect first time through ball in between two slow and lumbering Fulham defenders who were dozing in the sunshine blithely unaware of the danger, like a pair of wildebeest in the Serengeti totally oblivious to the presence of a lioness lurking in the long grass. Scott Hogan was too quick in thought and action for both of them, he was switched on and alert and ran on unopposed and finished perfectly and without fuss into the corner.

Fulham were stunned and out for the count and spent the remainder of the half passing the ball sideways and backwards, going absolutely nowhere. Brentford pressed, harried and defended in numbers and never gave an inch and it came as little surprise when they stretched their lead from their first corner when Field's perfect inswinger was thrashed into the roof of the net by the predatory Hogan – who else?

McCormack might have made a game of it right on halftime but squandered an excellent opportunity, hitting Button's post when given a clear sight of goal and Fulham heads went down even further and their players left the field to a deafening crescendo of boos and jeers.

Hogan had taken some knocks and sensibly was not risked after the break and he has now scored an impressive and unlikely five goals from eight attempts at goal in little more than ninety minutes of action, and yet despite his absence there was no respite for Fulham who were as yellow as their shirts, as Canos went up top and ran his opponents ragged.

Fulham had most of the possession as the home team invited them onto them, but it was the Bees who created the best chances when they repeatedly used their pace and cohesion to create havoc in a demoralised defence. Kerschbaumer and Canos both might have scored twice but for Bettinelli who also saved brilliantly from O'Connell's rising effort.

All three substitutes, Jack O'Connell, Andy Gogia and Josh Clarke played a full part in the victory and Gogia joined Kerschbaumer in coming so close to his first Brentford goal when he curled an exquisite late effort inches wide.

All fourteen Bees were heroes with Field making an exceptional debut before suffering a calf injury, and he was given support and encouragement by all his teammates who talked him through the game. Both Dean and Barbet were peerless and largely snuffed out the threat of McCormack and second half substitute Dembele, and Max Colin was also back to his imperious best. Woods, Saunders and Yennaris dominated the midfield and Alan McCormack's physicality was barely missed.

Unfortunately this might well be the last that we see of Sergi Canos at Griffin Park and if so, he will have left on a high, as he has been wonderful for us and we have been equally good for him. He can hardly have expected to have played thirty-seven times in the Championship as a nineteen year old and with six goals, including that incredible effort at Reading, his contribution has been immense and he has lifted everyone with his coltish enthusiasm and all he lacks is a tail to wag.

Fulham were rightly described as an *embarrassment* and *shameful* by their manager, Slaviša Jokanović and I suspect that there will be a clear-out at Craven Cottage given how narrow has been their escape from relegation to League One. In contrast, Brentford played as a team and this was their sixth win in a magical month that has seen them gain the incredible tally of nineteen points and score the same number of goals and also rise from the edge of the relegation zone to the dizzy heights of tenth place in the Championship.

This is an incredible achievement and so much credit is due to everyone at the club, as well as the fans for the way in which we have all pulled together, and this unity has been rewarded with a resurgence in results, performances and confidence despite the nagging and ever-present problems caused by injuries and exhaustion.

The squad has been tested to its fullest extent and every player has responded brilliantly and risen to the challenge, and nobody has been found wanting, and despite the recent loss of one of the best players in the Championship in Alan Judge, we have clearly demonstrated a grim determination to succeed and have fully deserved to rise up eight places in the league table.

We cannot match the likes of Fulham for the time being in terms of our income, squad numbers and, indeed, overall quality, but where we leave them trailing far behind us in our wake is in our spirit, shape, effort, planning, organisation, energy, ethos and determination never to give in, plus of course our exceptional team behind the team.

Brentford are a club to be proud of and Fulham, for all their riches, heritage and tradition could not live with us.

Kings Of West London! – 3/5/16

I would like to start today's article by expressing my heartfelt congratulations to Burnley who sealed their fully deserved promotion to the giddy heights of the Premier League by narrowly defeating Queens Park Rangers in a tense encounter at Turf Moor yesterday afternoon.

Burnley possess the perfect blueprint for what is required to achieve success in the Championship, a mean defence which has conceded only thirty-five goals, experience throughout the squad exemplified by the enigmatic Joey Barton, who has proved to be an absolute inspiration, a hard-working midfield which never allows opponents any time to settle on the ball, the inventiveness and trickery of George Boyd and of course the unselfishness of the battering ram Sam Vokes and the predatory instincts of Andre Gray upfront. All in all, a winning combination which has now received its just reward.

Brentford have made a massive contribution to their success by providing them with Andre Gray, scorer of twenty-two goals for his new club in forty matches, and James Tarkowski who only appeared four times but provided additional strength in depth.

At first sight it would appear that Burnley obviously got the better end of both deals given their promotion and the undisputed fact that they now possess two appreciating assets who could both flourish next season in the Premier League.

A close examination of the facts from a Brentford perspective, however, tells a different story.

Neither player wanted to remain at Griffin Park once their heads had been turned by the Siren Song emanating from the lips of their potential new employers and Tarkowski, in particular, made it totally impossible for the Bees to keep him after his toxic and inexcusable behaviour resulting in his downing tools and refusing to play against Burnley in a televised Championship encounter in January, something that I have never seen before and hope very much never to experience again as it left an extremely bad taste in the mouth.

Our hands were tied and we had no option but to sell particularly given the need to remain Financial Fair Play compliant and it was therefore simply a matter of extracting as much money as possible for the pair of them, and in my opinion we certainly did so.

At the time of his leaving Burnley fans were stunned and bemused and openly carped at the size of the fee that their team was reported to have paid for Gray, which will now increase to around nine million pounds given their ultimate success. I suspect that they are feeling somewhat different now.

Given that Tarkowski was definitely damaged goods, only wished to return to his native North West which narrowed his options, and that there did not appear to be a queue of teams competing for his signature, to receive an initial fee of around three million pounds from Burnley represented exceptional business on the part of the Bees.

As if that was not enough we will now be receiving another three and a half million pounds in additional bonus payments given Burnley's promotion. And it does not end there as there will be even more money owing should Burnley avoid immediate relegation back to the Championship, as well as generous sell-on fees if either player is sold at a profit as Gray assuredly will be at some point in the future should he maintain his massive progress.

Both Gray and Tarkowski perfectly exemplify the Brentford strategy and approach – in other words, identify young talent ahead of our rivals, buy low, give them an opportunity as well as the platform, support, coaching and encouragement to improve and then, when the time comes, sell them on at the top of the market given that for the time being at least we are unable to hold onto them given our lack of financial clout.

The missing part of the equation is how well we replace our departing stars, as for our business model to succeed and for us to maintain our place at the top end of the Championship we need to keep replenishing our talent pool, and again, I believe that we have not missed either Gray or Tarkowski nearly as much as I am sure most supporters would have either feared or expected.

A few weeks ago I would have conceded that we did not possess any player with the potential to replace Gray, but now with the emergence of Scott Hogan who has made a totally stunning and barely believable return from his two career-threatening injuries with five goals in barely a full game's worth of action but has also demonstrated a clinical ability to take chances in the six-yard box, the situation has certainly changed.

Hogan is a year younger than Gray, possesses similar strength, energy and running ability and is perhaps a more composed finisher in front of goal. Assuming that he completes his recovery as anticipated, and much praise is due to the Brentford medical team for their dedication, we will see a talented and hungry young player who will be determined to make his mark next season.

Brentford are to be congratulated for extending his contract by a further year before he made his comeback and their loyalty appears certain to receive its reward. Now might not be a bad time to try and persuade Scott to sign on for yet another year before his value rockets sky-high.

As previously mentioned, Gray has scored twenty-two times for Burnley but our strikers have more than matched his total with Lasse Vibe finally proving his international ability by scoring six goals in April and surely being a serious candidate for Player of the Month. Throughout the season Lasse has notched thirteen goals, a more than reasonable total for somebody new to the English game, and Philipp Hofmann and Marco Djuricin, four each. Scott Hogan's five, all in April too, makes a total of twenty-six goals scored by our current strikers, not including the two that Andre managed at the start of the season for us before he left.

James Tarkowski was the epitome of Longfellow's *Little Girl With The Curl*: *She was very, very good, but when she was bad she was horrid.*

At times his play was sublime as he showed the genius of a thoroughbred, winning the ball in the air or on the ground and then he would effortlessly stride away from his opponents and set the Bees on the attack.

Unfortunately there were times when he overreached himself and took unnecessary risks and the cost would be immense with the ball invariably ending up in our net. But this was how he was encouraged to play and you cannot praise him when things work out and excoriate him when they don't, you just have to take the rough with the smooth.

It will be fascinating to see how he adapts to the Premier League, if he indeed manages to win a place in their starting eleven, and I suspect that his seemingly casual style of play will probably prove to be a success at the highest level.

His lack of respect towards his head coach, teammates and supporters makes it impossible for me to mourn his departure and the emergence of Yoann Barbet has also meant that we have replaced him with a young player who possesses the potential to become even better than his predecessor.

Since receiving his opportunity Barbet has rapidly gained in confidence, has pace and aggression, reads the game well, loves a slide tackle and possesses a wand of a left foot which can ping the ball fifty yards directly to the feet of a waiting teammate.

He cost around half a million pounds from the lower divisions in France and has already proved to be a marvellous signing. He, Jota and Maxime Colin are three players who perfectly personify our use of proprietary stats and analytics as we plucked all three of them from obscurity without a whisper of interest from any other English club. Brentford at its best!

So thank you and well done to Burnley and also many, many congratulations to Brentford who last night sealed their position as the *Kings of West London* given that QPR are now five points behind us with one game to go and Fulham are trailing eleven places beneath us and have obtained fourteen points less than us.

Another amazing achievement by the Bees who are heavily outgunned by both of their rivals in terms of income and turnover but we totally outclass them both on and off the pitch, and our success is a confirmation of just how far you can go on hard work, creativity, original thinking, teamwork and planning plus a course the ability shown by a talented and committed group of young players.

I did some research this morning and this is only the sixth season ever when all three West London teams have been competing against each other in the same division, and it is the first time since 1948/49. This is now the third time in those six seasons that the Bees have come out on top, a feat that they also achieved in 1930 and 1931 and the Bees went on to win promotion to the top division a mere four years later. Hopefully a precedent for us to follow.

What a great time it is to be a Brentford supporter!

What A Game To Miss! – 8/5/16

I was fully prepared to get up at the crack of dawn yesterday and *schlepp* up the M1 to Huddersfield. Twelve-thirty is an ungodly hour to start a football match, particularly if it first necessitates a three-hour crawl up a crowded motorway riddled with a frustrating series of speed restrictions.

Dead rubber it might well have been, but it would also be the last opportunity for me to get my football fix for a couple of months or so, as well as to pay my own personal homage to a team that had put so many seemingly insurmountable problems behind them and whose dedication, perseverance, commitment and no little skill, now looked likely to be rewarded with a top ten finish.

Everything changed on Thursday with my wife's out-of-the-blue suggestion that we take advantage of the favourable weather forecast and go away for the weekend.

Football and Brentford's irresistible call, invariably take precedence over all other matters throughout the long and interminable Winter months, and home games are sacrosanct, but given the circumstances, would it hurt so much, would it be such a bad thing to, just this once, put the wishes and considerations of my family first and make the supreme and ultimate sacrifice?

My answer to that interesting philosophical question can be ascertained by the fact that Saturday lunchtime found Miriam and I ensconced on the beach at Poole Harbour and my knowledge of events at Huddersfield was confined to listening to the silver tongue of Mark Burridge on *Bees Player*.

So what happens? We only go and score five times away from home for the first time since, I believe, Plymouth in 1994, earn our best ever away victory in the second tier of English football, and the Bees put on a massively composed and vibrant performance that simply emphasised the confidence coursing through their veins, and the final five-one score line by no means flattered them. Indeed one of my spies at the match commented to me that *we should have scored eight*.

Scott Hogan - so much to look forward to next season

That's just how it is and my missing this mauling is surely punishment enough for my obvious lack of commitment and dedication to the cause, although it must be said that our weekend has been as pleasant and relaxing as we expected, and one has simply to weigh up the benefits and advantages of both options!

So the season finally ended in triumph and many of us perhaps wish that it could go on for a few weeks yet given the incredible happenings of the past month, but legs and minds alike are weary and badly need a rest if they are to come back recharged and re-energised for the start of next season.

Let's just take a moment to reflect on the immensity of our achievements:

- Brentford have finished in ninth position in the Championship, our second-best finish ever at this level after last year, and one previously matched only in 1950 and 1951

- 2015/16 is therefore our equal third most successful season since the end of the Second World War (and our most *successful* saw us relegated from the First Division)

- By ending the season as the form team in the league with an unparalleled run of seven wins and a draw in our last nine games we have risen nine places in the table and scored twenty-four times in that period

- We ended up a mere ten points away from the playoffs, so keep thinking about Fulham away and Middlesbrough, Charlton and Blackburn at home and what might have been

- With a highly creditable seventy-two goals we were equal top scorers in the Championship

- We were top scorers away from home with thirty-nine goals, including fifteen in our last five matches

- Brentford were the *Kings of West London*, finishing comfortably ahead of rivals Fulham and Queens Park Rangers for the first time since 1948/49

- Scott Hogan is perhaps the most prolific Brentford marksman in living memory as he played a total of one hundred and seventy-two minutes of football all season and scored seven times, an average of less than twenty-five minutes per goal

As for yesterday's game, the Bees always had far too much in their locker for a poor and dispirited home team which gifted Brentford a goal after twenty-one seconds when Cranie underhit his backpass and Sergi Canos was onto the error in a flash and finished perfectly past Steer, who then saved brilliantly from Barbet's header before being forced off by injury as the Bees threatened to run riot.

For the second time in three away matches a callow, young replacement keeper faced us, this time in Lloyd Allinson, who was to make a torrid debut.

He started well by foiling Hogan who actually missed a presentable opportunity before shooting narrowly wide of the near post as Brentford went into the interval only one goal up having hardly been bothered at the back.

That was all to change when Huddersfield equalised straight after the break when a quickly taken short free kick caught our back line dozing and Jamie Paterson, reputedly a Brentford transfer target, danced through a static defence, left Harlee Dean, otherwise imperious on his two-hundredth appearance for the club, on his backside and scored calmly and efficiently.

Rather than demoralising the Bees, this unexpected and totally undeserved goal roused them to new heights and Brentford simply stepped up the pace, went up a gear, and blew Huddersfield away, scoring five times for the first time this season.

Scott Hogan scored twice, each time finishing simply and without any flourishes or fuss after Kerschbaumer put him clean through with astute through balls. Hogan lasted sixty-four minutes before being replaced by Vibe and the watching Roy Keane left soon afterwards. Surely Scott's fairytale month couldn't end with an international call up, or could it? Stranger things have happened and in-form strikers are always in great demand.

Good man management again by Dean Smith who has ensured that Hogan is being nursed back into action and also kept hungry for next season.

For the first three months of the year we could barely buy a goal and now Vibe highlighted our amazing recent transformation and newfound confidence and capability upfront by scoring within three minutes of his arrival with a venomous shot perfectly drilled inside the hapless Allinson's near post after an incisive pass from Canos, who departed soon after to a hero's reception.

Lasse's seventh goal in as many games ensured that he joined Alan Judge on fourteen goals and he finished an excellent first season in English football as our joint top scorer once we had finally learned how best to utilise his ability to run in behind opposition defences.

Vibe then became the provider when he set up late substitute John Swift for a comfortable close range finish, which was his seventh goal of an eventful season. A more than creditable tally from a highly promising young player.

Swift barely celebrated his goal, which was scored right in front of the Brentford hordes and I wonder if his mind is already on his next move rather than contemplating a potential return to Griffin Park?

Five goals almost became six as Vibe went close right at the death, and the season ended on a massive high for everyone concerned with the club.

There has been a definite change of style lately as Dean Smith has made us far less gung-ho and we now sit back more often and attempt to use our pace and incision to pick teams off on the break.

I well remember the new Head Coach's first two away games late last year at Fulham and Cardiff when we scored four times and yet only came away with one point owing to our own *kamikaze* approach and defensive shortcomings. It finally looks like we have learned our lesson.

Now we are far more solid and organised defensively with Colin, Dean, Barbet and Bidwell forming an impressive and cohesive back four which is well protected by the speedy, mobile and combative Woods and Yennaris.

Suddenly there is pace coursing throughout the team with the likes of Colin, Yennaris, Canos and Hogan, and we are a real force to be reckoned with.

Konstantin Kerschbaumer too has finally proved his worth with assists for three of Hogan's last four goals and he also showed a welcome and unsuspected strength and determination to shake off an opponent before setting up Scott's opener yesterday.

What a rollercoaster and topsy-turvy season this has been for the Bees and their supporters and we can now all relax and take a break before the serious business starts again.

There will be much hard work taking place behind the scenes throughout the close season but the foundations are firmly in place for a successful campaign next season.

As for the squad, I am led to believe that their ninth place finish ensures that they qualify for a bonus payment and few would begrudge them their reward.

The Highlights Of The Season – 10/5/16

What a season that was and here are my highlights which I will replay in my mind throughout the close season and please accept my apologies for any omissions:

- Appointing a new Head Coach in Marinus Dijkhuizen who seemed to tick all the boxes

- Paying a new record transfer fee for Andreas Bjelland

- The excitement at signing a potential star in Chelsea's Josh McEachran

- Bringing in exciting young foreign prospects in Konstantin Kerschbaumer, Yoann Barbet and Andy Gogia

- Hoping that Ryan Williams might turn into our set piece secret weapon

- Buying two international strikers in Lasse Vibe and Philipp Hofmann

- Andre Gray's brilliant goalscoring form in preseason

- Jermaine Udumaga scoring his first goal for the club in preseason against Sporting Clube Farense

- Courtney Senior and Aaron Greene impressing against Boreham Wood

- Giving Stoke City a football lesson with Gogia running them ragged

- Thinking for a few weeks that we might manage to hang onto all our stars

- The injury time comeback against Ipswich and James Tarkowski's ninety-sixth minute equaliser

- Youngsters Josh Clarke, Josh Laurent, Jermaine Udumaga and Courtney Senior all making the starting eleven in the Capital One Cup tie against Oxford United

- Scoring four times at Bristol City with Gray and Hofmann combining menacingly up front and Philipp Hofmann scoring a goal of true international class

- Konstantin Kerschbaumer's back heel at Bristol City which helped set up Alan Judge's first goal

- Sticking four goals past our former loanee Ben Hamer

- Max Colin's eye-catching debut as a substitute at Burnley

- Lasse Vibe's twenty-five yard curler against Reading - what a way to score your first goal for the club

- Sam Saunders making his comeback from injury against Reading

- Signing Sergi Canos and Marco Djuricin on loan

- Djuricin's coolly-taken debut goal at Leeds

- Taking the lead for the first time all season at Leeds

- Uwe Rösler reacting to the attention of the Brentford fans at Leeds

- Goalkeeper Mark Smith making the bench at Middlesbrough

- Sergi Canos turning the game as an impact substitute against Preston

- Marco Djuricin turning his marker and scoring the winner against Preston

- The first win of the season at Griffin Park

- David Button's perfect assist for Alan Judge's brilliantly taken equaliser against Sheffield Wednesday

- The perfectly timed October international break which allowed Lee Carsley to put the squad through a mini boot camp

- Beating Rotherham through two wonderful Alan Judge goals

- Switching my mobile phone back on to learn about our unexpected win at Wolves

- Our first clean sheet of the season at Wolves

- Nico Yennaris seizing his opportunity at right back after Max Colin's injury

- Playing Charlton off the pitch after an uncomfortable first twenty minutes

- Alan Judge's goal and assists at Charlton

- The first win over QPR for fifty years with Marco Djuricin becoming an instant Brentford legend

- Substitutes Kerschbaumer, Vibe and Hofmann all playing their part in the QPR triumph

- Lee Carsley reviving our fortunes, leading us to four consecutive wins and winning the October Manager of the Month Award

- Alan Judge winning the October Player of the Month Award after a series of inspirational displays

- Brentford's exceptional first half display against Hull

- Kerschbaumer's bending shot against the post versus Hull

- Sergi Canos's first goal for the club against Nottingham Forest

- Philipp Hofmann's triple ricochet ninety-sixth minute winner against Nottingham Forest

- John Swift's Premier League class goal at Bolton

- Dean Smith's appointment as Brentford's Head Coach

- Playing MK Dons off the pitch at Griffin Park in Dean Smith's first game

- Outplaying Fulham at Craven Cottage

- Sitting in the Hammersmith End with the Fulham fans and trying not to cheer us on

- The deafening noise made by nearly five thousand Brentford fans at Fulham

- The glorious moment when we thought that Jota had scored a deserved winner at Craven Cottage

- Josh McEachran making his Brentford debut at Cardiff and instantly looking at home in our midfield

- Jake Bidwell's first goal for the club in his one hundred and eighty-sixth game

- Forty-five minutes of perfection against Huddersfield

- Lasse Vibe's thunderous volley against Huddersfield after Tarkowski's perfect chip forward

- Totally outplaying Brighton, but the ball refused to go in

- Our amazing support from three thousand fans at Reading rewarded by Ryan Woods's first goal for the club from twenty-five yards and the Goal of the Season by Sergi Canos

- Michael Hector's second yellow card for an embarrassing dive

- Nemesis Keith Stroud sending off two opposition players this season

- Thinking that we had sneaked a point at Birmingham when Hofmann equalised late on

- Totally outplaying Middlesbrough in the first half at Griffin Park

- The second half display against Burnley – forget about the first half

- Yoann Barbet's pass and Alan Judge's cool finish at Preston

- THAT save by David Button at Preston which ensured our victory

- Josh McEachran selling the Leeds attack a dummy and clearing the danger in our penalty area

- Sam Saunders running at the Leeds defence before scoring

- The first five minutes at Sheffield Wednesday

- That wonder goal by Alan Judge against Derby

- Putting Wolves to the sword again

- John Swift's two-goal performance against Wolves

- Josh McEachran's slide rule pass to Jake Bidwell before our second goal against Wolves

- Yoann Barbet's first goal for the club against Charlton

- The anticipation and excitement leading up to the visit to Loftus Road

- Another international break, another opportunity to regroup

- International caps for Daniel O'Shaughnessy, Alan Judge and Lasse Vibe

- The relief at winning again after losing four in a row, and celebrating Vibe's opening goal at Nottingham Forest

- Confidence returning to the squad with a wonderful first half performance against Bolton

- Nico Yennaris dominating the midfield and demonstrating his quality

- Lasse Vibe – *Goal Machine*, after we finally learned how to play to his strengths

- Alan McCormack and Ryan Woods ensuring that Luke Hyam finally got his just deserts at Ipswich

- Two brilliantly taken goals by Lasse Vibe at Ipswich

- Scott Hogan's return and first goal for the club against Bristol City – another last minute equaliser

- Hogan winning us the Cardiff match with two more late goals

- Sergi Canos's wonderful curling effort at MK Dons

- Watching Jake Bidwell's late free kick dribble through the MK Dons defence and bounce perfectly into corner of the net

- Losing at Hull City – and not really caring as it was simply a match too far

- The first seven minutes against Fulham

- Sam Saunders's lung-bursting run to score the first goal

- Konstantin Kerschbaumer growing into his role and his perfect through balls for three of Scott Hogan's goals

- Totally embarrassing Fulham and comprehensively beating them

- Tom Field's remarkably composed debut and assist against Fulham

- A twenty-one second opening goal at Huddersfield

- Putting Huddersfield to the sword – yet again

- Scott Hogan's clinical finishing with seven goals in under two full games

- Roy Keane leaving the stadium as soon as Scott Hogan was substituted at Huddersfield

- The massive improvement in our set pieces

- The *renaissance* of Josh Clarke

- Youngsters James Ferry and Reece Cole making the substitutes' bench

- Josh Bohui playing for the England Under 17 team

- Our last nine matches, which netted us twenty-two points and twenty-four goals

- Becoming a real team again on and off the field with club and supporters reunited

- The influence of Dean Smith and Richard O'Kelly taking effect on the squad

- Playing beautiful pass-and-move football the Brentford way again

- Two top nine finishes in our first two years back in the Championship

- Never being in the bottom three of the league table

- Looking forward eagerly to next season and what it has to bring

- Our foreign signings developing into excellent players once they had finally adapted to the league and their new environment

- Harlee Dean proving to be a real leader and reaching the two-hundred game mark for the club

- Maxime Colin and Yoann Barbet settling in so well and promising so much

- Jake Bidwell's consistency and composure and also reaching the two-hundred game milestone

- David Button – ever-present again and a massive influence

- Lewis Macleod finally getting onto the pitch, albeit briefly

- Andreas Bjelland getting close to a full recovery

- Sam Saunders and Alan McCormack earning new contracts and being a massive positive influence on their less experienced teammates

- Anticipating the goals Scott Hogan will hopefully score next season

- Everything about Alan Judge, a career year and such a wonderful player, and rightly named as one of the top three players in the Championship and in the Team of the Season

- Ryan Woods quietly going about his business and impressing everyone

- John Swift scoring seven goals in his first real look at the Championship

- Sergi Canos – an inspiration and a perfect example of how a loan player should conduct himself

- Finally getting the CPO verdict that helps bring the new stadium at Lionel Road even closer

- Finishing as *Kings of West London* and the leading London club outside the Premier League

- Mark Burridge and his *Bees Player* team

- Poetic justice as James Tarkowski did not receive a medal at Burnley's trophy presentation

- Matthew Benham, Cliff Crown, Mark Devlin, Phil Giles, Rasmus Ankersen, Robert Rowan and their teams working so hard, effectively and creatively to ensure that we maintain our edge

- On a personal level, having Richard Lee and Cliff Crown very kindly attend book signings and the fantastic response to, and reviews of, my book

Please Do Your Homework Mr. Samuel! – 11/5/16

I had not planned to write anything today as I had work to do and a book to finish, but that all changed when I opened a copy of *The Daily Mail* at my breakfast table and my blood immediately started boiling to the extent that I wished the cover of the newspaper had contained a health warning.

Martin Samuel is an extremely well-regarded and deservedly much-lauded journalist who writes a column every Monday and Wednesday giving his take on the latest major happenings within the world of sport.

I have to make a confession at this point and say that I generally look forward to and enjoy his work, as he certainly has a way with words, can turn an elegant and pithy phrase and enjoys exposing cant and hypocrisy wherever he finds it, as well as puncturing inflated egos and unjustified feelings of self-regard.

Given his exalted and rarefied position and consequent concentration on the bigger fish, Brentford rarely come within his purview as we are far too insignificant and lowly to catch his regular attention. Today though was different as he let fly with a broadside that was as ill-conceived as it was ignorant and as lacking in logic as it was inaccurate. He really let us have it with both barrels, and here is what he had to say:

As everything at Brentford is put through the analytics wringer, one presumes statistics do not just govern recruitment, but player sales. So it must have been some set of numbers that persuaded them to sell Andre Gray to Burnley – even for a club record six million pounds. Gray has scored twenty-three goals in forty-one league games as Burnley returned to the Premier League.

Brentford, meanwhile, have fallen from fifth to ninth, collecting thirteen points fewer than last season. With promotion worth in excess of one hundred million pounds, Brentford's computer might need a reset.

Brentford first caught the eye of the national media late in 2014 as a team of plucky underdogs who were over performing to challenge at the top of the Championship, and had come from nowhere to compete with fellow blue-eyed boys, AFC Bournemouth, for a most unlikely promotion to the Premier League.

Timesgate and the botched announcement of the parting of the ways with Mark Warburton last February put us on the back foot and changed matters totally, as the media unsurprisingly turned on us and then tried to devour us whole given our stated strategy of relying on statistical analysis and mathematical modelling.

Nobody bothered to take the time to discover what that really meant and we were convicted out of hand, and perhaps out of our own mouth, as faceless robots and automatons who would make every major recruitment decision on the basis of *Computer Says,* and were no longer relying in any way, shape or form upon the human element.

As we all know there is nothing that makes people feel more uneasy than new thinking and ideas and doing things differently to the norm, and the natural and default reaction is to mock, jeer, find fun and criticise rather than examine and analyse what is being mooted in a deep, thorough and analytical manner. That would be boring and require some effort, something nobody has the time to do, and journalists would far prefer the cheap headline and easy dig. And boy did we suffer, and continue to do so, as everyone from Martin Samuel, Daniel Taylor, Adrian Durham, Tony Cottee and pretty much the entire team of *Sky Sports* analysts have lined up to take cheap potshots at us and our perceived approach.

What is so galling is that we are really doing nothing very different to the overwhelming majority of Premier League and Championship teams who rely to a great extent upon the use of statistics and data.

Where we differ is that in the normal Brentford manner, we are putting our own unique spin on things rather than just subscribing to the plethora of scouting and player analytical databases that are readily available. We have also developed our own proprietary systems for how we both analyse and use the raw data, developed by Matthew Benham's *Smartodds* company.

Analytics are used to identify and shortlist potential transfer targets, but this is combined with physical scouting which also plays a crucial role in the recruitment process as former manager Andy Scott oversees a number of scouts who watch prospects in the flesh before any decision is made, and the recruitment process for a new Head Scout is also currently underway.

Given the tone and tenet of Mr. Samuel's article it is both interesting and relevant to consider the words of *Stats Guru* Ted Knutson, until recently employed by Brentford, who wrote about his experience on his acclaimed *StatsBomb* website, and I hope he doesn't mind my reproducing his words:

With a small recruitment team of two stats and six part-time scouts, we evaluated over one thousand players in a year for the first teams of Brentford and Midtjylland.

Yes, but were you successful? This is the most important factor, and obviously it depends on how you look at it.

After a disastrous start in the first nine games due to a poor manager choice, Brentford earned points at nearly a playoff pace, despite awful injuries in the first half of the season. The team also led the league in goals scored and avoided an FFP-related transfer embargo.

And most importantly, they did it with one of the lowest wage budgets in the league and my estimate of a ten to eleven million pound transfer fee surplus in the year we were involved in recruitment.

I'm going to notch that up as success, while admitting that at the start of the season, I was hoping for promotion just like the owner and every other Brentford fan out there.

I wonder what Martin Samuel would make of that response as I feel strongly that he has been totally simplistic and superficial in his mocking words about the club?

Without wanting to repeat my normal mantra I would state that it was not Brentford's desire or wish to sell Andre Gray to Burnley, or indeed anybody else. We had no option but to sell him as well as other leading players such as Moses Odubajo, Stuart Dallas and James Tarkowski because they all wanted to leave the club.

Their heads had been turned by bigger and richer clubs, generally swollen and inflated with massive Parachute Payments who were able to offer our best players mind-blowing salaries in a totally different stratosphere to what we could possibly afford. Odubajo also had a contractual release clause that was met by Hull City.

There is absolutely no point in keeping an unhappy, unsettled and dissatisfied player and Brentford have simply had to accept that for the foreseeable future that they are a stepping stone club which has to sell its best players whenever the predators come bashing at the door.

The club's turnover and attendances are in the bottom three of the Championship and they are therefore competing with one hand tied behind their back. The dictates of Financial Fair Play have also necessitated the sale of players such as Gray who has now earned us the best part of nine millions pounds rather than the six erroneously mentioned by Mr. Samuel in his column.

To finish fifth and then ninth in such a competitive division, which is otherwise awash with money, is surely an incredible achievement given the restrictions and handicaps that we currently face?

Brentford were well aware of Andre Gray's potential but had to sell him and could only ensure that they received their full valuation for him, which they did. Burnley have also just had to stump up a further promotion bonus payment with additional monies due should they survive next season in the Premier League, as well as a handsome sell-on percentage.

That has to be the Brentford way of doing business for the time being given a stadium that barely holds twelve thousand spectators. We buy low and sell high whilst punching way above our weight and playing attractive pass-and-move attacking football. There are already several other players in the squad from both at home and abroad, identified through our combination of stats and physical scouting with as much potential or more than Gray.

As expected, Gray scored freely for his new club and his goals led them to promotion, but we replaced him with Lasse Vibe for a mere fraction of the cost and he scored fourteen times as we finished with seventy-two goals, equal top scorers in the division, ironically enough alongside Burnley.

All in all our four strikers scored twenty-nine times between them (more than Gray managed) with the amazing Scott Hogan returning from two serious cruciate injuries to score seven goals in less than two full matches.

Of course a player of Gray's calibre was missed, but we did a pretty good job of replacing him whilst still living within our means and finishing in a highly creditable position in the table with which every Brentford fan is delighted considering from whence we came.

Please Mr. Samuel do your homework next time and give some credit where it is due rather than take cheap shots which are totally unmerited.

Surely you are far better than that?

The Lowlights Of The Season – 13/5/16

What a strange, but in the end, extremely positive season for which the term *rollercoaster* could have been invented. There were so many ups and perhaps an equal number of downs too and here are my personal lowlights, many of which, it must be said, were cancelled out by equally positive events:

- Losing so many key players so late in the preseason after the new Head Coach had almost finalised his preparations
- Realising the realities of our financial situation and where we sit in the food chain
- Player power and accepting that is not worth keeping unsettled players
- The unsettling situation of not knowing anything about our new foreign signings
- Having to throw so many of them into the Championship before they were ready or acclimatised
- Allowing Jonathan Douglas to leave with no obvious replacement
- The frustration of losing our record signing Andreas Bjelland to serious injury before he could make his league debut
- The total embarrassment of *Pitchgate*

- Injuries, more injuries and yet more injuries – a constant theme throughout the season

- Being unable to develop a settled team on account of so many serious injuries

- Josh McEachran's training ground injury

- Losing Jota in the season opener after a tackle from ex-Bee, Douglas

- Marinus Dijkhuizen struggling to make his mark

- Totally underestimating Oxford United and deservedly paying the price

- Jack Bonham's struggles against Oxford United and the lack of sympathy he received from the supporters

- Throwing Clarke, Senior, Udumaga and Laurent to the wolves against Oxford United

- Getting hit by the ball again at halftime against Oxford United – thanks Alan McCormack

- Realising that we were not as good as we either hoped or expected

- Newly promoted Bristol City taking us apart until Freeman's red card

- The unrealistically raised expectations after the far too positive messages emanating from the club

- The horrific elbow on Tarkowski at Bristol City

- Andre Gray finally leaving the club and joining Burnley

- The lack of strength and experience of our substitutes' bench at Burnley

- Lasse Vibe proving that he should not play marooned out on the right wing

- The continued absence of Lewis Macleod

- Being totally outplayed by Reading at Griffin Park despite our constant changes of formation

- Throwing away a victory at Elland Road through a careless Ryan Woods error in the dying minutes

- Having to put goalkeeper Mark Smith on the substitutes' bench at Middlesbrough and only being able to name six subs

- Throwing away the chance to allay our Middlesbrough bogey through profligate finishing

- Our terrible start at home to Preston

- Lasse Vibe missing a great chance to win the home match against Sheffield Wednesday

- Losing in the last minute to Sheffield Wednesday after a rebound off Jack O'Connell's backside

- The Fans' Forum Fiasco

- Having to sack our new Head Coach Marinus Dijkhuizen after only nine matches

- Losing a goal to a free header at a corner against Birmingham City after we had over five minutes to prepare for it after Alan McCormack's injury

- The appalling performance against Birmingham City which lacked any energy or ambition

- Alan Judge's brilliant late effort against Birmingham clanging off the crossbar to safety

- Lee Carsley's unsettling post-match revelations after losing his first game to Birmingham City

- Being overpowered and outclassed by Derby County

- Lasse Vibe still lying on the ground at the other end of the pitch screaming for a foul when the ball entered our net for Derby's second goal

- The abusive and aggressive behaviour of some appalling so-called Brentford fans at Derby

- Dropping my car keys out of my pocket and fearing I would be stuck in Derby

- Alan McCormack's rasping twenty-five yard effort coming back off the bar at Charlton Athletic

- Getting stuck in appalling traffic on the North Circular Road on my way to the QPR local derby and worrying that I would not arrive in time

- Marco Djuricin's injury at Blackburn – he was never the same player afterwards

- The death of Martin Lange

- The Pep Clotet will-he, won't-he saga

- Lee Carsley and Paul Williams leaving the club

- John Swift's ridiculous booking for an alleged dive at Bolton

- Alan Judge's one-on-one miss against MK Dons

- James Tarkowski's needless own goal at Fulham which revived the home team when we were totally dominating the match

- Jota's contentiously disallowed goal at Fulham

- Allowing a last minute sloppy winner at Cardiff after recovering from a two-goal deficit

- The second half non-display against Huddersfield

- Allowing yet another sloppy last minute winner at Birmingham City after fighting back to equalise

- Jota's personal problems forcing his return to Spain

- The frustration that is Philipp Hofmann – so much ability but so little end product to date

- The week from hell when we lost three home games and our season began to fall apart

- Not taking the FA Cup seriously

- *Button Fingers* against Middlesbrough – losing a game we should have won

- James Tarkowski's behaviour before the Burnley game and the effect it had on us

- Our first half non-performance against Burnley

- Allowing another late and daft equaliser against Leeds when we desperately needed a victory to help boost flagging confidence

- Losing George Evans to Reading – he would have suited us

- Losing Tarkowski, Diagouraga and Jota in January without bringing in any replacements

- The *Sky Sports* team putting the boot in during their live coverage of the defeat at Brighton

- Lewis Macleod falling foul of the injury hoodoo yet again after finally making his debut for the club

- The capitulation at Sheffield Wednesday after Yoann Barbet's early red card

- Missing Alan McCormack through injury just when his influence was most needed

- Our appalling run of results from January until the beginning of April when we won two, drew one and lost ten of our thirteen games

- Waiting for our luck to change

- The schism between different groups of supporters and the incessant bickering and arguing that further drained morale

- The constant and unfair criticism of Konstantin Kerschbaumer

- Capitulating late on against Derby County when an unlikely win seemed on the cards

- Losing to two relegation threatened teams in Rotherham and Charlton Athletic

- David Button's hesitation gifting Charlton the winning goal at Griffin Park

- The strange formation against QPR with no striker in the starting eleven

- Everything that happened both on and off the pitch at Loftus Road

- The unconscionable abuse directed at young loanee, John Swift

- Leaving the QPR local derby early to escape the humiliation on the pitch and our supporters' behaviour off it

- Finally bringing in a loanee in Everton's Leandro Rodríguez and losing him to a hamstring injury in only his second game

- Not taking advantage of Blackburn Rovers going down to ten men and losing to a late sucker punch

- Josh McEachran's second fractured foot of the season

- Worrying all the way through the March international break about the possibility of our dropping into the relegation zone

- Willing Rotherham to start losing and sticking pins into an effigy of Neil Warnock after their amazing run of victories

- Alan Judge's broken leg at Ipswich

- Luke Hyam's appalling challenge on Judge and the unsympathetic and unfeeling post-match reaction of Mick McCarthy

- Alan Judge missing the chance to play at Euro 2016 after so deserving to be selected for the Eire squad

- Scott Hogan missing his late penalty kick against Bristol City and fearing that we would have to wait until next season for him to score his first goal for the club

- Losing at Hull City with a weakened and exhausted team

- Jake Bidwell missing his first game of the season against Fulham through injury

- The closing of the Academy

- Martin Samuel's ignorant and uncalled for criticism of the club in *The Daily Mail*

End Of Term Report - 14/5/16

Now that the season is finally over the time has come for me to give my brief verdict on every player, how they each performed last season and what the future might hold for them:

2. Maxime Colin. We were all concerned about how well we would be able to replace the talented Moses Odubajo and the biggest compliment that I can give Max Colin is to state that Moses's name has barely been mentioned for many months now, so well has the newcomer done. Signed in mid-August from Anderlecht for nine hundred thousand pounds, he impressed on his debut as a substitute at Burnley and just got better with every game. Strong in the tackle and good in the air, his defensive positioning improved with experience and only Brighton's Jamie Murphy and Josh Murphy at MK Dons gave him the runaround. He had the pace and ability to rampage forward and dribble past opponents at will and his cross led to a classic headed goal by Lasse Vibe at Ipswich. Knee ligament and groin injuries cost him nearly half the season and led to the threat of an operation. Hopefully he will return for the new season fit and ready to go as he is an exceptional player who has already proved to be a bargain signing.

3. Jake Bidwell. At only twenty-three years of age Jake has already made over two hundred appearances for the club and proved to be a popular team captain. He is so unobtrusive it is easy to take him for granted and fail to recognise just how good he is. Unfortunately he suffered a hamstring strain at Hull and lost his ever-present status, missing the local derby win over Fulham. He also finally broke his scoring duck in his one hundred and eighty-sixth game for the Bees and obviously enjoyed the feeling so much that he scored twice more before the end of the season. He was cool, calm and collected and always very tough to beat and when he did make a mistake against Leeds which cost a late equaliser it stood out all the more because of its rarity. He was always eager to overlap and his accurate crosses led to four assists and his left footed curling corners and free kicks also improved throughout the season. The only problem with Jake is persuading him to sign a new contract as his current agreement expires at the end of next season. If he doesn't, what then? We would either look to sell him knowing that his former club, Everton, would benefit from a large sell-on percentage, or consider allowing him to run his contract down before leaving on a Bosman free at the end of next season.

4. Lewis Macleod. Another injury-wrecked season for Lewis and we still remain totally in the dark about his capabilities. His deep-rooted hamstring injury finally cleared up in late 2015 and allowed him to show his ability in the Development Squad and score eye-catching goals against QPR and Bristol City which clearly demonstrated his quality and whetted our appetite for more. He finally made his long-awaited and much-delayed debut for the Bees with an eight-minute run out at Brighton before succumbing to the injury hoodoo yet again, suffering a medial ligament injury in training. Next season perhaps? Surely he deserves some luck and the chance to show us what he can do?

5. Andreas Bjelland. There was palpable excitement and perhaps some disbelief amongst the Brentford supporters when the club smashed its transfer record by paying two million three hundred thousand pounds to sign Danish international central defender Andreas Bjelland from FC Twente. His preseason was hampered by a groin injury and he was given a run out on a terrible Griffin Park pitch in the Capital One Cup tie against Oxford United and must have wished he hadn't as he suffered a serious knee ligament injury and missed the entire season, which was a terrible blow for the club and player alike. He is now back in training and hopefully will be fit for selection at the beginning of next season. But where will he play given the recent success of the Dean/Barbet partnership? Midfield perhaps? What a wonderful problem for Dean Smith to have.

6. Harlee Dean. What a turnaround for the defender who ends the season with two hundred appearances for Brentford under his belt and a new two-year contract safely signed. How things have changed for the central defender who at one time looked certain to walk away on a Bosman free transfer. He came of age throughout the season and allowed his feet to do the talking rather than behave like a loose cannon, ever-ready to shoot off at the mouth if something upset him. He visibly matured, got a lot fitter, benefited from the long-term injury to Andreas Bjelland and the transfer of James Tarkowski, to become an automatic selection, a team leader, a captain in all but name and a tower of strength. He would not have been Harlee if there had not been one *faux pas*; in his case, the ridiculous red card he brought upon himself against Nottingham Forest. He read the game well and the blend of a tough traditional defender like Dean alongside a ballplayer like Tarkowski and subsequently Barbet, worked a treat. He won most of his challenges both in the air and on the ground, rarely dived in, showed far more mobility and also demonstrated an unexpected ability to play the ball accurately out of defence. His main weakness was in the opposition penalty area where he showed an infallible tendency to misfire or head the ball miles wide of the goal. He fully recognises this shortcoming stating: *I need to score goals. The manager is going to work with me in the summer.* At twenty-four his best is yet to come and he is finally playing for a Head Coach who believes in him and that has made a real difference to him.

7. Sam Saunders. After two injury-wrecked seasons it seemed that Sam might well be on his way out of the club and indeed it appeared likely at one time that he would move to America and play for Tampa Bay. Fortunately Sam chose to remain at Brentford and he more than justified his contract extension with a series of exceptional performances that ensured that he is about to enter his eighth season at Griffin Park. Dean Smith rightly valued his experience and leadership plus his ability to help his less experienced teammates and Sam rose to the challenge as well as scoring three beautifully taken goals against Leeds, Ipswich and, most memorably, his lob against Fulham, which highlighted his talent and growing confidence. He reads the game so well, finds time and space in the crowded midfield area and his bubbly enthusiasm, knowledge of the game and ability to keep possession is of massive value to the team.

8. Marco Djuricin. But for an ill-timed injury at Blackburn a mere eight days after his goal won the long-awaited West London derby against QPR and gave us our first win over the old enemy for fifty years, Marco Djuricin might have ended up as one of the stars of the team, but fate was against him and his season, and almost certainly his Brentford career fizzled out in frustration and disappointment. The Austrian international striker signed on loan from Red Bull Salzburg in late August although his arrival had been rumoured back in January 2015. He made an excellent initial impression, scoring a coolly taken goal within twenty-nine minutes of his debut against Leeds United and made it two goals in three games when he scored the winner against Preston a week later. Another goal arrived soon afterwards at Wolves and when he scored the winner against QPR, running adroitly to the near post to convert a Judge cross, it appeared that we had a new hero in our midst. He played on the shoulder of the last defender, was sharp in front of goal, eager to shoot rather than pass and was beginning to adapt to an unfamiliar role as a lone striker. A serious ankle ligament injury was the beginning of the end for him as he was forced to miss two months of action and never regained his fitness or sharpness on his return and soon drifted out of contention. This was a real shame, as Marco possesses a striker's instinct, something that cannot be taught, and will certainly come again, but not at Griffin Park, although his status as a Brentford legend is assured.

9. Scott Hogan. Sometimes people do get what they deserve and receive due reward for all their effort, dedication and determination not to give in when everything appears to be against them. Finally the Gods are smiling down upon Scott Hogan after he suffered and then overcame two career-threatening cruciate injuries and missed the best part of two seasons' worth of football. Much was expected of Hogan when he was brought in to play ahead of Andre Gray at the beginning of the 2014/15 season and now he finally has the opportunity to show us why we signed him. He has certainly been a man on a mission since he was introduced as a late substitute on the nineteenth of March against Blackburn Rovers. Further short run-outs followed against Bolton and Ipswich before he finally made his mark by winning and then missing a penalty kick against Bristol City, before netting his first goal for the Bees with a last-gasp predator's header which earned us a point. Two more clinical finishes against Cardiff made us understand that he was a really special player who was single-mindedly determined to make up for lost time. He was being carefully managed by the medical team and his time on the pitch was strictly rationed, but Lasse Vibe's injury meant that Scott was named in the starting eleven against both Fulham and Huddersfield and he rewarded Dean Smith's faith in him with four more goals. He ended up playing less than two full matches, one hundred and seventy-two minutes in all, and yet he scored an incredible total of seven goals and clearly demonstrated that he is a cool, calm and deadly finisher who has the rare ability to ghost in behind defenders and find time and space within crowded penalty areas. He has been compared in style and approach to Jamie Vardy and has already attracted the attention of the Eire selectors. Brentford have certainly been rewarded for their faith in Scott and for extending his contract for another year before he made his comeback and next season cannot come soon enough for him. What a prospect he is and if he can stay fit we will have a magnificent striker on our hands.

10. Josh McEachran. There was much excitement when we signed Josh McEachran from Chelsea for seven hundred and fifty thousand pounds. He seems to have been around for ever but is still only twenty-three years old. But scratch beneath the surface and his CV was slightly concerning as he had already had five loan spells at clubs like Middlesbrough and Watford without establishing himself, and he desperately needed a home and a role as his career appeared to be drifting. Unfortunately nothing has gone right for him since he joined Brentford. The first half of his season was ruined by a training ground collision with Toumani Diagouraga which resulted in a fractured foot, and, incredibly, he suffered a similar injury in March which ended his season. In-between he managed fifteen appearances without really making too much of an impact. He describes himself as *a holder and a passer, dictating play* and his approach should have suited our play given the manner in which we always try to play through the midfield, but despite showing glimmers of his ability with a dummy here and a perceptive pass there, it never really happened for him and his passing generally lacked incision or penetration and too often went sideways or backwards and he generally hung out a foot rather than tackle properly. Perhaps he was simply lacking in match fitness and confidence? We can only hope that he recovers in time for the start of next season and that he can then show us what he is capable of.

11. Philipp Hofmann. The enigma that is Hofmann. So much ability but so little end result to date. Expectations were high when we signed the massive German Under 21 international striker and it was hoped that he could provide us with a different type of option upfront given his size and strength. His progress was hindered by a series of niggling injuries and he seemed to find the Championship a massive learning curve and did not appear ideally suited to the lone striker system employed by the club. He did not have the pace or mobility to run the channels and, despite his height, he was not strong in the air. What he did have, though, was an unsuspected ability, strength and trickery on the ball and a real subtlety of pass. He only started six games all season but still managed to score four goals, including a wonderful finish at Bristol City, a calm dribble around a stranded goalkeeper at Wolves and that triple-ricochet winner at home to Nottingham Forest. He also missed a simple headed chance to win the home game against Brighton. I hope that next season he proves that he has a real future with us and that he relishes the challenge of adapting to the Championship. The jury is out.

12. Alan McCormack. The departure of Moses Odubajo saw McCormack given an immediate opportunity to replace him, and he started the season at right back where lack of any defensive cover from Andre Gray saw him given the runaround at Bristol City. The arrival of Max Colin saw him moved back into midfield where he remained an integral part of the team until he suffered niggling groin and calf injuries. Alan provided a much-needed calming influence and he cajoled and encouraged his less experienced teammates and ensured that they showed the necessary organisation and commitment. His passing also improved and became subtler, and we missed him badly during his injury absences. A goal proved elusive although he came desperately close against both Charlton and Bristol City. We keep writing him off and he stubbornly keeps proving us wrong and Alan's performances totally warranted his contract extension until the end of next season. Despite his ten bookings, he always knew exactly just how far he could go and he has still to see red whilst playing for the Bees. In an inordinately quiet, small and well-behaved team, McCormack was one of the few to speak up on behalf of his teammates and attempt to *manage* referees.

15. Ryan Woods. Woods first caught my eye as a skilful and tenacious right back playing for Shrewsbury at Griffin Park in 2013 and quickly developed into one of the best midfielders in the lower divisions. I was delighted when *The Ginger Pirlo* signed for us for one million pounds at the end of the August Transfer Window, a fee that looks an absolute bargain now. He took a few games to settle down and force his way into the starting eleven and was caught in possession on his debut, a costly error that denied us a victory against Leeds, but he is now an automatic choice. He is still developing as a player and possesses all the qualities required to become a complete midfield player. He can spray the ball around and I can still picture that long pass over the defender dropping perfectly into the stride of Sergi Canos before he scored the Goal of the Season at Reading. Ryan also scored a wonderful long-range goal in the same game and matched it at MK Dons. He can tackle, press and dribble and never stops running. What a player he is already, and there will be so much more to come from him as he gains further experience in the Championship.

16. Jack Bonham. This was another year of treading water for the reserve goalkeeper who sat on the bench undisturbed for every match apart from the Capital One Cup disaster against a rampant Oxford United team. Marooned behind an experimental defence, a drastically weakened side subsided to an embarrassing four-goal defeat that could and should have been even more. Bonham hardly shone on the night and looked a nervous presence in goal and was beaten by Roofe's exquisite forty-yard lob. He has obviously learned a lot from training with David Button and Simon Royce and at twenty-two is still very young for a goalkeeper. As things currently stand, he is there simply to sit on the bench and replace Button in an emergency with, in all honesty, little chance of being named to start a Championship match if Button was unavailable. That might suit Brentford, who, of course, pay his wages, but the situation is of no benefit at all to Bonham if he is to develop as a footballer. Nobody knows if he has what it takes to have a successful career and nobody ever will until he sees regular action at a lower level of the game. He has two more seasons on his contract but desperately needs to go out and play some football next season and demonstrate his worth.

17. Konstantin Kerschbaumer. Nobody I knew had ever heard of the Austrian midfielder when he signed for us from Admira Wacker Mödling for a reported quarter of a million pound fee, but then again we had known absolutely nothing about Jota either! He was reputed to be a speedy and tenacious box-to-box player and he made a massive first impression when he dominated the midfield in the preseason friendly match against Stoke City. The departure of Jonathan Douglas opened the door for him but the Championship was another matter and he struggled from the off to cope with its pace and physicality and was a peripheral influence, easily knocked off the ball, regularly caught in possession and tentative with his passing. He never hid and joined in where he could but he was totally out of his depth and sometimes I got the unworthy impression that his teammates were loath to pass the ball to him in tight situations. Lee Carsley mercifully took him out of the firing line as soon as he took charge, commenting: *He needs a lot of coaching. He runs as fast as he can everywhere without being effective* which was a tough but accurate assessment of his initial contribution. He gradually improved in short spells coming off the bench and soon there were small shoots of recovery, an excellent shot against the top of the post against Hull, an effort cleared off the line by a desperate MK Dons defence and a decent hustling performance at Craven Cottage. He featured in every match day squad from the end of January as he slowly came to terms with what was required of him, and by the end of the season he had shown such improvement that he fully deserved his starting role. With growing confidence and time on the ball he started to reveal his true ability, in particular his energy and effortless close control and he combined brilliantly with Scott Hogan as his defence splitting through balls led to three goals for the striker as well as the award of a penalty kick. Konstantin is proof of the strength and weakness of our stats and analysis based system. We certainly used our data to identify a promising young player who was not on the radar of our competition, and signed him for a relatively low sum, but he was thrown in far too soon owing to the prevailing circumstances and not given the time he needed to adapt to his new surroundings. He suffered unfairly and cruelly at the hands of the boo-boys who are only now beginning to recognise his undoubted ability, and I fully expect that his second season at the club will be far more productive for him.

18. Alan Judge. It is impossible to write about Alan Judge without feeling a combined sense of anger, frustration, disappointment and sadness at how the season ended for him, and how cruelly he was denied the opportunity to showcase his formidable talent on a global stage at Euro 2016 thanks to the unforgivable actions of an Ipswich Town player whose name I will not deign to mention here. At twenty-seven, Alan was approaching his peak and was in the form of his life all season, scoring fourteen times and assisting on eleven more goals and he was our main source of inspiration. His achievements were marked by his being shortlisted in the top three for Championship Player of the Year, and he was named in the Football League Team of the Year and the Championship Team of the Year. He was also the Championship Player of the Month for October, a month in which his form touched previously unseen heights. With the loss of the likes of Gray, Pritchard and Jota, Alan almost singlehandedly took over the mantle of providing our creativity and goal threat and he was more than up to the task. He generally played in a free role as a *Number Ten* behind the main striker, but he also drifted wide and on one bizarre afternoon at Loftus Road, of all places, played as our lone striker. After only scoring three times in 2014/15, the goals flowed this season – and what brilliant goals they were. A curling effort from a seemingly impossible angle against Sheffield Wednesday, a looping twenty-yard volley and rare header to beat Rotherham, a stupendous shot arrogantly bent into the far top corner in front of the worshipping Brentford supporters at Charlton, instantaneously and effortlessly controlling a long pass from Barbet before slotting the ball home at Preston, a goal which even drew applause from the home fans, and an amazing solo goal when he ran half the length of the field against Derby before scoring from way out on the right flank. He was quite simply touched by genius, and even managed to convert all three of his penalty kicks after his adventures of the previous season when he missed three out of his four attempts! It was no surprise that other clubs coveted him, but unlike a certain former teammate of his, he simply got his head down and did not allow the constant speculation to affect his performances. He was deservedly rewarded with his first international cap for Eire and was well in the frame for inclusion in their final squad for Euro 2016 when tragedy befell him with his double leg break. What happens now is anybody's guess. It was expected that with only one year remaining on his contract, and it being highly unlikely that Alan would sign an extension, that he would be sold this summer, and no Brentford fan would have begrudged him leaving for bigger and better things, such has been his brilliance, commitment and dedication to the Brentford cause. The club too might well have been banking on the anticipated fee in order to subsidise our own transfer budget. Now, all bets are off until we find out how long Judge will take to return to action. I would not expect that we will see him much before Christmas and it will then take him time to regain both form and sharpness. Perhaps he will be sold in the January Transfer Window; maybe he will stay for the entire season, hopefully play well for us, and then leave on a Bosman free? Could he even sign a new contract? Who knows, and all will be revealed over the coming months. In the meantime the memories are still totally clear in my mind of his brilliance, tirelessness and consistency and the sheer joy and bubbly effervescence he demonstrated in playing the game of football – the effortless dribbles past opponents, his non-stop energy and commitment, the quality of his passing, both long and short and his shoot-on-sight policy. He was the complete player for Brentford last season and we were privileged and fortunate to be able to enjoy performances of such quality, and he was by some distance the best player that I have ever seen perform in a Brentford shirt. Praise indeed, but fully merited in my opinion.

19. John Swift. You are just twenty years of age, on loan from a Premier League team with minimal experience of the Championship. You muck in, play twenty-seven games in all, score seven goals from midfield and also get picked for the England Under 21 team. Not bad, and surely the fans will be purring with delight at your contribution, chanting your name and begging you to join the club on a permanent basis next season? You would have thought that would have been the case, but unfortunately John Swift totally polarised opinions amongst Brentford supporters and was the recipient of much unwarranted, unpleasant and totally unnecessary and unjustified abuse from some quarters. He was too languid and lazy, they said, he went missing from time to time, he did not do his fair share of defensive donkey work, and tackling and pressing were an anathema to him. Maybe some of these criticisms had credence, but better that they had made some allowances for his youth, immaturity and inexperience and instead given credit to him for, and taken pleasure from, his many very real attributes. He had the natural ability to glide past opponents at will and was a wonderful exponent of the lost art of dribbling. He moved the ball quickly and accurately and specialised in making late runs into the box which led to his most of his goals, and he also scored with a perfectly executed long-range curler at Bolton which was much admired by the *Sky Sports* commentary team. Swift also had to cope with the difficulty and upheaval of learning a new role as he was often played on the left side of midfield rather than in his more accustomed central position. There was so much to admire in his ability and in many of his performances, and yet he failed to connect with many of the supporters who treated him appallingly and cut him no slack, and I would be surprised if John will wish to return to Griffin Park next season even should the opportunity arise, which is a terrible shame as he would add immeasurably to our midfield resources.

21. Lasse Vibe. Danish international striker Lasse Vibe signed for the Bees for around one million pounds from IFK Göteborg shortly before the beginning of the season and went straight from playing in the Swedish *Allsvenskan* to the Championship without the benefit of any preseason break. He found a place in the team playing firstly on the right flank where he was a peripheral influence, but he scored his first goal with a stunning long-range curling effort against Reading when moved into a more central role. He played alongside Marco Djuricin but won a regular place in the team as the sole striker after Djuricin's injury against Blackburn. From then on Vibe pretty much trod a lone furrow up front until Scott Hogan's recovery from injury late on in the season and eventually the pressure told on him and his effectiveness greatly diminished as the effects of fatigue and overwork slowed him down. After scoring with a fulminating volley against Huddersfield in mid-December he went over three months without scoring and clearly demonstrated that he was not best suited to the physical demands of playing as a target man. Smash the ball at or over his head and he would always come off second best against giant central defenders who totally outmuscled him and invariably won the physical battle, and with his confidence shot to pieces, he went on a ghastly run of poor performances marked by a series of missed chances and scuffed shots. He had hit the wall and the Championship was proving a tough learning curve for him. No striker scored for the Bees from the second of January until the second of April, a run of twelve matches that saw only eleven goals scored by Brentford and the abyss was beckoning until everything changed after the March international break. Vibe went away with the Danish squad and returned a new man, apparently revitalized and re-energised by his international recall. Suddenly there was a spring in his step and his luck finally turned. Firstly when loanee Leandro Rodríguez suffered a hamstring injury, which necessitated his withdrawal from the fray at Nottingham Forest and his replacement by Vibe, and then when home defender Kevin Wilson's horrendous gaffe gifted him a goal. Finally the floodgates opened as with confidence restored he went on a wonderful run of seven goals in seven games, and what goals they were. Close range tap-ins, flying headers, sumptuous outside of the foot finishes and long-range rockets. Everything he touched flew in and he ended up as equal top scorer with the highly creditable total of fourteen goals. More importantly, we learned to play to his strengths as his pace and vision enabled him to time his runs and get in behind defenders, and he looked twice the player he had been just weeks earlier. The fans took to him from the beginning because he never let his head go down even when things were not going well for him and he was always a chaser of lost causes. He played with a smile on his face and the crowd responded to him. How far has he come in so short a time? A few weeks ago and I would not have been too upset if he had decided to leave at the end of the season, now I can't wait to see if he can improve even more next season.

22. Jack O'Connell. Jack had a frustrating season as he was never able to establish himself in the team but at times he certainly looked the part in our central defence. He enjoyed runs of four and then three consecutive matches after Dean and Barbet's red cards but he was unable to keep his place given the strong competition he faced. He scored a goal from a corner against Fulham and, unlike our other central defenders, he always looked dangerous at set pieces, and but for a brilliant save he would have repeated the dose in the home match against our old rivals at Griffin Park. At twenty-two he is still a youngster and he could yet develop into an excellent defender and a real asset. He lacks pace but reads the game well, is strong in the air and is no mug with the ball at his feet. I hope that he is patient and that we find a role for him next season.

23. Jota. Who could ever have imagined Brentford doing so well despite Jota starting only one game all season? Jonathan Douglas's rugged challenge cost Jota damaged ankle ligaments which required surgery to repair and he had barely returned to the substitutes' bench in December when personal issues forced his return to Spain, initially on loan to Eibar. Brentford treated him with sensitivity and compassion given the circumstances and we will simply have to wait and see whether he will be in a position to return within the next year or if we have seen the last of the Spanish maestro. I personally doubt that he will play for us again and, if so, we will need to maximise our return for him which will not be easy given that he will, I am sure, only wish to sign for a Spanish team. As for replacing him, you can't, as how do you find another genius?

24. Akaki (Andy) Gogia. Andy Gogia was another foreign prospect signed on a free transfer from the lower leagues in German. The early indications were highly promising for the quick and tricky winger, as he impressed with his pace, skill and energy in the preseason friendly against Stoke and scored with a deflected long-range effort. He started the season in the first team but it soon became clear that he needed time to get used to the pace and physicality of the Championship and also become more accustomed and attuned to living and working in a foreign country. His cause was also hindered by some niggly injuries and he never started a match after the beginning of October. He impressed in the Development Squad and looked more direct and effective when coming off the bench late on in the season. Hopefully he will be one for next season and he will surely receive another opportunity given that we will be looking for a new winger.

27. David Button. At twenty-seven years of age, and coming off his second consecutive season as an ever-present in the Brentford team, David Button is probably not yet at his peak and might improve even more, but he has firmly established himself as one of the most consistent and talented goalkeepers in the Championship. What a bargain he has proved to be since we rescued him from the depths of the Charlton Athletic reserve team for a mere one hundred and fifty thousand pounds. He certainly received sufficient practice last season as he faced more shots on goal than any other keeper in the league and he invariably met and overcame the challenge. He was directly responsible for only two goals, at home to both Middlesbrough and Charlton but otherwise he was reliable, dependable, consistent and also inspired and brilliant on occasion. His save from Garner at Preston was stupendous and one of the moments of the season, and at times he seemed to be playing Derby County on his own at Griffin Park. He can still sometimes be tentative and vulnerable when dealing with crosses but he is otherwise technically extremely sound and invariably gets the basics right. His use of the ball when in possession was as calm and accurate as ever and he started so many of our attacks as well as providing a wonderful assist for Alan Judge's goal against Sheffield Wednesday. Button now has a tough decision to make given that his contract expires at the end of next season. Should he seek pastures new or extend his contract at the club? He is guaranteed first team football in a young and improving team at Griffin Park, but could he do better professionally and financially elsewhere? I suspect that he could, as goalkeepers of his quality are not easy to find. It is too soon to be sure but the latest indications are that he might possibly decide to leave and every Brentford fan will fervently hope that this is not the case as we are very fortunate to have him.

28. Nico Yennaris. Last season was a coming of age for Nico whose career at Brentford had appeared to be drifting into oblivion, and many were surprised when his loan move to Wycombe Wanderers was not made permanent. Maxime Colin's injury changed everything and Lee Carsley gave him the opportunity to deputise for him. Nico played like a man inspired, tough and tenacious in the challenge and eager to overlap, he ensured that Colin was barely missed and Nico was unfortunate to lose his place when the Frenchman recovered. His consistency was rewarded with a new three-year contract, a controversial move that initially attracted much criticism from some Brentford supporters who felt it lacked ambition, but Dean Smith knew exactly what he was doing and the decision is now looking an extremely good and eminently sensible one. He believed in Nico who was converted into a highly effective defensive midfielder who played a massive part in our late season success. He was all-action and all-energy, relentless and tenacious in his tackling and pressing but he also showed his great ability on the ball and he passed it quickly and accurately. Nico was ideally suited for

Brentford's pass-and-move approach and he also scored two well-taken goals. From a player who at one time seemed to be going nowhere except out of the exit door, Nico proved to be a revelation and ended the season as the most improved player in the team and enjoying life playing for the first time for a Head Coach who believed in him. Of all the stories of the season, Nico's was perhaps the most positive, surprising and satisfying.

29. Yoann Barbet. The best that I can say about French central defender Yoann Barbet's progress is that the departed James Tarkowski has barely been missed. Signed from Chamois Niortais for a fee of around half a million pounds he was another unknown player from abroad who was definitely seen as one for the future. He impressed in his initial first team appearances as he vied with Jack O'Connell to be the deputy for the first choice partnership of Dean and Tarkowski, but his big opportunity came with the departure of Tarkowski, and he certainly seized it. He received a temporary setback after an unfortunate red card at Sheffield Wednesday when he was caught on the wrong side of an opponent, but he learned from his mistake and soon scored his first goal for the club against Charlton. He proved to be a rugged defender who loves a slide tackle and he showed a good turn of pace. He also demonstrated great skill on the ball and sprayed long and accurate passes out to the right wing, memorably assisting on a wonderful goal for Alan Judge at Preston. He has adapted quickly and well to his new surroundings and is another star in the making for the Bees.

36. Josh Clarke. Josh certainly made the most of the opportunity given him to develop his skills as a fast, overlapping fullback and fought his way into the first team. Everybody loves a local boy made good, and his pace, enthusiasm and attacking brio shone through. He obtained some valuable experience on loan at Barnet, started four matches for Brentford and also impressed when coming off the bench, helping to make Scott Hogan's late equaliser against Bristol City. He has been offered a new contract for next season and I hope that he decides to remain at the club, as at only twenty-one years of age there is still time for Josh to emerge and develop into a regular first team player.

37. Courtney Senior. Still only eighteen, Courtney Senior impressed in the preseason friendly at Boreham Wood showing pace and skill on the right wing. He made his first team debut against Oxford United and twice was an unused substitute before returning to the Development Squad for the remainder of the season. His time has yet to come, but he is a real talent.

39. Tom Field. Tom made an assured and highly competent debut as a nineteen year-old deputy for the injured Jake Bidwell in the local derby against Fulham. He showed great composure and an excellent temperament. He was never overawed by the occasion, defended well and also swung in a perfect right wing corner which was thrashed into the net by Scott Hogan. Another one for the future, and, better still, he comes from a Brentford supporting family.

47. Sergi Canos. A total breath of fresh air, Sergi arrived on loan as an unknown eighteen year-old from Liverpool via Barcelona's academy. He left the club with his head held high as a firm fan favourite having scored seven times in thirty-eight games. He totally surpassed expectations and proved to be a massive success. He so obviously loved every minute of his stay and played with enthusiasm, a smile on his face and with a real *joie de vivre*. Unsurprisingly, given his age and lack of experience, he was inconsistent but he possessed the ability to turn a game on its head as both Preston North End and Nottingham Forest discovered to their cost, and he was always full of tricks. He worked hard and learned how to track back but he had the pace, dribbling ability and sheer talent to create havoc at the other end of the pitch, netting after a mere twenty-one seconds at Huddersfield and scoring unforgettable goals at Reading and MK Dons. He made a massive impression on everybody at the club and we all took great pride and joy in his achievement when he made his Premier League debut for Liverpool on the last day of the season. Have we seen the last of him? Maybe, but perhaps not, as if he is not considered good enough for Liverpool's squad next season or does not agree a new contract, then perhaps he might yet return to Griffin Park and thrill and inspire us once more?

Andre Gray, Toumani Diagouraga, James Tarkowski, Ryan Williams, Josh Laurent, Leandro Rodríguez and Jermaine Udumaga all made appearances for the Bees this season before leaving the club. It was a forgone conclusion that Gray would move up the food chain as he was a star in the making and coveted by clubs who could pay him far more than us, and we also had to sell him in order not to fall foul of Financial Fair Play restrictions. He played twice for us, firstly as a late substitute against Ipswich where he helped turn the match in our favour and scored a well-taken goal, bursting down the middle at pace, which put us back into a game that seemed lost. He and Philipp Hofmann also played together at Bristol City and terrified the opposition with Gray scoring with a perfect half volley at the near post as well as contributing to two other Brentford goals. He clearly demonstrated that he was a man in form and one who would take the division by storm – but unfortunately it was for Burnley and not us. Toumani Diagouraga was a wonderful servant of the club but we did well to extract a half million pound fee from Leeds for a player whose performances had declined from their impossibly high level of the previous season. He was no longer such a dominating influence on proceedings and his game suffered from the absence of Douglas alongside him, which forced Toumani to attempt tackles far more often, something that was not one of his strengths. He left with our gratitude and best wishes. The same cannot be said for James Tarkowski who acted in a totally unprofessional manner by virtue of his decision to down tools before the Burnley home game. As with Gray, we extracted a high fee for him, and the progress made by Barbet means that he has hardly been missed. Tarkowski was his normal frustrating self, combining moments of brilliance both in defending and on the ball with times when he lost concentration, over-reached himself and cost us dear. Leandro Rodríguez was a loan signing from Everton who was brought in to support the flagging Lasse Vibe. He pulled a hamstring in his second match before he really had the chance to show us anything and returned to his parent club. Laurent, Williams and Udumaga all made brief appearances without convincing the club that they had what it takes to merit further opportunities. Reece Cole and James Ferry were also non-playing substitutes and await their chance next season.

My Not So Beautiful Laundrette – 19/5/16

Ian Westbrook is an old friend of mine and we have been exchanging Brentford memories and war stories for more years than I, and I suspect he, would like to remember. He and his brother Hugh, as well as their late father, David, have been fervent Brentford supporters for decades now and the baton has also been passed down to the next generation with Ian and Hugh's children too.

Ian has provided today's article which deftly provides his answer to the difficult problem I am sure most of us have faced at some point. How are you supposed to keep in touch with the Bees when you are not at the match and marooned abroad? I hope you enjoy reading about his adventures which clearly demonstrate his ingenuity and determination not to miss out:

Where is the weirdest place you have been to follow a Brentford game that you were unable to attend?

I have kept in touch with the Brentford's progress in all the usual spots when I have had to miss a game – listening to Bees Player at home or at work, following scores on BBC Radio London and Beesotted's excellent Twitter service while on the move, via Soccer Saturday or thanks to text updates from friends who had been there.

But the start of this season provided me with a new dilemma because we had to take our family holiday straight after the opening match against Ipswich. Our two weeks in the USA, split between New York and Boston, covered the away games at Bristol City and Burnley, both due to start at ten o'clock local time, and, at a quarter to three, our time, the home matches with Oxford and Birmingham and I was the only person who wasn't too unhappy when that one was called off.

Clearly we weren't going to be sitting in our hotel room until midday waiting for the Saturday matches to finish, or staying in all afternoon for the evening games, so I accepted that we would have to wait to learn the scores while out and about. First up was the Capital One Cup tie with Oxford. As the game kicked off, my wife, son and I were enjoying one of the best touristy things we did on our holiday – walking across the Brooklyn Bridge back into Manhattan. My son and I noted that the match was under way, but didn't worry ourselves too much while we enjoyed the skyscrapers becoming ever bigger as we approached one of the main parts of the Big Apple in hot sunshine.

Once over the bridge and around half an hour into the game, we spotted a Starbucks and nipped in to use the Wi-Fi to check up on our progress. The first score we saw was three-nil to the visitors and I was relieved we hadn't known that while halfway across the bridge, or who knows what we may have done!

Next up Bristol City – and a relaxed start to the day meant that we could enjoy the kick-off and dulcet tones of Mark Burridge in our New York hotel room. We went out after that to a street festival and were out of touch with proceedings in the West Country until around twenty minutes from time when my son and I persuaded my wife and daughter that it would be good to spend some time in a café, which just happened to have Wi-Fi. We were inside in time to hear Philipp Hofmann seal the points and celebrated with iced coffee!

A week later we were in Boston – and following the match at Turf Moor proved a whole lot harder. We managed to grab an early update, including Burnley's goal, while in a shop but a tram journey and walk through the boiling hot streets were enjoyable but football-free. The match was well into the second half by this stage and we had no way of knowing whether we had got back into the match as we strolled through a suburb. But suddenly we found a small parade of shops and on closer inspection one had Wi-Fi – not the lovely baker with the smell of fresh bread wafting out on to the pavement, but the laundrette next door.

Unattractive it may have been but it had the connection I needed – and it worked too, and I settled down to watch other people's clothes spin round in the massive machines as Mark Burridge's voice finally filled my headphones.

It was a frustrating final fifteen minutes as Brentford tried and failed to snatch a point and my emotions as Konstantin Kerschbaumer shot over the bar and then a Harlee Dean header was blocked must have looked very strange to the woman emptying clothes into a basket, and even stranger when I showed my disappointment as Burnley cleaned up to take the points.

There were a couple of other matches during 2015/16 that I also followed from afar. At the end of October, my son did his now annual race in the junior Great South Run in Portsmouth. We have been to this event on numerous occasions, usually having to miss a Bees home game in the process. We had never been able to get our football fix as Pompey had always been away – but as luck would have it, this year they were due to play at home to Mansfield. With my son's race finishing at two – far too late to get to The Valley to cheer on the Bees – we walked over to Fratton Park, had the luxury of paying on the day and found ourselves in the end split between home and away fans. The game finished goalless but on at least a couple of occasions we drew odd glances as we started celebrating when not much was going on in front of us – because we'd found out that Brentford had scored at Charlton!

More recently, I had to follow some of the Huddersfield game on the final day of the season via London Underground Wi-Fi on the way to work. The Wi-Fi works at lots of the stations on the tube – but it disappears in tunnels so it needs firing up each time the train is at a platform. I'd followed the first half and early stages of the second with Bees Player at home – and on my five-minute walk to our local tube station heard both the home team's equaliser and then Scott Hogan restoring our lead. As the reception cut out when we moved into our first underground tunnel – the commentary remarkably kept on going, so while I was a long way under the city itself I heard Hogan making it three-one as it happened! I also heard Lasse Vibe's goal while connected at another station but missed John Swift's effort.

Our USA trip wasn't the first time we had been away during the football season. In December 2002, we made a trip to Australia to visit family – missing several Brentford games. I can remember receiving a phone call from a now dearly departed friend with the result of our LDV Vans Trophy match against Kidderminster whilst in view of Sydney Harbour Bridge.

But the strangest way, in the pre-Bees Player and Wi-Fi days, that we found out a result during the holiday occurred on the weekend before Christmas. We had driven halfway along the famous Great Ocean Road and were spending the night in an amazing bungalow close to a town called Apollo Bay. The accommodation was a long way up a hill – so high in fact that when a mist rolled in across the ocean at a rapid rate, we were above the band of cloud which appeared. Family at home knew that my Leyton Orient-supporting father-in-law and I were keen to find out our Saturday results so had arranged to have them phoned through to the complex.

First thing on Sunday morning, we had a knock on the door from a member of hotel staff clutching a piece of paper in her hand with a message that meant absolutely nothing to her – but everything to us! It was from that handwritten note that we learned the Bees had drawn at Loftus Road and Orient had won at Swansea's Vetch Field.

Novel as all these result-finding methods are – I can honestly say that I still prefer actually being at the game itself!

You Are A Long Time Retired – 21/5/16

I make a point of reading *The Football League Paper* every Sunday and I always make a beeline for the *Where Are They Now* column. Every week it features a grainy black and white team photograph dating back up to forty years or so and provides an update on what the players have been getting up to since they retired. Some, but a very small minority remain household names to this day, predominantly as managers and coaches, but the overwhelming majority have faded away into relative obscurity, their glory days long-since passed and they now work in a variety of common-or-garden or mundane jobs.

A worrying number have also passed away and I find it hard to realise or accept that a gnarled veteran in his early thirties when I first started watching the game fifty years ago is now in his dotage – or worse. I well remember researching the whereabouts of some of our former Brentford heroes from the sixties when working on the *Big Brentford Book* series and making the shocking discovery of how very few players from that era still remained with us.

So what happens to footballers when they retire and how do they cope with being out of the spotlight and no longer being a global, national or local hero? What happens when they have to adapt to the dull and prosaic reality of having to manage their own affairs, make their own travel arrangements, find alternative employment, adjust to a massive reduction in their earnings and even look after their passport rather than having it held for safekeeping by their club?

Retired footballers have on average around sixteen thousand days to fill from the time of their retirement until their death and it is not surprising that many former footballers find this transition difficult if not impossible to manage. Many fall upon hard times and the results of the loss of their former fame, glory, stature and even sense of purpose can be drastic and catastrophic with over one hundred and fifty ex-footballers ending up in prison, predominately for drug offenses. Others suffer from mental health issues and bankruptcy. Divorce is rife with a staggering one third of all footballers ending their marriage within a year of hanging up their boots and, tragically, suicide is also all too common.

Writer and award-winning stand-up comedian Alan Gernon has now produced a well-researched, thought-provoking and comprehensive book that is certainly not a barrel of laughs. *Retired* provides a disturbing analysis of the never-ending variety of troubles and problems that footballers can face once they stop playing; what can and does happen to them, and what support and help are available to them when things begin to go wrong as they attempt to readjust to normal life.

Liberally illustrated with a plethora of case studies of ex-players whose difficult and sad stories are either already in the public domain or who have been brave enough to go public with their recollections within this book, *Retired* is a much-needed and long-overdue cautionary tale of the problems and pitfalls that can await every footballer once he leaves the spotlight.

Mr. Gernon has ranged far and wide in his research and has obtained insights, some of them almost excruciating in their honesty, from former players such as David Bentley, Lee Bowyer, David Busst, Geoff Thomas, Jody Craddock, Mark Ward, Richard Sadlier, Gary Stevens and John Newsome, amongst others, who between them have suffered from a myriad of problems since the end of their glory days.

Some of the statistics are mind-blowing. Research undertaken by *XPRO*, a charity set up to help, support and advise former professional footballers highlights the following:

- There are over sixty thousand former players living in the UK and Ireland

- Two out of every five Premier League players, who earn an average of forty-two thousand pounds per week, face the threat of bankruptcy within five years of ending their career

- One third of footballers will be divorced within a year of retirement

- Eighty percent of retired players will suffer from osteoarthritis

World players' union *FIFPro* also revealed that thirty-five percent of former players faced problems with depression and anxiety, particularly if they had suffered serious injuries during their playing career, more than double the figure for the general population.

What about the young kids who dream of becoming footballers but have their hopes and dreams shattered? The odds are heavily weighted against them. According to the *PFA*, the average career span for a professional footballer is only eight years – and that is just for the lucky ones who make it. Former Liverpool schoolboy player Michael Kinsella's story is typical of so many like him. Thirteen members of his schoolboy side joined professional clubs with only two enjoying long-term careers. Six ended up in prison, with Kinsella himself receiving a ten-year sentence for drug offences.

Some players are fortunate enough to become managers or coaches, others seek the Holy Grail of a pundit's role within the media but these opportunities are few and far between with demand massively exceeding supply. There are nowhere near enough jobs to go round and most go to the biggest names.

Some players even die early from the effects of heading the old-style heavy leather football which resembled a cannonball when wet. Chronic traumatic encephalopathy (CTE) is a brain condition sadly becoming more common among footballers. Jeff Astle, a renowned header of the ball for West Bromwich Albion and England in the sixties and early seventies died tragically young in 2002 and the coroner concluded that he had suffered neurological damage from heading a football and his illness was later diagnosed as CTE.

Former West Ham player Mark Ward struggled after retirement and turned to alcohol and was short of cash. He rented out a property that was used to store drugs and he ended up in prison. Michael Branch was a special talent at Everton who ended up serving a seven-year sentence for supply of Class A and B drugs.

The book is relentless, featuring tale after tale of players who have fallen foul of a variety of problems and pitfalls and it can be so hard for footballers who can resemble *thirty-seven year-old newborns* emerging from what Niall Quinn has so memorably described as *an adults' playground* to adapt to what they have to face in the real world. Thankfully there is now far more support at hand and it is no longer considered a weakness to cry for help.

I showed this article to former Brentford striker Richard Poole whose career was ended so cruelly by injury almost before it had begun and it touched a chord with him:

You have touched me deeply with this article in more ways than one as my dreams were ended because of my injury and I was also isolated in France, which made things even tougher.

Most of the players mentioned in the book are quite well known but for those who played lower league football it was even harder.

In my time there was nothing in place for former players like myself who had been forced to pack the game up early and we were left to pick up the pieces of our lives as well as we could, and I can tell you that so many doors stayed shut and bolted, but that's life.

Hopefully this quite brilliant book will help raise awareness of the seriousness of the situation and reinforce the fact that there is now expert assistance available whenever it is required.

This is help that perhaps former Southampton player Bobby Stokes could surely have done with. Never a star, but a solid, dependable, all-action midfield dynamo whose place in Southampton legend is assured by virtue of the dramatic and unforgettable winning goal he scored in 1976 to win the FA Cup for The Saints against Manchester United. He was the toast of the town and became that rarity, a Portsmouth boy who became a hero for their hated rivals in Southampton. He died far too young in straightened circumstances and life after football was not kind to him.

Mark Sanderson has lovingly recorded his life and achievements in *Bobby Stokes: The Man from Portsmouth Who Scored Southampton's Most Famous Goal.*

It is a biography that has been written with sympathy, affection and respect by a man who has a light and deft touch with words and possesses an immense knowledge of his subject.

Both books are highly recommended.

"Retired" by Alan Gernon, and "Bobby Stokes" by Mark Sanderson, are both published by Pitch Publishing.

Shopping List – 23/5/16

The old season might only just have ended but there is already frenetic speculation on the fans' message boards as well as on social media about the identity of the players who Brentford FC might be looking to bring into the club in order to strengthen the squad for next season.

I am not sure if I have very much to add to the debate and anything that I write is, of course, pure speculation as unfortunately I am not now nor have I ever been, a fly on the wall in the room where the Brentford Brains Trust congregates in order to discuss potential signings.

Let's imagine, just for a moment or two, unlikely though it might be, that I did have a seat at that table and was asked for my opinion. If so, what suggestions would I make about the moves that we should make?

OK then, here goes:

Starting in **goal**, everything is totally up in the air until David Button's future is decided once and for all. He only has one year remaining on his contract and should he decline to sign a new deal he is far too valuable an asset to be allowed to run his contract down and leave on a Bosman free transfer next summer. The bottom line is that if he does not extend his contract shortly, then he quite simply has to be sold before the start of the next season. The key question though is what is best for him?

On the one hand he is the established first choice in a top ten Championship team and has not missed a league game for over two seasons. He and his family are also settled not too far away from the club. It just depends on what else might be on the table for him. At twenty-seven he is still improving and is not yet at his peak. As we are all well aware, he could very likely earn far more money elsewhere but if he went, would he play every week, something that I am sure is crucial to him?

I believe that Button is just as good as many goalkeepers already playing in the Premier League and teams such as AFC Bournemouth, Everton, Crystal Palace and Middlesbrough are considered likely to be looking to strengthen in that department. Button could well feel that now is his best and perhaps only opportunity to play at that level and I am sure that he and his agent at *Key Sports Management* are currently exploring what might be out there for him.

A couple of weeks ago I felt that the odds were on Button remaining at Brentford, but now I am not so sure. There has been no suggestion that talks between the club and his representative have been taking place, but there again, why on earth should I know if they have or haven't?

If we are to lose a key player this summer then I suspect that it will be David Button and should that come to pass, then he would ideally justify a fee of at least ten times what we paid Charlton Athletic for him and massively in excess of what we received from Cardiff City for Simon Moore whom Button replaced.

If he does leave Griffin Park then he will need replacing by somebody who is considered capable of fitting into the way that we play, in other words, acting as a sweeper keeper, being totally comfortable with the ball at his feet and distributing the ball to defenders quickly and accurately.

It is no great secret that we are one of many teams who have shown interest in Southend's Daniel Bentley who seems certain to be on the move this summer. He has had three seasons as first choice at Roots Hall, is confident and accomplished and will not come cheap. There will also be a lot of competition for his services from clubs with greater resources than ours but we would be able to offer him first team football. He would certainly be my number one choice to replace David Button should that become necessary, but I very much hope that David will still decide to re-sign for us.

Irrespective of what happens with Button I am sure that we will also be looking to bring in a young number three keeper to replace Mark Smith who has left the club, and several trialists received auditions in the Development Squad last season.

As for Jack Bonham, I feel strongly that he needs to go out on loan and play some first team football, as sitting on our bench game after game is doing nothing for his development as a goalkeeper. Whether that happens or not totally depends on who comes in as third choice, and whether he is considered capable of acting as substitute keeper with the possibility of some emergency action.

Moving further upfield, on the surface we are looking particularly strong in **defence** but does that view survive deeper scrutiny? Let's take a good look at our resources and then come to a final conclusion.

Maxime Colin, Nico Yennaris, Alan McCormack and Josh Clarke can all play right back with Jake Bidwell and Tom Field available on the other flank. Yennaris is more likely to be needed to play in midfield where he established himself late on last season and at the time of writing Clarke has yet to sign a new contract. Should he do so and Colin returns fit and well and fully recovered from his niggling groin injury then we have more than sufficient cover at right back.

Left back is another matter given that Jake Bidwell, like David Button, is entering the final year of his contract. He has even more in common with Button, sharing the same management company, and I wonder if he is receiving similar advice to his teammate?

Again, does Jake feel that the time has come to move on from Brentford FC given the long and loyal service he has given us? He has massive experience given his relative youth, has adapted well to the challenges of the Championship and must surely be coveted by many for his tenaciousness, consistency, calmness and overlapping ability.

He too might well feel that he could do better elsewhere and seek pastures new. If that is the case and he will not sign a new contract, then how does the club respond? Sell him now and pay Everton a hefty sell-on percentage from the proceeds, or continue to play him, allow him to run his contract down and face the risk of him leaving for nothing in the hope that he changes his mind and re-signs at some point during next season?

Not an easy choice, but whatever happens, a new left back who can challenge, or indeed replace, Bidwell, is an imperative. Given our style of play, he will need to be somebody who can both attack and defend as Jake snuffs out so much danger when other defenders are caught upfield.

Scunthorpe's Conor Townsend is a name that has been bandied about and he certainly impressed when on loan at Grimsby Town. He gets forward well and has a wand of a left foot and is deadly from set pieces, a skill that always comes in handy. I am not too sure about his defensive capabilities and he is also not the tallest and he therefore would not be able to act as our goalkeeper's out-ball when he is unable to pass the ball to one of the centre halves. Tom Field enjoyed a wonderful debut against Fulham but he is one for the future and his time will come, but probably not next season.

Matthew Benham and Phil Giles discussing the way forward for the club

We are currently extremely well-served at centre half with Harlee Dean, Yoann Barbet, Jack O'Connell and Andreas Bjelland. But again, all is not what it seems. Dean is our only natural right-sided defender and Bjelland is a question mark as he is only now approaching full fitness, having missed the entire season as a result of his serious injury received against Oxford United in August.

It currently seems likely that Gillingham's excellent right-sided defender John Egan, will join us this Summer and if the deal is concluded, perhaps after a tribunal ruling on the transfer fee, then he will certainly put pressure on Harlee Dean as he is reputed to be quick, good on the ball and also dangerous in the opposition box, as is evidenced by his more than impressive tally of six goals last season. If Egan does join us we will have more than adequate options and cover on both sides of the pitch and the only problem might be how to keep everybody happy.

Jack O'Connell is still only twenty-two and has two years remaining on his contract but he only started eleven times last season and I do wonder if he might be looking to move on, perhaps initially on loan? I would like us to keep hold of him as he showed some promise last season and could yet develop into a real asset.

So, to summarise, our defensive options are plentiful, and we possess some extremely talented players, but some tinkering will definitely be required this summer.

It really will not take too long to consider the **wingers** that we currently possess in Andy Gogia and Sam Saunders. Someone very closely connected to the club told me late last Summer that Gogia was a player who was considered highly likely to impress and quickly attract serious attention from other clubs. So far that has yet to happen, although there were signs by the end of last season that, like several others of our foreign contingent, he was slowly beginning to acclimatise to the unfamiliar conditions he faced both on and off the pitch. He will certainly get the opportunity to prove himself next season given the paucity of our resources.

Sam Saunders can certainly still play wide and provide good service from the flank. He has always depended upon guile rather than pace and he proved far more effective when playing in a more central role where he had more influence on the proceedings. Sam will doubtless more than play his part next season but I would be surprised if he is a regular starter.

Now that Sergi Canos has returned to his parent club, Liverpool, we lack a winger with pace, drive, incision, the ability to turn defence into attack in an instant, score and make goals and provide the odd moment of genius and inspiration. Not too much to ask for in one player, surely, and we will need to find somebody suitable on either a permanent or loan basis. We all live in hope, or is it merely wishful thinking, that Sergi will return to us, and he would certainly be my first choice, but if not we could be struggling to find a homegrown player who can provide the impact that we need.

Jamie Paterson, who played for Dean Smith at Walsall has been mentioned as a possibility but his situation is fairly complex as he is still under contract at Nottingham Forest who are currently without a manager and are therefore unwilling to make decisions about players until an appointment is made, and Huddersfield Town, for whom Paterson impressed whilst on loan last season, including scoring against the Bees, are also hovering in the wings as they want to sign the player on a permanent basis. Perhaps this might be an area where we look abroad for a suitable signing? Who knows, but this is a crucial gap to fill.

The two **defensive midfielders** play a vital role in the team, covering the back four, snapping into tackles, ideally winning the ball and also taking it off the goalkeeper or defenders to set us off on the attack again. They also need to make lung-bursting box-to-box runs, weigh in the odd goal or two, as well as getting back to cover when our attacks break down. Perhaps we will be looking to bring in a replacement for the departed Toumani Diagouraga but Dean Smith might well feel that there are other more pressing needs elsewhere given the presence of Ryan Woods, Nico Yennaris, Alan McCormack and Josh McEachran. Konstantin Kerschbaumer can also play there at a pinch.

Woods and Yennaris combined superbly in a defensive midfield partnership at the back end of last season and were tenacious and rugged and also used the ball excellently, and it could well be their position to lose. Alan McCormack will provide his customary aggression and organisational skills when required, but the real conundrum is Josh McEachran. Will be recover full fitness from his second long-term injury in time to make a real contribution and how will he fit into the team shape? He showed glimpses of his undoubted ability, particularly against Cardiff, Leeds and Wolves, but was otherwise a peripheral figure who lacked confidence, strength, fitness and sharpness. Given the impact that he was expected to have, and might well still, I really doubt if the club will make a serious investment in this area until Josh is given another chance to make the position his own.

Two seasons ago we had an embarrassment of riches in midfield and we could choose from players of the quality of Pritchard, Judge and Toral alongside Jota and Dallas on the flanks. Last season we ended up scoring twenty-four goals in our last nine games with the likes of Saunders, Kerschbaumer and Woods pulling the strings as our **attacking midfielders** with Canos on the wing. Judge missed the last six matches and Swift barely featured. The team ethic prevailed and these unheralded and unfancied players gelled together magnificently into a cohesive and successful whole.

Next season we will certainly start without Judge and probably Canos and John Swift too, and we will be looking to recruit a winger, as previously mentioned, as well as one or perhaps even two attacking midfielders of whom Romaine Sawyers will ideally be the first. He excelled for Walsall last season, as he is an elegant player who always has time and space on the ball, and he possesses the ability and vision to cut opposition defences apart. He enjoyed playing for Dean Smith previously and given our previous failure to sign George Evans, it is important that we manage to get this deal over the line.

The decision regarding whether Brentford sign one or two attacking midfield players might well hinge upon Lewis Macleod's availability. What a boost it would be for everybody if he returns to preseason training fit and raring to go and I see no reason why he won't.

As for Judge, he will eventually need replacing, but not until his future is decided on his eventual return from injury. Jota remains in limbo and, genius that he is, is totally irreplaceable anyway.

With Marco Djuricin having left the club at the end of his loan spell, Scott Hogan, Lasse Vibe and Philipp Hofmann are the three **strikers** who remain under contract. Hogan and Vibe were revelations in the final part of last season and we all hope that they can both pick up where they left off.

Hofmann is another matter as he was rarely fully fit, only started six matches all season and struggled to make an impact. I simply hope that last season was a learning curve for him and that he comes back in July totally determined to make a go of it in English football. The jury is still out on him and it is entirely possible that he might decide to cut his losses and return home and if so he will need replacing, assuming we are then able to sell him, however I can see something in him and expect that he will prove to be far more successful next season as he acclimatises to this country.

Assuming we have three main strikers to choose from and rotate where necessary, there may be no need to bring in a young loan striker unless we feel that given the change in the emergency loan rules we should have someone waiting on the sidelines who can fill in as necessary.

So, to recap, I would expect us **definitely** to sign:

- A third string goalkeeper
- A left back

- A right-sided central defender

- A winger

- An attacking midfielder

- In addition, depending upon whether some of our current contracted players leave or lack fitness, we might **possibly** sign:

- A first choice goalkeeper

- A second attacking midfielder

- A first choice striker

- A young loan striker

I have nailed my colours to the mast and I wonder how many, or more likely, few, of these predictions will come true?

Position	Team	P	W	D	L	F	A	GD	Pt	Form
1	Burnley	46	26	15	5	72	35	37	93	W W D W W W
2	Middlesbrough	46	26	11	9	63	31	32	89	W W D D D D
3	Brighton and Hove A	46	24	17	5	72	42	30	89	W W W W D D
4	Hull City	46	24	11	11	69	35	34	83	W W D W L W
5	Derby County	46	21	15	10	66	43	23	78	W W W D D L
6	Sheffield Wednesday	46	19	17	10	66	45	21	74	L D D D W L
7	Ipswich Town	46	18	15	13	53	51	2	69	L D D D W W
8	Cardiff City	46	17	17	12	56	51	5	68	L D L W L D
9	Brentford	46	19	8	19	72	67	5	65	D W W L W W
10	Birmingham City	46	16	15	15	53	49	4	63	L L D D D D
11	Preston North End	46	15	17	14	45	45	0	62	L D D L W D
12	Queens Park Rangers	46	14	18	14	54	54	0	60	W D L D L W
13	Leeds United	46	14	17	15	50	58	-8	59	W W W D L D
14	Wolverhampton Wndrs	46	14	16	16	53	58	-5	58	D L L D D W
15	Blackburn Rovers	46	13	16	17	46	46	0	55	D L D D W W
16	Nottingham Forest	46	13	16	17	43	47	-4	55	L D D W D W
17	Reading	46	13	13	20	52	59	-7	52	L L L D L L
18	Bristol City	46	13	13	20	54	71	-17	52	W D L D W L
19	Huddersfield Town	46	13	12	21	59	70	-11	51	D W D D L L
20	Fulham	46	12	15	19	66	79	-13	51	W L D L L W
21	Rotherham United	46	13	10	23	53	71	-18	49	W D D D L L
22	Charlton Athletic	46	9	13	24	40	80	-40	40	L L D L W L
23	Milton Keynes Dons	46	9	12	25	39	69	-30	39	L D D L L L
24	Bolton Wanderers	46	5	15	26	41	81	-40	30	L L D L W L L

[Final Table]

Afterword | Greville Waterman

I was just about to start writing a long and detailed review of last season's remarkable happenings as well as attempt to look into my crystal ball and give you all my own predictions for the 2016/17 season, when I had a *Eureka* moment.

Surely I have written more than enough already and anyone who has taken the trouble to read this book has a pretty good idea of all my views on these crucial subjects and really does not want or need to hear anything more from me?

I therefore decided to create my own All-Star team of eleven experts from both inside and outside Brentford FC and ask them to provide their views instead.

Thankfully everyone accepted my invitation to write something for the book and I hope that you all enjoy the fascinating, illuminating and thought-provoking comments that follow throughout the **Afterword** section and I am so grateful to all of them for their kindness and dedication.

Brentford fans **Stephen Burke** and **Paul Grimes** have provided their own memories and review of last season.

My fellow Brentford author and historian, **Mark Croxford**, has looked in great detail at our injury crisis and compared it to similar situations in previous years.

Renowned journalists **Jim Levack**, **Tom Moore** and *BBC Radio London's* **Billy Reeves** and **Phil Parry** have all provided their own informed view from the inside on Brentford's progress, the personalities involved, as well as their predictions for the future.

I have done my best throughout the season to explain the realities of Brentford's financial situation and how it has affected us, but hopefully it will be far more valuable and convincing to read an impartial and expert outsider's view, and I am grateful and delighted that **Kieron O'Connor**, author of the acclaimed *Swiss Ramble* blog has allowed me to reprint his recent forensic and comprehensive analysis and explanation of Brentford FC's finances. Thanks also to everyone at *Beesotted* for kindly allowing me to reproduce the Matthew Benham quotes from within Kieron's article.

Personally I have taken great pride and pleasure in the success that our former manager Mark Warburton has achieved over the past year at Rangers FC, and lifelong Rangers supporter **Jordan Campbell** has provided an in-depth analysis of the massive impact that Mark has had since joining the club.

Finally we end with the views from the inside as Brentford's Co-Director of Football, **Phil Giles** and Chairman, **Cliff Crown** have both penned specially commissioned articles which provide their own in-depth insights on the last season and the problems everyone at the club had to cope with, as well as their hopes and aspirations for the future.

Fascinating reading – I hope that you all agree.

Raised Expectations – And Reasons To Be Cheerful | Stephen Burke

2015/16 was the season that had everything for Brentford fans – the good, the bad and the ugly. Fortunately, things came good for the Bees at just the right time in a glorious April, despite the loss of our best outfield player to an ugly tackle.

For many people, much of last season was a disappointment - or rather an anti-climax after 2014/15 when we reached the playoffs. Expectations at the start of 2015/16 had, not surprisingly, been high with a new Head Coach and management team to build on Mark Warburton's achievements.

But those expectations were quickly dispelled as star players were sold, new and established players were injured, and our Head Coach (and signings) from elsewhere in Europe struggled to get to grips with the English Championship. Marinus Dijkhuizen didn't last long as one thing after another seemed to go pear-shaped.

Luckily, Lee Carsley stabilised the ship before jumping off. Then our new Head Coach, Dean Smith, had a rocky start to 2016 before things finally came good. Strangely both these purple patches came after the dreaded international breaks, which showed their value in enabling the team to regroup, if nothing else.

Off the back of six wins and a draw in April, the sun was shining again at Griffin Park. Trouncing Fulham in our last home match of the season was the icing on the cake, followed by the cherry on top with our best win of the season away at Huddersfield.

So after the lows and highs of 2015/16, I am a little nervous suggesting that expectations are high again as we look forward to 2016/17 and beyond. But here are my reasons to be cheerful.

Firstly football is, above all, a team game. In 2015/16 several of our stars from the previous season moved on to other clubs, mainly richer competitors in the Championship. We also lost several key players to injury, including our top scorer and main goal creator, Alan Judge.

It forced the Bees and Head Coach Dean Smith to go back to basics at the end of March. Sort out the defence, make the midfield more direct and incisive, and top it off with a couple of strikers who could actually score goals. No stars, just a group of players who knew what to do, played professionally, did their job, and became a team in every sense of the word.

If the Bees can continue the run of form that saw them take twenty-two out of twenty-seven points in the last nine games of the 2015/16 season, then we must be extremely optimistic about the future. The return of some players from major injuries with others regaining form, boosted the squad and the team at just the right time. And scoring twenty-four goals in every nine games would certainly keep the fans very happy indeed!

So what we do need to do to further strengthen the team in the close season? This is Dean Smith's big chance to show us his plans and ambitions for the Bees. What will Dean's Brentford look like and how will they play?

After leaking a lot of goals in mid-season, the defence now looks much stronger with competition for places in most positions and record signing Bjelland also set to return. David Button had an outstanding season, making more saves than any other keeper in the Championship. We must do our utmost to ensure he stays for at least another season, as well as find another young reserve keeper.

Up front we have two strikers in Vibe and Hogan who both know how to score goals. It will be interesting to see if they ever start together at some point. We need a third finisher to support them who will probably come from outside the current squad, replacing those who have failed to convince.

It's midfield where I think we need to invest most. We have not really replaced the 2014/15 stars who have left the club, and some of the current squad are either nearing the end of their playing days or haven't yet played to their full potential.

It would be great if we could keep Sergi Canos for at least another season. And in our glorious April, Konstantin Kerschbaumer began to show us what he is capable of. A couple of new buys to complement the excellent Ryan Woods in midfield could transform the team both in front of the defence and out wide.

So the second reason to be cheerful is that we have the basis of a strong spine to the team, capable of scoring goals and ideally not conceding so many.

Thirdly, the promotion of Burnley, Middlesbrough and Hull City means that we will not have to compete against the league's three best teams. They have all been bogey teams for the Bees and we should be more than a match for the other teams left in the league although there are some really big clubs coming down from the Premier League.

Fourthly, after a season of massive turbulence, it feels like Brentford both on and off the pitch is finally a much more calm and settled place. Players and coaching staff need time and space to show what they can do and for the best to be brought out of a squad when money is spread thin and cannot be used to buy everything.

Talking of which, Bees fans continue to be massively grateful to Matthew Benham for investing so heavily in the club and all its operations. We are totally unrecognisable in every way from a mere five years ago. I would just call on him to be more open in communicating with supporters about his vision and plans. Better communication during 2015/16 would have allayed much of the fear, vitriol and even worse that emerged during the first three months of 2016.

Fifthly, we are now hopefully just three years away from our new ground at Lionel Road. The ambition the move represents must be matched by ambition on the pitch to create a team that can attract a bigger fan base. Our new ground merits Premier League status.

For many of us, Griffin Park is Brentford. For me, that means almost fifty years of regular pilgrimage to TW8, first to stand in Braemar Road, then standing and now sitting in New Road. It's hard to imagine watching the Bees at home anywhere else, let alone not having a pub on every corner.

Our travels, particularly in the Championship, show how new stadiums with excellent facilities can and do work. Having a successful team on the pitch is key to filling the new stadium. But we also need to ensure that the ground has atmosphere and noise and becomes an intimidating place for away teams to visit.

So there is much to look forward to. My expectations are high - bring on 2016/17. I have a tenner on the Bees emerging as Champions come May 2017.

I wonder what odds Mr. Benham can give me?

Optimism For The Future | Paul Grimes

Well who could possibly have predicted that finish to the season or the amazing run of form in our last nine matches?

Well I guess Matthew Benham and his two Co-Directors of Football is the answer to that question, and I for one am delighted to be congratulating them for believing that we would come good when others, like me, felt that we were way short of a highly creditable ninth place finish. I certainly wouldn't want to play poker against Messrs. Benham, Giles or Ankersen.

Also there are two others that have come out of this run with a lot of kudos in my eyes and they are Dean Smith and Konstantin Kerschbaumer! It is well known I am not the biggest fan of either, but Smith in particular fully deserves a few extra words of praise.

I feel the majority of supporters will look at the form of Scott Hogan in that incredible run after the international break and that his goals and those of Lasse Vibe were the main catalyst for the successful run but I also think that something major happened to improve our defensive record.

I don't think that any of our five defensive mainstays were away during that critical March international break and I think it was clear that Smith made some tweaks in that period which laid the foundations for a tighter defence in front of the potent attacking force that we all knew we possessed, even if their goals had dried up since the turn of the year. Yennaris, Woods and McCormack also provided the solid shield in front of the back four that had been previously missing all too often.

Twenty-four goals scored but only eight conceded in our last nine matches suggests that whilst it was predominantly about the goals, to concede less than a goal a game in that period was just as impressive in my eyes as finishing joint top goal scorers in the division.

A lot of that has to be down to the team of Dean Smith and Richard O'Kelly for their coaching ability and for getting the squad to buy into their methods and totally believe in what they were doing.

So what did they do? They made us less gung-ho in our approach so that we sat back more and picked teams off on the break using our pace and ability to play quick and accurate passes and cut through the opposition. The midfield ensured that the back four was always well protected and Vibe and Hogan timed their runs perfectly to get in behind square defences.

Konstantin Kerschbaumer also deserves a lot of credit as he finally began to find his feet and confidence and got on the ball more often and with greater confidence. He started to make his presence felt with three incisive through balls all leading to Scott Hogan goals that looked so simple but were in reality brilliantly carved out and created.

Josh McEachran would also do well to note that passing the ball forwards can be far more effective than moving it sideways and backwards!

If you try to make the pass and it fails nobody complains because fine margins are sometime the difference, and so it proved for KK who ended the season with a handful of assists, which did not go unnoticed.

So what does the preseason hold for us in the transfer market? Ideally there will be a concentration on obtaining more homegrown talent rather than what I felt was the terribly risky approach of last summer's European trolley dash. Ultimately the gamble (and our due diligence) just about paid off as Colin and Barbet were massive successes, Vibe came good towards the end of the season, Kerschbaumer, likewise, but the jury is still out on Gogia, Hofmann and of course, the injured Bjelland.

My guess is that we will have a few additions and it will be extremely interesting to see if we concentrate on Bosman free transfers or pay fees for emerging young talent; this year's versions of Gray, Hogan and Odubajo from the Summer of 2014.

Given the likely loss of the anticipated Alan Judge transfer fee I suspect that money will be tight and we will need to prospect carefully.

I would also like us to consider bringing in a couple of carefully selected players with more experience and greater knowledge of the Championship who can act as leaders to the youngsters around them.

Henri Lansbury at Nottingham Forest is a very talented player who will drop deeper in his later years and when necessary in the short term, and he is someone who has the ability to control a game, make an incisive pass, score his fair share of goals and he can also put his foot in when needed. He is rumoured to be available for transfer but I suspect he will be miles out of our price range.

Kevin McDonald has fallen out of favour at Wolves but on form he is an elegant player who can dominate the midfield, win the ball and use it effectively and he would be a wonderful addition to our squad as at twenty-seven he is approaching his peak.

I well suspect that Darron Gibson's days at Everton are probably numbered. He is a combative midfielder who possesses similar attributes to Jonathan Douglas and I think he could be an inspired signing if we could afford his wages, as he could turn out to be as influential for us as Joey Barton was at Burnley.

Speaking of the youth in the side, I was delighted to see Tom Field make his full debut and I think he could be a great understudy to Jake Bidwell next season. I have really high hopes for him ahead of the likes of Bohui, Ferry, Cole and Westbrooke and I think he will go on to replace Bidwell when Jake eventually leaves the club.

Off the field I would like Matthew to dispense with the joint Director of Football set-up as we seem to have too many chiefs, and with the closing of the Academy and the new Elite Development Squad set-up I can only wonder if there is a need for all the current senior staff, particularly given the need to conserve funds wherever possible?

I would like to see Kevin O'Connor left alone now to work alongside Dean Smith and Richard O'Kelly perhaps with Alan McCormack assisting him with the development of young players who would be inspired by the example set by these experienced and exceptional professionals.

In summary, I am really looking forward with great anticipation to the preseason and our anticipated transfer activity almost as much as I am excited about next season, our third consecutive season in the Championship, and what a massive achievement that is given our size and resources.

An Injury-Hit Season | Mark Croxford

What a terrible season it was for injuries – a striker ruled out for the majority of a second season following a serious knee injury, a key defender incurring serious knee ligament damage and having to sit out the whole year, and another important squad member suffering a recurrence of an injury picked up during the previous campaign and being sidelined for the season.

No, I don't mean this year and I'm not talking about Scott Hogan, Andreas Bjelland and Lewis Macleod. I'm looking back at 2000/01 where the players in question were Derek Bryan, Ijah Anderson and Danny Boxall. Add to that list Darren Powell with a serious hamstring injury, which meant that he missed the first twenty-three league games, Lloyd Owusu dislocating his shoulder and being sidelined for thirteen matches and Paul Gibbs missing two months with a hairline leg fracture. Not to mention new signing Eddie Hutchinson being diagnosed with a shin splits problem, which kept him out of action for eight months, and goalkeeper Jason Pearcey failing to play a game before announcing his retirement after the medical experts told him he would never be able to play at a professional level again.

That year, so the management team said at the time, must have been unparalleled as far as injury bad luck was concerned. Maybe - but then again, maybe not. It wasn't difficult to think back to 1989/90 when the list of woes included Keith Millen being sidelined for three months, firstly with a foot injury and then picking up a knee injury in a reserve game, Gary Blissett slipping downstairs at his home, Simon Ratcliffe incurring a fractured cheekbone, Eddie May's hernia ruling him out for the last two months of the season and a thrombosis in the leg forcing Tony Parks into a lengthy period of rest. Throw in a host of additional injury problems for other first teamers and the season wound down with early league appearances for new young professionals Robert Peters, Marcus Gayle, Jason Cousins, Paul Buckle, Andy Driscoll and Ashley Bayes.

When talking about campaigns wrecked by injuries, what about 1992/93 and the opening day knee injury incurred by Terry Evans which saw him sit out seven months alongside two other experienced colleagues in Wilf Rostron and Bob Booker – meaning that more than eleven hundred games-worth of expertise missed out on our ultimately unsuccessful battle to stave off relegation?

So yes, this season has certainly been a miserable experience as far as injured players has been concerned but is it unique? Let's look at the facts in a bit more detail.

Excluding the *fringe* players who've made just a token number of league appearances such as Jermaine Udumaga and Josh Clarke plus Andre Gray, along with the long-term injury victims, we've used twenty-two players who have reached double figures in appearances for the first team in the Championship. That figure is pretty much par for the course in recent years.

Of those twenty-two players, twelve of them have either not missed a single game as result of injury or been absent on just one or two occasions at most. That's a pretty impressive record too and one which stands up well to scrutiny when compared to other seasons.

Before scaling the wall of Griffin Park midway through the season, James Tarkowski sat out a couple of early season matches, both within the space of seven days, and until the closing weeks both Alan Judge and John Swift had remained almost injury-free whilst a very late-season niggling injury for Lasse Vibe meant that his ever-present record as a member of the match-day squad was only ended with only three games to go.

Only Jake Bidwell and the ever-present David Button better Lasse Vibe's run of forty-three consecutive appearances in the matchday squad. Even Sam Saunders, whose early-season problems meant that he sat out thirteen games, can claim a high ranking place in the consecutive games chart, with a run of twenty-eight successive appearances in the eighteen-man weekly squad. Injury-prone? Says who?

So who has had their campaign *wrecked* by injuries?

Philipp Hofmann had two spells on the sidelines with back problems, missing around ten games as a result. But as he started only five times out of the thirty-three occasions he was named in the squad, perhaps his loss wasn't hugely significant? Maybe something similar could be said about Marco Djuricin whose longest spell out of action was for nine games, spanning two months, with his overall tally of absences pretty much equating to the number of games he actually started.

The *big hitters* could be classed as Alan McCormack, missing out fourteen times during his two-month absence, and Maxime Colin whose total of twenty games for which he was deemed unavailable meant that he missed exactly half of the matches he could played. A very big loss indeed. Not to mention the unfortunate Josh McEachran who sat out thirty-two games, five of which were on the bench, leaving him to make a contribution to the cause on just fourteen occasions.

Jota, such a star last season, practically disappeared from sight as his Douglas-inflicted injury on the first day of the season necessitated his missing the next seventeen matches. He was then named in the squad for the next six matches before leaving *pro tem* for pastures anew.

That of course, leads to the key statistic which undoubtedly ensures that the *injury-plagued* headline will always be tagged on to the 2015/16 season: three of our potentially most valuable players, including our record signing, starting just two games between them!

Regardless of the impact the presence of Scott Hogan, Andreas Bjelland and Lewis Macleod may have made on the team itself, and that three such prominent and significant players were all ruled out with long-term and serious injuries before being able to make any impact at all is unprecedented. The fact that all three will have been at the club for more than one year before making their league debuts is even more astonishing.

Three signings, a four million pound outlay – two starts and one hundred and ninety-seven games missed as a result of injury!

With all due respect to the likes of Ijah Anderson and Terry Evans, that's a real injury disaster!

Adapting To Change | Jim Levack

If ever a season epitomised the fickle nature of football, and in particular, Brentford fans, then the one just gone was it.

Despite its positive finale and the accompanying warm wave of optimism and harmony for next season, it was arguably one of the toughest ever seasons to be a Bees fan.

Managerial upheaval, fans fighting fans, rifts between friends, grave question marks over the club's structure, doubts over signings and the sale of firm favourites all contributed to a feeling of unease even among the most myopic.

It all started what seemed like a lifetime ago with hope, a raft of exciting continental signings and a new Dutch Head Coach espousing what we hoped would be total football TW8 style.

Expectations were realistic among most right-minded Bees fans that this would be a season of consolidation after the incredible playoff fairy tale of the preceding one.

But as the heroes of that Mark Warburton-led campaign slowly but inexorably drifted away from Griffin Park one by one, swayed by the lure of big money and bigger teams, the grim realisation that all might not be well in our brave new stats-driven world began to dawn.

Marinus Dijkhuizen departed with the admission that mistakes had been made in the appointment process, raising further doubts amongst the cynics that all was not well deep inside the Griffin Park database.

The for and against statistics lobbies were at loggerheads as the dismantling of the previous season's side continued, with the bargain and some argued, needless, sale of Stuart Dallas to rivals Leeds raising further doubts about the behind the scenes machinations.

Lee Carsley stepped in and history will show that his presence helped steady a ship that looked like it had hit an iceberg with a calm assuredness that comes only with four hundred and seventy-one league appearances and forty international caps.

His remit was clear - do whatever it takes to stabilise and turn things round. In a handful of games his wit, focus and *one of the lads* banter proved the turning point in a rollercoaster season and earned him a deserved Manager of the Month award.

He was a proper football bloke, so when he announced to a shocked press room that he had never wanted the job and didn't intend to take it, it seemed like just another in a growing list of PR own-goals unfolding before our eyes.

The Brentford fans took to Carsley, whose honesty was a breath of fresh air. He rested players who clearly weren't ready, added steel to the midfield and got the players playing for him.

For those who doubted the benefits of the statistical approach, he was proof that nothing will ever beat a combination of science and numbers twinned with a good old-fashioned football man who lets his side play with freedom, expression and passion.

That was always my personal view and I stand by it now that history has proved me right. Those closer to Matthew Benham's camp will argue that it was ever thus, and they may well also be correct.

For statistics to work you also need a football man respected within the game and by the players capable of having input into the acquisition process… someone like Warburton, Carsley or Smith, in fact.

To my mind though, Carsley was – like Warburton – the right man at the right time and played a pivotal part in the evolution of the club, as he helped Matthew Benham realise that a more considered and less radical balance between the two approaches needed to be found.

Benham found that with the excellent appointment of Dean Smith, a manager who repeatedly rebuilt a Walsall side shorn every summer of its brightest talent at the hands of predators. His reputation for bringing youngsters through, signing raw untested talent and growing a team from nothing, chimed perfectly with the blueprint Matthew Benham had drafted.

But what looked like the perfect appointment was soon to become another cause for division amongst supporters as Smith's tenure began with a whimper amidst a flurry of defeats and draws.

Knee-jerk reactions were rife, with usually measured fans insisting Smith was definitely not the answer and consigning him to the scrapheap. Anyone with more than a passing knowledge of his history in the West Midlands knew that he'd be the perfect man for the medium to long-term – given time and some patience and understanding.

But as setback followed setback even the most optimistic could be forgiven for fearing the worst as the relegation trapdoor beckoned.

The rifts evident between different factions, websites and even terrace neighbours at the start of the campaign, but which subsided during Carsley's reign were back with a vengeance, as the spotlight once again fell on the statistical side of things.

Then, as if by magic, everything clicked into place and win followed win and smiles replaced furrowed brows. Brentford were flying again.

There are a lot of thin lines and imponderables involved in winning football matches, but Smith worked hard on finessing the defensive side of things to make his side hard to beat, confidence grew and formerly hesitant players started to flourish.

Much has been made about Brentford's desire to pass their way around sides, to out-football the opposition without the need for big, physical specimens and to win through technique and guile rather than brawn.

But to my mind it's no coincidence that the Brentford revival coincided with the return from injury of Alan McCormack, who gave the side the bite and snarl they'd been sorely missing all season.

Carsley and Smith both knew what was needed so it was a surprise that the January Transfer Window slammed shut without the arrival of a steely midfielder, but presumably they knew McCormack was on his way back. That's why they're managers and the best I achieved was an Under 18 title spot managing my lad's team. It was a tough Coventry league though!

Humility has also been a big word for me this season and I was delighted to see Matthew Benham and the club acknowledging and conceding that mistakes had been made and tweaks added to the system to ensure that we learn from what went wrong at the start of the campaign.

All the best managers tell their players that there's nothing wrong with making mistakes on the pitch but it's when you don't learn from them that it rankles.

Brentford as a club has, in the past decade at least, strived to be progressive and admitted its shortcomings and I like that because it's what makes us special and unique.

The decision to downsize the mission statement from *Big New Ambitions* to *Believe in Brentford* is a good and encouraging example and will help set us up for next season with more realistic expectations.

Momentum is massive in football as Leicester and Orient have proved in the past, so if the finale of this season is anything to go by then the next could be one to look forward to as long as all those imponderables like luck, new signings, balance, morale, team spirit – the list goes on - slot nicely into place.

Whatever happens, a third season in the Championship will most likely see us even more firmly established in our new exalted position, and if my dear old Dad were still with us he'd be absolutely chuffed with that.

Why Next Season Will Be One To Look Forward To | Tom Moore

Brentford are certainly in a much better position to challenge at the top of the Championship than they were at this time last year.

If you look back to July 2015 when the Bees squad first reported back to preseason training, it was a step into a brave new world.

Mark Warburton had gone with Marinus Dijkhuizen, along with his assistant Roy Hendriksen, taking charge at Griffin Park without the benefit of any previous experience of management in England.

Phil Giles and Rasmus Ankersen had replaced Frank McParland and split their roles as Co-Directors of Football. Robert Rowan took over the position of Head of Football Operations having previously worked for Celtic.

Bartek Sylwestrzak had been promoted from working with the youth team to be a technical coach working with players on striking the ball. Paul Williams was added to the staff as Logistics Manager. Gianni Vio joined the club from Italian giants AC Milan to provide much-needed assistance to the squad on set pieces while Tom Bates also arrived from West Bromwich Albion, where he was coach and performance psychologist.

On the playing front, the Bees had signed Andy Gogia, Ryan Williams, Konstantin Kerschbaumer and Yoann Barbet, with Andreas Bjelland and Josh McEachran soon to arrive, while Tony Craig was set to depart for Millwall. The Bees still had Will Grigg, Andre Gray, Moses Odubajo, Stuart Dallas and Jonathan Douglas on their books, but by the end of August they had all departed.

The first week and the training camp in Portugal were more about getting to know each other and remember everyone's name and help blend in the new members of the squad rather than getting on with the critical job at hand.

Indeed, Phil Giles told me that next preseason will be entirely different:

Last summer, it wasn't just a question of Rasmus Ankersen and I coming in new and Marinus and Roy also coming in new. There were also new support staff and new players. This year we won't have the first part of preseason as a getting to know each other period. We'll be cracking on straightaway.

When making so many changes it is virtually impossible to get everything right and the Bees sacked Dijkhuizen and Hendriksen in September.

Williams departed before the end of the year, albeit in different circumstances; as he moved to Nottingham Forest in December after a successful spell as number two to Lee Carsley whilst Vio also left in May.

The club's signings, especially from Europe, needed time to settle into the English game and they won't have to do that this time around.

Konstantin Kerschbaumer struggled to adapt to English football, while Lasse Vibe also had a hit-and-miss season, as much due to the fact that he'd not had a break from the game in over twelve months and that he too was new to English conditions and the rigorous demands of the Championship.

The club has learned from those mistakes and ideally will not be repeating them during the 2016 off-season.

Giles added: *It was always the case that they'd all need time to bed in. The mistake we made wasn't so much in buying players and not giving them time to bed in. It was more that there were so many at the same time and it was unfair on them to expect them to hit the ground running.*

Coupled with injuries which meant that they had to play. They had to adapt in the job, so to speak, rather than being given time to settle down.

Yoann Barbet was given more time, because we had Harlee Dean and James Tarkowski, so he played in Development Squad games.

He had more time to adjust and other players had to come in and do it straight away. We always said it would take time for players to adapt. It takes time and it always will.

Supporters sometimes fail to take into consideration the huge problems that foreign players face in getting accustomed to living in a strange and alien country, sorting out the needs of their family, finding somewhere to live and also getting used to a new style of football.

A constant stream of serious injuries, players leaving in various circumstances and *Pitchgate* were all difficult issues the club had to deal with over the course of the campaign.

For Brentford to finish ninth, despite all of these shenanigans on and off a pitch that had to be relaid after two competitive games, is a remarkable achievement.

Now the club is on a much more even keel and it is the settled sides that generally have better and more successful campaigns.

Dean Smith has started to repay the faith the club showed in him when they appointed the former Walsall boss at the end of last November.

Signings like Kerschbaumer have shown that they have more than enough ability to succeed in the second tier, whilst the departures of the previous two transfer windows which hit us hard, appear unlikely to be repeated.

It means that when the players report back to preseason training, they will be fully aware of their roles and the new signings can just stand on a chair, sing their songs and bed in.

Captain Jake Bidwell told me after the five-one win at Huddersfield:

I think Brentford have a head start compared to last year. The building blocks are already in place.

I can't imagine there will be much change. The things that have worked will stay in place and the things that haven't will get addressed. We're much further down the line.

Of course there will be challenges to overcome. Brentford's budget will be much smaller than the majority of Championship sides and the stringent Financial Fair Play rules mean the club must keep their costs down.

Newcastle will probably be the favourites to win the league, particularly with Rafa Benitez likely to remain in charge, and will be the big draw for many fans.

Aston Villa need to rebuild under their new owners but they have the budgetary capacity to be challenging at the top of the division.

Norwich are likely to have a similar squad to the one relegated from the Premier League and will also be contenders.

Derby, Brighton and Sheffield Wednesday will be challenging again after missing out in the playoffs and it would not be a surprise to see all three sides at the sharp end of the Championship.

You have bigger budget sides currently rebuilding such as QPR, Fulham, Reading, Blackburn and Nottingham Forest and, to a lesser extent, Huddersfield.

There are also teams such as Wigan, Preston, Leeds, Birmingham, Cardiff, Ipswich and Wolves who are more than capable of challenging for honours, while Bristol City, as demonstrated by their attempts to sign Andre Gray last Summer, have the funds to compete with the cream of the crop.

Burton, Rotherham and Barnsley will be the lower budget sides in the second tier but it is not beyond the realms of possibility to see them also pull off a surprise or two.

This is the exciting and unpredictable nature of the Championship, in that there will always be a surprise team challenging at the top, such as the Bees in 2015, or a fancied and moneyed one that ends up suffering relegation, like Wigan also did that year.

The feeling I've got from speaking to people connected to the club is that the coming season is going to be one to remember for Brentford fans.

What a nine months we have to look forward to!

Men At The Top | Billy Reeves

I'm not chums with football managers or players: I leave that to my commercial rivals.

In a very pompous way, I am the representative of the fan, asking awkward questions when things go awry.

And there was plenty of that last season.

There's three ways of dealing with my probing. Be brutally honest, or be positive and defend the players no-matter-what, or speak a lot without saying too much. All three of Brentford's Managers, or Head Coaches, to be more accurate, throughout the (ultimately historic) topsy-turvy 2015/16 season fell into one of the three.

Marinus was as open a character as you'll ever get in English football: a very tall country-boy (I was always terrified he'd bang his head in the broadcast area underneath the Brook Road stand) he was so chilled-out there were a couple of occasions when I thought he was going to offer me a cup of green tea rather than an analysis.

Of course, describing the pitch as an *embarrassment*, and the recruitment policy as *not my job* sounded a little perfunctory when taken out of context, but we kind of knew he didn't mean it to sound flip. I reckon he left with us all being very fond of him.

Lee Carsley, also taken out of context, left a few red faces: my initial interview with him didn't run on air until the following morning; I had asked him to explain exactly why he didn't *want the job*, i.e. *I'm not celebrating – two people have lost their job* and he wanted to make it clear that he hadn't done anything to cause Marinus and Roy, his assistant to be sacked.

Unfortunately the press deadline, now it's all online, spread the quote that evening, and the *I don't want the job* comment was twisted by Brentford's enemies into a comedy that it very much wasn't. Lee is very serious about coaching (the reason he prefers his role with the England set-up is for family reasons) but I can only describe the atmosphere during his tenure as *madcap*, he was very much one of the lads and perhaps that's what the squad needed at that point. After the draw at Blackburn the post-match resembled the Keystone Cops!

Dean, naturally, falls into the final category. My colleague Nick Godwin gently ribbed me on air for using the cliché *Football Man* to describe the no-nonsense former defender; but this is perfect shorthand for the way Dean deals with the media; he stays positive and doesn't fall into any of my little traps.

Even during his poor run, one could see he wasn't under pressure and that he was just going about his business. His record in April was fantastic, a punishing schedule, having to use fringe players and first-year pro's he changed personnel and tactics to fit each situation. Tellingly, in an unusually frank moment he said he felt that League One is more challenging tactically, and the Championship is much more physical.

My favourite quote of his, however, claimed the moral high ground back for us Bees after Ipswich: *We have to play our way, to make sure that's the way that wins out.*

Carso, wonderfully summed up the Brentford philosophy, ethos and business model: *We buy technical players then put meat on the bones.*

Last season Andre Gray was, arguably, bought in as third-choice striker and, due to injuries, had to play - and the team was built around his strengths.

Dean had to play in several different ways to combat the constant change in line-ups, and his experience and flexibility is what got us through this season.

He's a clever lad.

A Football Man.

He's not my chum though.

The View From The Press Box | Phil Parry

So there we were, sat in a bar in a hotel in Darlington, it was late and one of our party had sportingly offered to go and get the second round of drinks and the topic of conversation was about to shift from what had just come to pass to what next, and let's face it that was a topic which could take up most of the night if none of us had had alarm calls to worry about.

In short, after the glorious forty-six game marathon the final one hundred metre sprint had ended in heartache with a metaphorical hamstring pull leaving just Middlesbrough and Norwich with an opportunity to dip for the line.

We had conducted our final post-match interview with Mark Warburton, shaken hands with him for the last time, and thanked him for his willingness to help us do our jobs, the memories he had created and the dignified way that he had conducted himself in the last few difficult months of his tenure. With that, a wave and a trudge to the car park for the short trip along the A66 from the windswept, barren landscape of the Riverside Stadium car park to the warm embrace of a sympathetic bar.

It was in the car where we dealt with the what-ifs, the what-might-have-beens and all the missed opportunities, points gone begging and bad luck stories. But such talk was only an act of therapy and by the time a first comforting jar had been consumed, progression became the watchword. What was going to happen next, what did it mean and most importantly would it work? Well the conclusive answer to that final question would need time to become apparent.

From the moment that Warbs's summer departure announcement was made, regardless of how it was handled, the eyebrows were being raised and questions asked around the football village. Enquiries that continued and even became more intense as the close season progressed and further developments occurred. In the office, in the pub, talking to people in the game the entreaties remained the same, why change a system that seemed to work, what's with all this statistical stuff, why do they need so many different types of coaches and will this new system work?

The growing consensus, perhaps out of confusion and ignorance, was that there had been a bit of a handbrake turn and the club was now pointing down a lane that did not appear on too many maps or sat navs. And the fear was that it would prove to be a bit of dead end.

Some evangelists of the new direction may have been proclaiming that the doubters and naysayers had their own agenda. If this *radical* alteration was seen to work it would perhaps turn the perceived old order on its head and that would not sit comfortably with the so-called traditionalists.

Admittedly there are still some out there in the world who would like football to return to the halcyon days when centre forwards could bundle goalkeepers into the back of the net with impunity, the ball, when wet, weighed as much as a cannonball, and there was hardly any grass on pitches come March. But in reality it's tough to find those recidivists, as anyone who fails to see the need for progress often gets left behind in the pub that time forgot nursing a glass of brown and mild.

The fear with regard to Brentford's apparent aspirations and intentions was the rapidity and scale of all the changes. Two Co-Directors of Football with little or no experience of working in the sport, and a range of specialist coaches including someone in charge of *Football Philosophy*. Then into the mix was thrown a new Head Coach with very little experience, eighteen months as a gaffer in the professional game, and the levels of trepidation expressed to me increased even more.

The other major change in the summer of 2015 was of course the makeup of the squad of players. Some of the key elements of the side that got the Bees to that night on the banks of the River Tees were on their way and replacements were being found from some interesting sources and using some reportedly unusual scouting techniques.

If I was to be honest my concerns were raised when I attended the press conference to unveil (football cliché) Marinus Dijkhuizen as the new Head Coach. He struck me as a really decent family man who would treat players as human beings, but he looked nonplussed and surprised by the level of interest being shown in him and his arrival in West London. I feared for his longevity and those worries were not eased when I bumped into a Dutch film crew at the opening day fixture who said that there had been a deal of surprise in the Low Countries at Marinus's appointment.

So the club had gone about doing things in a slightly different way, but did that necessarily mean that they would fail to hit the aims being set? And in all honesty were they really striking such a novel and revolutionary rallying call or just combining some new ideas with a solid foundation?

Personally I think the regime did themselves no favours by early on in the campaign suggesting that they should aim to better the final league position obtained in the previous season. It's laudable to want to progress, but after the most successful campaign in well over half a century, to make wholesale alterations to the club's approach and not expect or allow time to settle was at best naïve. My interpretation of many supporters' expectations was that a top-half finish with a possible late push for the playoff zone would be just fine.

Regarding the alterations made and the different approaches taken it is not as if they were out of left field or totally innovative or unique within the football world. However it is in the actual application of ideas and plans and not necessarily the ideas themselves that can prove to be a root cause of difficulty and misunderstanding.

Let us now just analyse one of two of the changes.

Using statistical evidence for transfers: Long gone are the days of traditional squad building where a manager watches a grainy video of an Eastern European starlet and then signs him on a whim and a prayer. Clubs up and down the land will do as much research as possible including the use of statistics, Leicester City are just one of many clubs who now work this way. But scouts and coaches I know tell me that statistical analysis is just one part of the research and due diligence required and generally provided when considering a potential new signing. A character analysis, observation in the flesh and a full medical history are all part of the mix. As is the overall opinion of how a certain player is likely to fit into the squad dynamic. As the sport evolves, transfers will increasingly involve a collation of many types of information, knowledge is after all a powerful tool, but it's how to wield that power which counts the most.

Specialist coaches: Years ago I remember talking to Bob Primrose Wilson, yes that is his middle name, about his transition from double-winning goalkeeper to goalie coach at Arsenal. He believes that his ascension to specialist coach was an epochal moment in football when the importance of the custodian and his specific individual needs were finally recognised. He is, of course, correct and there is nothing wrong with having a coach to work on certain facets of the game. A good friend of mine, who is as UEFA A Licence coach and has worked at various levels of football, reckons that specialist positional coaching is inevitable. However the autonomy of the specialists has to be held somewhat in check by the overall boss, because again, as many have proven, a team needs to exceed the sum of its parts in order to succeed. And he asserts that there's absolutely no point in having great corner taking routines if a side's pressing patterns or counter-attacking ploys are shocking.

Co-Directors of Football: Oh dear isn't this a really thorny issue in the sport? Well, yes and no, and that comes down totally to how a club's structure works, the roles people play and the experience and knowledge people bring to the job. Most clubs have within their structure someone, maybe more than one person, who is responsible for overseeing the bigger non-day-to-day footballing issues. These of course range from overall club structure to recruitment and ethos. At Tottenham Hotspur it is not Mauricio Pochettino who gets in amongst the wheeling and dealing when it comes to transfers or even wage negotiations, Daniel Levy appears to be very good at that, and dealing with agents, and moving players in or out is a particular skill. But Pochettino will certainly be involved in selecting the players he would like and making his case for them.

Some years ago Swansea's board of directors, led by Huw Jenkins set a style marker in the sand, decreeing that the Swans would play their football in a certain way and incoming managers would be appointed because they fit that style and would adhere to the ethos. There are many other examples where Directors of Football do the bits of the job that they are adept at, then place trust in the people they appoint to get other elements of the club right.

When admissions of errors finally emanated from the boardroom at Griffin Park, that was a bold acceptance that perhaps the focus should have been on the evolutionary aspects of change rather than revolutionary. Recent developments have certainly indicated that following the appointment of Dean Smith, a modern farsighted manager with knowledge combined with an open mind, some of the radicalism of last summer is finally being tempered. The Head Coach's opinion appears to hold a greater sway, recruitment may be more focused and less left field and the word from people I speak to in the game is that Brentford appear to have got their feet firmly back on the ground.

There is a lot of affection and admiration for what the Bees have achieved over the last few years both in journalism circles as well as in the world of football. And the questions that were asked last year were not as a result of behind the hand chuckling, it was genuine perplexity. The fact the club still finished ninth after a rather tumultuous season speaks volumes of the work that has gone on and is an indication of the influence that Dean and Richard have had.

As we stood outside The Griffin after the last home game of this season there was still talk of what-ifs and what's next and that is the prerogative of all football fans. Some things have worked, others not, and that ultimately is how evolution progresses, is it not? So, moving forward, if Matthew, Phil, Rasmus, Dean *et al* take the best bits, and discard the dodos then why not think positively about the future?

Brentford - Methods Of Dance | Kieron O'Connor

It is a sign of how far Brentford have progressed that many of their supporters were somewhat disappointed with their ninth place finish in this season's Championship. The Bees reaching the playoffs the previous campaign, which Chairman Cliff Crown described as *our most successful in living memory*, had raised their expectations.

This was fair comment, given that Brentford had finished fifth in their first season in the Championship for twenty-two years, and were plying their trade in League Two as recently as 2009. In fact, Brentford had been languishing outside the top two divisions for the best part of sixty years before gaining automatic promotion from League One in 2014, which amply demonstrated the club's ability to bounce back after the heart-breaking defeat to Yeovil Town in the previous season's Playoff Final.

As Brentford owner Matthew Benham noted: *We have come a long way in a fairly short space of time and that can't be forgotten.* Crown, in turn, described the 2015/16 season as one of *consolidation, before we kick on again.* That seems reasonable enough, considering Brentford's impressive finishing run, when they won seven of their last nine games although that did follow a less enjoyable run of ten defeats in thirteen games.

On the face of it, the reason for Brentford going backwards was fairly straightforward, namely the departure of manager Mark Warburton, who had seemed to be working a minor miracle by guiding the club to an impressive fifth place the previous season. A former city trader, Benham had promoted Warburton from his former role as Brentford's Sporting Director to manager, but his contract was not renewed following a disagreement about the future philosophy of the club.

Warburton was replaced by Marinus Dijkhuizen, the Excelsior manager, in June 2015, but he left just four months later after a miserable time with Benham himself admitting: *On the pitch, the level of the team is not where it was 12 months ago.*

He added: *Very quickly we realised that he wasn't going to be our guy. But to be fair to Marinus, he was also dealt a bad hand. Such a vast turnover of players. Massive upheaval.* However, he did also note: *There was a huge cultural divide between him and the players.*

In fairness to the Dutchman, not only did he lose star striker, Andre Gray, who was sold to Burnley, but he also had to cope with a disastrous, newly-laid pitch that contributed to injuries to a number of players, including record signing Andreas Bjelland, who was ruled out for the season.

Lee Carsley, the Development Squad Manager, was briefly promoted to Head Coach, before making way for the current incumbent, Dean Smith, who arrived from Walsall in late November. Despite losing a couple of key players in the January transfer window in James Tarkowski to Burnley and Toumani Diagouraga to Leeds United, Smith led the team to a top ten finish.

Given all the issues experienced this season, there is cause for optimism in the future. As Co-Director of football Phil Giles put it: *There's been so much happening this season with injuries, pitches, three managers, players striking, broken legs; all this kind of stuff. It can't happen every season surely?*

Overall, it does look like all the millions invested by Benham are beginning to pay off. He is a lifelong Brentford fan, who owns two betting and statistic companies, *Smartodds* and *Matchbook*. His initial involvement came in 2006, when the supporters trust, *Bees United*, needed another half a million pounds to complete their takeover.

At that time, Brentford were in deep financial trouble. As former Chairman Greg Dyke said: *It is fair to say that without Bees United there would probably not have been a club for Matthew to take over.*

That said, Benham is the man that has brought financial stability to Brentford, first by pledging to inject a minimum of £5 million of new capital between 2009 and 2014, then by taking full control in June 2012, when he took over Bees United's 96% shareholding.

Dyke again: *The days of spending monies that we did not have and borrowing monies that we could not repay are long gone for this club. Matthew's monies have removed us from the hand-to-mouth existence that we endured.*

In fact, Benham's financial commitment to Brentford was up to £76 million as at June 2015. The long-term aim is clearly to create a sustainable club, but for the time being its ability to maintain a competitive challenge in the Championship is almost entirely reliant on the owner's generosity.

In addition, Benham's background has led to Brentford being regarded as England's prime exponents of statistical analysis. This approach was pioneered at FC Midtjylland, who won the Danish league in 2015, where Benham is the majority shareholder.

Benham himself does not appear completely comfortable with the *Moneyball* label being applied to this strategy, as it is so often misused and misunderstood: *Everyone came to the conclusion that our methods consisted only of maths and nothing else. However, there has always been a mix between maths and traditional coaching. Analytics have been responsible for identifying some of our most successful players. But analytics are one part of a very big process.*

The approach was further explained by Rasmus Ankersen, Brentford's other Co-Director of Football: *We really believe analytics can make a difference and have a role to play in football and will have a bigger role to play in the future. But no matter how many times we say we also do all the traditional stuff, people don't listen because the narrative is set. We don't disrespect or disregard traditional scouting or coaching at all.*

He added: *Brentford and Midtjylland are small clubs with small budgets and that means you've got to think differently. If you just do the same as the other team then money becomes the decisive factor and we will lose, so we have got to take a different approach. Analytics are a different weapon. We had to go down that route to find an edge.*

Brentford's challenge was highlighted by their 2014/15 financial results, which saw their loss nearly double from £7.7 million to a hefty £14.7 million, despite revenue rising by £5.5 million to a record £10.0 million following promotion to the Championship.

All three revenue streams increased: (a) broadcasting rose £3.4 million from £1.1 million to £4.4 million, thanks to the higher TV deal in the Championship; (b) ticketing shot up £1.4 million (81%) from £1.7 million to £3.1 million; (c) commercial was up £0.7 million (44%) from £1.7 million to £2.4 million.

However, wages also surged by £7.8 million (78%) from £10.0 million to £17.7 million, which the club said was *required to not only ensure survival but also compete in the Championship.* In addition, a significant element was *as a result of bonuses paid out based on the first team's league position.*

In addition, player amortisation was £1.8 million higher at £2.1 million, while other expenses climbed £1.1 million to £7.3 million.

Profit from player sales increased by £1.4 million from £0.6 million to £2.0 million, but other operating income (unexplained) fell by £3.1 million from £3.9 million to £0.9 million.

It should be noted that Brentford have changed the way that they account for player trading. In the past, the club wrote-off transfer fees as they occurred, but they now capitalise player registration costs and amortise charges over the length of the contract, as do the vast majority of football clubs. This has resulted in a restatement of the 2014 comparative, but, interestingly, this does not explain why the revenue figure has also changed.

Although Brentford's £15 million loss is clearly not great, it is by no means the worst in the Championship, having been *beaten* by Bournemouth - £39 million, Fulham - £27 million, Nottingham Forest - £22 million and Blackburn Rovers - £17 million. The harsh reality is that hardly any clubs are profitable in the Championship with only six making money in 2014/15 – and most of those are due to special factors.

Ipswich Town were the most profitable with £5 million, but that included £12 million profit on player sales. Cardiff's £4 million was boosted by £26 million credits from their owner writing-off some loans and accrued interest. Reading's £3 million was largely due to an £11 million revaluation of land around their stadium. Birmingham City and Wolverhampton Wanderers both made £1 million, but were helped by £10 million of Parachute Payments apiece.

So the only club to make money without the benefit of one-off positives was Rotherham United, who basically just broke even – and ended up avoiding relegation to League One by a single place.

Of course, losses are nothing new for Brentford, though there has been a clear willingness to accept higher losses since Benham came on board. In the five years up to 2010, the annual losses were kept down to £1 million or lower, but in the five years since then Brentford have reported aggregate losses of £36 million, averaging £7 million a season.

The approach was outlined by Crown in 2013: *The board continues to run the club with a level of losses commensurate with the capital injections by Matthew Benham. We believe that this is the correct strategy in a results-oriented business and one which involves a prudent approach to the level of risk to the financial security of the club. The continuing losses are accepted by Matthew and your board as the price to pay to reach our goals.*

That said, Benham explained that *it wasn't sustainable for us to continue making such heavy losses as we were last season. But off the pitch, we (now) have a more sustainable structure. The club isn't operating anywhere near the loss it was operating at twelve months ago.*

Part of that improvement will have been due to profits made from player sales. These can have a major impact on a football club's bottom line, but Brentford only made £2 million from this activity in 2014/15, presumably for the sale of Adam Forshaw to Wigan Athletic.

In fairness, this is not an enormous money-spinner outside the Premier League, though some clubs made a lot more than Brentford here: Norwich City - £14 million, followed by Ipswich - £12 million, Leeds United - £10 million and Cardiff City - £10 million.

Actually, that £2 million was the highest amount that Brentford have made from player disposals for ages, accounting for almost 50% of the profits from player sales in the last nine years.

That is all going to change in the 2015/16 accounts with the lucrative sales of Andre Gray, Moses Odubajo, James Tarkowski, Stuart Dallas, Will Grigg and Toumani Diagouraga, which should bring in at least £15 million of profits.

Crown explained the thinking behind these departures: *Sometimes we lose players that we would rather keep – whether for offers that the leaving players feel they can't refuse, and more recently for the slightly more practical purposes of complying with the League's Financial Fair Play (FFP) regulations.*

Benham echoed this: *We have to cut our cloth accordingly, which unfortunately includes having to accept big bids for our best players from time to time.*

At least players are now leaving for big money rather than peanuts. The club has also got smarter about structuring its transfers, as it has been reported that they will earn around £3.5 million in add-ons on the Gray/Tarkowski deals as a result of Burnley's promotion to the Premier League.

To get an idea of underlying profitability, football clubs often look at EBITDA (Earnings Before Interest, Depreciation and Amortisation), as this strips out player trading and non-cash items. Again, Brentford had one of the lowest with their minus £14 million EBITDA only better than Bournemouth minus £25 million, Nottingham Forest minus £20 million and Blackburn Rovers minus £15 million.

To be fair, only three clubs had a positive EBITDA in the 2014/15 Championship (Wolves, Birmingham City and Rotherham) and none of those clubs generated more than £1.5 million. In stark contrast, in the Premier League only one club (QPR) reported a negative EBITDA, which is testament to the earning power in the top flight.

Brentford's revenue has increased in line with the club's rise through the divisions: £3.0 million in League Two in 2009, £4.4 million in League One in 2014, and £10.0 million in the Championship in 2015. As Crown said after the promotion to League One: *It was important for the club's long-term future to get promoted as soon as possible.*

One other important driver for revenue movements before promotion to the Championship was progress in the Cup competitions, e.g. 2013 was boosted by taking Chelsea to a replay in the fourth round of the FA Cup.

However, Brentford's revenue was nowhere near the big hitters in the Championship. In fact, it was the smallest in the division in 2014/15 at £10 million. To place this into perspective, four clubs enjoyed revenue higher than £35 million (over £25 million more than Brentford): Norwich City - £52 million, Fulham - £42 million, Cardiff City - £40 million and Reading - £35 million.

Benham is acutely aware of this structural imbalance: *You have to remember, our revenue is very low. So we can't spend, spend, spend like other teams do. We have to be realistic. We have the lowest revenue in the Championship by far.*

This alone explains Brentford's desire to find an edge by better use of analytics, as it's a competitive necessity. Given their revenue level, Brentford have punched well above their weight in finishing fifth and ninth in their two seasons in the Championship.

Of course, these revenue figures are distorted by the Parachute Payments made to those clubs relegated from the Premier League, e.g. in 2014/15 this was worth £25 million in the first year of relegation.

If we were to exclude this disparity, then the revenue differentials would be smaller, but Brentford would still be rock bottom of the league table, behind the likes of Wigan Athletic, Huddersfield Town, Rotherham United and Millwall – and two of those clubs ended up being relegated.

The increasing importance of TV revenue higher up the football pyramid is seen by Brentford's revenue mix. In the Championship, broadcasting accounted for 45% of their total revenue, compared to just 24% in League One. As a result, match-day's share fell from 38% to 31% and commercial decreased from 38% to 24%.

In the Championship most clubs receive the same annual sum for TV, regardless of where they finish in the league, amounting to just £4 million of central distributions: £1.7 million from the Football League pool and a £2.3 million solidarity payment from the Premier League.

However, the clear importance of Parachute Payments is once again highlighted in this revenue stream, greatly influencing the top eight earners, though it should be noted that clubs receiving Parachute Payments do not also receive solidarity payments. As a comparison, Brentford's broadcasting income was £4.4 million, while Fulham earned nearly £30 million.

Looking at the television distributions in the top flight, the massive financial chasm between England's top two leagues becomes evident with Premier League clubs receiving between £65 million and £99 million, compared to the £4 million in the Championship. In other words, it would take a Championship club more than 15 years to earn the same amount as the bottom placed club in the Premier League.

The size of the prize goes a long way towards explaining the loss-making behaviour of many Championship clubs. As Benham observed, *if we get into the Premier League, things become easier because of the TV deal money.*

This is even more the case with the astonishing new TV deal that starts in 2016/17, which will be worth an additional £30-50 million a year, to each club depending on where they finish in the table. For example, I have (conservatively) estimated that the club finishing bottom in the Premier League next season will receive £92 million, which is £86 million more than a Championship club not receiving Parachute Payments.

From 2016/17 Parachute Payments will be higher, though clubs will only receive these for three seasons after relegation. My estimate is £75 million, based on the percentages advised by the Premier League (year one – £35 million, year two – £28 million and year three– £11 million). Up to now, these have been worth £65 million over four years: year one – £25 million, year two – £20 million and £10 million in each of years three and four.

There are some arguments in favour of these payments, namely that it encourages clubs promoted to the Premier League to invest to compete, safe in the knowledge that if the worst happens and they do end up relegated at the end of the season, then there is a safety net. However, they do undoubtedly create a significant revenue disadvantage in the Championship for clubs like Brentford.

Crown has openly stated that Brentford's goal is *sustainable Premier League football*, but Benham's ambitions don't stop there, as he has noted that the new deal *to an extent levels the playing field*, as seen by the improved performances this season of clubs like Southampton, West Ham and, of course, Leicester City.

Despite rising 81% to £3.1 million, Brentford had one of the lowest match-day incomes in the Championship, only ahead of Huddersfield Town - £3.1 million, Rotherham - £2.6 million and Wigan Athletic - £2.4 million. This was far lower than clubs like Norwich City - £10.7 million, Brighton - £9.8 million and Leeds United - £8.8 million.

This was even though attendances increased from 7,715 to 10,700 in 2014/15 with the sale of season tickets almost doubling to 5,641. This was 140% higher than the 4,469 average in League Two in 2007/08. There has been a dip in attendances 2015/16 to 10,310, which was only ahead of Rotherham – and some 2,300 behind Huddersfield Town, the next lowest club.

So Brentford's average attendance is still one of the smallest in the Championship, though it is a similar level to Bournemouth who managed to gain promotion despite this disadvantage. Interestingly, the south coast club operated a similar strategy to Brentford, effectively speculating to accumulate, as the club's owner heavily financed their attempts to go up.

Brentford have some of the lowest ticket prices in the Championship, especially at the important cheaper end, as explained by the board: *We took a conscious decision to keep season tickets and match-day prices to a level that would reward all those who had supported us through so many previous seasons.* Moreover, season ticket prices have been frozen for the 2016/17 season in line with the club's views on affordability.

The club's income is clearly limited by the 12,300 capacity of Griffin Park, hence the plans to build a new 20,000 capacity stadium at Lionel Road. The club has acquired the site and has planning permission, but needs to buy one remaining piece of land before any work can start.

This is subject to a Compulsory Purchase Order, but the tribunal still needs to set the price. Even though the land is only valued at £2.5 million, Brentford have offered £6.25 million in an attempt to accelerate the process, the owners are apparently looking for £8.5 million.

The club has admitted that this is a very complex development, including not only the construction of a new stadium, but also a hotel and over nine hundred apartments that will help fund the development along with the sale of Griffin Park.

Benham has already provided around £25 million of funding for the new stadium, though the final cost could rise to £45 million to overcome all the challenges. In particular, three railway lines surround the site, which pose *unique problems*, including the construction of a bridge across one of the lines.

This is another sign of the owner's commitment, though the delays have been frustrating for Benham: *When I first became involved with the club, around ten years ago, we were talking about the new stadium possibly being used as a venue for the 2012 Olympics, but it has drifted further and further away.* Nevertheless, the club remains confident of being in the new stadium ready for the 2018/19 season.

Once again, despite rising 44% to £2.4 million, Brentford's commercial income was also among the smallest in the Championship, way behind Norwich City - £12.8 million, Leeds United - £11.3 million and Brighton - £8.9 million. In fact, it was only higher than Millwall - £1.9 million and Wigan - £1.5 million.

Brentford's shirt sponsor is *Matchbook*, the global sports betting exchange and one of Benham's companies. The deal was extended for the 2015/16 season with an option to extend for one more year. The partnership also sees *Matchbook* branding on the roof of the New Road Stand.

In 2014 Adidas extended the kit supplier deal by four years until the end of the 2018/19 season.

Brentford's wage bill shot up by 78% (£8 million) from £10 million to £18 million in 2014/15, though this was impacted by bonuses for finishing in the playoff positions. Effectively, Brentford have increased their wage bill in order to get out of League Two and League One, and then upped it again in the Championship.

This has resulted in a fairly horrific wages to turnover ratio of 178%, though this was actually better than the 224% in League One.

Of course, wages to turnover invariably looks terrible in the Championship with no fewer than 10 clubs *boasting* a ratio above 100%, but Brentford's 178% was only surpassed by Bournemouth's 237% - and that was inflated by substantial promotion bonus payments.

However, Brentford's £18 million wage bill was still in the lower half of the Championship. On the fairly safe assumption that Bolton's wage bill was higher than Brentford's, the Bees only had the 15th highest wages in 2014/15.

Of course, this was still ahead of many other clubs, which might surprise some Brentford fans, as Benham noted: *The big myth of last season was the squad was run on a shoestring. In reality, the total first team budget was mid-table.*

That said, Brentford will always struggle to keep its top talent, as there are some clubs that will pay players a lot more. The impact of Parachute Payments is again felt keenly here with the highest wage bills found at Norwich City - £51 million, Cardiff City - £42 million, Fulham - £37 million and Reading - £33 million.

Benham appreciates this point: *It comes back to budget. Once we went up, and the players became aware that if they were playing for any of our Championship rivals, they would get paid more money, we had a job on our hands keeping certain players happy. Our structure is much more bonus-heavy, which hasn't helped us.*

This is likely to mean a fairly frequent turnover of players, as those departing will need to be replaced by new recruits, who, if they do well, will almost inevitably be sold. Many clubs have to follow this strategy, but it's a difficult one to successfully execute.

Another aspect of player costs that has risen is player amortisation, which is the method that most football clubs use to expense transfer fees and was adopted by Brentford this season. This has grown by £1.8 million from £0.3 million to £2.1 million in 2015.

As a reminder of how this works, transfer fees are not fully expensed in the year a player is purchased, but the cost is written-off evenly over the length of the player's contract via player amortisation. As an illustration, if Brentford were to pay £5 million for a new player with a five-year contract, the annual expense would only be £1 million (£5 million divided by 5 years) in player amortisation (on top of wages).

Brentford's £2.1 million is towards the lower end of the Championship, significantly surpassed by most other clubs, especially those relegated from the Premier League in recent times, i.e. Norwich City, Cardiff City and Fulham. Of course, this expense will have grown considerably in 2015/16 based on the much high transfer expenditure recently.

For many years, Brentford spent hardly anything on player recruitment, but have averaged gross spend of around £5 million in the last two seasons. This season alone included the following purchases: Andreas Bjelland (FC Twente) - £2 million, Lasse Vibe (IFK Göteborg) - £1 million, Maxime Colin (Anderlecht) - £0.9 million and Josh McEachran (Chelsea) - £0.8 million.

However, as a result of the high player departures, Brentford actually had £12 million of net sales over the last two seasons. Benham argued that this was a necessity: *With FFP we were always going to have to sell players.* This meant that they were comfortably outspent by the likes of Derby County - £29 million and Middlesbrough - £23 million.

It's a challenge to sign players, but Brentford can offer certain advantages, as Benham explained: *What we can demonstrate to potential new signings is that if they come to Brentford, and excel, then it can be a springboard for their careers. Look at what it did for Andre, Moses and Forshaw. When they come to a team like us, they also have more chance of getting regular first team football.*

Brentford have also made good use of the loan system, e.g. last season their loans included Sergi Canos from Liverpool, Marco Djuricin from Red Bull Salzburg and John Swift from Chelsea.

Brentford's net debt more than doubled in 2015 from £19.2 million to £43.5 million, as gross debt rose by £23.8 million from £22.7 million to £46.4 million and cash fell £0.5 million from £3.5 million to £3.0 million.

Most of the debt (£43.4 million) is owed to the club's owner, Matthew Benham, and is interest-free, though secured by a legal charge over the club's freehold property. In addition, there are £2.9 million of other loans, while the club has a £500,000 overdraft facility.

Brentford's was by no means the largest debt in the Championship, being lower than nine other clubs. In fact, four clubs had debt over £100 million, including Brighton - £148 million, Cardiff City - £116 million and Blackburn Rovers - £104 million. Bolton Wanderers have not yet published their 2015 accounts, given their much-publicised problems, but their debt was a horrific £195 million in 2014.

That said, the vast majority of this debt is provided by owners and is interest-free, so the amounts paid out by Championship clubs in interest is a lot less than you might imagine.

Even after adding back non-cash items such as player amortisation and depreciation, then adjusting for working capital movements, Brentford have made substantial cash losses from operating activities, e.g. £10.8 million in 2015. They then spent a net £3.2 million on player recruitment and a hefty £16 million on infrastructure investment, i.e. stadium development. This was funded by £23.7 million of loans and £5.9 million of new share capital.

Since 2009 the club's only real source of funds has been money pumped in by Matthew Benham. This has been used to cover operating losses (£30 million) with a further £24 million spent on infrastructure investment (stadium and training ground) and £8 million on acquiring a subsidiary (for the Lionel Road site). Only £4 million went on player purchases (net), made up of £8 million purchases and £4 million sales.

Benham's total commitment was up to £76 million as at 30 June 2015, comprising £43 million of loans, £25 million of non-voting preference shares, £5 million of new share capital and £2 million of working capital loans. This included £24.5 million on the Brentford Community stadium.

With some justification, the Chairman described this as *magnificent financial backing*, while even Mark Warburton, who has more reason than most to criticise the owner said: *You have to respect the fact that someone's put so much money into the football club and put it into this state of health.*

Of course, the long-term aim would be to reduce this reliance on Benham. As far back as 2013, the Chairman said: *We believe as a board we should be striving to be breaking even on a sustainable basis, without the requirement for substantial cash injections from our owner.*

Being so dependent on one individual can be a concern, but Benham has to date been willing to provide substantial funding. However, Brentford will not be able to simply buy success, as they will need to continue to comply with the Financial Fair Play regulations.

Under the rules for 2014/15, clubs were only allowed a maximum annual loss of £6 million (assuming that any losses in excess of £3 million were covered by shareholders injecting £3 million of capital). Any clubs that exceeded those losses were subject to a fine (if promoted – like Bournemouth) or a transfer embargo (if they remain in the Championship – as was the case with Fulham, Nottingham Forest and Bolton Wanderers).

It should be noted that FFP losses are not the same as the published accounts, as clubs are permitted to exclude some costs, such as youth development, community schemes, promotion-related bonuses and infrastructure investment (such as stadium improvements and training ground). This latter expense in particular will help Brentford's FFP calculation, as they have spent a lot in these areas.

From the 2016/17 season the regulations will change to be more aligned with the Premier League, so that the losses will be calculated over a three-year period up to a maximum of £39 million, i.e. an annual average of £13 million. This will likely encourage clubs to *go for it* even more.

Recently the club announced that they would close their Academy, which has come as a major surprise, given that they had attained the coveted Category Two status. This is once again about finding an edge in order to compete and progress as a Championship football club, as Brentford *cannot outspend the vast majority of our competitors*, though it will undoubtedly hit the affected youngsters hard.

The club statement explained their decision thus: *This philosophy is particularly relevant with regards to the future of the Brentford FC Academy. As a London club, there is strong competition for the best young players, and the club's pathways to First Team football must be sufficiently differentiated to attract the level of talent that can thrive in a team competing towards the top end of the Championship.*

Moreover, the development of young players must make sense from a business perspective. The review has highlighted that, in a football environment where the biggest Premier League clubs seek to sign the best young players before they can graduate through an Academy system, the challenge of developing value through that system is extremely difficult.

There's no doubt that Brentford have come a long way, but the club is still far from breaking even, so continues to be reliant on Matthew Benham to a large extent. The owner has invested heavily to give the club the best possible chance, but there is no guarantee of success, especially with big clubs like Newcastle United and Aston Villa joining the fray next season.

It will be important that the transfer budget is spent well in the summer. According to Co-Director of Football, Phil Giles, there should be money available after the January sales: *The money will be reinvested in the Summer. I believe we're fine for FFP this season.*

Although Brentford is clearly a club with ambition, they have to strike the right balance off the pitch. A couple of years ago, Benham gave some idea of the long-term vision: *Every club in the Championship would like to get to the Premier League at some point, so we are no different. But we are not going to put a timeframe on it. At some point we are going to try to make a push for it... in x years. I don't want to say publicly. But yes it is achievable within a few years.*

At the time that seemed extraordinarily bullish, though Bournemouth and Burnley have shown the way for *small* clubs. These days, the owner is keeping his feet on the ground: *Brentford is a long-term project, and we are a team in transition at the moment.*

In a recent interview, Benham beautifully summed up Brentford's dilemma: *We will give it everything to go up – as long as it makes financial sense of course.*

*

This analysis of Brentford's finances was written by Kieron O'Connor, the author of the respected *Swiss Ramble*, a blog focusing on the business of football. Kieron has twice won the Football Supporters' Federation's Blogger of the Year award and is regularly quoted by the media, including the *BBC, The Guardian, The Times, Daily Telegraph, The Independent* and *The Economist*.

You can find Kieron's blog here: *http://swissramble.blogspot.co.uk* and he is on *Twitter* at *@SwissRamble*.

Kieron would like to point out that many of the Matthew Benham quotes in this piece came from a rare, lengthy interview that the club's owner granted to the excellent fan site *Beesotted*.

Warburton's Revolution: How A Blank Canvas Became A Blueprint To Champagne Football | Jordan Campbell

Before the arrival of Mark Warburton, Rangers had experienced the pain of four years of continued corporate rape, abetted by the incompetence of the national game's governors.

Since he took over Mark Warburton has galvanised an entire support of millions worldwide and has engendered a massive change in morale and mind-set.

Arriving on the fifteenth of June 2015, Mark Warburton was appointed as the fifteenth permanent manager of Rangers Football Club. Flanked by his trusted aide and club legend Davie Weir, the walk up the famous marble staircase and into his first press conference heralded the dawn of a new era.

The environment they were entering was tough, there's no getting away from it.

The first team squad that had so massively underachieved had been decimated, the club had been operating without a scouting structure for three years too, and, to make matters even more testing, preseason training was scheduled to start in just twelve days' time, allowing little time to assess the existing squad and bring in a new players ahead of the upcoming campaign.

Rangers faced arguably its most pivotal season in its entire history. Supporters worried that the off-field tribulations would result in the loss of a generation of supporters and feared that another year of Championship football would see operations scaled back to a level never seen before. So, the importance of identifying the right man for the job had never been greater given that he was inheriting the worst Rangers team in living memory.

In his first press conference Warburton presented himself as both professional and articulate, an immaculately dressed man who possessed a breadth of knowledge, which far surpassed that of any other football manager I had ever witnessed.

Like many, I had been doing my homework on his methods and inspecting his CV. Naturally I was impressed with his background as a stock market trader in London, but I was slightly taken aback by the sheer amount of passion and ambition that must have been behind his decision to give up that lifestyle for a crack at football, notwithstanding the belief and conviction he must have had in his ideas.

The innovation of the *NextGen* series, along with the progress he had made at Brentford in winning promotion from League One and then securing a place in the Championship playoffs were tremendous achievements, yet, for many, he was seen as a gamble, inexperienced and not boasting a track record worthy of being given the Rangers hot seat.

This was a natural reaction and confirmed the pressure he would be under to deliver from the off. There is no honeymoon period in the goldfish bowl of Glasgow. He had gone from the City of finance to the City of football.

However, the challenging circumstances didn't prevent him from starting the rebuilding job at quite a pace.

It soon became apparent that Warburton's extensive knowledge of the English game would be an invaluable tool, as Wigan trio Rob Kiernan, Martyn Waghorn and James Tavernier were brought in for a combined fee of around six hundred thousand pounds.

Joining them on Bosman deals were Swindon's Wes Foderingham, Bradford's Andy Halliday and Danny Wilson from Hearts, a former Rangers youth product. Jason Holt followed suit from Tynecastle and North London youngsters Gedion Zelalem and Dominic Ball arrived from Arsenal and Spurs respectively.

Stressing the benefits of having a *lean squad* in terms of the number of bodies at his disposal was something he was quick to make clear. Ensuring youngsters have a pathway to the first-team and that peripheral members of the squad feel they are still in with a chance of playing on any given Saturday are crucial to ensuring the balance between competition and opportunity if these calculations are weighed properly.

Warburton, though, isn't your average football coach, either in how he progressed to his current position or in the way he views the game. He manages to meld together a perfect blend of traditional values such as a strong work ethic, a desire to succeed and a never say die attitude whilst taking a clinical but calculated approach to his decision making and in the footballing blueprint he has constructed and refined.

It was abundantly clear that this forward-thinking attitude extended to the conditioning side of the game.

I was shocked when Warburton confirmed that it would just be himself and Weir taking on the coaching mantle, as he stated he liked to be in control of everything himself.

Darren McGregor was allowed to join Hibs on a free, but before his departure, he highlighted the main themes of the preseason programme and how it differed from previous years.

A lot of preseasons can comprise aimless running. Whereas the gaffer is all about keeping us on our toes, keeping everything short, sharp, dynamic. Everything has been with the ball; it's all been small-sided games and possession so I definitely think that's transferred onto the park.

Ten months later, and *short, sharp* and *dynamic* are the exact three adjectives most Rangers fans would use to describe the team Warburton has created.

Dean Shiels, the Northern Irish midfielder, stressed how, unusually, he had looked forward to what is traditionally billed as the most gruelling period of the season, saying: *It has been the most enjoyable preseason I've had. I think of years gone by when you used to get run ragged round a pitch and didn't see a ball for a week. But this preseason everything we've done has been with the ball, technical stuff, and tactical stuff. Even though the running has been tough at times, it's always been with the ball. The lads have enjoyed it. They prefer it that way.*

Warburton constantly stresses the need for the players to enjoy coming to their work and, if it wasn't already evident a month or so into the training camp, then the messages coming from the dressing room throughout the campaign about the spirit and the bond between the players and the fans confirmed it.

The decision to allow the players to devise their own code of conduct was another way of empowering the players and instilling a sense of discipline which has always been one of the staples of being a true Ranger.

The tradition of every Rangers manager wearing a suit and tie pitch-side has been embraced by the gaffer too, but he has too much class that I struggle to contemplate him being a tracksuit manager regardless of where he was based!

The biggest off-field coup has undoubtedly been in bringing in chief scout Frank McParland from Burnley, a man who Warburton regards as *the best in the business*. Warburton's close relationship with Sean Dyche smoothed this process, and the contacts and knowledge of the English market he has brought looks to be paying dividends.

Neil McIlhargey was brought in from Brentford as Head of Analysis and quickly compiled a database detailing every single player in the Scottish Championship and Premiership.

There has been an attitude change in how the youth teams are viewed. Most of the eighteen to twenty-one year-olds have been loaned out to lower division Scottish clubs rather than playing in the Under 20s squad as Warburton doesn't view this as beneficial to their development as many of them have been playing against the same boys for the best part of a decade.

He has come under fire in the tabloids for expressing his opinions on such things, including his opposition to artificial surfaces in the aftermath of Waghorn's injury against Kilmarnock, which was exacerbated due to the unforgiving nature of the plastic pitch.

His media persona is so polished that for many Rangers fans, the weekly press conferences have become a must-see event. Unfortunately, he faces the exact same questions every week which means he has been painted as robotic and a purveyor of clichés, but that is more due to the journalists looking to trip him up and create a sensationalist headline.

He is far too intelligent to fall into that trap, but it is a worry for many that the intense scrutiny he comes under could lead to him leaving sooner than hoped.

He said: *It's intense, I have to say. It's the one area that jumps at you compared to down south. Here, it's just the constant scrutiny. You find yourself being very careful on every single response. You have to think it through; one loose statement, one flippant remark, one remark taken out of context can be so damaging. So, for me, you have to be on your guard 24/7.*

I thought London was a football city and then you come to Glasgow and really they live and die for their football. There are so many pages every day in the papers, there are radio shows every evening, and it's scrutiny beyond belief. The fans phone in and it fuels the fire.

As the season has progressed, appearances on *talkSPORT* with Adrian Durham and Jason Cundy, and in-depth interviews with Rob Wotton on *Sky Sports News* have become more frequent. This is good for the club in terms of raising its profile down south and gaining further exposure but paranoia dictates that many cynically view it as putting himself in the shop window.

There was a lot of hype around Warburton from the fans who had read into his past but, equally, a lot of scepticism as to whether he just talked a good game.

The scale of the transformation and at the rate in which it had been achieved at the start of the season was nothing short of remarkable. This was a completely new group of players that had been blended together in a few weeks but looked as if they had been playing together for a lot longer. In a preseason friendly Rangers outplayed Burnley and *dominated the ball*, a phrase often uttered by Warburton, against a side which would eventually go on to win the Championship.

Chances were created and wasted, and Foderingham's goal was breached via the heart of the defence – a sentence which would become a microcosm of the negatives of the season, however negligible. However, the dedication to playing the ball out from the back and building between the lines gave the support confidence that these were principles that would be improved upon. A one-nil defeat was inconsequential to the bigger picture.

The opening game of the competitive season against Hibs in the first round of the *Petrofac* cup clearly demonstrated what was to come when Rangers fought back after trailing and when the teams re-emerged after the break, the floodgates opened. There was a tempo and verve to the passing that had been missing for years; an insatiable thirst to extend the lead rather than sit back and rest on their laurels.

It finished six-two to Rangers and the swashbuckling manner in which the hounding was carried out signalled the start of a magnificent run in the league campaign, with Rangers winning their first eleven games of the season.

Sandwiched in between that was a sobering reverse at the hands of St Johnstone in the third round of the league cup, where the cavalier tactic of having both fullbacks bombing on at the same time left the two centre halves fatally exposed. Tommy Wright had sussed out how to overcome the system: sit deep, stay compact and leave two up top who can get in-behind at pace.

It was simple, but effective, and gave those in the Premier League the chance to ridicule the strength of the side. What it didn't take into account is that Rangers were still the dominant side and, over the course of the season would have won more of these types of games than they lost. Warburton was only two months into a rebuilding job so it was natural that it would take time for the back four to gel as a unit.

With the team fully embroiled in a title race, the game against Hibs, three days after Christmas, in front of a sold-out Ibrox, had all the ingredients needed to be a memorable match and was set-up to be a massive indicator as to whether the trophy would be heading west to Glasgow or east to Edinburgh.

Rangers duly stepped up to the plate and delivered a magnificent performance, running out convincing winners. Even when reduced to ten men, Warburton remained on the front foot and altered the shape to a 4-3-2 formation.

This relentlessly positive mentality was typified by Waghorn who, with only a few minutes left on the clock, broke away and instead of heading for the corner, he drove at the defence and slid the ball in at the near post to seal the points and make Ibrox erupt once again.

Top division teams, Kilmarnock and Dundee were swept aside in the Scottish Cup before they were drawn against Celtic for the Old Firm tie that everyone had hoped for.

That would have to wait though, as league duty had to be taken care of first.

In the league, at one stage, Rangers had created a seemingly unassailable lead of seventeen points. But in the end it would be fair to say that Warburton's charges limped over the line.

Rangers eventually won the title in front of their own supporters. It was a nervy affair as Dumbarton proved resolute opponents but James Tavernier got the decisive goal in the second-half and when the final whistle went the relief was palpable. Rangers had secured their top-flight status after a four-year absence and could now solely focus on the cup competitions.

Warburton's first trophy came in the *Petrofac* Cup final with a comfortable four-nil win over Peterhead.

But the real test was going to be Celtic and as the game approached you could feel the atmosphere in the city building throughout the week. Celtic were in a no-win situation. If they won they wouldn't receive any plaudits unless it was by a big margin due to the gulf in finances and class of player available at their disposal far outweighing what Rangers had. If they lost though, the manager Ronny Deila would almost certainly be sacked and panic would set in.

Warburton excelled at Brentford whilst working with the underdog tag but it was a different kettle of fish at Rangers; however, this was the one game where Rangers were the outsiders. With the stadium packed half an hour before kick-off the atmosphere was at fever pitch.

Warburton didn't alter a thing. No defensive mindset was adopted, no tinkering with personnel; he believed in his philosophy even if it was being knocked as being too idealistic in the press.

The players responded better than anyone could have envisaged. They came flying out the traps, showing a composure on the ball and an intensity off it which Celtic were unable to match, and Kenny Miller scored early on.

I bumped into a friend at halftime and we were in disbelief at just how superior we were in every department. It would have been naïve to expect this to continue for the whole game though and, as expected, Celtic came out with a sense of purpose which had otherwise been missing, and equalised straight away.

Rangers could have folded but, instead, they persisted with what had brought them joy so far and retook the lead in extra time through the outstanding Barrie McKay, whose transformation under Warburton has been sensational. Unfortunately Celtic substitute Tom Rogic guided the ball home superbly with his left foot to tie the score at two apiece. Rangers had looked fitter the whole game but injury had ruled out Waghorn and ex-Bee Harry Forrester, while Kiernan had limped off, meaning this was more of a second-string side than anything.

The game went to penalty kicks and the nerves were shredded and after six penalties each the two teams couldn't be separated.

Law made his way to the spot and sent Gordon the wrong way. Rogic looked assured. But as he planted his standing foot, a divot underneath the ball popped up as he made the connection with the ball. Foderingham dived to his left and the ball went high over the bar.

Such is the bond between the players, their first thought was to run straight to the fans and celebrate with them. Forrester was raising his crutches aloft as the *bouncy* got into full swing. The stands were still full twenty minutes later as *Warburton is Magic* reverberated around the stadium.

This wasn't just your average celebration, this was four years' worth of pent-up emotion being released as most supporters had doubted whether Rangers would ever get back to days like that, so they were entitled to bask in the glory.

Rangers had a three-week gap in which to recover after the exertions of the season and then prepare for the Cup Final against Hibs, who still had the playoffs to occupy their minds. It was a dilemma for Warburton in terms of getting the balance right between recharging the batteries and maintaining match-fitness.

He took the team south to Spurs' training ground where they played a select XI. Rangers won while Hibs were beaten by Falkirk in the semi-finals courtesy of a last minute sucker-punch.

In the end what was a classic Scottish Cup final - thanks to the open nature in which it was played – paled into insignificance due to the disgraceful scenes that followed the final whistle.

Hibs thoroughly deserved their win; their 3-5-2 formation nullified our fullbacks and stifled our fluidity, while they had an intensity that was entirely missing in the Rangers ranks. The failure to defend the two late corners has been a problem all season, while Tavernier and Kiernan's horrendous displays allowed Anthony Stokes to run amok. If it wasn't for Foderingham it may well have been more.

You would have looked twice at someone if they had asked you about the Rangers and Brentford connection just eighteen months ago. But Lewis Macleod's forced transfer to the Bees, and Warburton's subsequent arrival in Govan just six months later established the link.

Since then, there have been two more links in the shape of Kiernan and Forrester, courtesy of the gaffer's prior knowledge of working with them.

Warburton's recruitment has been tremendous so far and these two players are no exception to that. Kiernan has played the vast majority of the games this season and his best spell was from January through to March where he and Wilson looked impenetrable for much of that time – credit here goes to Warburton who realised the weaknesses in the system and rectified it by dropping the defensive line deeper, alternating which full-back rampaged, narrowing the shape and reigning in Halliday who sits in front of the defence.

While he is dominant in the air from a standing start, possesses a decent enough turn of pace and has two good feet for a centre-half, his tendency to go to ground needlessly and get attracted to the ball instead of spotting the immediate danger and tracking his runner are his most obvious flaws. Whether these are chinks in his armour that can be eradicated through working with Davie Weir remains to be seen.

Harry Forrester joined on the last day of 2015 to a relatively muted reception. This was not in any way a judgement on his ability; rather, it was the left field nature of handing him a six-month contract and the fact that he was unable to break into the Doncaster team, which raised eyebrows.

This is probably more of a reflection on the minority of fans who hadn't faced up to the reality that the days of lavish spending are long behind us, and that a bit of creativity is needed to make the most of our limited budget nowadays.

A quick look at his pedigree, which boasted a hefty transfer fee at Aston Villa as a teenager as well as the offer of a contract later at Ajax, reassured me that this would be another inspired signing, another gem plucked from obscurity and his form rediscovered once reunited with his former coach.

Three games into his Rangers career, however, and I was sceptical as to whether he offered anything different to what we had. He had looked very busy and got himself into good positions but was snatching at chances, something he put down to *trying too hard to impress*.

Once he scored his first goal though, he never looked back. A last gasp winner against St Mirren, a beautifully curled finish against Raith, and a scorcher fourteen seconds into the Scottish Cup quarter-final against Dundee, endeared him to the crowd. He was becoming our creative hub in the month of March only for it to be curtailed by an impact injury sustained in the *Petrofac* Cup final against Peterhead, which ruled him out for the remainder of the season.

Clearly the thinking behind the signing had been that the short-term contract would motivate Forrester to produce the goods in order to win himself a longer stay in Glasgow, a wish he expressed within his first fortnight at the club. He penned a three-year contract in April and it is anticipated he will play a prominent role next year, using his guile and roaming presence to manufacture scoring opportunities, whether that be out wide or in a more central role. Warburton describes him as a *street footballer* due to his instinctive hunger for the ball and reliance on intuition rather than physicality.

What makes the job Warburton is doing even more fascinating is when you look at the climate in which he is trying to operate.

While Rangers will generate around twelve million pounds in season ticket revenue next year, Warburton is expected to only have a wage budget of around nine million pounds to work with.

Currently, it is believed he has built a squad for around the same wage bill costs as the one listed in the last financial accounts, just over six million pounds. That is still by far the second biggest in Scotland, with Celtic's sitting at around sixteen million pounds for first-team wages alone. When you factor in non-football staff it is around thirteen and thirty-three million pounds, respectively.

With the increased revenue that will derive from TV income, SPFL competition money, improved season ticket sales and potential European football, there is scope for considerable more investment in the playing squad even though Rangers cannot compete with the financial packages on offer in England. That's why Warburton has made it clear that it is the club, its history, the stadium, the facilities, the fans, the derby and the route to European football that sells Rangers, not the money on offer.

A video of the pre-match atmosphere at Ibrox in the penultimate Old Firm game before their financial implosion, shown to him by his son, was when he himself knew he couldn't turn down such an opportunity.

The structure of contracts is another area where he has interesting views. Preferring to keep a relative parity when it comes to the base-rate of pay in order to not upset dressing-room harmony, he prefers to use performance-based bonuses as incentives.

This Summer's Transfer Window will be pivotal if Rangers are to complete the last stage of their journey back to reclaiming their position at the apex of the Scottish football pyramid.

It is expected that Rangers will continue to do the bulk of their shopping in the English Football League with Accrington Stanley midfield duo Josh Windass and Matt Crooks arriving on pre-contracts, whilst Liverpool academy graduate, Jordan Rossiter, joined the ranks for just a quarter of a million pounds followed by Joey Barton.

Other big names such as Nico Kranjcar, Grant Hanley, Danny Graham and Graham Dorrans have all been linked, showing that adding experience to a young squad and strengthening the spine of the team are major priorities.

In less than a year Warburton has caught the imagination of the Rangers faithful, as shown by the fact that they had the highest average attendance in Scotland this year at over forty-four thousand. He has made it a pleasure to support the team again rather than a chore performed out of a sense of duty.

Rangers fans are expecting title number fifty-five to be delivered next year and, even with Brendan Rodgers taking over at Celtic, there is the utmost belief that Warburton will be at the helm when it arrives – and that he won't need a second bite of the apple.

Let's just hope that talk of a new contract materialises as Rangers are on the cusp of building something special, mainly thanks to the influence and achievements of Mark Warburton.

*

Jordan Campbell is a lifelong Rangers supporter. He was formerly a youth player at Hamilton Academical FC and is now pursuing a career writing about sport.

He regularly contributes to a Rangers fanzine, *WATP Magazine*, and has also written for the *Rangers Report*.

Jordan can be found *@jordanc1107* on *Twitter* where he will inevitably be writing about all things Rangers and he hopes that in next year's review we will all be talking about the exploits of Lewis MacLeod.

Looking Forward And Back | Phil Giles

About two weeks before the end of the season I went for lunch with our Chief Executive, Mark Devlin. I asked Mark if he'd ever known a season with so many ups and downs and with such a variety of different situations to manage and cope with. Mark has been in football a lot longer than me and he replied that it was definitely the most unusual season he had ever been through. This was my first season as one of the Brentford Directors of Football - it has been quite an experience and a steep learning curve from the first day.

Having overcome the challenges of the last twelve months, I believe that we have ended the season in a strong position to build further and to try to get back into the top six in the division next year.

We took a conscious decision in January 2016 not to pay over the odds for players and instead give match time to the existing squad players and in particular those players who were brought in during the previous summer. I was particularly pleased with how the second half of the season saw some of those players develop and show what good players they are.

Nico Yennaris was excellent after moving into midfield during the latter part of the season. Konstantin Kerschbaumer adapted to the pace and physicality of the division and demonstrated his passing ability when playing behind the striker. Yoann Barbet was patient through the first part of the season, which allowed him the time to train hard and get used to English football, before taking his chance when it presented itself.

The squad has therefore had an opportunity to grow together over the course of the year and the players who came from overseas are now better adjusted to the division than was the case nine months ago. With a bit more luck with regards to injuries and a good preseason I'm certain we will be able to make a better start to the next season than we did the last.

Speaking of injuries, I'm sure that for most Brentford fans one of the highlights of the 2015/16 season was the return of Scott Hogan from serious injury. One of my first acts in the job last year was to spend an evening in a restaurant in Chiswick with Scott and learn about his recovery and the second knee injury which had just been sustained. He was going in to hospital the following morning for another operation and yet he was in good spirits and ready for another long period of rehabilitation. Matthew Benham was also present that evening and he was keen to keep faith with Scott and make sure that he had the time to recover and get back playing. So it was decided that we'd extend his contract for an additional year, a decision that I hope was a good one for all concerned.

If I had one wish for next season it would be that both Lewis Macleod and Andreas Bjelland make a similar impact to Scott when they finally return from long absences. Both have worked incredibly hard to get back playing and deserve some luck over the next twelve months.

The same could be said of Alan Judge. The injury he sustained at Ipswich was a particular low point of the last twelve months. I was sitting not too far away from where the tackle took place, and it was fairly clear right away what had happened – Alan's reaction was distressing and told the whole story. I thought the medical team did a great job in getting Alan to hospital as efficiently as possible. I left the game at half time to go to the hospital. Matthew and some of the coaching staff came down soon after as we all rallied around Alan and offered our support.

Out of a difficult afternoon came a moment of amusement as we planned how to drive Alan back to London that evening. I was keen to offer to help, as was Alan's agent, Barry, who had driven to the hospital immediately after being informed of what had happened. When the doctors pointed out that Alan had been on the laughing gas for quite some time and could potentially be quite sick on the way home, both Barry and I were quick to withdraw our services and suggest the other might be a preferable chauffeur. Thankfully Barry drew the short straw although I'm told that the upholstery of his Range Rover escaped quite lightly!

I'm sure that despite missing out on the Euro's this summer, Alan will be targeting the even bigger prize of World Cup qualification in 2018.

The appointment of Dean Smith brought with it some stability with regards to the long-term Head Coach position. That allowed my fellow Director of Football, Rasmus Ankersen, and I to concentrate on some longer term planning at the Club. We have taken several decisions in the latter part of the season which I hope will give us a solid foundation to achieve our promotion ambitions in the coming seasons.

The biggest decision was that we will focus only on developing players from the age of seventeen rather than the full age spectrum in our Academy. This was a difficult decision but one that we thought was necessary for the long-term progression of the club. Further restructuring decisions were also taken, including the creation of a Head of Athletic Performance to oversee the conditioning of the players, and a new Chief Scout to lead our innovative scouting team.

We have invested both time and money into the training ground, installing a new *Motz* pitch that is identical to that at Griffin Park and also attending to several other pitches. The main building has been renovated and we've employed a new Head Chef to provide us with the highest possible quality of food with a focus on the nutritional requirements of top athletes.

The upshot of these changes is that our training ground is now an environment that is completely focused on the requirements of our first team and Development Squad. It is also an environment, which I hope is more befitting of a team that has finished in the top ten of the Championship in the last two seasons.

Dean has done a fantastic job in challenging circumstances since joining the Club towards the end of 2015. On his first day in the job I collected Dean and Richard O'Kelly at Euston station before driving straight to the training ground, passing the cameras from *Sky Sports News* as we entered. Richard insisted that we stop at the gates, wind down the windows and speak to the staff who do a terrific job monitoring who is entering and leaving the site – we have had to increase security this year owing to a number of incidents at the training ground. It is a measure of both Dean and Richard that they were keen to get to know everyone from day one. They are first and foremost good people and it's been brilliant to have their family at our games, both home and away.

Dean, Rasmus and I have spent lots of time planning what we need to add to the squad over the Summer to give us the best chance of promotion next year. Performances and results at the end of last season show that we are not that far away from a team that is highly competitive at this level. That being said, we have already lost Sergi Canos, John Swift and Marco Djuricin who are all attacking players, so we will most likely need to reinvest in this area if we are to retain our status as the joint top scorers in the division next year.

Recruitment is always challenging, especially to get the balance right between players who can have an immediate impact and those who will be developed for the future. It is essential that we mainly focus on younger players since we need to maintain resale value in the playing squad. Selling players is an important part of our business strategy since the revenues generated by the club in other areas are restricted by our lack of facilities.

I believe that we will focus more heavily on the English market this summer than we did a year ago. That's not to say that we haven't acquired good players from overseas and will continue to do so in future. Rather, we think that it is more likely that English players will adapt more quickly to playing at Brentford and in the Championship, which will mean we can start next season in the strongest possible way. Ryan Woods is a good example of how that happened this season, although it should also be pointed out that some of the overseas players like Maxime Colin also took to English football like a duck to water.

When asked last season for our targets for 2015/16, I replied that we should look to improve on our fifth place finish in the previous season. In hindsight, given the turnover of staff and players and the long injury list, that was a target which was almost impossible to achieve. For the coming season, I think that we should have similar ambitions – we should certainly look to improve on the previous season and if we can then that would push us close to the top six in the division again.

Ultimately we will look to win every game that we play, and if we can play each game as we know we can, then with the usual backing of our fervent and loyal fans I'm sure that an exciting and successful season awaits.

Growing Pains - A Reflection On 2015/16 And A Look Forward To 2016/17 | Cliff Crown

I think it's fair to say that was one rollercoaster of a season! Certainly not one for the faint-hearted and whilst I can't promise it won't be just as hectic, I do believe the coming twelve months will be less eventful for all of us. We are pointing in the right direction and are as strong as we have ever been.

If there is one thing I have learned from this season it is that football is a crazy business and totally and utterly unpredictable!

So with that in mind here's my summary of the year just gone and my look forward to 2016/17.

The previous season was always going to be a hard act to follow! Deep down we all knew that with the substantial changes which were made last summer it wasn't going to be easy. We had raised the bar and the level of expectation and if that wasn't hard enough, we lost amongst others Gray, Odubajo and Dallas in August as well as seeing Pritchard return to Spurs. When you consider and analyse the contribution that Gray, Pritchard and Jota in particular made in 2014/15 it's no surprise to find that we struggled initially compared to the previous year. Replacing those three alone would have been a tall order for any club!

Injuries aren't an excuse as every club suffers some. But the number and seriousness of injuries we have been afflicted with this year has been way more than any club deserves. I can only salute the professionalism of all the players, and frankly there are far too many to mention by name, for the dedication and hard work they put in to get back to full fitness.

And our grateful thanks goes to the medical team who have been incredibly busy this season and worked so hard to get players back to full fitness as quickly as possible! When it comes to injuries, none was more painful to witness than that of Alan Judge. *Judgey* was our talisman and I know everyone at the club is with him every step of the way and believes, just as he does, that he will come back even stronger

What is really important to me is that everyone who reads this understands that the owner and the people running the club want success just as much as you, the fans do.

Football is a complex business and whilst we are constantly striving to make the right decisions, things do not always pan out the way that you expect or intend. Our experience over the last nine months has shown that even with careful and thorough planning, detailed research and clear communication things can still go wrong! And we made mistakes. You don't get to be better and to change the way you do things without risking error but what is vital is that you learn from those changes, and I believe we have.

Along with mistakes, I believe we have made some very good decisions. We wouldn't be about to embark on an historic third year in the Championship having finished in the top half again, unless a lot of things had gone very well.

So what were the highlights?

Our first win over QPR in 50 years. Nothing was more satisfying than enjoying that moment at Griffin Park in front of our own fans. And also finishing as London's top club outside the Premier League.

The six wins and nineteen goals in April after the disappointment of the January to March period. I recall clearly the concern expressed by some at the prospect of having to play eight games in twenty-eight days but my, how we performed! The brilliant goals and assists from *Judgey* throughout the season and, of course the fantastic last game of the season in glorious sunshine when we won by five goals to one at Huddersfield to record our largest ever away victory at this level and finished as joint top scorers in the division.

Having had the time to settle and gel, we saw in our last nine games this team play the kind of exciting football we believed they would be capable of, and with great leadership from Dean and Richard, I believe they will achieve even greater things next season.

Before I look forward to next season I'd also like to take this opportunity of thanking everyone else at the club for all their efforts in helping us secure Championship football for a third consecutive season. It's been a real team effort across the football and non-football sides of the business and everyone has played their part.

The truth is we are still a work in progress, and there is bound to be yet more change in the summer. However I can assure all fans that we are very happy with the management team. I have got to know Dean and Richard as well as Flemming and Tom over the last six months and to a man they are really great guys and I am delighted that the very significant improvement in performance and results towards the end of the season bodes extremely well for next year.

I also want to acknowledge the important work done by our Co-Directors of Football – Rasmus and Phil and everyone in their teams who have worked tirelessly to help us through what has undoubtedly been a season of transition. They are top guys with a clear vision as to what we need to be successful.

And of course I must extend thanks to the rest of the staff at Brentford. Mark Devlin and everyone who works with him have continued to work tirelessly to make sure the rest of the business continues to develop and improve the way we do things and in particular the work we have carried out to improve the fan experience.

This time last year we knew we had to sell players to meet the requirements of Financial Fair Play and it was inevitable that Andre Gray, in particular, would leave because of the difficulty of competing with clubs with huge Parachute Payments. Frankly, all we can do is to ensure that the players we sell are sold on our terms and that we receive by way of initial fee and add-ons what we consider to be an appropriate fee.

This year we are in a totally different position - we are well within the boundaries of the Financial Fair Play regulations and so we do not have to sell players. However that's not to say that players won't be sold.

Virtually every club in the land is a selling club and we won't shy away from selling and re-investing in new talent – we have done that before, and finished up even stronger, and I won't pretend we won't do it again. In spite of everything no one can say that we have not brought some new and exciting talent to our club this season.

Matthew's investment is huge, and we are all extremely grateful for it, but it is not all on players. He is also funding the club's push for a more suitable home. On that front we were delighted to receive confirmation that the Compulsory Purchase Order had been successful on the first of April 2016 and so we can finally move onto the next stage. I appreciate it has been a long and slow process but it is football, so there will undoubtedly be some more twists and turns along the way.

What we have achieved to date has been significant despite many obstacles, but there is still a long way to go and many hurdles to overcome, and some of them we aren't even aware of yet! This is another example of a complex business where we need to carefully consider what is best for Brentford FC and we shall not waver from our determination to secure a sound future for this great football club.

We are continuing to grow as a business whilst remaining friendly and family orientated. Our community is inextricably linked to the football club and we are once again indebted to Lee Doyle and his team at the Community Trust who continue to promote the club in our local communities and do us proud.

So what can we look forward to?

As you will already know ticket prices have been frozen as we continue to recognize the importance of keeping football affordable for our loyal fans.

More change; because change and evolution are both necessary in the long-term and if we get it right, change brings improvement and with that greater success - well at least that's the theory!

A new *Motz* pitch at Jersey Road so that conditions there can replicate the new playing surface at Griffin Park. We might not have shown our best side with the pitch last August, but I am delighted to say that laying the new *Motz* pitch in record time in September was ultimately one decision we definitely got right.

Consolidation in the Championship. When we won our final game in 2013/14 if I'd have offered our fans at least the next three years in the Championship without ever being in the bottom three I think they would have bitten my hand off. Just look where we have come from and everyone can see how much progress we have made. You only have to look at Yeovil and Doncaster in particular and to clubs like Wigan, Bolton and Blackpool to truly understand what we have achieved. And long may that continue!

A settled management team committed to growing our business both on and off the football field.

An owner and a board who all want the best for Brentford FC and who won't be afraid to make tough decisions if we believe it is in the club's best interests.

Of course we won't always get the decisions right and yes we have learned a lot. And will continue to learn as we face the challenges that we come across but what I can say is we are far more settled today than we were one year ago and we are in good shape to build upon this season and go again!

We've got some extra big games coming up – Aston Villa and Newcastle are clubs we could only have dreamed of playing just three years ago so let's enjoy those games and all the others, get behind the team and see what we can achieve!

I really hope you enjoyed reading Greville's book!

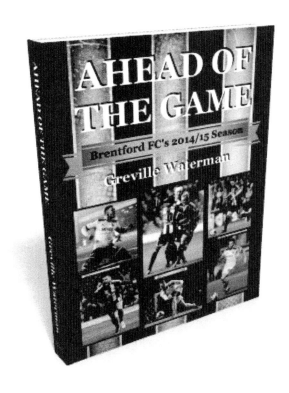

Ahead of the Game: Brentford FC's 2014/15 Season

Greville Waterman

In May 2014, Brentford FC were promoted to the Football League Championship. It was only their second season at such a level, in sixty years, and many asked how the newcomers would cope against the so-called massive clubs Norwich City, Blackburn Rovers, Cardiff City and Leeds United. Would they survive? Would they thrive? Or, as many expected, would they fall short and crash back to Division One at the first time of asking?

The 2014/15 season answered these questions in emphatic style with Little Old Brentford - the perennial underachievers - displaying a vibrant brand of positive, attacking football that took the Division by storm and rocketed the Bees into the playoff places. Under the visionary ownership of Matthew Benham and the ultimate man-manager, Mark Warburton, the club had created a new and different way of doing things that piqued the interest of the Football World. Rather than look downwards, the disbelieving but delirious Brentford supporters began to harbour dreams of reaching the Promised Land of the Premier League.

In Ahead Of The Game, long-established supporter and blogger, Greville Waterman, puts together selected articles from his blog, alongside new content, to detail Brentford's journey. He offers a fascinating and incredible inside story of how this unfancied team defied expectations, overcame the unforeseen break-up of the successful partnership between Benham and Warburton, did the double over Fulham, and came within a whisker of promotion.

This book is a must-read for any Brentford fan and includes guest contributions from Cliff Crown, Richard Lee, Billy Reeves and Jim Levack. Whatever the future holds, it is clear that The Bees are truly Ahead Of The Game and the best is yet to come!

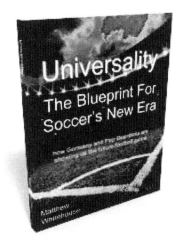

Universality | The Blueprint for Soccer's New Era: How Germany and Pep Guardiola are showing us the Future Football Game by Matthew Whitehouse

The game of soccer is constantly in flux; new ideas, philosophies and tactics mould the present and shape the future. In this book, Matthew Whitehouse – acclaimed author of The Way Forward: Solutions to England's Football Failings - looks in-depth at the past decade of the game, taking the reader on a journey into football's evolution. Examining the key changes that have occurred since the turn of the century, right up to the present, the book looks at the evolution of tactics, coaching, and position-specific play. They have led us to this moment: to the rise of universality. Universality | The Blueprint For Soccer's New Era is a voyage into football, as well as a lesson for coaches, players and fans who seek to know and anticipate where the game of the future is heading.

The Bundesliga Blueprint: How Germany became the Home of Football by Lee Price

In this entertaining, fascinating, and superbly-researched book, sportswriter Lee Price explores German football's 10-year plan. A plan that forced clubs to invest in youth, limit the number of foreign players in teams, build success without debt, and much more. The Bundesliga Blueprint details how German fans part-own and shape their clubs, how football is affordable, and the value of beer and a good sausage on match days. The book includes interviews from Michael Ballack, Jens Nowotny and Christoph Kramer, and the movers-and-shakers behind Germany's leading clubs including Schalke, Dortmund, and Paderborn.

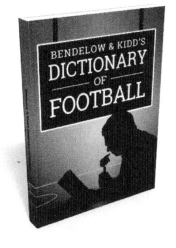

Bendelow and Kidd's Dictionary of Football by Ian Bendelow, Jamie Kidd

Over time, the language of football has developed into something quite unrecognisable, a melting pot of hyperbole, idioms and exaggeration. Many of football's terms would be seen as bizarre in any other walk of life; a doctor would never diagnose a patient with having the dreaded metatarsal, and only commentators seem to feel the need to tell us who was at number one the last time a team won at a certain ground.

Join Bendelow and Kidd as they produce a barnstorming run through some of the best-loved (depending on how you look at it) phrases and sayings which come out of the mouths of players, managers, pundits, journalists and of course, you, the fans.

From trigger happy chairmen to the want-away striker, football offers us a unique language which can be amusing, and at other times simply infuriating. That's right, the lads really did give it 110% out there today, as they silenced the boo boys, in the relegation six-pointer.

A book which will make you laugh out loud, nod your head in agreement, and hopefully offer a few surprises, Bendelow and Kidd's Dictionary of Football should have its place on every true football fan's bookshelf.

Tragic Magic: The Life of Traffic's Chris Wood by Dan Ropek

Traffic was the most enigmatic British band of their day. Formed in early 1967 by Chris Wood, Steve Winwood, Jim Capaldi and Dave Mason, they rejected the bright lights of London, in favor of a run-down, supposedly haunted, cottage in the country – a place to live communally and write music. With Chris especially intent on channeling the vibes of England's landscape into their sound, days would be spent getting high, exploring, playing and working in varying proportions. Against all odds this eccentric model paid off – songs such as "Dear Mr. Fantasy" and "John Barleycorn Must Die" would lift Traffic into the upper echelons of the rock world.

As they brushed shoulders with Jimi Hendrix, The Beatles and the Grateful Dead, and with Dave dropping in and out of the band, Traffic's music evolved from a synthesis of Steve's innate musicality, Jim's atmospheric lyrics and Chris's special brand of congenial mysticism. Record sales boomed and tours carried them back and forth across the Atlantic, everything seemed to be going to plan – a dreamlike fairy tale come true.

But for Chris, a toll would be exacted.

Amid the clashing egos, wearing road trips, stressful break ups and a complex personal life, he vacillated precariously between bursts of exquisite creativity and torrents of self-destruction; a paradoxical dance which continued until his death in 1983. For a man who found artistic expression everything, and for whom suffering for it was an expectation, Chris would stare fully into the Medusa's face of the music industry, paying a higher price than perhaps any of his contemporaries.

Researched and written over a ten-year period, "Tragic Magic" offers the only definitive account of Traffic's story and Chris Wood's quietly extraordinary life.

Wolfram Wars: Exposing The Secret Battle in Portugal by Rod Ashley

Wolfram – also known as Tungsten – is about more than electric light bulbs. Its more deadly claim-to-fame rests in its armour-piercing qualities. During WWII, Wolfram was in great demand with both the Allies and Axis powers who scoured the globe for the precious material; indeed, they deployed huge resources to secure supplies whilst simultaneously doing their best to sabotage and undermine one another.

The greatest beneficiary from these shadowy dealings was Portugal, a neutral country, under the control of the mercurial António de Oliveira Salazar. The sudden surge in demand created great wealth and bustling 'gold rush towns' deep in Portugal's remote mountainous interior, but threatened to undermine Salazar's grand vision for his country. *Wolfram Wars* examines the role of Portugal in the Wolfram trade, alongside the exploits of its British, American and German customers. It takes in the glitz and glamour of wartime Lisbon, the mischievous dealings of intelligence services, and includes some of WWII's most interesting spies – spies with code names such as Garbo, Tricycle, and Treasure. A certain young intelligence officer and creator of James Bond – Ian Fleming – also has a role to play.

Appealing to connoisseurs of WWII history, Wolfram Wars is a story that offers adventure, intrigue and espionage, and a fascinating insight into this little-known but hugely important aspect to the war.